THE CHILDREN'S ENCYCLOPEDIA

ORIGINATED
AND EDITED·
by
ARTHUR MEE

VOLUME TWO

THE EDUCATIONAL BOOK COMPANY, LIMITED,
TALLIS HOUSE, TALLIS STREET, LONDON, E.C.4

CONTENTS OF THIS VOLUME

THE CRUMPLING AND WEARING OF THE EARTH

THE GREAT CRUMPLES AND FOLDS IN THE EARLY CRUST OF THE EARTH, WITH MOLTEN IGNEOUS ROCK
FORCED INTO THEM, AND IN ONE PLACE BURSTING THROUGH

THE FOLDS SOME MILLIONS OF YEARS LATER WHEN RAIN, RIVERS, FROST, AND WIND HAVE GREATLY
WORN THEM DOWN

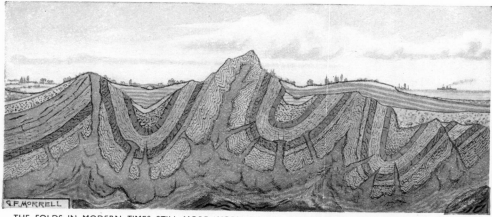

THE FOLDS IN MODERN TIMES STILL MORE WORN DOWN, SHOWING VALLEYS HILLS SEA, AND SOIL

25

The Story of the Boundless Universe and All its Wondrous Worlds

Some of the oldest rocks of England peeping out of the sea at the Lizard

THE FOUNDATION STONES OF BRITAIN

WE have seen how the mud in the bottom of the sea was raised to form most of the present solid surface of the Earth, and how the various layers have been named and dated by the fossil plants and animals they contain, and we have briefly described the age and contents of the main layers or strata from the Cambrian rocks up till the present time.

Now, Britain has been in existence for many ages, and mountains have been washed away here and there, and plains made valleys, and valleys made into arms of the sea, so that at different places different layers of rock have been laid bare, and the general surface has become a tessellated pavement or patchwork of strata of all kinds and ages. Over this rock may have crawled or swum trilobites of Cambrian and pre-Cambrian times. Along that road giant lizards may have waddled. Above that field the archaeopteryx may have flown. In the soil of that garden there may be dinosaurs.

By studying our maps every child may know the age and the geological history of the soil of his garden, whether he lives at Land's End or John o' Groats, in Inverness or in London.

The oldest rocks that contain recognisable fossils are the rocks called the Cambrian; but in a few places in Britain the Cambrian rocks have all been worn away, and we can see rocks millions of years older—rocks that were there probably millions of years before life appeared.

The island of Lewis in the Hebrides, for instance, is one of the oldest pieces of land in existence. The rock there is the rock known as *gneiss*.

This is crystallised rock, and presents a great problem to geologists. It is possible that, like the rock above it, it is mud or sedimentary rock, and has been crystallised simply by heat and pressure. It is even possible that it has never yet been worn down into mud, and that it represents some of the actual material of which the crust of the Earth was already made, and many geologists believe that it is really lava which had been forced through earlier sedimentary layers of the crust. Anyhow, it is the deepest part of the crust of the Earth that Nature has allowed man to penetrate, and the gneiss may be considered as the foundation stones of Britain.

Gneiss, as we have said, is found in Lewis. It is found also in other islands of the Hebrides, and a great belt of it runs through Sutherland, Ross, Cromarty, and Inverness, from Cape Wrath to the islands of Rona and Ramsay. It occurs also in

ASTRONOMY · GEOLOGY · GEOGRAPHY · CHEMISTRY · PHYSICS · LIFE

THE FACE OF OUR MOTHERLAND AND THE AGE OF THE PLACE YOU LIVE IN

Geological map of Great Britain in six colours and tints, showing the rocks at or near the surface everywhere, and so enabling any inhabitant of our island to fix the period of time when the site of his home was laid down. Local maps for the various geological ages appear elsewhere.

This is the first map of the Children's Encyclopedia Picture Gallery. It shows the whole country. There follow in this series maps for the great geological ages covering the areas in which the rocks of these ages are seen on the surface. From this series of maps, therefore, we are able to trace the place in time of the place we live in, and the chapters of geology accompanying the maps enable us to realise something of the nature of the world in those days. This map shows the geological areas represented in various parts of Britain. The Primary or Palaeozoic area is shown dark grey ; the Secondary or Mesozoic in the middle tint of grey ; the Tertiary or Cenozoic (Kainozoic) in light grey. The red patches show where volcanoes have burst through the crust at various times, and where quantities of basalt and other lavas have poured over the land. The Archaean rocks—the gneiss rocks—are shown in greyish pink. The masses of granite thrown out by volcanoes are marked pink with white dots. The section at the bottom of the map shows how various rocks overlie one another and emerge to the surface in different parts of the country.

Anglesey, in Shropshire, and in the Malvern Hills. The gneiss is often mixed with granite and other igneous rocks which have been forced into it. It is particularly interesting in its character as the oldest uncovered rock in the world; but at the time it came to the surface there was probably no life on the Earth, and so it lacks the interest of fossils.

We say *probably* there was no life, for graphite and lime have been found in some gneiss rocks, and some geologists think that these were of organic origin—possibly the remains of sea vegetation. In some of the Canadian gneisses, too, certain curious objects were found which were thought to be fossils, and the name *Eozoon* was given to the sea-creature whose remains they were supposed to be, and, though most geologists are not convinced that the object is really a fossil, it is just possible it may be.

Gneiss, then, may be regarded as the backbone and framework of modern Britain, and, though it is probably not part of the original crust of the Earth, it is probably not unlike that crust in its general make-up. It will be interesting, therefore, to see what it is made of.

When we analyse it we find that it is made chiefly of silicon and oxygen, and that in its purest form it occurs as quartz.

THE WONDERFUL TRUTH ABOUT A PIECE OF QUARTZ

One of the most interesting and extraordinary things about quartz is the fact that it usually contains vast numbers of minute cavities filled with water. There may be thousands of millions of such cavities in a single cubic inch. Despite its cavities, it is one of the hardest and most enduring of rocks, and even after it has been broken down it persists as pebbles, granite, and sand. All the sandstone mountains are built of grains of quartz, and most of the sand is quartz sand.

Amethyst, cairngorm, chalcedony, opal, jasper, agate, and some other precious stones are forms of quartz, and chiefly to the silicon in quartz we owe flints and prisms, eye-glasses, and lenses. So that we have every reason to be pleased with the foundation stones of our island.

Millions of years have, of course, elapsed since the surface of England was gneiss. Since that time tremendous masses of the original gneiss have been worn down by rain, rivers, and frost, into gravel and sand and mud. During the millions of years that have intervened the land has periodically been washed into the sea, and the mud in the sea has risen again as mountains and solid land. In the sea, too, little sea creatures have collected the silica and the lime from the ancient rocks, and so have separated them from the rest of the mud, and the collected separated lime has risen from the sea as new land—as the limestone of Derbyshire, as the white cliffs of Dover.

The land has been continually moulded and remoulded. Here a mountain has been rubbed away; here a new country has been plastered on; here a volcano has poured forth its basaltic lava; here the lava has been worn away into causeways and columns. So now we have the surface of England, as we said, piled deep with recent rocks in one place, and rubbed down to pre-Cambrian rocks in another.

THE PICTURE GEOLOGY AND THE GREAT TALE IT TELLS US

The story of each great sedimentary layer and what it has to teach us of the life and conditions in England during that particular geological period is told in the great series of pictures and maps to which we now come in our geological study of the Earth. The course of our very rapid survey will cover perhaps hundreds of millions of years.

This picture geology opens with the colour plate facing page 765, on which are three pictures. The first picture shows the tremendous folds into which early stratified rocks of the Earth were thrown as the crust cooled and crumpled.

The second picture shows the folds after millions of years of rain, and wind, and frost have worn them down into rugged mountain ranges. At some such stage as this, Life appeared.

The third picture represents the condition of things still later in modern times. Now the Sun, wind, rain, frost have worn down the folds into the hills and valleys.

THE HISTORY OF OUR LAND THAT LIES UNDER OUR FEET

Britain is a splendid country geologically, for almost the whole geological record, from the oldest to the earliest rocks, can be studied on its surface. Every one of us who has a garden and a home has a museum and a book of geology at our door, and by looking at our picture maps, we can find out what age or page in the geological history of Britain lies under our feet.

The Story of Immortal Folk Whose Work Will Never Die

Little Marco Polo sees the wonders of the East

MEN WHO MADE THE WORLD KNOWN

THERE may still be a few people in Britain who have never visited a foreign country, never looked upon the sea, never travelled in a train, never left their native village. They may have read of the outer world, and friends may have told them, but from personal experience they have no knowledge of affairs beyond their own parish limits.

Once upon a time all mankind was as stationary. Each tribe believed its own country to be the habitable world. The rest was supposed to be the domain of evil spirits, of fiery air not to be breathed, atmosphere solid with frost, and the seas like an icy ooze.

Had there not been valiant roving exceptions many lands would have remained unpeopled. For the human family was once confined to a small area, and the world at large had to be discovered and colonised, peopled, as our British Isles have been.

A marvellous little picture of the arrival of a people is given us by Bede, the early historian of England. That saintly old scholar, living 1300 years ago in an age of ignorance and barbaric terrors, wrote a book which we would not lose for all the world's gold, for it tells of the travels and toils of the peoples who made British history down to the eighth century.

No story of fairyland adventure is better than this old historian's wonderful account of the arrival of the Picts. Such adventure, such an astounding find ! The Picts came, he says, from Scythia, and here is his account of what happened.

They arrived in their long ships on the northern coasts of Ireland, where, finding the nation of the Scots, they begged to be allowed to settle among them, but could not succeed in gaining their request.

The Scots answered that the island could not contain them both; but, " We can give you good advice what to do," said they. " We know there is another island not far from ours to the eastward which we can often see at a distance when the days are clear. If you will go thither you will obtain settlements; or if they oppose you, you shall have our assistance."

Now, the island to the eastward which the Scots thus described and gave to the Picts was England, Wales and Scotland ! The wandering savages had stumbled by accident upon a northern fringe of Ireland, and had missed the 90,000 square miles of Great Britain.

Such a mischance seems hard to believe today; but we shall find the same thing happening far later, when men equal in daring and with more knowledge took to the seas again as explorers. Columbus set

EXPLORERS · INVENTORS · WRITERS · ARTISTS · SCIENTISTS

out to reach the East by sailing on and on to the West. He found his path barred by a land totalling nearly 17 million square miles, a country more than four times the size of Europe. But he thought he had reached his goal.

He called his new-found islands the West Indies. He died in the belief that he had discovered the unknown shore of India, and never heard that it was the New World, an unguessed continent, America, that he had introduced to the knowledge of mankind.

EARLY EXPLORERS AND THEIR THRILLING ADVENTURES

Long after his day the mystification lasted. When La Salle, the French explorer, reached America late in the seventeenth century, he was still in quest of that East-in-the-West which Columbus thought he had reached.

He sailed up the St. Lawrence River in Canada till he came to a great waterfall. " This is the waterway to China; it lies beyond these falls," he said; and he gave the falls a name that lives on the map today, Lachine Rapids, or China Rapids.

Now, these errors were made by men who had at their service much knowledge stored from adventures earlier than their own. How did the men fare who sailed without knowledge and without charts? Herodotus, who lived nearly 500 years before Jesus, and was the first traveller to write the record of his adventures, tells us that the Greeks of his day never sailed even by daylight out of sight of land, and always spent the night on shore.

THE VERY BEGINNING OF THE HISTORY OF TRAVEL

But there were travellers thousands of years before the Greeks who as far excelled them as Columbus did later. No book on history or geography tells the story of the men who first crossed the trackless wastes of the huge Pacific and peopled its thousands of isles, enormous distances apart, in their frail boats, the prey of any storm that might arise.

Known Vikings were in America 500 years before Columbus; but unknown men were there thousands of years before the Vikings. Lands were always before men, but wherever civilisation has gone, it has found other men already in possession of big countries. The Maoris, who reached New Zealand nearly 600 years ago from Polynesia, were preceded by other natives.

If the truth could be known the Eskimos and Laplanders would count among the hardiest of travellers, for they forsook sweeter, greener lands and wandered on in pursuit of independence, up into the dreaded Arctic. It is certain that they were there a thousand years before Caesar came to England, for Homer has a thrilling passage in the Odyssey which describes how his hero visits a land where the summer Sun shines by night as well as day, " When a sleepless man might have earned a double wage, the one by day, the other by daylight night, so near are the outgoings of the night and of the day."

But the more we learn of the past, the more we realise how tremendous was the loss of knowledge borne later for long centuries by the world. We may never know the truth of the marvels of India and China, but we reach safer ground for history on coming nearer home, when we cast the eye over the map of the Mediterranean countries. It is there that detailed history of travel begins.

BOLD MARINERS AND MERCHANTS WHO CAME TO BRITAIN

We cannot trace any influence of Babylonian voyaging, but we know the Egyptians carried their rites and culture across the sea into Europe; we know that a superb civilisation, with far-reaching sea trade, sprang up in the island of Crete, only to be blotted out by some barbarian invasion from the North as utterly as Pompeii was buried by Vesuvius.

Then there arose that wonderful seafaring people the Phoenicians, who were friends of David and Solomon, and furnished materials for the building of the Temple at Jerusalem. Bolder mariners never existed. They found their way to India, Persia and China; they established trading centres in Greece and Spain. There seems little doubt that they also came to Britain.

A daughter colony of Phoenicia was Carthage, which, becoming powerful by about 850 B.C., sent seamen out to the west coasts of Africa and Europe, and furnished perhaps the first reliable description of Britain, its foggy seas, and its illimitable ocean lying to the West.

One of the grandest of all recorded expeditions was a little Phoenician venture of 600 B.C. Necho, King of Egypt, said to them: " I believe it is possible to sail round Africa; go and do it."

They went. They sailed out of the Red Sea and down the east coast of Africa until the autumn. Then they camped and sowed corn, and when it was ripe, harvested it and continued their voyage. They sailed round the Cape of Good Hope; they sailed up the west coast of Africa, and noted that whereas on starting the Sun had always risen on their left-hand, it now rose on their right. The voyage

perished, and it fell to a boy to revive the love of travel. That boy was Marco Polo, born at Venice in 1254, who, when everything about the East had been forgotten, save that it was a place of fabulous splendour and terrors, calmly walked to China.

Marco Polo, immortal hero of the greatest of all romantic explorations on foot, was but 15 when he set out on his travels with his father and uncle.

MAGELLAN'S LITTLE BOAT BRINGS THE FIRST NEWS OF THE DISCOVERY OF THE PACIFIC OCEAN

was triumphantly completed three years after setting forth.

Greece and Rome greatly extended our knowledge of geography, but Rome, mistress of the world, as she called herself, did not know of China, and the Chinese, who considered all the rest of mankind barbarians, did not know of Rome.

Rome followed Greece into desolation ; barbarism reigned ; books and knowledge

They had to go over mountains, and across terrible deserts, through hot, burning lands, and places where the cold was terrible. Poor Marco was made ill by hardships, but he kept bravely on.

At last they came to China, where a great king, called Kublai Khan, was very pleased to see them. Marco grew up at the Court, and became a prime favourite of the king. Marco learned to speak several languages, and was so clever that the king sent him as his ambassador to Cochin China, to India, and to other lands.

Each time he came back Marco was able to tell the king not only the answer to the message with which he had been sent, but all about the countries themselves : how the people lived, what their trades were, and what were the big cities and rivers and mountains wherever he went. The king had never had so clever an ambassador before.

At last the Polos wanted to return to Venice, from which they had been absent for twenty-three years. The king was very sorry to let them go, but at last consented, and they came back. Marco remembered all he had seen and learned, and afterwards he had it all written down.

For long people did not believe his story to be true. They could not think it possible that there were such great lands as China and India, with millions upon millions of people. And the talk of silks and jewels and beautiful foods and scents of which he told seemed just as untrue.

MARCO POLO'S THRILLING STORY OF HIS JOURNEY IN THE EAST

At last, when men began to know more, they saw that there was some truth in this book. It set men studying and making bold plans for discovery. The great Columbus, who lived some two hundred years later, was one of those who studied the book, and it helped him greatly when he was making up his mind to try to find India by sailing over the sea to it.

To see how hard Marco Polo found it to make people believe the account of his travels, we must read the story of what happened when his father and uncle got back to Venice. Nobody knew them. Nobody would believe that the little Marco Polo who had gone away as a boy had become a great traveller and come back a rich man. So the Polos asked their old friends to a great feast. First they appeared in robes of crimson satin ; then they changed these for other robes, and at last they came into the room wearing the torn, soiled clothes which they had worn in their wanderings. Their friends stared in surprise, and were still more startled when the three men cut open the patches of the old clothes and showed that these were filled with jewels. Then the people believed that the strangers were the Polos, back from the far-off lands.

The effect of Marco Polo's book was not immediate, but it was lasting and progressive once it was tested and its truth established. The East ceased to be regarded by the rest of the world as a fantastic unreality, such as the mysterious lands supposed to be visited by Lemuel Gulliver are to us.

AN ARAB'S WONDERFUL RECORD OF THIRTY YEARS OF TRAVEL

It was an actuality, this great East, noisy with nations and kings, and Ibn Batuta, a learned and intrepid Arab, spent thirty years, between 1304 and 1378, in travelling over a route which included Mecca, Persia, Mesopotamia, Arabia, Africa, Asia Minor, Bokhara, India, China, and Sumatra. That was a wonderful record for days when half the ships at sea were pirates, and many of the men on the roads were brigands.

The first condition made honest seagoing a peril; the second made overland trade increasingly hazardous and unprofitable. Goods from the East had to be carried by land to the Levant, or up the Red Sea to Egypt. In either case all had to go to Marco Polo's home, Venice, for distribution to the rest of Europe. Oh, for a seaway to the East ! was the cry.

The discovery of Madeira, in 1420, by João Gonçalves Zarco and Tristão Vaz, 535 miles from Lisbon, took Portuguese ships south-west, but it was a step toward more distant goals, for it encouraged Bartholomew Diaz, another Portuguese, to test the possibilities of the African coast.

Let us remember that the ships of the period were only little half-decked boats carrying at most 36 men, with bad and insufficient food. And let us not forget that mariners' terrors of aerial fire, the breath of death in the vicinity of the equator, were real and tragic.

A PERILOUS VOYAGE TO PENETRATE THE GATEWAY TO THE EAST

Diaz overcame them. Setting sail in 1486, he took two little vessels down the west coast of Africa, sailed through the latitudes said to be fatal to life, reached the Cape of Good Hope, and at its foot he reached Algoa Bay, without quite knowing how great was his feat. Before he could realise that the gateway to the East had been penetrated, his crew mutinied and forced him to return home.

Fate was hard to poor Diaz. When the next Portuguese expedition set out he was

THE MEN WHO MADE THE WONDERFUL JOURNEY

THE PHOENICIANS AND THE KIND OF BOAT IN WHICH THEY SAILED ROUND THE AFRICAN
CONTINENT TWO THOUSAND YEARS AGO

placed under Vasco da Gama, and the prize of the golden East fell to his leader. Diaz was turned back by Da Gama from that memorable voyage and died, in 1500, in a ship which became a wreck.

Between the feats of Diaz and Da Gama came Columbus's immortal first three voyages across the Atlantic and Cabot's discovery of the North American mainland. The Spanish success in the West caused Portugal to redouble her efforts toward the East, and it was in 1497 that Da Gama was sent forth with three little ships to double the Cape of Good Hope and strike out for India.

VASCO DA GAMA FINDS THE WAY TO INDIA BY SEA

His men were just as frightened as those of Diaz and Columbus had been. But he kept on and on, and at last reached the Cape of Good Hope, and found that he could get round to the other side of Africa. Terrible storms seemed likely to swallow up his ships. His crew begged him to go back. " I will never go back until I have set foot in India," he said. Some of the men made up their minds to kill him, but he put these men in irons, and himself took command of the steering of the ship. They reached the Indian Ocean, and, sailing along the east coast of Africa, found great cities. At one of these they were able to get a pilot who knew his way across the waters. They reached Calicut, in India, at last, and tried to make friends with the King of Calicut. He was a bad man, and, after taking their presents, tried to kill them. They managed to return to Portugal, having found out one of the most important things in the world—the way to India by sea.

TRIUMPHS OF DISCOVERY THAT LED TO THE EXPANSION OF TRADE

So in five years there came two of the most memorable of triumphs. The attempt to find India in the West produced America; the attempt to find India by sea in the East succeeded, and less than a quarter of a century later Cortes had entered Mexico, Pizarro was engaged in the conquest of Peru, and trade was streaming East and West.

We read elsewhere of the great deeds of Columbus. Here we must note a consequence. There was a scramble for territory between Spain and Portugal. The Pope decided that all the newly-found lands in East and West should be divided between the two countries, and a dispute arose as to whom the Moluccas belonged. Portugal claimed these islands, but Ferdinand Magellan, who had quitted his native land for Spain, declared that they belonged to that country, and was equipped by Charles the Fifth to sail round the world and take the Moluccas and anything else he might succeed in discovering.

The ships went out from Seville to the West on September 20, 1519, and returned from the East on September 8, 1522, three years all but twelve days. But when they got back, instead of the five ships and 270 men with which they had started, they had only one ship and 18 men. Sebastian del Cano was in command; the brave Magellan was dead. Let us see what had happened to him.

He struck out boldly for what we now know as South America. Nobody had ever been able to get to the end of it ; nobody could tell whether it was possible to get round or through it. Some of his men rose in mutiny, and one ship left him because the crew were too frightened to go farther. Del Cano, to his eternal shame, was among the mutineers. He, like the rest, was mastered and forgiven.

THE INTREPID MAGELLAN DISCOVERS THE MIGHTY PACIFIC

Magellan explored all down the coast, and at last came to a great opening. He sailed up it, hoping it would go right through. No; it was only a great river. He came back, and went on until at last the coast seemed to break in two. He sailed in through heavy waves into a channel which ran between great precipices. He was the only man not afraid. His men almost died of fright when a great storm arose. He managed to calm their fears, and at last they got through the strange channel. And then a magnificent open ocean appeared before them. It was smooth and calm, and he called it the Pacific, the "peaceful" ocean. That is how the great ocean was named.

He had come through a strait which he called after his own name. The Magellan Strait had shown him the way through South America. To get through it had taken him thirty-eight days, so it is not surprising that his men were afraid. He now sailed half-way round the world, and reached the Philippine Islands, where he was killed in a battle with the natives. It was when Magellan died that Del Cano,

MAGELLAN'S SHIP WAS THE FIRST TO GO RIGHT ROUND THE WORLD, BUT POOR MAGELLAN DIED ON THE WAY, KILLED IN THE PHILIPPINE ISLANDS BY NATIVES

taking the only ship fit to sail in, continued the voyage, still in strange waters, but knowing that he was steering for home. He came back round the Cape of Good Hope as Da Gama had come round from India. When he got home people saw that, as he had gone out by one way and come back by another, the world really was shaped like a ball, and that Del Cano had been round it.

Many attempts were made to follow Magellan, and after fifty years Sir Francis Drake sailed round the world.

THE SECRET OF THE WINDS AND HOW IT HELPED THE SAILORS

Now comes a strange story from the Pacific. All the early voyages were in one direction. The winds carried the little ships forth, but did not bring them home unless the tour of the world was completed. Magellan died at the Philippines in 1521. Forty-eight years later there arrived an expedition from Mexico to take the islands in the name of Spain.

It was commanded by Andreas de Urdaneta, a Basque, and he, with a touch of true genius, solved the secret of the seasonal direction of the winds. He discovered that the same force that blew him from east to west would at the right time turn and blow him back from west to east again. He for the first time recrossed the Pacific, and all navigation of that ocean was based on his grand revelation until steam came to make us independent of winds and currents.

The world was now an open map, but the details remained to be filled in. How this was done we shall read in stories dealing separately with America, Australia, Africa, the Arctic, and Antarctic. Many glorious names shine from those maps, which were wrought in tears and paid for with noble lives.

TRAGIC MYSTERIES OF GLORIOUS FIGURES ON THE WORLD'S MAP

Outstanding figures are Jacques Cartier, a French navigator, who did much exploring in Canada in the middle of the sixteenth century; Sir Hugh Willoughby, who perished in the Arctic with his 62 men in 1554 on the expedition which led to Richard Chancellor, his lieutenant, in another ship, discovering the White Sea and the ocean route to Russia; Davis, who discovered the strait bearing his name; Hudson, doomed to death with his little son by the desertion of his crew in Hudson Bay, in 1611; Bering, who found the way between Asia and America in 1728; Hartog, Dampier, and Cook in Australia, and the martyrs to Polar Exploration.

A name which still brings a sigh to the lips is that of Jean François de Galaup la Pérouse, a knightly figure of France, who in 1788, after a world voyage, arrived in Botany Bay to claim Australia for France. He found the English had beaten him by less than 40 hours.

With the grace of the chivalrous hero he turned away to sea—and vanished. During nearly 40 years every sea was sought for him by British mariners. At last, in 1826, the truth came by chance to light. Two little wrecked ships were found in dismal ruin upon a coral reef north of the New Hebrides. They were La Pérouse's. He and his crews had perished in warm southern seas as Willoughby had been frozen in the north.

THE WONDERFUL THINGS A RUSSIAN DID IN SIBERIA AND CENTRAL ASIA

Ferdinand Richthofen, of Karlsruhe, Silesia, must be noted for 12 years of splendid travels in Asia and America in the nineteenth century, yielding us a monumental work on China. We must close with Nicholas Prejevalski, the Russian who did wonders in Siberia, Central Asia, and Tibet. He discovered the wild descendants of camels which had escaped from the storms that wrecked a once thriving civilisation in Central Asia, and brought back to Europe the wild horse, parent type of every existing domesticated species. His discoveries date from the last quarter of the nineteenth century.

We live in a great and wonderful world, teeming with marvels, beauty, and terrors, and we see that from the dawn of humanity down to the present time there has always been someone ready to venture his comfort, health, and life in order to banish doubt and dispel mystery, and to found in their place knowledge of what lay across an ocean, what secrets a mountain hid, what treasures were contained in the darkest continent.

Few of the explorers have profited, but they have left names that live for ever. Those who died, those who suffered, knew that they would not die or suffer in vain. There is something of the poet, the artist, the prophetic seer in these heroic souls, and to such come intimations of immortality.

BARTHOLOMEW DIAZ REACHES THE CAPE OF GOOD HOPE WITH A MUTINOUS CREW

ST. GEORGE AND THE PRINCESS LEAD THE DRAGON TO THE MARKET-PLACE. See page 781

The Great Stories of the World That Will Be Told For Ever

THE CAT AND THE PARROT

MADAME THÉOPHILE was a sandy cat of whom the French writer Théophile Gautier tells this charming story.

She had a white chest, a pink nose, and blue eyes; she was called Madame Théophile because she dwelt with me on the most friendly terms, sleeping at the foot of my bed, dreaming on the arm of my chair while I wrote, descending to the garden to follow me in my walks, assisting at my meals, sometimes even intercepting a morsel of food which I might be carrying on my fork to my mouth.

One day a friend of mine who was going away for a few days confided to my care his parrot. The bird, feeling himself transported to a strange land, climbed by means of his beak to the top of his perch, and sat there silent and trembling.

Madame Théophile had never seen a parrot, and this creature, so new to her, evidently caused her immense surprise. As motionless as an embalmed cat from Egypt, she regarded the bird with an air of profound meditation, putting together all the notions of natural history which she had been able to gather on the tiles, in the courtyard, and the garden. The shadow of her thoughts passed across her blinking eyes, and I could read there, quite as well as if she had spoken out with her voice, this summing up of her examination.

" Decidedly this strange creature cannot be a green fowl."

Arrived at this decision, the cat got down from the table where she had established her observatory, and went and crouched in a corner of the room, stomach on the ground, the elbows protruded, the head low, the spring of the spine extended —like a panther watching gazelles quench their thirst at a lake.

The parrot followed these movements with a feverish anxiety; he bristled his feathers, rattled his chain, lifted an agitated foot, and sharpened his beak on the edge of his feeding-tin. Instinct told him than an enemy was contemplating some kind of wickedness.

As for the eyes of the cat, fixed upon the bird with a fascinated intensity, they said, in a language which the parrot perfectly well understood, and which had nothing in the least uncertain about it: " Although green, the chicken ought to be good eating."

I followed this scene with interest, ready to interfere when occasion called. Madame Théophile had drawn nearer to the parrot; her pink nose quivered, she half-closed her eyes, opened and shut her claws. Little thrills ran up and down her spine ; like a greedy man sitting down before a delicious truffled pullet, she delighted

IMAGINATION · CHIVALRY · LEGENDS · GOLDEN DEEDS · FAIRY TALES

herself with the thought of the succulent and rare meal which she was about to make. This foreign dish, so new to her and yet so tempting, tickled her appetite.

Suddenly her back bent like a stretched bow, and one elastic jump took her to the foot of the perch. The parrot, realising his danger, with a voice low and solemn, said suddenly:

" Have you breakfasted, James? "

This phrase caused the cat an indescribable terror, and she sprang back. A flourish of trumpets, a smash of plates and dishes, a pistol fired at the ear, could not have given her a more frantic terror. All her ideas of birds were reversed. Her face expressed clearly the staggering thought that had suddenly come to her.

" This is not a bird; this is a gentleman. He speaks! " one imagined her saying.

Then the parrot began to sing, with a great shout in his voice, for he had realised that the fright caused by his speech was his best means of defence.

The cat threw toward me a hurried glance of interrogation, and, my reply not satisfying her, she buried herself under the bed, from which it was impossible to make her move an inch all the day long.

Next day, a little more courageous, Madame Théophile ventured to make another timid attack, but with the same fortune as had met her the last time.

From that moment she threw up the sponge, accepting the green bird as a man who must be treated with respect.

THE TALE A BABY TELLS

No Indian brave was so great a warrior, no medicine man was so strong an enchanter, as Glooskap.

He cleared the Earth of evil as a gardener clears a garden of weeds. When he had overthrown tyrannical chiefs, fierce animals, wizards, giants, goblins, and demons, he said he should soon sail away to some other world, and find more work that he could do.

When people heard that the mighty one was leaving them they flocked to his wigwam with requests.

One day four men came. The first was so poor that he hardly knew how to feed his children; he asked to be lucky with his crops and hunting. The second was of low estate; he asked that he might become honoured in the tribe. The third man wished to cure his violent temper. The fourth, who was dressed as carefully as a bride and had stuffed his moccasins to make himself look tall, asked that his height should surpass that of all others.

Glooskap gave each of them a little box of ointment, bidding them rub it on their bodies when they got home. This the first three faithfully did. In course of time the poor man became rich, the lowly man great, and the ill-tempered man gained perfect self-control.

But the fourth man could not wait; he anointed himself in the forest on his way home. No one ever saw him again. Next day a hunter was puzzled to see, in a clearing that had been empty last evening, a pine that surpassed all others in height.

Another day a woman came to see the wonderful Glooskap.

" Mighty sir," she said, " you are leaving the Earth, and yet there is one thing you have never conquered here."

" What is it? Where is it? " cried Glooskap, starting up.

" It is Wasis, my baby," the woman replied. " You can never force him to obey you; it would be useless to try."

Glooskap knew nothing of babies. He was a solitary warrior. He prepared at once to meet this strange monster.

The woman led him to her house, and there was the baby sucking its thumb.

Glooskap smiled to see how small it was, and laughed to think that such a helpless creature could be supposed to defy his all-powerful self.

He told the baby to come to him. Wasis began to play with his own toes.

Glooskap was amazed at this insolence. He repeated his order in tones of thunder, whereupon Wasis set up such a wail that the warrior was almost frightened. The more he threatened and commanded Wasis to be silent, the louder did the baby cry. Then he began to recite incantations and curses which would have made any adult drop dead from sheer terror. But Wasis simply continued his melancholy howls, till Glooskap could endure the noise no longer, and fled from the house.

Babies remember the victory to this day, and if we only had the wit to understand them they are trying to tell us about it when they crow " Goo, goo! "

SAINT GEORGE AND THE DRAGON

Saint George of Merry England was the youngest and the bravest of the seven champions of Christendom. Clad in bright armour, with his magic sword Ascalon by his side, he used to travel on his war-horse in far countries in search of adventures, and many were the perils he encountered.

One day, as he was riding across a marsh in the land of the pagans, he saw a noble and lovely maiden walking all alone toward the sea-shore.

She was dressed in beautiful robes, like a bride on her wedding-day, but her face was pale and sorrowful, and she stared in terror at the sea.

St. George rode quickly up to her. On hearing the sound of his horse's hoofs the girl turned and cried:

" Flee, young knight; flee, or you will perish also! "

" God forbid that I should flee when a maiden is in peril ! " said St. George.

As he spoke the sea in front of him began to rise up in great waves, and from the waves there came the sound of roaring. At the same time he heard a noise far behind him. He turned and saw that the walls of the city on the hills above the marsh were crowded with people, who were shrieking and wringing their hands.

" The dragon, the dragon! " cried the maiden. "Flee, or it will be upon you! "

The sound of roaring grew louder.

" Flesh and blood cannot withstand the burning flame that comes from its jaws," said the maiden. " It has destroyed two armies of soldiers; it has eaten up all our sheep and cattle, and laid waste my father's kingdom. Escape while you can, and do not risk your life by staying to defend me!

" Every year a young virgin comes to this marsh to be killed and eaten by the monster in order to prevent it from rushing upon the city and slaying all the people. I am Princess Sabra, the daughter of the king, and the lot has now fallen upon me. Oh, horror! You are too late! "

While Princess Sabra was speaking the sea had risen up in greater waves, and from the waves there came the sound of loud and angry roaring, which increased in volume every moment.

St. George had scarcely time to clutch his spear and lift up his shield before the dragon was upon him.

It was the most terrible monster ever seen on Earth. It was an enormous serpent with two great wings and four strong feet armed with cruel claws, and in its tail there was a long, poisonous sting.

It rushed through the air upon St. George, and a burning flame came from its jaws. With a sudden stroke of its wing it nearly felled him to the ground. But as it passed he gave it so fierce a thrust that his spear broke into a thousand pieces. Swinging back, the dragon again struck at him with its tail, and knocked him from his war-horse.

The fire of its breath made him faint and dizzy. He rose up, reeling like a dying man; but his strength returned in a marvellous way when he drew his magic sword Ascalon.

In trying to strike him once more the dragon exposed the tender part of its body beneath its wing, and there St. George wounded it. So deep was the wound that the dragon stood still and trembled. St. George then knelt down and prayed.

" Undo your sash and tie it about the dragon's neck. It will not harm you," he said to Princess Sabra.

The princess did so.

" Now lead it to the market-place in the city," he said.

The dragon followed the princess as meekly as a lamb.

When they reached the city all the people ran away; but St. George told them to have no fear, the dragon was now quite harmless, and with a blow of his magic sword Ascalon he killed the monster in the market-place.

" I did this," he said to the pagans, " to show to you the power of God, and to convert you to the true faith."

When the pagans learned that it was a Christian knight who had subdued the dragon and made it as meek as a lamb they gave up their false idols and became good Christians.

Princess Sabra was the first to be baptised, and it was not long before she was married to her true knight, the brave St. George of Merry England, who had saved her from such a terrible death.

THE BOY WHO MIGHT NOT GO WEST

In the woods of North America there lived an Indian boy and his grandmother. Whenever he went out to play she said to him: "Be sure to go to the East; never go West."

The boy grew up, and learned to use his bow and arrows. Every time he went hunting she said the same thing to him: " Never go West."

" Why may I not go West? " he asked. " Other boys go East or West as their heart or the chase leads them."

Still she would give him no reason, and only cried, " Never go West."

At last he plagued her into telling him the truth.

In the West there lived a mysterious being who had hated the boy's father and grandfather before him. If the boy fell into his power there would be no mercy. " And without you," said the old woman, " I should die of grief."

The boy thought to himself, " The worst enemy in the world shall not stay me from going where I please."

Next morning he got up while his grandmother slept and went westward. When he had been walking for some hours he came to a lake fringed with gloomy trees. He lay down to drink, and suddenly a great voice cried: " How dare you come West, you pygmy, you red doll! "

The boy could see no one anywhere.

" Go home and see what I shall do with your grandmother," called the voice from nowhere. " I will tear down her hut with a hurricane! "

" That will be a blessing," said the boy. " It will save me the trouble of going to fetch firewood."

The boy returned. As soon as he was out of sight of the lake he ran like a deer. As he drew near his grandmother's hut the leaves began to whistle with the hurricane's approach. He dragged the old woman out, and they crouched for shelter in a cave near by, while the tempest burst upon the forest, tearing up trees, and crushing their hut as if it were a handful of twigs.

" This is not fair fighting," said the boy.

Next morning he built his grandmother a new hut, and then he went East, to a man who practised magic in the hills. There, for a bearskin, and a handsome pipe, the boy bought a little pebble.

Once more he went West.

As he approached the lake a voice screamed: " What, have you dared to come back? I shall——"

Before it could finish its threats the boy called: " Come out and show yourself, and fight me."

" Do you think I will obey a snippet like you? " howled the voice. " I will send a forest fire to burn your grandmother to a cinder! "

Then the boy threw his pebble into the lake. Instantly the waters began to boil like a kettle. The boy snatched up his bow and kept a sharp watch.

He saw a great frog crawl out on the opposite bank. The next moment an arrow pierced the creature's body; it gave a shrill human cry, and then the voice in the lake was never heard again.

Thenceforward the youth and his grandmother lived in peace and prosperity, walking to all points of the compass at their own free will.

THE TIGER WOMAN OF THE JUNGLE

In Burma there are two races of people. One race lives in villages and tills the ground; the other race lives among wild beasts in the jungle on the hills.

One day a villager set out for the hills, where he found a beautiful hill woman, whom he led to his village and married. For a time they lived happily and had a little baby girl. But the baby died, and the villager began to neglect his wife.

Coming home very late one night he found his hut empty, and about it were the marks of a tigress' feet. He knew what had happened. His wife had changed into a tigress and gone back to the jungle.

All his deep love for her returned, and he set out again for the hills, taking with him the clothes of his dead baby. He followed the tracks of the tigress until he came to a cave, and there he saw the eyes of the wild beast blazing in the darkness.

He was not afraid. He put down the baby's clothes at the mouth of the cave, and the tigress leaped out upon him. But when she saw the clothes of her little dead girl her heart was melted. Instead of killing the villager she suddenly changed into a woman, flung her arms about his neck, and went back joyfully with him to their empty hut.

TOM THUMB

Not far from Fairyland lived a man and his wife who were often sad because they had no child.

They looked so gentle and kind-hearted that the wizard Merlin thought he would go and see if they really deserved to be happy. So one day he dressed himself in an old, ragged coat and knocked at their door.

"Come in," said the old woman. "Won't you sit down and rest a little? We are very poor, but I am preparing some bread and milk for my husband's dinner, and I will make you some, too."

"That is very kind of you," answered the old man, throwing off his cloak.

them he would never grow any bigger, so they gave him the name of Tom Thumb.

Tom was so small that his godmother had to call for the help of the other fairies to make him a suit of clothes.

They made him a shirt out of a cobweb, a coat of a beetle's wing, shoes of the skin of a mouse, and a cap out of an oak-tree leaf. When everything was ready Tom's godmother gave him a little magic sword, which she told him he must be sure always to wear.

Tom was a good boy, but he had one bad fault; he was very inquisitive. One day, when his mother was making a pudding, there came a knock at the door,

TOM TOLD HIS STORY TO THE KING

"I am the wizard Merlin, who can do all things, and because you have been generous and thoughtful for others I will make you a gift. You may choose what it shall be."

"Oh, please," cried the old woman, "we want a little child! Even if it were no bigger than my thumb we should be quite content."

"Very well," said the wizard, smiling; and he went away.

When the man and his wife woke up the next morning there lay beside them a little child, a boy, so tiny that he really was no bigger than his mother's thumb. When the fairy godmother came she told

and she went to see who was there. She was away so long that Tom began to wonder what was inside the bowl.

He got off his chair, which always stood on the table, and walked round and round the basin, wishing that he could see over the top. By the basin lay a fork.

"Hurrah!" cried Tom, seizing the fork. "This will make a capital ladder."

And he climbed up the prongs until he could reach the top of the basin. But even then he could hardly see in, for his head only just reached the top.

"I know," said he. "I'll jump."

Tom put both hands on the edge of the basin and jumped. He jumped once, but not quite high enough; he jumped again, but still he could not see. So he jumped a third time, and this time he jumped right into the basin.

At this moment his mother came back, and, taking up the big wooden spoon, was about to stir the pudding when she saw something moving in the basin. This so frightened her that she took up the basin and threw everything in it as far as she could out of the window.

Underneath the window flowed a river, and as Tom tumbled out headlong a big fish came swimming by. The fish opened his mouth, and in fell Tom.

The fish was caught, and it was so fine a fish that it was taken to the palace for the king's dinner. As the cook cut open the fish out jumped Tom upon the table. When the king heard of it he ordered Tom to be brought before him.

"Where do you come from, and what is your name?" asked the king.

Tom told his story, and the king was so pleased that he allowed Tom to stay with him and live in the palace.

It was all very splendid, and for a long time Tom enjoyed himself and was very happy. When the king went for a ride Tom went too, only, instead of a horse, Tom rode on the back of a rat.

As they were riding in the forest one day a big cat sprang out, and, pouncing on the rat and its rider, carried them off into a tree. Tom took out his magic sword, and after a brave fight he killed the cat. Then he turned and began to climb down the tree. But it was a long way for little Tom's legs, and he had not gone far when he felt his foot slipping.

Just then, however, the king missed Tom, and, looking round, he was just in time to catch him as he fell.

Tom had had such a fright that when he got back to the palace he felt quite ill, and had to go to bed. In the morning the king came to his bedside and found him very miserable.

"What is the matter with you?" asked the king.

"I want to go home!" sobbed Tom.

"Nonsense!" said the king. "You have everything you can ask for, and you ought to be very happy."

"I want my mother! Please let me go home!"

"Certainly not!" said the king. "You must stay till I am tired of you."

"Oh dear!" sighed Tom. "And when will that be?"

"I don't know," said the king. "I like you very much at present."

All that day Tom wondered how he could get away without being caught; but the more he wondered the more miserable he became.

He worried so that he became thin and ill, and at last his fairy godmother, thinking that he had been punished enough for his inquisitiveness, determined to help him. So she went to Tom's bedside, and Tom, jumping for joy, begged to be taken home.

The carriage was waiting on the window-sill. They got in, and away they sailed over the house-tops till they came to the cottage where Tom lived.

When they saw Tom again his parents cried for joy, and they all lived happily together for the rest of their lives.

THE KNIGHT AND THE WONDERFUL STONE

A BRAVE English knight in the Holy Land was captured by the Saracens and thrown into a dungeon to die. But a nightingale came and perched on the window of the dungeon and cheered the knight with her song; and the knight fed her with some of his scanty food and made a pet of her. He used to talk to her as if she were a human being, and one day he said: "Ah, sweet bird! If only you could help me to escape!"

The nightingale at once flew away, and as she did not return for three days the knight thought she had been killed by some hawk. But on the night of the third day she flew back to the dark dungeon once again, carrying in her beak a stone.

The knight took the stone, and by accident touched his fetters with it; to his astonishment and delight they fell off. He then went to the dungeon door, and touched that also with the magic stone, and the door opened.

The knight lost no time in leaving his prison, and he managed to escape to England, to which country the nightingale followed him. There the knight showed his gratitude to his little feathered friend by building her a golden cage, with an open door, in the garden of his castle.

Nature's Wonderful Living Family in Earth and Air and Sea

A Black Bear from the Rocky Mountains has a game with a Syrian Bear

THE BEARS AND THEIR COUSINS

Time brings great changes. When a naturalist from Rome visits us today we take him to our splendid London Zoo and show him bears of many lands. When his ancestors came here nearly 2000 years ago there was neither a London nor a Zoo, but there were many bears roaming about the land.

Droves of these British bears were captured, carried alive to the arenas of Rome, where they were cruelly baited to amuse the heartless mob. Bear-baiting was very popular in England in Queen Elizabeth's time. A captive bear was chained to a stake and fierce bulldogs set to attack it. In time, however, cultivated people became disgusted with the barbarities of the bear-garden and the famous diarist Evelyn, in 1670, called it "a rude and dirty pastime." It was abolished in 1835. Today, outside our Zoos, we have nothing of bears but their skins. But though Britain knows them no more they are a widespread family.

Before civilisation was fully established here famine often ravaged our land, and British bears increased existing distress by taking toll of British cattle and also of human life. It is not known when the last of our bears vanished. They saw the earliest Briton steal in from the sea to possess the land; they saw the Picts and Scots arrive; they were present when the Roman legions dashed through the surf with their eagles held high; they saw Saxon and Dane break in; and they certainly witnessed the Norman Conquest.

They hunted, and were hunted by, men who used stones as weapons, then bronze, then iron; and probably they went down finally before missiles in the discharge of which gunpowder was used.

We have only to cross into Europe today to find bears exactly like those whose hides had to be furnished as tribute each year to English kings, down to the time of Edward the Confessor. It is the same species, the brown, that we find in the Pyrenees, in Germany and Hungary, in the three Scandinavian countries, in Russia, right through Asia as far as Kamchatka in Eastern Siberia.

The brown bear is a lord of the wilds north of the Himalayas; it ranges the hills from Afghanistan to Nepal, has its place in the scheme of things in Sumatra, and is even found in the less inhabited parts of the Japanese islands. The Alaskan brown bear is a monster exceeding all bears in size, with the exception, perhaps, of the Polar species which are so familiar to us. This immense territory of a single

PREHISTORIC LIFE · MAMMALS · BIRDS · REPTILES · FISHES · INSECTS

species, differing here and there in local racial peculiarities, is a testimony to the excellence of the brown bear's natural equipment. Brain is not at its brightest in the skull of a bear, but there is sufficient of it to house much natural cunning. Sight is poor; but the sense of smell is perfect, a faculty which detects the presence of an enemy and leads unerringly to food.

THE BEAR THAT HAS THE ACTIVITY OF A STEEPLEJACK

On the physical side there are great strength and huge claws, which can strip the flank of an ox and climb a tree as a steeplejack climbs a spire. Added to this the bear has superb teeth, which can not only devour flesh, but roots, fibres—anything eatable—as the teeth of the great cats cannot. Fish, mouse, horse or honeycomb, are all equally acceptable to Bruin.

A further feature is that where we have a species of bear spreading from the far North away to warm latitudes, those in the frigid winter sleep through the cold, fasting, as still as a tortoise.

This does not apply to Polar bears but to other species, and it is a wonderful thing that so huge an animal should have this power of suspending life, as it were, and lie foodless and unconscious for months, like the chrysalis of a moth.

If man could do such a thing we should forthwith colonise Antarctica, sleep the winter away and spend the summer blasting ice to get at the gold and coal hidden beneath the frozen soil.

Why the Polar bears do not hibernate is a mystery. The males positively do not, for they can be seen all the winter, roaming hungry and grim down at the edge of the ice-field, where seals may be caught, and where dead whales and sharks lie stranded, awaiting the great scavenger.

Unless attacked or rendered fierce by hunger, it rarely attacks man, but Eskimos are often met who have been clawed by coming to close quarters with it. Such a programme accounts for the activities of the male Polar bear in winter.

DEVOTION OF THE MOTHER BEAR TOWARD HER LITTLE ONES

The case of the female is different. As winter approaches she begins a pilgrimage of devotion through the icy night. She marches inland and buries herself in deep snow, and never moves from hiding till spring and the Sun return. Then she goes out to meet her lord—but not alone. She takes with her her new cub, or two cubs, born during the months of seclusion.

Baby bears are not like spiders which voluntarily pass long spells without food. No; baby bears need constant food, and their mother's milk is the only source in that little white home in the North.

If the mother hibernated all bodily operations would practically cease. Hibernation is an absolute trance, the nearest approach to death that flesh and blood can sustain. A bear in a deep trance could not suckle her babies. Therefore we are compelled to believe that this devoted mother lies in her snowy pit all the long winter fasting, dozing perhaps, yet ever alert to the needs of her little ones.

There is nothing in life to equal this sacrifice; yet if we note the passionate eagerness with which a common hen broods her eggs in darkness for three long weeks we can understand the instinct, if not the ability, of a conscious creature so long to abstain from food while exhausting herself for the nourishment of her young. Motherhood, with its selfless love, is the supreme marvel of all the instinctive emotions, and the most beautiful.

THE VALOUR OF THE MOTHER BEAR IN FIGHTING FOR HER OFFSPRING

Bears have long been hunted by man. For not only do the hunters relish bear steak—which in the case of a Polar bear tastes like something between pork and beef—but Bruin's thick coat is a very valuable article of commerce. When the hunter meets the bear nowadays it is claws and teeth against the rifle and the expanding bullet, and only in the hundredth case does the artificial weapon fail before the natural weapon.

In such contests the mother bear, striving for the safety of her cubs, is a model of quick and anxious genius and pathetic valour. In one case, although wounded, the mother urged and drove her two cubs before her, and when they lagged she gave each a mighty thrust with her paw, sending them gliding fast ahead. They understood her plan, ran as hard as they could until she overtook them, placed themselves in position for another push, and so, between their own efforts and hers, escaped.

For sheer pathos, however, turn to an adventure of the crew of Captain Phipps' ship and the mother bear and two cubs which approached the fire lighted on the

PORTRAITS OF THE BEAR FAMILY

THE BLACK BEAR   THE HIMALAYAN BEAR

THE SPECTACLED BEAR ROAMING THE ANDES IN SOUTH AMERICA

THE SKUNK

THE KINKAJOU

THE RING-TAILED COATI

THE POLAR BEAR

COMMON RACCOON

THE WEASEL ON THE PROWL

THE FERRET LIES IN WAIT

THE SLOTH BEAR TAKES A STROLL

THE GRIZZLY BEAR THINKS IT OVER

THE GLUTTON
OR WOLVERINE

THE SEA-OTTER

THE LITTLE SKUNK

THE RUSSIAN BEAR ASKS FOR MORE

THE STOAT OR
ERMINE

THE RATEL

THE BEECH MARTEN

THE BADGER ON THE ALERT

THE POLECAT LOOKS SURPRISED

THE ISABELLINE BEAR OF INDIA

THE GREAT PANDA OF N.W. CHINA AND TIBET

THE AMERICAN BADGER

THE TAYRA

THE MALAYA BEAR

THE SLOTH BEAR

THE ZORILLE

THE PANDA

THE PINE MARTEN

THE OTTER

These photographs are by Miss Frances Pitt, Messrs. F. W. Bond, W. S. Berridge, and C. Reid, and the American Museum of Natural History

ice to burn blubber. The men retreated as the ravenous animals came up, and let them draw pieces of blubber from the fire, then two shots stretched the cubs dying on the snow, and the third mortally wounded the mother.

Only just able to crawl to where they lay, the mother carried each a piece of flesh, then perceiving that they could not eat, tried to raise them with her feeble paws, crawled a little way ahead, and with mournful cries sought to incite them to follow her out of danger.

THE PATHETIC STRUGGLE OF THE BEAR FOR LIFE

She returned, licked their wounds, and again endeavoured to lure them to rise and follow. Once more she went back and, though her own life was waning fast, she pawed her little ones with incredible tenderness. Slowly it dawned upon her dim mind that her babes were dead and that the sailors were the cause.

She raised her head, they say, and growled at them, to receive in return a merciful volley of shot, when she fell to rise no more, dying in the act of licking the wounds by which the lives of the cubs had ebbed.

" It would have drawn tears from any eyes to see it all " was the comment of those hard-pressed adventurers, and we can believe it.

The remoteness and rigours of their dismal domain, their majestic size—they are nine feet long and weigh as much as twelve men—render

The white bears all in a dim blue world
    Mumbling their meals by twilight,

the most fascinating of all the tribe. One has seen over 60 of them perform together in a modern arena, and very dull and depressing it was to witness the melancholy inertia of such superb creatures.

HOW THE BEAR HOLDS ON WITH HIS CLAWS IN A FIGHT

But in the wilds they are impressive in the extreme. The hairs on their enormous flat feet are a wonderful asset in enabling them to grip the ice, and they lumber along in an inelegant gallop which runs down the swiftest man that ever fled for his life. Their very gait seems to harmonise with the rude horror of their surroundings.

So does another masterly form of approach which Polar bears alone have acquired, because they alone need it. It is a gliding sprawl, effected by the bear lying flat with its four limbs outspread and kicking itself along with its hind paws. This method distributes its weight, and allows it to cross thin ice which it would shatter were that weight applied only at four points by a bear's feet.

No bear hugs. That is a fable. What they do is to strike, and then endeavour to hold with their claws while they bite. There is not much hope for the unarmed man in such an encounter.

One bear had a desperate fight with a fine Bengal tiger in a menagerie at Edinburgh a few years ago, and though Bruin was frightfully lacerated it was the tiger that died, with three ribs broken, and bitten through and through the throat before the end came.

Not many such encounters occur in the wilds, for the weaker there can fight and run away. In a confined space, however, even play may lead to disaster. All animal play is mimic battle, and one such game began one morning at the London Zoo between a big brown bear and one of a smaller species.

The little fellow dealt a few shrewd nips, and then the big bear became enraged, seized the other by the throat, and, partly by biting and partly by holding it down in the water, killed it. Then it dragged it off to its den and began to eat it.

THE GRIZZLY BEAR WITH ITS FIERCE AND APPALLING TEMPER

We have noted that there are several local races of the far-spread brown bear, so must remember that the famous grizzly bear, formerly included in the group, is now marked off as a separate species. Its name covers two meanings. It describes its more or less grey " grizzled " coat, and its grisly or fierce and appalling temper when disturbed.

In Alaska the grizzly is believed to have branched out into two species, monsters both. In the Hudson Bay district there is the smaller variety known as the Barren Ground grizzly; but the common grizzly spreads terror throughout the Rocky Mountain range. Some of these brutes weigh half a ton!

It is thought that a big Central Asian bear is a true grizzly; and names would suggest that the American black bear and the black bear of the Himalayas are of the same species. They are not; the Himalayan bear can always be distinguished by the white inverted crescent on its breast which the American lacks.

Similarly, the so-called blue bears of Tibet and of British Columbia are distinct. The spectacled bear of the Andes, so named from the tawny spectacle-like rings round its eyes, is black, but not a black bear by title. Nor does the curiously white-patched, white-muzzled black-bodied Bruang or Malay bear come into those known as the black species.

The most interesting of less familiar bears is the sloth bear of India. Like the Himalayan black animal it has the white chevron on the chest, but its snout is a dingy grey. Its hair is excessively long and coarse, and its weight does not exceed 350 pounds. Its habits are quite without parallel in the animal world.

HOW THE SLOTH BEAR OF INDIA GETS A DINNER

Like other bears it will kill and eat anything; it will take honey and vegetation, and it is also a great ant-hunter—especially of the strongly-fortified termites. With its powerful great claws it rips the side out of such a fortress. Then " it huffs and it puffs " till it blows the dust away inside, draws in mighty breaths, and in so doing draws the insects and their grubs into its mouth. That is a unique manner of getting a dinner, and the sloth bear has profited mightily by its invention.

We must pass from the bears to their nearest kin, the raccoons. The living bridge leading to this family is the panda group, two genera, each of a single species.

The great panda of North-Western China and Tibet is marvellously bear-like, but its cousin, the long-tailed panda, with its long slim body, its bushy tail, its claws which can be moved a little in and out of their sheaths, suggests an animal as to which Nature has two minds.

She began a bear and left the creature almost a cat, so that men call this common panda the cat-bear—a very helpful description.

The raccoons are an American creation. Broad-headed, with a fox-like snout, with fine climbing feet, thick fur, handsome ringed tail, an appetite for anything, not excepting freshwater tortoises and cray-fish. The coons are shy, tree-haunting creatures, which sometimes leave the woods to call on a poultry farm. After such a visit the farmer has need of a new stock of birds for his pen.

The nearest ally to the coon is the cacomistle. It is cat-sized and almost entirely a flesh-eater. Next comes the bassaricyons of Central America; the coatis, with such fantastic long snouts that they are called proboscis-bears; and finally the kinkajous of the same great land, with tails which cling, with an expression like a lemur, and an amiable nature which admits of their being readily tamed.

THE ANIMALS THAT ARE HUNTED FOR THEIR VALUABLE FUR

Following established practice we must, for the sake of convenience, class the weasel family among cousins of the bears. That has always been done, but recent discoveries suggest that the group really developed from the same branch as the civets. It is an important family, including the weasels, the badgers, and others. So valuable is the fur of some of the species that pursuit has led to almost as much exploration as unknown lands of gold.

First come the tayra and grison of tropical and South America, and in the case of the grison, Mexico as well. The larger of the two, the tayra, sometimes hunts in little packs in wood and on plain; the grison might be a stoat from its habits, especially where poultry bring dinner to its mind.

Martens are known to us in Britain from the presence of that bloodthirsty little beauty, the pine marten. At home in the forsaken nest of a crow, it descends at night to rob a roost, or to slaughter half the lambs penned in a fold. But pine martens are rare enemies to rats and mice. The beech marten does not come so far west as its fellows, but it ranges away from Central Europe and Italy far into Asia, and, though eager for blood, has such a passion for fruits that tree-trunks in its neighbourhood have to be spread over with some offensive fluid.

THE FERRET SHOWS ITS VARYING TEMPERAMENT AND ITS TEETH

The extreme richness of its splendid fur makes the sable the most famous of all the marten group. Eastern Siberia and Kamchatka are its last strongholds, and there rodents, fish, and berries are the materials out of which the precious fur that wraps a lithe and nimble form is developed. Largest of all the martens is the fisher marten, whose name indicates its favourite food, yet snakes and even the prickly porcupine serve to stay its healthy appetite.

Shorter in the leg, longer in the body, and smelling abominably, the polecats are widely distributed, and in England have given us a species for domestication in the ferret, a rare ratter and rabbiter which has helped man to make domestic history.

Ferrets are of varying temperaments. In the writer's own family many have been fondled like white rats; and there was one which, having been lost, came home in the possession of a person who shouted hysterically, " I've got Charlie! " And he had—with Charlie's teeth fastened through his thumb!

We also remember the Maidstone rat-catcher whose ferret jumped at his face, seized him by the tip of the tongue, and held there till killed.   Ferrets are ferrets!

The minks are in Europe, America, and Asia, while the weasel proper is all over Europe, Central Asia, and North America. It has a body length up to eight inches and a tail of two inches or a little more.   The stoat, turning white during winter in its northerly range, is then called the ermine, and furnishes the Crown, the Law, and fashion with its beautiful fur. It is stouter and stronger than the weasel, measuring up to eleven inches, with a tail up to five inches.

THE AMAZING SKILL OF THE POWERFUL WOLVERINE

Big as he is, with powerful claws and teeth as potent as a small hyena's, the glutton or wolverine, found in the north of the New World and the Old, is a weasel. Trappers who cannot catch him, but whose beaver-snares he robs with amazing skill, call him names which are not his nor deserve to be.   He is a greedy genius.

Ratels follow.   These are badger-like animals confined to India and Africa. Their love for the product of the bee gives them the name of honey-badger.   As pets they have the startling habit of throwing the nimblest somersaults, revealing a latent talent for acrobatics which would make their fortune in a jungle gymnasium.

The most impressive weasel, in an offensive sense, is the skunk.   It has the power of offending men and animals by the overpowering foulness of a fluid which certain glands enable it to squirt out. Even the boldest-hearted hunting dog will howl and lie down, or run away and hide, if set to face this unsavoury beast.

Cape polecats, or zorilles, employed as friends in Boer households, where they are called mouse-dogs, link the skunk with ferret-like curiosities whose outlines also suggest little badgers ; and they in turn provide the link associating badgers with the rest of the group.

Our badger is a grand, courageous Briton, ancient, honest, inoffensive; so powerful of jaw that he can eat anything that contains nourishment, so sturdy a digger that he builds himself a subterranean fort-city.   He takes an occasional bird, but think of the rats and mice and food-destroying rabbits that he eats !

THE OLD BADGER THAT DECKED ITS HOME WITH BLUEBELLS

One badger which was suspected of poaching rare water-birds at Kew was tracked to his lair.   The gallery leading to it was like a giant's charnel house, white with dead birds' bones.   But the old badger was an artist—his home was all decked with bluebells ! The trackers caught him, but, fine to relate, he was released, far out in the country, where food abounds, but where water-fowl are sufficiently cautious to keep away.

Half a dozen species of badgers repay study in various parts of the world; but our last word is for the otter, the splendid creature which miscalled sport seeks with hounds and with spears in the hands of a multitude to exterminate from our rivers.   Their brilliant swimming and tunnelling, their fine teeth which grip fishes that elude fingers, their extensive travels when food or water fails, make otters very efficient in the struggle for life, and they are at home wherever the dog tribe is found.

Of nearly a dozen species the sea-otter is the most famous, partly because its fur is so luxurious, partly because a craze for that fur has caused men to hunt it almost out of existence.

TWO FIGHTING OTTERS THAT PUT A MAN TO FLIGHT

But our own delightful otter is supreme in our affections.   How is it possible not to like an animal which constructs slides on a steep river bank and toboggans down them like a laughing child ?

The much-hunted otter is a warrior at will.   Two of them put to flight a man who attacked them with a pitchfork, and another killed and ate an impertinent ferret which sought to drink its blood.   Brer Bear could not have been more judicial, more fitly final.

THE BEAUTY OF A LOST CIVILISATION

THE FIGURE THAT HAS STOOD NEARLY 5000 YEARS IN THE RUINS OF A TEMPLE IN CRETE

A KING'S DRAUGHTBOARD FROM OLD CRETE ON WHICH A KING PLAYED PERHAPS 4000 YEARS AGO

The upper photograph is by Messrs. Boissonnas et Cie., Geneva, the lower picture is reproduced by courtesy of Sir Arthur Evans from his book "The Palace of Minos at Knossos."

The March of Man from the Age of Barbarism to the United Nations

Vases buried at Crete for thousands of years

A CIVILISATION WIPED OUT

IF men were not very slow to learn the lessons of history, there is a little island in the Aegean Sea which might have saved the world from many calamities and dreadful disasters long before Jesus was born in Bethlehem.

This island is called Crete, the scene of a heroic defence by our soldiers in 1941, but 2500 years before Christ it was a land of lasting peace.

It was a country inhabited by men and women who had no fear of war. It was an island of peace. In the midst of a savage and barbarous world, engaged century after century in killing, burning, destroying, and enslaving, this little island shone upon the waters of the Aegean like an oasis in the desert. No war meant peace, and peace meant civilisation.

Men had only to look at Crete to see the open road to happiness; but they turned their eyes away from that suburb of Paradise, and, taking axe and torch in their hands, set their gaze eagerly toward the battlefield.

We should be wiser. Look at Crete, and learn one of the greatest lessons which history has to teach. It is now not quite two thousand years since the birth of Jesus. Carry your mind back to that marvellous moment in the destinies of the human race, pause there awhile, and then go on, backward and backward, backward for a

thousand years, backward for another thousand years, and then backward still into the savage past of humanity for half a thousand years more—carry your mind back as far as that, a journey of nearly forty-five centuries, and then see what the human mind can do when it has peace.

As long ago as that, 4500 years before our time, the Cretans had a great city called Knossos, and many other cities as well, all unfortified—for they feared no enemies—and all devoted to the joys of existence. One of the most striking facts to be learned from Knossos is this: that as soon as the mind is delivered from the fear of starvation or war it turns to the creation of beautiful things.

We are inclined to believe that love of beauty is something we learn after centuries of brutality or arduous work, something rather unnatural or artificial to which we climb with difficulty; or we think it is a mark of cultured people, setting them apart from and high above the common people. But this is a false belief.

Born in us, born in the darkest savage, is an instinct for beauty, an apprehension of the great difference which exists by natural law between what is lovely and what is hideous. The savage sticks feathers in his hair, and however comical or ugly we may deem some of his decorations to be all of them, in his eyes, are

MIGHTY EPOCHS OF THE WORLD & MAN'S WONDERFUL ADVENTURES

beautiful, that is to say, are things which create admiration. Very early in man's history there was an effort toward decoration, and we may well believe that one of the first movements in the minds of the first human beings who ever breathed on this planet was a feeling of admiration for sunrise and sunset, for the Moon, the stars, for the sea, and the flight of birds, for the glow of flowers, and the sound of the wind as it passed through the trees.

THE CRETANS WHO STUDIED THE BEAUTY AND NOBILITY OF LIFE

But Knossos takes us much farther than admiration of beauty or wonder at the glory of Creation. The people who lived there felt within themselves the godlike instinct of creation. They did not merely say, " How beautiful !" or "How wonderful !" but, "Let us make beautiful things; let us do wonderful things." Their minds, freed from the fear of want and war, turned instantly to creative work.

Life at once appeared to them as the opportunity for doing lovely and noble things. They had time on their hands, and what could they do with time but turn it to the happiness of human life?

Do not think that these Cretans were different from other men. Do not say that they made lovely things because they were specially gifted. There were Cretans who did not live in Crete and who were wholly different from the peaceful islander. From these Cretans of the mainland came, strangely enough, the name of Palestine, for the Israelites called these fighters Philistines, from which word the name Palestine comes. It was because they were always at war that these Cretans of the Syrian mainland were barbarous, and it was because the island Cretans were free from the horrors of war that they could turn their minds to higher things.

WHERE THE PEOPLE FIRST DREAMED OF FLYING

The consequence was that they built a great city, beautiful in design, curious in character, and crowded with inventions. They made a labyrinth, and they built bathrooms. They had wonderful gardens, and water-pipes running under the ground. They had gymnasiums, and every kind of pots and pans we can think of. Their women wore clothes very like the clothes women wear in our own day, and their young men were as keen on athletics as the young men of modern England. Hair-pins like those of today were worn in those far-off days, and many of the handsome vases found in Egypt are now known to be the work of these Cretans.

But something more; there seems to be evidence for the belief that the Cretans were the first people in the world to dream of flying, and that their mechanical skill turned itself, many centuries before the birth of Christ, to the conquest of the air. The legend of Daedalus and his wings comes from Crete.

How great would have been the progress of the world, how very different the state of our knowledge today, if the Cretans had pushed forward along this road of mechanical invention and artistic creation! But, alas, they lacked one thing without which even the blessing of peace may turn to a nation's destruction. They were without the inspiration of a moral ideal.

We may see at once the conditions of their minds when we know that one of their favourite sports was bull-fighting. The inclination toward cruelty is found in all savage people, and is born of fear, the fear of ferocious animals and tyrannical enemies; but security and education ought to tame this dreadful instinct, and we feel that there must have been something bad in Cretan nature for its persistence so late in their civilisation.

THE WRECK OF THE SPLENDOUR OF CRETAN CIVILISATION

Perhaps they thought little of it, and perhaps their politicians would have laughed at everyone who said that such a flaw in the Cretan character would wreck the whole splendours of Cretan civilisation. But such was actually the case. This one sin against the moral law plunged Crete into the abyss of desolation.

To be cruel toward animals is to be cruel toward men, and the Cretans saw no harm in making marauding expeditions into other lands for the purpose of taking slaves. Many a little home in Greece was raided by these ruthless Cretans; many a father and mother was broken-hearted at the awful sight of sons and daughters carried into slavery. Often these humble Greeks must have gnashed their teeth and vowed terrible vengeance against the grand islanders of Crete; and one day the hour struck, and all the glory that was Crete was swept off the face of the Earth by lowly peasants destined to raise up a glory far higher and more lasting, the glory that was Greece.

But, before the moral law was thus terribly vindicated, the Cretans flourished in a prosperity unknown among other peoples. The climate lent itself to luxurious agricultural production. The surrounding sea tempted fishermen far away from the island shores and encouraged shipbuilding. The peace and prosperity of their political life inspired each generation of sculptors and painters, craftsmen and engineers, to surpass the achievements of their ancestors.

THE LONG REIGN OF PEACE IS ENDED BY THE SCOURGE OF WAR

There was soon so much wealth in this island that the Cretans were able to carry a part of it across the sea to other lands. The wonder of their workmanship, and the number of their ships, excited not only admiration, but envy, among Greeks, Egyptians, and Phoenicians. Perhaps the Cretans bore away from every shore to which their sails carried them youths and maidens to be slaves, as they certainly did in the case of Greece. But, however that may be, envy presently joined hands with hatred, and one day a fleet appeared off the coasts of Crete, not laden with merchandise, but filled with fighting men.

The long peace was ended. The scourge of war, destroying all that was evil in Crete, destroyed also all that was good. A civilisation as wonderful as any so far seen in the world was burnt out of existence, like a gorse-bush; was wiped off the face of the Earth like a sum on a slate.

The earth, as if it would make itself the grave of that noble effort of the human mind, closed over the city of Knossos, and hid it from the sight of men for three thousand years. All that Crete might have taught mankind was hidden from knowledge. It simply vanished. History went forward as if there had never been a city of Knossos, and civilisation fell into a thousand blunders which any Cretan beggar boy might have told its statesmen would assuredly bring ruin and death.

A MIGHTY CIVILISATION THAT HAD A TRAGIC ENDING

On this journey of ours from the far past to the present, we shall see more than once that a mighty civilisation can vanish from the face of the Earth, and remain for centuries as if it had never been. This is one of the most curious facts in the progress of mankind.

We should all say that a mighty civilisation would at least leave something of itself to help and inspire succeeding ages, that it could not possibly fade into nothingness, like a phantom, like a mirage, like a mere shadow. But we should be wrong. Behind civilisation there is something which hates it, something always creeping up behind it with the dagger of the assassin; something which loves the works of darkness; something which does not wish to press manfully forward, but longs to sink back into barbarism, torpor, and chaos. Let the opportunity occur, and the most towering civilisation may fall like a pack of cards to this enemy of man's soul, and be lost to the world.

Such was the fate of Crete. Such, for a long period, was the fate of Greece. Such was the fate of Rome. A candle was blown out, and the Earth plunged into darkness. It is a tragic tale, and a dreary chronicle, and yet no tale in the whole world is so impressive or inspiring.

PEACE AND MORAL ENTHUSIASM IN THE PROGRESS OF THE WORLD

For if evil can pull down the towers of knowledge, and bring the golden palaces of prosperity to the dust, goodness can yet keep its candle burning in all the tempests of calamity, and show a light, however dim and wavering, to those whose souls can never rest in darkness.

If Crete had loved mercy, if Greece had loved honour, if Rome had loved simplicity, and if the so-called Christian Empire had truly loved its Master, the world would now be thousands of years ahead of its present tragic plight.

History teaches us, if we have the ears to hear, first, that peace is essential to civilisation; and, secondly, that without moral enthusiasm no civilisation can endure.

Look back on Crete. Does it not strike us, after all, as something splendid and uplifting that Life should sweep away all the grandeur of that marvellous civilisation with a gesture of contempt, and an utter carelessness as to how long its relics should remain buried under the Earth, because the only civilisation Life is seeking is the civilisation of man's soul?

To the universe our palaces and spreading cities are nothing more than so many sand castles, so many molehills; what it requires of us is a humble spirit in love with the Divine.

THE WOOL ARRIVES FROM ACROSS THE WORLD

THE BUSY SCENE AT A SOUTH AFRICAN DOCK AS BALES OF WOOL WHICH CAME FROM AUSTRALIAN
SHEEP HALFWAY ACROSS THE WORLD ARE UNLOADED ON THE QUAY

The Story of the Things We See About us Every Day

Merinos on an Australian sheep station being brought in for shearing

WOOL AND ITS STORY

WHEN we see a picture of a savage clothed in a leopard skin, or of an English lady wearing a sable coat, we quite understand that both these people, so far removed in character and country, are clothed in the coats of animals ; but when we put on our ordinary clothes in the morning do we remember that we also are putting on an animal's coat?

Our outer clothes and often our inner ones are made of wool, and wool is a product of the sheep. Though we can imitate its appearance we cannot find a real substitute for it.

It is estimated that there are about 500 million domesticated sheep in the world, and all these are producing wool that is taken from them once a year and woven into cloth to keep us warm. This involves no cruelty to the sheep, for it is the same thing for the animal as hair-cutting is for us.

As man, by careful selection and breeding, has produced hens that lay several hundred eggs a year in place of the few laid by the original jungle fowl of India from which our hens are descended, so he has carefully selected sheep with the best coats and has gradually produced a race of animals that now yield on an average twice as much wool as sheep yielded little more than half a century ago.

That is a great triumph of scientific stock-breeding, and means not only that we get more and better wool, but that wool is made cheaper, because when the quantity of anything is greatly increased its price always falls.

All sheep do not yield the same quality of wool, and even the same kind of sheep will produce better wool in one country than in another. The difference is caused by climate and soil. Sheep reared in Australia produce a finer wool than the same kind of sheep brought up in England.

Australian wool is now among the finest in the world, and there is a great demand for it. Australia possesses more sheep than any other country, and she produces a thousand million pounds of wool in a year, or about a quarter of the entire world output. The United States and Argentina and Uruguay are other large wool producers. In quantity and quality however Australia is easily the first wool-producing country.

How long the sheep's wool has been woven into fabric we cannot tell, but the practice is very old. Though the ancient Egyptians as a race did not wear woollen

INDUSTRIES · HOW THINGS ARE MADE · WHERE THEY COME FROM

garments, because their climate was warm, we know that some of them did wear wool. As far back as history goes, and still farther, the production of wool has been a great industry, for almost from the beginning men have kept large flocks of sheep as part of their wealth. Virgil, the Roman poet, knew all about the ins and outs of sheep-farming, and his descriptions of the work of the shepherd might almost have been written today about the big sheep stations of Australia.

THE DAYS WHEN SHEEP FARMING WAS ENGLAND'S CHIEF INDUSTRY

England's prosperity in the Middle Ages was largely built up on wool, as sheep farming was the principal national industry. English sheep produced fine wool that was exported to the Continent and there woven into cloth, chiefly by the skilled weavers of Flanders.

Later, Flemish weavers came to England and the woollen manufacture grew up here, encouraged and protected by our kings as a source of revenue. Edward the Third, for instance, prohibited the export of wool from England, and he also forbade the importation of fine woollen cloths from Flanders, his purposes being to deprive foreign competitors of their raw material, and to encourage the English weavers to produce the better and finer kinds of cloths they had before neglected.

After a time the weaving industry became very important, and the splendid parish churches of East Anglia, almost like cathedrals, are a testimony to the wealth and prosperity of that part of England, which was the first seat of the woollen industry.

Now, another Britain across the seas—Australia—is the great wool producer of the world, and it has become in reality what Colchis, corresponding roughly to the modern Georgia, was in ancient fable, the Land of the Golden Fleece.

THE DIFFERENCE BETWEEN WOOLLEN CLOTH AND WORSTED

Wool is woven into two distinct kinds of cloth, one called woollen cloth, and the other worsted. The difference is due to the way the thread or yarn is prepared. Each has its advantages. The woollen cloth is closer in texture and warmer, and worsted is finer and more handsome in appearance. In worsted manufacture the three operations of combing, spinning, and weaving are carried on in different factories, whereas in woollen manufacture there is no combing, and the spinning and weaving are both carried out in the same factory.

There are now many hundreds of woollen factories in England employing more than a quarter of a million people, but the very first factory was started by the Romans, at Winchester, in the year 80, for the making of warm garments for their soldiers, who found the changeable and damp climate of Britain very different from the warm and genial climate of their sunny native land.

The question is sometimes asked why a woollen garment keeps us warm when a cotton or a linen one does not. There is always a great deal of air between the hairs or wool-strands on an animal's back, and the fluffier the wool is the more air is held by it. Heat finds it very difficult to get across a layer of air, because air is a bad conductor, and so whether the wool which holds a layer of air is on the animal's back or on our back in the form of clothes, it keeps the body warm by the way it prevents the heat from passing off into the atmosphere.

WHY THE MERCHANT COVERS HIS ICE WITH A THICK BLANKET

As a matter of fact a woollen garment will keep us cool in summer as well as warm in winter, for just as it prevents the heat of the body passing out, it prevents the heat of the Sun and air passing in. That is why the ice merchant sends his ice through the streets covered with a thick blanket. He thus saves it from being melted by the Sun.

It is not sufficient, however, that a material should prevent heat passing through it—rubber would do that—but it must be porous so that the outside air and the inside air can mingle to some extent. In this way the perspiration produced when we exert ourselves at work or play evaporates slowly.

In a changeable climate like that of the British Isles, it is important we should wear wool next to our bodies to save us from the sudden chills that are so harmful to health. Let us remember, many of us owe our health and our lives to the sheep that supply us with wool, the best substance ever found for making clothes for human beings.

PICTURE-STORY OF HOW WE GET WOOL

Sheep suffer from a skin disease known as scab, and, to keep the animals healthy, the State insists that all sheep shall be disinfected twice a year with a germ-killing liquid known as " dip."

There are two ways of dipping sheep. The picture at the top shows the older method : completely immersing the animals in a race, or trough, filled with liquid. But spraying, as seen here, has now largely superseded ducking.

25 c 2

SHEARING THE WOOL FROM THE SHEEP

Each sheep yields about ten pounds of wool a year. Here we see lambs being separated from ewes before shearing begins. The sheep are graded before being shorn, coloured chalk marks on the nose indicating the classification.

The men who cut the wool from the sheep's backs use mechanical shears. Shearing by hand is practised only on very small sheep stations, for mechanical shearing is not only quicker but it cuts the wool far more closely.

SORTING THE WOOL FOR THE MARKET

When the wool is sorted it is arranged on tables in a sale room, each lot being marked in readiness for the auctioneer. The buyers inspect the wool, and then the sale begins. In this picture the wool is shown spread out before the sale.

Here is a scene at a wool sale in Sydney, Australia. Buyers from all over the world gather together to bid for the fine wool of the merino sheep. As much as £500,000,000 has been realised by the sale of one year's wool.

SENDING THE WOOL TO THE SHIPS

A MOTOR LORRY AND TRAILER LOADED WITH 30,000 POUNDS OF VALUABLE WOOL

A FLAT TRUCK WITH BALES OF WOOL ON A SIDING IN SOUTH AUSTRALIA

BALES BEING TAKEN ABOARD A SHIP IN AN AUSTRALIAN PORT

All the wool that is in excess of Australia's own needs is shipped to England and other countries, and to get it to the ports where it is placed on board the liners it is baled and often carried for long distances by road or by rail.

PREPARING THE WOOL FOR SPINNING

When the wool arrives at an English mill, sorting is the first process in the making of wool cloth. Every sheep grows wool of different qualities on different parts of its body, and the wool sorter examines each fleece and separates the various qualities or sorts. To enable him to sort the wool properly he must work in a good light.

Next the wool is scoured with hot, soapy water to remove grease and dirt. The wool feeds in little by little over the escalator band, and is pushed through the tanks by the rows of forks.

This is the carding engine, a series of rollers set with bent wire pins. As the wool passes over and under these rollers the fibres are teased and opened, and all felted lumps are promptly removed.

COMBING AND DRAWING THE WOOLLEN FIBRES

Now comes the division between the woollen and worsted branches of the industry. Before being spun into a worsted yarn, the wool is combed to separate the long fibres (or tops) from the short fibres (or noil). This picture of the Noble Comb shows the wool being fed into the teeth of the comb. It is pressed home by the dabbing brush ; then some of the long fibres are drawn off by the teeth of the inside circle. The sliver of " top " is shown on the left.

After the combing process the slivers of wool pass through machines such as this, which is one of a series of "drawing boxes," and at each stage they are gradually made thinner and thinner. The picture shows three slivers being drawn out to form one thin final " roving." The roving passes forward to the spinning frame.

SPINNING THE RAW WOOL INTO YARN

When the sliver is sufficiently drawn out, it is spun. This is a cap spinning frame. The bobbins rise and fall inside the caps, which distribute the yarn evenly, as it winds on. Wheels have been removed to show the roving passing through.

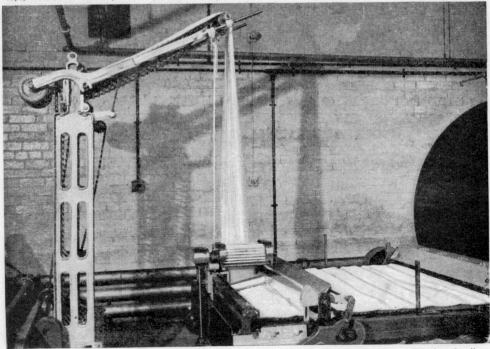

To make the woollen yarn, the sliver from the first card is run through a second set of card rollers. This time the sliver is fed on to the second half of the card at right-angles to the wool flow, to give a criss-cross distribution of fibres.

THE WOOL IS READY FOR THE WEAVER

As the wool comes off the second card it is divided into narrow strips, and reeled on to long bobbins.

These bobbins are placed in the mule spinning frame, which draws and twists the slubbings into yarn.

Woven cloth has warp and weft. The warp runs lengthways through the piece, the weft crosses the width. This man is building the warp on a warping mill. The threads must be arranged very carefully according to the required design.

WEAVING THE SPUN WOOL INTO CLOTH

This is the loom which weaves the cloth. The wooden frames which hang from the overhead bar are the healds. They raise and lower different series of warp threads, making a shed for the shuttle to pass through. The shuttle carries the weft.

The woven piece is now scoured with soap and water to remove all traces of the oil which is used during manufacture. Hard rubbing must be avoided.

Then it is dyed. The pieces run through the dyestuff in an endless rope, sometimes for many hours until they take the shade the dyer wants. With care, level dyeing results.

RAISING THE NAP AND CROPPING THE CLOTH

This is a teasel gig, in which actual teasels are used. They brush up the surface to give a " fuzzy " finish to woollen cloth and raise the fibres to make a fluffy blanket. The teasel gig is used in the West of England.

The cropping machine, with spiral blades something like a lawn mower, shears away the surface fibres, making the cloth smooth. The revolving blades must be carefully set, to avoid damaging the cloth which is continuously passing beneath it. The guard has been lifted and the fluffy fibre can be seen on the blade.

THE CLOTH IS READY FOR US ALL

Here the cloth is folded between hot cardboard press papers. The piles of cloth are weighted, and when they are unfolded the cloth is found to be quite smooth. This process is like ironing. A full press is seen on the right.

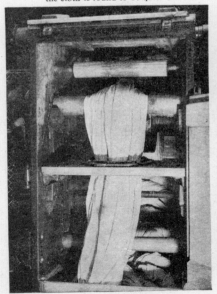

Milling is one of the oldest finishing processes. The well-soaped cloth rotates between heavy rollers to shrink, thicken, and firm it.

The machine in this picture is blowing steam through the cloth which sets it and gives it a good finish. Careful finishing at all stages makes all the difference to the final appearance of the cloth.

The pictures on these pages are by courtesy of the Australian Government and the International Wool Secretariat

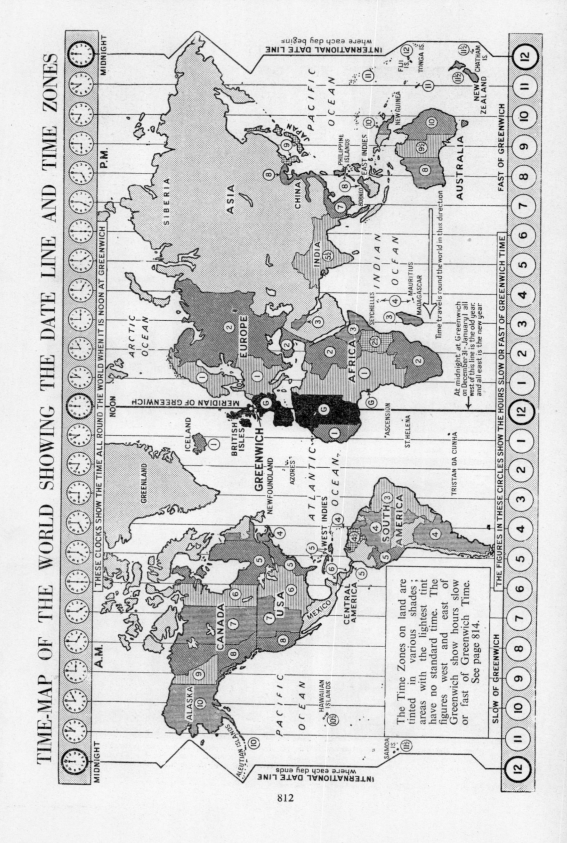

TIME-MAP OF THE WORLD SHOWING THE DATE LINE AND TIME ZONES

The Time Zones on land are tinted in various shades; areas with the lightest tint have no standard time. The figures west and east of Greenwich show hours slow or fast of Greenwich Time. See page 814.

Plain Answers to the Questions of the Children of the World

WHERE DOES A THOUGHT COME FROM?

THIS is the question of questions. We know certainly that thoughts depend on the brain. If we are to do our duty to ourselves, we must regard the brain as the place where the real self lives. The brain thrives on work, but we must not abuse it by depriving it of sleep, and we should even think of every one of the other parts of our body as no more than its servants. The brain is the house of thought, but it is not thought itself; and though there is no harm in saying for convenience that the brain thinks, that will not really do as an answer to our question.

There is a Something that thinks, a Something that knows. We cannot feel it, or see it, or cut it up; for it lies underneath all that we can see and cut up. The word substance means a standing underneath. And so when you ask where the thoughts come from, we can only reply that they come from the thinking substance—the Something that thinks.

When you ask where thoughts go in sleep, it is, perhaps, as if you had asked "Where does the music go when the violin or the organ is not being played on?" When we are asleep the brain—or, rather, the highest part of the brain—is not acting. It remains alive, of course, and has the needs of a living thing. It requires pure blood, which is one reason why we should sleep in pure air, but it is resting as a fiddle rests in its case; so no thought comes from it.

We are never wholly asleep, however; part of our bodies is always working, and even part of the brain. Sometimes we can be sure that, though the Self we know is asleep, part of the Self we do not know so well is not asleep, for men have awakened with the answer to questions which they could not answer the night before. Many cases like this show that sometimes a certain amount of thinking goes on in our brains even when we are asleep—or when, at any rate, the greater part of us is asleep.

We think because it is our nature to think, and this it is which distinguishes us from all other creatures.

We should always make a point of using the word Thought in the strict way to mean the putting together of two ideas. "Tom is good," is a thought. It puts together the idea of Tom and the idea of goodness. We say that there is a relation between Tom and the state of goodness. "Tom is not good" is another thought, asserting another kind of relation between Tom and goodness.

SUN · MOON · STARS · FIRE · WIND · WATER · LIFE · MIND · SLEEP

Why Does Iron Float on Mercury and Not on Water?

All questions of floating and swimming and flying depend on the comparative differences between various things as regards gravitation. Iron is heavier than water, or, as we say, its specific gravity is greater than that of water. Iron must therefore sink in water. Mercury is heavier than water, and therefore mercury must sink in water. But mercury is heavier than iron, and it must therefore sink in iron, which is just a peculiar way of saying that the iron must float on the mercury. The thing with the highest specific gravity is the thing for which the Earth has the strongest pull. It therefore gets nearest to the Earth, and anything else must float on the top of it.

Where Does the Day Begin?

The Sun is always seeming to rise somewhere, because at some place or other the Earth is just spinning round so as to face it, and the Sun is always seeming to set somewhere, because at some place or other the Earth is just spinning away from the Sun.

And, of course, whatever we call *now*, whether we call it six o'clock or twelve o'clock, *this now is now everywhere.* The present moment *is* the present moment here and on the farthest star. Only when just opposite the Sun *we* call that midday, whereas the people on the other side of the world are then away from the Sun, and call it midnight.

But, simply because the Earth goes on spinning, and the Sun is always shining, the day is dawning somewhere always, and *really*, therefore, the answer to the question, " Where does the day begin? " is that the day is always beginning somewhere or other.

Since people live in different parts of the world, what we call night (when it is our night) will be someone else's day, and our midnight, when a new day begins for us, as we reckon, will not be the midnight of other people in other parts of the world, so that what we *call* Monday they may *call* Tuesday, yet we and they are both talking about the same moment!

In order that we shall not get more mixed than we can help we have agreed that we shall take a line exactly on the other side of the Earth from the Greenwich line, and this we call the Date line.

When it is midnight on the Date line, what is called Monday on one side of the line is Tuesday on the other side. Fortunately the Date line scarcely touches any land at all, and the little it does touch is very unimportant land. The line passes across the ocean. It makes one or two deviations from the straight for the sake of convenience. The Aleutian Islands, for instance, are placed on the same side of the line as Alaska, and Fiji is on the same side as New Zealand.

What is a Time Zone?

When calculated from the Sun's position every place in the world has its own local time, which is different from that of every place east and west of it. Thus, Bristol time is slow of London time.

But when railways and bus services run it is convenient for a country to have a uniform system of time throughout all its territory, and thus throughout the British Isles Greenwich time is observed.

Not only so, but different countries that have constant dealings with one another find it extremely inconvenient to have differences of time that involve an odd number of minutes and seconds, and the chief countries have, therefore, agreed to form *time zones,* in each of which there shall be a standard time based on Greenwich, and varying from it only by hours and half-hours, and not by odd fractions.

Some countries, however, like the United States, Canada, and Brazil, are so wide from east to west, that they divide themselves into several zones. The whole Earth is divided into 24 equal zones of 15 degrees each, corresponding with the 24 hours of the day, and at sea these are rigidly observed by ships. But on land the boundaries of the zones are varied, and become irregular so as to include in the same zone certain areas closely connected for commercial purposes. A glance at our time zone map on page 812 shows how irregular these boundaries may become.

The convenience of this system of standard time zones is clear when we compare countries that have adopted it with those that have not. Thus Peru with zone time is exactly five hours slow of Greenwich, whereas if it had not adopted zone time it would be some 14 minutes more than five hours slow of Greenwich. A few parts of the world have no standard zone time.

Why Does the Hair Stand on End With Fright ?

We know that both in ourselves and in many of the lower animals the hair can, and does, stand on end with fright, almost " like quills upon the fretful porcupine," as Shakespeare says. It is also true, as he says, that it is possible for " each particular hair to stand on end," for we find that every hair has the power to do this, and that what happens is not that several hairs stand up together as the result of pulling on the skin. At the root of the hair we find a tiny muscle so arranged that, while the hair usually lies slantwise, when this muscle is set working the hair stands upright.

The best reason we can give for this peculiarity is that the instinct of fear, acting through the unconscious mind, stimulates the nerves which control these tiny muscles, which in turn raise the hairs. The creature thus affected appears more formidable; a cat, when its hair is standing on end, looks very much bigger and more terrible to an enemy.

What Makes the Poison in a Snake's Fang ?

A snake's fang is an eye-tooth, or canine tooth, as it is called, corresponding to the sharp pointed teeth that we have at the corners of the jaw between the front teeth and the back teeth. In the case of the poisonous snakes the tooth has a special channel in it through which the poison can run when the snake bites. The snake has certain glands like the salivary glands which in man produce saliva and assist in the mastication and digestion of food.

In the snake, however, these glands do much more than that, and especially the gland which corresponds to the one we have in front of the ear, the one which gets so big and painful when we have mumps. In the snake the business of this gland is to produce the poison. It runs along a little tube from the glands on each side of the mouth to the poison teeth. When the snake bites, the muscles of the jaw, which make the teeth meet, also squeeze upon the glands in these tubes in such a way that a little of the poison is forced through the channel in the fang, and left in the victim's body.

The amount of poison thus injected is, as a rule, exceedingly tiny, but the venom, or poison, of many of the venomous snakes is among the most deadly of all poisons, and a mere portion of a drop will kill. This is a deeply interesting question from the widest point of view, because it is so remarkable to discover that, in certain kinds of animals, parts of the body which are possessed by so many other kinds of animals, and which were certainly evolved for one purpose in the first place, are turned to a quite new and special purpose in these particular cases. In non-poisonous snakes, these same glands, which are so poisonous in the venomous snake, look just the same, yet produce nothing to hurt anyone.

Why do we not see our Breath on a Warm Day ?

We know that our breath is warmer than the air outside; but though the breath coming out of our bodies is always of very much the same temperature, the air outside varies very much. Sometimes the air outside is so warm that it does nothing in particular to that gaseous water—or water in the form of a gas—which is always in our breath; and so we see nothing.

But on a cold day this gaseous water, as it leaves our bodies, is suddenly turned so cold that it forms a little cloud, made, like other clouds, of drops of water. That is what we see when we say that we see our breath. It is the water in our breath that has been turned liquid by the cold. There is just as much water in our breath on a warm day, but then it remains in the form of a gas as it comes from our bodies.

Why must a Diver have Lead on His Boots ?

The diver would certainly sink without the lead on his boots. His body itself is heavier than water, and though the small quantity of air between himself and his case tends to make him float, yet the metal round his head makes him heavier still.

The point about the lead on his boots is that it makes him sink in the right direction. If it were not for that he might sink head first or sideways, and might find it exceedingly difficult or impossible to right himself. The lead serves, in a way, the same purpose as a piece of lead placed at the bottom of those little toys which cannot be upset. A closer parallel is the case of the balloon, which is kept the right way up by having its heaviest part below.

THE PATHS OF ALL THE ECLIPSES OF THE SUN FROM 1936 TO 1968

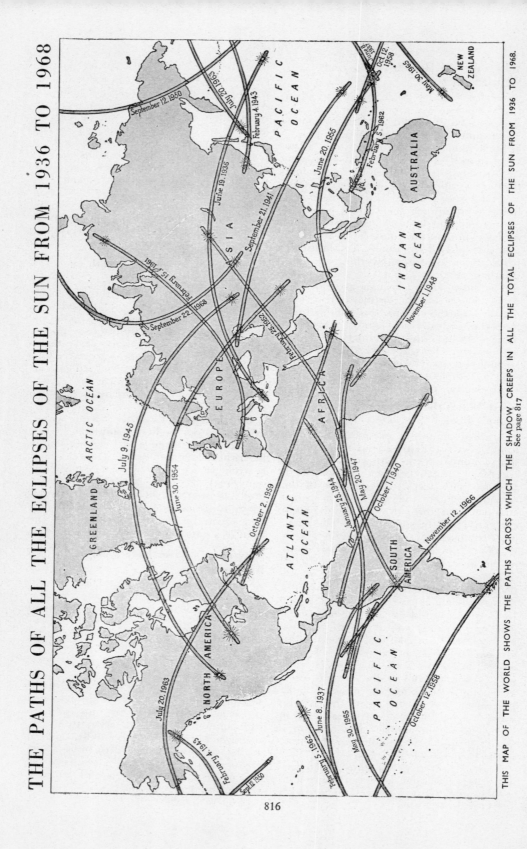

THIS MAP OF THE WORLD SHOWS THE PATHS ACROSS WHICH THE SHADOW CREEPS IN ALL THE TOTAL ECLIPSES OF THE SUN FROM 1936 TO 1968.
See page 817

Why is the Surface of Water always Level ?

Water, like everything else, is under the influence of gravitation. All the parts of it must therefore get as near as possible to the centre of the Earth. In the case of a solid thing, those forces which hold it together partly oppose the force of gravitation, and so an indiarubber ball, for instance, will remain as a ball, though if it were melted it would run flat out on the table as water would. But when we come to consider what the shape of the Earth is, we shall see that our question is not quite right if we are to read it strictly. The Earth is a ball, and if water is to obey the law of gravitation and get as near the centre of the Earth as possible, it follows that the surface of water must always curve, and its curvature, as we say, must be the same as the curvature of the Earth. The water in the smallest pool or basin must obey this law, but, of course, the curve is so slight that we cannot see it.

If, however, instead of a pool we take a huge lake or the ocean, we can see for ourselves that the surface of the water is curved, because we can see how a ship leaving us gradually disappears, or a ship coming over the horizon rises up as it approaches us. So the real answer to this question is that the surface of water is *always* curved ; and it is always curved in one way—the way in which the Earth itself is curved.

How can we Foretell an Eclipse of the Sun ?

We can predict the movements of the heavens because they move to order, and we can time the progress of the planets as we time our movements by the help of a watch.

While the Earth goes round the Sun, the Moon goes round the Earth, and at certain times the Moon comes between the Earth and the Sun during daytime on one hemisphere, and cuts off the sunlight from certain places on that hemisphere as it passes along.

Twelve or thirteen times in the year the Moon is, in a way, between the Sun and Earth, but not directly between, and not always in such a position as to cause an eclipse, for the Earth goes round the Sun in one plane and the Moon round the Earth in another plane, and unless the planes intersect or nearly intersect, the shadow of the Moon does not fall on the Earth. We must have Earth, Sun, and Moon almost in a straight line, with the Moon in the centre, before we can have an eclipse of the Sun.

The times at which Sun, Moon, and Earth are so placed can be found out by astronomical calculations, and thousands of years ago the Chaldaean astronomers discovered that each eclipse recurs at intervals of 18 years and 10 or 11 days. If, then, we note the exact time of the middle of any eclipse and count forward 18 years and 10 or 11 days we shall find another eclipse of *exactly the same kind* and visible in the same latitude though not in the same longitude. There are many total eclipses over a period of, say, 30 years.

The period of 18 years and 10 or 11 days was called by the Greeks " the saros," and the name is still used. As an example of the saros we may notice that a total eclipse was seen in America and Spain on July 18, 1860, and again in Colorado and on the Pacific Coast on July 29, 1878. On our map opposite this eclipse is shown in the path it took in 1950 and the path it will take in 1968.

Is a Fly Stronger than a Man, Comparing their Size ?

What the question really means is this : "Is a fly really stronger than a man relatively to its size, or in proportion to its size ? " The answer is certainly yes. The last thing in the world that distinguishes man is bodily strength of the kind which is shown in lifting weights, and so forth. It is by *skill*, made not by the muscles but by the brain, that man lives on the Earth —skill, not strength. If we weigh the proportion of the bodies of different animals that is made of muscle, and if also we weigh the proportion that is made of brain, then we learn how muscle has been getting less and less important, while brain, with all that brain means, has been getting more important.

Not only a fly, but animals in general are the superiors of man so far as muscular strength is concerned ; but then the question of muscular strength is an inferior one, and man is master because of what really matters, which is mind. The race is not to the swift, nor the battle to the strong, but to the wise, who use their brains to good advantage.

How Does the Milk Get into the Coconut ?

The stuff that we call the milk of coconuts is not milk, and has nothing about it at all like milk, except its appearance. It would be a puzzle, indeed, if real milk were found in coconuts, for milk is formed only by the milk-glands of certain animals called mammals. If you tried to feed a baby on the milk of coconuts instead of real milk, you would very soon learn the great difference there may be between things that look the same, only it would be a very wrong thing to do, for the baby would very soon die. Various plants besides the coconut produce fluids that look milky, and are often called milk simply because they look like it ; but no plant produces anything at all the same as real milk. The milk of the coconut is simply a fluid formed by the tissue or substance of the nut, and so we need not ask how it gets there.

Why Do Lobsters Turn Red in Boiling ?

The red colour of a boiled lobster is simply due to a chemical change that occurs in the brown colouring matter of the shell when it is heated. It is curious that red colouring matter, such as the haemoglobin of our blood, turns brown when it is heated, but the brown of a lobster's shell turns red. If the lobster were red in the sea he would be too easily seen, and would not be able to catch his food unawares, so he would die of starvation.

Are There People on the Moon ?

Well, we have only seen one side of the Moon because, as it goes round the Earth it turns slowly on itself, so as always to keep the same side turned toward us. But we are all quite sure that there are no people on the Moon, either on this side of it, or on the other side, which we have never seen. People could not live on the Moon because its surface has no air or water. Even if people could live there without air or water, they would probably be burnt to death in the daytime, having no air to protect them from the heat of the Sun, and they would be frozen to death at night, having no air to keep in the Sun's heat. There are certainly no people on the Moon, and never were.

But possibly at one time there may have been humble forms of plant life on the Moon, and some people suppose that there may be a little of this even now, for it is just possible that there may be a very tiny amount of air and water still left at the bottom of some of the deepest valleys in the Moon. If there was a building on the Moon as big as St. Paul's Cathedral, we should quite easily be able to see it through our biggest telescope, but there is not the slightest sign that intelligent beings have ever made a mark of any kind on the Moon.

Why is the Fire Hot ?

The heat that we feel when we stand opposite a fire is of two kinds. Partly it is the heat in the air which the fire has made warm, and which we feel against the skin. That heat has flowed into the air from the hot fire, but by far the greater part of the heat we feel opposite the fire is what is called radiant heat, a thing which is exactly of the same nature as light, only that instead of *seeing* it we *feel it hot*.

So our question is : What happens in the fire that makes it produce the heat of both kinds that we feel ? It will be quite plain to us that when heat is being produced something is being done, something is being made, and we know that the power has to come from somewhere. It comes from the carbon in the coal and the oxygen in the air.

They have energy and power locked up in them which are, so to speak, released when the carbon and oxygen combine to make the fire. The potential energy of the carbon and oxygen are changed, when they combine, into heat energy. This heat shows itself in a rapid motion, we suppose, of the matter in the fire. This communicates itself to the atoms of the air, and sets up the waves in the ether which we call radiant heat.

Why Cannot We Wash the Colour Out of Soap ?

We often notice that the colour comes off things, and the reason, of course, is that the colour is only on the surface, and if the surface is scraped, or rubbed, or worn away, the colour goes with it. But many things are coloured all the way through. We might say why does not the colour come off a brass fender, or off a silver spoon, or off a gold ring ? The colour does not come off in these cases for the same reason that explains why it does not come off soap. The soap is made throughout of coloured material.

The Story of the Beautiful Things in the Treasure-House of the World

A Raphael fresco in the Vatican

RAPHAEL AND HIS TIME

WHILE Michael Angelo was working at his immortal frescoes and statuary, and attracting the attention of beauty-loving people to Rome, two other artists, also born in Florence, were continuing the traditions of the famous town.

They were men who would have dominated a smaller period; had Leonardo da Vinci and Michael Angelo never been born, Fra Bartolommeo and Andrea del Sarto would themselves, in the same generation, have made the name of Florence memorable.

During the two centuries of development of Tuscan art, painting, as painting—that is to say, the technique of the art apart from the subject painted—had passed through a curious change.

We see the bodiless shapes of Duccio, the more vigorous work of Giotto marked by his pale, water-colourish tones ; the dear and lovely saints of Fra Angelico and Botticelli—sinners in technique, for whom spirituality and temperament accounted for righteousness ; Cosimo with his growing strength and great sweetness; Masaccio, who made men stop to think because he painted definite, vigorous persons and situations with definite strokes; and then Leonardo, whose technique was both pliant and strong, who was the first

to introduce into painting what is called chiaroscuro—light and shade in colour. A natural outcome of these changing styles was the work of Fra Bartolommeo and Andrea del Sarto.

Fra Bartolommeo, who lived from 1475 to 1517, stands out both as a wonderful colourist and a remarkable master of composition. He built up masses of figures as an architect throws out buttresses and towers from a central body of stone. This faculty is shown in almost all the artist's work. There is the fine painting called The Virgin Appearing to St. Bernard, now in the Florence Academy, where the figures are piled up on either hand from an almost empty central space. In the picture called Madonna della Misericordia, in the gallery at Lucca, groups of people are arranged in a truly monumental fashion.

The painter monk got through a great deal of work in his short lifetime—altar pieces, frescoes, a great many smaller pictures, chiefly of the Holy Family and the Madonna, examples of which are in the National Gallery. Raphael's attention was caught by a fresco of Bartolommeo's, painted in the hospital of Santa Maria Nuova in Florence. Both in colour and composition Raphael was

PICTURES · STATUES · CARVINGS · BUILDINGS · IVORIES · CRAFTS

impressed by the monk's work, and sought to learn some of his secrets of technique.

Had Bartolommeo possessed in even the smallest degree the secret of delineation of character and individual beauty which characterised Leonardo, he would have been counted among the great masters. His genius lay in the grouping of his figures; the people he painted, beautiful shapes though they may be, lack vitality; and in his later work, in an effort to imitate the strong light and shade of Leonardo, he spoilt his own naturally clear and beautiful colour.

THE MEN WHO MADE THE NAME OF FLORENCE FAMOUS FOR EVER

A very different person was Andrea del Sarto—he lived from 1486 to 1531—in a way the rival of Fra Bartolommeo. His technique and charm were such that he was known as the faultless painter. In a generation of geniuses Andrea was much thought of—according to the later judgment of history, a little more than he deserved. When Michael Angelo was in Rome, talking to Raphael one day he said, "There's a little man yonder in Florence, who, were he employed on such great works as these, would bring the sweat to your brow." But we ourselves reserve the heat of feeling Michael Angelo spoke of for his own work; the "faultless painter" leaves us pleasantly interested.

Andrea del Sarto had in his best work an extraordinary suavity and sweetness. His weakness was in his imitativeness. He followed Leonardo's skilful blending of light and shade with colour, but he had none of the great master's genius of insight into character; he aspired to Michael Angelo's rugged grandeur, and only succeeded in getting into a habit of making heavy draperies. His ideals were never lofty, for his mind had a common touch, but his painting, as painting, was exquisite. All his figures were bathed in a beautiful soft light.

ANDREA DEL SARTO SHOWS THE RARE SWEETNESS OF FLORENTINE ART

To study the work of this man is to realise how far Florentine art had gone in the journey away from archaism to sweetness and human freshness and lovableness. Religion still has a considerable place, but happiness has come into art to stay, we hope, for ever.

There are two paintings of Andrea del Sarto's in the National Gallery, one a Madonna and the other a portrait of a sculptor, which give us an idea of the artist's charm of treatment.

Two fine groups—Charity, and The Holy Family—are in the Louvre. But his work should be studied in Florence, where so much of it is treasured. There is a fresco of the Last Supper, at San Salvi, which draws the eye even after looking at Leonardo's master work on this subject ; several frescoes in Santissima Annunziata, such as the Birth of the Virgin, show his skill in composition.

Like most Italian artists, Andrea del Sarto painted a number of Madonnas, and he stands out a little from his fellows in having created a new type of face for the mother of Christ. Two fine specimens are The Holy Family, in the Pitti Palace; and the Madonna delle Arpie, in the Uffizi. The faces in these pictures are characterised not so much by saintliness as by sweetness, charm, simplicity.

For most of them he used as a model his lovely and wayward wife, whose facial beauty was not the outward sign of a beautiful spirit. Whether we look at them from the point of view of the painter's rather unhappy attachment for an unscrupulously selfish and hard woman, or from the point of view of beautiful portraiture, or as pictures of the Virgin, they claim our admiration and mark a stage in the innumerable repetitions of the little Jesus and his mother.

WANDERING ARTISTS WHO GAVE BEAUTY TO THE TOWNS AND VILLAGES

Another Florentine painter who was busy about this time was Bronzino. He lived from 1502 to 1572, and is chiefly remembered for his portrait work.

One of the pictures by Bronzino in the National Gallery is an allegory called Venus, Cupid, Folly, and Time; it is a brilliant example of his work.

It is the habit to speak of Italian art in various "schools" of painting—the Sienese, Florentine, Umbrian, Venetian. These are, however, merely broad definitions. We should not necessarily think that artists worked wholly in the town or state to which accident of birth or the style of their work allotted them. Quite a number of them were wandering artists, going from town to town to see the work of other men, intensely curious, and eager to share the ideas of their neighbours. They would undertake a piece of painting

THE MADONNA DEL GRANDUCA, IN THE PITTI GALLERY, FLORENCE

THE SISTINE MADONNA, IN THE ROYAL
GALLERY, DRESDEN

CATHERINE OF ALEXANDRIA, BY PINTURICCHIO,
IN THE NATIONAL GALLERY

POPE JULIUS THE SECOND, IN THE NATIONAL
GALLERY, LONDON

THE MADONNA AND CHILD, IN THE PRADO
GALLERY, MADRID

THE MADONNA AND CHILD, IN THE
MUNICH GALLERY

LA BELLE JARDINIÈRE IN THE
LOUVRE, PARIS

THE HOLY FAMILY, IN THE PITTI GALLERY,
FLORENCE

FERDINAND DE' MEDICI, BY BRONZINO, IN THE
UFFIZI GALLERY, FLORENCE

THE GRAND DUCHESS ELEANOR,
BY BRONZINO, IN DRESDEN

PORTRAIT OF BALTHASAR
CASTIGLIONE, IN THE LOUVRE

PIERO DE' MEDICI, BY BRONZINO,
IN THE NATIONAL GALLERY

THE MADONNA IN THE CHAIR, IN THE
UFFIZI GALLERY

THE VIRGIN AND CHILD, BY PERUGINO,
IN THE LOUVRE, PARIS

SAINT JOHN THE BAPTIST, BY
ANDREA DEL SARTO, FLORENCE

RAPHAEL, BY PINTURICCHIO,
IN SIENA CATHEDRAL

SAINT JOHN IN THE DESERT,
IN THE UFFIZI, FLORENCE

here, a fresco there, often finishing the work of a man whom death had claimed.

The authorities of the towns and villages, generally speaking, were just as eager to have their walls painted and buildings decorated as the artists were to do them. People cared intensely about beautiful things. A number of these artists have never attained to any fame; some are what we might call half-great. Many well-known names are among the company of artists who worked here and there, going from town to town—Giotto, Fra Angelico, Gozzoli, Uccello, Filippo Lippi, Gentile da Fabriano, Piero della Francesca, Signorelli, Pinturicchio.

One of these, Gentile da Fabriano, who lived from 1360 to 1428, is known as the first painter of any merit of the Umbrian school. The artists of this little colony were very much akin in spirit to the Sienese; they were more swayed by feeling than by thought. Fabriano was what one might call a happy painter, loving to portray the joyous element in the life of the Middle Ages. Although his subjects are religious, his pictures really show knights and ladies, lovely dresses, flowers and plumes, pleasant fields and sunny skies. His best known picture is the Adoration of the Magi, in Florence.

THE TWO MEN WHO PREPARED THE WAY FOR RAPHAEL

After Gentile da Fabriano the men of the Umbrian school became indifferent, uninspired. A number of second-rate artists lived and worked in the district, such as Boccati, Lorenzo di Viterbo, and Niccolo da Foligno, who was a pupil of Gozzoli.

Fiorenzo di Lorenzo is another Umbrian artist of this class. He was much influenced by the Florentines and at one time in his life did some good painting in Perugia, the capital of Umbria. He is chiefly to be remembered through his two famous pupils, Perugino and Pinturicchio, who prepared the way for the man who was the glory of Umbria, Raphael.

Perugino, who lived between 1446 and 1524, was the elder of the two by a few years. He is chiefly famous for his graceful, airy compositions and mastery of space management—essentially Umbrian qualities. There is a glow, a clear colour in his work, a restfulness, a peace, which throughout a long life-time of painting were never quite lost. For vigorous movement he had no aptitude whatever, but he

atoned for that lack by his remarkable restraint and delicacy.

There are pictures or frescoes by him in almost every gallery in Europe, and a great number in his native Perugia. Two of his most famous works are the triptych —The Madonna Adoring the Child— in the National Gallery, and The Holy Family, in the Louvre.

Pinturicchio has all the grace of the Umbrians but little vitality. Like his fellow artists, he painted an enormous number of religious subjects, and he attained to a certain prettiness without much strength. Fine examples of his pictures are in the National Gallery—St. Catherine of Alexandria, and a Madonna—and The Return of Ulysses, a fresco.

THE ARTIST WHO CREATED A NEW AND LOVELY TYPE OF MADONNA

Like Andrea del Sarto the Florentine, Pinturicchio painted lovely women as Madonnas, and stands out in the history of Umbrian art as a creator of a new type of this eternal subject. There are some large compositions of Pinturicchio's in the Libreria of Siena and the Borgia Rooms of the Vatican, which show that, like Perugino, had the artist only possessed vigour equal to his grace, he would have been numbered with the great.

It is strange that about Raphael, at one time the brilliant follower of these two Umbrian masters, the judgment of history should not yet be finally pronounced. A very great deal has been written and said about the " divine painter," and until the mid-nineteenth century a kind of hysterical worship was accorded him. The men who know most about art today are trying to judge him on the merit of his work, apart from the traditions clinging to his name.

RAPHAEL REVEALS THE GREATNESS AND BEAUTY OF HIS ART

There is no doubt that Raphael was a very great artist, but not in the sense that Michael Angelo and Leonardo da Vinci were great. He had no share in the grandeur, the Titan-like vigour of Michael Angelo; he was incapable of the profound insight into men and women that makes Leonardo's few remaining masterpieces treasures of all mankind. But he was the greatest illustrator, the greatest space composer, the world has ever known.

He saw figures of men and women in masses as beautiful patterns against the sky, the landscape, the pillars, arches, and walls of a building. He had genius for shaping vast spaces, and filling a picture in such a masterly way that, while containing scores of figures, it had a leisurely air—the leisureliness of time and eternity.

This, his peculiar greatness, the art of composition, was undoubtedly born in him; his styles of painting he owed to many men in turn. Raphael was extraordinarily receptive, sensitive to impressions, a born imitator; he could seize on the best in another man's work, and in this way he drew to himself, as to a magnet, the most alluring qualities of Italian art.

RAPHAEL'S WONDERFUL ACHIEVEMENTS IN A SHORT BUT BRILLIANT CAREER

In the year 1500, when Raphael was 17, he entered the studio of Perugino at Perugia, where Pinturicchio was head assistant. For four years he worked in the studio, very much influenced by the paintings of the two Umbrian masters.

In 1504 he produced the masterpiece of his early manhood, The Marriage of the Virgin. This picture shows his growing genius for " piled-up " compositions, his sense of the beauty of space, his love for arched buildings as a background to groups.

It is almost impossible to estimate the value of the space management of the famous painting. The group in the foreground would make a very different effect without the mounting steps in the middle distance, the domed temple surmounting the picture, the tiny figures quietly coming and going.

By this time Raphael's fame was established and he entered on to the years of crowded work that only ended with his death at the age of 37. Even allowing for the fact that his pupils and assistants helped largely in many of the pictures which bear his name, Raphael produced an astounding number of pictures and frescoes. His achievements are the more remarkable because he was something of a social " lion," the favourite of the great.

HOW RAPHAEL FOUND SCOPE FOR HIS GENIUS AT THE VATICAN

It soon became the fashion to talk about Raphael, admire him, follow him about. The inevitable result of this hero-worship was that the artist had to spend much time in society, away from his work.

After his period of work in Perugino's studio Raphael went to Florence for four years, and during that time fell under the influence of Leonardo da Vinci, Michael Angelo, and Fra Bartolommeo. While at Florence he painted a great number of his exquisite pictures of Mary and the Child. There is an unearthly sweetness in these heads of Mary, something that appeals to the emotion and is only saved from oversweetness by Raphael's exceeding grace.

In 1508 the artist was called to Rome by Pope Julius the Second, and from that time found it almost impossible to cope with commissions for work which came to him. He was obliged in very many cases to content himself with making the cartoon for a picture, leaving his assistants to " paint it in," and then giving the finishing touches himself.

His great work on becoming artist to the Papal Court was the decoration of some of the Vatican apartments—the Stanze—and the Loggie of one of the courtyards. Here Raphael's genius at composition had full scope. When we consider the numerous pictures in the Stanze, it would seem that any one of them might almost have been the work of a man's lifetime. Hundreds of figures are grouped and painted, all looking as if they could not possibly have been placed anywhere else, and yet each subordinate to the magnificent whole.

THE PAINTER WHO BLENDED THE PAGAN WORLD AND THE CHRISTIAN STORY

You know that there are crowds of people in these pictures, but your eye seeks the one place and person, or two persons, it was the artist's intention you should seek; and that is the final genius of figure management in a composition.

The subjects of the Stanze were taken from historical, allegorical, and religious sources. In the Loggie are frescoes mainly from Old Testament history. They are affectionately known as Raphael's Bible, but we know now that the master was not responsible for very much of this work.

There was something miraculous in the energy of this young man. In the midst of almost inexhaustible demands on his time he succeeded in finding leisure to paint some very fine portraits.

It is probable that as time goes on Raphael will be chiefly remembered for his Vatican pictures and his lovely Madonnas. By these he is for ever set apart. No other painter has blended so marvellously the pagan world and the Christian story, or thus brought the spirit of the whole Renaissance to rest within one lifetime.

The Wonderful House We Live In, and Our Place in the World

These pictures show an amoeba throwing out two "arms" to seize a particle of food. The arms gradually surround the particle and draw it into the substance of the amoeba.

THE VERY SEAT OF LIFE

EVERY creature that exists, a moss, or a man, or a microbe, or a monkey, or a fish, is made of living cells.

We are all alike in this, all living things; but if we survey the whole world of life in this fashion we find that a very great division can be made. In the one division are creatures made simply of one cell, and in the other are those made of more than one cell. The one-celled creatures were certainly the first to appear on the Earth, and we have already learned a good deal about them. We need the microscope to see them with.

The many-celled creatures are all the visible world of life, animal and vegetable; but though there is such a vast difference between, shall we say, an oak tree and a microbe—the first made of billions of cells, and the other made of only one—yet we find that the living cell in each is astonishingly similar, whether it is the single cell of a microbe, or a cell in the leaf of an oak tree, or in the skin of your hand, or anywhere. If we could learn the secret of the cell, we should have the secret of life; but a lesson we can learn from it is the lesson of oneness in different things.

Already we have studied a number of cells closely resembling one another, which we call microbes. Wherever we turn in the world of life we find cells and yet more cells. Having looked at the cells which form the bodies of the simplest plants, we may now look at the simplest kind of animal, especially because the cell which makes it is what we call a typical cell— that is to say, it has all the characters of cells in general.

This humblest of animals is called the amoeba, and is readily found in ponds; it simply consists of a single cell which has no cell-wall. If we watch it under the microscope we shall see a very good reason why it should not have a cell-wall. The amoeba is just a round speck of living matter, but it can move of itself, as we say. You know already that movement is usually a mark of living things, and this amoeba, like most cells, can move itself bodily about. It does this by crawling. It swells out one side of its body, and then pulls the rest of its body after it.

Of course, if the amoeba had a stiff wall round it, it could not crawl; to crawl, it is bound to change its shape, and so, though we call it round, when the amoeba is active and looking for something to eat, it is not round, but has an irregular shape which changes from moment to moment. It is only round when it is starved and almost dead, or perhaps when it has had plenty of food, and is resting after a meal.

We now know that there is a very simple way of making an amoeba stop moving and become quite round, and this is very interesting because it teaches us that all life is the same everywhere.

BODY, MIND, AND SOUL · CITIZENSHIP · ECONOMICS · GOVERNMENT

You will have heard of chloroform. This is a liquid, looking rather like water but with a curious smell, which is given to people to smell at when perhaps they have had a finger crushed, and the tip of it has to be taken off. It sends them to sleep in a peculiar way, so that they feel no pain. This is because the chloroform acts on the cells of their brain and makes them stop working; but in most respects all cells are really the same, and all true poisons, like alcohol, chloroform, prussic acid, and so on, are harmful to them.

WHAT HAPPENS TO LIFE WHEN WE GIVE IT CHLOROFORM

So, if you are watching an amoeba crawling under the microscope, and add the very tiniest amount of chloroform to the water in which it is moving, it is poisoned; it stops moving, and curls itself into a round ball.

Of course, if you give too much chloroform the amoeba will be killed, just as a man would be killed if you gave him too much chloroform. But do you not think it is very interesting that the same stuff should act in the same way on every kind of living cell? We are not to imagine that the cells in our brain look like the amoeba, or that they crawl about; they have a very different business. Nevertheless, they are alive, and the point is that all living cells everywhere, whatever their business is, have their life arrested if they are chloroformed, because in reality all life is one and the same.

THE MOST REAL PART OF THE CELL WHICH IS THE ABODE OF LIFE

Now let us look more closely at the amoeba, and see whether we can find different parts in it. Is it just a round speck with no features; or has it different parts, just as our bodies have different parts? The answer to this is that the amoeba has two parts, and that this is the general rule with all living cells.

Somewhere about the centre of the amoeba, this tiny speck, there is a still tinier speck, which is not an accident, but is found in all amoebae. It looks a little denser than the rest of the amoeba, doubtless because it has not quite so much water in it, and it has a special and very important name—important because the little speck of living stuff is typical of the living cell everywhere.

It is called the nucleus, which is from the Latin word for a nut, which is *nux*, and means simply the kernel. This is a very good name, for the kernel of a nut is the real part of it; the rest exists for the sake of the kernel. And, just as the cell-wall is not the real cell, so the outer part of the cell itself is not the real cell. The most real part of the cell, as we shall soon see, is the nucleus, which is the very abode of life But we may first of all say a word or two as to the rest of the cell which is of far less importance.

In the case of the amoeba and many other cells, the outside part of the cell is rather like our bodies as compared with our brains. It is by movements of the outer part of the cell that the cell moves.

So we may say that it serves the cell for legs. Then, of course, the amoeba has to take in its oxygen through the outer part of the cell, which thus serves it for nose and lungs. Remember that every living cell in our own bodies is also breathing in the same way.

THE NUCLEUS IS REALLY THE BRAIN AND THE MASTER OF THE CELL

Like every other living creature, the amoeba has to feed. No living thing can make its life and movement out of nothing. The amoeba has no hands, no mouth, and certainly no knife and fork, but it has to get food into its body somehow, just as we have to. When it meets a tiny speck of something it can eat, it slowly throws out from itself two little projections, one on each side of the speck of food. These gradually enwrap or flow round it, until at last it is enclosed inside the body of the amoeba—that is to say, inside the cell.

The pictures show us exactly what the amoeba looks like when it is taking a meal, and how it makes arms and mouth for itself. Then, just as we have to digest our food, the amoeba has to digest its food; and so the outer part of the amoeba, or, rather, the whole amoeba except for the speck in its centre, may play the part of a stomach. You never find a speck of food inside the nucleus, any more than you would find a trace of milk inside the human brain.

All the work of digestion and preparing has to be done outside the nucleus. The nucleus is the master, and all the work has to be done outside it and for it, so to speak ; just as in our own bodies the brain is the master.

When we come to look at the white cells of our own blood, we see that they are able to pick up and carry away particles of smoke that we have breathed into our lungs, and that they are even able to catch and kill microbes and other living cells which might hurt us. But you will never find a speck of coal-dust or a microbe inside the nucleus of a white blood-cell, unless the cell is killed by the microbe and is falling to pieces.

THE NUCLEUS OF THE CELL ON WHICH THE LIFE DEPENDS

If we look at the cell apart from the nucleus, we are very uncertain as to how it is made. It is certainly not transparent, though it lets a good deal of light through it ; it looks rather like a half-transparent jelly. Indeed, if you can imagine a jelly looking like ground glass, that would be very much what the body of a cell looks like.

Not only is the nucleus the essential part of the cell, but the life of the body of the cell depends upon the nucleus. If one of your fingers were cut off it would die ; your finger is alive, but it cannot live by itself. In the same way, if we cut off any part of the body of a cell from the rest of the cell, it will die ; or, to put it another way, if you cut a cell into two parts, one of them containing the nucleus and the other not, then the part which contains the nucleus will go on living, will mend itself, will recover its former shape. But the part which does not contain the nucleus will die. This always happens ; no exception to it is known anywhere. It is true of the amoeba, but, if we take the case of a cell more unlike the amoeba than anything else we know, we find that the same is true.

THE WONDERFUL LIKENESS BETWEEN THE AMOEBA'S LAWS OF LIFE AND YOURS

The nerve-cells in our bodies are at first very like the amoeba, but when they are fully formed they are vastly different. Like the amoeba, they have a nucleus. But the cell-body is prolonged in one or more directions in the form of a long thread, which is what we call a nerve. That thread is really part of the cell-body of the nerve-cell from which it springs. So if you were to cut a nerve across, the experiment would really be the same as the experiment of cutting the amoeba

into two pieces, one containing the nucleus and the other not ; and the result is the same in both these different cases.

The part of the nerve still in connection with the nucleus remains alive and unchanged, but the other part of the nerve, on the far side from where the cut was made, dies. It seems very wonderful indeed that it should be possible to take such a cell as this tiny amoeba of the ponds on the one hand, and one of the nerve-cells in the human brain on the other hand, and to prove that the laws of their lives are one and the same.

The laws of any life are the laws of all life, however vast the difference may be between one kind of living creature and another. If, after an accident where a nerve has been cut, a clever surgeon sews the two cut ends of the nerve together, then, through the power of the nucleus, which may be two or three feet away, as in the case of the nerves of our legs, new living nerve matter will grow down from the cut place into the sheath of the old nerve, and take its place again ; just as the piece of the amoeba that contained the nucleus soon grows into a whole amoeba once more.

PROTOPLASM, THE WONDERFUL MATTER IN WHICH ALL LIFE LIVES

The nucleus, then, is the centre of the life of the cell ; apart from the nucleus the body of the cell cannot live. The cell's power of repairing damage depends entirely upon the nucleus.

Furthermore, we have learned also that the character of the cell depends upon the nucleus. Boys and girls differ in character, as we know ; though their bodies are very much alike, their brains are very different. Probably all cell-bodies are made of very much the same stuff—arranged, if it is arranged at all, in very much the same way ; but it is the nucleus of one kind of cell that differs from that of another, and so gives the cell its character.

Though the body of a cell cannot live without its nucleus, yet the body of the cell is truly alive, and will live—for a very short time—even when separated from the nucleus. The stuff, then, of which the body of the cell is made, and the stuff of which the nucleus is made, is living stuff. As we are beginning to understand that all life is really the same, we shall not find it difficult to believe that all living matter, wherever it is found, whether in a lily or in a fish or in a man, has certain common properties which make it different from matter that is not alive. This is certainly so, and we must clearly understand the wonderful stuff which we may call living matter, or, at any rate, matter in which life exists. The name for this particular kind of matter in which all life lives is *protoplasm*. The word really means the first building-stuff. All the life we know is lived in protoplasm, and the living part of all living cells is made of protoplasm, both the cell-body and the nucleus.

THE THINGS THAT MAKE UP WHAT WE CALL PROTOPLASM

Now, all matter is made up of various kinds of elements, such as carbon, silver, oxygen, and so on ; and the first thing we have to ask about protoplasm is, What elements does it contain ? The answer to this is certain. Protoplasm is made up, *somehow*, of certain elements which we are perfectly familiar with in the world in general. Nor are they even rare elements ; they are among the commonest and most widespread of all the elements that we know. This is a very important fact. Even the most wonderful kind of living cells there are—the nerve-cells of the highest part of the human brain—are made up, so far as their elements are concerned, of the stuff that is all around us.

We must notice exactly what the elements found in protoplasm are. Two of them, at any rate, we know already, for we know that all protoplasm contains water, which is made of the elements oxygen and hydrogen. It would be more correct to say that protoplasm is contained in water, rather than that protoplasm contains water. Live things cannot live without liquid water.

THE FIVE GREAT ELEMENTS THAT ARE NECESSARY TO ALL LIFE

We have also learned, however, that this statement is not quite the whole truth. It must not be taken to mean, for instance, that if a living thing is frozen, or if it is made quite dry, it must die. That is not so. In these cases the living creature stops living *always*, but it does not necessarily die ; it stops growing, it stops breathing ; it shows none of the characters of life, which are only shown in the presence of liquid water.

Yet, though it cannot be said that it is living, it still has in it the power to live if it gets liquid water ; it cannot be called living, and it cannot be called dead. The processes of life do not go on except in the presence of liquid water, and it is probably right to say that liquid water is one of the things which make protoplasm.

Besides oxygen and the hydrogen of the water, in which all protoplasm lives, there is a great deal more of both oxygen and hydrogen in it ; not combined, however, to form water, but combined in different ways with various other elements, and with each other. The elements invariably found in protoplasm, elements without which protoplasm cannot exist, are *carbon, oxygen, hydrogen, nitrogen, phosphorus,* and *sulphur*. There can be no protoplasm without the six elements we have named. In addition a number of others are required, such as copper and iron, but they are all common elements, and there is nothing rare about any of them. Living protoplasm could not be spread through the world as it is if the things it needs for its life, and for remaking itself as it goes on living, were not to be found almost everywhere. Life, then, is made out of common things.

THE GREAT POWER OF PROTOPLASM TO MAKE NEW THINGS OUT OF OLD

Now, if we have got that clearly understood and remembered, we can go on to another great fact which must always be remembered along with it. It is that while, on the one hand, the elements of protoplasm are common and familiar, the ways in which they are combined in protoplasm are unlike anything else.

You remember that what we call the elements often combine with each other to form what we call compounds. The simplest instance is the compound water made by a combination of the elements oxygen and hydrogen ; and water is found in protoplasm. But the compounds of which protoplasm is really made, though they are compounds of familiar elements, are utterly different from any compounds found anywhere else. This, then, is the power of protoplasm, to take common, ordinary things, and make them, as it alone can, into things which are utterly new and different. Life does this with the common elements of the world, building them into protoplasm, out of which are built the bodies of all the varied and beautiful living creatures that live, and have lived, and are yet to live.

The Story of the Marvellous Plants that Cover the Earth

The loveliness of the wild foxglove which produces a million seeds in a summer

FLOWERS AND FRUITS

THE end of the flower is to produce seeds, and seeds are young plants just beginning their careers. We saw that in the picture-story of a buttercup on page 334.

But we have already seen that the flower first makes spores—little spores called pollen-grains and big spores called embryo-sacs. The transformed leaf-structures that make the pollen-grains are the *stamens*, and the transformed leaf-structures that make the embryo-sacs are the *carpels*. A male-cell in the pollen-grain fertilises an egg-cell inside what is called the embryo-sac; and so it is one of the uses of a flower to secure that the pollen-grains are scattered, and that some are dusted on to the stigma or carpel-tip.

The poet Goethe was one of the first to see clearly that a flower consists in ordinary cases of four tiers (or whorls) of different leaf-structures which have been changed for different purposes. It is Nature's way to make apparently new things out of old things, and the flower consists of four whorls of transformed leaves. These are :

1. The sepals which protect the bud and steady the blossom.
2. The petals which shelter the more important parts and also attract insect-visitors.
3. The stamens that make pollen.
4. The carpels that make embryo-sacs, within each of which there is an egg-cell.

That the parts of a flower are transformed leaves may be seen in a case like the water-lily, where the green sepals pass quite gradually into white petals, and these into yellow stamens. It is difficult to tell where one stops and the other begins. Again, when flowers " go double," this means in most cases, as in a wild rose becoming a garden rose, that what should have developed into stamens have sunk back into parts nearer leaves— the parts we call petals. One sometimes finds a canterbury bell in which the whole flower has become a crowded tuft of green leaves. This may happen when a plant is too well fed; it ceases to be floral and becomes more leafy. It will be understood that sepals and petals are nearer to leaves than can be said of stamens and carpels, which are leaf-structures transformed in connection with spore-forming or seed-forming.

" You will find," John Ruskin said, "that all plants are composed of two parts:

The leaf and the root, one loving the light and the other darkness; one liking to be clean, the other to be dirty; one liking to grow for the most part up, the other for the most part down; and each having faculties and purposes of its own. But the pure one which loves the light has, above all things, the purpose of being married to another leaf, and having child-leaves, and children's children of leaves, to make the Earth fair for ever. And when the leaves marry they put on wedding-robes, and are more glorious than Solomon in all his glory, and they have feasts of honey, and we call them flowers."

This is finely said, but we should be careful to notice that stamens are not really *male* parts, nor the carpels *female* parts. They are spore-making organs, and the spores are made in the pollen-sacs and ovules. So when a flower has stamens only, and another carpels (with ovules) only, it is better to call them *staminate* and *pistillate* flowers, rather than male and female flowers.

THE WAY POLLEN IS CARRIED ABOUT FROM FLOWER TO FLOWER

The pollen-grains are of different colours and shapes and sizes, but they are usually yellow and dry; and we may speak of them as grains of golden dust. What is important is that they should reach the usually moist and sticky tip (or stigma) of the pistil. There, each sends out a delicate pollen tube which contains the male-cell, and makes its way down the interior of the carpel (the style) to reach the egg-cell within the embryo-sac, which is within the ovule, which is within the ovary ! The union of the male-cell and the egg-cell is called fertilisation; it is the beginning of a new individual life. But the dusting of the tip of the pistil with pollen is called *pollination*, and it is brought about in one of three chief ways.

Sometimes, as in grasses and sedges, alders and birches, oaks and elms, the pollen is carried by the wind from flower to flower. This is the oldest method, which lasted for ages; but it is very wasteful. Thus, in the pine-forests there is sometimes so much pollen that it is borne up by the wind like clouds of smoke, and when it sinks to the ground—as much of it does—people talk of a sulphur shower.

THE BUSY BEE PAYS ITS CALLS IN THE GARDEN

The second method, which is seen in most flowering plants with notable blossoms, is by means of insects or some other flower-visiting animals. The visitors, such as bees, come for the sake of the nectar and the pollen itself; and the colour and fragrance may be useful advertisements. They get dusted with pollen and land some of this on the pistil of a neighbouring flower of the same kind, for they often pay many consecutive visits to the same species. If the humble-bee is visiting, let us say, aconite one forenoon, it will keep to aconite for a while, so that the pollens are not so much mixed as one might expect.

It has been shown for various insects that they can distinguish different colours, and not only colours but different degrees of brightness; and it is likely that in the course of their individual experience they learn that the colour and brightness of certain flowers mean plenty of nectar and pollen. As we say, they learn to *associate* certain flags of colour with certain feasts of honey. The same applies to the fragrance of some flowers; it appeals to the sense of smell, which is very keen in some insects, such as bees. Some odours that are repulsive to us are attractive to insects, and thus we find that some flowers with an evil smell are eagerly sought by certain flies, which lay their eggs in them and bring about pollination in so doing. In South America many flowers are pollinated by humming-birds, and even the slow-going snails may dust pollen on the flowers they visit. This happens, for instance, in the little golden saxifrage of damp woods.

HOW NATURE PROTECTS THE SEEDS OF THE PLUM AND CHERRY

In a small number of plants, such as the common pea and the wheat, self-fertilisation occurs. The pollen-grains from the stamens of a flower land on the stigma of the same flower, and send out their pollen-tubes. In such flowers it looks as if there had been a slipping back to an old-fashioned state of affairs. It is interesting to note that in some cases, where pollen-grains pass from stamens to stigmas of the same flower, they do no useful work, for they do not send out pollen-tubes.

Now let us consider the fruit.

The fruit consists of the ripe seed-box or seed-boxes, to which may be added some extra parts, such as an expanded flower-stalk (as in the rose-hip), or a fleshy flower-stalk and green sepals (as in the strawberry). When we use the word fruit we think at once of something juicy, but we cannot separate dry fruits from soft fruits, and even the fruiterer's shop window shows many dry fruits.

If we look at such a common kind of fruit as a plum or a cherry, we distinguish at once the firm outer skin, the juicy pulp, and the stone. The last contains the seed, or kernel, and being hard and

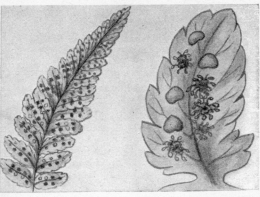

2. The under-surface of part of a frond dotted with little spore cases called sporangia.

3. Part of the frond magnified to show spore cases, some with their wax-like covering.

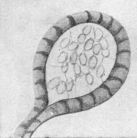

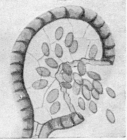

1. This is part of the front side of a frond of the Male Shield Fern, which propagates itself by spores. In one year this fern will scatter 1000 million spores.

4. An unripe case with the spores inside before the wall bursts to release them.

5. A spore case discharging the spores, which are carried away by the wind.

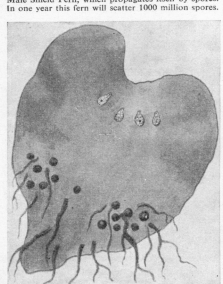

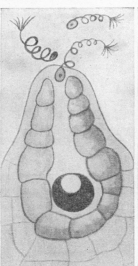

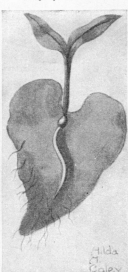

6. The spore falls to the ground, where with moisture it swells and bursts its case. It sends down a rootlet and forms a thin, flat, green expansion called the prothallium. This picture shows the under-surface. At the top are the egg-cells, and at the bottom the male organs.

7. Enlarged view of female organ. The spiral bodies with tufts of hair called cilia are from the male organ and are attracted to the female cells which they fertilise.

8. As a result of the union of the cells the young fern begins to sprout. It draws nourishment from the prothallium, and before very long develops roots.

woody, it protects the very young plant inside from being digested in a bird's food-canal or frost-bitten in the soil. It also keeps the seed from sprouting too soon.

The use of the juicy pulp, which is sheer loss to the plant, is to attract birds and beasts that eat the fruit but at the same time scatter the seeds.

The outer skin prevents the fruit from drying in the Sun, and it keeps out bacteria and moulds unless it is in some way broken. Everyone knows how quickly a plum goes bad if the skin is pierced by a bird's peck or a wasp's bite. The " going bad " means that bacteria have got in at the wound.

There are three great kinds of dry fruits and two great kinds of soft fruits. The first set of dry fruits includes the box-fruits (capsules), which liberate the seeds by bursting or gaping or opening in some way, as in the case of pea-pods, turnip-fruits, and poppy-heads. The second set, known as splitters, divide into pieces, each enclosing a seed which is not liberated till it sprouts in the ground. We see this kind of fruit in all the members of the hemlock order, in mallows, and in plants like the white dead-nettle. Thirdly, there are all sorts of nuts and nutlets, which do not split or liberate the seed till the time of sprouting. These may be illustrated by hazel-nuts, by green fruits of the buttercup, and by grains of wheat.

HOW THE STRAWBERRY, THE RASPBERRY, AND THE FIG ARE FORMED

The soft fruits are either stone-fruits with the seed inside the hard innermost layer, as in plum, peach, and cherry, and berries which have the seeds embedded in a juicy pulp, as in grapes, gooseberries, and currants. The hard thing in a cherry is the stone ; the hard thing in a mistletoe berry is a seed. So, looking backward, we have box-fruits, splitters, nuts, stone-fruits, and berries. To these, however, must be added a number of complicated fruits. Thus a strawberry is a collection of tiny yellowish nutlets on the rounded red surface of the fleshy top of the flower-stalk. A raspberry is a collection of little stone-fruits perched on the soft, conical tip of the stalk. More complicated is the fig, where a whole group of fruits, each from a separate flower, is enclosed in a fleshy cup.

The uses of the fruit are all bound up with the seeds. Some fruits protect the seeds from frost and seed-eating enemies; some attract the attention of fruit-eating birds and mammals, and that is profitable when the visitors do not digest the seeds; some scatter the seeds by explosion or by forming parachutes; and some prevent the seed sprouting too quickly in the ground. These are the ordinary uses of fruits, but perhaps they may be more clearly understood if we keep in mind the following facts.

THE SUGAR FACTORY WORKING INSIDE A GREEN PLANT

1. Fruits are usually built up of trans-formed leaf-structures, or carpels, which naturally tend to dry and die. This throws light on the splitting of dry fruits.

2. Many juicy fruits are rich in sugar, and the green plant is a sugar-factory. It is natural that after the nectaries of the flower close up—having played their part in attracting insect-visitors—there should be a re-direction of the surplus sugar into the fruit.

3. Many soft fruits have at least 75 per cent of water. This must come, of course, from the soil, and we can understand better how it can be spared if we remember that the leaves are no longer using or losing so much water.

4. Seeds are rich in nitrogenous food-stuffs of great value as nourishment which form a legacy for the next generation. But what is in the fruit is not handed on, and is so much loss to the plant. We understand, therefore, why the fruits contain comparatively little in the way of protein, but often much in the way of sugar, which is less nourishing.

5. Everyone is familiar with the extraordinary difference between an unripe apple or plum and a ripe one. This is due to the chemical changes of ripening, such as fermenting starch into sugar, making ethers and oils of fine fragrance, and also in many cases making colouring matter, as in the apple's rosy cheeks.

FRUIT AS A LINK BETWEEN PARENT AND SEED

6. As we have just said, the treasures of fruits, so precious to man in apple and orange, grape and banana, and scores of other cases, represent so much loss to the plant, but in some plants the fruit is the link between the parent and the developing seeds which are laying up stores for the growing time.

SIMON DE MONTFORT COMES TO ROCHESTER

SIMON DE MONTFORT, THE PATRIOT WHO FOUNDED PARLIAMENT IN ENGLAND, STARTLES ROCHESTER
BY RIDING INTO THE CATHEDRAL ON HORSEBACK

instead of round, and with much higher walls, columns, and roofs.

We can still go and look at this beautiful work of more than six centuries ago. Only part of the splendid tomb Henry set up in it for the body of Edward the Confessor now remains. The golden shrine, and golden statues, and precious stones are all gone. We may think it looks dusty and dingy now, as we look close into it to see the mosaic or inlaid pattern of tiny pieces of glass; but it has stood there for hundreds of years, and round it have passed not only generation after generation of quiet folk who came to pray in the holy place, or to admire its beauties and read the story of the past, but also rough soldiers and thieves, who tore down the ornaments and jewels, and made sad havoc with what had been the pride and joy of their forefathers.

SIMON DE MONTFORT, THE PEOPLE'S LEADER AGAINST THE KING

It has been said that the great result of Henry's long reign was the giving back of England to the English. It was possible for a poet who lived toward the end of this reign to sing:

Now England breathes in the hope of liberty,
The English were despised, but now they have
    lifted up their head.

We remember that William the Conqueror claimed all the land as his own, and parcelled it out as he pleased; and when he wanted money he extorted it. Two centuries later, when Henry the Third wanted money for his wars, his buildings and his foreign favourites, the people were strong enough to refuse to give it to him unless he promised to rule by the law of the land. In the great fight between Henry and the people the name of a great patriot stands out—Simon de Montfort.

HOW THE BISHOPS FLUNG DOWN THEIR CANDLES AT THE KING'S FEET

" I fear thunder and lightning not a little, Sir Simon," said Henry to him one day when caught in a bad storm, " but I fear you more than all the thunder and lightning in the world." And well he might, for this Simon feared nothing. He once rode into Rochester Cathedral, it is said, on his horse.

Before the actual fighting began, Henry made promises over and over again, only to be broken. Let us see and hear how these promises were made on one occasion.

A great procession of bishops and clergy, with splendid silk robes, carrying lighted candles in their hands, arrived at the Great Hall at Westminster, where Henry awaited them. Then, standing round him, they spoke strong and terrible words as to what would happen to the king who took away any of the freedom of the land. As their voices died away—can you almost feel the hush after the loud, passionate talking?—they flung down their candles, saying:

" May all those who take away our rights perish as these lights perish !"

The king made solemn promises as the candles were relit, and the bells rang out joyfully to tell the news to the people waiting outside.

But the king's promises were broken, and the country had to fight again, and Henry was forced to draw up new laws and add to the good old ones. *The new laws were written in English for the first time since the Norman Conquest.* Again the king broke his word, and more fighting went on, till at last Simon succeeded in forming a talking place, called a Parliament after the French word *parler*, meaning to talk.

THE CHILDREN'S ENCYCLOPEDIA OF HUNDREDS OF YEARS AGO

This was even more useful than the old Assembly of the Wise Men had been. In it not only barons and bishops could discuss what was best for the country and the people, but knights from every shire had the right to come and talk; also citizens from the towns, and these, too, had a voice to say what the people in their part of the country wanted done, and how they wished the money to be spent which they paid in taxes.

The battle of Lewes was the crowning victory of the barons under Simon. When Henry was taken prisoner did he think one wonders, of the words he had said long before about fearing his conqueror?

It was three years after this battle that a great thinker named Roger Bacon wrote a book about every sort of knowledge which has been called the encyclopedia of the thirteenth century. He speaks of geography, grammar, music, languages, arithmetic, and many other matters. The story of how hard he worked, how he collected his materials, how poor he was, how kind he was in teaching others as poor as himself, is of great interest.

SCENES OF OUR BEAUTIFUL HOMELAND

THE LOVELY RIVER DART REACHES THE SEA

A MOUNTAIN STREAM TUMBLES DOWN INTO LAKE DERWENTWATER, CUMBERLAND

THE SNOW-COVERED CAP OF BEN NEVIS RISES LIKE A SENTINEL ABOVE THE QUIET VALLEYS

PERHAPS THE MOST BEAUTIFUL STREET IN
BRITAIN—PRINCES STREET, EDINBURGH

THE OLD WORLD VILLAGE OF CADGWITH
IN CORNWALL

THE PLACID WATERS OF THE NORFOLK BROADS

THE RIVER DART FLOWS THROUGH DITTISHAM IN DEVON

THE SHAMBLES, AN ANCIENT
STREET IN YORK

QUEEN ELEANOR'S CROSS
AT GEDDINGTON

A GLIMPSE AT RIEVAULX ABBEY
IN YORKSHIRE

THE MEDIEVAL BRIDGE ACROSS THE RIVER TORRIDGE
AT BIDEFORD IN DEVON

THE ROCKY COAST OF OLD ENGLAND AT
KYNANCE IN CORNWALL

NEAR HILLTOWN IN ULSTER, WITH THE MOUNTAINS OF MOURNE IN THE BACKGROUND

THE HILLTOP RUINS OF CORFE CASTLE IN DORSET

THE OLD TUDOR HOUSE OF IGHTHAM, KENT

RUGGED HEIGHTS OVERLOOKING ABERGLASLYN
PASS IN WALES

SUNSHINE AND SHADOW IN THE SURREY
VILLAGE OF SHERE

One Thousand Poems of All Times and All Countries

THE QUEEN AND THE FLOWERS

For several centuries England has had a Poet Laureate. Originally he was chosen from the poets of the day to celebrate the great events in the history of the country, but he is no longer under any such obligation. The following poem, from "Fortunatus, the Pessimist," is written by a Victorian Poet Laureate, Alfred Austin, who retells in simple, tuneful verse an old and beautiful legend.

THERE was a king in olden days
   With black heart, scowling forehead.
The mighty trembled at his gaze,
   And his sceptre was abhorred.

Alike to burgher and to boor
   His grasp was hard and greedy;
He had no pity for the poor,
   Indulgence for the needy.

Beside him sat a gentle queen,
   Compassionate and holy,
Who fed the hungry, clad the mean,
   And comforted the lowly.

Till with harsh words he her forbade
   To visit, cheer, or aid them.
Then meekly, though her heart was sad,
   She listened, and obeyed them.

It happed one day, in hovel rude,
   A leper lay a-dying;
And there was none to take him food,
   And none to soothe his sighing.

Forgetting all, with bread and meat
   She filled a little wallet,
And, sallying out into the street,
   Made haste to reach his pallet.

When lo! the king, with courtiers girt,
   Came riding through the city.
The queen in terror raised her skirt
   To screen her work of pity.

Seeing her shrink and bow her head,
   His brow began to pucker;
"Now show me what it is," he said,
   "You hide below your tucker."

She spoke not, but uncovered it,
   And look what it discloses!
Not wheaten loaf and dainty bit,
   But mrytles, pinks, and roses.

"What gauds are these?" he fumed and cried,
   "And wherefore were they hidden?"
" I disobeyed you," she replied,
   " And trembled to be chidden.

" Food I was taking where, ah, me!
   A lonely leper cowers;
But the Lord Jesus, as you see,
   Has changed them into flowers."

The king dismounted from his horse,
   First smelt pink, rose, and myrtle;
Then knelt, and, smitten with remorse,
   Kissed her white hands and kirtle.

Henceforth he held no sumptuous state
   In courtyard, hall, or stable;
The poor were welcomed at his gate,
   The hungry at his table.

When died his queen, and in the tomb
   Was laid with pomp and wailing,
Myrtle at once began to bloom,
   And climb round slab and railing.

And even when the snow lies white,
   And frosty stars are shining,
Clove pinks about her grave are bright,
   And round it roses twining.

POEMS · SONGS · BALLADS · VERSES AND RHYMES WITH MUSIC

ETERNAL RULER OF THE CEASELESS ROUND

Some of the finest poetry is found in hymns. This noble prayer was written by an American minister, John White Chadwick, who was born in 1840 and died in 1904. He published several books of verse and was a very just critic.

ETERNAL Ruler of the ceaseless round
    Of circling planets singing on their
        way,
Guide of the nations from the night
    profound
  Into the glory of the perfect day,
Rule in our hearts that we may ever be
Guided and strengthened and upheld by
  Thee.

We would be one in hatred of all wrong,
    One in our love of all things sweet and
      fair;
One with the joy that breaketh into song,
    One with the grief that trembles into
      prayer;
One in the power that makes Thy children
  free
To follow truth, and this to follow Thee.

O clothe us with Thy heavenly armour,
  Lord,
    Thy trusty shield, Thy sword of love
    divine;
Our inspiration be Thy constant word;
  We ask no victories that are not Thine.
Give or withhold, let pain or pleasure be,
Enough to know that we are serving Thee.

ROBIN REDBREAST

One thing always to remember about poetry is that it can express the feelings of the heart far better than prose. You will feel this when you read this sweet poem about Robin Redbreast and the coming of winter by William Allingham. How surely the poet expresses in warm and friendly words his love for Robin Redbreast! Such feeling could not be put into words but for the power of poetry.

GOOD-BYE, good-bye to summer!
    For summer's nearly done;
The garden smiling faintly,
    Cool breezes in the sun;
Our thrushes now are silent,
    Our swallows flown away;
But Robin's here, in coat of brown,
    With ruddy breast-knot gay.
    Robin, Robin Redbreast,
      O Robin dear!
    Robin singing sweetly
      In the falling of the year.

Bright yellow, red, and orange,
    The leaves come down in hosts;
The trees are Indian princes,
    But soon they'll turn to ghosts;
The scanty pears and apples
    Hang russet on the bough;

It's autumn, autumn, autumn late,
  'Twill soon be winter now.
    Robin, Robin Redbreast,
      O Robin dear!
    And wellaway! my Robin, Robin,
      For pinching days are near.

The fireside for the cricket,
    The wheat-stack for the mouse,
When trembling night-winds whistle
    And moan all round the house;
The frosty ways like iron,
    The branches plumed with snow—
Alas! in winter, dead and dark,
    Where can poor Robin go?
    Robin, Robin Redbreast,
      O Robin dear!
    And a crumb of bread for Robin,
      His little heart to cheer.

TO A MOUNTAIN DAISY

This beautiful poem, by the great Scottish poet Robert Burns, contains a few words of his native tongue which English boys and girls may not find it easy to understand. These are maun (must), stour (dust), wa's (walls), bield (shelter) and histie stibble (dry stubble). Few of the other words that are used vary much from ordinary English.

WEE modest crimson-tipped flower,
    Thou's met me in an evil hour;
For I maun crush amang the stour
    Thy slender stem;
To spare thee now is past my power,
    Thou bonnie gem.

Alas! it's no thy neibor sweet,
The bonnie lark, companion meet,
Bending thee 'mang the dewy weet
    Wi' speckled breast,
When upward springing, blythe, to greet
    The purpling east.

Cauld blew the bitter-biting north
Upon thy early humble birth;
Yet cheerfully thou glinted forth
    Amid the storm;
Scarce reared above the parent earth
    Thy tender form.

The flaunting flowers our gardens yield
High sheltering woods and wa's maun
  shield,
But thou beneath the random bield
    O' clod or stane
Adorns the histie stibble field,
    Unseen, alane.

There, in thy scanty mantle clad,
Thy snawy bosom sunward spread,
Thou lifts thy unassuming head
    In humble guise;
But now the share uptears thy bed,
    And low thou lies!

CORONATION

The purpose of this poem, written by Helen H. Jackson, is to illustrate the ancient truth that an earthly crown may only be the symbol of a slave, while true freedom may be clothed with the poorest and humblest raiment.

At the king's gate the subtle noon
  Wove filmy, yellow nets of sun;
Into the drowsy snare too soon
  The guards fell one by one.

Through the king's gate, unquestioned then,
  A beggar went, and laughed: "This brings
Me chance at last to see if men
  Fare better being kings."

The king sat bowed beneath his crown,
  Propping his face with listless hand;
Watching the hour-glass sifting down
  Too slow its shining sand.

"Poor man, what wouldst thou have of me?"
  The beggar turned, and, pitying,
Replied, like one in dream, "Of thee
  Nothing. I want the king."

Up rose the king, and from his head
  Shook off the crown and threw it by.
"O man, thou must have known," he said,
  "A greater king than I."

Through all the gates, unquestioned then,
  Went king and beggar hand in hand.
Whispered the king, "Shall I know when
  Before *his* throne I stand?"

The beggar laughed. Free winds in haste
  Were wiping from the king's hot brow
The crimson lines the crown had traced.
  "This is his presence now."

At the king's gate the crafty noon
  Unwove its yellow nets of sun;
Out of their sleep in terror soon
  The guards walked one by one.

"Ho, there! Ho, there! Has no man seen
  The king?" The cry ran to and fro;
Beggar and king, they laughed, I ween,
  The laugh that free men know.

On the king's gate the moss grew grey;
  The king came not. They called him dead;
And made his eldest son one day
  Slave in his father's stead.

THE NIGHTINGALE AND THE GLOW-WORM

William Cowper, like all gentle and tender natures, not only hated to see any cruelty by mankind to dumb creatures, but was sorry to contemplate the cruelty of these creatures to each other, though they are really never cruel, and seldom kill except for food. In this poem he imagines a glow-worm giving a nightingale a good reason why he should leave him alone. Certainly, if a glow-worm could think and speak, he might have done as the poet describes.

A nightingale that all day long
  Had cheered the village with his song,
Nor yet at eve his note suspended,
Nor yet when eventide was ended,
Began to feel, as well he might,
The keen demands of appetite;
When, looking eagerly around,
He spied far off, upon the ground,
A something shining in the dark,
And knew the glow-worm by his spark;
So, stooping down from hawthorn top,
He thought to put him in his crop.

The worm, aware of his intent,
Harangued him thus, right eloquent:
"Did you admire my lamp," quoth he,
"As much as I your minstrelsy,
You would abhor to do me wrong
As much as I to spoil your song;
For 'twas the self-same Power Divine
Taught you to sing and me to shine,
That you with music, I with light,
Might beautify and cheer the night."

The songster heard this short oration,
And, warbling out his approbation,
Released him, as my story tells,
And found a supper somewhere else.

HOW SLEEP THE BRAVE

These lovely verses were written by William Collins, a poet whose life was very sad. He was born on December 25, 1721, educated at Oxford, and afterwards lived and wrote in poverty in London. Later an uncle left him sufficient money, but his health and mind failed, and he died at the age of 38 (June 12, 1759) without knowing that his "Odes" had won a lasting place in our literature.

How sleep the brave who sink to rest
  By all their country's wishes blest!
When Spring, with dewy fingers cold,
Returns to deck their hallowed mould
She there shall dress a sweeter sod
Than Fancy's feet have ever trod!

By fairy hands their knell is rung,
By forms unseen their dirge is sung;
There Honour comes—a pilgrim grey—
To bless the turf that wraps their clay;
And Freedom shall awhile repair
To dwell—a weeping hermit—there!

THE SPACIOUS FIRMAMENT ON HIGH

We give here Joseph Addison's paraphrase of the Nineteenth Psalm. In its Bible version this psalm was a great favourite of St. Augustine, and Addison has skilfully retained all the teaching of the original while expressing it in the modern poetic form with a great and solemn dignity.

THE spacious firmament on high,
    With all the blue ethereal sky
And spangled heavens—a shining frame—
Their great Original proclaim.
The unwearied sun, from day to day,
Doth his Creator's power display,
And publishes to every land
The work of an Almighty hand.

Soon as the evening shades prevail
The moon takes up the wondrous tale,
And nightly to the listening earth
Repeats the story of her birth;
Whilst all the stars that round her burn,
And all the planets in their turn,
Confirm the tidings as they roll,
And spread the truth from Pole to Pole.

What though in solemn silence all
Move round this dark terrestrial ball?
What though no real voice nor sound
Amidst their radiant orbs be found?
In reason's ear they all rejoice,
And utter forth a glorious voice,
For ever singing as they shine:
The hand that made us is Divine.

A MAN'S REQUIREMENTS

These simple lines are full of charm. They picture for us true love in many phases, and they are, of course, true poetry because they are written by a true poet—Mrs. Browning.

LOVE me, sweet, with all thou art;
    Feeling, thinking, seeing;
Love me in the lightest part,
    Love me in full being.

Love me with thine open youth
    In its frank surrender;
With the vowing of thy mouth,
    With its silence tender.

Love me with thy azure eyes,
    Made for earnest granting;
Taking colour from the skies,
    Can Heaven's truth be wanting?

Love me in thy gorgeous airs,
    When the world has crowned thee;
Love me kneeling at thy prayers,
    With the angels round thee.

Love me pure, as musers do
    Up the woodlands shady;
Love me gaily, fast and true,
    As a winsome lady.

SLEEP, BEAUTY BRIGHT

William Blake, the strange and mystic poet, as we have seen, could write simple lays of country life, and here we have him crooning a pretty little cradle song tender as a mother's, except that in the last lines he has a sudden fear for the dangers of life which the child, as it grows older, will have to face.

SLEEP, sleep, beauty bright,
    Dreaming in the joys of night;
Sleep, sleep; in thy sleep
Little sorrows sit and weep.

Sweet babe, in thy face
Soft desires I can trace,
Secret joys and secret smiles,
Little pretty infant wiles.

As thy softest limbs I feel,
Smiles as of the morning steal
O'er thy cheek and o'er thy breast,
Where thy little heart doth rest.

Oh, the cunning wiles that creep
In thy little heart asleep!
When thy little heart doth wake
Then the dreadful light shall break.

A SONG OF THE NIGHTINGALE

The poets have always heard an under-note of sadness in the nightingale's song, and indeed it seems to be tuned to the pensive beauty of the night. This is brought out strongly in the comparison made here with the lark's exultant day-song by Hartley Coleridge. Hartley was the eldest son of Samuel Taylor Coleridge, a far greater poet. The son, like his father, lived much in the Lake District. Wordsworth loved him as a child. He died in 1849, at the age of 53.

'TIS sweet to hear the merry lark,
    That bids a blithe good-morrow;
But sweeter to hark in the twinkling dark
    To the soothing song of sorrow.
O nightingale! What doth she ail?
    And is she sad or jolly?
For ne'er on earth was a sound of mirth
    So like to melancholy.

The merry lark, he soars on high,
    No worldly thought o'ertakes him;
He sings aloud to the clear blue sky,
    And the daylight that awakes him.
As sweet a lay, as loud, as gay,
    The nightingale is trilling;
With feeling bliss no less than his
    Her little heart is thrilling.

Yet ever and anon a sigh
    Peers through her lavish mirth;
For the lark's bold song is of the sky,
    And hers is of the earth.
By night and day she tunes her lay
    To drive away all sorrow;
But bliss, alas! tonight must pass,
    And woe may come tomorrow.

THE STREAM AND THE OCEAN

Victor Hugo was one of the great poets and novelists of France. Most of his stories have been translated into English, but not all his poems. These short verses have not the grand roll and the passion of his great poems as those would not suit the subject he has here chosen; but they make a charming little poem which was specially translated into English for our book by Mr. Harold Begbie.

THE streamlet down from the moun-
    tainous glen
  Fell drop by drop to the roaring sea;
And the ocean, strewn with the wrecks of
    men,
  Cried: " Whimperer, what dost thou
    want with me?

" Lo, I am the terror that none may fence,
  I drive to the edge of the sky my way;
And can I, who am terrible, strong,
    immense,
  Have need of thy trickles of dew and
    spray? "

Then the streamlet answered the ocean
    back:
  " O bitter sea, to your furious brink,
Without glory or noise, I give what you
    lack—
  A drop of water that men can drink."

THE COUNCIL OF HORSES

John Gay, born at Barnstaple in 1685, died in London on December 4, 1732. He was a poet who had much success in his own day and, although his works as a whole are now but little read, many of his songs and shorter poems have enduring merit. While best known as the author of the Beggar's Opera, his Fables are perhaps the most quoted of all his writings, and of these we have selected the following example, which is very familiar in style and moral.

UPON a time a neighing steed,
  Who grazed among a numerous
    breed,
With mutiny had fired the train,
And spread dissension through the plain
On matters that concerned the state.
The council met in grand debate.
A colt whose eyeballs flamed with ire,
Elate with strength and youthful fire,
In haste stept forth before the rest,
And thus the listening throng addressed:
" Goodness, how abject is our race,
Condemned to slavery and disgrace!
Shall we our servitude retain
Because our sires have borne the chain?
Consider, friends, your strength and might;
'Tis conquest to assert your right.
How cumbrous is the gilded coach!
The pride of man is our reproach.
Were we designed for daily toil,
To drag the ploughshare through the soil,
To sweat the harness through the road,
To groan beneath the carrier's load?

How feeble are the two-legged kind!
What force is in our nerves combined!
Shall, then, our nobler jaws submit
To foam and champ the galling bit?
Shall haughty man my back bestride?
Shall the sharp spur provoke my side?
Forbid it, heavens! Reject the rein;
Your shame, your infamy, disdain.
Let him the lion first control
And still the tiger's famished growl.
Let us, like them, our freedom claim,
And make them tremble at our name."
A general nod approved the cause,
And all the circle neighed applause.
When, lo! with grave and solemn pace,
A steed advanced before the race,
With age and long experience wise;
Around he cast his thoughtful eyes,
And to the murmurs of the train
Thus spoke the Nestor of the plain:
" When I had health and strength like you
The toils of servitude I knew;
Now grateful man rewards my pains
And gives me all these wide domains.
At will I crop the year's increase;
My latter life is rest and peace.
I grant, to men we lend our pains,
And aid him to correct the plains;
But doth he not divide the care
Through all the labours of the year?
How many thousand structures rise
To fence us from inclement skies!
For us he bears the sultry day
And stores up all our winter's hay.
He sows, he reaps the harvest's gain;
We share the toil and share the grain.
Since every creature was decreed
To aid each other's mutual need,
Appease your discontented mind,
And act the part by Heaven assigned."
The tumult ceased, the colt submitted,
And, like his ancestors, was bitted.

STUPIDITY STREET

This fine little poem, by Ralph Hodgson, is a parable, meaning that people perish for the want of vision.

I SAW with open eyes
  Singing birds sweet
Sold in the shops
  For the people to eat,
Sold in the shops of
  Stupidity Street.

I saw in a vision
  The worm in the wheat,
And in the shops nothing
  For people to eat;
Nothing for sale in
  Stupidity Street.

THE HUMMING TOP

Here is another poem by that favourite children's poet, Eugene Field, for of his delightful verses we can never tire.

THE top it hummeth a sweet, sweet song
  To my dear little boy at play;
Merrily singeth all day long,
  As it spinneth and spinneth away.
    And my dear little boy
    He laugheth with joy
When he hears the monotone
    Of that busy thing
    That loveth to sing.
The song that is all its own.

Hold fast the string and wind it tight
  That the song be loud and clear;
Now hurl the top with all your might
  Upon the banquette here;
    And straight from the string
    The joyous thing
Boundeth and spinneth along,
    And it whirrs and it chirrs
    And it birrs and it purrs
Ever its pretty song.

Will ever my dear little boy grow old,
  As some have grown before?
Will ever his heart feel faint and cold
  When he heareth the songs of yore?
    Will ever this toy
    Of my dear little boy,
When the years have worn away,
    Sing sad and low
    Of the long ago,
As it singeth to me today?

THE SEA

The spirit of freedom which one seems to absorb when on a voyage has never been better rendered than in this poem by Barry Cornwall. In this case it is supposed to be an old sailor who was speaking, but the salty breeze, which the poet has so cleverly suggested by the swift movement of his verse, is familiar to us all. There is a certain infectious quality of actual pleasure in this song of the sea that makes us for the moment sharers of the old sailor's love for the life of the ocean, though we may be conscious that there is another side to it less attractive.

THE Sea! the Sea! the open Sea!
  The blue, the fresh, the ever free!
Without a mark, without a bound,
It runneth the earth's wide regions round;
It plays with the clouds, it mocks the skies,
Or like a cradled creature lies.

I'm on the Sea! I'm on the Sea!
I am where I would ever be—
With the blue above, and the blue below,
And silence wheresoe'er I go.
If a storm should come and awake the deep,
What matter? I shall ride and sleep.

I love—oh, *how* I love—to ride
On the fierce, foaming, bursting tide,
When every mad wave drowns the moon,
Or whistles aloft his tempest-tune;
And tells how goeth the world below,
And why the south-west blasts do blow.

I never was on the dull, tame shore
But I loved the great Sea more and more,
And backwards flew to her billowy breast,
Like a bird that seeketh its mother's nest;
And a mother she *was*, and *is* to me,
For I was born on the open Sea.

The waves were white, and red the morn,
In the noisy hour when I was born;
And the whale it whistled, the porpoise rolled,
And the dolphins bared their backs of gold;
And never was heard such an outcry wild
As welcomed to life the Ocean-child.

I've lived since then, in calm and strife,
Full fifty summers a sailor's life.
With wealth to spend, and a power to range,
But never have sought nor sighed for change;
And Death, whenever he come to me,
Shall come on the wide, unbounded Sea.

QUIET WORK

These verses, by Matthew Arnold, take the form of a sonnet, or a little poem of fourteen lines, in which the last six lines are not merely a continuation of the first eight, but have a change of thought, which is proper to this form of verse.

ONE lesson, Nature, let me learn of thee,
  One lesson which in every wind is blown;
One lesson of two duties kept at one
Though the loud world proclaim their enmity—

Of toil unsevered from tranquillity!
Of labour, that in lasting fruit outgrows
Far noisier schemes, accomplished in repose,
Too great for haste, too high for rivalry!

Yes, while on earth a thousand discords ring,
Man's fitful uproar mingling with his toil,
Still do thy sleepless ministers move on,

Their glorious tasks in silence perfecting;
Still working, blaming still our vain turmoil,
Labourers that shall not fail when man is gone.

LITTLE VERSES FOR VERY LITTLE PEOPLE

A CRADLE SONG

WHAT does little birdie say
  In her nest at peep of day?
Let me fly, says little birdie,
Mother, let me fly away.
Birdie, rest a little longer,
Till the little wings are stronger.
So she rests a little longer
Then she flies away.

What does little baby say
In her bed at peep of day?
Baby says, like little birdie,
Let me rise and fly away.
Baby, sleep a little longer,
Till the little limbs are stronger,
If she sleeps a little longer
Baby, too, shall fly away.

Tennyson

GOOD-CHILDREN STREET

THERE's a dear little home in Good-
  Children Street—
My heart turneth fondly today
Where tinkle of tongues and patter of feet
  Make sweetest of music play;
Where the sunshine of love illumines each
  face,
And warms every heart in that old-
  fashioned place.

For dear little children go romping about
  With dollies and tin tops and drums,
And, my! how they frolic and scamper
  and shout
  Till bedtime too speedily comes!
Oh, days they are golden, and days they
  are fleet,
With little folk living in Good-Children
  Street.

See, here comes an army with guns painted
  red,
  And swords, caps, and plumes of all sorts;
The captain rides gaily and proudly ahead
  On a stick-horse that prances and snorts!
Oh, legions of soldiers you're certain to
  meet—
Nice make-believe soldiers — in Good
  Children Street.

And yonder Odette wheels her dolly
  about—
  Poor dolly! I am sure she is ill,
For one of her blue china eyes has dropped
  out,
  And her voice is asthmatic'ly shrill.
Then, too, I observe she is minus her feet,
Which causes much sorrow in Good-
  Children Street.

'Tis so the dear children go romping about
  With dollies and banners and drums,
And I venture to say they are sadly put out
  When an end to their jubilee comes.
Oh, days they are golden, and days they
  are fleet,
With little folk living in Good-Children
  Street.

But when falleth night over river and town
  Those little folk vanish from sight,
And an angel all white from the sky cometh
  down
  And guardeth the babes through the
  night,
And singeth her lullabies tender and sweet
To the dear little people in Good-Children
  Street.

Though elsewhere the world be o'er-
  burdened with care,
  Though poverty fall to my lot;
Though toil and vexation be always my
  share,
  What care I—they trouble me not!
This thought maketh life ever joyous and
  sweet:
There's a dear little home in Good-
  Children Street.

Eugene Field

WISHING

DO you wish the world were better?
  Let me tell you what to do:
Set a watch upon your actions,
  Keep them always straight and true;
Rid your mind of selfish motives,
  Let your thoughts be clean and high:
You can make a little Eden
  Of the sphere you occupy.

Do you wish the world were wiser?
  Well, suppose you make a start
By accumulating wisdom
  In the scrap-book of your heart.
Do not waste one page on folly;
  Live to learn, and learn to live.
If you want to give men knowledge
  You must get it ere you give.

Do you wish the world were happy?
  Then remember day by day
Just to scatter seeds of kindness
  As you pass along the way;
For the pleasures of the many
  May be oft times traced to one,
As the hand that plants an acorn
  Shelters armies from the sun.

Ella Wheeler Wilcox

Hushaby, babby, lie still with thy daddy,
  Thy mammy is gone to the mill
To get some wheat, to make some meal,
  So pray, my dear babby, lie still.

Old woman, old woman, shall we go
    a-shearing?
" Speak a little louder, sir, I'm very thick
    of hearing."
Old woman, old woman, shall I kiss you
    dearly?
" Thank you, kind sir, I hear you very
    clearly."

Little Tommy Tittlemouse
  Lived in a little house;
He caught fishes
In other men's ditches.

I have a little husband
  And he is two feet four;
So he can reach the knocker,
  And ring at our front door.

But when we want our dinner
  He must take it down himself;
It's really very awkward
  When a wife can't reach the shelf.

Perhaps I shall grow bigger,
  But this I surely know:
I cannot love him dearer
  If I grow, and grow, and grow!

Hush, baby, my dolly, I pray you don't
    cry,
And I'll give you some bread and some
    milk by and by;
Or perhaps you like custard, or maybe a
    tart?
Then to either you're welcome, with all
    my heart.

Birds of a feather flock together,
  And so will pigs and swine.
Rats and mice will have their choice,
  And so will I have mine.

There's a neat little clock,
    In the schoolroom it stands,
And it points to the time
    With its two little hands.
And may we, like the clock,
    Keep a face clean and bright,
With hands ever ready
    To do what is right.

If you are to be a gentleman, as I suppose
    you be.
You'll neither laugh nor smile for a tick-
    ling of the knee.

Peg, Peg, with a wooden leg,
  Her father was a miller;
He tossed the dumpling at her head,
  And said he could not kill her.

Daffy-down-dilly has come to town
    In a yellow petticoat and a green
gown.

The gossips of the village—see,
  Their fine lace caps are wearing.
They sip their dainty cups of tea,
  White sugar they are sharing.
Their fingers shine with golden rings,
  But—duty never matters!
Nothing is ready for the men,
  And under—they are tatters!

Peter White will ne'er go right;
  Would you know the reason why?
He follows his nose wherever he goes,
  And that stands all awry.

I often sit and wish that I
  Could be a kite up in the sky,
And ride upon the breeze, and go
Whatever way it chanced to blow;
Then I could look beyond the town,
And see the river winding down,
And follow all the ships that sail,
Like me, before the merry gale,
Until at last with them I came
To some place with a foreign name.

What is the news of the day,
    Good neighbour, I pray?
They say the balloon
    Is gone up to the moon!

The Story of Where Power Comes From, What It Does, & How It Works

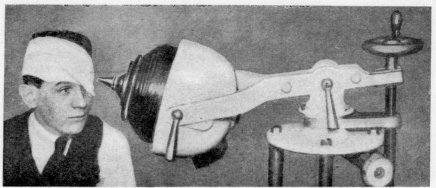

Removing metal from an injured man's eye by means of an electric magnet

WHAT ELECTRICITY DOES FOR US

THE more we study the subject of electricity the more remarkable do we find the numberless ways in which it can be made of use to us.

The steam of a boiler can be sent through pipes and radiators, and made to warm a room, or it can be made to drive a steam engine. Petrol and oil can be mixed with air and exploded in a cylinder and made to drive a motor-engine; oil can be burnt to make heat. But beyond these simple and direct means of using the power of steam and oil, they have not much adaptability.

If, on the other hand, we make use of electricity there are a thousand and one ways in which it can help us; all sorts of ways in which even the tiniest quantities of it can be made to do valuable work for mankind.

The thousand-horse-power motors of a powerful electric locomotive are of no greater use in the service of man than the infinitely feeble current that creeps across the sea through two thousand miles of submarine cable. The huge electric magnet in the steel works which will lift ten tons of iron has its counterpart in the little electric magnet which tinkles a bell when a button is pressed. An electric current can be made with equal ease to heat a

huge mass of molten metal in a furnace, to boil an egg, or warm the gloves of an airman.

It is the greatest power in the world because it is so pliable, so adaptable, so easily apportioned to the task for which it is wanted. It travels so easily and with such incredible swiftness along wires or conductors that it can be supplied instantly over vast distances.

Thus the early dreams of water-power engineers to drive huge dynamos by the water-power of Iceland falls, and transmit the current across the sea to the manufacturing districts of Scotland, is by no means impossible, though not at present feasible. But generators driven by water-power today supply electricity to places a hundred miles away over land; and electricity can be actually stored up in the chemical plates of an accumulator and carried by road, train, and ship to the farthest ends of the Earth.

Pass an electric current along a wire made of some material which offers great resistance and the wire will become hot. In this simple way we get heat from electricity. The heating "units" that are used in an electric iron, an electric oven, an electric stove, are nothing more than lengths of highly-resisting metal wire

ELECTRICITY · WIRELESS · OIL · GAS · MOTORS · ENGINES · SHIPS

which become red-hot when a current is passed along them.

Now, if we heat a resistant wire still more strongly it becomes white-hot, or incandescent, and in this state it gives out light. See, then, how easily we can obtain light or heat from this wonderful power. The electric bulb or incandescent lamp is nothing more than a little filament, or wire, of very highly resisting material enclosed in a glass bulb from which the air is exhausted, so that there is no oxygen present in which it could burn away.

Thus, electricity gives us heat and light, both depending on the resistance of certain substances which become hot to a more or less degree when a current passes through them. The electric motor, driven by the current from a battery or dynamo, turns the current into power; and here, again, it is just as easy to drive a tiny motor that will work a dentist's drill or a toy machine as to drive a heavy train at sixty miles an hour.

THE ELECTRIC MOTOR TURNS THE ELECTRIC CURRENT INTO POWER

If we go into a busy factory we shall see dozens of motors of various sizes at work, ranging perhaps from the tiny motor of the desk-fan to giants of a hundred horse-power. Electricity is everywhere ; it comes into the factory through limp-looking cables which lead to a switch-board or distributing arrangement, and from there is meted out to the various motors, the electric lights, the radiators; and each single thing is under the control of a simple switch that can be turned on or off at will.

Power, light, and heat are probably the most familiar every-day evidences of the place that electricity takes in our life. But the telegraph and the telephone play parts just as intimate, though in turning to them we leave the big forces of electricity and deal with currents of infinitely small magnitude. The telephone has become such a familiar instrument that many of us are apt to forget the telegraph; yet each time we go into a post-office the little ticking instrument away at the back might remind us of its existence. For in spite of the universal application of the telephone in all our big towns and cities, and even in our villages, the telegraph remains at work all day.

The telegraph carries our words round the world. The operator presses a key in London and simultaneously a delicate recording instrument marks a paper ribbon in Lisbon, New York, Teheran, or Bombay. It enables a man to express a thought aloud, as it were, to someone five thousand miles away. It has annihilated space.

THE TELEGRAPH AS THE NERVE SYSTEM OF THE BRITISH COMMONWEALTH

The telegraph may be described as the very nerve system of the British Commonwealth, uniting the brains of the great rulers of our sister nations with those of our own Government in London.

As in all other things electrical the telegraph is merely a means of transference of electric power. Suppose we were to crowd a lot of glass beads on a knitting needle so that there was no room for one more from end to end. Suppose, then, we tried to force another bead on at one end; what would happen? A bead would be forced off the other end. The power we exerted at one end of the needle would in the same instant accomplish something at the other end.

We may regard a long telegraph line in much the same way. The surface of the metal wire is crowded with electrons—particles of negatively-charged electricity. The telegraph operator, in tapping his key, is applying to the line an electric current which forces, as it were, more electrons on to the line. The line being already full a corresponding number of electrons are "pushed off" the other end of the line, and instantly make the telegraph give a signal.

AN ANSWER TO LONDON RECEIVED IN A MINUTE FROM A PERSIAN CITY

Here is the answer to the question so often asked, How is it that electricity travels so fast ? The transmission of the current is so rapid that we can sit in a London office and ask a question of a man sitting in an office in some Persian city, and in a minute or so we shall get his answer.

Half the business of the world is done with the telegraph. When our great-grand-fathers went on business to New York we heard nothing from them for two months or more. Today the man going to New York telegraphs by wireless from mid-ocean to say that he is having a fine passage; sends a telegram by cable to say he has safely arrived at New York, and inquires at his office in London about his business. The man in New York is *still with his friends in London.* The electric nerve is a link between people; they can exchange thoughts, for the distance between them has been conquered.

Such progress has been made in this connection that it is now possible to talk as well as to telegraph. Today a man in London can ask for a number in New York, and within a few minutes be connected up with that number and be holding a perfectly natural conversation.

A MAN IN THE EIFFEL TOWER SIGNS HIS NAME IN AMERICA

Everyone uses the telephone today. Business without it would be impossible; home life would in many cases be difficult. The manager of a big store today does not have continually to go the rounds of the various buildings. He talks to any one of his workmen over the telephone lines fitted throughout the works. The activity of commercial life as it is today could not go on without this advantage.

Yet every time we take up our telephone we bring electricity into play. How little do we think as we begin our conversation that we are marshalling together the wonderful discoveries of the ancient shepherds, the far-Eastern spinning women, the laborious researches of Galvani, Volta, and the hundreds of pioneers that followed them down to the time of Bell, Edison, and Thomson?

Even more wonderful are the modern inventions by which pictures, signatures, and photographs can be sent by electricity to one country from another. For nearly three years a picture was telegraphed every day from Paris or Manchester to London by the *telectrograph* invented by Thorne Baker. At a later date the French inventor Edouard Belin sent by wireless the signature of the French premier from the lofty aerial of the Eiffel Tower to the receiving station in the United States.

PICTURES SENT BY WIRELESS FROM CONTINENT TO CONTINENT

When a picture is sent by telegraph it is divided up into thousands of tiny parts. Each piece is given its own value in the form of electricity; and these currents, each one varying in strength with the light and shade of the photograph, are sent through the ether, and arrive, still as electricity, at some distant receiving station where the ingenuity of man once again turns them into light or dark spots which a machine pieces together to form a facsimile of the original picture.

Pictures of topical events are sent every day from one continent to another by electricity. Every big newspaper has its own special department for the transmission and reception of telegraphed photographs. A newspaper reporter can take a photograph to any central telephone office and wire it to his editor.

Electricity is used in a great many devices where signalling is concerned. The simplest form of a signal that we know is, of course, the electric bell. It is easy to understand how a distant signal can be given by electricity if we try to think of a current as always trying to flow round a circle, or closed loop of wire, but being quite unable to do so if there is a break in the wire. Thus, we might join a wire to the positive pole of a battery, run the wire along from London to Edinburgh, and back to London again.

The electricity from the battery charges the whole wire—no matter how long—and the instant the free end of the wire is joined to the negative pole there will be a continuous, or "closed," circuit, round which the current can flow. While the end of the wire was left unjoined to the negative pole of the battery no current could flow—the circuit was "open."

OBJECTS COATED WITH GOLD AND SILVER BY ELECTRICITY

But we can think of the whole length of wire bristling with the energy of the battery, and always waiting to yield up its power as soon as there is a complete circuit of metal round which to circulate. A good example is seen in a big ship, where several miles of electric wires may be used in order to connect the various signalling devices and controls, the telephones and the lights, and the radio.

We can see there how the electric fire alarm operates. A form of alarm, also used extensively in factories and offices, is an electric bell connected through a battery to a *broken circuit.* As long as the circuit is broken the bell does not ring. But the free ends of the circuit are connected with a device in which a piece of metal would, on becoming hot through a fire, expand and so lengthen as to touch a metal contact, thus completing the circuit and making the bell ring. In the case of fire alarms in our streets the handle which is pulled after the little glass window has been broken closes the circuit of a bell and battery in the fire station. When we take the receiver off a telephone instrument in an area where there is no automatic exchange two contacts come together whereby a current flows through a circuit running to the exchange, and lights a lamp in the operator's signalling apparatus, showing that a call is required.

Another thing of vast use to us which electricity accomplishes is the covering of metals with beautiful, fine deposits of silver, gold, nickel, and so on. The process of electro-plating is one of the most widely used in the world. It has a very real importance, for it enables us to coat metals which are easily affected by the air with a cheap covering that protects them. Iron in particular easily rusts if exposed to the air, and in course of time it practically crumbles away.

But if a piece of iron be well cleaned, connected by a wire to the negative pole of a battery and placed in a bath of water containing a salt of nickel, and the positive pole of the battery be joined to a piece of nickel also immersed in the liquid, ions of nickel will travel along through the liquid in an endless procession and deposit themselves upon the piece of iron in the form of an infinitely thin layer of nickel metal, and this coat of nickel metal, as most of us know, can be beautifully polished and will not allow the iron to rust.

THE MAKING OF NITRIC ACID FROM THE NITROGEN OF THE AIR

In similar ways the jeweller can plate objects with gold; the silversmith can make table silver of some cheap white metal afterwards plated with silver; and all kinds of objects can be plated with chromium, which is the most resistant of all the metals.

This power of the current to undo the bonds of Nature and resolve substances into their elements is of great value, for when electricity gives us a metal out of some metallic compound it gives it to us in a marvellously pure state. Copper, for instance, of extraordinary purity is made in this way, and is spoken of in commerce as electrolytic copper.

Electricity is used in hundreds of industries, and employed in a myriad ways by the engineer and chemist. Nowadays immense quantities of nitrogen gas are actually manufactured by electricity for use in the manufacture of artificial fertiliser for agricultural purposes.

Artificial fertilisers must contain nitrogen, and enormous quantities of nitrogen compounds—such as sulphate of ammonia, nitrate of ammonia, and so on—have to be used by farmers, especially in the less temperate countries.

FERTILISER FOR OUR CROPS MADE BY AN ELECTRIC SUN

Priestley, the English chemist who discovered oxygen, noticed in 1779 that an acid was produced when an electric spark passed through the air ; and a few years later the famous Cavendish proved that it was nitric acid, an acid composed of nitrogen, hydrogen, and oxygen. Nitrogen had first been obtained, in the form of nitric acid, from the air! Today huge water-power electric plants are in use for extracting this valuable gas from the atmosphere.

A well-known method invented by Birkeland and Eyde consists of passing air over a brilliant sheet of intensely hot flame which is called an electric sun. This flame, a huge electric arc light in reality, is spread out by the help of magnetic force to a length of about six feet. It plays upon the air in a brick-lined furnace, and the nitrogen is passed into milk of lime, with which it helps to form the fertiliser.

Today *air mining*, both for nitrogen with which to feed the crops and for oxygen for commercial purposes, is a great industry. Nitrogen which is distilled from liquefied air is used in electric lamps together with argon; the bulbs are first exhausted to a high vacuum and then traces of these gases introduced, giving the "gas-filled" incandescent lamps which are in almost universal use.

We could go on giving one example after another of the extraordinary general use which is today made of this power.

ELECTRICITY THAT WILL RECORD A HEARTBEAT OR DRIVE A BATTLESHIP

It is of immense use in the science of healing, where the X-rays have almost revolutionised medical work. It can operate a delicate instrument that records the faintest beats of the heart, the feeble ebb and flow of a current sent beneath an ocean, and it can equally drive a battleship or melt a thousand tons of rock.

Imperishable Thoughts of Men Enshrined in the Books of the World

William Shakespeare with some of the great men of his time

A SHINING SPLENDOUR COMES

WILLIAM SHAKESPEARE, quite the most famous Englishman throughout the world, gained his fame not by deeds of heroism but by hasty writings which he did not preserve with any care. Through his natural genius, unhelped by trained study, English literature in its choicest forms burst, almost suddenly, into its brightest splendour.

The chief form of writing used by Shakespeare was the drama. But the English drama, as we now understand it, had only been invented during the life-time of Shakespeare's father. The first English comedy, called Ralph Roister Doister, was written by Nicholas Udall for a company of boys only eleven years before Shakespeare was born; and the first tragedy, Gorboduc by Thomas Sackville and Thomas Norton, was acted in the Temple only three years before Shakespeare's birth.

So steep was the ascent from the time when there was no English drama to the perfecting of dramatic art. It was an outburst of intellectual energy at which the world has wondered ever since.

Long before Shakespeare there had been, at first under the supervision of the Church and later by the Guilds of Workmen, acting of a rude kind in England in the so-called Miracle Plays, representing Scripture scenes and lives of the saints, and in versions of romantic traditions, like Robin Hood's adventures; and they were followed and accompanied by Moralities, in which the characters were not human beings but Virtues and Vices, with comical Interludes thrown in to raise a laugh. These merrymaking scenes have left us relics to this day in the antics in panto- mimes of the clown and harlequin.

We know quite well what the Miracle Plays, Moralities, and Mysteries were like, for numerous examples have been pre- served, as in the 49 Mysteries of York, 32 of Wakefield, and 25 of Chester. We know that, though they created an interest in a rough form of acting, in days when reading was comparatively rare, they were not dramatically conceived, but were rather tableaux connected by rhymed talk.

The first theatre was built near London when Shakespeare was 12, none being allowed in the city till many years had passed. With the theatre came pro- fessional actors and professional writers for the stage, and the first group of them were men ranging from ten years older than Shakespeare to his own age. It was these men, John Lyly, Thomas Nash, Thomas Lodge, George Peele, Robert

ROMANCE · HISTORIES · DRAMAS · ESSAYS · WORLD CLASSICS

Greene, and above all Christopher Marlowe, since known as the University Wits, who first began to write true plays and who were the real preparers of the ground for the work of Shakespeare. They were men whom he knew, and who knew him.

THE DAWN OF A NEW AGE OF SPLENDOUR AND ROMANCE IN LITERATURE

"These spacious times of great Elizabeth," from which Shakespeare rises as a lasting king of men, were great in changeful wonders to a degree only paralleled in the nineteenth and twentieth centuries when steam power on land and sea, the conquest of the air, and the miracle of wireless brought all parts of the Earth close together. These modern discoveries, revolutionary as they have been, have not had deeper significance than the changes that aroused men to wonder and activity in the time of Shakespeare. A number of new prospects lately unfolded then spread wide and fair before the gaze of man.

The whole round Earth had become vaguely known, and it was felt to be rich in romance. The charms of the ancient life of Rome and Greece were breaking through the mists of ignorance that had clouded the Middle Ages. Printing was spreading in all countries tales of all other countries, gathered from long vistas of time. And, above all, the minds of men were being freed to think as they would about whatever concerned their welfare and happiness. Our English language, too, had become rich in words that would express all thoughts and feelings. "Lo, Creation widened in man's view," and records of mind-stirring thought were pouring in upon our nation through translations from other tongues.

THE GLOWING GENIUS OF THE STRATFORD TRADESMAN'S SON

What was needed was a man who could gather up and record for after times, somehow, the vast interest in life felt by these alert, quick-minded, Elizabethan lovers of the romance that came surging afresh over the world. Who could that man be? How could he find an adequate form of expression? Would he be a man packed with learning and writing history, grave and gay?

No. He was not that kind of man at all. He did not write in that way. He chose the new style of writing plays—the drama —as his method of expression, moulding it to suit his purpose. The knowledge he had he was obliged to find in English; in translations if it came from foreign sources. He was an English country youth, who in his early twenties went to London and became an actor; a tinkerer and improver of plays by the University Wits; then a writer of plays written around borrowed plots; then a writer of lively comedies, of splendid histories more fascinating than all the books of history; of delicious poetical fantasies, of sweet romances, and of noble, heart-moving tragedies. He became a picturer of all the romance of life, past and present, as if it were being lived again before the eyes of the people of his day, and of all who follow after. Also he was much more than a mere playwright, Woven into his plays are the proofs, in haunting words, that he was a profound thinker and a poet for every mood.

It was William Shakespeare, the Stratford tradesman's son, who at first, when he came among them, was sneered at by the University Wits as "an upstart crow beautified with our feathers," yet so ministered to the Elizabethan mind in the plays he wrote that his great friend, Ben Jonson, hailed him as "not of an age, but for all time."

THE POEMS THAT BROUGHT WILLIAM SHAKESPEARE HIS FIRST FAME

Why Shakespeare was so careless about his plays, which the world now thinks are supremely great, and why he apparently thought more about his poems, Venus and Adonis, Lucrece, and his sonnets, we shall understand if we realise the poems based on old-world myths and stories were fashionable. They were supposed to be the kind of writing in which poets should excel. Shakespeare, by writing them, proved that he could write the poems that were in fashion better than the best. As a poet he gained his earliest fame.

On the other hand plays, though popular to see, were not rated so highly as poems in literature. Indeed, that is still true, unless the plays are great in thought and feeling. Besides, Shakespeare had overhauled many plays written by other men, correcting something here and adding something there, and how was he to claim these as his own? So, of the 37 now attributed to him, only 16 were published in his lifetime. Yet it is the plays that establish his greatness, and, contain his choicest poetry.

To the plays we shall come in due course; here a glance must be given to the poetry which he gave to the world as poetry.

The Venus and Adonis and the Lucrece are only interesting to us now as fashions of verse that have passed away, and because they show Shakespeare's mastery of flowing rhyme, and echo his early acquaintance with animal life in country surroundings, while in Lucrece there are some passages of fine writings on serious themes of a kind that the people of his time greatly admired. Even in the plays

poet was writing before the years when he produced his greatest works. He gives more than twenty illustrations, most of them in a single line, of the slow power of remorseless Time.

> Time's glory is to calm contending kings,
> To unmask falsehood and bring truth to light,
> To stamp the seal of Time in aged things,
> To wake the morn and sentinel the night,
> To wrong the wronger till he render right,
> To ruinate proud buildings with thy hours,
> And smear with dust their glittering golden
>   towers;

AN EVENING AT THE MERMAID TAVERN WHERE SHAKESPEARE AND BEN JONSON USED TO MEET

of the period it was expected that, now and then, a chief actor would recite impressively an eloquent passage as a soliloquy—that is, as a man might talk to himself while he was thinking deeply.

The fine reflection beginning, " To be or not to be," in Hamlet, and the pleading beginning, " The quality of mercy is not strained," in The Merchant of Venice, are instances; and in the same way we find in Lucrece the three stanzas on Time which show how thoughtfully the

> To fill with worm-holes stately monuments,
> To feed oblivion with decay of things,
> To blot old books and alter their contents,
> To pluck the quills from ancient ravens' wings,
> To dry the old oak's sap and cherish springs,
> To spoil antiquities of hammered steel,
> And turn the giddy round of Fortune's wheel;
>
> To show the beldame daughters of her daughter,
> To make the child a man, the man a child,
> To slay the tiger that doth live by slaughter,
> To tame the unicorn and lion wild,
> To mock the subtle, in themselves beguiled,

To cheer the ploughman with increaseful crops,
And waste huge stones with little water-drops.

In these verses there is a poetic vision of impressive happenings condensed into a few wonderfully chosen words that must have convinced all readers that a great poet was among them. And the sonnets were more haunting still.

Many books have been written on Shakespeare's 154 sonnets, with the object of showing who the people were about whom he wrote these pithy poems—the two men who were his friends, and the woman whom he loved and who deceived him; but the books do not prove much with certainty about either Shakespeare or the friends he claimed to be making immortal by his descriptions of them. The explanations are nearly all guess-work, and it is better to read the sonnets as poems of varying quality, and not as forming a complete scheme or design.

EXQUISITE BEAUTY AND SWEETNESS OF SHAKESPEARE'S SONNETS

Many of them are exquisitely beautiful, with a cadence that haunts the mind, and imagery enchanting in its sweetness and simplicity, so that they set a standard by which great poetry may be for ever judged. They were written comparatively early, before the poet had reached 30, and full twenty years before he died, old at 52.

Though now we have no care for the phantom-like people in flattery of whom Shakespeare wrote his sonnets, into them he wove such phrasing and such thought as will preserve the sonnets fresh as long as the English language is read. It was a braggart whim of poets of that time to suppose their verse was preserving remembrance of the people they enshrined in verse, but when Shakespeare said the same thing he prefaced it with lines like these, which made the boast true:

Shall I compare thee to a summer's day?
Thou art more lovely and more temperate;
Rough winds do shake the darling buds of May,
And summer's lease hath all too short a date.
Sometime too hot the eye of heaven shines,
And often is his gold complexion dimmed,
And every fair from fair sometime declines,
By chance, or Nature's changing course untrimmed.
But thy eternal summer shall not fade,
Nor lose possession of that fair thou owest,
Nor shall death brag thou wander'st in his shade,

When in eternal lines to time thou growest.
So long as men can breathe, or eyes can see,
So long lives this, and this gives life to thee.

The personal aspect of these sonnets is lost in their beauty, in the sounding of the depths of thought, and the picturing of Nature's fairness with inimitable art. Such phrasings as " the prophetic soul of the wide world dreaming on things to come," are indeed everlasting possessions. So are splendid lines like these:

When to the sessions of sweet silent thought
I summon up remembrance of things past;

such descriptions as

Full many a glorious morning have I seen
Flatter the mountain-tops with sovereign eye,
Kissing with golden face the meadows green,
Gilding pale streams with heavenly alchemy;

such word pictures as

That time of year thou mayest in me behold,
When yellow leaves, or none, or few do hang
Upon those boughs which shake against the cold,
Bare ruined choirs, where late the sweet birds sang.

Sometimes the intensely personal and the beautiful are gloriously intertwined, as in the sonnet bewailing the absence in Springtime of one loved.

From you have I been absent in the Spring,
When proud-pied April, dressed in all his trim,
Hath put a spirit of youth in every thing,
That heavy Saturn laughed and leaped with him.
Yet nor the lays of birds, nor the sweet smell
Of different flowers in odour and in hue,
Could make me any Summer story tell,
Or from their proud lap pluck them where they grew;
Nor did I wonder at the lily's white,
Nor praise the deep vermilion in the rose;
They were but sweet, but figures of delight
Drawn after you; you, pattern of all those,
Yet seemed it Winter still, and, you away,
As with your shadow I with these did play:

In these earlier and slighter poetical writings of Shakespeare, apart from the mighty dramas in which he pictured

All pains the immortal spirit must endure,
All weakness that impairs, all griefs that bow,

we see the qualities that led the next greatest poet of the English race, John Milton, so different from Shakespeare in his life story, to say of him,

Thou, in our wonder and astonishment,
Hast built thyself a live-long monument.

The Great Words that Stir the Hearts and Minds of All Mankind

SPACE

ONE of the earliest games played by children is seeing how far they can throw a stone or a ball. Another good game, but not so often played, is seeing how far we can throw our thoughts. Try it; you will be surprised to find how very small is the distance.

For example, there is this matter of space. You know the word as well as you know any word in the dictionary, but have you got inside your head any words which will explain what you think about the matter—about this matter of space? Before we go a step farther, close your eyes for a moment, repeat the word to yourself two or three times, and then see how far you can throw your thoughts into the thing you call space.

You will probably find that you cannot throw your thoughts an inch, that they remain where they are, just as a ball made of glue would stick to your hand however hard you tried to throw it. Space! What is it? Is there such a thing? If so, it is something nobody can understand.

A moment ago we decided to try this matter on a very intelligent little girl 10 years of age. We said to her : "What do you mean when you use the word space?" She replied "The hole in my stocking."

It was not a bad answer. For when we speak of space we very often mean the distance between two objects. We say that So-and-So has a good broad space between his two eyes; or that the space in a room between door and window is not big enough to permit of swinging a cat.

But there is another kind of space—the space of vast distances which Addison had in mind when he exclaimed :

The spacious firmament on high,
With all the blue ethereal sky,
And spangled heavens, a shining frame,
Their great Original proclaim.

What do we really know about this kind of space ? How far can you throw your thoughts into that abyss of distances which no man can measure?

Now, a very interesting discovery comes our way in merely answering the question, What do we know about space? We discover that men of all nations have invented a language which nobody but themselves can understand, and that only in this mysterious language, which is far worse than Double Dutch to the ordinary person, can the word space be reduced to a rational meaning. You can *feel* some dim meaning in the word space, you can let your brain become dizzy by the mere effort of thinking about it; but until you learn the mysterious language of mathematics you will never be able to think as clearly about space as you think about cricket.

LIBERTY · JUSTICE · SPACE · DISTANCE · MOVEMENT · TRUTH · FAITH

Now, this leads us to another very interesting discovery. It shows us that ordinary language is no good at all for defining the mysteries of life, yet that one of its chief uses is to give some kind of expression to our feelings. Astronomers could not tell us anything about the stars if they had not first of all talked of those heavenly bodies in the universal language of mathematics. But the poet can make us feel the glory, the majesty, and the sublime mystery of the firmament by using the language of sensation, that is to say, the language which utters feelings.

Some men have said that there is no such thing as space, that it is simply an idea in the human mind, and this was long the opinion of many able men. Now there is a change, and philosophers are telling us that space must be thought of in relation to time, and that the universe is finite but boundless—striving, not very successfully, to translate into the language of feeling discoveries made by men who use the language of mathematics.

THE FLIGHT OF IMAGINATION THROUGH THE STARRY HEAVENS

But space is something that can be felt, and it is well worth seeing how far we can express our feelings of so great a mystery in the ordinary language of sensation.

Perhaps you will say, What is the use of feeling about space if I cannot understand it ? What is the good of using the language of feeling about a thing which belongs to mathematics? We should answer to that objection, Nothing belongs to mathematics. You do not deny yourself the pleasure of paddling in the sea or swimming through the waves because you are not a physicist or a navigating officer. Think of music. It is one of the greatest of our delights, and if anyone attempted to reduce that delight to a scientific explanation we should laugh at him. The language of feeling has its logic in the happiness of human life. Let us see what the language can tell us about space.

There is a beautiful definition of God which says that "His centre is everywhere and His circumference nowhere." Think of a vast circle. Its centre is your heart. Pin your thoughts to that centre, and then let your imagination fly away with a thread to discover a point in distance where it can sweep round in a circle. Your imagination reaches Venus or Mars, but cannot stop there because it

perceives Saturn in the far distance; or it must fly with its thread trailing from the thought-pin fixed in your heart, and even as it flies it discerns more planets and more suns, planets and suns dimly discernible to the biggest telescopes on Earth ; but beyond all reach of our knowledge no hope presents itself that the circumference of the circle is at last coming into sight.

WHERE THOUGHT CAN LOSE ITSELF IN A BOUNDLESS EXPANSE

But suppose that at last your imagination did reach some sort of end, a wall or a precipice, would you not say to yourself: "There must be another side to this wall," or "I wonder what lies beyond this precipice?"—knowing that something cannot end in nothing, feeling perfectly certain that there is no such thing as nothingness.

It is in this sense that poets use the term space. They mean by the word a boundless expanse, a place where thought can lose itself. They do not know whether it is occupied for ever and ever by the same ether which appears to occupy all the distances of our great starry space; they do not tell us that they know anything at all about it; but they make us feel that it is far easier for us to think of this space going on for ever and ever than it is to think of a space which has borders and shores beyond which there is nothing.

Who can think of nothing ? Who can imagine a circle beyond which the almighty power of God cannot extend? Who can think of the Creator of the universe knocking at a door which is for ever fastened against Him, *and by whom ?*

THE VISION OF THE POET AND THE MYSTERIES OF THE UNIVERSE

When people say to us that it is impossible to think with real intelligence of space or of God, we should reply to them that it is impossible for some of us to think without them. The mind seems to be utterly incapable of thinking of a beginning to space or a beginning to Life. Something in our very nature rebels against any notion of a time when there was nothingness. Space ! Is it a vast circle of ether ? But a circle swimming in what? Outside this gigantic world of ours is ether; outside the stars is still ether. If that ether end, if there be a final curve in space making the whole universe a circle, what is beyond it ? You say it is finite, yet you are forced to say it is boundless. The poet will reply to you that if the universe is finite it is bounded, and that if it is boundless it is infinite. The poet uses his imagination; the philosopher restrains his reason. In this matter it is easier to follow the poet.

Because you cannot put your feelings about space into very clear language, you must not cease to let your feelings go in that direction. When a man says to his thoughts, "You shall only work at things I can understand," his own work is done.

THE MISERY THAT COMES IF WE BANISH WONDER FROM OUR MINDS

Many a great man of science has found himself miserable in old age because in youth he stopped his ears to music and poetry, and because for the sake of his reason he vigorously banished wonder and imagination from his mind. Moreover, and this is a most important matter, the long road of scientific exploration is strewn with theories once thought by men who expounded them to be gospel truth, but discarded later as incorrect and sometimes even ludicrous, even though they may have served a useful purpose in their turn. Reason alone is thus a dangerous guide to truth.

We need never be overawed by science. The very latest science may be wrong. Think of the theory of Democritus, who considered the atom was a mere hard particle ; as late as the age of Newton this belief held, yet how different is our conception of the constitution of the atom today! Even the best of our guesses and the greatest and truest of our discoveries are only victories in the field of partial truth.

Always remind yourself that we can only understand bits of things. If we understood all there is to understand of the Earth our knowledge would be only of a bit of the universe. Add all our bits together, and how small is the sum.

THE UNIVERSE AS A PLAYGROUND FOR THE HUMAN SOUL

The great Goethe once wrote that to everyone who seeks to explain the universe he was entitled to say, "Dear friend, it is with you as it is with me: in the particular you feel yourself grand and mighty, but the whole goes as little into your head as into mine." The whole of the universe—that is the playground for every human soul.

Cultivate your imagination. Feel the beauty of moonlight on a wind-swept ocean, even if you are quite certain that the moon is a dead and meaningless world; feel the glory of sunrise, the loveliness of rose and violet, the inspiration of music, the exaltation of poetry, and the inexpressible dearness of domestic happiness, even if you have mastered all the theories of science, and can direct your thoughts of the universe in the language of geometry.

A word like space may drive you almost frantic if you shut yourself up in a room with a book explaining the newest theories of Einstein; but that same word may break like a great chord of music in your heart if you go out into a moonlit garden and look up at the starry heavens, feeling in your soul that no language of any kind can ever fathom the ultimate mysteries of the universe.

You may, if you like, say that the hole in your stocking is a part of space, but never be so foolish as to assert that it is the whole of space. You may think, if you like, that the physical universe is finite, not boundless, but never be found so wanting in imagination that you will be led to assert that beyond this finite universe there is nothing.

A GREAT MYSTERY, AND ITS INFLUENCE ON THE MIND

Think of space as you think of eternity, as that which not only has neither beginning nor end, but by its very nature can have neither beginning nor end. Use the thought of space to deepen your sense of humility and to intensify your feeling of wonder. Employ it to strengthen and develop your imagination, so that you feel yourself to be a child of infinity and an heir of eternal life. Remember that you are always standing at the centre of a circle, the circumference of which is never to be reached. And remember also that this boundless region of space is everywhere penetrated by the same laws which we observe in the universe, that reign of law which one of Earth's greatest thinkers has said gives "sanity to the mind and a joyous satisfaction to the heart."

Everywhere there is a power ruling over all things, and however unthinkable the immensity in which we find ourselves, it is governed by the same law which rules the heart of a mother, and gives beauty to flower and bird. Space does not crush us; it humbles our heart, inspires our mind, and thrills our dreams.

JACOB MEETS RACHEL AT THE WELL

JACOB KISSED RACHEL, AND LIFTED UP HIS VOICE, AND WEPT.   From the painting by H. R. Mileham

The Story of the Most Beautiful Book in the World

JACOB THE WANDERER

JACOB set out from his father's house to escape the anger of his brother Esau. He had deceived Esau, and was afraid.

Jacob believed in God, or else he would never have schemed to get his father's blessing. As he went away from his home, and began his long and perilous journey, he must have thought to himself, " I have done a wicked thing. I have deceived my own father. I am running away from my home like a guilty thief. What does God think of me?"

This burning thought of shame must have made him sad. He was all by himself. There was no one to whom he could talk. He had only his own guilty thoughts for his companions. Think how full of fear and regret he must have been when the sun sank slowly in the west, the shadows lengthened on the way, and the night wind blew through the solitary trees.

As night came on he drew near the city of Luz, but he was either afraid to enter it or too footsore and broken to go farther. He took some stones that were in the valley, piled them together for a pillow, and then, casting himself down with his long cloak wrapped about him, composed himself for sleep.

His last thought was surely one of bitter and aching repentance. Yesterday he had been a loved and honoured son in the house of his rich father. Now he was a wanderer upon the face of the Earth, a fugitive from the wrath of his own brother. Between those two days stood the black shadow of a single wicked act.

His repentance, we may be certain, was earnest and sincere, for while he slept there came to him a vision. Jacob saw a wonderful golden ladder rising from the bare rocks of the valley where he lay and reaching up into the golden glory of Heaven. On this ladder was a great company of angels, some ascending to Heaven, some descending to Earth. Even from these bare, cold rocks there was a way to Heaven, and even from Heaven to these bare, cold rocks God sent down the comfort of His love.

While Jacob gazed entranced at this dazzling ladder, there came to him a voice, saying, " I am the Lord God of Abraham thy father, and the God of Isaac," and a promise that God would be with him. Refreshed by his vision, Jacob rose up early in the morning, and pressed forward on his journey. He knew now that there is forgiveness of sin.

When he had come into " the land of the people of the East," he saw before him shepherds watering their flocks at a well. He came up to them just as they

GREAT FIGURES OF THE OLD TESTAMENT · THE LIFE OF JESUS

had finished, and had rolled the stone over the mouth of the well. He asked them whence they came ; and they said Haran. He asked if they knew a man there named Laban; and they answered Yes. " Is he well ? " asked Jacob. " He is well," they replied. " And behold, Rachel his daughter cometh with the sheep."

JACOB MEETS A BEAUTIFUL MAIDEN AT THE WELL

Jacob looked up quickly and saw a beautiful dark maiden approaching him in the golden dust raised by a flock of sheep. This was his cousin, the daughter of his mother's brother. He was amazed by her beauty, and at that instant loved her tenderly. While she was yet a little distance away he rolled the stone from the well, and waited for her to approach.

Then he told her who he was, and broke down—so weary and sad was he after his long journey. Rachel bade him be happy, and hurried on to tell her father of his nephew's arrival.

Laban, with his two daughters, Leah and Rachel, received him kindly, and, made him feel at home in this strange land ; and Jacob stayed with him as a guest for a month.

After that time Jacob offered to work for Laban, and Laban cordially accepted his services. But what wages should he pay his nephew ? Jacob answered " I will serve thee seven years for Rachel, thy younger daughter." And Laban agreed.

Jacob loved Rachel with a noble and heroic love. No longer did he think of returning to his home in a few days. He was content to wait in this strange land working night and day for seven years that he might win Rachel. At last the day broke when the wanderer, now a changed and upright man, was to receive his bride.

THE BITTER DISAPPOINTMENT OF JACOB THAT ENDED THE FEAST

Laban prepared a great feast, and Jacob rose up in the midst of much company to welcome his bride. But when the marriage ceremony was over, and the veil was lifted from the bride, Jacob saw that he had married not Rachel, but Leah. Laban made light of his disappointment and said churlishly that in that country it was not proper for the younger daughter to wed before the older. " If you would have Rachel for your second wife," he said, " you must serve another seven years."

Jacob's love for Rachel was so great that he submitted to Laban. As we already know, it was permitted to men to have more than one wife in those days.

At last the day of his happiness dawned, and Rachel became his wife. Jacob was now full of happiness, and he longed greatly to take Rachel to the home of his childhood. Laban stood in his way for a long time, and poor Jacob actually had to steal secretly away from this hard taskmaster, just as before he had stolen away from the wrath of his brother Esau.

Jacob succeeded finally in coming to an arrangement with Laban, and then pressed forward with his wives and servants, and his flocks and herds, on his great journey to the west.

HOW JACOB AND ESAU MET AGAIN AFTER MANY YEARS

As he drew nearer and nearer to his loved home, he became oppressed by the fear that Esau's anger might yet burn hotly against him. Therefore he sent messengers ahead of him to tell Esau of his coming.

These messengers returned saying that Esau was advancing at the head of four hundred men. Jacob was afraid, and sent forward more messengers with presents for Esau. After that he assisted his wives and sons, and all the company, to cross the ford called Jabbok, and then withdrew himself to pray.

On the morrow the Sun shone upon Jacob, and when he encountered Esau his brother, instead of angry words and blows between them, there were greetings of love and kisses of affection.

It was a pleasant sight to see these two men—the one headstrong, noble-hearted, and bold; the other worn and broken by his exile of repentance—greeting in the midst of the multitude of their servants, surrounded by Jacob's flocks and herds.

With Jacob, whose name we must henceforth call Israel, was his little son Joseph, the son of the lovely Rachel. Another son, named Benjamin, soon after was born to Rachel, but at his birth Rachel died, and Israel was heartbroken, for he loved her dearly. But he found comfort in his sons, particularly in Rachel's sons, Joseph and the little Benjamin, and these brothers grew up in a great love. His other sons were strong and vigorous lads, while Joseph played before the tent-door with his little brother.

JACOB'S LIFE DRAWS TO ITS CLOSE

JACOB SEES HIS BROTHER ESAU COMING TO MEET HIM

JACOB'S LAST HOUR WITH HIS SONS

The pictures on this page are from the well-known Bible paintings by J. James Tissot

CAN YOU MAKE THESE INTO PICTURES?

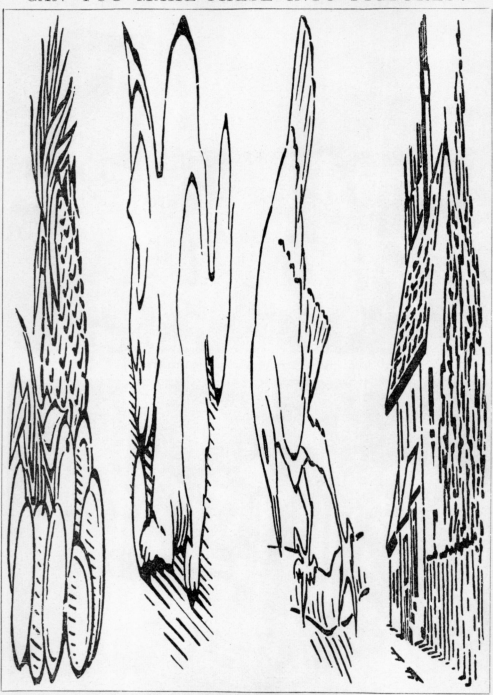

It is difficult to recognise these objects if you look at them in the ordinary way, but anyone can make them into pictures by looking at them properly. Hold the page horizontally some distance away, on a level with your eyes, so that you look along the page, and you will see some fruit, a kitten playing with a ball, a bird, and a house. The reason for this is that the pictures are drawn with the perspective wrong.

The Interests and Pleasures of Life for All Indoors and Out

A LITTLE SHADOW THEATRE

By means of scissors, paste, cardboard, paper, and a piece of wood, it is very easy to make this amusing shadow puzzle game which is as interesting for grown-ups as it is for children, and will provide plenty of fun for a Christmas or New Year party. For this simple toy take some stout and stiff cardboard, and cut out two pieces 15 inches high by 6 inches wide. Then cut another piece 15 inches high and 18 inches wide, and from the middle of this cut a piece about 12 inches high and 12 inches wide, the shape left being very much like the wings and curtain of a theatre, as in the picture overleaf.

With two strips of gummed paper fasten the two narrow pieces of card to the larger piece, one on each side, so that the paper will form hinges, and the side pieces can be turned at right angles to the middle card. Strips of linen pasted or gummed on to the card make even better hinges than the gummed paper.

The picture on the next page shows how this screen-frame will look. To make it neat, cover one side of it with black paper—not the side on which the linen or paper strips are pasted. Then, turning the screen over, paste over the opening which has been cut out, a piece of ordinary semi-transparent tracing-paper. The paper should be as white as possible. The screen is now ready, and can be put aside while the rest of the toy is made.

Cut out four figures in stiff cardboard, each about 3 inches high. and these should be, if possible, rather fantastic and humorous, as that will add to the fun of the game. Any kind of upright figures will do, and may be copied from books, but if there is any difficulty about drawing people, four upright pieces of

card can be cut into any kind of irregular shapes, and will serve for the purpose of the game, though, of course, it is much more fun to have real figures.

A piece of wood 12 inches long by about 6 or 7 inches wide and ¾ of an inch thick, is wanted for a stand for these figures. Running the whole length of this board, cut six grooves at regular intervals, just wide and deep enough to hold the figures upright when they are placed in these grooves.

Now take some stiff paper and make four extinguishers by rolling up the paper like a dunce's cap, sticking down the edge and cutting the opening evenly all round. Then sew a little ring in the top of each. The extinguishers should be about 4 inches high and 2 inches in diameter at the bottom.

Next get a thin stick about 2 or 2½ feet long, and in the end put a nail, and to this fasten a straight piece of wire about 12 inches long with the end turned up slightly to form a hook. The wire should be stout enough to remain stiff and straight. All that is wanted now for the game is an ordinary candle placed in a candlestick.

Any number of people may play at puzzle shadows. Stand the screen on the table, with the wings folded at right angles, and put a lighted candle some distance at the back of it. One who does not take part in the game acts as master of the ceremonies. He puts the wooden stand between the screen and the candle, and then places the four figures in any of the grooves—not, of course, all in the same groove.

All other lights in the room except the candle are turned out. The first player now

CRAFTS · GAMES · NEEDLEWORK · PUZZLES · SCIENCE EXPERIMENTS

takes his place before the screen, and he must on no account look over it to see what is behind.

Hooking the wire holder into the ring of one of the extinguishers, he lifts this over the top of the screen, and, guided only by the shadows of the figures and the extinguisher on the paper front of the screen, he tries to put the extinguisher over one of the figures. So long as the shadow of the extinguisher is above the shadows of the figures, it may be moved about in any direction. but directly it touches or begins to cover the shadow of a figure, it must be let down.

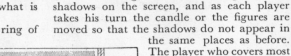

THE FRAMEWORK OF THE THEATRE

Then the holder is gently unhooked, and another extinguisher is lifted over the screen in the same way. This is done until the player has tried to cover all the figures by using all four extinguishers. He is then allowed to go behind the screen, and see how far he has succeeded.

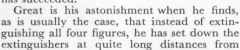

THE LITTLE MEN FOR THE SHADOW THEATRE

Great is his astonishment when he finds, as is usually the case, that instead of extinguishing all four figures, he has set down the extinguishers at quite long distances from them. Nothing is more deceiving than the shadows on the screen, and as each player takes his turn the candle or the figures are moved so that the shadows do not appear in the same places as before. The player who covers most figures wins the game, or, to prolong the game, points may be given for each figure covered, and these points added up at the finish.

It is essential that the master of the ceremonies gives no indication either by word or by the expression of his face as to how a player is succeeding while he is trying to cover the figures; and it is important, too, that the candle be kept well back, so that the extinguishers, as they are moved about, cannot possibly get into the flame and catch fire.

After playing the game like this, a variation can be tried. The board and figures are removed, and each player in turn tries to let down the extinguishers with the holder so that they will be in a line between the screen and the candle. The one who puts the four extinguishers in the straightest line is the winner.

A FIRESIDE GAME FOR WINTER EVENINGS

THERE is a certain kind of sentence known as a palindrome, a word that means " running back again." The particular kind of sentence to which this curious name is given is one that can be read backward as well as forward, and is the same either way; the letters run back again in the same order as they run forward. Of course, it is fairly easy to make such sentences if only words are considered, but a palindrome sentence must read backward, letter by letter, the same as forward.

A very good game for a winter evening is to sit round the fire, and try to make up some palindromes.

Perhaps the best known of all such sentences are these two, the first being Adam's supposed remark to Eve:

Madam, I'm Adam;

and the second, Napoleon's statement:

Able was I ere I saw Elba.

But many other sentences can be made up to read backward and forward alike.

Snug & raw was I ere I saw war & guns.
Repel evil as a live leper.
Egad, a base tone denotes a bad age.
Red root put up to order. (This is a reference to a beetroot.)
Put it up but not on tub, put it up.
Stop, Rose, I prefer pies or pots.
Draw no dray a yard onward.

In building up such sentences we must, of course, work from the beginning and end at the same time—that is, directly we have chosen a first word, we must write it backward at the end of the sentence; then a second word is treated in the same way, being reversed and placed as the second from the end. In this way we can see if our sentence is making sense as we go along. The best way to begin building up a palindrome is to get a good number of palindrome words, such as madam, level, noon, and so on. These give a good foundation to use with other words that are not palindromes, but make true words when reversed, such, for example, as was, saw ; den, Ned; ton, not.

THE RIGHT WAY TO COOK VEGETABLES

VEGETABLES get their name from the Latin word *vegere* meaning animating—having the power to impart life—and this valuable quality, which chiefly exists in Vitamin C, can be destroyed by careless treatment. To preserve it as much as possible, cook all vegetables, other than dried ones and potatoes, by the fast steam-boiling method. This is done with either fat or water in the bottom of a saucepan with a close-fitting lid.

Most vegetables—though not asparagus, potatoes, and globe artichokes—are delicious eaten uncooked when they are fresh and young, and all vegetables, except shelled peas and broad beans, need washing, but none should be soaked in water for long. A teaspoonful of vinegar in a basin of cold water soon lures out insects and dirt, after which a rinse beneath running water should finish the job.

Root vegetables should be scrubbed, scraped, and, if old, should have their outer skin peeled off before they are sliced or diced (which means cut up into small cubes), ready for putting into the pan. Greens need shredding with a very sharp knife, and cauliflowers breaking into sprigs, before cooking.

To steam-boil in fat, heat sufficient cooking-fat, lard, dripping, or a mixture of all three, to cover the bottom of the saucepan. When it is hot, but not smoking hot, put in the vegetables with a teaspoonful of salt for every pound, quickly put on the lid, which should be hot, and cook for 10 to 15 or 20 minutes, over moderate heat, according to the age and tenderness of the vegetable. Shake the pan occasionally to make certain every bit of vegetable gets its fair share of cooking.

To cook in water, follow the same method, but have boiling water instead of fat in the pan, a half to three-quarters of a pint according to the breadth of the pan's base. The chief thing to remember when cooking in this way, is that unless the lid of the pan fits perfectly the steam that should be keeping the vegetables moist escapes, and the pan and its contents burn. When tender, drain the vegetables, keeping the water, which is full of goodness, for making gravy.

Serve all vegetables in well-heated dishes with warmed lids, adding more salt, if necessary, a little pepper, and, to water-cooked vegetables, a knob or two of butter or margarine, or a little sour cream. Time the

Correct storing of vegetables is as important as good cooking, and an airy rack like this is ideal.

cooking of all vegetables so that they are served immediately they are ready.

To prepare asparagus, scrape the ends of the stems and wash in cold water. Tie into bundles of about 12 stems of equal length and thickness, cutting the stems level when necessary, and cook, standing upright in a deep pan, with boiling water reaching about half way up the stems, for 10 to 15 minutes, with the lid on.

Old beetroots may need as much as eight hours baking, unpeeled, in a slow oven, or two to three hours boiling or steaming. Young tender beets are better wiped with a damp cloth, sliced thinly and cooked in a covered preserving jar, standing on a cloth in a saucepan of boiling water, till tender, usually about 30 minutes.

Celery and leeks require much washing and scrubbing to clean them, and their tops can be cooked and eaten, hot or cold, as well as used for soup stock. Curled uncooked celery makes a pretty garnish. Cut, clean, tender white celery in two-inch lengths and fringe the ends with a sharp penknife, leaving a short connecting space in the centre. Place in iced, or very cold water till the ends curl.

Buy small dried peas, beans, or lentils rather than large, for they are likely to be younger. Cover with boiling water and soak for 12 to 24 hours. Cook with a few bacon rinds in a lidded pan, in the water in which they soaked. Bring the water gently to the boil and simmer till tender—one to two hours. Add a broth posy (see Index), or dried mint, and either leek or onion green, for the final half hour, and keep all the liquid for stock.

Except for frying, never skin a potato before cooking it. For boiling, choose potatoes of the same size, and scrub well. Salt (with one tablespoonful of salt for every pound of potatoes) sufficient water to cover the potatoes and bring this to the boil; then put the potatoes in, boil up quickly, and then with the lid on cook more gently till testing with a fork shows the potatoes are tender.

Potatoes for mashing, or for a potato salad, should be peeled and have added while they are still hot the hot milk for mixing the mash, or dressing cream for the salad. Potatoes are full of a natural starch which hardens the surface as it cools, and so anything added after a potato is cold does not mix well with it.

Vegetables make a meal, but a complete dinner includes meat or fish, as on page 997.

LITTLE PROBLEMS FOR ODD MOMENTS

THESE problems are continued from page 750, and their answers, together with more questions, will be found on page 998.

57. How Much Money has Each?

Hugh and Harry decide to run a race, the loser to pay the winner 5s. If Hugh loses he will have just as much money as Harry, and if he wins he will have three times as much.

How much money has each?

58. What are Their Wages?

Thomas Bull and his two sons, John and Henry, work together. John and his father earn 30s. a day, Henry and his father earn 27s. a day, and the two sons together earn 21s. a day.

How much per day does each earn?

59. How Much was the Waistcoat?

A man's coat cost seven times as much as his waistcoat, but the bill for the two together was £9 14s. 8d.

How much did the waistcoat cost?

60. What is the Length of the Cloth?

A piece of cloth measured with a yard-stick an inch short is 36 yards long, reckoning the yard-stick as being right.

How long was the cloth really?

61. How Many Miles a Day?

A schoolmaster went for a walking tour, and for seven days his average walk a day was 15 miles. His average for the first four days was 18 miles a day.

What was his average for the other three days of the tour?

62. What Could the Barrel Hold?

A barrel was exactly two-thirds filled with oil. The oil merchant took out one gallon less than half of the contents, and then one gallon less than one-third of what remained. He had 15 gallons left.

What was the capacity of the barrel?

63. How Many Calves and Sheep?

A farmer sold an equal number of calves and sheep, and received in all the sum of £72. For the calves he received £5 15s. each, and for the sheep £6 5s. each.

How many of each kind did he sell?

64. What was the Rent?

Jones was on his way to pay his quarter's rent, when he met Smith to whom he said, " I am going to pay my rent, and the money is all in half-crowns. If it were in florins, instead of half-crowns, I should have 12 more coins."

How much was the rent per annum?

THE ANSWERS TO THE PROBLEMS ON PAGE 750

47. At noon on August 30th. For 10 seconds an hour is 4 minutes a day, and at the end of each day the clock and the watch will be 8 minutes farther apart than before. They will thus be 12 hours apart and show the same time again in 90 days, for ninety times 8 minutes is 12 hours. In 90 days the watch has gained 360 minutes, or 6 hours, and the clock lost 6 hours, so that each points to six o'clock ; 90 days from noon on June 1 is noon on August 30.

48. 30s. The difference in the prices was 6s., equalling half the value of the frame used, which cost thus 12s. ; and as the frame and picture were 42s. the picture itself was 30s.

49. Yes. Joan had enough money. If they had £9 between them, and Joan had £2 2s. more than Janet, Joan must have had 21s. more than half of £9, and Janet 21s. less than half. Thus, Joan had £5 11s., and Janet had £3 9s.

50. If he sold one house for £990 and made a profit of 10 per cent., the house must have cost him £900, because the difference between these two sums—£90—represents 10 per cent. upon the price paid for the house originally. If he sold the second house at a loss of 10 per cent. he must have paid £1100 for it, as £110 is 10 per cent. of £1100, the sum paid for it. Thus he lost £20 exactly on the two transactions.

51. Divide £9 19s. 6d. by 10s. and the result is 19. Nineteen half-guineas were charged for 12 visits. We have to find two numbers which, when added, make 19, and when one is added to half of the other make 12. The easiest way is to try several numbers. The number that we divide must be an even number. 18 and 1 make 19 ; but 9 (half of 18) and 1 make only 10. 16 and 3 make 19, but 8 (half of 16) and 3 make 11. 14 and 5 make 19, and 7 (half of 14) and 5 make 12. So 14 half-guineas, or £7 7s., were charged for seven night visits, and 5 half-guineas (or £2 12s. 6d.) for five day visits—that is, £9 19s. 6d. altogether.

52. The cyclist lost the train by 20 minutes, and was misled by reckoning the average by distance and not by time. If he took an equal amount of time in walking, riding, and coasting, the average would have worked right. As it was, the 4-mile walk took 1 hour, the 4 miles of level road took ½ hour, and the 4 miles of downhill took 20 minutes—in all, 1 hour and 50 minutes, while he had only 1½ hours in which to catch the train.

53. The easiest way to do this is to subtract amounts with the pounds, shillings, and pence all equal—£1 1s. 1d., £2 2s. 2d., £3 3s. 3d., and so on, from £34, and see if any of them yield, as a result, a sum the shillings in which are double the number of pence, and the pounds in which are double the number of shillings. The two sums were £5 5s. 5d. and £28 14s. 7d., which, added together, make £34.

54. Evans does one day's work more than half the field, and Watson would take two days to do this piece, so that Evans does as much in one day as Watson does in two days. Thus, if they work together, Evans will mow two-thirds of the field, and Watson one-third. Thus, Evans mows one-sixth more than half the field, and does this in one day ; so that Watson mows one-twelfth of the field in one day. Together they will do one-sixth added to one-twelfth, which is one-quarter, and will take four days for the whole field.

55. The first day he reached 3 feet high before he slipped back, the second he reached 4 feet before he fell. Thus, on the 27th day, he reached 29 feet before he slipped back to 27 feet, and on the 28th day he reached 30 feet, but as he was at the top he did not slip back again.

Thus, he took 28 days to climb to the top.

56. One-third and one-fourth, when added together, make seven-twelfths, and the difference between seven-twelfths and one, which is twelve-twelfths, is five-twelfths. Thus, five-twelfths of the trees in the orchard were cherry trees, of which we know that there were 30. If five-twelfths of the trees were 30, the entire number must have been 72.

MAKING A WONDERFUL TOP

A MAGNETIC top is not only amusing to play with, but is also interesting to make.

First of all the lid of a small tin such as baking-powder, coffee, and other household foods are packed in, is required. It should be about 2 or 2½ inches in diameter. Then take a round cardboard box of the same diameter as the tin from which the lid came, so that the lid will fit on to it tightly. Now carefully cut off a part of the round cardboard box so that it stands about 1½ inches high. In the middle of the tin lid punch a small clean hole, ³⁄₁₆ of an inch in diameter. If there is any difficulty, get an ironmonger to do this. Now put the lid on the section of the box that was cut off, so that this part of the toy appears as in picture 1.

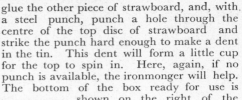

1. THE BODY OF THE TOP.

Next get a round, smooth disc of heavy wood, about 1¾ inches in diameter and ⅜ or ½ inch thick. In the centre bore a hole, and through the hole pass a small iron rod, so that it will fit very tightly, and not move up or down in the hole. This iron rod should be a trifle more than ⅛ of an inch in diameter, and should be sharpened to a smooth point at one end. The ironmonger would do this, too, if it cannot be managed at home. The rod must now be magnetised. This can be done by passing a strong magnet along the rod again and again in one direction.

Anyone who deals in electrical appliances would magnetise the rod. The rod is put through the hole in the disc, so that the point projects on one side for about ⅜ inch, and the whole forms a little top, as seen on the left of picture 2.

Next prepare a bottom for the section of cardboard box on which the tin lid was placed. This bottom should be of cardboard, and the bottom of the original box from which the section was cut will do very well. Cut two round pieces of thick strawboard a little smaller than this. Fasten one of these pieces firmly with glue to the bottom which we are preparing; then place on the centre a small piece of tin about ½ inch square. On top

glue the other piece of strawboard, and, with a steel punch, punch a hole through the centre of the top disc of strawboard and strike the punch hard enough to make a dent in the tin. This dent will form a little cup for the top to spin in. Here, again, if no punch is available, the ironmonger will help. The bottom of the box ready for use is shown on the right of the second picture, the tin under the strawboard being indicated by dotted lines.

One other thing is needed, and that is a small piece of wooden or stiff card tubing, about ¾ inch high, and ¼ inch diameter inside. Take the top and place over the handle the tubing. Now put the top inside the box, with the handle A sticking through the hole B. Hold the box upside down with the top in it, and place the bottom which has been prepared, in position, so that the hole C punched in the strawboard is over the point of the top, and the point rests in the dent, or cup, in the square of tin.

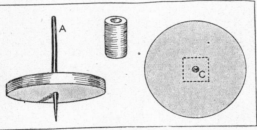

2. THE INSIDE PARTS OF THE TOP.

Hold this bottom on firmly, turn the box up the other way, and give the handle of the top, which will stick out at the top of the tin lid, a few twists to see that it spins easily and evenly in the little tin cup at the bottom. If it does, all that is necessary now is to stick the bottom into the box with strips of paper. Next paste round the box a piece of ornamental coloured paper or black leatherette, to give a tidy appearance, and the top is ready.

But to get interest and amusement out of the top, obtain some thin steel or iron wire. Cut this into short lengths and, with a pair of pliers, twist it into different shapes. Then, spinning the top by the handle that projects, place

3. DANCING FIGURES FOR THE TOP.

against the twisting handle a piece of wire shaped like that at the top of picture 3. The wire moves backward and forward again and again across the tin top of the box. The length of wire, when twisted, should be about 2½ inches. Another way is to form a spiral of wire, or make a little man with a flag, as also shown in picture 3.

A TUMBLER SUPPORTED BY THE AIR

WE know by the strength of the wind the force that the air can exert when it is in movement. If a hurricane is blowing, we have to bend forward and use a great deal of energy to move against the wind ; and in America and some other countries the atmosphere, when it is moving at great speed, can even hurl a train off the track.

It is difficult, however, to realise that the air has great power even when it is still. There is a simple experiment that shows how the air can sustain a comparatively heavy object, which, having no visible means of support, appears to be hanging by magic. The experiment is an excellent one from a scientific point of view, and it will cause a good deal of surprise and wonder if it is done as a trick to show the skill of an amateur conjurer.

For the experiment two tumblers, a small piece of candle, and a square of rather thick paper, large enough to cover the open end of one of the tumblers, are required. The top edges of the two glasses must be the same size, and must be so level that when one is stood upside down on the other the edges exactly touch all round.

First saturate the paper with water, taking care not to tear it in any way. If by any chance it should get torn, soak another piece, or it will be impossible to do the trick.

LIFTING THE
TUMBLER

Then place the small piece of candle inside one of the tumblers and light it, waiting a moment or two for the wick to burn up. When the flame is burning brightly, place the wet paper over the mouth of the glass and invert the other tumbler over it, as shown in the picture. The candle will go out after a moment or two ; then raise the top tumbler gently, and it will be discovered to be holding up the lower one, too.

The explanation is that the burning of the candle rarefies the air in the tumbler, and the pressure of the air outside being greater than that inside, it holds the two glasses together firmly. When the upper tumbler is raised, the other one is drawn up and supported by the pressure of the atmosphere below.

In performing this experiment it is well to choose tumblers that are not too heavy, and they should be perfectly clean and dry before using. Any failure to carry out the experiment will be due to the instructions not being followed or to irregularity in the surface of the glasses.

As can be easily understood, it is essential that the edges should be close together, in order that there may be no opportunity for the outside air to rush in as the air in the glass becomes rarefied.

THINK OF A NUMBER

TAKE six pieces of card, and copy on to them the six sets of figures printed below, putting one set on each card. With these six cards it will be possible to tell a number that a friend may have thought of, without a moment's hesitation.

First ask the friend to think of a number between one and sixty ; then show him the six cards and ask him to point out on which of these cards his number appears. In a moment we tell him the number he had in mind, much to his astonishment.

3	5	7	9	11	1
13	15	17	19	21	23
25	27	29	31	33	35
37	39	41	43	45	47
49	51	53	55	57	59

5	6	7	13	12	4
14	15	20	21	22	23
28	29	30	31	36	37
38	39	44	45	46	47
52	53	54	55	60	13

9	10	11	12	13	8
14	15	24	25	26	27
28	29	30	31	40	41
42	43	44	45	46	47
56	57	58	59	60	13

3	6	7	10	11	2
14	15	18	19	22	23
26	27	30	31	34	35
38	39	42	43	46	47
50	51	54	55	58	59

17	18	19	20	21	16
22	23	24	25	26	27
28	29	30	31	48	49
50	51	52	53	54	55
56	57	58	59	60	31

33	34	35	36	37	32
38	39	40	41	42	43
44	45	46	47	48	49
50	51	52	53	54	55
56	57	58	59	60	46

results is the number thought of. Thus, suppose that the friend thought of 47. It is on the first, second, third, fourth, and sixth cards. The figures in the top right-hand corners of these are 1, 4, 8, 2, and 32, which, added together, make 47—the number thought of. From this very simple set of figure cards even more fun can be got by guessing people's ages, which is, of course, done in the same way.

Some people may already know of figure cards by which a number can be guessed,

The explanation is very simple. Merely add up the figures that appear on the top right-hand corners of the cards upon which his number appears, and the total that but these are usually arranged so that the top *left*-hand figures have to be added to give the solution, while here the *right*-hand numbers are the ones which must be added.

SIMPLE TRICKS WITH A PENNY

HERE is a very simple trick which usually surprises and puzzles an audience. Undertake to pick a marked penny out of a hat without seeing it. First of all borrow a hat, and then ask three or four members of the audience to put a penny each into it. Next cover this with a pocket-handkerchief, and talk to allow the coins to get cool.

Now ask any member of the audience to take one of the coins from the hat and put a mark upon it, after which he is to return it to the hat and cover the whole with the handkerchief again.

Then comes the climax of the trick. Approaching the hat without looking at it, talk of the wonders of magnetism, and, putting the hand under the handkerchief into the hat, extract the marked coin.

The explanation is this. In marking the penny, the member of the audience handled it for some few seconds, and the heat of his hand was communicated to the penny.

When feeling the coins in the hat, the warmth of the one that has been handled is quite perceptible, and so it is easy to identify it and bring it triumphantly from the hat.

To be still more certain that the penny selected and marked shall be warm, ask the one who marked it to hand it round among the other members of the audience so that they may all examine it thoroughly and be able to recognise it again when they see it a second time.

For a change, collect the coins on a plate, then ask an onlooker to choose one and pass it round for its date to be noted by everyone, the last person mixing it up with the others again. Immediately cover all the money with a handkerchief, and feel this to find the selected coin which will be warm as before.

Before starting, place ready and unnoticed on the first and second fingers a light coloured rubber band, and now slip this over the coin in the handkerchief—it can easily be done without being seen while apparently feeling for the correct penny. Then lift up the handkerchief, saying the selected one cannot be found, and give the others back to their owners, counting them. Naturally there will be one missing.

Ask for a glass, spread the handkerchief over this, placing one hand on top, while the other hand pulls the sides of the handkerchief. The coin will then drop into the glass which is handed to the audience for them to see that the original penny is inside.

A WORD GAME WITH SKITTLES

AN interesting word game can be played with skittles and ninepins. Print on each skittle the letters of the alphabet, no letter appearing twice on the same skittle. It is wise to give rare letters, like q, x, z, only once, and to make up the necessary number of letters with those that are more often used.

When the skittles are ready, stand them up in three rows, the skittles being about six inches apart, and the rows also six inches apart. Then take the two balls, and, from a distance of about twelve feet, bowl them in succession, seeing how many skittles can be knocked

THE SKITTLES ARRANGED FOR PLAY

over. Now see what letters are on the skittles that have been knocked down, and from these make up words. Sometimes it is scarcely possible to make one word, while at another quite a number of words will come easily.

In marking the skittles see that there is at least one vowel on each skittle. Every letter of the alphabet should be given at least once, the additional number required to make up four on each skittle may be any letters, such as three or four a's, or e's, and so on. The player who makes most words in a given time is the winner of the game.

HOW TO TIE UP A BROWN PAPER PARCEL

IT is always useful to be able to tie up a brown paper parcel neatly, and yet there are many who do not know how to do this.

Stand the box or article that is to be tied up in the middle of the paper, bringing the two edges together so that they overlap on top of the box, and then neatly turn in the ends so that there is a pointed flap, which is folded up as in the

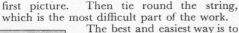

first picture. Then tie round the string, which is the most difficult part of the work.

The best and easiest way is to fold the string double, and lay it on the table with the box on top of it. Then slip the two loose ends of the string through the loop, draw this loop up on top of the box, and turn the ends to right and left, as in the second picture; now take them round and tie on the other side.

A KALEIDOSCOPE THAT A BOY CAN MAKE

THE kaleidoscope is one of the most interesting of scientific toys, and there are few boys and girls who have not had a kaleidoscope at one time or another.

The name is made up of three Greek words which mean, " I see a beautiful image," and by means of the instrument an endless number of patterns, all beautiful in form, and all different from one another, can be made. As a matter of fact, far from being a mere toy, the kaleidoscope is sometimes used by artists and pattern-makers to obtain new designs.

The usual form of kaleidoscope, which was devised by Sir David Brewster early in the nineteenth century, is a tube in which two mirrors are arranged at an angle to one another ; and between these mirrors a number of coloured fragments are free to move about as the tube is turned round. Whatever position these coloured pieces take up they are reflected in the mirrors, and the multiplication of the pieces by reflection forms a regular design which, however irregular the coloured fragments themselves may be, becomes very artistic and pleasing to the eye.

The tube, with its arrangement of mirrors inside, is not essential, and here is a much simpler form of the kaleidoscope which can be made with very little trouble.

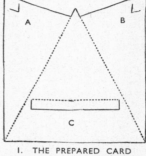

1. THE PREPARED CARD

First of all take a piece of white cardboard, fairly tough in substance, 4 inches by 4¼ inches, and at one end of its greatest length cut it to the shape shown at the top of picture 1. Then at A and B cut small V-shaped nicks as marked in the diagram, and an inch from the bottom, at c, cut a line 2½ inches long, with a line of ⅛ inch at each end, at right angles to the longer line.

On the opposite side of the card, with a penknife, lightly score the cardboard along the directions marked by dotted lines in picture 1. This is done so that the card may be easily bent along these lines. The diagram shows exactly how to cut and score the card. The dotted lines are where to score, and the black lines show where to cut right through. The card will form the body of the kaleidoscope.

Now for the mirrors. A looking-glass is not really necessary, for tin can be used and does just as well. Take two pieces of perfectly smooth and flat tin, 3 inches by 1½ inches, and, with an ordinary metal polish that may be in the house, rub them until they shine brightly and reflect nearly as well as looking-glass. Now, with a slip of gummed paper, join the pieces of tin by hinging together two of their ends so that they can be opened at any angle, as in picture 2, taking care, of course, that the paper is stuck on the dull sides of the tin, and not on the sides which have been so carefully polished.

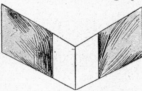

2. THE MIRRORS HINGED

Now the kaleidoscope can be put together and this is how to do it. Place the white card on the table in the position shown in picture 1, with the scored lines on the underside. Then push up the little ledge c that has been cut in front, and turn up the two triangular flaps on each side along the scored lines, thus forming upright sides. Now take the folded metal mirror, and, opening it at an angle of about sixty degrees, place it inside the card, so that the two nicks A and B in the cardboard sides come over the metal and hold it in position. The turned-up ledge in front prevents the mirror from closing up.

Now place some tiny pieces of stiff, glossy coloured papers and metallic papers of various shapes on the white card between the mirrors, and, holding the kaleidoscope as shown in picture 3, let a good light fall upon the mirrors, when a beautiful design will be seen.

As the coloured fragments are shaken about, the design ever changes. No matter how irregular the coloured pieces may be, a geometrical design will be formed, but this will be prettier if the fragments of coloured papers are themselves cut into some regular shapes, such as circles, rings, triangles, s's, x's, and so on.

With a little practice the cards can be cut to hold the mirrors at various angles, and this adds greatly to the interest, for according to the angle of the mirrors, so the number of times that the objects are reflected varies.

3. THE KALEIDOSCOPE COMPLETE

Simple Learning Made Easy For Very Little People

READING—THE WORKING LETTERS

JOHN and Jennifer did not have to "learn" their alphabet, for when they were tiny children Mother used to sing it to them.

They also had a picture book of capital and small letters, which Father Christmas had given them when they were three years old; and now that they were five they easily remembered the names of all the letters, for when they had made their word books, Mother had told them the names.

They were really interested in reading, and Mother said she would teach them the sounds the letters said ; then they would be able to find out words for themselves. First of all, she said, they would learn the sounds of the five letters that did all the hard work. They were called working letters, but their proper name was vowels.

The five letters are **A E I O U.** We will make up some words in which are these letters ; first of all, some words that begin with A:

Apple. Annie. Alphabet.

Now some words that begin with E:

Engine. Egg. Edward.

These are some words that begin with I:

Indian. Ink. Indiarubber.

These are some words that begin with O:

Omnibus. Orange. Ostrich.

These are some words that begin with U:

Ugly. Uncle. Umbrella.

" Now," said Mother, " we will learn some words with A E I O U in them.

We'll make up rhymes. I will make up a rhyme and you can tell me the word I want at the end of each line. First we will find some A words:

A fish was caught in a frying pan—
Get it out as fast as you can.

John wears a dark blue cap.
Jennifer wears a scarlet hat.

" Now let's think of some E words:

Timothy paddled and got very wet,
But caught a minnow in a net.

Daddy uses a fountain-pen
Like those used by gentle-men.

" Now some I words:

The soldier, he was made of tin,
For a sword he carried a pin.

The piper's son who stole a pig,
On the way home danced a jig.

" Here are some O words:

The treacle pudding is very hot
Because it came straight from the pot.

Daddy bought John a jumping fox.
Mother bought Jennifer Jack-in-the-box.

" Now some U words," said Mother:

The dirty clothes go in the tub,
To get them clean we give a rub.

A bee can fly and he can hum.
He cannot help me count my sum.

One day Mother came in and gave John and Jennifer two envelopes, one to each. Inside were some slips with a question, and some little cards with YES or NO written on them.

" Now," said Mother, " here is a picture for each of you; everything in the picture has its name printed underneath.

READING · WRITING · ARITHMETIC · MUSIC · DRAWING · FRENCH

You must get out a question slip, read it, look at the picture, and put the right answer slip by the side of the question."

THE POSTMAN

THE POSTMAN

Is the postman running? No
Is he walking? Yes
Has he a lot of letters? Yes
Has he any parcels? No
Is he dressed in red? No
Does he carry an umbrella? No
Does he carry a bag? No
Does he carry a sack? Yes
Has he any letters? Yes

NUMBERS—ADD, MULTIPLY, SUBTRACT

Multiplication. John and Jennifer were fond of counting and threading beads in 2's and 3's, and Mother said they could now learn what × means, and learn their tables. She wrote down for them:

One 2 is 2
$1 \times 2 = 2$
Two 2's are 4
$2 \times 2 = 4$

Then they strung their beads in 2's with numbers in between:

After that John and Jennifer learned lots of tables by stringing their beads in 3's and 4's, and so on.

Mother then showed them how we write multiplication sums:

For working these sums she made them some table boards like this:

$$\begin{array}{r} 4 \\ \times 4 \\ \hline \end{array}$$

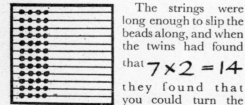

The strings were long enough to slip the beads along, and when the twins had found that $7 \times 2 = 14$ they found that you could turn the sum round and that $2 \times 7 = 14$ was just the same. Ten Times table was

easy, because they knew that 10 meant 1 ten, 20 meant 2 tens, 30 meant 3 tens, and so on.

When they threaded their beads in 10's they had such a long string that Mother let them stop at 10 tens, and said they had made a 100 chain. It was great fun.

Mother made them a few sum cards with what she called mixed-up sums, and the twins had to look very carefully, to see whether they had to add up the figures, subtract, or multiply them.

$$\begin{array}{r} 5 \\ +4 \\ \hline \end{array} \qquad \begin{array}{r} 6 \\ -3 \\ \hline \end{array} \qquad \begin{array}{r} 3 \\ \times 2 \\ \hline \end{array}$$

$$\begin{array}{r} 9 \\ -1 \\ \hline \end{array} \qquad \begin{array}{r} 8 \\ +8 \\ \hline \end{array} \qquad \begin{array}{r} 5 \\ \times 5 \\ \hline \end{array}$$

Taking away EVERYTHING and NOTHING were two easy things the twins learnt. If John was greedy and had 6 sweets, and ate them all, he would have none left. So Mother made this quite plain for them by writing down:

$12 - 12 = 0$
$17 - 17 = 0$
$100 - 100 = 0$

If John had 6 sweets, and did not eat any, he would have 6 left. So:

$$6 - 0 = 6$$
$$29 - 0 = 29$$
$$80 - 0 = 80$$

Adding on ones was easy, too, because it was always the next number, and taking away ones was easy also—once he had learned to say his numbers backwards!

Hard Addition. Mother then showed them how to do hard adding-up sums with tens and units:

$$
\begin{array}{cc}
t & u \\
2 & 7 \\
+4 & 7 \\
\hline
\end{array}
$$

" Now, a unit is one," said Mother, " and if we add 7 and 7, we have 14, which is a ten and a four, and, as we cannot put a ten and a unit in the unit answer, we put the ten underneath the

$$
\begin{array}{cc}
t & u \\
2 & 7 \\
+4 & 7 \\
\hline
7 & 4
\end{array}
$$

10's side—and, whatever we do, we must not forget to add it in."

Equal Addition—method for subtraction. One day Mother showed the twins a big sum:

$$
\begin{array}{cc}
t & u \\
8 & 4 \\
-2 & 8 \\
\hline
\end{array}
$$

" We have to take 28 away from 84, and that is not easy! Let us do the units first:

" Take 8 away from 4, we cannot! So we give the 4 a 10, and make it 14, and find we can take 8 away from 14, and the answer is 6. Now, we must be fair to the tens, too, so we give the smallest ten another ten, and then we can work the sum."

$$
\begin{array}{cc}
t & u \\
8 & 4 \\
-2 & 8 \\
\hline
5 & 6
\end{array}
$$

Which is not so hard after all.

WRITING—QUESTIONS AND ANSWERS

JOHN and Jennifer found that writing helped them with their reading. Mother said that writing long and hard words would help them, and a question-and-answer game would help them to remember the queer marks they knew.

One morning the postman brought a catalogue from the stores, and it had lots of pictures. Mother did not want the catalogue, and said the twins might cut out the pictures and paste them in plain books, and copy the names underneath. John and Jennifer found a lot of pictures with really hard words to copy underneath. They made a page for the house; a page for the garden; a page for Mother; a page for Daddy, and a page for each of themselves, as well as one for their school:

THE HOUSE PAGE
cupboard refrigerator radiogram
fireplace electric iron saucepan

THE GARDEN PAGE
lawn mower shears wheelbarrow
sprinkler cloche syringe

MOTHER'S PAGE
umbrella gloves shoes
cardigan handkerchief slippers

FATHER'S PAGE
raincoat walking-stick suit
muffler attaché case pullover

JOHN'S PAGE
jersey blazer cricket-bat
knickers football-boots overcoat

JENNIFER'S PAGE
dressing-gown tunic stockings
party frock pinafore petticoat

SCHOOL PAGE
reading arithmetic painting
writing drawing dancing

Another day Daddy had a gardening catalogue full of lovely pictures of people working in their gardens and allotments, and of flowers, fruit, vegetables, seeds, and all kinds of gardening tools.

This time Mother chose the pictures for them and wrote questions. The twins looked up the words they wanted and wrote the answers, not forgetting the capital letters, commas, and full stops.

WHAT FLOWERS GROW ON THE ROCKERY?

Daffodils, hyacinths, scillas, and snowdrops grow on the rockery.

WHERE ARE THE APPLES ?

On the apple tree.

WHAT HAS DADDY PLANTED ON HIS ALLOTMENT?

Daddy has planted potatoes, peas, beans, and carrots.

WHAT IS BEHIND THE HEDGE ?

The tool shed is behind the hedge.

WHAT RED THINGS CAN YOU SEE IN THE CATALOGUE ?

I can see red holly berries, red poppy flower, and a red flower-pot.

MUSIC—TIME-KEEPING

WHEN we hear music to which people are dancing, it is not the tune we notice so much as the rhythm. It is time that we learned more about rhythm.

The sounds which make melody are either high or low, but if we listen carefully we notice that they have other qualities as well. A man may be tall or he may be short ; he may also be fat or thin, fair or dark, and in describing him to someone else it is not sufficient to say merely that he is tall. Musical sounds are very similar to people. We can pick them out and describe them.

In the Londonderry Air, one of the most familiar and loved of all melodies, there is one note near the end which impresses us more than the others:

In the square box is the important note. It is a high note, the highest note in the melody, and it sounds even higher than it is because it follows three rather low notes which are all on the same level.

If we make up a tune for our own pleasure we need not write it down ; we can remember it. If we want little children to learn our tune we still need not write it down. We can sing it to them and they can sing it after us. But suppose we want others to learn our tune.

We must show how high the notes are so that there will be no mistakes with the pitch. We therefore either give the sol-fa names of the notes or draw a plan of the tune, using lines and spaces to measure the ups and downs. But we have to find some way of showing how much time each note is to take. Fortunately this has been worked out for us.

Feel your heart beating, *Thud, thud, thud, thud* . . . each beat being quite regular. Put your hand to your heart and sing to successive beats : *doh, re, mi, fa, soh, lah, te, doh.* And now : 1 2 3 4 5 6 7 8. We might make this game more interesting:

There we have the beginning of a hymn tune: O God our help in ages past. We can show the ups and downs quite easily, and so long as we have the same shaped note for each sound we can show that each lasts for the same length of time as its neighbour. The one-beat note, going at the same rate (more or less) as a heart-beat, is shown like this: This sign with the black head and the stem is called the *crotchet* (or we may also call him *taa*). We can now write the first line of our tune:

But we are making a mistake. The last note is more important than the others. It comes at the end of a phrase. When we say:

" O God our help in ages past," we wait here and then go on:

" Our hope for years to come."

Where music fits words it tries to stop where the words stop. If this were not the case songs would make nonsense.

Put your hand to your heart again.

Beats 1   1   1   1   1   1   1   1   2

O God our help in ages past. Two heart-beats sound while we hold to the last note and word. So we need a note which will tell us to wait for twice as long as on a crotchet. Here it is: ♩ (*minim* or *taa-aa*).

We have not finished with this melody yet, for, when singing or playing, we must do exactly as the composer tells us. Dr. Croft, who composed this hymn tune, discovered, as did many other cathedral organists like himself, that congregations are often slow in starting. So, very thoughtfully, he started his tune with another long note—another two-beat note.

Beats 1 2   1   1   1   1·   1   1   1 2

taa-aa taa taa taa taa taa taa taa-aa

Hymn tunes are one side of music—the dignified side. They must, because they are dignified, frequently employ the one- and two-beat notes. We started, however, by talking about dance music. Dance music does not want to have so much to do with stately notes as a rule. It wants gay, carefree, quick-moving notes, which can patter along.

Read these words:

" Baa, baa, Black Sheep! "

Clap the rhythm. Clap, clap, clap, clap. Four steady beats which are crotchets— ♩ ♩ ♩ ♩. Then we go on to the next line:

" Have you any wool? "

Say those words to crotchets— ♩ ♩ ♩ ♩. Now put both lines together ♩ ♩ ♩ ♩ — ♩ ♩ ♩ ♩. What we have seems wrong. It sounds heavy and uninteresting. We want some quicker notes to fit the quicker moving words. We use some notes which last only half as long as the crotchets. These notes are called *quavers*, and when we see two quavers (for they often move in pairs) we can say *taa-tai*.

Let us look at the melody of Baa, baa, Black Sheep. As it is the F stave which is used by men, you had better ask Father

to sing it. Perhaps you can teach *him* something about crotchets and quavers!

Doh —

Now look at the beginning of two melodies. You will see how much you can manage in the way of reading music:

That, light hearted because of its quavers, is one of the songs from the children's opera Hansel and Gretel, an opera by a German composer with the musical-sounding name Humperdinck. If you ever have the chance you must see this opera. And here is the solemn opening of the children's evening hymn from the same opera:

Doh—

These two tunes, from the same opera, show how necessary is contrasting music.

We will look at one more tune, this time not a song but a dance for fairies. The fairies are those which we meet in A Midsummer Night's Dream by Shakespeare, and also in an opera based on Shakespeare's play, by Henry Purcell. This opera is The Fairy Queen.

That lovely, quiet, swift movement, played by the strings of the orchestra, is surely one of the most perfect pieces of fairy music ever composed.

At the beginning of the melody there are groups of notes within two brackets. Compare these two groups. What do you notice? First, the shape of group A is the same as that of group B. Both phrases go up and down in the same way, although group B begins one note higher than group A. Then let us look closely at the note values of the two groups:

A

B

The two phrases match each other in rhythm. This teaches a very important lesson. Interest depends on melodic shape, rhythmic shape, and the *repetition* of both melodic and rhythmic patterns.

Let us go back to our railway journey. Just out of a big station we noticed the engine making this sort of noise—*sh, sh, sh; sh, sh, sh;* and so on. We listened and listened and found the noise turning into—*one, two, three; one, two, three* . . . A little later on when we were running very smoothly we heard the wheels—*rat, tat, tat, tat; rat, tat, tat, tat* . . . *one, two, three, four; one, two three, four.* We had found two different rhythmic patterns, the first based on three-beat groups, the second on four. But do not let us forget the lady with the knitting needles. *Click, click; click, click* . . . *one, two; one, two* . . . *crotchet, crochet; crotchet, crotchet.* For every *click, click* (1, 2), we heard *rat-tat-tat-tat* (1 & 2 &), all *quavers.* In musical notation we could write what we heard:

KNITTING
  NEEDLES
CARRIAGE
  WHEELS

The downward lines help us to see the way in which the notes are grouped. Like the divisions on a ruler they give us exact measurement.

With the help of these lines players are enabled to keep together. They are called bar lines. The space between one bar line and another is called a bar. What a help it is to a conductor to be able to say, if he wishes to repeat a passage in rehearsal, " We will go back, please, to the tenth bar."

Bar lines do more than that. They show whether the notes are grouped in twos, in threes, in fours, or what you will.

To make quite certain that the player or singer knows as much as possible about the music he is going to play or sing before he starts, figures are put at the beginning of each piece of music— *time signatures.*

Music with *two* crotchets in a bar is shown

Music with *three* crotchets in a bar is shown

Music with *four* crotchets in a bar is shown

Of the music we have been looking at in this chapter the merry song from Hansel and Gretel should have the signature 2/4; the evening hymn 4/4; the dance 3/4.

Copy the melodies and add the time signatures. Also put in bar lines. Each begins on the first beat of the bar (not all melodies do).

Remember that a ♩ can also be represented by ♫ and the time taken by ♩♩ can also be shown by ♪. A bar of 2/4 time has not always two crotchets, but it always has notes which add up to the value of two crotchets.

Rhythm is important in music, but it is also important in life. An engine runs rhythmically when it is in good order. A horse trots rhythmically. If you want to run or to swim well you must learn to use your arms and your legs rhythmically.

All this means that if you learn rhythm from music, which asks for great precision in its rhythmic patterns, you will be more useful at many other things.

ART—MATERIALS FOR CARVING

WHEN walking on a shingle beach we may have suddenly caught sight of a large stone which made us think of an animal or a person. Again, perhaps we have seen the shapes of things in an old tree trunk or a broken piece of rock. It is very much in this way that sculptors have had ideas for their sculpture, for the shape of the material does help to decide what they are going to carve, and what the carving will look like when it is done.

If we look at an African wood carving we see at once that it was cut from a round log of wood, and the sculptor or carver has enough cut away to show the figure of a god whose image he was making.

Some sculpture is life-like and realistic, while other is more imaginative or grotesque, like the wonderful gargoyles through which the water pours from the roof of a cathedral, or heads like the copper lion from Ur (see Index); but in both cases the sculpture should look like the material in which it is made. It should express an idea and the material in which it is made. What can be carved in ivory, like the ones shown on page 70, could not be carved in hard, brittle stone.

To begin carving we need some fairly soft materials which can be cut with a penknife or an old broken dinner-knife, or even proper stone carving chisels. A large block of salt is very good for the purpose. A lump of chalk, such as is put on the fields in some parts of the country, is equally good and can be kept longer than salt. A block of soap will also do to practise on and will look something like ivory when finished. Odd pieces

CARVED FROM BRICK

of soft stone or soft brick can be shaped by tapping the surface with another piece of harder stone, or a hammer, or with chisel and mallet. The hammered part comes away as dust.

Mixed plaster of paris, just as it is about to set hard, can be poured on to a board in a pile like an old stone boulder, and when set can be carved with penknife or hammer and chisel. We can also pour the plaster into a cardboard box made watertight with strips of gummed paper; and when set, and the box removed, we have a grand block of plaster to carve.

11TH CENTURY CHESSMAN—FRONT AND BACK

If we go to the Science Museum we can see a model of a flint knapper at work, and from it we realise just how pieces flake off when the hammer is used the right way. In some places we can go into a stone quarry and see how with mallet and chisel the stonemason shapes his stone.

CARVED FROM SALT

If we go to the Diploma Gallery of the Royal Academy we can see an unfinished roundel by Michael Angelo. We see how the great sculptor chipped away the marble in shaping the pattern of his figures and gradually led up to the finishing and smoothing of the carving.

While we cannot expect to carve in such difficult material without a great deal of experience, we can successfully carve in salt, soft brick, chalk, or plaster fairly easily. Alabaster too is a possibility, and odd lumps of it are quite cheap.

Any experience we may gain in carving will help us greatly in our understanding and appreciation of sculpture, whether ancient or of our own time. We come to realise that, as in any other form of art, we must create in the material in which we express our ideas. Sculpture is not an imitation of something, but a sculptor's ideas expressed in the material carved. The figure of a man carved in a 22-inch block of salt was done by a boy of 12. He used an old dinner knife, a potato peeler, and a large palette knife, such as cooks use, for carving it. The figure is in a sitting position, just like the scribe and his wife in the statue 7000 years old illustrated on page 3897.

When we look at any of these figures we feel their solid, block-like character. The idea has been expressed in a block, and the simple block shape has been kept at the same time.

The half brick carved like a corbel head from a cathedral was done with stone-carving chisels and a mallet. It was carved by a boy of 12, and shows how much the material in which we work affects the result. The finely carved lines of the hair could not have been done in salt, but they could in brick, and they could be made even finer still in ivory.

Our other illustration is of an Isle of Lewis chessman carved in ivory about the eleventh century. It is one of a king, and is very beautifully carved from every point of view. The shape is roughly that of the ivory tusk, tapering upwards, and is pleasing to handle, as it was meant to be handled while playing chess.

FRENCH—THE PARTY ON THE BOAT

THIS part of our story gives an account of the little family party on the boat. The first line under each picture is the French; the second line gives the English word for the French word above it; the third line shows how we make up the words in our own language.

Nous quittons l'Angleterre.
We leave the England.
We are leaving England.

Maman n'aime pas la mer.
Mamma likes not the sea.
Mamma does not like the sea.

Elle descend dans la cabine.
She descends into the cabin.
She goes down into the cabin.

Nous croisons un bateau à voiles.
We cross a boat with sails.
We pass a sailing boat.

Il y a un homme dans le bateau.
There is a man in the boat.
There is a man in the boat.

Nous restons sur le pont avec papa.
We stay on the deck with Papa.
We stay on deck with Papa.

Nous aimons beaucoup la mer.
We like very much the sea.
We like the sea very much.

Le perroquet est tout seul.
The parrot is all alone.
The parrot is all alone.

Nous courons à la cage.
We run to the cage.
We run to the cage.

Quelqu'un dit: "La terre est en vue."
Somebody says: "The land is in view."
Somebody says: "Land is in sight."

Il y a beaucoup de falaises.
There are many of cliffs.
There are many cliffs.

Jeannette voudrait voir des poissons.
Jenny would like to see some fishes.
Jenny wants to see some fishes.

Maman se sent beaucoup mieux.
Mamma herself feels much better.
Mamma feels much better.

The Story of the Boundless Universe and All its Wondrous Worlds

The peak of a Cambrian rock in Wales

THE WORLD OF THE CAMBRIAN AGE

Far down under most of the surface of England and a large part of Wales and Scotland lies a vast sheet of slaty rock only a mile or less beneath us in some places, but probably more than five miles down in others.

This great bed of rock is nearly three and a half miles thick, and is known as the Cambrian formation, after the ancient name for Wales, because these wonderful rocks were first found in that country.

In the bold and rugged mountainous masses of Carnarvon and Merioneth, the forces at work in the Earth's crust had split the colossal sheet of Cambrian rock, had exposed its ends at the surface of the Earth, and in places had raised it into mountains nearly three thousand feet high. In the Isle of Man, too, and in the North of Scotland, as shown on the accompanying map, other portions of this immense layer of rock are found forced up to and above the Earth's surface.

In these places geologists were able to make a thorough examination of the rock, and it was discovered to have the wonderful and curious property of splitting into the very hard, smooth thin sheets called slates, which are now used so extensively for roofing and other purposes.

Most of the slates we use, and most of the best slates, come from quarries in Wales.

Not all of this Cambrian layer is composed of smooth and fine grained sheets of slate; it contains strange things and records, remains of great masses of rock that existed before it was formed, ripple-marks of the waves that beat on those shores many millions of years ago, pebbles worn smooth and round by long years of tossing about by the breakers of those far-off days, even marks of rain-drops that fell on the soft, sandy mud, and sun-cracks which formed when it had partly dried, are found in this wonderful rock that now lies so far down beneath our country.

But this is not all. Forms of curious creatures, utterly unlike the life of our day, are found preserved in the Earth. Many of these are shown in the pictures. The upper picture on page 887 shows them as they are believed to have existed; the lower picture shows them as they are found at the present day, embedded in the slaty Cambrian rock.

It is thus easy to see that this colossal bed of rock, deeper than the loftiest mountain in Europe is high, and now many thousands of feet below most of our country, was once at or near the surface. But it was worn down or sunk below sea-level, and thousands and thousands of feet, even miles, of other strata were piled

ASTRONOMY · GEOLOGY · GEOGRAPHY . CHEMISTRY . PHYSICS . LIFE

THE CAMBRIAN & SILURIAN AGES IN BRITAIN

This map shows the rocks of the Cambrian and Silurian Ages where they are now seen on the surface of Britain. The pictures of the Cambrian Age appear opposite and those of the Silurian Age will be found on page 1010.

LIFE AND REMAINS OF THE CAMBRIAN AGE

A VIEW OF THE WORLD IN THE CAMBRIAN AGE, WITH A SECTION THROUGH THE SEA SHOWING SOME OF THE CREATURES OF THE PERIOD—ANCESTORS OF SHRIMPS, PRAWNS, AND LOBSTERS

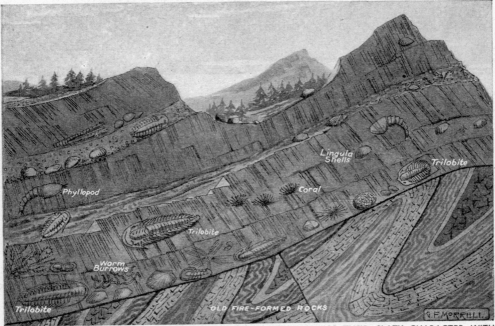

A SECTION THROUGH THE ROCKS OF THE CAMBRIAN AGE, SHOWING THEIR SLATY CHARACTER WITH FOSSILS (GREATLY ENLARGED) IMPRISONED IN THE CRUMPLED-UP STRATA

on it in places. The terrific weight pressing on it from above and the expansive forces due to the great internal heat of the Earth pressing on it from below, bent and twisted the great bed of rock in various ways, transforming it into the hard slates that resist fire and water.

Careful study by geologists has revealed the amazing fact that this hard, smooth slate was once mud, and that it was deposited on the shores and bottom of a large shallow sea. We see, therefore, that nearly all England and Wales, the Lowlands of Scotland, and most of Ireland, was once the bed of a vast sea.

It was millions of years before most of the kinds of life we are familiar with had come into existence. There were then no creatures with backbones. There were not even insects. There were no trees, nor palms, nor flowers, nor ferns; on flora at all to adorn the land, except possibly mosses and lichens, the lowliest

shell nor backbone—came into existence. During the Cambrian Age however, life made enormous strides, and creatures wonderfully made—such as the curious little phyllopods, ancestors of our shrimps, prawns, and lobsters—flitted about. But the most remarkable of all were the trilobites. These strange crustaceans, for they were not fishes, were in those times the lords of creation, great things as much as two feet long, and swarming everywhere. They did not reign long, however; many millions of years ago they died out, yet through all the long ages that have intervened there is one family, that of the crab, which has descended directly from the trilobites, and still shows traces of its ancestry. The king crab of China and the East is the nearest living relative although now most unlike a trilobite in appearance.

The trilobite was a soft-bodied creature enclosed in a shell of many sections, each section being divided into three lobes, so

THE KING CRAB OF CHINA, THE NEAREST LIVING RELATIVE OF THE TRILOBITE OF THE CAMBRIAN AGE

forms of vegetation. There was neither the song of bird, nor the hum of insect, nor the rustling of leaves, to break the stillness of those far-off days—only the everlasting beat of the waves on the shore, or the sound of the rushing rain and roaring wind that wore or tore away those earlier rocks out of which the Cambrian rocks were made.

The sea, on the other hand, was teeming with life even at this early period of the Earth's existence, and there is no doubt that it was in the sea that the first forms of life—probably organisms with neither

giving the creature its name. It had a great shovel-like head enabling it to penetrate the mud in search of food and shelter, and it could roll itself up into a ball—as we see in the accompanying pictures—like that curious insect found in our gardens still—the little wood-louse, known to children as "rolley-ups." The eyes of the trilobites were most wonderful, some having as many as fifteen thousand facets. The presence of creatures with so many elaborately-developed characters at such a remote period is evidence that life must have existed long ages before.

The Story of Immortal Folk Whose Work Will Never Die

Mazzini   King Alfred   Andreas Hofer   Boadicea   Kossuth

Garibaldi   Miltiades   Bolivar   Themistocles   William Wallace

THE CREATORS OF LIBERTY

MAN, the highest of living creatures, is very old in human reckoning, but very modern in comparison with other forms of life; and by far the greatest part of humanity's career has been little more exalted than that of the brutes.

Civilised man is the youngest child of ancient parents who were savage and lawless robbers and murderers by nature and practice. The terrible deep-rooted instincts of that untamed ancestry are constantly thrusting through the thin, modern wrappings with which civilisation invests us.

The Ten Commandments are but as laws given yesterday, but they are an everlasting reminder of our imperfections, of our greed and passion, our wrongdoing and tyranny.

Every age has its Goliaths—single Goliaths and communities of Goliaths. It is only when the challenge of Goliath is answered by an enlightened and valiant David that the grinding tyranny of the giants is defeated and mankind is permitted to struggle some few steps toward the distant goal of perfection. The history of mankind could be written around these heroic souls who have withstood ruthless wrong, who have died for freedom, and, sometimes a harder thing, lived for it.

A shining example gleams among the earliest records, when two men saved the world for liberty and learning. It was five centuries before the birth of Jesus, when the Empire of the Medes and Persians, founded upon pitiless might, upon superstition and the folly which accompanies blind brute power, aimed at the mastery of Europe.

Greece lay across the path. The little nation was a military barrier. Worse still, she was a danger to all that held the intolerable Empire together; for independent thought travelled from Greece into the realms of King Darius, voices which talked of culture and human rights and liberties. Greece must be crushed.

So a great army of those formidable Medes and Persians of whom the Bible tells us, marched into Greece, and drew up on the plain of Marathon, near Athens. No nobler picture exists than that of the devoted little Greek nation facing the Eastern Goliath. The hour brought the man. Miltiades was undismayed. He counselled, exhorted, directed. Under his leadership this little David nation attacked its formidable giant.

There is no clue as to exact numbers. Greece could not have had more than 10,000 fighting men all told, but at the battle of Marathon in 490 B.C. she

EXPLORERS · INVENTORS · WRITERS · ARTISTS · SCIENTISTS

overthrew more than 50,000 men who had marched to trample her out of life.

The peril was not yet ended. The enemy slowly re-armed. Themistocles, who had fought under Miltiades, foresaw with wonderful insight that the next battle would occur at sea. By ten years of teaching and preaching he overcame furious opposition, got a fleet organised, and was ready when King Xerxes, successor to Darius, brought his hosts against the devoted land.

THE BATTLE OF SALAMIS WHICH SAVED THE WEST FROM THE EAST

The battle of Salamis was the battle of Themistocles. Nominally, a Spartan general commanded the united forces of Greece and Sparta, but Themistocles was the guiding spirit. His allies proposed to retreat and leave their land to be overrun. Themistocles said that this would be fatal to Greece. So by an audacious trick he caused word to be conveyed to Xerxes that flight was intended. During the night Xerxes moved his forces into the bay, and in the morning the Greeks found their ships surrounded.

They had to fight then and there as Themistocles desired; and, put to the test, they won an annihilating victory, as his brave spirit had foreseen would happen.

After twenty-four centuries, we still recognise that Miltiades and Themistocles at Marathon and Salamis saved the world. The supremacy of the West was established in that vital contest with the silken barbarism, the luxurious tyranny of the East. Had Greece fallen the story of the world would have been fatally different.

Miltiades and Themistocles, who have all posterity in their debt, suffered the fate not uncommon to heroism. Miltiades, first of historical martyrs, perished in the prison into which his ungenerous countrymen flung him. Themistocles perished as a hunted fugitive from the people he had saved from bondage and death.

THE LITTLE ARMY THAT ROUTED THE GREAT HOSTS

The saviours of a cause may die that a people or a principle may live, and in their death may be the seeds of victory. An illustration occurs in Jewish history. A mighty kingdom arose in Syria, and one of its kings, named Antiochus, who ruled over Palestine as a part of Syria, resolved to make the Jews give up worshipping God according to the Hebrew law, and to offer sacrifice to false gods. Then there arose Mattathias who, with his sons, refused to obey the orders of King Antiochus. Among the sons of Mattathias the most skilful warrior was the second, whose name was Judas, surnamed Maccabaeus.

Judas gathered together a troop of Jews who were ready to die for faith and freedom; and though they were few in number, yet they routed utterly great hosts which the King of Syria sent to subdue them, and won back Jerusalem from his soldiers.

When men saw this small band making havoc of vast armies, they gathered to Maccabaeus, nor could the Syrian generals in any way subdue them. And though Judas himself was at last slain in a battle where his followers were so few that they were overwhelmed by the numbers of the enemy, yet it was indeed he who at that time won freedom for the Jewish people.

In our own land, the torch of liberty has passed through many hands, none fiercer than those of Boadicea, Queen of the Iceni in what is now Norfolk and Suffolk. Her husband died a king, with the promise that his widow and heirs should inherit his kingdom.

BOADICEA AND HER FIERCE FIGHT FOR FREEDOM AGAINST THE ROMANS

Rome, however, proved faithless. Boadicea was defeated, and treated like a serf. When she protested she was publicly scourged, and her two lovely daughters were submitted to treatment which almost broke her proud heart.

But it did not break; instead, it caught fire. Boadicea raised an army of Britons, and fell upon the Romans and upon all Britons friendly to them. The slaughter was horrible, in keeping with the pagan times. It is curious that London, nurse of freedom, comes into history for the first time in Boadicea's rebellion of A.D. 60, when in the name of liberty and right it was sacked and its people massacred.

Boadicea was ultimately defeated, as she was bound to be, and died, like Cleopatra, by her own hand. She was a tigress in her hour of trial, and sought by savagery to redress barbarism, the only method of retaliation known to the age. But the agonising lesson she taught was never forgotten. Rome, mistress of the world, was shown that wronged weakness may rise to maddened strength and become an instrument of terrible retribution.

The feats of Boadicea are commemorated in noble poetry and statuary. She looks from her lofty pedestal at the Houses of Parliament in which are administered the affairs of an Empire embracing realms that Caesar never knew; a reminder that even the mightiest of human forces must observe justice to the lowliest of its citizens.

We look forward in the history of our land, and a figure beckons us to the finest story in our annals. Alfred the Great stands out as the noblest soul that ever

scholarship claimed his attention. Half his life was given to fighting. During his first 35 years London lay a waste, despoiled by the foe, and nearly all England was prostrate before those fierce and terrible hordes.

The valiant king put heart into a few troops and gained small victories, and from that, with larger forces, he gained great battles. But all seemed lost in a defeat which drove Alfred to hide and entrench in the marshes. He came forth

THOMAS THORNYCROFT'S FINE STATUE OF BOADICEA, AMID STREAMING LONDON'S CENTRAL ROAR
" Regions Caesar never knew, Thy posterity shall sway "

graced our land. He had all the fiery courage of Boadicea, but refined by a beauty of spirit such as comes to mankind but once in a millennium. He was born, in 849, into an England of which practically all north of the Thames was in possession of the ferocious Norsemen. When he died in 901 there was not a Norseman in the land who was not a citizen or a prisoner in English hands.

The fifth and youngest son of Ethelwulf, Alfred was educated in Rome, but had to distinguish himself as a soldier before

again undaunted, resumed his campaigns, fought from sea to sea right across England and was never again defeated.

The Vikings came with horses; Alfred raised his own cavalry. They had much-dreaded war-galleys. He built bigger and better galleys, and created our first navy; he swept the Vikings from our seas, and sending his ships afar, met and defeated the foe on their own coasts, so that they could not attempt invasion.

The Danes who remained in England he caused to swear fealty to him. He

THREE CHIEFTAINS OF MANKIND

THE BRAVE NEGRO CHIEF WATCHING THE
COMING OF THE FLEET SENT BY NAPOLEON

GARIBALDI, THE FOUNDER OF MODERN ITALY,
LOOKS OUT FROM HIS ISLAND HOME

ALFRED THE GREAT UNDER THE ENGLISH OAKS HE LOVED SO WELL

BUILDING ALFRED'S FLEET. FROM THE PAINTING BY H. R. MILEHAM

settled them on the land, gave peace within our borders, rebuilt and fortified London and the coast, and then, after being the greatest warrior of his age, became the greatest friend of peace.

HOW ALFRED WARMS THE HEART AFTER A THOUSAND YEARS

To redeem the land from ignorance, that sinister enemy, he with his own hands translated history, religious discourses, and philosophical works from Latin into English, and sent copies throughout the land. He fixed in writing the best of the old laws and established new, but always with the approval of his Parliament.

Much of his writing still exists, and warms the heart and imagination after a thousand years. Alfred was greater and nobler than all the mythical heroes of legend and poetry, the purest and sweetest spirit that England ever cradled. Alexander the Great as conqueror and educator of peoples, Caesar as conqueror and just law-giver, moved in greater spheres, but Alfred outshone both for the sublimest human qualities, saviour of his land, teacher of his people, father of English prose, a hero and saint who thought himself neither, but tried to make all his countrymen both.

Time passed and the ideals of kingship changed. We had to defend ourselves against lawless encroachment, and at times we were guilty of trespasses as unpardonable. No Scotsman forgets that this was the case when our Edward the First sought to conquer all Scotland.

WILLIAM WALLACE GATHERS HIS MEN TOGETHER IN THE HILLS

When the young Queen of Scots, called the Maid of Norway, died, the Scots were divided as to who should be king, and they asked Edward to judge between the men who claimed the throne. One of these men, John Baliol, said that he would own Edward for his overlord, and so the king gave judgment in favour of Baliol. But afterward he said that John Baliol, having sworn to be loyal to him, had broken his promise, and he drove Baliol from the throne, and sought to rule Scotland with English officers.

Then there appeared a young man named William Wallace who was strong and skilful with all manner of weapons, and when some English soldiers tried to rob him, he turned on them and slew them with his staff, though they were armed. The English set a price upon his head, and he fled to the hills, and there gathered round him men determined to rid their native land of foreign masters, Then the English governor gathered an army, and Wallace awaited him by the bridge near Stirling.

The English army began to march across the bridge, but while a part of the army was on one side of the river and a part on the other, Wallace set upon them suddenly, and put them utterly to rout. The fame of this exploit stirred up many more of the Scots to join Wallace, and the English were driven out.

After this, Edward, who had been abroad, came back to England, and marched into Scotland with a strong army, having many mail-clad horsemen and archers. The Scots lords held aloof from Wallace, for they were unwilling to be led by a captain who was not of noble birth. Nevertheless, Wallace gave battle to King Edward at Falkirk, having his men all on foot and armed with long spears. He and his men fought stoutly till Edward bade his archers send a storm of arrows among them. Then, great gaps being made in the ranks of the Scots, the English charged through and routed them.

THE SAD BETRAYAL OF THE NATIONAL HERO OF THE SCOTS

But, even after this, Wallace, having escaped, went on fighting against the English ; till one day a false knight betrayed him into the hands of English soldiers, and he was taken a prisoner to England. King Edward, instead of treating Wallace as an honourable and valiant foe, put him to a shameful death.

The freeing of France from the interference of English kings by the exalted action of the peasant maiden, Joan of Arc is described fully elsewhere.

In Austria is a land called Tirol, and Napoleon caused the Austrian emperor to give Tirol to the King of Bavaria, who was always ready to do his bidding. But when the Austrians went to war again with Napoleon, the Tirolese rose up under Andreas Hofer, who was an innkeeper, and drove the French and the Bavarians out of the country, though they themselves were only peasants. For a short time Hofer was made their ruler, as a loyal subject of the Austrian emperor, though he would not obey the Bavarian king and the emperor of the French.

A NOBLE PATRIOT WHOM NAPOLEON SHOT

ANDREAS HOFER IS APPOINTED GOVERNOR OF TIROL. "I AM ANDREAS HOFER, THE PEASANT," HE WOULD
SAY WHEN THE PEOPLE CALLED HIM "YOUR EXCELLENCY"

ANDREAS HOFER AMONG HIS FRIENDS IN THE LAST FEW DAYS BEFORE NAPOLEON ORDERED
HIM TO BE SHOT

But the French armies defeated the Austrian armies, and the Tirolese could not openly resist the power of Napoleon unaided. Then, though the brave Hofer hid among the mountains, a traitor was found who showed the French where he was. He was taken prisoner, and condemned and shot as a rebel. Yet the stand that Hofer made helped to give heart to the other nations of Europe to rise against the rule of Napoleon, and so in due time Napoleon was overthrown, and the Tirol was restored to its old freedom, for which Hofer had fought and died.

THE SAD STATE OF ITALY UNDER HER FOREIGN RULERS

We turn next to Italy, once the mistress of the world, and find her depressed and degraded by ignorance and by servile consent to foreign rule. The once great land had passed into the possession of foreign enemies—Spaniards, Austrians, and French—so that she was split up into many little states and duchies, each with its own tyrannous and hateful form of government. The spirit of all was expressed by the Austrian emperor, who said to the people of the Lombardy-Venetian provinces, " You belong to me by conquest, and you are to forget that you are Italian."

Education was suppressed, ignorance fostered, every uplifting influence was stamped upon, and encouragement was given to conflicts between Italians, which weakened all except the foreign invaders. The grossest cruelties and barbarities marked the system, and provoked the creation of secret societies desperately resolved to destroy oppression.

Two of the leaders of the movement were Giuseppe Mazzini, born in 1805 at Genoa, and Garibaldi. One of the few Italian patriots fortunate enough to gain a sound education, Mazzini burned to redeem his country, but he was seized, imprisoned, and sentenced to death.

HOW MAZZINI PLANNED THE REDEMPTION OF ITALY IN HIS PRISON CELL

It was while he was awaiting execution that a great idea dawned upon him—that all the forces of disorder and destruction now arrayed against oppression should be combined and organised for the purpose of regeneration. He saw it was not enough to destroy oppression, but the spirit and practice of liberty must be re-created. To this task, after he escaped death, he devoted all his energies.

Italy became too dangerous for such a man, and he fled, first to France, and then to Switzerland, and finally to England, where at last he found safety. Mazzini was the mind, Garibaldi was the sword which won back Italy's unity and freedom.

Again and again Mazzini appeared secretly in Italy to counsel, encourage, and direct. It was death to give him shelter; but he came and went unbetrayed. His marvellous career was brilliantly successful for his country. His plans prospered. Italy was redeemed, and Mazzini died in his bed in Pisa.

Great as were his talents, Mazzini would never have carried his noble schemes to success without the aid of the lion-hearted Giuseppe Garibaldi, a romantic and inspired sailor two years his junior. The same pure fervour of patriotism which animated Mazzini burned clear in the breast of this born leader of men. Garibaldi was the great heroic fighter of the cause which Mazzini shaped.

GARIBALDI, THE FISHERMAN'S SON WHO STIRRED ALL ITALY

While he was still a very young man, Garibaldi was already a skilful sailor, for he was a fisherman's son. He joined in a revolt against the Austrians which was easily crushed, and he had to flee to South America. There he became famous as a leader in local wars, but after a time he returned to Italy and joined in a fresh revolt, gathering men who were ready to fight, because Garibaldi filled them with his own great love of their cause. Yet they were still not strong enough to overthrow the Austrian rule, and again he had to go away, to the United States. Yet again he returned, and once more the men of North Italy arose. This time they were victorious, and before long all Italy became one nation, certainly in great part because of the power that Garibaldi had of filling those about him with his own courage and enthusiasm.

Of similar spirit was Louis Kossuth, who set himself to win freedom for Hungary from the rule of Austria at the time when the Italians were seeking their own liberty. He was not a soldier, but a writer and orator, and a statesman whom the Hungarians accepted as their leader. They were defeated at the time, and Kossuth had to flee the country, but later the Hungarians agreed to own the Emperor of Austria as their king if they could have

GARIBALDI ON HIS HILLTOP MONUMENT LOOKING DOWN ON ROME

certain rights of governing themselves, and this they owed, in the first place, to Kossuth. But Kossuth himself was not content with this. He would not own allegiance to Austria, and he died some years later, not in Hungary, but in Italy.

Kossuth did not live to see his dreams realised as Mazzini and Garibaldi did; but we have seen it. The Austrian Empire has perished. Italy, which she ground into the mire of ignorance and misery, later attained power such as not even Mazzini dared to hope for, while Austria went down in a welter of agony, at which even those who overthrew her could scarce forbear to weep.

There is a great lesson in this for those who think. Liberty is the most precious of the rights to which man aspires. It comes to those who oppose courage and persistence to difficulty and danger, in its march overwhelming those who have held it back. The tyrant may flourish on wrong-doing for a while, but the men who strive for liberty win in the end, and their names are hallowed for evermore.

SIMON BOLIVAR, WHO SPREAD THE GOSPEL OF LIBERTY IN SOUTH AMERICA

Two of the world's supreme defenders and creators of freedom—George Washington and Abraham Lincoln come into a story elsewhere; here we may touch on the great South American patriot and hero, Simon Bolivar.

Of noble birth, wealthy, son of a slave-owning family, he went to Madrid to study, saw the closing scenes of the French Revolution, and returned to his native Caracas, in Venezuela, to spread the gospel of liberty in South America. Venezuela declared her independence of Spain, but an earthquake destroyed 8000 of her population, and the survivors regarded the catastrophe as an act of Divine vengeance upon them, and repented of their act of revolt. Bolivar escaped, but returned with a little army and gained the name of Liberator.

Again disaster attended him, and he had to fly to Haiti in the West Indies, there to meet that astounding Negro Toussaint l'Ouverture. The help he received from Haiti enabled him to return and free Venezuela; and remembering Haiti and its Negroes, he liberated his own slaves and beggared himself.

By great courage and persistence, Bolivar drove the Spaniards from point to point, and formed one great republic of Colombo, Venezuela, New Granada, and Ecuador. He ruled Peru, and from Upper Peru the state of Bolivia was formed in his honour.

The man who befriended Bolivar in Haiti was a pure-blooded Negro, a former slave, named Toussaint L'Ouverture, born in 1746, and therefore 37 years the senior of Bolivar. In the world struggle of the period, the Negroes of Haiti rose against French rule, and sought to establish their independence. Toussaint was called upon to lead them.

TOUSSAINT, THE BRAVE NEGRO CHIEF WHO REFUSED TO BE A KING

Spain held the eastern half of Haiti, where Toussaint made the Negroes take service with the Spaniards against the French. At once he proved himself a born leader. But the French Revolution decreed the freedom of all its slaves, so Toussaint formed a republic of Negroes. The English to spite the French, offered to make him King of Haiti, but he refused. He as sternly declined to have the former rulers ill-treated; and he impartially protected white from black, and black from white.

This poor slave, transfigured by freedom, was a born leader of men in war and peace. For seven years he ruled in righteousness and equity. Then Napoleon sent an army to reconquer Haiti. Toussaint was taken prisoner and carried captive to Europe, where he died in 1803 from the rigours of a vile imprisonment.

THE IMPERISHABLE SONNET WORDSWORTH WROTE FOR POOR TOUSSAINT

Wordsworth has outlined his fate in an imperishable sonnet:

Toussaint, the most unhappy man of men!
Whether the whistling Rustic tend his plough
Within thy hearing, or thy head be now
Pillowed in some deep dungeon's earless den;
O miserable Chieftain! Where and when
Wilt thou find patience? Yet die not; do thou
Wear rather in thy bonds a cheerful brow:
Though fallen thyself, never to rise again,
Live and take comfort. Thou hast left behind
Powers that will work for thee; air, earth, and
    skies;
There's not a breathing of the common wind
That will forget thee; thou hast great allies;
Thy friends are exultations, agonies,
And love, and man's unconquerable mind.

Napoleon committed many crimes, but none more ignoble than that which sent this heroic black genius to a miserable death. But poor black Toussaint is one with the immortals.

The Great Stories of the World That Will Be Told for Ever

LITTLE RED RIDING HOOD

A LITTLE girl once lived in a cottage at the edge of a great wood. Her mother had made her a pretty little red cloak with a hood to fit over her fair curls, and she was so fond of it that she hardly ever wore anything else. And therefore she was known to everybody as Little Red Riding Hood.

At the other side of the wood was a tiny house among the trees where Little Red Riding Hood's grandmother lived all alone. One fine afternoon Little Red Riding Hood's mother said:

"Your grandmother is not very well. In this basket I have put some eggs, a jar of honey, and some butter. Put on your cloak and take them to her, with my love. But be sure that you do not stay long on the way, because it will soon be dark, and then, you know, the wolves come out."

So Little Red Riding Hood put on her cloak, and away she went.

But the wild flowers were very beautiful in the wood, and she put down her basket on the trunk of a tree and began picking a large bunch of them.

Little Red Riding Hood was very fond of flowers. She knew all their names, and all about them, and she loved them so that when she spoke to them she thought they understood all that she was saying.

The little red squirrels, with their funny long tails, darted out from the bushes and ran up the trees; and Little Red Riding Hood forgot all about the wolves.

Soon it began to grow dark, and, remembering what her mother had said, she jumped up, and was picking up her basket when there bounded up to her a great wolf!

"Where are you going?" asked the wolf. He spoke so kindly in his big, gruff voice that Little Red Riding Hood thought he could not possibly hurt her. So she told him she was carrying some eggs and honey and butter to her grandmother, who lived in the little house at the edge of the forest and who was ill.

"Oh," said the wolf, "I know where that is!" And he ran on and was soon completely out of sight.

The wolf ran very fast, and did not stop until he came to the little house. He knocked at the door, and the grandmother called out: "You must pull the bobbin, and then the latch will go up."

He pushed open the door, and, going straight to where the old lady lay in bed, opened his mouth and devoured her! Then he put on her nightdress and cap, jumped into the bed, and cuddled down among the clothes. Presently there came a tap at the door.

IMAGINATION · CHIVALRY · LEGENDS · GOLDEN DEEDS · FAIRY TALES

"Pull the bobbin, and the latch will go up!" called out the wolf in a voice like the grandmother's.

Little Red Riding Hood walked in.

"Draw up a chair," said the wolf, "and tell me what you have in your basket."

Little Red Riding Hood got a chair and sat down by the side of the bed.

"I have brought you something nice to eat, Granny," she said, as she bent over the bed. "But what great ears you have, Grandmamma!"

"All the better to hear you with," said the wolf.

"What great eyes you have, Grandmamma!"

"All the better to see you with."

"And, oh, what great teeth you have, Grandmamma!"

"All the better to eat you with!" cried the wolf, jumping out of bed.

Little Red Riding Hood ran screaming to the door. The wolf ran after her, and had almost caught her when a shot from a gun was heard, and the wicked wolf dropped down dead.

A woodcutter who was passing had heard the cries of Little Red Riding Hood, and popped his gun through the window in time to save her.

Little Red Riding Hood was very grateful to the woodcutter, but she had been so frightened that she ran all the way home. When she came to the cottage she found her mother waiting for her at the door.

The mother drew Little Red Riding Hood in, and listened to her story of all that had happened. She was delighted to have her little girl home again, and Red Riding Hood was so happy to be out of danger that she promised her mother never to be disobedient any more.

THE HARE AND THE HUNGRY MAN

Indian children declare they can see a hare on the face of the Moon, and this is the story of how they imagine the hare came there.

In India long ago animals were as wise as men; they could speak and, what is more, they could reflect—which cannot be said of every human being.

There were four creatures in particular —a hare, a jackal, a monkey, and an otter—who were very pious. They lived like hermits in a wood near Benares. They never thought of worldly excitements or selfish pleasures. They gave alms and kept the fast days like good Brahmins.

One evening a poor man came through the wood, and found the jackal sitting on a log, deep in meditation.

"Good beast!" whined the man, "of your charity give me a little food!"

"With joy!" cried the jackal, jumping up. "How fortunate it is that I had luck in my hunting. I will fetch you the meat from my cave."

"I do not eat meat," said the man, and he passed on.

Presently he saw the otter sitting on a stone in mid-stream, deep in meditation. When he begged the creature gladly offered him some fish, but this, too, he refused, and went his way.

By and by he encountered the monkey swinging from a bough by one hind leg, deep in meditation. The beggar had hardly begun his request before the animal offered him some mangoes; but the man would not eat fruit either.

Lastly he found the hare, lying in the dewy grass with the moonlight shining through his pink ears, deep in meditation.

"Charity, good sir!" whimpered the man. "I am famishing."

All that the hare had to give was grass, and what use would that be to a hungry man? He thought "I will give myself."

The charitable animal said: "Make a fire, sir, and you shall soon have a meal."

The man made a fire of twigs on large stones, and when they were red-hot the hare threw himself upon them.

But instead of being burned he felt as if he lay on a bed of cool water-lilies. He lifted his head and asked the beggar: "What is this? Kindle your fire again. I do not scorch."

Suddenly the beggar shot up past the tree-tops, gigantic in height and splendid in appearance.

"Oh, noble little beast," he said. "I only sought to test your charity. It is boundless. I will set your seal on the skies so that Man may for ever remember your example."

So saying he tore up a mountain, and squeezed it till its juice ran out. Then, using its peak as a pen and the juice for ink, he drew a picture of the hare on the full moon. Indian children point it out to each other to this day.

THE MAN WITH A HUNDRED SONS

A CERTAIN Serbian had a hundred sons, and the cost of their clothes, toys, and sweeties was very great.

Still, he never grumbled, and looked forward to the day when they would be grown up. Ah, but he was worse off then! One after the other they said to him: "Father, I am old enough to be married; please find me a good wife."

The poor old man got on a pony and rode off on his quest. He had very little luck till one day he saw another old man ploughing, and his tears dropped on the newly-turned earth.

"What is the matter, brother?" asked the traveller; "you weep like a cloud."

"So would you," replied the ploughman, "if you had a hundred daughters to provide for, as I have."

"We are well met!" cried the old man, jumping from his pony.

The two became friends. The sons and daughters met and fell in love with each other in the most lucky fashion. They agreed to be married on the same day.

Well, there was more work for the old man, for a Serbian wedding is a very magnificent affair. The bridegroom comes in procession to fetch his bride, with two bride-leaders, with witnesses, running footmen, standard-bearers, and guests. The old man had to find these people a hundred times over. No wonder that he was tired and confused on the day of the wedding; no wonder that he did not miss one person in that huge crowd.

The procession reached the brides' home in safety, and after exchanging gifts, and feasting they set off on the return journey. It was now growing dusk, but they had no mishap till they reached a wide river called Luckless. There was a broad bridge over it. When the procession was halfway across, the sides of the bridge began to draw together. Horses neighed, brides screamed, men shouted angrily.

All at once a voice called from the other bank: "Who is the head of the procession?" and the party saw a black giant towering up in the gloom.

"I am the head of the procession," cried the old man. "If this is your bridge, sir, for mercy's sake let my guests come across."

The giant replied: "I will do that if you promise to give me what you have forgotten at home. If you can recognise it in three years' time you shall have it back. Is it a bargain?"

"Yes, yes!" cried the old man; and immediately the bridge expanded, the procession passed over, and the giant vanished from sight.

As the wedding party drew near home they saw a solitary figure coming to meet them. It was one of the hundred sons!

"Oh, my child," wailed the old man, "I never missed you! How did this happen? Where have you been?"

"I crave your pardon, and my bride's," said the son. "I was so weary with the work we had overnight in preparing for the wedding that I never woke till noon."

Then a dreadful silence fell. Presently, in a voice broken by sobs, the old man told the boy what had happened.

In three days the monster came to carry him off. As they parted the father and the bride called to the prisoner: "Keep a good heart! We will come for you in three years' time."

How long it seemed! At last the time was up, and the poor old man set out for River Luckless again.

The black giant came to meet him. He carried a pole on which was perched a sparrow, a dove, and a quail.

"If you can say which is your son you may keep him," he said.

The old man gazed and gazed, but he could not tell, and at last he stumbled away. As he went he began to think that the sparrow had looked at him very hard, so he ran back and begged the giant to let him try again.

The giant smiled and brought out a partridge, a titmouse, and a thrush. But still, stare as he might, the old man could find no clue. He went off weeping. But as he reached home he thought, "I will choose one and risk all!"

Again he returned, and asked for a last chance. The giant showed him a sparrow, a dove, and a woodpecker. As the old man looked intently he saw a tear gathering in the dove's eye.

"That is the bird with a human soul!" he thought, and seized it.

Suddenly he found that he was grasping his son's shoulder and that the giant had once more vanished.

The feast of a hundred weddings was as nothing compared to the feast of one joyous home-coming.

THE COMING OF RUSTEM

THERE once lived in ancient Persia a good and trustworthy chieftain named Zahon. He was the confidant and friend of the Shah, had great riches and honour, and was a very envied person. But Zahon had a great trouble. Unfortunately he was childless.

As the years went by, however, he prayed and prayed that the gods would grant him a son; and at last, in his old age, his wish was realised. But when the child was born the trouble of the old chieftain increased tenfold. The baby was beautiful and strong, but his hair was snow-white; and the news of the marvel spread over the land as a thing of very evil omen. It was said that sorcerers had effected this wonder.

The comments of the people and the fears of his own superstitious heart quite unmanned the good old Zahon. At last he could bear it no longer. He took the white-haired baby in his arms, bore him away into a wild, unpeopled spot, and left him there to die.

Now, on the top of a mountain in that country dwelt a Wonder-bird in a sandal-wood nest. This Wonder-bird, soaring in the clouds, spied the little helpless babe in a solitary spot below, and, descending, bore him in his strong talons toward his nest. But as he flew up the rocky peak a voice in the air spoke to him:

" Hurt not the child thou bearest, O Wonder-bird, for great destinies await him. His son will be the light of the East, the star of Persia, the champion of the world."

Upon hearing that, the Wonder-bird bore the little one carefully to his nest, and sheltered and fed him. The years passed, and the child grew old enough to play about the mountain-top and was dimly seen by those below; and the tale ran rapidly among the people that up on the mountain-top the Wonder-bird guarded a living boy.

In the meantime, Zahon, old and disappointed, was living a life apart, caring for nothing. He was haunted by the thought of the helpless babe left to perish. The cloud never entirely left him; but one night he had a strange dream, wherein a voice spoke with such reality that he awoke with its sound in his ears. The voice bade him go and seek the child he had so cruelly abandoned. Hither and thither he wandered, finding nowhere a white-haired boy, until at last, coming into the regions of the Wonder-bird, he heard of a child living in a bird's nest on the high mountain-top, and hope revived in his heart. But when he came to the mountain the old man was sorely tried. He scaled the lower flank, only to be met with steep walls of granite.

The Wonder-bird, however, who was watching from above, flew down to meet the sorrow-stricken chieftain with the white-haired boy in his hold.

" Here is he whom thou comest to seek, whom thou didst so hardly leave to perish," said the Wonder-bird. " Guard him well."

The boy, however, did not wish to leave his strange foster-parent, and touching was the scene of parting when the great Wonder-bird solemnly blessed him and bade him never forget the home of his childhood and the nurse who had loved him. The strange guardian then took from his breast three feathers and gave them to the boy.

" Take these," said he, " and whenever thou art in direst distress cast one of these on the fire, and I will come to thine aid."

Then the Wonder-bird went back to his sandal-wood nest and the stars and the winds, and Zahon tenderly bore his son back home, clothed him, and named him Zal.

Now, as time went on, no one in the country was more beloved or more universally praised than white-haired Zal. His strength and fighting skill were extraordinary. There appeared to have entered into his being in those early days on the mountain-top a strange power which seemed to foreshadow a great and splendid future.

When he was grown to be a young man he was sent by the Shah into a neighbouring country on a mission of war. Everywhere he was a noticeable figure, partly because of the white hair surmounting the beautiful young face, and partly because of his strange personal power. Now, in that country to which he had journeyed lived a king's daughter named Rudabeh, and one day into the court and chamber of this Princess penetrated tales of the white-haired Zal, and she fell deeply in love with Zal before she had even seen him.

The young hero, on the other hand, heard nothing but the praises of Rudabeh.

Many political circumstances, however, hindered the meeting of the hero and the beautiful Princess. But Zal was determined it should be. One night the Princess was in the tower of her summer house, and there Zal sought her, and implored her to let down a rope by which he might climb to her tower. Then the lovely Rudabeh unwound the braids of hair from her shapely little head, where they had

After a short time of marriage, however, Rudabeh was stricken with a great illness, and it was feared she would die. All the physicians of the land were summoned to her aid, but to no purpose. Then one night, as Zal sat by the pale Princess, there came to him suddenly the thought of the Wonder-bird and the magic feathers.

With hope again in his heart he threw one on the little charcoal brazier, and

THE WONDER-BIRD FLEW DOWN

made a dusky crown, and let the longest braid fall down into the garden below. The Princess fastened the hair to a ring in the wall, so that no tension should come upon herself, and, guided upward by this priceless rope, Zal reached her balcony.

Later on, after much trouble and political dissension, the barriers that lay between the marriage of these two romantic beings were removed, and Zal bore off his beautiful wife to his own home.

waited at the open window. Soon the air was heavy with rushing, mighty wings, and the Wonder-bird alighted. He gave a healing potion to the dying Rudabeh, so that she recovered from her illness, and, again blessing his foster-child, disappeared.

Some time after, a babe was born to Zal and Rudabeh, who was called Rustem, and he grew to be such a wonderful warrior that he was soon known as the Shield of Persia.

THE MAN WHO MADE TREES TO BLOSSOM

A DOG was heard whimpering outside a cottage door in Old Japan.

The old woman who lived there let the creature in. It was a wretched cur, but she fed it, and in a day or two she and her husband came to love it like a child.

Their neighbours, however, had nothing but kicks and abuse for the mongrel.

One day, as the good old couple sat in their garden at twilight, they saw the dog digging in an excited manner, giving little cries as he worked.

"I must see what he's after," said the old man, "for he's an intelligent fellow."

He got a spade, and very soon he came on a coffer of gold pieces. The dog wagged his tail, and the old couple almost cried with delight. They all three had a good supper that evening.

Next day the old couple went round to give a share to all their poorer neighbours, and they told the story freely.

The disagreeable couple next door soon sent round to borrow the wonderful dog, to see if he would bring them fortune also.

For some time he did nothing but sit and stare at the sky. Then he trotted off to a corner and began to dig. Alas! when the man took his spade to the place he found nothing but bones and broken crockery! In his rage the man lifted his spade and killed the dog. Then, growing afraid of its master's anger, he buried it at the foot of a pine tree.

The old couple were very sad when their pet did not return. But in the night his spirit came trotting into their room, and said : " Master, cut down the pine tree and make a mortar of the wood, and think of me whenever you use it."

Next day the old man obeyed, but when the old woman began to grind rice in the mortar the grain turned to gold!

They made no secret of their good fortune, nor did they refuse to lend the mortar to the wicked neighbours. But when these people began to grind the rice became evil-smelling mud!

The angry couple carried the mortar outside and burned it on a bonfire.

That night the dog's spirit appeared again, and said: "Master, take up the ashes from the bonfire and sprinkle them over your withered cherry tree; it will blossom again."

The old man gathered up the ashes, and threw a handful on the dead tree. It immediately burst into radiant blossoms. After that he went up and down the country, restoring poor people's withered trees for them, till the story of his fame reached the emperor.

He was commanded to perform the miracle in the royal gardens, and was afterwards loaded with gifts and honours.

When the bad couple heard this they gathered up the remaining ashes from the bonfire, and set out for the Court. The emperor and his courtiers assembled to watch the performance. But this time the tree remained dead in every twig, and the ashes had been thrown so clumsily that they half-blinded the emperor below.

The bad man was beaten for being an impostor, and crept home to seek the charity of his good neighbour.

THE KING WHO CAME TO CASHMERE

MANY years ago a Prince and a Princess in India fell in love ; but their fathers were at war and would not let them marry. So the lovers ran away together and hid in a great forest.

But in the evening, as the Prince was looking for food, a robber rode away with the Princess. He put her in a cave, and went to sleep, and the Princess then arose and bound him, and, dressing herself in his clothes, mounted his horse and went in search of the Prince.

Instead of finding him she came in the morning to the city of Cashmere.

All the streets were crowded with people who were anxiously watching an elephant. The king of the city and all his family were dead, and the people desired to find a new king to reign over them. Now, everybody in India believes that an elephant can tell who is of royal blood, so the people had let an elephant loose, and they were waiting to see whom it would acknowledge as master.

To their surprise it ran up to the disguised Princess, and knelt down before her. The people shouted for joy, and carried the Princess to the palace, and crowned her, duly robed, as king.

But when the Prince at last came to the city in search of her she told the people that she was a Princess, and so they made the Prince their king, and she married him and became queen.

Nature's Wonderful Living Family in Earth and Air and Sea

Fur-seals of the Arctic

THE GREAT SEA HUNTERS

WHEN that great man and prince of naturalists, Cuvier, was chancellor of the University of Paris, his students, to whom he was as dear for his humour as for his genius, determined to play a trick on him.

Their leader arrayed himself in the guise of an ox, and conducted the laughing conspirators to the professor's bedroom. They crept on tiptoe to the bedside, with a lighted candle, and woke him.

" Professor," said he of the disguise, in a hollow voice, " we have come to eat you."

Cuvier blinked for a moment, ran his eye swiftly over the figure before him, then like lightning he answered:

" Eat me ! Horns and hoofs ! Pooh, you can't ; you're graminivorous ! "

The evidences which served instantly to reveal to Cuvier that a grain-eater proposed to play the impossible part of flesh-eater have their counterpart in other aspects of animal life. Its birthright is written on every animal.

Were it not so we might be troubled at times to resolve whether certain forms are flesh or good red herring. We find the waters teeming with creatures which live and have their being in the sea, fish-like in their tapering outline, with fin-like flippers in place of normal limbs, eating the same food as the big fishes, passing months at a time in the sea, and crossing the world by great ocean corridors.

But as we glance at their physical features we can ignore their habits, and in the strain of Cuvier we reach our answer.

" What, air-breathing, clad with fur and charged with warm blood ! You are not fishes, you are seals, sea-lions, sea-bears, and walruses. You are flesh-eating land mammals, but you have gone back to the waters from which we have all come."

That is our answer to the fishlike seals.

They are simply fin-footed mammals, whose homes are in the deep, but whose cradles are on shore. The story of how the change was made is a long one.

Long, long ago, it must have been millions of years, mammals were much less specialised than they now are. A huge group, which we call the Creodonts, was the prevailing type. They must have been as fitted to eat foods of all sorts as men, pigs, and baboons are today.

The plan did not content Nature. She has always urged advance along special—rather than general—lines. Her rewards have been given to individual merit and to success, by whatever means they have been attained.

The oft-told tale was repeated at the expense of the Creodonts. The Jack-of-all-

PREHISTORIC LIFE · MAMMALS · BIRDS · REPTILES · FISHES · INSECTS

26 F 2

trades type slowly succumbed to the specialised type. The animal family ceased to be all brothers and sisters, and branched out into more remote relationships.

When today we see animals of very different kinds possessing certain features in common, that does not mean these different animals are closely related. They may have inherited these features from that far-away type of animal from which all later kinds have arisen.

THE FOUR-LEGGED CREATURES THAT LEFT THE LAND LIKE LIVING SUBMARINES

Remembering this, we no longer puzzle over certain resemblances between seals and land bears and sea-otters. Bear-like and otter-like animals belonged to that huge Creodont group and the seal tribes sprang from the same strain when the great branching-off into fresh families began

But how come they to the waters? It is impossible to say today what exactly was the nature of the competition which impelled them to sacrifice a land career. Perhaps it was not a surrender but a triumphant adventure. Who can guess?

There may not have been enough herb-eaters to satisfy the flesh-eaters ; perhaps certain flesh-eaters took to catching fish in shallow water and thus ventured deeper and deeper in pursuit of their prey. We cannot tell why those distant founders of the families of the water-animals forsook the land.

Certain it is that four-legged creatures which once romped and rummaged on shore took the great plunge, passed from land locomotion to the condition of living submarines, and have been ever since more and more perfecting themselves in their new element.

THE ODD THINGS THAT HAPPENED TO THE SEA-LION'S FINGERS AND TOES

Today the hind limbs of the true seal are united with the tail and stretch in a rigid line backward. The sea-lion can still turn the hind limbs beneath it, the toes directed toward the head, and so employ them not so much as legs and feet but as levers to propel itself forward over the ground. It moves like a lame horse hobbled.

The original five fingers and five toes per hand and foot are there, but they are all enveloped in skin, so that the four limbs are paddles. Eyes have been enlarged and brightened so that the faintest peep of light serves in the liquid gloom. Lungs have been given increased capacity for storing oxygen and checking its issue to the blood ; and in calm and storm, in hot weather and cold, the seals are now as perfectly adapted to life in the sea as land animals could hope to be.

Born on the dry land, they learn, like boys and girls, to swim as their mothers teach, and then an old-new realm is theirs :

> Where the sea-beasts, ranged all round,
> Feed in the ooze of their pasture-ground;
> Where the sea-snakes coil and twine,
> Dry their mail and bask in the brine;
> Where great whales come sailing by,
> Sail and sail, with unshut eye,
> Round the world for ever and aye.

Such is the life of the seals, except that ice and murk of frigid waters are more commonly their lot than the sunny waters where the sea-snakes glide.

The group is divided by science into three families, of which the eared seals consisting of the sea-lions and the sea-bears rank first.

THE SEA-LION THAT CAN CARRY A LIGHTED LAMP ON ITS NOSE

The extraordinary intelligence of these creatures has led to their becoming familiar objects to people who have never visited the sea. Every zoological garden has examples, and public entertainments regularly include performances by seals. How it happens that sea-lions should be masters of unparalleled feats of balancing passes understanding, but, as we all know, they can carry lighted lamps unerringly upon their noses, and by the same means balance balls and other articles with the certainty of a human juggler whose skill is gained by many years of training.

The big sea-lion is a hair-seal ; the smaller species are sea-bears, and, carrying a beautiful undercoat of soft, thick fur, are the ones most sought by hunters whose business lies with furs.

Both varieties have well-defined external ears, but the true seals, while their hearing is so acute that they can be lured to ship or shore by the sound of music, are without the outer conch which marks the ears of the other variety.

Another distinction is that the hair-seals go more to land than the earless seals, which are at home, for rest or for nursery engagements, upon an ice floe or any site which invites when absence from the water is desirable.

QUEER HUNTERS OF THE SEA

THE SEA-LION

THE BULL WALRUS

THE SEA-ELEPHANT

SEA-LIONS AT THE LONDON ZOO

A FAMILY OF NORTHERN SEA-BEARS

THE SEA-ELEPHANT COMES ASHORE

THE SEA-LION OF CALIFORNIA

Some of the photographs on these pages are by Messrs W. S. Berridge, H. Irving, H. Wright and F. W. Bond ; others
are from Sir Ernest Shackleton's books published by Messrs Heinemann

The sea-lion's land home is called a rookery, from the enormous numbers of animals which collect, or did collect in happier days, to rear their babies in company. The males arrive first, the females later, and as each male desires to become the lord of a harem, there are terrific battles for the opposite sex.

Rival bulls seize each other with their formidable teeth. They rive and rip and tear till flesh is bitten away in masses, till flippers are torn to shreds, and hides reveal the greater part of their blubber lining. When the contest is ended and each has the ladies of his choice, the mothers settle down to nurse their babies, while the males stand vigilant to repel enemies.

As the she-bear fasts in the snow with her babies, the male sea-lion remains foodless by his. Singular is the fact that he never drinks, except such moisture as accompanies the fish which form his food. The bull sea-lion now undergoes a fast on land which extends in some quarters to four months. Four months without bite or sup! We need no longer marvel that salmon going up a river to spawn eat nothing till they return to the sea.

THE WONDERFUL LOVE OF A SEA-LION MOTHER FOR HER LITTLE ONES

The mother sea-lion, however, does feed. She goes forth to sea and swims out 200 miles and more, to secure food with which to nourish her little one.

She returns to find all the pups gathered together in mobs of thousands. The young ones do not recognise their mothers. Any matronly seal with milk to yield seems a mother to them. But trust maternal love. There is something distinct for each mother in the plaintive bleating of one little infant she knows. One voice among ten thousand is identified; it is her baby's!

"How did you find your way home?" a little girl was asked after having been lost in the streets.

"I don't know how I did it ; I knew there was a house with a little yellow bedstead upstairs belonging to me, so I went to it," was the child's delightful explanation. There is the equivalent of that little yellow bedstead in a seal mother's imagination, and she goes to it without error, pushing her way through the mass of clamouring babies to her one and only love.

The southern sea-lion, whose home address is the coasts of South America

from Peru and Chile on the Pacific side, and from the River Plate on the Atlantic coast south to the Falkland Islands and Tierra del Fuego, and who is met also at the Galapagos Islands, was first identified by Magellan on his world voyage. Later he was seen in great size and numbers by Captain Cook.

The northern species, a giant weighing over half a ton, is also associated with a memorable name. Bering, who found the waterway between Asia and America, was the first to see in it an animal previously unnamed in science.

THE TERRIBLE CRUELTY THAT FOLLOWED A HUNT FOR FUR

California gives its name to another species. New Zealand has a local variety. Australian waters are the home of a species which is specially interesting from the fact that the young have the close furry undergrowth of the fur-seal, only to lose it and turn hair-seal when they attain maturity.

As we have noted, it is the sea-bears which help to clothe women who like sealskin. The history of this animal makes us blush for humanity. Once the fur-seal was one of the most numerous of all sea animals, but the craze for its fur led to a horrible system of persecution. It was stabbed or shot at sea when its babies were starving for food on shore. On land it was butchered in tens of thousands, with every conceivable element of cruelty, even to the flaying of the poor creatures before life was extinct or sensation numbed. Herds numbering over two millions were reduced by this brutal and hateful system to a few score thousand.

THE SAD STORY OF 700,000 SEALSKINS AND A GREAT WASTE OF LIFE

Then a notable thing happened. The approaching extinction of the species led to an international agreement. Great Britain, Russia, Japan, the United States, and Canada decreed by treaty that for a term of years there should be no more slaying of these seals at sea. In order to compensate the Powers which could catch seals at large but were debarred from going to their breeding grounds, Russia and America agreed to pay them 15 per cent of their annual gains in sealskins. This applies only to the fur-seals.

The fur-seal story is one of marvel as well as cruelty. Pursuit of the animals has led men far and wide into uncharted

A GROUP OF ODD AMPHIBIANS

CRAB-EATER SEALS AT HOME ON THE ICE OF THE FROZEN NORTH

THE SOUTH AFRICAN SEA-LION

THE WALRUS LOOKS AHEAD

SEALS BASKING IN THE SUNSHINE ON THE ROCKS

THE MONK-SEAL LIES IN WAIT

THE HOODED OR BLADDER-NOSED SEAL

seas, and into privations such as only heroism allied to the love of gain could encourage. In one year Russian sealers, in order to keep up prices, threw into the sea 700,000 sealskins, a waste of life which might have produced millions from the animals so wantonly butchered.

But look at the map. Look at Alaska, that land of gold mines and other metals dear to commerce, a land of wonderful animals and untold treasures. America bought it, nearly 600,000 square miles, seals and all, paying Russia £1,500,000 for it in 1867. Within 40 years America received twice that sum from State duties paid by her hunters of seals.

So fur-seals, when they left dry land for the water, were destined to have greater influence upon international events ashore than the animal's mind could conceive.

At present the position is that fur-seals may be killed only by licensed hunters at their rookeries, and the majority taken must be males, which greatly outnumber the females. This prevents the loss of 75 per cent of seals formerly attacked at sea, for of every four killed there, three sank from sight. Each female caught on her way to or from the rookery left a pup to starve, and was prevented from bringing into the world another little one of which, in the course of Nature, she should have been the mother.

THE GIANT WALRUS THAT CHARGES LIKE A SUBMARINE

Classification places the walrus next to the sea-lions and sea-bears, so we must do the same. After the whales and sea-elephants these are the giants of the sea mammals, though not in length, for a 13-feet sea-lion is their equal in that respect. But in bulk the walrus excels. A bull walrus in its prime is not far short of two tons in weight, and specimens exceeding a ton are not at all uncommon.

Their superb ivory tusks are less weapons of offence than implements employed in obtaining food. The walrus dives and rakes in the ooze for shellfish. He is not such a terror to other animals as the polar bear is on land, or the grampus in the waves. His diet is innocent, and when he is captured alive the great difficulty is to make him eat even the delicate fish that would nourish a human invalid.

The Eskimos know walrus habits, and when they kill one, they first explore its stomach to obtain there the clams and other varieties of shellfish which the poor beast has eaten.

But though the walrus is peaceful enough in his haunts if left undisturbed, when he is wounded or when his friends or family are attacked, he is fury embodied. What a hippopotamus is in an African river, that the walrus is in an Arctic sea. It is then that the second service of the tusks is made manifest.

The walrus charges like a submarine intent on ramming, and he drives those ivory sickles of his through the timbers of a boat like a spoon through an egg-shell. Many walrus adventures attended the sea passage of Peary on his perilous way to the North Pole.

HOW A WALRUS SHATTERED THE STOUT TIMBERS OF A WHALING BOAT

One giant bull succeeded in getting home a blow in full force at a great stout whaling boat. The timbers were shattered as if they had been paper! Had Peary met walruses all the way instead of when he went out to convert them into food, the North Pole would have been left for Amundsen to find, for he learned that walruses can be terrible foes to those who challenge them.

Great ungainly animals, they are intensely interesting studies as living object-lessons in Nature's art of favouring bizarre developments of features helpful to a given method of life. But because they bear ivory, and their bodies contain blubber that can be rendered into oil, men have been as merciless as hyenas to them, and as greedy as vultures.

The men who hunt for ivory would beggar the world of its finest animals. One example shall suffice. It is from an official statement laid before an important congress at Quebec.

THE SEAL THAT SOBS AND CRIES AS IF IT WERE A HUMAN BEING

Whalers discovered a herd of walruses and coveted their tusks and hides. They knew that this herd afforded the only food of a tribe of Eskimos ashore. But they slaughtered every walrus there. Government explorers, following later in the train of these cruel men, found the Eskimos where the hunters had left them. But every one of them was stark and silent—men, women and children had been starved to death!

We are more familiar with true seals than with walruses in England, though a baby walrus has been to town, only to drown itself in a little bath after braving the perils of an entire ocean. Seals do not do that.

Much as seals love the sea, the rivers, and certain inland stretches of water, they thrive delightfully as pets. More intelligent friends no man ever had than these hoarse-voiced, sinuous, waddling creatures from the deep sea.

When we see them active and clever in a state of nature, or at close quarters as our companions, we cannot believe that animal minds rise no higher in consciousness than that of a muddled man when he walks in his sleep. Indeed, there are many instances of their high intelligence.

When a seal is hurt or grieved it sobs and cries. When its little one is injured the mother gives vent to desperate wails of misery, and tears stream down her poor face as if she were human.

THE SEALS COME UP THROUGH A HOLE IN THE ICE

With intelligence so highly organised the seal naturally reveals first-class tactics as a hunter. It is wonderful to see half a dozen of them neatly drive a shoal of salmon or other fish into shallow water or into a bay, and then snap them up as dogs snap up meat.

Like all living creatures the seal has its enemies. Man is now the worst, but natural conditions produce the bear on ice or island and the shark and the grampus in the sea. The grampus takes seal after seal for his dinner, and a shark, when a fishermen went to the rescue of a seal which the fish was attacking, bit the animal in two, disappeared with one half and left the remainder floating before the eyes of the astonished rescuer.

There are nearly a score of species of true seals. The grey, the Greenland, the bearded, the monk-seal, the crab-eating seal, the fierce leopard-seal, which attacks less powerful members of the seal family, the Weddel, the Ross, and the crested seal are the species with which people who frequent the sea are best acquainted.

None of them has ceased to enjoy the sunshine from which the sea hides them. On ice floe or sandy strand they derive as much delight from sunlight and air as can be felt by the weariest of men released from a gloomy city.

This very fondness for sandy conditions is the undoing of many seals. They frequent sandy rookeries where deadly parasites abound. These attack the young, impoverish their blood, sometimes kill them outright, or leave them only to be saved from death by the restoring effects of a grand sea change.

The adults suffer in the griefs of their offspring, but their minds are not equal to the one solution of this problem of life and death. If they went to rocky shelters they would escape the deadly parasite which assails them. But they still go to their favourite haunts.

If there were time Nature would evolve a seal which would take to the rocks for its nursery. But will there be time? Men kill these poor seals for the sake of their blubber and skins at the rate of a million and a half annually, and Nature is not reproducing at that rate!

Captain Frank Wild, who brought the "Quest" home after the death of Sir Ernest Shackleton, would give the seal tribe a testimonial as life-savers. On the voyage which cost Shackleton his ship in the Antarctic ice Wild was left in charge of the men marooned on Elephant Island while Shackleton did his great boat journey through mountainous seas in search of some vessel that might bring relief.

Food was terribly short on the island, and the shipwrecked mariners were almost at their wits' end, when one day, like a gift from the fairies, up sailed two or three seals to the beach. They were not only meat and oily drink in themselves; they brought food with them.

In their stomachs were the fish they had just caught and eaten at sea. And these were now eaten a second time by the men whose very lives depended upon a minimum quantity of food day by day.

One other species we must note. It is the weirdest of all—the mighty elephant-seal, or sea-elephant. The name arises not only from the gigantic dimensions of the animal, but from a curious bladder-like formation about the nose. This hangs loose and limp as a rule, but when the animal is excited it is inflated and gives the seal the appearance of bearing about a fair copy of a trunk. The nostrils pierce the appendage, and the whole appearance of the creature is impressively grotesque.

The animal is another example of a species which has waxed gigantic without obvious profit. A male sea-elephant ranges up to close on 20 feet in length. In the water they are as agile as you please, but on land they are sloth itself. They assemble in herds, and though they roar as loudly as Bottom the weaver desired to, they are quite harmless.

THE GRACEFUL WAY IN WHICH THE SEA-LION USES ITS FLIPPERS

No seal has quite lost the hand-like use of its flippers. The sea-lion is specially apt in their employment. With his front flippers he will guide a current of air to his head and body as we do with a sheet of paper. With his hind limbs he fans himself with quite artistic grace.

The sea-elephant also uses his front pair as entrenching tools. He excavates a hollow in the sand in which his great body can lie. Stranger still, just as a real elephant picks up dust and scatters it over his body, so this titanic seal flicks up sand with his flippers to guard his ponderous frame against the excessive heat of the Sun. An animal protected with blubber representing 250 gallons of oil may well fear heat from without.

Such then is a little of the harvest of interest we gather from a visit to a fascinating group of creatures that once took the line of least resistance and followed it into the sea. They are mariners without superiors, superb navigators of the wide free ocean. But they can adapt themselves to new conditions today as they did in the long ago.

Some of them can make themselves happy in fresh water, which few ocean fish can do. There are true seals in Lake Baikal, a huge fresh-water sea in Siberia; and also in the salt inland Caspian Sea. The presence of sea animals in these surroundings is evidence that not long ago, as geology reckons time, these waters had free communication with the ocean.

THE SEAL THAT TRAVELLED THIRTY MILES OVERLAND IN A WEEK

It must be so. We know that some of the fur seals travel far inland when driven by hunters; we know that a common grey seal has done an overland journey of 30 miles in a week in Norway. But that does not alter the probabilities as to Baikal and Caspian seals. They do not leave the sea and cross a country to landlocked waters. They went there when the way to and from the outer seas was open. A rising of land shut them up and made them prisoners for ever. But they settled down and made the best of their lot and there are as fine seals in those two stretches of water as can be found anywhere.

It was to be expected that these animals might take kindly to fresh water and its fishy products, although themselves bred in the sea, for their ancestors made the greatest change of all in giving up the world which we ourselves inhabit for one of storm and tempest, deep unlighted abysses, and food which is always fish.

But they have remained mammals in every particular. Brains have grown in the best of them, and, with brain added to muscle and bone, flippers may serve quite well as feet for sojourns on land, and eclipse them completely for making progress in the water.

A TALE OF AN OLD SEAL AND HOW IT THROWS PEBBLES

They tell a tale in North Devon of a bit of coast visited from time to time by a " demon," a black and bulging demon which throws showers of pebbles at anyone who approaches, and then vanishes during the confusion.

" I don't believe it is a demon, not really," explained a native to the writer. " I think it is an old fat seal scattering pebbles with its fins as it goes. But, sir, how it breathes so long out of the water is a caution to me! "

We who have now run through this story together could tell him the reason, could we not?

The March of Man from the Age of Barbarism to the United Nations

Michael Angelo's picture of Ezekiel, in the Sistine Chapel, Rome

THE MAN WHO DREW THE FIRST MAP

WHILE Thales in Anatolia was studying Nature for an answer to the riddle of life, a very remarkable man in Babylon was searching his own soul for the source and origin of all existence.

The Israelites were captives in Babylon, and among them was this man of great original genius, whose name was Ezekiel. Before his time the priests in all countries had been looked upon as the guardians of old memories, called traditions, and a priest used to shut himself up in his temple, surround himself with an air of mystery, and perform ceremonies which were full of superstition. Ezekiel, searching his own heart, saw that Israel was losing its faith in the spiritual life, and was beginning to live like all the heathen nations surrounding it, chiefly because there were no teachers to proclaim the truth of God—the one true God of righteousness.

So he stood forth, in the midst of that sorrowful captivity, and cried out : " Thus saith the Lord God, Woe be to the shepherds of Israel that so feed themselves ! Should not the shepherds feed the sheep?"

He declared that the great mission of a priest was to look after the lives of people, to guard the soul of Israel, to feed the spiritual life of Israel. The greatest achievement of man, in his opinion, was holy living.

A prophet is not a person who foretells the future, but a man who speaks out concerning the present. The word may mean many things, but in Israel, and among the Arabs, and to the Early Christians, a prophet meant one who interpreted God's will and spoke out boldly as an inspired person concerning things of that time.

Such a prophet was Ezekiel. His interest for us lies in the fact that, while Thales was turning the attention of men outward from themselves, Ezekiel was turning that attention away from all *things*, and inward to the soul. Let the soul think constantly of God and it will live in the atmosphere of truth.

These two movements of thought continue to the present hour. From Thales we learn to seek for Nature's laws by observing her various movements; from Ezekiel we learn to feel the power of God in our souls by prayer and meditation.

To see the romance of this double movement in the mind of man, we must remind ourselves that up to this moment the human race had received all its ideas about God and the world from priests who practised superstition, and that its chief interest in life had been fighting

MIGHTY EPOCHS OF THE WORLD AND MAN'S WONDERFUL ADVENTURES

enemies and getting food. Man was a warrior in constant dread of slavery and starvation. How marvellous, then, this passion for truth in Greek and Hebrew ! They were looking in opposite directions, but their search was for the same thing.

We are reading of a time when savagery was still a tremendous power in the world, and when the learning of the few was almost entirely coloured by superstition. We are five centuries and more before the time of Jesus. Marvellous, then, is it to find that at one and the same moment a Greek shepherd and an Israelite should suddenly shake off this superstition, and direct the minds of men into two channels, altogether different, yet both necessary for the progress of the human race.

We must not wonder when we find that both Thales and Ezekiel moved only a few paces forward on these new lines. Thales made wrong guesses about Nature, and still clung to the substance of Greek paganism ; Ezekiel taught that the priest was the great ruler, and tried to draw up a set of hard-and-fast rules for the perfect State. Nevertheless, both men set thought stirring in new directions, and presently Greece was to produce Aristotle, and Israel was to give a Good Shepherd to the whole world.

ANAXIMANDER, THE MAN WHO THOUGHT THE EARTH WAS FLAT

For us the chief line to follow at the present moment is the line taken by Thales—the line of science and philosophy. When he was dead another Greek named Anaximander carried his work a step farther. This brilliant man drew the first map of the world. It was a queer sort of map, but it was a map. He did not know that this world is a globe; he did not know that this globe turns its face first toward and then away from the Sun, nor that it swings through ether in a circling movement round the Sun. This was a discovery hidden from him in the night of the future. To him, as to every other being then on the Earth, our planet was a flat and stationary thing composed of land and water, over which balls of flame were for ever moving like fireworks.

Therefore his map was ridiculous; but, nevertheless, it witnessed to something that was not at all ridiculous—it witnessed to the faith in the man's mind that he could understand the Earth and the heavens. Anaximander drew that first map not to help sailors in their journeyings across the sea, but to help those who should come after him to understand *the origin of the world.*

Notice at once a decisive difference between the Greek and the Hebrew intellect. The Hebrew was always looking forward to a perfect State. The Greek was always looking back to the beginning of Creation. The Hebrew wanted to make the world perfect. The Greek wanted to know how there was any world at all.

STRIVING TO SOLVE THE RIDDLE OF THE UNIVERSE

This curiosity of the Greek about the origin of life is still, 2500 years afterward, a driving force in the minds of the greatest European thinkers. Our politicians say, "Let us make the world better"; our engineers say, "Let us make better ships, better locomotives, better aeroplanes"; our doctors say, "Let us produce a stronger and a healthier race." They are all looking forward to the future, like Ezekiel and Isaiah. But our physicists, geologists, anthropologists, astronomers, and philosophers are still *thinking backward*, are still looking back into the far past of the universe, striving, like Thales and Anaximander, to discover the causes of Creation. How did it come into being, this stupendous universe of stars and suns, of mind and feeling?

Anaximander said that all about this world of ours was the Infinite, and that this Infinite had produced the world out of something that was everywhere. Thales, we remember, had taught that the world was made of water. Anaximander refused to think it was made out of anything to be found on its surface. He looked much farther afield than Thales did; he looked into Infinity; he talked about a substance which was everywhere in boundless space, and said that the world had been made out of this something.

THE FIRST THINKER TO STUDY THE MYSTERIOUS CHANGES OF LIFE

You will feel the wonder of his thought when you remind yourself that this idea of his is still the idea of modern science. By inspiration, Anaximander reached the same point at which European thought now stands after centuries of most careful observation and deduction.

He was the first man in the world, so far as we know, to think deeply about

OLD IDEAS OF WHAT THE EARTH WAS LIKE

ONE IDEA IN THE VERY LONG AGO WAS THAT THE EARTH WAS SURROUNDED BY WATER

THE HINDUS USED TO THINK THE EARTH WAS BORNE ON THE BACK OF A TORTOISE

AN EARLY GREEK MAP OF THE WORLD, THOUSANDS OF YEARS AGO

decay. He saw the bud become the tender green leaf, watched the greenness of the leaf change to yellow, and marked the dried leaf fall to the ground. He saw the child grow to the youth, the youth to manhood, the man to old age. What did it all mean? Why was this eternal coming and going? Birth and death, and all things changing and dying—why? At one moment there was something; at the next moment, nothing. A father took his child into his arms, kissed it, and then passed into the night. Whence came he? And whither did he go?

ANAXIMANDER'S OPTIMISM AND THE NEW IDEAS OF LIFE IT INSPIRED

There are poets living among us now who see this same coming and going, and who tell us mournfully that life is a tragedy, a meaningless tragedy. Anaximander was of sterner stuff. He saw that this coming and going was good, because it was necessary. Death made room for others. Life renewed its strength in the young. The tree did not die because the leaves fell. He was an optimist because he felt the power of the universe on this Earth and in his own mind.

This is a most important matter for us to remember. All the thinking of men up to this time was Oriental, or Eastern; and the whole tone of Oriental thought was pessimistic. If the Greeks had thought as the Indians thought, or the Persians, or the Egyptians, human progress would have been wholly different from what it is now. But the Greeks did not say that life was sad and depressing; they did not feel that the great thing for a man to do was to fold his hands, close his eyes, and dream of nonexistence. They said that life was good because it was a riddle challenging an answer, and they came to believe that all creation can be explained in terms of morality. Let us see what this means.

THE GREEK MIND SEARCHING OUT FOR THE MORAL TRUTH

We are now approaching a very striking turn in human thought, and one that the world seems inclined to overlook. We must see that we do not make this foolish mistake. To the Greek thinker, free as he was becoming from all religious superstition, there was one thing in Nature to which his daring soul was fast anchored, and this was the Moral Law. He made many bad shots, many wrong guesses; but he never talked absolute nonsense. His philosophy was always concerned with conduct. The greatest thing of all for him was to know how to live. All Greek science, all Greek philosophy, and all Greek art were governed by the passion to discover rightness. The entire search of the Greek mind was for moral truth.

Anaximander looked beyond this Earth for its origin, but he never overlooked the Moral Law. Everything about him declared it. This very fact of coming and going was part of the Moral Law. Things came into existence and went out from existence because it was necessary. The Infinite was at work. The Earth was not to be considered as something apart from this Infinite; it was to be seen as belonging to the whole.

Greater Greeks were to come, carrying the crude guesses of Anaximander to greater heights of speculation; but it was Anaximander who first assisted the human mind to see the natural laws which govern our planet as part of the great Moral Law which governs the universe.

HOW ANAXIMANDER'S TEACHING HAS INFLUENCED HUMAN PROGRESS

Out of nothing, nothing can come, as another great Greek thinker said. The universe is something; therefore it proceeds from something. It is not a chaos, or an anarchy; therefore its origin is order and law. Never mind what the priest tells you about gods and goddesses; they are useful only if they help you to live rightly. Study the laws of Nature and you will discover the Moral Law of the universe. You will be foolish if you break that Moral Law, for it is greater than you; you will be a coward if you fear it, for it is framed for your well-being. No; study Nature, discover the Moral Law and obey it gladly.

Vast is our debt to the ancient Greeks, but perhaps the greatest part of this obligation is to be found in our conviction that the universe is governed by Moral Law. We may not see much farther into the mystery of life than Thales or Anaximander; but at least we feel that everything here on Earth belongs to a mighty universe, and that the laws of the universe are the will of a great Intelligence. It is by following this clue that we can escape all forms of anarchy and advance with confidence to the truth which makes us free.

The Story of the Things We See About us Every Day

A diver going down to the sea-bed of the Gulf of Mexico for sponges

THE SPONGE AND WHAT IT IS

THE common bath sponge is a familiar object, yet very few people know what a sponge really is, and most people wrongly imagine that it is a sort of sea-weed. Nor is it very strange, perhaps, that people should not know its true nature, for it was formerly one of the puzzles of science, and even yet it is in some ways rather a problem.

One old writer imagined that sponges were made out of the foam of the sea ; another thought they were worm houses, built by worms much as bees build honey-combs, and wasps nests; and another thought they were half-bird half-animal. As a matter of fact, the sponges are really very lowly animals.

Animals are divided into two great classes—those made of single cells, and those made of more than one cell; and the sponges are the lowest form of the second class. They consist of many cells, and the dry material we use for the bath is the horny skeleton of the cell which holds them together and gives them shape.

The fibrous skeleton is made in such a way, with tiny cells plastered all over its surface, that it forms a porous mass with mouths and tiny pores on the exterior leading into a network of tubes large and small. The cells set round the pores and mouths, and lining the passages have,

each, little finger-like processes which all move together and cause a stream of water to flow in at the pores and out again at the mouths; and in this way food and the gases in the water are made to circulate to all the cells.

There are male and female sponges, and the female sponges produce eggs that develop into single cells, which at first go swimming through the water, but afterward take root and form such elaborate compound structures as we have described.

Most of the sponges of commerce which are used for washing and surgical purposes come from Turkey, Greece, and Florida; but the bath sponges are not the only sponges. There are sponges of all shapes, sizes, and colours, some the size of a pin's head, some as tall as a man; some fan-like, some tree-like, some cup-like, and some basket-like; some built on a horny framework, some made of lime, some with a glassy frame. Some are snow-white, some grass-green, some sky-blue, some red, and some yellow.

In recent years artificial sponges made of rubber and other substances have come into general use. In some respects they have advantages over natural sponges, for they are very durable, of even texture, and can be moulded into regular shapes.

INDUSTRIES · HOW THINGS ARE MADE · WHERE THEY COME FROM

PICTURE-STORY OF A SPONGE

This diver is at work with his fork and basket on the sea-bed off the Florida coast. A sponge-fishing crew usually consists of six, and the American fleet is manned principally by Greeks. In some parts of the Mediterranean sponges are still gathered by swimmers without diving suits.

Here the sponges are being roughly cleaned after being brought ashore by the boats. There is a thin skin over the sponge, and in all the pores and canals is a slimy, sticky substance, which is the life-matter of the sponge and must be removed.

In Florida sponge culture is carried on artificially. Small portions of sponge are strung on a wire made of lead with a copper core, and this is suspended in shallow water from two posts. In six months the fragments have grown into sponges six times their bulk when planted. Sometimes the pieces are nailed down to cement slabs and placed in the sea.

DRYING THE SPONGES IN THE SUN

Here are the sponges brought in from the fishing ground at sea by the two boats which we see on the left and right of the picture. They are big, good sponges which have been gathered by hand from the bottom of the sea.

The sponges, having been washed and cleaned, are put out to dry on wooden racks, and are then sorted into baskets ready for transit. Later they are graded according to size and quality. Sponges are valuable not only in the bathroom, but for use by doctors and nurses in treating patients.

THE SPONGES AS WE FIND THEM

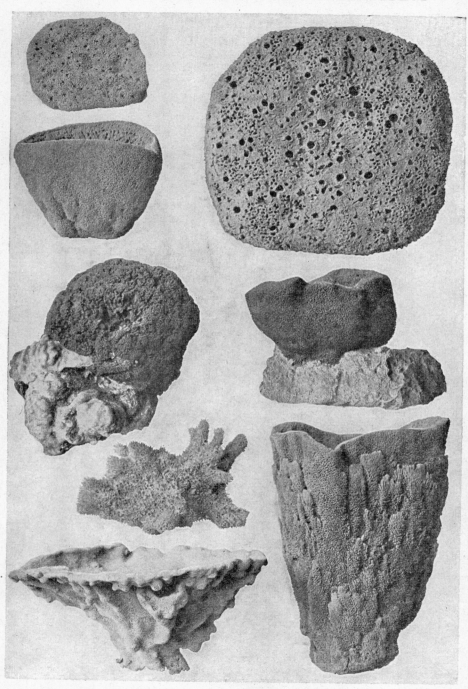

It is odd to think that the sponge we use in the bath was once alive, and is an animal product, not a vegetable growth as it seems to the eye. The sponge lives in the sea, breathing oxygen like a fish. Water is drawn into it through little pores, and the food the water contains is devoured by cells, the water passing out by the big holes. The holes are really canals, and in them sea-worms and tiny shell-fish, and even small crabs, make their homes.

Plain Answers to the Questions of the Children of the World

Signs and symbols made on the rocks by the Stone Age men of Australia

WHO BEGAN TALKING AND WRITING ?

SOME people have supposed that there must have been a time when man did not talk, and so they have given a special name to men of that period. But we may be almost sure that they are wrong; we may believe that human beings have always been able to talk. The lowest kinds of human beings now living certainly talk, though they are much higher than the first men were.

But we know the highest kinds of apes have a sort of language, and this makes it probable that the earliest men had a language, too. Indeed, many people think that language, or speech, is exactly the thing that makes man what he is, and that mankind, therefore, came into existence exactly when the ancestors of men became developed into beings that could talk. Another way of saying this is that we could not call beings human who had not the power of speech in some form or other. Such beings could not teach each other from generation to generation as human beings do, and, in a word, they would only be animals.

But of course men did not always write. Writing is a form of speech, only written instead of spoken, but it is very much more difficult to learn, as we all know; and if we think for a moment we shall see that it must have been much more difficult to invent than speech. Indeed, a simple kind of speech scarcely required invention at all, for it could grow out of mere noises that meant pleasure, or anger, or distress. But writing requires invention. It needs people to agree with one another that certain marks shall mean certain things; and this is true even though we know that writing grew out of simple pictures of things like the eye, or a man standing, that anyone could recognise.

We do not think there can be any doubt that, just as we all can talk and understand what other people say long before we can write, so mankind could talk long before writing was invented. Who first began to write, however, nobody can possibly say. We have evidence of the existence of human beings who have left us rude pictures scratched on bones, for instance, but no signs at all of any kind of writing. Indeed, " man before writing " was, until lately, supposed to have lived in Europe not many thousands of years ago; and though we now know that writing goes back much farther than we used to think, we can guess fairly well about the time that it was invented. Many people will agree that it was easily the most wonderful invention of all time.

SUN · MOON · STARS · FIRE · WIND · WATER · LIFE · MIND · SLEEP

Do Animals Talk to one Another?

People used to think that only human beings could talk to each other, and there is no doubt at all that no other creatures can talk one thousandth part as well as we do. But no one who knows animals now doubts for a moment that many kinds of animals can talk to each other—only they do not use our kind of talking.

Monkeys, for instance, make many kinds of sound with their mouths which have different meanings ; only they do not make assertions but they express their feelings. A baby expresses various feelings with its mouth long before it can talk, and so many animals can express fear, joy, anger, and many other feelings with their voices, and their fellows can understand them. That is talking of a kind.

But though monkeys probably come nearer to us in talking—though still very, very far away—than any other animals, many insects, which are very simple and humble creatures compared with monkeys, can talk wonderfully in their own way, especially the social insects, like ants and bees and wasps. If they could not tell each other what they felt and wanted, they could not live together in societies as they do—societies, remember, from which human beings have a lot to learn yet. The insects have long " feelers," with which, as it seems, they can touch each other, and say what they want to do or how they feel.

Has the Earth a Light of its Own Like the Sun?

There is no doubt that the Earth had a light of its own long ago, and this thoughtful question very rightly suggests that the other planets, too, must surely have had a light of their own at one time, just as the Sun has, because the Sun and the planets were all made from the same hot cloud, or *nebula*.

But the Earth has now no light of its own because it has become cool, while the Sun remains hot, so that the Earth cannot give out any light of its own, but can only reflect the Sun's light. The reason is that the smaller a thing is, the more quickly does it lose its heat. The heat escapes from the surface, and the smaller a thing is, the larger is its surface in proportion to the amount of stuff in it. If we go to a

place where people are making glass, and get them to make us three or four balls of glass of very different sizes, we shall find that the little one is quite cool when the biggest one is still too hot for us to touch it.

A baby needs warmer clothing than a grown-up, and small and thin people need more clothing than large people, because they have such large surfaces to lose their heat by in proportion to the mass of their bodies. As regards the solar system, we can learn especially from the Moon and from Jupiter. The only reason why the Moon should have become so much cooler than the Earth, though it is made of the same stuff, is that it is so much smaller. On the other hand, Jupiter is very large, and it has been suggested that the giant planet may still be hot enough to give out some light of its own.

Do Animals Dream As We Do?

As we cannot ask animals the answer to this question, we must find it out as best we can by arguing from other facts we know. The case is the same regarding babies and very small children before they can speak. But in all these instances we have quite good reason to believe that dreams occur, just as they occur among ourselves as we grow up.

As regards babies and animals, we know that their brains or senses are made on the same principles as ours in every respect. They are exposed to the same influences as ourselves, and so it would be very curious indeed if the same results, such as dreams, did not follow from what are practically the same causes.

In dreams we have feelings of various kinds, and just as our faces largely express our feelings when we are awake, so they do when we are asleep. If we observe how a dog, for instance, expresses feelings when awake, we may look out to see whether it ever shows the same sort of expression when it is asleep—perhaps only for a very brief moment, but clearly, nevertheless.

We do find signs in animals which plainly show that they are having feelings of one kind or another—and that means that they are dreaming. Of course, their dreams will differ from ours, just as ours differ. A musician and a painter have very different dreams, and we should expect a dog, in which the smell part of the brain is very important, to dream smells, just as we dream sights and sounds.

HOW THE WATER COMES OUT OF THE PUMP

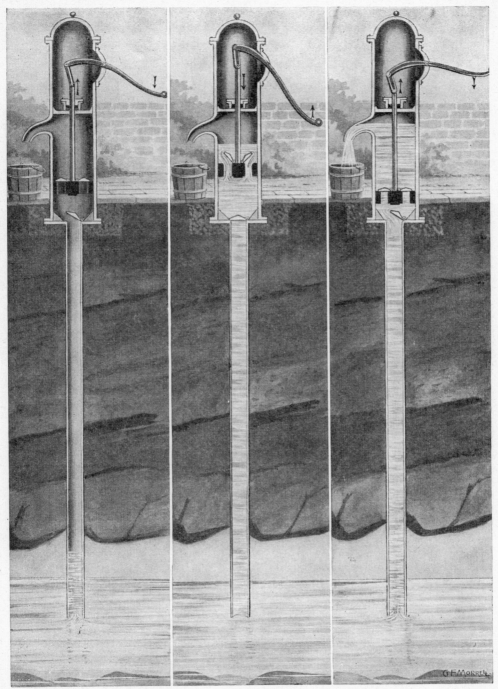

A suction pump raises water by suction much as we suck fluid through a straw. These pictures show how the suction is applied. In the first picture we see a piston beginning to move upward. As it ascends its suction opens a valve and begins to suck water up the tube. The water sucked up is seen in the second picture rushing to the upper side of the descending piston through two valves in the piston's head. In the third picture we see the valves closed by the weight of the water, and the water being forced out of the spout as the piston again ascends.

HERALDRY AND WHAT IT MEANS

HERALDRY is a survival from the days of long ago, when the social life of the people was very different from the life we live. The country was organised then, not for the general good of the majority, but for the benefit of the few—for the king with his princes and a small number of chiefs or lords acting under him and responsible to him.

It was the duty of the chiefs when the king was attacked to go to his aid, taking with them a band of retainers; and in order that among the many bands assembled in the king's army, the members of each might be able to distinguish their own leaders and comrades, each lord had an emblem or symbol embroidered on his garments and trappings, and on a banner borne aloft, and at a later period on the coats of his followers.

Very often the chosen symbol would have some direct reference to the lord who wore it. Thus, if an ancestor had been killed in a fight with a lion, the lord would perhaps choose a lion as his emblem; if he himself were famous in falconry he might choose a hawk; if he were of a humorous turn of mind he might select for an emblem something the name of which was a play or a pun on his own name, such as, for instance, a castle near a ford or a river for the name of Castleford.

In course of time the symbol became the distinguishing sign of the lord and his family, to be used on all occasions. It would be painted on his ceilings and sculptured on his walls, but its first use was in battle, and as it was a part of the armament of the lord it came to be known as his arms. Being embroidered on his surcoat it was called a coat-of-arms, and as the shield bearing the emblem was a prominent part of his outfit in war it came to be the custom, wherever the arms appeared, to draw them inside a shield.

When members of one family with a coat-of-arms married into a family with a different coat-of-arms, the two arms were combined, and as this needed a good deal of ingenuity there gradually grew up a science of Heraldry, which arranged these things according to certain rules; and regulations were made to prevent unauthorised people from using coats-of-arms. The possession of a coat-of-arms thus became a badge of birth and breeding; it was a hall-mark of importance.

Many of the symbols used for arms were quaint and homely—birds, lobsters, beehives, acorns, wheels, and so on. As family after family combined their arms, complicated and beautiful designs grew up.

Heraldry is very useful today in unravelling the past, for it enables those who understand it to trace the history and pedigree of ancient families and important personages. It is in many ways the handmaid of history and has always occupied the attention of the learned.

Nobody can say exactly how far back it goes, but from the very earliest period we find it was the custom for individuals and communities to be distinguished by some sign or device, and this is the origin of Heraldry. It is because war and the chase were the chief business of men in olden days that these things have provided so large a part of the symbols used and have given their vocabulary to the science.

So far as English heraldry is concerned, this grew up chiefly during the time that the Normans and their successors were in power, and as a result many of the words used in Heraldry are Norman French.

The general use of armorial devices in the strict sense on shields and banners is supposed to have begun about the middle of the twelfth century. In the first Crusade the shields of the Christian knights seem to have been plain and they had no designs emblazoned on their banners, and in the second Crusade we are not sure that there were armorial bearings.

But, as we can see for ourselves in the coloured pictures of the Bayeux Tapestry on page 709 of this book, the idea was beginning to germinate at the time of the Norman Conquest, for on the shields of both Saxons and Normans there are simple figures something like armorial bearings, including dragons and crosses. These seem to have been the early stages of Heraldry as we understand it today. Tournaments, of course, with all their pageantry helped to bring armorial bearings into general use, and arms soon became one of the characteristic features of the Middle Ages.

What looks to us the left-hand side of the shield is called the dexter or right-hand side, and what looks like the right is the sinister or left. The reason is that the shield is regarded from the point of view of the man who carries it.

Are Ear-Rings Good for the Eyes?

We do not know anything good that can be said of ear-rings; but, of course, we must not say any evil of them that is not true. It is utterly untrue that piercing the ears, with or without the wearing of ear-rings, has any effect at all upon the eyes. There is no reason whatever why it should have such an effect, and hundreds of thousands of cases every day prove, of course, that it has not. Perhaps, if we want to say the best we can for ear-rings, we may add that, at any rate, they do less harm than nose-rings, which are worn for the same reason—that is to say, for ornament—by many savages.

Has Each Planet a Law of Gravitation?

The law of gravitation is not a question of any planet or star. It is a universal law. It is equally and strictly true of every particle of matter everywhere, and applies strictly between that particle of matter and every other particle, whether near or far. For us on the Earth, the most important kind of gravitation is the Earth's gravitation; that is simply because the Earth is so near. But a book, which rests on a table under the pull of the Earth, is also being pulled toward the Sun, and the Moon, and every star in the sky. Only the Earth, being near, has the advantage, and that is why it is the downward pull we know so well, and usually call gravitation.

In the case of any of the bodies of the heavens, this downward pull depends upon its mass. Thus, if we could exist on the surface of the Sun, we should find the downward pull vastly greater than here; on Mars, less than here; on the Moon, still less; and so on. But if we think this over, we shall see that it simply means that gravitation is true everywhere, and that it is not the best way of putting it to say that each planet has its own law of gravitation.

Can We Think about Things that Do Not Interest Us?

No. We simply cannot think of things that do not interest us; it is interest that starts us thinking. And so everyone who studies the human mind likes to see a child who is interested, wants to know, and thinks over things by himself sometimes. It is that, and not the look of him,

which proves that he is a human being and not just a nice little animal.

The grown-up people who are wise, and who discover new truth, are those who do not stop thinking when they grow up; and this is because they have not lost their interest in things. It will not do to say that we cannot help being interested or not interested, for everything is interesting if we will only give it a chance. We have only to begin to think about the world in which we live to find that the more we think the more interesting the things we think about become.

How is it that a Worm Lives when Cut in Two?

All animals except the very lowest depend on what we call a nervous system, which controls the power of movement, and so forth. Now, when this nervous system is all heaped together in the form of the brain, as it is in man and the higher animals, the life of a creature depends upon that brain being uninjured. But in lower creatures, like the worm, the arrangement of the nervous system is different. It is more scattered over the body, and so, when a worm is cut in half, there is enough nerve matter in either half to enable it to keep living.

Does a Fish Feel?

Certainly. Everything that lives, from a microbe up to a man, has some kind of feeling. The power to feel and to respond to what is felt is a mark of all living matter everywhere, and its disappearance without return is the mark of death. But the amount and the quality and the clearness of feeling differ widely in various living things. So the fish does feel, but it does not feel as we do.

Seeing is a kind of feeling, and perhaps a fish sees quite as well as a young baby does. A fish hears, too, and smells and tastes. Also, a fish certainly has the sense of touch. It can suffer a kind of unpleasant feeling, too, and must do so, for instance, when it has a hook in its mouth; but it would be a great mistake for us to fancy that it feels sharp pain as we should if we had a barbed hook in our mouths.

A fish has only a very simple kind of brain, and cannot feel so keenly as we do. So as to whether it is right to fish, we should decide for ourselves and then act accordingly.

Where do Flies go in the Winter?

Most flies live their lives in spring and summer, then die. Some of them are fortunate enough to find a place where they can hide and obtain warmth.

They hide in quiet places about the house, in outbuildings, in the fields and stables, where we should never dream of looking for them. They do not feed. They simply lie dormant, sleeping the cold days away.

But an unexpected warm day in winter comes. The extra warmth wakes him, makes him hungry, and sends him forth to seek food. The warm day passes, and he may get back to safe hiding; but most likely he will not. Very few flies manage to get through the winter. If they are not worn out and ready to die at the end of the summer, many of them are killed by a fungus which, floating in the air, settles on their bodies, drives roots into their insides, and destroys them.

What is a Corn?

A corn is a hard growth which occurs on the toes or some other part of the feet, and is generally the result of wearing a shoe too small for the foot.

The corn itself is composed of the outer part of the skin; and the overgrowth of this skin in a lump, which produces the corn, is caused by the pressure of the shoe at the spot. But the corn would not result unless the pressure was taken off at intervals, and this, of course, is done when we take the shoe off. If the pressure were kept applied to this spot all the time continuously, the skin, instead of overgrowing at that point, would waste away.

It was once the custom in China to place a very tight bandage round the feet of girls, with the result that the feet did not grow to their proper size. So that the result of the pressure on the skin depends entirely upon whether it is continuous, and whether it is severe. The overgrowth of the skin is due to the irritation produced by the pressure.

How Does Oil Make a Rough Sea Calm?

The explanation of this lies in one of the contrasts between oil and water, which we can readily observe for ourselves even when we have a small quantity of the two liquids in a couple of bottles.

If we shake the bottle of oil, we notice how slow its movements are, and how difficult it is to make it splash. It is what we call a viscous liquid. Water moves much more easily, and we call it a mobile—that is, movable—liquid. Oil calms troubled waters because it is so viscous. But it is very difficult to understand what it is that makes one liquid viscous and another mobile. Partly it has something to do with the size of the molecules of the liquid. In the case of oil of any kind, the molecules are very large.

How Far Off is the Sky?

What we call the sky is nothing but the appearance of blue that we get on a bright day, owing to the fact that solid particles in the air reflect the blue part of sunlight to our eyes, and also to the fact that nitrogen gas is itself blue.

When we see the blue sky, then, what we really see is air. The height of the particles that reflect this blue light to our eyes is perhaps 50 or 60 miles at most, and, compared with the size of the universe, that is almost nothing at all. But by the sky we may mean the great space around us that we may see on any bright night. We see vastly farther then than in the daytime, because we can see right through the air out to the stars; while in the daytime the Sun is lighting up all the air around us, so that, though we seem to see a long way, we really cannot see past the lit-up air—except when there is something very bright beyond it, such as the Sun itself, and sometimes even the Moon.

How Do Men Find Where a Fault Is in the Atlantic Cable?

We must imagine that, instead of an electric cable having a copper wire in the middle, we have a long tube, into which we pour water. We must imagine, also, that the end, or bottom, of the tube is hundreds of miles away, much farther than we can see. Even then we can tell how far off the bottom of the tube is if we know how much water will fill it.

Just in this way clever men have found out how to tell the length of copper wire in an electric cable. They have instruments by which they can tell how much electricity has been put into a wire when it is full, and as they know how much electricity one mile or one yard of wire will hold, they can tell how far off is the end of the wire—that is to say, they can tell the place where it has broken.

The Story of the Beautiful Things in the Treasure-House of the World

A National Gallery picture by Bernardino Luini, showing Jesus among the Doctors

VENICE RISES AND ITALY WANES

It would seem that when Leonardo da Vinci, Michael Angelo, and Raphael had made their supreme gifts to the world's store of beauty, great Italy had done her share of giving and doing; she might well fold her hands and rest.

But one of the most amazing features in the history of painting in that glorious country is the rise of the school of Venice, the lovely, haunting city set like a jewel on an arm of the sea.

The early art of Venice centres round two men, one an artist and the father of artists, Jacopo Bellini, and the other a dealer in antiques, Squarcione. In Padua, neighbour to Venice, a second Florence for culture, Squarcione had his shop, and round him gathered a group of artists. Squarcione may indeed be called the founder of the Paduan school, from which Venice gained her first lessons in painting.

Squarcione, a strange and eager man with an overwhelming love for beautiful things, had travelled a good deal in Italy, and also spent some time in Greece. The result of his wanderings was a collection of works of art, among them some fragments of Greek sculpture, which were the source of an intense interest to the Paduan group of students. One of these, Mantegna, Squarcione presently adopted as his son,

and through this young and powerful genius the Paduan school learned to love Greek art. Through all the work of Mantegna the pursuit of the classic ideal can be seen. His sense of form is that of a sculptor, his art is one of the loftiest, and perhaps the coldest, that Italy produced.

Mantegna's greatest works are his wonderful frescoes in Padua and Mantua. He left also a collection of pictures, drawings, and engravings which are treasured in various towns of Europe. There are some five cartoons of his, The Triumph of Caesar, at Hampton Court, and in the National Gallery five paintings, Madonna with Magdalen and John Baptist, The Triumph of Scipio, Summer and Autumn, Samson and Delilah, and The Agony in the Garden. The Scipio picture, like The Judgment of Solomon, in the Louvre, and Judith, in Dublin, are specimens of Mantegna's later work, where he allows his feeling for shape and line to override any sense of colour he may have possessed, and produces rather a monochrome effect.

Jacopo Bellini, of whose work little remains, is overshadowed by his sons, Giovanni and Gentile, who were the first great masters of Venice. But, although through the Bellinis Paduan art became the inspiration of Venetian, another slight

PICTURES · STATUES · CARVINGS · BUILDINGS · IVORIES · CRAFTS

influence was at work in the paintings of artists on the island of Murano.

The best men of this little colony were the Vivarini family. Alvise Vivarini worked as a pupil in the studio of his father Bartolommeo, and the style of the two men was very akin in spirit to the Sienese. There is a picture by the elder Vivarini in the National Gallery called Madonna with Saints Paul and Jerome, but his greatest work, and that of his son, is at Venice. A pupil of Alvise's was Lorenzo Lotto, three of whose pictures are in the National Gallery. Lotto's paintings show something of the Sienese spirit, and a peculiar gentle sadness which perhaps we may say was the outcome of his own temperament.

THE MAN WHO GAVE VENICE THE IDEA OF PAINTING IN OILS

During the time the Bellinis were working, an artist called Antonello da Messina, brought to Venice from Flanders, where he had been working, the method of painting in oil, an innovation of the highest importance to Venice. Antonello was a painter who, in an epoch less crowded with great men, would have gained all the distinction he merited. His best work is portraiture. The finest examples are the Condottiere, in the Louvre, and Portrait of a Man, now in a private house in Milan. Another of his portraits—supposed to be himself—is in the National Gallery, together with a picture which is his earliest signed work—The Saviour—a painting of the Crucifixion, and another of St. Jerome in his Study.

The Venetian artists, adopting oil as a medium, did not use it as we understand it now. They still painted in tempera, where the pigment is mixed with white of egg, and when the picture was fully worked out, and almost finished, they added the final coat in oil. This method, however, made a vast difference to the progress of painting in Venice, where damp and misty airs played havoc with exposed fresco and pure tempera.

THE MEN WHO GAVE VENICE ITS FINE PICTURES OF PAGEANTS

The careers of Gentile and Giovanni Bellini together cover the great years of Venetian painting. In the work of these two men, with Crivelli, another pupil of Alvise Vivarini, we see the growth of the peculiar qualities which were to mark Venetian art for another 150 years. For the first time in the history of Italian painting colour was considered as part of the making of a picture, and not added as an afterthought.

With the Bellini school began the pageant pictures so natural to a city where civic and religious processions of an amazing brilliance took place, when the Doge and his followers showed themselves as a mass of bewilderingly beautiful colour against the fair and lovely background of Venetian streets and waterways. This was the kind of picture the people of Venice hailed with great delight. They gloried in the pageantry of pictures like Gentile Bellini's Corpus Christi, or Preaching of St. Mark, or the St. Ursula pictures by Carpaccio, a pupil of Gentile.

The Bellinis and their friends were not concerned with the meaning of things, rather with their nature and beauty. Some of their portraits are magnificent, such as the Loredano, by Giovanni, in the National Gallery. They painted religious subjects rather because they made great pictures than that they had a spiritual significance.

THE BEAUTIFUL PICTURES THAT STILL STIR THE HEART AFTER 500 YEARS

Only a few pictures by Gentile Bellini are left in the world, and the best of those are at Venice. The National Gallery owns four : Adoration of the Magi, Portrait of a Mathematician, Sultan Mohammed II, and a monk as St. Dominic. Of Crivelli's pictures the National Gallery owns a good many, mainly religious subjects. The bulk of Crivelli's work is at Milan.

It has been said that Giovanni Bellini was a whole school in himself. He went through many stages, absorbing and showing in his work the various changes through which, during his long lifetime, and in different men's hands, from Mantegna to Titian, Venetian art passed. He painted chiefly religious subjects and allegories. Inability to express movement was perhaps his notable weakness.

Giovanni's influence stirred all the neighbourhood, rising in a crescendo of greatness to Titian, his immortal pupil. Many smaller men owed their training and ideals to him, including Carpaccio and Cima da Conegliano. Nine pictures of Cima are in the National Gallery, many in Venice and Milan. Carpaccio is remarkable as a great illustrator, a story-teller,

PICTURES FROM ITALY'S GREAT DAYS

DOGE GIOVANNI MOCENIGO
BY GENTILE BELLINI

THE MADONNA OF THE BASKET
BY CORREGGIO

A PORTRAIT OF HIMSELF
BY ANTONELLO DA MESSINA

THE THREE SISTERS—BY PALMA VECCHIO

ARIOSTO—BY TITIAN, IN
THE NATIONAL GALLERY

THE MARRIAGE OF THE TWO
ST. CATHERINES—BY BORGOGNONE

SULTAN MOHAMMED II
BY GENTILE BELLINI

Many of the paintings in these pages are from photographs by Messrs. Alinari, Anderson, Hanfstaengl, and Bruckmann

and Cima as a painter of gentle, charming women who happened to be saints.

Other artists, followers of Giovanni Bellini, were Giorgione (1477–1510), Palma Vecchio (1480–1528), and Sebastian del Piombo (1485–1547). The first of these is far the greatest and had a considerable effect not only on the other two but on many other artists of the day.

In Giorgione's work all the light and colour and richness of the Venetian school ran riot. Giorgione had discovered the witchery of Nature's loveliness. He has nothing to do with the asceticism underlying the work of many other Italian schools of painting, nothing to do with the fine seriousness of his master Giovanni Bellini. He is completely satisfied with the beauty of life in Venice, drenched in colour, haloed by the Sun, girdled by the sea. The paintings of Titian and Giorgione stand out in this great period because of this quality. Even after the passage of five hundred years, during which time their colour and radiance have suffered, these pictures stir our hearts.

THE MARVELLOUS ART AND INDUSTRY OF THE GREAT TITIAN

Giorgione died of plague in Venice while still in his early thirties, and there are only about fifteen pictures of his in existence now. The Piping Shepherd in Hampton Court is a rare and lovely piece of work, as are the Fête Champêtre in the Louvre, and the Virgin and Child and Saints, in the church of Castelfranco, the town where he was born.

The Bellinis and their followers are sometimes spoken of as the youth of art in Venice, Titian as its vigorous young manhood, Giorgione as an exuberance natural to both, Tintoretto as Venetian art in its glorious prime.

Titian, who began as a pupil of Giovanni Bellini, would have soared to greatness in whatever country and generation he had been born. He lived from 1477 to 1576. He had the vigour and elasticity, the combined egotism and impressionableness, that stamp genius in all ages.

He could watch and admire the work of other geniuses and could imitate it, but in doing so he would make the quality he sought irrevocably his own. All through his long lifetime he was working, experimenting, trying this style and that subject, and was always supremely great. If it had not been for his industry we might have thought that his greatness grew like the lilies, without taking thought. When we look at his work, we realise that almost every picture was a separate adventure into which he flung the power and ardour native to him. There was nothing of the sorrowful gift of temperament, such as clouded Michael Angelo's life with grey, in Titian. He was a born pagan, and, though he did much work of a religious character, he died a pagan, full of the happiness that the keen vision of beautiful things provokes.

THE MAN WHO COULD NOT HELP PAINTING LOVELY THINGS

We can realise for ourselves, by walking about for a few minutes in the National Gallery, just what it is that makes the appeal of Titian—not the appeal of genius to genius, not the reason why artists worship the great Venetian, but the reason why he appeals to ourselves, those who are not artists and can only look on.

We go first to the Sienese, and see what the first painters of Italy were about, see their bad drawing, their self-consciousness, the simple joy in painting which makes their wry-necked saints so nice. Then we go to the Florentines, and see how carefully they were studying all the time, a little cold, deadly sure of their lines when once they had got them. If we are quite honest we must confess that we like many of these great men because we think we ought to, but when we get to the Venetian painters we are suddenly at home ; we should like their pictures even if we were not taught that they were great ; and Titian is the genius who in that way is at once our friend.

THE SPACIOUS PAINTINGS AND INSPIRING WORK OF THE FAMOUS TINTORETTO

Titian left a great pile of work for the joy of mankind, and it is now scattered all over Europe. There are so many of his pictures in Madrid and Vienna that here is another reason for wanting to visit these great cities. Venice, of course, and Florence, are rich in treasures of Titian's work. Paris owns about a dozen, Dresden eight; in the National Gallery we have a fine group which includes The Holy Family and Shepherd, Venus and Adonis, the famous Bacchus and Ariadne, Christ and the Magdalen, and a Madonna with St. John and St. Catherine.

Tintoretto, called the Michael Angelo of Venice, is not so near to everyday human liking as was Titian even in the gravity of his old age. Tintoretto sought huge and baffling problems in his work and seemed self-consciously to measure them with his own strength. Many of his pictures are large piled-up compositions, in which space, figure-drawing, colour, and light and shade, make difficulties which only a genius could overcome. Two such pictures are the Massacre of the Innocents and the Presentation in the Temple—both in Venice.

THE TREMENDOUS WORK DONE BY THESE OLD ARTISTS

The colour has faded in most of his larger pictures, and only in some of his portraits and small sketches do we get an idea of his palette. He turned away a little from the glowing warm colour usual to Venetian painters, and worked in the silvery tones in which Titian himself, in his old age, was beginning to find pleasure.

As in the case of Titian, the number of paintings in existence by Tintoretto make one wonder how these artists contrived to find time to eat and sleep. There are over a hundred of Tintoretto's paintings in Venice, twenty in Vienna, ten in Florence, and dozens scattered about in other towns of Europe. Among the fine examples of his work to be seen at the National Gallery are St. George and the Dragon, Christ washing the feet of the Disciples, Origin of the Milky Way; and four at Hampton Court—Esther before Ahasuerus, Nine Muses, Portrait of a Dominican, and the Knight of Malta.

THE VERONA SCHOOL OF ARTISTS AND THEIR INFLUENCE

Tintoretto shared with an artist from Verona, Paul Veronese, the last honours of sixteenth century art in Venice. Verona was a dependency of Venice, and for three or four generations artists had been working there, affecting very much the art life of neighbouring towns. Paul Veronese, son of a sculptor, was the outcome of this movement. He saw subjects more as pictures and less as figure studies than did most of the painters of his day. He had a freshness and a serenity of his own, and though classed with the Venetians and imbued with their love of light and brilliant costume, he retained throughout his own personality. Italy was now under the Spanish domination, and in Paul Veronese's work is reflected a little of the Spanish ceremonial and style of dress.

Several fine pictures by Paul Veronese are in the National Gallery.

Here the great period of Venetian painting came suddenly to an end. In the eighteenth century there was in Venice a strange and brief revival of Renaissance art, most beautifully born out of due time, in the work of Giovanni Battista Tiepolo, who really belongs to the sixteenth century. Venice was very little changed, still gay, pleasure-loving, rioting in colour and sunlight, and this artist threw all her magic qualities into his pictures. A very fine specimen of his painting is the Adoration of the Magi, now at Munich. Two other artists who were working at about the same time were Guardi and Canaletto. They painted beautiful pictures of the city of lagoons, full of light and space.

There were several minor schools in North Italy similar to those of Verona and Padua, and artists in these communities maintained a steady activity, even if they did not rise to great heights.

THE GOOD PAINTERS WHOSE PICTURES ARE PERHAPS TOO PRETTY

The Milanese school as a whole erred on the side of prettiness. Ambrogio Borgognone (about 1455-1523) is not so much open to this charge as many other artists of Milan. He painted some very fine religious subjects and a number of low-toned, beautiful landscapes with figures. Two of his Madonna and Crucifixion pictures are in the National Gallery, together with a painting of the marriage of the two Saint Catherines.

The Milanese school seemed to suffer from Leonardo da Vinci's visit to the town, as the Great Master's work was the cause of imitators who could not aspire to his greatness and only parodied his style. Luini was perhaps the weakest of these followers. His pictures are too finished, too charming. A characteristic example of this work is Christ among the Doctors, in the National Gallery. Some frescoes which Luini painted in the church of Saronno showed that he was capable of good painting, but for the most part he was merely " pretty."

The school of Brescia produced, among many artists of indifferent merit, two painters—Moretto and Moroni. Moretto's St. Justina is a very beautiful picture in quiet tones. Moroni's outstanding gift was in portraiture. His masterpiece is the Tailor in the National Gallery.

Correggio, who lived from 1494 to 1534, exercised on the Italian of his own and the next century an influence almost as powerful as that of Michael Angelo. He had the great Florentine's passion for form without his solemnity and grandeur, and he had a fatal facility—a kind of easy knack—for showing movement and foreshortening in figures which was only just counteracted by his genius. This is shown in the wonderful painting of the Assumption, in the dome of Parma Cathedral, and in the Virgin and Child with St. George, in Dresden Gallery.

THE STRIKING OF THE DEATH-KNELL OF ITALIAN ART

Correggio was, above all, a painter of beautiful women. His Madonnas are very lovely, a little too lovely, perhaps. He is happiest in his pictures of women of classical story. In the National Gallery are several of Correggio's paintings.

In the late sixteenth century and the early seventeenth art in Italy centred in Bologna. There, a number of painters, headed by members of the family of Carracci, formed a school whose principle was that each artist should imitate the best qualities of the greatest Italian artists. Although some of the work of the Carracci themselves was notable, and showed instinctive greatness, their followers struck the death-knell of Italian art.

In painting there are always certain problems to be dealt with after a student has mastered drawing: colour treatment, space composition, and perspective; and to solve these problems for himself is essential to a true artist. If he looks at the work of another and greater man, learns how *he* has solved them, and takes his methods as a short cut to save himself trouble, any natural skill he may possess dies out. Late Italian art is strewn with these corpses.

THE EMOTIONS AND THOUGHTS THAT GREAT ART REPRODUCES

Instead of strength we get prettiness; instead of portraits which show in a face the soul of a man or woman, we get a pleasing expression, a passing feeling—a smile, a frown, happiness on the surface, pain of the passing moment. Great art does not aim at easy effect; it is impersonal, beyond the touch of the accident of the hour. It reproduces those emotions and thoughts which are fundamental, embedded in a person's character, which in time can make a beautiful face repulsive and a plain face lovely.

If you see a portrait which reminds you of a photograph, as of a lady with a charming smile, and all the lines of age carefully " touched " out, be sure that portrait is poor art. Leonardo's famous Mona Lisa does not come under this ban, because in her subtle, enigmatical smile was expressed the woman's character, history, and destiny. A face like Guido Reni's Ecce Homo, which appeals to a cheap emotion without appealing to reason and thought, is poor art.

The best men of the Carracci school of Bolognese art were Albano, Domenichino, Guido Reni, and Guercino. In spite of their other weaknesses some of these artists were excellent decorators. Domenichino's Last Supper, and Guido Reni's Aurore, both in Rome, are sufficient proof of that.

HOW WE KNOW THE TRUE FROM THE FALSE IN ART

Presently an artist called Caravaggio came into prominence, and he turned his fellow workers away from copying the ideals of the great and taught them a rather brutal realism. From saints and pagan goddesses he went for his models to low and vulgar people; he painted inn brawls and rather ghastly scenes. He and his followers worked in dim rooms lighted by a single small window; their pictures show the violent and striking effect which these working conditions would produce.

An artist of Naples, Salvator Rosa, was a fine painter of landscape and war pictures, and he stands out as being stronger than the rest.

Unhappily, the artists of the decadent period in Italy produced an enormous number of pictures. They are seen in almost every gallery in Europe, and they have an easy triumph with people who have not had the advantage of learning to know the true from the false in art. This is not easy to know. The only way we can guard ourselves from idols in the world of beauty is to go back and worship the great. If we have once learned to love Michael Angelo and Beethoven, we need not be afraid of liking other music and pictures; sooner or later the anchor will pull; Beethoven and Michael Angelo will set us right.

THE PORTRAIT OF A TAILOR, BY MORONI, AT THE NATIONAL GALLERY, LONDON

25 F 2**

THE EMPRESS ISABELLA, BY
TITIAN, AT THE PRADO, MADRID

A PORTRAIT BY ANTONELLO DA
MESSINA, AT ANTWERP MUSEUM

THE MADONNA AND CHILD, BY
GIOVANNI BELLINI, AT VENICE

THE HOLY FAMILY WITH ST. PAUL AND ST. GEORGE, BY GIOVANNI BELLINI, AT VENICE ACADEMY

AURORA, BY GUIDO RENI, FROM A PALACE
IN ROME

THE MARRIAGE AT CANA, BY PAUL VERONESE,
AT DRESDEN

LA FORNARINA, BY PIOMBO, AT
THE UFFIZI, FLORENCE

LAURA DE' POLA, BY LORENZO
LOTTO, AT THE BRERA, MILAN

FLORA, BY TITIAN, AT THE UFFIZI
GALLERY, FLORENCE

THE MADONNA AND ST. JEROME, BY CORREGGIO, AT THE PARMA GALLERY

THE HOLY FAMILY WITH ST. CATHERINE,
BY TITIAN, AT THE NATIONAL GALLERY

THE MEETING OF JACOB AND RACHEL,
BY PALMA VECCHIO, AT DRESDEN

ST. GEORGE, BY MANTEGNA,
AT VENICE ACADEMY

THE VISION OF THE CROSS, BY
PAUL VERONESE

A NOBLEMAN, BY MORETTO,
AT THE NATIONAL GALLERY

THE MADONNA AND THE CUCCINA FAMILY, BY PAUL VERONESE, AT THE DRESDEN GALLERY

THE TRANSFIGURATION, BY GIOVANNI BELLINI,
AT THE NAPLES MUSEUM

THE MARRIAGE OF ST. CATHERINE,
BY TINTORETTO, AT VENICE

The Wonderful House We Live In, and Our Place in the World

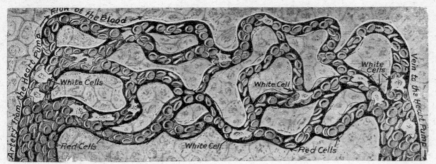

Through these thread-like pipes, called capillaries, blood runs to every part of the body, carrying its red cells, which bring oxygen, and its white cells, the wandering chemists that keep microbe burglars away.

THE RED CELLS OF THE BLOOD

WE have been talking about living cells, which are the simple units of all living creatures, as atoms are the units of the elements of matter. We have read of some of the simplest of these living cells, those which are complete creatures in themselves, such as microbes, the amoeba found in ponds, and so on.

This prepares us now to study the most wonderful fluid in the world—the red blood which is found in the bodies of all the higher animals, and which we know so well in ourselves. Though we think of the blood as a fluid, it is really crammed with living cells, red and white, upon the health of which our own health depends.

The gaseous part of the blood is a matter of life and death for us. We breathe in order that its composition shall be kept right—in order that the poisonous gases produced by the body and carried by the blood shall be got rid of ; and in order that the life-giving gas, oxygen, shall be supplied to it in proper quantity. All these three parts of the blood—the cells, the fluid, and the gases—are absolutely necessary for life. We may begin here with cells, and, on the whole, we may say that cells are of two kinds, known as red cells and white cells.

The red cells are much the more numerous, and the easier to understand.

In a volume of blood the size of about two pinheads, there should be millions of these red cells. We can count the number by taking a very small drop of blood, dropping it into a little well made in a glass plate, and covering it up and looking at it through the microscope. We know exactly how deep the well is, and the floor of it is ruled in both directions with tiny lines of which we know the distance apart, so that if we count the number of cells in each of these squares we can reckon the richness of the blood in cells.

This takes a very long time and is very difficult to do, expecially as the blood has to be diluted first ; but it is very well worth doing, both for the red cells and the white cells, because their number changes very much in different states of health, and very often the doctor knows how to treat a patient just because he is able to watch these changes in the number of cells in the blood.

All the colour of the blood is due to the red cells. When we look at a single cell by itself, however, it is not really red, but yellow. It is the great number seen together that makes the blood look red.

When you prick your finger, the drop of blood should be of a rich red colour, but in people who are living unhealthy lives or who are not quite well the blood is

BODY, MIND, AND SOUL · CITIZENSHIP · ECONOMICS · GOVERNMENT

often too pale, and these people suffer in many ways, in consequence.

Eating wrong food is one of the chief causes of this paleness, for without iron and copper and other substances the red cells do not form properly, so that their numbers may fall to perhaps much less than half of what they should be. Also the number of cells may be quite up to the mark, but they may not contain the right quantity of the yellow or red stuff which it is their business to carry about.

THE CELLS THAT MAKE OUR BLOOD RED AND THE WAY THEY WORK

The red cells are round and flat, and thinner toward the middle than toward the edge. When a thing is scooped out in the middle, it is said to be *concave*, and when it is scooped out on both sides it is said to be *bi-concave* ; if it is rather flat it is called a *disc*. So we say that red blood-cells are *circular bi-concave discs*. Indeed, in shape they are rather like the glasses which short-sighted people have to wear in spectacles.

When the blood is healthy the red cells are all of the same size and shape. We cannot see any nucleus in them. But each cell had a nucleus when it was younger. When they are grown up, so to say, they lose their nucleus; they cannot divide into two, as many cells do, and they only live a short time in the blood—perhaps one to three months. Then they are broken down and disposed of. This is going on all the time, and all the time new red cells are being poured into the blood.

THE LIVING PILLARS OF OUR BODY AND THE WONDER THAT WORKS INSIDE THEM

The red cells are made inside our bones. This is one of the astonishing things which many people find it hard to believe; they think of bones as hard, dead things which exist merely for the same reason as the pillars of a building.

But these are living pillars, and the inside of them is filled with stuff called marrow, which is not only alive, but one of the most alive and most active tissues in the body. The cells in this red bone-marrow, as it is called, have the amazing power of making new red cells, which the blood picks up as it pours through the bones, unless, indeed, the red bone-marrow falls ill, as it sometimes does. There is nothing, perhaps, which upsets the red bone-marrow so certainly as having to breathe impure gases brought to it by the blood because we have been breathing foul or stagnant air.

As the blood flows in our bodies, the red cells are whirled along with it, but they do not move of themselves ; they are very passive things, as different as can be from the white cells. They do not change their shape; indeed, they seem to have an elastic covering which prevents them from doing so. They never eat up a microbe or an enemy in the blood. Sometimes we do see microbes in them, but that is because the microbes have killed the cells, not because the cells have eaten the microbes.

What, then, is the use of the red cells which exist in such billions and billions in our blood? The answer is that their use is simply as vehicles, as carriers of the precious colouring matter they contain. This yellow or red matter has a long name, but it is so important that we must try to learn it.

THE IRON THAT MAKES BLOOD RED AND GRASS GREEN

Its name is *haemoglobin*—the first half of this word is simply the Greek for blood. Haemoglobin is probably the most remarkable chemical compound in the whole world. It is also one of the most complicated. We have learned in another part of this book that such a compound as water consists of molecules, each of which is made of three atoms. It is probable that there are at least a thousand atoms in every molecule of haemoglobin. They are mostly atoms of carbon, hydrogen, nitrogen, and oxygen, but one of them—and it is absolutely necessary—is an atom of the metal iron.

So haemoglobin follows the rule that the compounds of iron are usually coloured. It is interesting to remember that, as iron is necessary for the most important coloured compound in the animal body, so iron is necessary for the most important coloured compound in the vegetable body.

That is to say, iron is one of the things that help to make colour in the world—not only the red in our blood, but the green colouring matter of leaves. It may be, then, that very humble forms of life can exist without iron, but at any rate we are certain that iron is necessary for the life of all higher animals and plants. This tells us something about our food, too. The red cells die, and are broken up after a time, and their iron is lost.

Iron is therefore a necessary part of our food; we should die without it. And perhaps it is interesting to know that the foods which contain iron, and from which we get it, include the best of all our foods, such as milk, eggs, bread, meat, potatoes, peas, rice, and oatmeal. The wines which are supposed to be rich in iron, and used to be ordered for this purpose, contain nothing like so much as is found in these common foods; and, to anyone whose blood is poor in iron, milk is worth all the wine in the world.

But we have not yet said why this haemoglobin should be so important. We know that it is important, since our bones are filled with material for making it, and since the blood is crammed with cells to carry it, and since we fall ill at once if the amount of it in our blood falls below the proper quantity.

It must have some great use, then, and it certainly has, for it is this haemoglobin that carries the oxygen, which we get from the air when we breathe, to every part of the body. We have learned that every living cell must breathe or die; every living cell of the body must get oxygen or die. Now, the only way in which it can get this

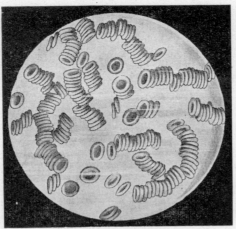
Red cells grouping together as they die

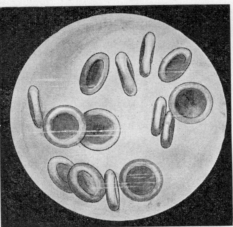
Red cells floating in the plasma

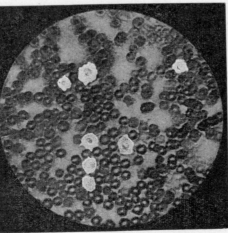
White and red cells of the blood
A DROP OF BLOOD SEEN IN THE MICROSCOPE

oxygen is through the blood, and the only way in which the blood can supply it is by means of this haemoglobin. Every few minutes — some say every four minutes — every red cell in the blood passes through the lungs, and after doing so it goes to various parts of the body again and again until its life is ended and a younger cell takes its place. The whole meaning of its passing through the lungs is that there it finds oxygen.

Now the special point to note is this: that the fluid part of the blood, and the white cells of the blood, cannot take up, as they pass through the lungs, anything like sufficient oxygen for the needs of the body. It is only the red cells that can do this, and it is only because of the haemoglobin in them that they can do it.

Sometimes there are plenty of them, but they do not contain enough haemoglobin, and when this is the case we suffer.

Each molecule of haemoglobin has the power of combining with itself a molecule of oxygen. Now, no one knows the exact composition of haemoglobin, but let us, for convenience, give it a name of its own, Hb. We cannot call it H, because that stands for hydrogen.

Now, a molecule of oxygen will be O_2. Well, when blood passes through the lungs, all the Hb of the red cells combines with the O_2 in the lungs, and makes a compound which we call HbO_2. This is simply haemoglobin and oxygen, and the long name for it is oxyhaemoglobin. In contrast with this, we sometimes call haemoglobin, when it is not combined with a molecule of oxygen, or when that molecule of oxygen has been taken away from it, *reduced* haemoglobin. We remember that when oxygen is taken from anything, that thing is said to be reduced.

WHAT GOES TO THE LUNGS WHEN WE BREATHE

What comes to the lungs, then, is reduced or simple haemoglobin—Hb; what leaves the lungs is HbO_2. This makes a remarkable difference of colour in the blood, for HbO_2 has a bright and cheerful red colour—the colour of life, as it has been called; while Hb itself has a much darker and more sullen colour. We have all probably observed this change in the colour of the blood. For example, the difference may be seen at once in anyone who has a choking fit, for his skin becomes dark and purple. All the blood in it is full of Hb instead of HbO_2, because he is not getting air into his lungs. When he gets right again the healthy colour will return, owing to the air getting into his lungs, and the blood in his skin has plenty of HbO_2 in it instead of having only Hb.

If you look at the back of your hand or at the front of your wrist you will see little blue lines. These are veins, and the blood in them is running up the arm. You can tell that it is doing so, for if you hang your arm down and run your finger firmly along one of those veins, say, on the back of your hand, running your finger downward toward the fingers, the blue line disappears. Then, if you take your finger off, you can see the blood run upward and fill the vein again.

THE CIRCULATION OF THE BLOOD THAT MEANS LIFE

The vein looks bluish because the colouring matter in the red cells of the blood is of the dark kind; it is Hb, not HbO_2; and this blood is rushing back up your arm as fast as it can in order to get to the lungs, where it will find fresh oxygen which you are breathing in to get ready for it at this moment; and there the Hb will be made into HbO_2, and the dark blood will turn bright again. This bright blood returns to the heart, and is pumped by it to every part of the body, where its business is to give up its oxygen so that the HbO_2 is reduced to Hb again, which is sent back to the lungs for more oxygen, and so on.

The most wonderful things about haemoglobin, then, is its power of picking up oxygen very easily and of giving it away again very easily, wherever it is required. Now we are able to understand the whole duty and purpose of these countless red cells in our blood.

If we are to be well and strong, and useful and happy, we must have a sufficient supply of red cells in our blood, and they must contain sufficient haemoglobin. So we must avoid anything that poisons them, or that poisons the bone-marrow which makes them, and so prevents it from supplying them to the blood quickly enough. Bad air from motor-car exhausts is an important poison we are likely to meet in this country; but in great areas of the world much the most serious poison of the red blood-cells is the tiny living creature which causes the disease malaria. Certain kinds of mosquitoes carry this creature, and, when they bite us, pass it into the blood, where it kills many of the red cells. We are beginning to abolish this disease by killing the mosquitoes that carry it.

WHY IS IT THAT MEN DIE IF THEY SWALLOW POISON?

The action of many poisons is due to the fact that they interfere with the work done by haemoglobin. The poison unites with the haemoglobin in the blood so that it can no longer take up oxygen, and a person so poisoned therefore dies of a kind of suffocation. The blood which is passing through his lungs is not able to pick up the oxygen in them.

If a man habitually drinks large quantities of alcohol, it makes him lazy and sleepy, and he does less work with his muscles. The tissues of the body are not exercised as they should be, with the result that they are thus not burnt up so well, and this is one of the reasons why people who take too much alcohol are inclined to grow fat. The fire of life cannot burn brightly with alcohol. It gradually destroys our ability to think quickly and clearly; we lose our appetite; and we are more likely to catch colds and chills.

The Story of the Marvellous Plants that Cover the Earth

Seeds of the hawkweed being distributed by the wind

THE FLOWER'S WONDERFUL SEED-BOX

WE have seen that the fruit of a plant is its wonderful seed-box. Let us now look more carefully at the precious contents of the box and see especially how the seeds are sown and distributed far and wide over the Earth.

Inside the flower's seed-box (the ovary) there are ovules, and these ovules are *possible* seeds. The ovule is the ripe seed ; but we do not get at the heart of the matter till we are clear that the seed contains a very young plant (the embryo). Besides this very young plant, which will develop into a seedling, there is a store of condensed food, as in a grain of wheat, and there are protective seed-coats, or husks. The store of food, which is a sort of legacy, may be outside the young plant, though within the seed-coats, or it may be in the young plant itself, as we see clearly in peas or beans.

The simplest way in which seeds are sown is by the cracking and bursting of the seed-boxes. Then the seeds tumble out, as we may see in the ripe pod of a pea or of a laburnum. The liberated seeds may be washed away by water, or swept along the ground by the wind, or buried in an earthworm's hole. Seeds lying loose may be collected by ants, as in the case of gorse and broom, and stored in the ant-hill. But an ant may lose the seed it is carrying, and this is another way in which seeds are scattered.

In some cases the seed-box bursts explosively, as we may both hear and see if we sit among the gorse on a warm autumn day. The seeds are jerked out to a little distance, for the drying of the wall releases certain springs in a Jack-in-the-Box fashion. In the balsam, whose Latin name is *Impatiens noli-me-tangere* (I do not wish you to touch me), the jerking out of the seeds is very effective indeed.

In this case five valves suddenly roll up like watch-springs and sling the seeds out ; the force is due not to a sharp release of dried-up fibres but to a layer of living cells very rich in water which expand suddenly when the trigger is pulled by touching the tip of the ripe fruit. The most famous explosive fruit is that of a tropical plant called *Hura crepitans*. It bursts with a report like a pistol shot and scatters the seeds for a few yards. Then there is the squirting Italian cucumber, where the fruit bursts and scatters the seeds along with its *liquid* contents.

The great advantage of explosion over simple breakage is that the seeds are thrown out beyond the immediate neighbourhood of the parent plant. Otherwise

BOTANY & ITS WONDERS · FLOWERS · TREES · HOW THINGS GROW

Medrik seeds with hooks
for catching in wool

Hooked herb
bennet seeds

Hooked seeds
of the orlaya

Cyperus-like sedge
with spiked seeds

The explosive squirting
cucumber seed

Philobolus fungus spores
scattered by explosion

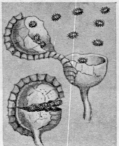

Male fern's spore case
bursts, scattering spores

Common wood sorrel
expels its seeds

Spring bitter vetch
seeds spring out

Violet seeds
thrown out

Cuckoo flower's
seeds spring out

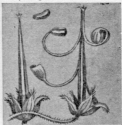

Expulsion of
crane's bill seed

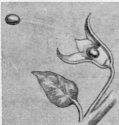

Germander's seed
hurled away

Castor oil plant throws
out the seed

Stork's bill seeds
parachute to earth

Feather grass's
feathered seeds

Spiked goat grass seeds
work along the ground

Starry scabious seeds that
hop along the ground

Starry clover's seed
that creeps along

Hard grass seed that
works its way along

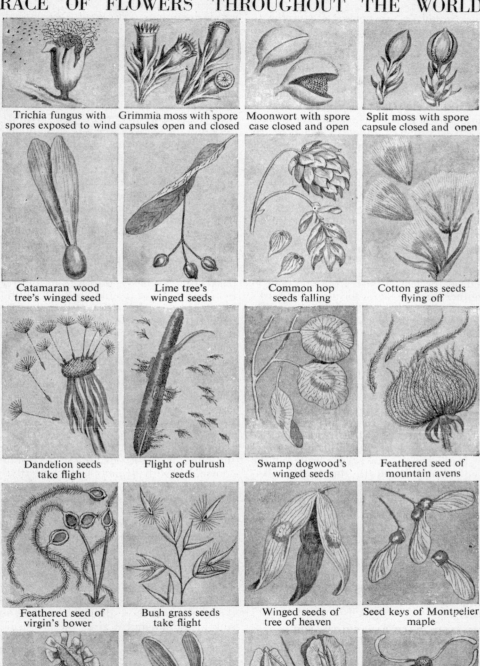

Trichia fungus with spores exposed to wind

Grimmia moss with spore capsules open and closed

Moonwort with spore case closed and open

Split moss with spore capsule closed and open

Catamaran wood tree's winged seed

Lime tree's winged seeds

Common hop seeds falling

Cotton grass seeds flying off

Dandelion seeds take flight

Flight of bulrush seeds

Swamp dogwood's winged seeds

Feathered seed of mountain avens

Feathered seed of virgin's bower

Bush grass seeds take flight

Winged seeds of tree of heaven

Seed keys of Montpelier maple

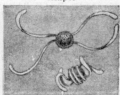

Winged seeds of artedia

Two-winged seed of triopteris

Winged seed of opoponax

Horsetail spores with spirals, rolled and unrolled

there would be unwholesome overcrowding among the seedlings.

Another way in which seeds are scattered is by the fruits becoming attached to passing animals, such as rabbits and sheep. They cling for a while by means of roughnesses, hooks, or bristles, and then fall off or are rubbed off. This is true of burdock, some grasses, and Jack-run-the-hedge, which is also well called "cleavers." In nutlet fruits and others which do not liberate the seed till it sprouts in the ground, there is very little practical difference between the fruit and the seed which fills it. Therefore we may include among the different kinds of seed-scattering the attachment of the dry fruit to the fur or fleece of animals.

THE WAY IN WHICH THE HUNGRY THRUSH SPREADS THE MISTLETOE SEEDS

The seeds of water plants may be carried on the feet of birds from one pool to another, and a clodlet formed on a bird's foot on a ploughed field may contain many seeds which will be sown elsewhere. Thus Darwin got no fewer than 82 seeds to sprout from a ball of earth that had formed on a partridge's foot, and that was after the ball had been kept dry for three years !

A peculiar kind of sowing is seen in the mistletoe. The white berry contains one seed embedded in glue-like pulp which hardens on exposure to air. Now the thrush likes the pulp but it does not like the seed. Yet it is a little difficult to reject the seed when swallowing the fruit, and the seed often adheres to the bird's bill— whereupon the thrush cleans it off by wiping its bill on a branch! In this strange way the seed is sown ; it remains glued to the branch till genial spring weather comes ; then it sprouts and fixes itself more firmly ; it is not till the second spring that it begins to grow vigorously. In the case of one of the tropical mistletoes the seeds are sometimes smeared by birds on to telegraph wires, where, of course, they die.

THE SEEDS WITH PARACHUTES FOR MAKING FLIGHTS IN THE AIR

It should also be noticed that when a thrush swallows the whole fruit, the undigested seed may be passed out none the worse for its journey down the food-canal, and this would be another kind of sowing.

What is unusual in the case of the thrush and the mistletoe berry is common among other fruit-eating birds and among fruit-eating mammals. The fruit is swallowed, its soft parts are digested, the stones or seeds are unharmed, and they are passed out again, it may be miles from the place where they were swallowed.

On the other hand, there are many birds and mammals that are able to digest the seeds they swallow. This is of some practical importance for man, as a creature digesting the seeds of weeds is, in so doing, helping the farmer by checking the spread of pests, while a creature that swallows the seeds and passes them out again undigested and unharmed is plainly scattering abroad what is injurious.

One of the most important agencies in seed-scattering is the wind, and this applies particularly to small fruits or seeds which have parachutes or floats of some sort. The fruit of the maple is a heavy nutlet borne at the end of a long blade-like parachute. When it is torn from the tree by a gust of wind it sinks with a beautiful twisting motion which often carries it far beyond the tree's shadow. If we throw it up into the air again we can watch its peculiar twisting flight as it sinks.

THE SEED THAT FLIES THROUGH THE AIR LIKE A BUTTERFLY

There are many other fruits with parachutes, such as elm and ash, and in some cases the parachute belongs to the seed itself. Thus the seed of a bignonia has broad glossy wings, and is so finely balanced that it " floats lightly along through the air in an almost horizontal course, and with the motion of a butterfly."

Very useful, too, is the down of fine hairs seen on many small fruits and seeds. Thistle-down and dandelion-down are fine examples, and the feathery plumes of the fruits of traveller's joy, or old man's beard, often entangle in long lines which float through the air with a beautiful wavy motion. The seeds are borne like gossamer-spiders on the wings of the wind.

They are scattered far and wide. The down makes it more difficult for them to sink in the air and it gives the favouring breeze something to grip. In the case of a very light fruit like that of the groundsel it has been suggested that the Sun's rays striking on the tuft of white hairs and warming the immediately surrounding atmosphere may produce a small eddy which lifts what is certainly "as light as gossamer" even when there is no breeze. They say that the groundsels had their original headquarters on the Andes, from where they have spread—thousands of different kinds—over the whole Earth; and part of the success of this journeying must surely be due to the parachutes.

What strikes one is the great variety of ways in which the sowing of seeds is brought about in Nature. Coconuts are floated by the currents of the sea to distant islands—what a contrast between this and

a ball which is torn up by the wind and rolled along the ground for great distances, scattering the seeds as it goes; and the same sort of thing occurs in the grass called spinifex and in some other cases. What a contrast between this and the liberation of seeds from neatly-made little holes at the top of a poppy head!

The meaning of the great variety is simply that plants have in different ways

Seeds of the balsam expelled from their case

The burst seed-cases and the flying seeds of the monkey's dinner bell

Bursting seed-cases of the thorn apple

A section through an ivory-nut

The long and spiky seed-cases of eschscholtzia

A much enlarged section of a rose-hip

THE WONDERFUL WAY IN WHICH NATURE PROTECTS THE SEEDS AND SENDS THEM OUT INTO THE WORLD

the groundsel's aerial journeys! The fruit-stalks of the ivy-leafed toadflax bend away from the light and poke the seed-box into a crevice of the wall—what a contrast between this and the way the seeds of the wild cherry are sown by birds! The fruit stalk of the pea-nut bends to the earth and pushes the fruit into a hole—what a contrast between this and the balsam's impatient explosion! The Rose of Jericho of the desert curls its dry branches into

counteracted their great handicap—that they are fixed to one place. Those have been most successful which have been best able to scatter their seeds, for, although many seeds come to nothing, wide scattering increases the chances of finding suitable and less crowded places where they may sprout and grow, where the seedling may become a plant which leafs and flowers, fruits and seeds, and resumes the journey over the Earth.

WILLIAM OF WYKEHAM AT WORK ON WINCHESTER CATHEDRAL

The Story of the Peoples of All Nations and Their Homelands

The Flemish woolworkers of the Fourteenth Century, who came over to England to teach their trade and founded the woollen industry of Yorkshire

FIGHTING FOR THE THRONE

WHEN Prince Edward left his old father Henry the Third to go and fight in the Crusade his young wife Eleanor pleaded to go with him. It was in vain that he told her how dangerous the journey was, and how uncomfortable she would be on board ship, or living in a tent. She only answered that " the way to Heaven is as near from Palestine as from England." So Eleanor had her way ; and the story goes that by gaining her way she was able to save her husband's life.

A man stole into his tent one hot day when he was resting with his heavy armour off, and, pretending he had a letter to deliver, struck at him with a poisoned dagger. Eleanor rushed forward and sucked the poison out of the wound, and had the joy of seeing her husband recover. After this they had to journey home again, for Henry was dead, and the prince was now Edward the First.

It was Edward who prepared the splendid tomb of marble for his father, once sparkling with gold and jewels, but now so dusty and grey, close by Edward the Confessor's shrine in Westminster Abbey. He also carried on his father's work by pulling down a piece of the old Norman Abbey and building it up again in the new style. Edward made many good laws, and arranged courts to deal with various matters of government. He also took care that real justice should be done, and sent away any judges he found to be dishonest.

Early in his reign he had bitter fighting with the Welsh. The Britons had found shelter among the western hills from both Romans and Saxons; and their children's children defied all attempts to join their land to England.

The English lords who lived on the borderland had great difficulty in preventing the Welsh from carrying off their cattle, and whatever else they could find, and followed them, when they could, back to their hills to punish them. There is a little railway now up to the top of Snowdon, and other lines wind about the valleys, and coaches run from place to place. As one travels about these hills, it is easy to understand what fine hiding-places the Welsh had, and how the beauty of the country and the splendid strengthening air made the Welsh owners do their best to keep it to themselves.

But Edward was clever and determined, and in the end succeeded in becoming master of the country, so that at last he

THE FIVE CONTINENTS & 100 NATIONS & RACES THAT INHABIT THEM

was able to hang up before the shrine of his namesake, Edward the Confessor, the crown of Llewellyn, the last Welsh prince.

When the nobles came to pay homage to Edward he promised to give them a prince as ruler, born in Wales, who could speak neither French nor English, and he fetched out to them his little son, born at Carnarvon Castle a few days before ! Ever since that time the eldest living son of the Sovereign has been created Prince of Wales.

HOW EDWARD TRIED TO UNITE ENGLAND AND SCOTLAND

Edward's great wish was to rule over the whole island of Britain. He wanted the Scottish king to do homage for all his kingdom, but the Scots steadily refused.

To try to make the kingdoms one by peaceful means, Edward proposed to marry his son to the Maid of Norway, whose mother was the daughter of the Scottish king, but the little girl, the last of her family, died on her way across the stormy North Sea. If she had lived it might have saved much misery during the years that followed, when Scotland was helped by France to resist England.

Disputes soon arose as to who should rule in Scotland after little Margaret died, and Edward claimed the right of settling them. Naturally, the Scottish people did not agree to this, and fought hard to get their own way. In ten years Edward made three conquests in Scotland. Many of the battles were fought near that narrow part of Scotland between the Forth and Clyde, now so busy with coal-mining and manufactures as we see in our Picture Atlas. Stirling, in the old time, was the key of the road to the Highlands, with its fine castle hill, and the Abbey Craig near by, now crowned with a monument to the great patriot William Wallace, who fought Edward and gained a victory over the English in the neighbourhood.

THE QUEEN WHOSE MONUMENT STANDS AT CHARING CROSS

In the same year that the Maid of Norway died, Edward lost his beloved Eleanor. To mark his grief, he built crosses wherever her body rested on its way from Nottinghamshire to Westminster Abbey. Three of these are still to be seen. The site of the last is quite near the Abbey. Green fields and a few country houses were its surroundings then ; now it lies in the midst of London.

The original cross stood where Charles Stuart now sits on horseback, and a copy of the cross stands in front of Charing Cross Station.

A few feet from where Edward lies in the Abbey is the ancient coronation chair made by him to enclose the famous stone that he brought from Scotland, on which the kings of that country had been crowned for centuries. Tradition associates it with the stone used as a pillow by Jacob at Bethel, and subsequently with the stone of destiny on which the kings of Munster in Ireland were crowned.

The chief battle in the reign of the son of Edward the First was fought at Bannockburn, within sight of Stirling. It was a wonderful day. Robert Bruce, the hero-king of Scotland, rode up and down on his brown pony—a battle-axe in his hand and a gold crown on his head—encouraging his soldiers. Robert had not half as many men as Edward, but before night fell the Scots were free once more; and Edward the Second left so much treasure behind that the Scots became richer, as well as freer, in this one day.

THE BATTLE AT WHICH ARROWS FELL LIKE FLAKES OF SNOW

Edward the Second ruled so badly that he was made to give up the crown, and his son of 14 was chosen king in his place. He was Edward the Third.

A great deal happened during the fifty years of his reign. He began by marrying Philippa when only 15 ! Her husband was away a great deal, for unnecessary wars with Scotland and France were incessant. He invaded Scotland again and again, and succeeded to a certain extent, till France helped the Scots. Then troubles broke out in that country, as Edward claimed to be the rightful king of France, through his mother.

One of the battles that followed was Crecy, in France, fought amid thunder and lightning and torrents of rain, and an eclipse of the Sun. It is said that the English had four cannon with them, and that this was the first time gunpowder was used in war. The arrows of the English fell fast and thick as flakes of snow; the men who came to help the French fell back, and soon all was in confusion. Edward's eldest son, a boy barely 16, led in the fight. You perhaps know the three feathers, with the motto, " I serve," used as a badge by

A KING IN WAR AND A KING IN PEACE

EDWARD THE FIRST, ON HIS WAY TO MAKE WAR ON THE SCOTS, DIES WITHIN SIGHT OF SCOTLAND

ROBERT BRUCE, KING OF SCOTLAND, GRANTS A CHARTER—FROM THE PAINTING BY
WILLIAM S. HOLE, IN THE POSSESSION OF EDINBURGH CORPORATION

the Prince of Wales. It was this Black Prince, so called from the colour of his armour, who took this badge to put on his shield at the battle of Crecy. According to old but untrustworthy tradition it had belonged to the blind old King of Bohemia, who cried, " I pray and beseech you to lead me so far into the fight that I may strike one good blow with this sword of mine," and was found dead on the field.

For nearly a year Edward tried to take the town of Calais, whose white cliffs we can see from Kent. Kent has been called the window from which we look out on Europe, and Calais has been called the door into France. Little wooden houses were built all round the town for the soldiers, and no one could pass food through. At last the people were starving, and had to give in to the English.

HOW QUEEN PHILIPPA SAVED THE SIX BRAVE MEN OF CALAIS

Edward said that six of the men of Calais must come and give their lives, and then he would let the rest go free; it was the sort of thing that peoples allowed kings to do in those days. So one after another brave man offered to go, and the six came to Edward with ropes round their necks. Can you imagine how the wives and children of these men felt as they saw them go to the English camp ? Edward would not listen when asked to spare them, but shouted, " Call the headsman! They, of Calais have made so many of my men die that they must die themselves." But then Queen Philippa herself knelt before the angry king, and with tears raining down her face, said to him, " Ah, gentle sire, from the day I passed over sea in great danger I have asked you nothing. Now I pray and beseech you, for the love of Christ, to have mercy on them."

The king kept silence for a while; then his heart softened, and he put the ropes of the six citizens into her hands. How happy Philippa must have been, as she cared for them, giving them fresh clothes and a feast, and presents before they went away!

You may see the six burghers as modelled by Rodin, the great French sculptor, close to the Houses of Parliament in London. A picture is on page 4647. But the war went on. Hundreds of soldiers crossed the Channel, to die away from home. Presently it became difficult to find enough men to till the fields, and there was poverty and discontent everywhere. A terrible sickness, too, called the Black Death, swept over the country, till nearly half the people died. The rich people did all they could to keep wages low, lest the poor labourers should cease to be their slaves.

THE MISERY OF A PEOPLE AND THE HONOUR OF A CAPTIVE-KING

The state of France was just as miserable, with land uncultivated and towns in ruins, for people were driven away from their homes, and many of their goods were taken by English soldiers. An old writer said that there was no woman who had not garments, furs, feather beds, and utensils from the spoils brought home by the army.

After the next great battle, at Poitiers, the Black Prince took the French king prisoner. The story is told that the captive was mounted on a fine white horse, while the prince rode beside him on a pony, and that he stood respectfully behind his chair at table. The king went home to try to collect the enormous sum asked for his ransom, and, being unsuccessful, came back, for he was an honourable man, to end his days in England.

Edward the Black Prince died before his father. He lies in Canterbury Cathedral, with his black armour hanging over his tomb. One good thing he did for England was to encourage the woollen trade. He found that sheep flourished well, and that there was plenty of water to be had, but that people sent away most of the wool to other countries to be made into cloth; and so he invited some clever workers to come over the Channel from Flanders— Philippa's country—to settle in the East of England and gather English people round them to learn to make woollen goods as well as they did. This was the beginning of the great woollen trade since carried on in Yorkshire.

WHEN WYCLIFFE GAVE ENGLAND HER FIRST ENGLISH BIBLE

We can gain a most interesting sight of these times from an old writer named Froissart. Chaucer, lived, too, at this time; we can see his tomb in the Abbey, and we read of him elsewhere in this book. Most amusing and delightful pictures of the people does Chaucer draw, and we learn much about the customs of the time from them.

TWO DRAMATIC SCENES OF LONG AGO

THE WARS OF THE ROSES BEGIN WITH THE PLUCKING OF THE ROSES IN TEMPLE GARDENS

MARGARET OF ANJOU, QUEEN OF HENRY THE SIXTH, FLEEING INTO A FOREST AFTER ONE OF THE
LAST WARS OF THE ROSES, WAS PROTECTED BY A ROBBER AND ALLOWED TO ESCAPE
From the painting by J. Doyle Penrose

Wycliffe lived also in this fourteenth century. He has been called the first Protestant. His title to fame lies in his having given to England the first English translation of the whole Bible. This he completed toward the end of his life. We see this " first complete Bible in the English language " among the manuscripts of the Bible in the British Museum, and notice that it belonged to Thomas, the youngest son of Edward the Third. He was the only one of their children, says Froissart, who was present when Philippa died. Holding the king's hand in hers, she told him her last wishes, asking that " when it should please God to call you hence you will not choose any other grave than mine, and will lie beside me in the Abbey of Westminster." So there they lie, near the Confessor's shrine, Philippa's tomb opposite that of Eleanor, her husband's opposite that of Henry the Third. It is thought that the faces of the sculptured effigies are portraits.

THE TROUBLED LAND IN WHICH A CHILD WAS KING

Round Edward's tomb were little brass statues of his twelve children, but only six are left. From them we can gather the ordinary costume of gentlemen of that day. They wore long outside cloaks, and tight-fitting jackets with belts beneath.

The son of the Black Prince, Richard the Second, followed his grandfather. He was only 10 when he came to the throne, and an old poem describing the times quotes the words with sorrow, " Woe to the land where the king is a child." The great nobles, especially the king's uncles, were always quarrelling, and the poor peasants who worked on the land could bear their poverty and hardships no longer, but at last broke into open revolt, marching to London, breaking into parks, burning and sacking houses. We have in an old poem a pitiful picture of the idleness of the nobles and clergy, and the sufferings and anger of the poor.

THE BOY KING WHO PLACED HIMSELF AT THE HEAD OF A MOB

Richard, when a boy of 15, showed great courage in meeting a mob of rioters, and placed himself at their head when the leader, Wat Tyler, was struck down. Springing to the front, he cried, " I will be your leader! " But the promises he gave were broken, and in the end the poor folk were none the better off.

Richard did a great deal toward making Ireland more peaceful, but the improvement did not last. He made his own people very angry by trying to govern without Parliament, and at last, after many troubles, he was forced to resign his crown, as Edward the Second had done before him. It was a sad ending to a brilliant beginning. When he was born his father was a powerful soldier and heir to the English throne, and the news of the boy's birth was received with shouts of joy from the soldiers assembled in the Great Hall of the Black Prince at Bordeaux. When Richard died he had lost all his inheritance and was in prison alone.

A distant cousin became king after him —Henry the Fourth. As Henry the Fourth had no real right to the throne, he was constantly in dread of losing it, and found it difficult to keep order in England and Wales. Scotland was afraid to do much against him because their Prince James was a prisoner in England. When this boy James was about 9 years old his father sent him to France to be educated, and to be out of harm's way. His ship fell into the hands of Henry the Fourth, who said, " His father should have sent him to me. I can teach him French as well as the King of France."

HOW THE BATTLE OF AGINCOURT WAS FOUGHT AND WON

All the years the lad spent in England he used for study. He was particularly fond of Chaucer, and later wrote very interesting poetry himself. Henry the Fourth little thought that James, before he returned to his own land and kingdom, would act as chief mourner at the funeral of the king's own son, Henry the Fifth.

Full of life and mischief was Prince Hal, as he was often called in his father's lifetime, and he got into many scrapes, one of which ended in his being sent to prison for striking a judge. As soon as he became king, his great ambition showed itself : he wanted to be king of France as well as of England. He had no real right to be so, but kings were little bothered by right, and Henry gathered a large force, crossed the Channel, and won a victory at Agincourt. One of the old Chronicles tells all about it :

Of the trumpets rending the air with tremendous clamour; of the fury of war and deadly spear-thrusts and eager sword-strokes; of the

THE MEN WHO FOUGHT AT AGINCOURT

THE SORT OF MEN WHO FOUGHT AT AGINCOURT IN 1415. A GROUP FROM A PAINTING
BY JOHN HASSALL

THE ENGLISH TROOPS AT AGINCOURT READY FOR BATTLE

wedges of archers and their piercing arrows ; of how that brilliant star of kings, the light and lamp of knighthood (Henry the Fifth), exposed that precious treasure of his person to all the chances of war.

After all this, and more, it was arranged that Henry should marry Katherine, the French princess, and that when the poor, mad old king, her father, died, his son should be passed over, and Henry was to reign with his daughter. France was in a state of chaos, with endless quarrellings among the nobles, or this arrangement could never have been made.

HOW A BABY KING WAS CROWNED WITH A BRACELET

But all Henry's plans came to a sudden end. He was a good soldier, was wise, and seemed born to do great things; but he died when only 35, leaving a little son of nine months as his heir. There is a picture of this child, crowned and wearing a long mantle embroidered with the Arms of England and France. He was crowned on his mother's lap, with her bracelet, it is said, as a crown for his baby head.

Henry (who had been a great friend of Dick Whittington) died near Paris, a long way from the coast, and the funeral procession went by Rouen at a slow pace in great state, Katherine, a widow at 21, following in deep grief.

Then, taking ship, the crossing was made, and the procession formed again, passing along in the same order till Westminster Abbey was reached at last. Henry's war-horses walked right up the nave of the Abbey, bearing the armour and helmet of the dead hero.

JOAN, THE BRAVE AND STAINLESS MAID OF FRANCE

Henry the Sixth had a long reign. First his uncles governed for him, and during this time the English lost what hold they had on France. This was chiefly through the efforts of one of the bravest girls who ever lived upon the Earth, the young French girl called Joan of Arc, who was bitterly sorry for the miseries of her country and longed to drive the English out. She dressed herself in shining armour and rode at the head of an army with a great white banner, cheering on the soldiers and making them brave like herself. At last she succeeded in leading them to an immortal victory, but she herself was betrayed to the English by her own countrymen, to their lasting disgrace, and was burned at the stake by the English, to their lasting shame and dishonour.

The influence of Joan of Arc led to the final failure of the English kings to retain rights of kingship in France, supposed rights which had caused wars to rage between Englishmen and Frenchmen during three hundred years.

Had the English nation any right to be engaged in the wars that are recalled to our minds by such victories as Crecy, Poitiers, and Agincourt ? If we think about this question carefully we shall see some very important facts, visible in much of the world's history, facts which show how man's wrong-doings do not prosper, but in the end are over-ruled for the world's good.

The world's good means the happiness, prosperity, and goodness of the many people who form nations. Too often the great enemies of mankind have been the ambition and self-seeking of the few who, having power, wished to obtain more.

THE COMING OF THE CONQUEROR AND THE TROUBLES THAT FOLLOWED

Those were the feelings that brought William the Conqueror to England, where nobody wanted him. But his coming made trouble for all his successors, into which he dragged their unfortunate people; for it was impossible that any king should rule, peaceably, Englishmen on one side of the Channel and Frenchmen on the other side. No one really succeeded in doing that. Such ambition led constantly to bitter failure, closely following what are called, in the usual way of reporting wars, " glorious victories."

Always the feelings of the people on either side of the Channel mastered and overthrew, sooner or later, the personal ambition of self-seeking kings. That overthrow did not come about through organised action by the people, but through the steady pressure of their unalterable wishes. William the Conqueror came with power, strength, and glory to master England. With him he brought the French language, and French ideas of religion, art, and manners. What was good in these changes was accepted, and proved a benefit to England ; but the rest was resisted and rejected ; and, indeed, in the end it was the invaders who were absorbed and conquered. They became Englishmen. They modified the English language usefully, but at last, after a couple of

THE STEEDS OF HENRY THE FIFTH PRANCE PROUDLY UP THE NAVE BEHIND HIS COFFIN

generations, they were speaking the new English, not French.

Then the invasion turned the other way across the Channel. Proud Englishmen tried to master parts of France, and sometimes all France. They won victories, but they never gained their ambitious aims. The general feeling of the French people rejected them. That feeling, as with English feeling against French ambition, was stronger in the end than any personal self-seeking of scheming kings. A strong undercurrent of commonsense leads people in the mass to bring to naught the gaudy ambitions of those who seek for glory rather than for the general good.

THE NOBLES WHO MADE WAR A FASHION AND A SPORT

But that is often brought about only after deep and wide-spread suffering. So it was with the wrongful invasion of France by English kings. Their foreign wars could only be carried on by the support of their powerful nobles. These nobles made war a fashion and a sport. When they were beaten out of France their habits unfitted them for peaceful life, and so at home they continued their habits by taking sides in the ridiculously trivial Wars of the Roses, to decide which of two families should provide English kings. They were called the Wars of the Roses because the Lancaster family wore a red rose and the York family a white one.

The punishment for this mistaken activity came in the form of extermination. Nearly all the great nobles who had begun the war were killed, either in battle or by execution, as first one side and then the other gained the upper hand, and this clearance of families delighting in war was in the end a good thing, for it had the effect of clearing the way for a wider public liberty, and the influence of finer types of active men. The country was prepared for a period of peaceful progress by the absence of those who had fomented trouble.

THE KING WHO FOUNDED THE FAMOUS SCHOOL AT ETON

This stupid conflict lasted thirty years and eleven pitched battles were fought. At last Henry the Sixth died miserably in the Tower. The poor man was often out of his mind after Edward the Fourth, of the House of York, first became king.

Henry was too weak to control others and to govern in such troubled times, but he was fond of scholars and teachers and books and pictures of all kinds. He founded the great school at Eton, and King's College at Cambridge. His wife Margaret of Anjou did her best to help him to keep the kingdom so that their son might have it after him; but the poor lad was killed, and the queen after being in prison for some time had to escape across the sea to France.

The wife of Edward the Fourth had many sorrows, too. At one time her husband had to leave England in great haste to avoid being taken by the Red Rose party, and she and her daughters had to leave the Tower, where they were living, and go to a safe refuge at Westminster. Here her eldest son was born.

When Edward the Fourth died, his son of 13 was the next king, but the boy was never crowned, being hurried off to the Tower by his Uncle Richard, who soon managed to get his little brother into his power, too. They both disappeared—it is believed that Richard had them suffocated in the Tower.

CAXTON, THE MAN WHO LEARNED TO MAKE A BOOK IN A FEW DAYS

He now became king himself as Richard the Third, and tried to please the people by calling Parliament together and setting many things in order. He also did a good deal for trade. But the people were so horrified at the death of the little princes that they turned against Richard, and in the battle of Bosworth Field, Richard was killed, and Henry Tudor, of the Lancaster family, was made king as Henry the Seventh.

He married the eldest daughter of Edward the Fourth, and so the two houses of York and Lancaster were united at last, the red and white roses mingling in one double flower, the Tudor rose.

During this time, close by the west door of the Abbey, there sat a man earning his living, busy from morning till night. He had learned while young, in Flanders, how to reproduce books in an easier and quicker way than the old way of copying by hand; in fact, how to begin and finish a book in a few days. He brought a printing press back to England, and, setting it up in Westminster, printed many notable books. The king and his nobles came to watch Caxton's work.

He was of more importance to the world than all the kings in this story, and we read of him elsewhere.

THE RUINED WALLS OF BRITAIN

THE RUIN OF CROWLAND ABBEY IN LINCOLNSHIRE

CAERPHILLY CASTLE, GLAMORGANSHIRE

DENBIGH CASTLE, DENBIGHSHIRE

THE WALLS OF CHEPSTOW CASTLE ON A CRAG ABOVE THE RIVER WYE

CARNARVON CASTLE, CARNARVONSHIRE

RHUDDLAN CASTLE, FLINTSHIRE

KIRKSTALL ABBEY, LEEDS

HASTINGS CASTLE

VALLE CRUCIS ABBEY, DENBIGHSHIRE

WHITBY ABBEY, YORKSHIRE

PEVENSEY CASTLE, SUSSEX

RIEVAULX ABBEY, YORKSHIRE

FURNESS ABBEY, LANCASHIRE

KENILWORTH CASTLE, WARWICKSHIRE

HARLECH CASTLE, MERIONETHSHIRE

CORFE CASTLE, DORSET   ROCHESTER CASTLE KEEP, KENT   SAINT MARY'S ABBEY, YORK

NETLEY ABBEY, HAMPSHIRE   GLASTONBURY ABBEY, SOMERSET

CARISBROOKE CASTLE, ISLE OF WIGHT   BOLTON CASTLE, YORKSHIRE

SAINT BOTOLPH'S PRIORY, COLCHESTER

HOWDEN ABBEY, YORKSHIRE

KNARESBOROUGH CASTLE

FOUNTAINS ABBEY, YORKSHIRE

BAYHAM ABBEY, TONBRIDGE

KIDWELLY CASTLE

CASTLE ACRE PRIORY, NORFOLK

SCARBOROUGH CASTLE

WEST MALLING ABBEY, KENT

WAVERLEY ABBEY, SURREY

BODIAM CASTLE, SUSSEX

BYLAND ABBEY, YORKSHIRE

CRICCIETH CASTLE

KIRKHAM ABBEY, YORKSHIRE

One Thousand Poems of All Times and All Countries

THE BALLAD OF AGINCOURT

Here, with quick and graphic touch, Michael Drayton describes the great battle of Agincourt, where, in 1415, the English army, led by King Henry the Fifth, won a great victory over the French after a closely contested battle. Drayton was a contemporary and a friend of Shakespeare.

FAIR stood the wind for France
　　When we our sails advance,
Nor now to prove our chance
　　Longer will tarry;
But putting to the main
At Caux, the mouth of Seine,
With all his martial train,
　　Landed King Harry.

AND taking many a fort,
　　Furnished in warlike sort,
Marcheth toward Agincourt
　　In happy hour;
Skirmishing day by day
With those that stopped his way
Where the French general lay
　　With all his power.

WHICH, in his height of pride,
　　King Henry to deride,
His ransom to provide,
　　Unto him sending;
Which he neglects the while,
As from a nation vile,
Yet, with an angry smile,
　　Their fall portending.

AND, turning to his men,
　　Quoth our brave Henry then:
Though they to one be ten,
　　Be not amazed;
Yet have we well begun—
Battles so bravely won
Have ever to the sun
　　By fame been raised.

AND for myself, quoth he,
　　This my full rest shall be:
England ne'er mourn for me,
　　Nor more esteem me:
Victor I will remain,
Or on this earth lie slain;
Never shall she sustain
　　Loss to redeem me.

POITIERS and Creçy tell,
　　When most their pride did swell,
Under our swords they fell:
　　No less our skill is
Than when our grandsire great,
Claiming the regal seat,
By many a warlike feat
　　Lopped the French lilies.

THE Duke of York so dread
　　The eager vaward led;
With the main Henry sped
　　Amongst his henchmen.
Exeter had the rear,
A braver man not there:
O Lord, how hot they were
　　On the false Frenchmen!

THEY now to fight are gone;
　　Armour on armour shone;
Drum now to drum did groan:
　　To hear was wonder;
That with the cries they make
The very earth did shake;
Trumpet to trumpet spake,
　　Thunder to thunder.

WELL it thine age became,
　　O noble Erpingham,
Which didst the signal aim

POEMS · SONGS · BALLADS · VERSES AND RHYMES WITH MUSIC

To our hid forces!
When, from a meadow by,
Like a storm suddenly,
The English archery
  Stuck the French horses.

With Spanish yew so strong,
Arrows a cloth-yard long,
That like to serpents stung,
  Piercing the weather;
None from his fellow starts,
But playing manly parts,
And, like true English hearts,
  Stuck close together.

When down their bows they threw,
And forth their bilboes drew,
And on the French they flew,
  Not one was tardy:
Arms were from shoulders sent;
Scalps to the teeth were rent;
Down the French peasants went;
  Our men were hardy.

This while our noble king,
His broadsword brandishing,
Down the French host did ding,
  As to o'erwhelm it;
And many a deep wound rent
His arms with blood besprent,
And many a cruel dent
  Bruisèd his helmet.

Gloster, that duke so good,
Next of the royal blood,
For famous England stood,
  With his brave brother
Clarence, in steel so bright,
Though but a maiden knight,
Yet in that furious fight
  Scarce such another.

Warwick in blood did wade;
Oxford the foe invade,
And cruel slaughter made,
  Still as they ran up.
Suffolk his axe did ply;
Beaumont and Willoughby
Bare them right doughtily,
  Ferrers and Fanhope.

Upon Saint Crispin's day
Fought was this noble fray,
Which fame did not delay
  To England to carry.
O, when shall Englishmen
With such acts fill a pen,
Or England breed again
  Such a King Harry?

TRUST IN GOD AND DO THE RIGHT

This plain, vigorous appeal to us all for faith and honest action, without any littleness, was written by Dr. Norman Macleod, a preacher much admired by Queen Victoria.

COURAGE, brother! Do not stumble.
  Though thy path is dark as night;
There's a star to guide the humble—
  Trust in God and do the right.

Let the road be long and dreary,
  And its ending out of sight;
Foot it bravely—strong or weary—
  Trust in God and do the right.

Perish policy and cunning,
  Perish all that fears the light;
Whether losing, whether winning,
  Trust in God and do the right.

Trust no party, church, or faction,
  Trust no leader in the fight;
But in every word and action
  Trust in God and do the right.

Trust no forms of guilty passion—
  Fiends can look like angels bright;
Trust no custom, school, or fashion—
  Trust in God and do the right.

Some will hate thee, some will love thee,
  Some will flatter, some will slight;
Cease from man and look above thee—
  Trust in God and do the right.

Firmest rule and safest guiding,
  Inward peace and inward light;
Star upon our path abiding—
  Trust in God and do the right.

ALADDIN

Imagination is Aladdin's Lamp, and castles in Spain are those built by the dreams of youth. Here James Russell Lowell, the famous American poet, tells us in a few lines that live for ever in our memory of the power of youthful fancy. To do this in two verses is true literary art.

WHEN I was a beggarly boy,
  And lived in a cellar damp,
I had not a friend nor a toy,
  But I had Aladdin's lamp;
When I could not sleep for cold
  I had fire enough in my brain,
And builded, with roofs of gold,
  My beautiful castles in Spain!

Since then I have toiled day and night,
  I have money and power good store;
But I'd give all my lamps of silver bright
  For the one that is mine no more;
Take, Fortune, whatever you choose—
  You gave, and may snatch again;
I have nothing 'twould pain me to lose,
  For I own no more castles in Spain!

PROSPICE

The facing of death by Robert Browning's strong man is one of the supremely noble possessions of our English tongue. It is the song of the hero who would die fighting. We think of our armies of heroes as we read this proud faith of a man looking out toward death. In this case it is the poet himself thinking of his wife, who has gone before, but Prospice, as the poem is called, meaning Look Forward, is the song of the brave spirit everywhere and always.

FEAR death?—to feel the fog in my
    throat,
  The mist in my face,
When the snows begin, and the blasts
    denote
  I am nearing the place,
The power of the night, the press of the
    storm,
  The post of the foe;
Where he stands, the Arch Fear in a visible
    form,
  Yet the strong man must go:
For the journey is done and the summit
    attained,
  And the barriers fall,
Though a battle's to fight ere the guerdon
    be gained,
  The reward of it all.
I was ever a fighter, so—one fight more,
  The best and the last!
I would hate that Death bandaged my
    eyes, and forbore,
  And bade me creep past.
No! let me taste the whole of it, fare like
    my peers
  The heroes of old,
Bear the brunt, in a minute pay glad life's
    arrears,
  Of pain, darkness, and cold.
For sudden the worst turns the best to the
    brave,
  The black minute's at end,
And the elements' rage, the fiend-voices
    that rave,
  Shall dwindle, shall blend,
Shall change, shall become, first a peace
    out of pain,
  Then a light, then thy breast,
O thou soul of my soul! I shall clasp thee
    again,
  And with God be the rest!

DUTY AND POWER

This is an epigram by Emerson. An epigram is a thought expressed in a very few lines, so pithily that we are not likely to forget it. It may be written either in prose or verse.

So nigh is grandeur to our dust,
  So near is God to man,
When duty whispers low, *Thou must,*
  The youth replies, *I can.*

INSCRIPTION ON A SILVER PLATE

These lines, written by Eugene Field for his little son, may be read with profit by many who are fathers of families. For, after all, the most necessary lessons in life and conduct require much repetition, and most of us will find much in poems for children that applies quite as well to grown-ups.

WHEN thou dost eat from off this plate
  I charge thee be thou temperate;
Unto thine elders at the board
Do thou sweet reverence accord;
And, though to dignity inclined,
Unto the serving-folk be kind;
Be ever mindful to the poor,
Nor turn them hungry from the door;
And unto God, for health and food
And all that in thy life is good,
Give thou thy heart in gratitude.

THE IVY GREEN

Charles Dickens we all know as one of the great English novelists, but we do not think of him as a poet. Though he wrote very little verse, this study of the creeping ivy shows he was not devoid of poetic gifts.

OH, a dainty plant is the ivy green,
  That creepeth o'er ruins old!
Of right choice food are his meals, I ween,
  In his cell so lone and cold.
The wall must be crumbled, the stone de-
    cayed,
  To pleasure his dainty whim;
And the mouldering dust that years have
    made
  Is a merry meal for him.
    Creeping where no life is seen,
    A rare old plant is the ivy green

Fast he stealeth on, though he wears no
    wings,
  And a staunch old heart has he.
How closely he twineth, how tight he
    clings,
  To his friend, the huge oak tree!
And slily he traileth along the ground,
  And his leaves he gently waves,
As he joyously hugs and crawleth around
  The rich mould of dead men's graves.
    Creeping where grim death has been,
    A rare old plant is the ivy green.

Whole ages have fled, and their works
    decayed,
  And nations have scattered been;
But the stout old ivy shall never fade
  From its hale and hearty green.
The brave old plant in its lonely days
  Shall fatten upon the past,
For the stateliest building man can raise
  Is the ivy's food at last.
    Creeping on where time has been,
    A rare old plant is the ivy green.

BOADICEA

This vigorous and stirring poem was written by William Cowper, a great English poet who died in the year 1800. It is a song of praise of Boadicea, the patriot queen who roused the people of England in revolt against their Roman oppressors, at first with victory, but later to suffer defeat from the veteran soldiers of Rome. Boadicea died A.D. 62.

When the British warrior queen,
    Bleeding from the Roman rods,
Sought, with an indignant mien,
    Counsel of her country's gods,

Sage beneath the spreading oak
    Sat the Druid, hoary chief;
Every burning word he spoke
    Full of rage and full of grief.

Princess! if our aged eyes
    Weep upon thy matchless wrongs
'Tis because resentment ties
    All the terrors of our tongues.

Rome shall perish—write that word
    In the blood that she has spilt;
Perish, hopeless as abhorred,
    Deep in ruin as in guilt.

Rome, for empire far renowned,
    Tramples on a thousand States;
Soon her pride shall kiss the ground—
    Hark! the Gaul is at her gates!

Other Romans shall arise,
    Heedless of a soldier's name;
Sounds, not arms, shall win the prize,
    Harmony the path to fame.

Then the progeny that springs
    From the forests of our land,
Armed with thunder, clad with wings,
    Shall a wider world command.

Regions Caesar never knew
    Thy posterity shall sway;
Where his eagles never flew,
    None invincible as they.

Such the bard's prophetic words
    Pregnant with celestial fire,
Bending as he swept the chords
    Of his sweet but awful lyre.

She, with all a monarch's pride,
    Felt them in her bosom glow;
Rushed to battle, fought, and died;
    Dying, hurled them at the foe.

Ruffians, pitiless as proud,
    Heaven awards the vengeance due;
Empire is on us bestowed,
    Shame and ruin wait for you.

TO THE CUCKOO

One of the most beautiful poems ever written about the sweet-voiced bird that comes with each returning spring was composed by a young Scottish student named Michael Bruce, though it has sometimes been claimed for another poet. Bruce died in 1767 at the age of 21.

Hail, beauteous stranger of the wood!
    Attendant on the spring!
Now Heaven repairs thy rural seat,
    And woods thy welcome sing.

Soon as the daisy decks the green
    Thy certain voice we hear;
Hast thou a star to guide thy path
    Or mark the rolling year?

Delightful visitant, with thee
    I hail the time of flowers,
When heaven is filled with music sweet
    Of birds among the bowers.

The schoolboy, wandering in the wood
    To pull the flowers so gay,
Starts, thy curious voice to hear,
    And imitates thy lay.

Soon as the pea puts on the bloom
    Thou fliest thy vocal vale,
An annual guest in other lands,
    Another spring to hail.

Sweet bird! thy bower is ever green,
    Thy sky is ever clear;
Thou hast no sorrow in thy song,
    No winter in thy year!

O could I fly I'd fly with thee!
    We'd make, with social wing,
Our annual visit o'er the globe,
    Companions of the spring.

THE ARROW AND THE SONG

In these simple verses by Henry W. Longfellow the poet's object is to illustrate a great truth. Nothing that we do, think, or say, though at the time we may not guess the consequence, is in vain. Just as the arrow shot in the air will somewhere fall to earth, so the deeds we do and the thoughts we express will make their mark, unseen by us.

I shot an arrow into the air,
    It fell to earth, I knew not where;
For, so swiftly it flew, the sight
Could not follow it in its flight.

I breathed a song into the air,
It fell to earth, I knew not where;
For who has sight so keen and strong
That it can follow the flight of song?

Long, long afterward, in an oak
I found the arrow, still unbroke;
And the song, from beginning to end,
I found again in the heart of a friend.

I HAD A LITTLE NUT-TREE

I had a lit-tle nut-tree, no-thing would it bear

But a sil-ver nut-meg and a gol-den pear. The

King of Spain's daugh-ter came to vis-it me, And

all for the sake of my lit-tle nut-tree.

THOMAS A TATTAMUS took two T's
To tie two tups to two tall trees,
To frighten the terrible Thomas à
Tattamus!
Tell me how many T's there are in all
that.

MOLLY my sister and I fell out,
And what do you think it was
all about?
She loved coffee and I loved tea,
And that was the reason we couldn't
agree.

LITTLE ROBIN REDBREAST sat upon a
tree;
Up went pussy-cat, and down went he,
Down came pussy-cat, and away Robin
ran;
Says little Robin Redbreast: "Catch
me if you can."

OH, my pretty cock! Oh, my hand-
some cock!
I pray you do not crow before day,
And your comb shall be made of the
very beaten gold,
And your wings of the silver so grey.

WASH me and comb me,
And lay me down softly
And lay me on a bank to dry,
That I may look pretty
When somebody comes by.

MR. EAST gave a feast;
Mr. North laid the cloth:
Mr. West did his best;
Mr. South burnt his mouth
With eating a cold potato.

OF all the gay birds that e'er I did see
The owl is the fairest by far to me;
For all day long he sits on a tree,
And when the night comes away flies
he.

THE white dove sat on the castle
wall;
I bent my bow, and made her fall;
I picked her up, feathers and all,
And I rode away from the castle wall.

Hick-a-more, Hack-a-more,
    On the king's kitchen door;
All the king's horses
And all the king's men
Couldn't drive Hick-a-more, Hack-a-
    more,
Off the king's kitchen door!

Poor old Robinson Crusoe!
    Poor old Robinson Crusoe!
They made him a coat
Of an old nanny goat,
I wonder how they could do so!
    With a ring a ting tang,
    And a ring a ting tang,
Poor old Robinson Crusoe!

I'll tell you a story
    About Jack a Nory,
And now my story's begun:

We are all in the dumps,
    For diamonds are trumps;
The kittens are gone to St. Paul's!
The babies are bit,
The moon's in a fit,
    And the houses are built without
        walls.

If the evening's red and the morning's
        grey
It is the sign of a bonnie day.
If the evening's grey and the morn-
    ing's red
The lamb and the ewe will go wet to
    bed.

I'll tell you another
    About Jack and his brother,
And now my story's done.

Solomon Grundy,
    Born on a Monday,
Christened on Tuesday,
Married on Wednesday,
Took ill on Thursday,
Worse on Friday,
Died on Saturday,
Buried on Sunday,
This is the end of
Solomon Grundy.

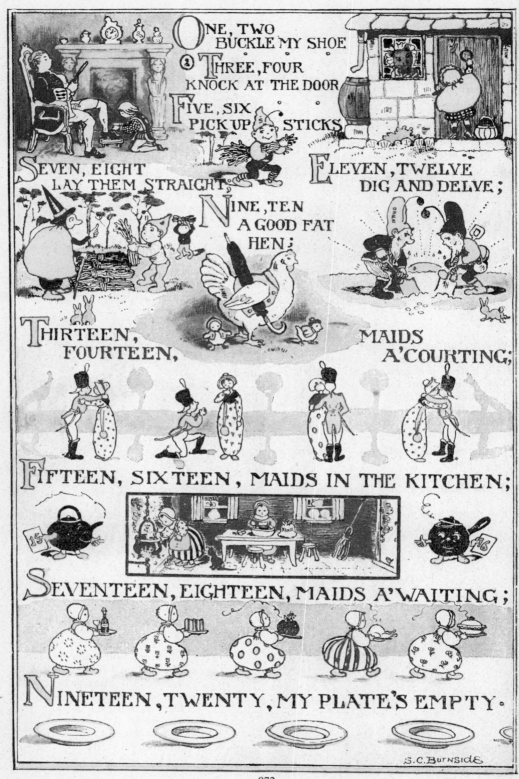

One, Two
Buckle My Shoe
Three, Four
Knock at the Door
Five, Six
Pick up Sticks

Seven, Eight
Lay them Straight;
Nine, Ten
A Good Fat
Hen;
Eleven, Twelve
Dig and Delve;

Thirteen, Fourteen, Maids A'Courting;

Fifteen, Sixteen, Maids in the Kitchen;

Seventeen, Eighteen, Maids A'Waiting;

Nineteen, Twenty, My Plate's Empty.

S. C. Burnside

972

The Story of Where Power Comes From, What It Does, & How It Works

Sir J. J. Thomson experimenting with the aid of the Ruhmkorff coil

WHAT A MAGNET CAN DO

EVERYWHERE in the big world of electricity where there is mechanical power at work there is sure to be an electric magnet.

We have seen how a coil of wire (wound round a pencil, for instance) becomes endowed with magnetic power when an electric current is passed through it. There is a famous law known as Ampère's Rule that tells us which is the north-seeking pole and which the south in such a magnet. The rule says that if you try to imagine yourself swimming with the current along the wire, the north pole will always be on your left.

Thus, there is something quite definite in what happens when a current travels along a spiral path, and something equally definite takes place if a bar of iron is placed inside the spiral or coil. The iron itself becomes a magnet, but of enormously greater power than that of the coil itself.

A simple electric magnet is very easy to make, and with it many interesting experiments can be carried out. If you magnetise a knitting-needle or a bar of steel by stroking it from end to end a few times with an electric magnet, this will convert the steel into a permanent magnet;

while the electric magnet itself, the moment you disconnect it from the battery, will lose its magnetism! Here is an interesting example of a temporary power or force creating a lasting one!

The power of an electric magnet can be very great. It is actually largest in proportion to the weight of the magnet when the magnet is very small. An electric magnet weighing only a few grains has been made to lift 2500 times its own weight. The great lifting magnets used in factories are made as large as five feet in diameter, and may weigh three or four tons. Their lifting power is only four or five times their weight, so that a four-ton magnet could not pick up more than about twenty tons. Such magnets are much used for loading and unloading pig-iron, steel ingots, girders, iron plates, and scrap as seen in the pictures on pages 359 and 361.

These huge magnets of industry are known as the iron-clad type, and are usually circular. The magnet is raised or lowered by a winder or a crane; it is dropped down on to a steel ingot, the current is switched on, and the magnet is raised. The ingot clings to it by magnetic attraction just as long as the current

ELECTRICITY · WIRELESS · OIL · GAS · MOTORS · ENGINES · SHIPS

flows through the coil. The magnet, with its load, is then gently slung over to a truck and lowered, and the current is cut off. The magnetic force vanishes, and the ingot has been gently transferred to its new position.

So tenaciously does a magnet hold its object that ingenious magnetic devices have been made to grip and hold pieces of crude metal which are being shaped by machinery. High-speed portable hammering machines are made, and other magnetic machines for chiselling and riveting. These are important labour-saving devices which work with great rapidity. There are a hundred other uses to which this power is put in modern factories.

HOW THE MAGNET HELPS THE WORK OF THE DOCTOR

Magnets have a special use in extracting splinters or bits of steel or iron from the body, and particularly from the eye, as shown on page 853. The attractive power of the magnet will draw to itself pieces of metal so small that their removal in any other way would be almost impossible.

One great advantage the electric magnet possesses is its instantaneous response to an electric current. When the current is switched on, the magnetism is produced at once, and in a well-constructed magnet its power ceases the instant the current is cut off. There is, however, such a thing as *residual magnetism*—a lagging behind of the power, known to electricians as hysteresis—and this effect is overcome by using a number of soft iron wires or thin iron strips, insulated one from the other, instead of one solid piece. With a magnet made in this way the magnetic power shows no sign of lagging behind, even for the thousandth part of a second, after the current has been cut off. As a result magnetic instruments and machinery can be worked at marvellously high speeds.

WHAT HAPPENS WHEN WE PRESS THE BUTTON OF AN ELECTRIC BELL

Perhaps the best-known device depending on an electric magnet is the ordinary electric bell. So accustomed are we to ring a bell by pressing a button that not one person in a thousand would ever bother his head to think how it is done.

Every electric bell, and every electric indicator, depends on an electric magnet; the magnet provides the power which moves the hammer which strikes the gong. If you follow the wires from the button,

you will find that they lead to the electric bell and a battery. The bell-push is nothing more than a simple switch, or contact-maker. On pressing the button a piece of spring metal is pressed against another piece of metal, so that a complete circuit is established, and the current from the battery is then enabled to flow through the coils of a small horseshoe electric magnet. Fixed to a small brass pillar is a piece of spring metal to which is fitted a small iron plate, which faces the poles of the magnet; in another pillar is a metal screw which just touches the back of this spring *armature*. The wires are joined up as shown in the picture on page 977 and by following the arrows it can be seen that the current travels from the carbon rod in the battery to the coils of the magnet, then to the armature, to the contact pillar and to the push, and, through the push, back to the zinc rod of the battery.

As soon as the magnet is energised it attracts the armature to it, and this motion makes the hammer strike the gong. But, in so doing, the armature will be drawn away from the contact-pin, and this means that the current is broken.

THE ELECTRIC MASTER CLOCK THAT KEEPS ALL THE OTHERS IN ORDER

When this happens the magnetism disappears; consequently there is nothing now to draw the armature, which springs back. It then again completes the circuit, and the magnet again pulls the armature toward it; so that again the circuit is broken. The same thing, in fact, happens over and over again, with the result that we have a rapid succession of taps on the gong, and this continues just as long as the button is pressed.

Something akin to the bell is the type of electric clock which is made to work by signals from a master clock. One type of master clock used is made to give a signal, really to make a contact effective, once or twice each minute. An electric current is then caused to flow through the coils of a small magnet fitted in each electric clock which it controls. The power of this magnet is used to work a little ratchet wheel, and to jerk it forward one tooth at a time. The wheel is geared in such a way that it actuates the hands of the clock, and at each contact it moves the hands through a space on the dial equal to half a minute, or a minute, as the

TELLING THE TIME IN A HUNDRED ROOMS

By the use of an electric current a hundred clocks in a hundred rooms can be so controlled, or synchronised, by a single pendulum, that all show exactly the same time. The diagram shows the synchronome system. The master clock consists only of a pendulum (A) which pulls round the wheel (B) once every half minute, causing the vane (C) to withdraw the catch (D) and allow the gravity lever (E) to fall. The roller (F) runs down the bracket (G) fixed on the pendulum-rod, pushes the pendulum aside, and forces the upright arm of the gravity lever to touch the point of the screw in the end of the armature (H). Thus the circuit of the coil electric magnet (J) is closed, and the current from the battery of cells (K) flows through the dials all over the building. The clock faces have no pendulums behind them ; they are known as impulse dials, and consist, as shown in the right-hand corner, of a large wheel actuated by a magnet to work other wheels. The pointers on these dials advance half a minute while the magnet (J) attracts the armature (H) and throws the lever (E) up on to its catch again. The magnet (L) behind the dial receives the impulses which attract the armature (M), moving the lever (N) so that the click (O) picks up another tooth of the wheel (P). In this way the spring (Q) propels the wheel, and the minute-hand attached to it, one half-minute. Thus every dial is affected by the master clock.

case may be. While the master clock is thus an ordinary timepiece, the hands of the electric clocks that it controls merely move forward in jerks at fixed intervals; anyone can see this by watching an electric clock for a minute or two. One master clock can control any number of electric clocks, which all keep exact time

A marvellously sensitive measuring instrument is used to make measurements of the muscular contractions of the heart, of which it makes, with the help of photography, an actual chart somewhat resembling that of a recording barometer. Between the poles of a very powerful electric magnet is stretched a delicate shaving

THE GREAT ELECTRIC MAGNET THAT TRAVELS ABOUT WITH ITS LITTLE HOUSE
This photograph is of an electric magnet made by Messrs. E. G. Appleby and Company

with it. A clock of this type is shown on page 975. The type of electric clock now used so largely in our homes is driven by a tiny motor supplied with power from the electric mains, but the driving force is still magnetic, though produced by the electric currents flowing through the rotating armature and field magnets.

of quartz, about a thousandth part of an inch thick, yet sufficient to bar the way to a tiny beam of light. The quartz is coated with a thin film of silver to make it a conductor. The feeble current caused by the heart-beats passes through the quartz which, as we have seen, makes it behave like a magnet. It is, of course, infinitely

WHAT MAKES THE ELECTRIC BELL RING

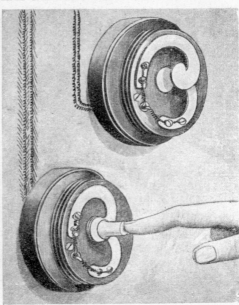

These pictures show us what happens when we ring an electric bell, such as we find at the front doors of most houses in these days. The pressing of the button, as seen here, brings two pieces of metal in contact and so, by setting up what we call a circuit, allows the current to flow through the wires shown in the right-hand picture.

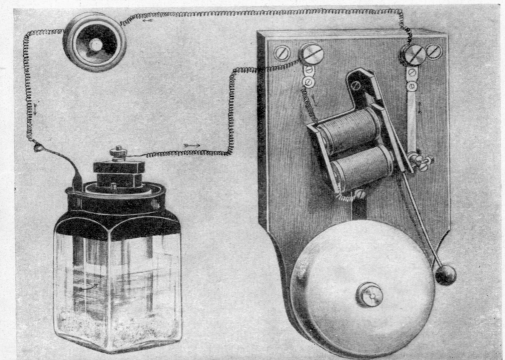

The current is generated in the cell on the left, which may be anywhere in the house. When the button is pressed the current flows from the cell, magnetises the two-coil magnet on the board, and so draws toward it the strip of soft iron carrying the hammer, which thus strikes the bell. This movement breaks the circuit at the contact between the spring and adjusting screw, causing the electro-magnet to release the hammer which immediately flies back and so completes the circuit again. This happens repeatedly until the button is released.

feeble, but the power of the electric magnet is so great that it repels the quartz, which moves to one side—about a thousandth part of an inch or so—and allows the beam of light to reach a moving band of photographic film. The heart-beats are thus recorded by photography, and the record reveals the condition of the patient.

THE SWITCH THAT TURNS ON HUNDREDS OF HORSE-POWER

All kinds of delicate instruments for measuring very small currents are based on the action of a magnet, which repels or deflects a fine wire or wire coil when a feeble current passes through it. Sometimes a little coil is suspended between the poles of a permanent horse-shoe magnet, and a tiny mirror is fixed to some part of the coil in such a way as to reflect a spot of light on to a scale. The smallest movement of the coil is then shown, greatly magnified, by the moving of the spot of light along the scale. Such an instrument is called a mirror galvanometer.

An important use of the magnet is seen in the " relay." Quite a small electric magnet, excited by a very feeble current, can be made to switch on a far heavier current. A man can press an ordinary electric bell-push on a huge machine; the press will make contact in a circuit which flows through the coils of quite a small magnet, but this magnet attracts a lever which throws in a heavy switch turning on hundreds of horse-power. When a telegraph current arrives at some distant office it is far too feeble to operate the Morse sounder or tape machine; but it can easily excite a small relay, the armature of which throws in the heavier current to operate the telegraph instrument.

HOW SPARKS ARE MADE TO FLY THROUGH THE AIR

A magnet plunged into a coil of wire will cause a current to flow along the wire. If two coils are placed side by side, whenever a current is sent through one of them an *induced* current will be set up in the other. If both coils are wound over a bar of soft iron, the induced current can be quite powerful. A typical example is what we call the Ruhmkorff coil, for many years used in wireless telegraphy. Little Ruhmkorff (or *induction*) coils are quite inexpensive, and many fascinating experiments can be performed with them.

A central magnetic " core " is made up of pieces of soft iron wire, and two layers of thick copper wire are wound round it; a simple electromagnet. Over the thick coil, called the primary, is wound a coil of very fine wire, often running into many miles; this is called the secondary. An electric current is passed through the primary, and interrupted several times a second by means of an arrangement very similar to that we have already seen in the electric bell, and at every interruption an induced current is set up in the outer secondary coil, of such high voltage that, if two wires leading from the ends are brought near together, intense sparks will fly across the gap, the current breaking down the resistance of the air that is between them.

The voltage of the secondary current depends on how many times the number of turns of wire in the secondary exceeds the number of turns in the primary. Thus, if twenty turns were wound round the magnetic core of soft iron, and twenty thousand turns round this in the form of the secondary coil, whatever *volts* were passed through the primary would be magnified a thousand times in the secondary. A boy with a four-volt battery could produce a current of four thousand volts with quite a small and cheap coil.

THE BEAUTIFUL EFFECTS POSSIBLE FROM AN ELECTRIC CURRENT

Large coils and transformers are used for producing X-rays which give a million volts, making a terrific spark that will jump across twenty inches of air. The spark from a small toy coil is of such intense heat that if a piece of thin paper be held between the wires carrying the sparks it will be perforated by numbers of tiny holes, which are burned through it. Beautiful effects can be obtained by passing a current from a coil through a glass tube filled with such a gas as nitrogen or helium in a rarefied condition.

Today the *transformer* is more important than the induction coil. Enormous numbers of transformers, made by winding two coils of wire of different numbers of turns over a soft iron " core " are now used to transform *down* the high voltages of alternating current generators to sufficiently *low* voltages for use in motors, electric lamps, and so on.

The magnetism obtained by the passage of an electric current round a soft iron core gives us power when and where we want it and at the required voltage.

Imperishable Thoughts of Men Enshrined in the Books of the World

Shakespeare reading one of his plays to Queen Elizabeth

SHAKESPEARE'S POEMS

PERHAPS it is not really wonderful that we do not know more about Shakespeare and his writings.

We must remember how differently actors and playwrights were regarded then. Today they are honoured members of the community; in Elizabeth's reign such men as Shakespeare were described as " low, common fellows."

His plays were written originally to be read by the actors, and not for publication in book form. There was no public eager to know all that could be found out about the most popular playwright of the day. No attempt was made to publish a collected edition of the poet's works till he had been dead seven years; and no full and separate Life of him was written till he had been dead 127 years.

All we know of him is derived either from brief official records; or from chance references to him in books or letters of his period; or by inference from his writings where they seem to suggest personal information.

The last source of knowledge is very important, for we know, broadly, in what part of his life Shakespeare wrote nearly all his plays. Though he is the least personal of men, and rarely seems to think

of himself, the tone of his mind at different stages in his life is reflected in his choice and treatment of his subjects; and so we can follow with confidence some changes, otherwise unrecorded, in Shakespeare's life. His plays throw light on the moods that passed over his spirit, though they do not disclose the details of his career.

As this is so, Shakespeare's plays should always be read with an understanding of when they were written, in relation to his growth in skill, character, and fortune. For not only did he choose widely different subjects for his purposes as a playwright, but his style of writing changed as his outlook on humanity altered with the years, and the high spirits of youth sank into the gravity of middle age, which changed again into the serenity of life's eventide.

Here, then, we must trace the succession of his plays, as, like the course of a stream, it reflects the scenery which determines its own changeful character.

Shakespeare's known writings were written in about twenty years. Eight of these years were before 1600, and twelve were after that date. He certainly wrote freely some years before 1592, and possibly after 1612, but we do not know

ROMANCE · HISTORIES · DRAMAS · ESSAYS · WORLD CLASSICS

clearly what his writings were at either of those periods. Most likely they were corrections and additions to other men's plays, suggested by his knowledge of the actor's art, for he had been five or six years in London when he wrote his first full play, Love's Labour's Lost. The four or five years before his death in 1616 were no doubt spent chiefly in his native town of Stratford-on-Avon, and as far as we know his writing was limited to helping younger writers like John Fletcher, who were his disciples in the dramatic art. Thus, the play Henry the Eighth is almost universally regarded as being written by Fletcher under Shakespeare's supervision, with some scenes by the older poet.

Between the writing of Love's Labour's Lost and of the play Henry the Eighth four periods can be clearly traced in Shakespeare, though they overlap to some extent. First there comes a set of plays that show light-hearted exuberant youth, which expresses itself in the forms that were popular at the moment. The most characteristic piece is Love's Labour's Lost, a fanciful exercise that changes frequently from rhyme to prose and then to blank verse, and is full of the trickery of playing a kind of game with words.

HOW SHAKESPEARE WITH HIS WONDERFUL POWER PUTS PICTURES INTO VERSE

No one could anticipate from such a play the greatness that was in Shakespeare. It is not till we reach the closing verses descriptive of winter that we recognise the wonderful pictorial power of the poet, and his gift of simple closely-knit expression.

When icicles hang by the wall,
    And Dick the shepherd blows his nail,
And Tom bears logs into the hall,
    And milk comes frozen home in pail,
When blood is nipp'd and way be foul,
Then nightly sings the staring owl:
Tu-whit-tu-who—a merry note,
While greasy Joan doth keel the pot.

When all aloud the wind doth blow,
    And coughing drowns the parson's saw,
And birds sit brooding in the snow,
    And Marian's nose looks red and raw,
When roasted crab hiss in the bowl,
Then nightly sings the staring owl:
Tu-whit,tu-who—a merry note,
While greasy Joan doth keel the pot.

A perfect miniature of winter in England at that time. Saw, of course, means saying, keel means skim, and crab means crab-apple.

Other plays of the time were The Comedy of Errors, in which the interest lies in the plot, and Two Gentlemen of Verona, which includes the first of the exquisite songs that adorn so many of Shakespeare's plays.

Who is Silvia? what is she?
    That all our swains commend her?
Holy, fair, and wise is she;
    The heaven such grace did lend her,
That she might admired be.

Is she kind as she is fair?
    For beauty lives with kindness:
Love doth to her eyes repair,
    To help him of his blindness;
And, being helped, inhabits there.

Then to Silvia let us sing,
    That Silvia is excelling;
She excels each mortal thing
    Upon the dull earth dwelling;
To her let us garlands bring.

PLAYS THAT REVEALED THE SWEETNESS OF SHAKESPEARE'S POETRY

The poetry that was inherent in Shakespeare from the first shows itself in sentiment mellifluously expressed in these early plays, written before he had attained his full strength of intellect. A tender example is this speech of Julia in the Two Gentlemen of Verona, when going on a pilgrimage of love.

The current that with gentle murmur glides,
Thou knowest, being stopped, impatiently
    doth rage;
But when his fair course is not hindered,
He makes sweet music with the enamelled
    stones,
Giving a gentle kiss to every sedge
He overtaketh in his pilgrimage;
And so by many winding nooks he strays
With willing sport, to the wild ocean.
Then let me go and hinder not my course:
I'll be as patient as a gentle stream
And make a pastime of each weary step,
Till the last step hath brought me to my love;
And there I'll rest, as after much turmoil
A blessed soul doth in Elysium.

THE PROUD NOTE OF PATRIOTISM THAT HAS SOUNDED THROUGH THE AGES

This period of youthful sweetness with growing strength covered the time when Shakespeare was writing his early published poems and probably some of his sonnets; and it included also his early historical plays and his first passionate tragedy, Romeo and Juliet.

In his early historical plays he followed the lead of Christopher Marlowe, who had made blank verse seem the natural metre for heroic and tragic scenes. Probably he worked with Marlowe; certainly he was greatly impressed by Marlowe's full-toned, high-sounding strain, and closely

SIR EDWARD POYNTER'S PICTURE OF HELENA AND HERMIA IN THE GARDEN—FROM A
MIDSUMMER NIGHT'S DREAM

imitated it, especially in Richard the Third, the most melodramatic of his plays.

For the historical foundation of his plays Shakespeare had few books on which he could rely. Indeed, almost his only source was Holinshed's Chronicle, but he so used it that he made his characters live vividly before the eyes of all who saw or read his acted histories, and millions have found a thrilling interest in our country's story through his presentation of it.

His love of England and his pride in her greatness struck a chord of patriotism that has resounded through the ages. First in point of time, though not perhaps in writing, is the proud boast with which the play of King John closes.

This England never did, nor never shall,
Lie at the proud foot of a conqueror,
But when it first did help to wound itself.
Come the three corners of the world in arms,
And we shall shock them. Nought shall make
    us rue,
If England to itself do rest but true.

And never, surely, was delight in all that England is to her children expressed with such passionate tenderness as in the speech given to John of Gaunt in King Richard the Second:

This royal throne of kings, this sceptred isle,
This earth of majesty, this seat of Mars,
This other Eden, demi-paradise,
This fortress built by Nature for herself
Against infection and the hand of war,
This happy breed of men, this little world,
This precious stone set in the silver sea,

Which serves it in the office of a wall,
Or as a moat defensive to a house,
Against the envy of less happier lands,
This blessed plot, this earth, this realm, this England,
This land of such dear souls, this dear, dear land,
Dear for her reputation through the world!

The same proud note was struck again as firmly in the six-years-later play of Henry the Fifth, when Shakespeare had passed out of the period of enthusiastic youth.

The weaknesses of Shakespeare's earliest period are perhaps most concentrated in his first tragedy, the passionate love-story of Romeo and Juliet, but its intensity of feeling has caused it to keep its place on the stage, though, when calmly examined on its merits as a transcript from real life, it has little to recommend it, unless it is used as a warning against the whirlwind feeling of youth. From that stage he passed, about the age of 30, into a second period when his genius developed on the lines of most delightful comedy, graceful poetical fancy, and graver and deeper reading of human character.

The plays of the period that show these qualities most clearly are The Merchant of Venice, Midsummer Night's Dream, and As You Like It, while to the same period belong the historical plays, Henry the Fourth, with its richly humorous relief in the character of Falstaff, and Henry the Fifth, where English nationalism reaches its greatest intensity.

THE LAUGHTER THAT PLAYS ROUND A FANCIFUL USE OF WORDS

Falstaff is a reminder that nowhere in English literature is there such an equal commingling of humour and seriousness as in Shakespeare, and the humour grew with the seriousness. In his earlier plays the poet was smart and witty, but his laughter was that which plays round a fanciful use of words. As his view of life became graver the humour deepened, and displayed with a rich humanity the strange incongruities of character. At no moment is humour far away, though often it raises the laughter which merges into a sigh.

In The Merchant of Venice Shakespeare's skill as a dramatist and student of human character reached its full balance. It is a mixture of comedy and tragedy. An undertone of sadness is heard from first to last. It begins with the merchant's misfortunes and is heard throughout the scorning of the Jew Shylock. That tone was never again to leave Shakespeare's

work entirely when he left the world of pure fancy and dealt with mortal things.

In The Merchant of Venice the richness of the poet's vein of pure poetry, already seen in his sonnets, was brought into his plays in fuller measure. He has begun to decorate his scenes with passages of sheer beauty, as in Lorenzo's enjoyment of the night, with music stealing in.

How sweet the moonlight sleeps upon this bank!
Here will we sit, and let the sounds of music
Creep in our ears; soft stillness and the night
Become the touches of sweet harmony.
Sit, Jessica; look, how the floor of heaven
Is thick inlaid with patines of bright gold;
There's not the smallest orb which thou beholdest
But in his motion like an angel sings,
Still quiring to the young-eyed cherubins;
Such harmony is in immortal souls;
But, whilst this muddy vesture of decay
Doth grossly close it in, we cannot hear it.

SHAKESPEARE'S STUDY OF CHARACTER AND HIS SPLENDID SPEECH ON MERCY

Now, too, the poet's study of human character is more subtle and complete, as in his delineation of the effects of persecution on the Jewish people, seen in Shylock; and at the same time his thought, when he concentrates on some definite subject, is more closely knit and its expression perfected, as in the fine discourse on Mercy.

The quality of mercy is not strained;
It droppeth as the gentle rain from heaven
Upon the place beneath; it is twice blessed;
It blesseth him that gives and him that takes:
'Tis mightiest in the mightiest; it becomes
The throned monarch better than his crown;
His sceptre shows the force of temporal power,
The attribute to awe and majesty,
Wherein doth sit the dread and fear of kings;
But mercy is above this sceptred sway,
It is enthroned in the heart of kings,
It is an attribute to God Himself;
And earthly power doth then show likest God's
When mercy seasons justice. Therefore, Jew,
Though justice be thy plea, consider this,
That in the course of justice none of us
Should see salvation: we do pray for mercy,
And that same prayer should teach us all to render
The deeds of mercy.

THE LULLABY THE FAIRIES SANG WHILE THEY WATCHED OVER TITANIA

A most delightful side of Shakespeare's genius was his power of surrendering himself to the sweetness of fancy as it visits nearly all young minds. That this happy playfulness was native to the man is shown by the fact that not only did he indulge it in his Midsummer Night's Dream when his mind was strengthening into full manhood, but he again gave it free play in The

AND THEN THE WHINING SCHOOLBOY, WITH HIS SATCHEL AND SHINING MORNING FACE, CREEPING
LIKE SNAIL UNWILLINGLY TO SCHOOL—FROM THE PICTURE BY HUGH THOMSON

Tempest, written in his maturer years. By the gladsome play of his dainty fancy Shakespeare is the poet of childhood as much as he is the poet of manhood and womanhood in all their moods.

Hear the lullaby of the fairies as Titania, their queen, sleeps while they watch.

You spotted snakes, with double tongue,
  Thorny hedgehogs, be not seen;
Newts and blindworms, do no wrong;
  Come not near our fairy queen.
Weaving spiders, come not here;
Hence, you long-legged spinners, hence!
Beetles black, approach not near;
Worm nor snail do no offence.
  Philomel, with melody,
  Sing in our sweet lullaby;
Lulla, lulla, lullaby; lulla, lulla, lullaby:
  Never harm,
  Nor spell, nor charm,
  Come our lovely lady nigh;
  So, good-night, with lullaby.

THE MOST CHARMING COMEDY THAT SHAKESPEARE WROTE

It is the very voice of Fairyland; and Shakespeare can recapture it at will. Of course we think differently of these lowly creatures now, some of them doing very little harm and much good, and all being interesting, but they were once feared, and the feeling remains here and there as an inheritance without the old belief that fairies might, if they would, guard us against them as they guarded Titania.

The open-air comedy of As You Like It remains the most charming, without the alloy of pain, that Shakespeare ever wrote. Its prevailing tone is heard in the song :

Under the greenwood tree,
Who loves to lie with me,
And tune his merry note
Unto the sweet bird's throat,
Come hither, come hither, come hither;
  Here shall he see,
  No enemy
But winter and rough weather.

Who doth ambition shun,
And loves to live i' the sun,
Seeking the food he eats,
And pleased with what he gets,
Come hither, come hither, come hither:
  Here shall he see
  No enemy
But winter and rough weather.

THE POET AND PHILOSOPHER WHO UNDERSTOOD THE INMOST SOUL OF MAN

Yet still, even here, the stress of life is not altogether excluded while the woodland company is singing " The life is most jolly." The mention of the weather introduces that most poignant strain that tells how the poet's spirit had been sobered and chastened by personal cares of which we know but little.

Blow, blow, thou winter wind,
Thou art not so unkind
  As man's ingratitude;
Thy tooth is not so keen,
Because thou art not seen,
  Although thy breath be rude.
Freeze, freeze, thou bitter sky,
Thou dost not bite so nigh
  As benefits forgot.
Though thou the water warp,
Thy sting is not so sharp
  As friend remembered not.

And again, into the midst of the gay-souled company, " fleeting the time carelessly as in the golden world," the melancholy Jacques brings the note of sadness, as he reminds them all, through his brief, yet full, sketch of the Seven Ages of Man, of the slow march of inexorable time.

All the world's a stage,
And all the men and women merely players:
They have their exits and their entrances;
And one man in his time plays many parts,
His acts being seven ages. At first the infant,
Mewling and puking in the nurse's arms.
And then the whining schoolboy, with his satchel
And shining morning face, creeping like snail
Unwillingly to school. And then the lover,
Sighing like furnace, with a woful ballad
Made to his mistress' eyebrow. Then a
  soldier,
Full of strange oaths, and bearded like the
  pard,
Jealous in honour, sudden and quick in quarrel,
Seeking the bubble reputation
Even in the cannon's mouth; and then the
  justice
In fair round belly with good capon lined,
With eyes severe, and beard of formal cut,
Full of wise saws and modern instances;
And so he plays his part. The sixth age
  shifts
Into the lean and slippered pantaloon,
With spectacles on nose and pouch on side,
His youthful hose well saved, a world too
  wide
For his shrunk shank; and his big manly voice,
Turning again toward childish treble, pipes
And whistles in his sound. Last scene of all,
That ends this strange eventful history,
Is second childishness and mere oblivion,
Sans teeth, sans eyes, sans taste, sans every-
  thing.

The obsolete *pard* mean leopard; *capon*, a chicken; *sans*, without.

We have in this sketch a full illustration of the serious mood that was settling on Shakespeare, and drawing from him deep thoughts that have added to his renown as the first among the singing poets and the large-hearted humorists, the crowning glory of being a profound philosopher, understanding the inmost soul of man.

The Great Words that Stir the Hearts and Minds of All Mankind

NUMBER

OF all schoolroom studies the most dull seems to be that which we call Arithmetic. Yet that study is concerned with one of the great mysteries of life, and for many years lay at the base of a philosophy which held the attention of famous and brilliant Athenians spellbound.

Before the invention of an alphabet came the invention of numbers ; before A B C came 1 2 3; before a child learned to spell c a t, it learned to count its toes. We may almost say that the first intelligent act of man lay in the perception that things can be separated and divided into parts. Yet the alphabet had long been invented, and men had already written books which will never die, before Pythagoras began those inquiries into Numbers which ended in Arithmetic.

Pythagoras borrowed from the Egyptians. He visited the priests, not to worship their gods, but in order to discover fragments of useful knowledge concealed in their mysteries. To be a Greek, we are told, was to seek to know, to know the substance of matter, to know the meaning of Number, to know the world as a rational whole.

The meaning of Number! We say of a book that it has so many pages, of a field that it has so many acres, of a ship that it has so many tons. We number the stars.

We number the electricity we consume in our lamps. We number the runs made by a batsman. We number the bones in our bodies, the teeth in our mouths, and the fingers on our hands.

"Number off!" cries the drill-instructor, and the squad, each man flinging his head to the left, calls out his number, One, two, three——. We go to a crowded hotel in a strange city, and are treated not as a person but as a number. We pay our bill by numbering the notes in our wallet or the coins in our pocket. A man considering a dangerous action counts up the number of things in his favour and weighs them against the number of things which are not in his favour. A boy opens an old book on science and learns that he is living in a wonderful world of three dimensions, with five senses to help him to understand it. A child soon wonders why it has two eyes and only one mouth.

Number enters into everything we do. Our heart is for ever beating time. The pendulum of our clock is for ever ticking. Our very thoughts are so many vibrations of the brain. We walk by taking a number of steps. We eat by taking a number of bites—sometimes two bites at a cherry. Our eyelids blink. Our breathing is twofold. The words of our mouth are units which can be added together. Our brain

DISCOVERY · WILL · HONOUR · HOPE · RIGHTEOUSNESS · REASON

has two hemispheres. We are three-in-one—body, mind, and spirit.

All this is a part of the mystery of Number. But perhaps the first aspect of this mystery to catch the attention of thinking men was that aspect of things which brings them to our minds in pairs of opposites. Men looked at the world and said : There is Light and there is Darkness. There is Male and there is Female. There is Resting and there is Moving. There is Straight and there is Curved. There is Right and there is Left. There is Finite and there is Infinite. There is Good and there is Bad.

THE WONDERFUL THING THAT CAME FROM THE STUDY OF NUMBER

So wonderful did this discovery seem to them that from the time of Pythagoras, right down the ages till Athens had ceased to be an influence in the politics of the world, almost all philosophy, including Aristotle's natural history, was sensibly governed by the method of counting things in twos, studying things in couples, each couple composed of opposites like Right and Wrong, Light and Darkness.

But a much more wonderful thing was to come of man's attention to Number. First of all it led to a breaking up of a single body to discover what it was made of, its parts or its elements. Instead of looking at a tree, an elephant, or a rock, and thinking of it as a tree, elephant, or rock, men asked themselves, " What is it made of ? Why is a tree different from an elephant, and an elephant from a rock ?" Thus began a method which presently taught mankind that rays of light might be split up so as to reveal the character of substances giving them forth, and that there is no element in the Earth which cannot be traced to the Sun.

THE EARLY GUESSWORK OF THE OLD PHILOSOPHERS

This *analytical method*, as it is called, is now part of all science. No one in these days thinks he can understand a mystery in the whole; every puzzle is split up or broken down, and the elements of which it is composed are sought for, examined, tabulated, and considered separately from one another, before the whole thing is labelled or defined.

Until this method came into being a man was free to speculate as he chose about the mystery of existence. All the early philosophies are merely guesswork.

A man might say what he liked. His only critics were those who tried to trip him up over his words. Even in Athens at its highest glory some of the theories concerning man and the universe are so absurd that they make us laugh. It was not until Number had given birth to the analytical method that philosophers were challenged to square their guesses at truth with the numbered and classified facts of physical science. It was no use to assert that the world was supported by an elephant standing on a tortoise. The critic demanded to be shown, if not the elephant or the tortoise, at least the reasons for believing in their existence. After many hundreds of years it became impossible for men to say that the world was stationary and flat ; science could prove that it was a revolving sphere that swung round the Sun like a ball at the end of a string. The method by which this revolutionary truth was made manifest is also a triumph for Number. Mathematics came from arithmetic.

HOW EUCLID HELPED TO BUILD THE FORTH BRIDGE AND THE STEAM ENGINE

Some three hundred years before the birth of Christ there was born a Greek whose name was Eucleides, or as we now spell it, Euclid. He, like Pythagoras, Plato, and Aristotle, was thrilled by the wonder of this mysterious thing called Number. But with his wonder there went something that none of the other three had possessed; it was a creative enthusiasm, a passion and a genius for what we now call mathematics.

This man went to live in Alexandria, and wrote a great work in thirteen books. It is said that no work except the Bible has had such a reign. He called it the *Elements*. In this book he used the language of common speech, but in reality he was using another language altogether, the language of Geometry.

Others before him had attempted to do what he so successfully did in these thirteen books, but it was he more than any man in the world who collected the broken alphabet of mathematics together and made it speak out a language common to all the races of mankind.

Because of this language of Number a bridge that astonishes the world strides across the Firth of Forth, and great ships of iron are driven through storm and tempest by engines so fine and perfect that some of their steel elements must be made to the thousandth part of an inch. There is no triumph of engineering which cannot be traced right back to the propositions of Euclid, and it has taken the brains of all Europe 2000 years to prove that this ancient Athenian was wrong in one place and perhaps only partially right in another.

THE LANGUAGE OF FIGURES IN WHICH WE READ THE MYSTERIES OF THE SKIES

The greatest and divinest achievement of Euclid, however, lies in another sphere. We say *divinest* with intent. In giving men an almost perfect language of geometry he gave them the language of the universe. In no other tongue could man have read the mysteries of the starry skies. In no other tongue could he have had speech with Jupiter and Uranus. By arithmetic Professor Ramsay discovered the unknown and unguessed gas called argon; by the processes of higher arithmetic Leverrier and Adams proved that an undiscovered planet was pulling at Uranus and were able to tell the astronomers exactly where to point their telescopes to find it—the planet now called Neptune. In no other tongue could man have asked questions of Space and Time, and brought back their answer to the philosopher.

Now, think of the wonder that has come from the first man who said, *One, two, three.* We have created a language which enables the mind of a man on this planet Earth to hold converse with the physical universe of God. Even in the infancy of this language, before it stammered its way out of its alphabet, Plato saw in it a proof of man's divine origin.

THE GREAT THINGS THAT HAVE FOLLOWED THE COUNTING OF THE FINGERS

For in this simple language alone could man spell out the secrets of the mighty universe, and man, having made this language himself, was therefore akin with that universe. How great had been his wonder if he had lived to our day, and read the latest page in this miraculous book of mathematics—the page which tells us that Euclid was wrong, that Newton was wrong, and that the whole universe is one tremendous curve !

This is the greatest thing that has come from the brain of that first man who counted his fingers and said *One, two, three.* But many other things of infinite importance to the history of mankind have come from that action.

Think of the commerce of the world. It is built up on Number. A vast host of the human race spends its whole working life in counting. There is scarcely an unlettered peasant in the most backward country on the Earth who is not harnessed to the chariot of Number. Look at the Chancellor of the Exchequer studying the page which tells him of the millions of pounds owed by England to America, and then look at this South Sea Islander counting the pearls in his hand, or at that coolie in China counting his baskets of tea. The whole world, we may truly say, is living by Number. The clerk in a bank is not more surely harnessed to this chariot than the wife of a field-labourer in the outer Hebrides who tramps five miles to a village shop and buys a yard of ribbon, a pound of soap, an ounce of tobacco, and twelve stamps.

THE MYSTERY OF NUMBER IN THE RELIGIONS OF THE WORLD

Think, too, of the great insurance offices of the world. They are all built up on Number. Men collect figures about human life which they call statistics, and on those statistics base a law which enables the insurance offices to work with mathematical exactness. Men arrive at definite results by poring over averages, and this same method is used by the statesman in calculating revenue, by the Darwinian in studying the data of evolution, and even by the student of the human mind.

Finally, the mystery of Number has entered into all the religions of the world. The circle stands for eternity, the triangle for the Trinity of the Christian Faith, and the number seven is regarded as sacred. Far back in the remotest antiquity we find men bowing their heads before the figure three, because it is the first of the numbers which has a beginning, a middle, and an end. Far back, too, in those mists of time men spoke of God as the One, and laid it down that human life was a return of the Many to the One; and this, we may say, is still the one really broad religion, the one religion believed by the vast majority of the human race—namely, that, though the elements of the universe are more in number than the sands on the seashore, they are in reality only one, and that One is God.

JOSEPH AND HIS LITTLE BROTHER BENJAMIN

JOSEPH CALLS HIS LITTLE BROTHER BENJAMIN TO HIM

THE BROTHERS ARE SENT AWAY WITH FULL SACKS

THE CUP IS FOUND IN BENJAMIN'S SACK

The Story of the Most Beautiful Book in the World

Joseph relating his dreams to his father—From the painting by H. R. Mileham

JOSEPH AND HIS BRETHREN

OLD Israel loved Joseph, the son of his beloved Rachel, more than any of his children and took pleasure in making this favourite child a coat so royal in its bright colours that his brothers became jealous and angry.

Then Joseph dreamed strange dreams and told them to his father and his brothers. He did not explain to them what those dreams meant, but the father and brothers saw plainly their significance. The dreams meant that Joseph was to be a great and mighty man. "Shalt thou indeed reign over us ?" cried his older brothers ; and they hated him.

Joseph would not explain himself to his simple brothers, for he saw that their world was different from his, and he knew that his thoughts would appear as madness to them. Perhaps he did not even tell his favourite brother, the little Benjamin, the mysterious stirrings which were so real to him in his soul. Perhaps he did not quite understand them himself.

One day Israel sent Joseph to see how his brothers fared with the flocks in a distant part of the country. As Joseph drew near to them one of the brothers said bitterly, " Behold this dreamer cometh ! " Then they plotted and agreed to kill him.

But Reuben pleaded for Joseph, saying, " Shed no blood, but cast him into this pit." Secretly in his heart the good Reuben determined to rescue Joseph when the angry brothers had gone. So they took Joseph, stripped him of his coat, and flung him into the pit.

Later, when Reuben was gone away, and as they sat eating bread, a company of Ishmaelites came by on camels, carrying spices into Egypt. Then one of the brothers suggested that Joseph should be sold as a slave to these merchants, and they lifted him out of the pit, and sold him for twenty pieces of silver. When Reuben returned and found that it was too late to save Joseph, he was very sad. The other brothers killed a kid, dipped Joseph's coat in the blood, and carried it to their father.

When Israel saw it he cried with a loud voice that an evil beast had devoured his son, his favourite son, Joseph, and when the others would have comforted him he put them by, saying: " I will go down into the grave unto my son mourning."

Joseph in the meantime reached Egypt, was sold by the merchants, and became a servant to the Captain of the King's Guard. Here he prospered exceedingly, and Potiphar, his master, trusted him and

GREAT FIGURES OF THE OLD TESTAMENT · THE LIFE OF JESUS

loved him. But Potiphar's wife, a deceitful woman, hated Joseph, because when she tempted him to do a dishonourable thing he remained faithful to his master and friend. So this unjust woman lied against Joseph to Potiphar, and Potiphar, believing dreamed dreams, and Joseph explained what those dreams meant. One servant, he said, would soon be restored to the king's favour. The other would soon die.

The interpretations came true, and one day, when Pharaoh was troubled by an

JOSEPH'S BROTHERS STAIN THE COAT WITH BLOOD TO DECEIVE THEIR FATHER JACOB

her story, had Joseph cast into prison.

In the prison his wonderful mind laid hold upon the keeper, and he made Joseph an overseer of the other prisoners. Now, in this prison were two servants of the great King of Egypt, Pharaoh, and they evil dream, the servant who had been restored to his favour remembered Joseph and spoke of him to the king.

Then Joseph was brought out of prison, and told the king the meaning of his dream. For seven years, he said, God would bless the land of Egypt with over-flowing harvests, and then for seven years Egypt would know drought and famine. Let Pharaoh learn of God, he said, and put over the land a man who would hoard the corn of years of plenty, so that the people might not die in the years of famine.

And Pharaoh brooded on this matter. He took off his ring and put it in Joseph's

a bitter famine, and his old father Israel, who had never ceased to mourn for him, hearing that there was corn in the barns of Egypt, sent his sons to purchase the precious food from the Egyptians. He sent all his sons, except the last-born, Benjamin, fearing some evil might befall him.

Can you not picture to yourself the moving scene when those ten sons of

THE COAT OF MANY COLOURS. From the painting by Ford Madox Brown, in the Walker Art Galley, Liverpool

hand, and arrayed him in vestures of fine linen, and put a gold chain about his neck, and he made him to ride in the second chariot which he had, and made him ruler over all the land of Egypt.

Thus was the man of genius lifted up from a prison and set upon a throne.

While he reigned in great glory and honour there came, as he had prophesied,

Israel, strangers from a far country, stood before the mighty Viceroy of Pharaoh, and knew not that he was their own brother ?

Joseph knew the land they came from and recognised them as his brothers. He steeled his heart against them, however, and pretended to treat them with sus-picion, as if he thought them to be spies, enemies of his country. He allowed them to fill their sacks with corn, but insisted that Simeon, one of the brothers, should remain while the others returned home and brought Benjamin.

On their way home the nine brothers discovered that the money they had paid for the corn was wrapped up in their sacks,

Once again the brothers stood before the great Viceroy. This time Joseph looked on the little brother he had loved so dearly. The brothers bowed themselves to the ground and presented their presents to Joseph. "Is your father well ?" he said graciously. "The old

JOSEPH SOLD INTO SLAVERY—FROM THE PAINTING BY H. R. MILEHAM

and they began to be afraid of a new disaster. Israel, their father, burst into tears, and would not let Benjamin go. But when the corn was eaten and starvation was staring them once more in the face the brothers persuaded the old father to let his youngest son go with them.

man of whom ye spake—is he yet alive?" And they answered, "Thy servant our father is in good health, he is yet alive."

Then Joseph, mastering the love that was breaking his heart, turned and looked at Benjamin. The sight was greater than he could bear. All the past rushed to

JOSEPH IN THE DAYS OF HIS GREATNESS

JOSEPH, OVERSEER OF PHARAOH'S GRANARY—BY SIR LAWRENCE ALMA-TADEMA

THE PROUD MOMENT WHEN JOSEPH BRINGS HIS FATHER TO PHARAOH—BY SIR EDWARD POYNTER

his eyes in "the water of his soul." He withdrew quickly into a private room and burst into tears. Afterward, when he had washed his face and recovered his composure, he returned to the brothers and invited them to eat with him. Greatly astonished, they sat down to eat, and their astonishment increased when they saw that the great Viceroy, who sat at the high table by himself, sent the richest of his dishes to Benjamin. They were returning early in the morning to Canaan, when one of Joseph's officers overtook them, and accused them of stealing his master's silver cup. The sacks were opened, and in the mouth of Benjamin's sack lay the missing vessel.

JOSEPH'S GREAT LOVE FOR BENJAMIN AND HOW HE BROUGHT HIM BACK

The brothers all returned to Joseph, and prostrated themselves before him in great fear. Joseph said they might return in peace, all except Benjamin, in whose sack the cup had been found ; he must remain and become his servant. Then one of the brothers stood up and said:

Oh, my lord, let thy servant, I pray thee, speak a word in my lord's ear, and let not thine anger burn against thy servant, for thou art even as Pharaoh. My lord asked his servants, saying, "Have you a father or a brother?" And we said unto my lord, "We have a father, an old man, and a child of his old age, a little one; and his brother is dead, and he alone is left of his mother, and his father loveth him."

And thou saidst unto thy servants, "Bring him down unto me, that I may set mine eyes upon him." And we said unto my lord, "The lad cannot leave his father: for if he should leave his father, his father would die." And thou saidst unto thy servants, "Except your youngest brother come down with you, ye shall see my face no more."

And it came to pass when we came up unto thy servant my father we told him the words of my lord. And thy servant my father said unto us, " Ye know that my wife bare me two sons; and the one went out from me, and I said: Surely he is torn in pieces; and I saw him not since. And if ye take this also from me, and mischief befall him, ye shall bring down my grey hair with sorrow to the grave."

Joseph could not bear any longer the sorrow of this appeal. Hastily he dismissed his retinue of servants, and stood alone in the great hall with his brothers.

Then he wept as a strong man weeps when he is stricken to the soul. And while his brothers marvelled to see this mighty Viceroy in tears, he lifted his face and looked upon them, and exclaimed, " I am Joseph! "

He reproached them not for their first cruelty, and bade them not to reproach themselves. He told them to hasten back to Canaan, to tell Israel that Joseph was yet alive, and to bring their father and all their people to Egypt. And after he had said these kind things he went forward to his brother Benjamin, the playmate of his childhood, and kissed him.

THE WANDERER GOES DOWN INTO EGYPT TO SEE HIS SON AND TO DIE

Pharaoh heard of this beautiful scene, and rejoiced again in Joseph. He sent wagons and rich presents to old Israel in Canaan, and bade him come down and live in Egypt. And Israel, the old, old man, who had once slept with stones for his pillow—Jacob, the poor exile and wanderer—had but one cry when he heard all this greatness: "Joseph my son is yet alive ! I will go down and see him before I die ! "

Joseph drove out in his chariot to meet his father, and they met on the frontier of Egypt—the old man and the young Viceroy. And we are told that Joseph " presented himself unto him," and he fell on his neck and wept. And Israel said unto Joseph, "Now let me die, since I have seen they face, because thou art yet alive."

Then Israel stood before Pharaoh and blessed the mighty king, and he settled in the land of Goshen, and Joseph cared for him, and the Israelites flourished exceedingly. Israel's death, after his long life of wandering, was full of peace.

HOW JOSEPH DIED AMID THE GREAT PROSPERITY OF HIS CHILDREN

But, at the death of their father, Joseph's brothers feared his wrath, thinking that now he would surely take revenge on them. But Joseph had no such thoughts in his great soul, and he comforted them and spake kindly unto them.

And so the dreamer's dreams came true. And when Joseph died, at a great age, he saw not only his greatness equal with Pharaoh's, but his children's children, to the third generation, living in prosperity among the Egyptians.

" I die," said Joseph, " and God will surely visit you, and bring you out of this land unto the land which He swore to Abraham, to Isaac, and to Jacob."

The Interests and Pleasures of Life for All Indoors and Out

KEEPING A FRESH-WATER AQUARIUM

THERE are few hobbies more fascinating than the keeping of an aquarium, which has the advantages of being amusing and instructive, and at the same time is quite an inexpensive pastime.

First of all there is the tank, and as it is very difficult for an amateur to make one so that the joints are quite watertight, it would be much better to get one ready made. The best shape is oblong, and one may occasionally be seen for sale at a second-hand furniture shop. Make certain before buying that the tank is not leaky.

But almost any kind of rectangular glass vessel will serve, and an accumulator jar makes quite a good tank.

Whether a small start is made like this, or a larger tank is bought, the aquarium must be placed where it can receive good light, without standing in direct sunlight all day. Some sunshine *is* necessary, though, or the water plants will not thrive, so let the tank get direct rays morning and evening, but screen it from the sun in the hottest part of the day in summer.

Having obtained an aquarium, the next step is to get it ready for its tenants. Put a little clean gravel in the bottom and cover this with a layer, just over an inch thick, of sand which has first been washed clean. Arrange this to look natural with small " hills " at the back or sides.

Then comes the stocking of the aquarium. First of all some place of retreat for the inmates must be provided. A quantity of willow moss or water soldier placed at the bottom will be very useful for this purpose. There should be some aquatic weed, which will give out oxygen and absorb the carbonic acid given off by the fish, and Canadian pond weed, found in most ponds and rivers, will serve very well in this way.

If there is a sufficient quantity of this weed the water very rarely needs changing; but a little fresh water must be added from time to time, as evaporation takes place.

The water plants should be set in the sand, and it is easier to do this if only an inch or two of water is put into the tank, which can be filled up afterwards. Water from a stream or a clean pond is the best, though if this is lacking, tap water can be used.

Scavengers are needed in an aquarium just as they are in a pond, and so place a few water snails in the water to eat up any decaying leaves and keep the inside of the glass clean. They also supply the fish with eggs for food, and here it must be distinctly understood that fish in an aquarium *do* need food. Many an inmate of an aquarium has been starved to death because the owner thought that all the food the fish required was contained in the water.

Where the water was obtained from the tap it has no food at all in it; even if it is pond water the stock of food needs supplementing, and a dealer will advise on the most suitable kinds to buy.

Another useful scavenger, which multiplies at a great rate and provides food for the fish, is the fresh-water louse. It is to be obtained by pulling up weeds from a pond,

CRAFTS · GAMES · NEEDLEWORK · PUZZLES · SCIENCE EXPERIMENTS

and picking the creatures out of the mud sticking to the roots.

Now we come to the fish themselves, and here remember to keep as close to nature as possible. The aquarium has stagnant water, therefore obtain the fish from standing ponds and not from running streams. Members of the carp and tench families are the most suitable, and if these cannot be found in ponds they can be bought from a naturalist's shop.

Goldfish are the most familiar inmates of aquariums, but they are best kept on their own, and there are a number of different kinds which make an attractive collection. The Prussian carp, the common carp—greyish brown in colour, with barbels adorning its upper lip—the mirror carp, and the leather carp, are all easily obtained, and easily kept. Of tench, the common or green tench is suitable, though it feeds by night and is very fond of concealing itself among the weeds in the aquarium.

The golden tench gives a pleasant variety to the bowl, its lighter yellow contrasting with the deep red-gold of the golden carp. One or two fish should be introduced at first, and if these thrive more may be added; but an aquarium must never be overcrowded, and the old rule of a gallon of water to every one-inch fish will serve as a rough guide.

If the fish swim along the surface of the water tail downwards it is a sure sign that they are being suffocated.

Absolute cleanliness is essential in the keeping of an aquarium ; any decaying matter must be removed at once or the fish will die. Take out also any unused food after feeding. A fungus disease frequently attacks goldfish in aquariums that are not kept perfectly clean. When this disease appears, all dead and infected fish must be at once removed, and the aquarium thoroughly disinfected with permanganate of potash solution, being well washed in clean water afterward.

To keep dust out of the water as much as possible, and also to prevent the fish from jumping out, a piece of glass may be placed over the aquarium like a lid, being slightly raised from the vessel by two pieces of wood laid across the top. This plan enables the air to get to the water.

Great care must be taken not to handle the fish, and should it become necessary to remove them from the aquarium, this must be done by means of a net, another vessel containing water being ready for them. A suitable net may be bought, though one to serve the purpose can easily be made by making a circle of wire and fixing it to a cane, a bag of gauze or fine network being sewn round the wire circle.

AN AQUARIUM COMPLETE

If the aquarium has to be cleaned owing to a green coating of vegetable matter obscuring the glass, the fish must first be removed as described, and then the water can be drawn off by means of a siphon, which is a bent tube with one end larger than the other. When the water has been emptied, the green coating on the glass can be removed by rubbing with a sponge, this being frequently rinsed in clean water during the process.

It is well to aerate the water from time to time, and this may be done by pumping air with an ordinary syringe or with a pair of bellows connected with a piece of indiarubber tubing leading into the water of the aquarium.

DRAWING A CAT WITH THE HELP OF TWO COINS

THE four little pictures shown here prove how very simple a thing it is to make amusing drawings. For these, only a sixpence and a halfpenny, a pencil and a piece of paper are needed. First put the sixpence on the paper and draw a circle round it; then place the halfpenny to the right, overlapping slightly, and run the pencil round its edge, being careful not to cut into the first circle.

The ears, eyes, nose, mouth, tail, and two curves for hip and leg joint are then put in to make pussy complete.

COOKING FISH AND MEAT

ONCE upon a time every good cook believed the only way to roast or " bake " meat was to put the joint with some extra fat in an open baking tin, then to place the tin in a very hot oven (500° F.) for 15 or 20 minutes to " brown " in the nourishing juices, and then to reduce the oven temperature and continue cooking the joint for 15 or 20 minutes for each pound, basting it frequently.

Modern scientific cookery research has proved that a casserole in which the joint is cooked slowly at a temperature between 180° to 250° gives equally nourishing results. For this slow method, a joint of beef weighing two to eight pounds would need 30 minutes for every pound and 80 minutes over, other meats requiring 35 to 40 minutes per pound and 65 to 70 minutes over.

Meat may also be Pot Roasted in a thick saucepan with a tight-fitting lid. Sufficient fat to cover the bottom of the pot about half an inch deep is needed, and directly this is hot the joint should be fitted in, the lid put on, and the heat reduced so that the meat cooks slowly. The joint will need turning once during cooking, and a few sliced onions placed around and seasoned with a teaspoonful of salt, will improve the gravy.

Fish can be cooked in similar fashion, allowing about 10 minutes per pound and 5 minutes over.

To cook fresh Meat Mince in exactly 5 minutes, rub the base of a clean, thick, frying-pan with dripping and heat the pan thoroughly. Then quickly turn in half a pound of lean raw mince seasoned with a teaspoonful each of salt, chopped parsley, and chives, and, if liked, about 6 drops of Worcester sauce. Rapidly stir the mixture till it loses its raw look, and be sure not to let it go on cooking until it turns dark brown. Within 2 to 3 minutes of putting it in the pan, the mince is ready to serve in several different ways—just as it is, with mixed vegetables and a piping of mashed potato ; as a Shepherd's Pie, mixed with a little sauce or gravy, and covered with mashed potato, which is then sprinkled with cheese and browned

Take trouble in dishing up a meal attractively like this—(above) meat mince rounds served with straw potatoes, halved tomatoes and watercress; (below) cooked fish flaked into hot, clean, scallop shells (or individual fireproof dishes would do), covered with browned breadcrumbs and decorated with lemon " butterflies " and a border of green peas.

for 5 minutes under the grill; cold as the foundation of a Salad; sandwiched, while still hot, between slices of bread for a Picnic; or as a filling for a Potato Duckling. To make this take a heaped tablespoonful of mashed potato, scoop out a little from the centre, replace with the same amount of mince, cover with more mashed potato and form into the duck's body, turning up the tail with the fingers; and then fasten on a mashed potato head with a used match, first taking off the burnt end. Put two currants for eyes, a split slice of carrot for the beak, and place the duckling on a " pond " of spinach.

With the exception of salted fish which should be put on in cold water, and Salmon which should be put into boiling salted water to preserve its colour, fish to be boiled should be put into warm water, brought to the boil, and then, with seasoning added, simmered gently till the bone separates easily from the flesh, which proves that it is cooked. Cook in as little water as possible, and to keep white fish a good colour, add a little lemon juice.

To broil fish between two plates standing on a pan of boiling water, rub the lower plate with butter, on it place a small flat fish, some fillets, or one or two small slices of cod or hake, seasoned with a good sprinkling of salt and pepper on both sides. Over this invert the other plate, which should be the same size, and cook for 15 to 25 minutes according to the thickness of the fish.

A delicious way of finishing off plate-cooked fish is to drain off all liquor for a sauce, sprinkle the top of the fish with a heaped dessertspoonful of toasted, salted breadcrumbs, dot with grated cheese, and put under the grill till lightly browned.

Salt fish, like Finnan Haddock or Kippers, can be grilled, or can be put in a pan, covered with cold water, and brought to the boil by which time the flesh will be flaking from the bones. Serve with a good knob of butter.

The cookery lesson to follow this is fascinating—cake-making and decorating—and will be found on page 1121.

LITTLE PROBLEMS FOR ODD MOMENTS

THESE problems are continued from page 872, and their answers, together with more questions, will be found on page 1124.

65. What were the Legacies?

An uncle left £420 to be divided in unequal proportions between three nephews named George, John, and Charles. George received one-seventh more than John, and John received one-sixth more than Charles.

How much did each receive?

66. How was the Tea Mixed?

A grocer sells a mixed tea at 3s. a pound, and has a profit of 20 per cent. upon his cost price. The tea is a mixture of two varieties, one of which he purchases at 2s. a pound, and the other of which he purchases at 2s. 8d. a pound.

In what proportion does he mix them?

67. How Many Apples were Bought?

A market woman bought equal numbers of windfall apples at four a penny, five for a penny, and six for a penny. She sold them all for five a penny, and lost fourpence over the transaction.

How many apples had she purchased in the first place?

68. Can the Division be Made?

" Look here," said Bob to Jennifer. " Can you do this? Divide 45 into four parts, so that if one of the parts is multiplied by two, another divided by two, another added to two, and another has two subtracted from it, the results will all be the same." Jennifer tried, and after a time succeeded.

How did she do it?

69. Who was Right?

" There is only one more wicket to fall," said a boy who was watching a cricket match, as the ninth man was going in. " No," said another, " there are two." " You are both wrong," said a third boy; " there are three."

Which of the three boys was correct?

70. What was the Sum?

On his way home, Harry realised he had forgotten to copy the long division sum on the blackboard into his exercise book, so he ran back to school only to discover that much of the sum had been rubbed out. With a × to represent each place where there was no figure, the sum looked like this:

$$2 1 5) \times 7 \times 9 \times (1 \times \times$$
$$\times \times \times$$

$$\times 5 \times 9$$
$$\times 5 \times 5$$

$$\times 4 \times$$
$$\times \times \times$$

Harry remembered that the sum ended without a remainder, and, being a clever boy, he filled in all the figures that had been erased.

How did he do it?

71. How Much were the Pens and Pencils?

" You may give me three dozen lead pencils and five dozen pens," said Uncle William, when he was purchasing prizes for the boys at a Sunday-school picnic. Each pen cost twice as much as each pencil. If he had bought three dozen pens and five dozen pencils he would have saved six shillings on the bill. What were the prices of the pencils and the pens?

THE ANSWERS TO THE PROBLEMS ON PAGE 872

57. At present Hugh has 5s. more and Harry has 5s. less than half the whole money. If Hugh wins he will have three-quarters of the whole money, so that 5s. is half the difference between half and three-quarters of the whole money. This means that 10s. is the whole difference, so that they must have 40s. between them. Hugh will have three-quarters of this 40s. (that is, 30s.) if he wins, so that he must have 25s. now, and Harry has the remaining 15s.

58. John and his father together earn 3s. a day more than Henry and his father, so that John earns 3s. more than Henry. As the two sons together earn 21s., John must earn 12s. and Henry 9s. Thus, the father earns 18s. a day.

59. If the coat cost 7 times as much as the waistcoat, the waistcoat must have cost one-eighth of the total sum paid for the two. The total sum paid for the two was £9 14s. 8d., and one-eighth of this is £1 4s. 4d., which was therefore the price of the waistcoat.

60. If the yard-stick was one inch short, the actual length of the cloth was 36 times 35 inches, instead of 36 times 36 inches. Thirty-six times 35 inches is 35 yards, which was therefore the actual length of the cloth.

61. If the average for 7 days was 15 miles, the total number of miles walked in the 7 days must have been 105. If the average for the first 4 days was 18, the miles walked in the first 4 days must have been 72. Thus there must have been 33 miles walked in the last 3 days, and the average is 11 miles a day.

62. Begin this at the end. The merchant had 15 gallons after taking out one gallon less than one-third of the quantity in the barrel. If he had taken out one gallon more, thereby leaving 14 gallons instead of 15, he would have had two-thirds of the quantity before he took out the last lot. Fourteen is two-thirds of 21, so that before the second withdrawal the barrel must have had 21 gallons in it. As the merchant took out one gallon less than half the quantity originally in the barrel and left 21 gallons, 21 gallons must be one gallon more than half of the original quantity. Half of the original quantity was therefore 20 gallons, and the whole original quantity was 40 gallons. As 40 gallons was thus two-thirds of the capacity of the barrel, the barrel must have had a capacity of 60 gallons.

63. The sheep and calves were equal in number and for one of each the farmer received £12. Dividing 72 by 12 we have 6, so that there were 6 sheep and 6 calves.

64. There are 10 florins in a pound, and there are 8 half-crowns in a pound. Thus, if the coins had been florins, Jones would have had two coins more for every pound. But we know that he would have had 12 more coins, so that the quarter's rent must have been £6—that is, £24 a year.

HUMPTY DUMPTY EGGS FOR EASTER

It is fun to have variegated eggs for breakfast on Easter Day, and very easy to make them. Just tie up each egg in the outer skins of onions, and boil it; the result will be surprisingly pretty. A breakfast any time of the year will be gayer, too, if a face is drawn on an egg, and it is then decked out smartly in a little hat. Make this from paper measuring six inches by four inches.

Fold the paper once so that it measures four inches by three inches, then bend both points of the folded edge evenly towards the centre till they meet and make a peak. Turn the paper below this backwards on either side, and tuck the ends in tidily. Trim with a parsley "feather," and the egg hat is ready.

An egg can be made into an odd fish by drawing a mouth and eyes on the rounded end

Use a fragment of a fringed paper cake frill to support Miss Humpty's mouth above the level of the egg cup, but make Mr. Humpty's collar of manly brown.

and attaching a tail and fins. The tail and fins are of stiff paper, and have—cut along one edge—hinges, by means of which they are stuck to the egg.

Hard-boiled eggs for a picnic look more exciting if each is decorated with a different design. Anyone clever with a paint-box can soon do this, and another idea is to stick on stars, half-moons, and other fancy shapes cut in different sizes from gold, silver, and coloured paper.

Dipping the eggs in cold-water dye prepared as directed gives further variety. The name of each guest could be brushed on first with melted candle-grease, which should be allowed time to harden before the eggs are dipped. Then, when the dye has dried, the wax can be removed and the names will show up clearly in white.

SOME GOOD CARD TRICKS

Tricks with cards always impress an audience. Here are a few which look clever, but are not hard to perform.

FEELING THE PIPS

Ask someone to choose a card. In taking this back, allow it to face the audience, then, holding it upright between the fingers and thumb of the left hand, " feel " its spots with the right. It is only necessary in doing this to bend the card slightly to be able to read the sign in the bottom left-hand corner. The exact position and distance away to hold the card so that the symbol on it can easily be identified will soon be discovered after a little practice.

READING THE PACK

This is one of the simplest of card tricks, but it can only be done if there is a mirror in the room. Stand to face the mirror and see that the audience have their backs to it. Then hold above the head a pack of cards—which have first been well shuffled by some of the onlookers, so that they shall know that the arrangement of the cards has not been faked—and one by one remove the cards, naming them as this is done and passing them on to someone in the front row of the spectators. This will give time to glance into the mirror to see what the next card is without making this too noticeable.

When there is no mirror in the room the trick can be performed in this way. After the pack has been shuffled by a spectator hold it in both hands and, chattering all the time to distract attention, turn the top card so

that it backs on to the pack, and notice what it is. Put the cards behind the back. Then bring them forward again with the turned-round card facing the audience, and call out what it is, at the same time memorising the card now exposed. Again holding the pack behind the back, remove this card, and put it *face outwards* on top of the card first named. Then bring the pack forward again, and repeat the process. Practise this trick a good deal before doing it in public, for there must be no fumbling, and all the card edges should be kept level or a smart onlooker might spot how it is done.

GUESSING A CHOSEN CARD

It is wise to borrow a pack for this trick, and as it is passed over spread the cards out fanwise with their backs uppermost. Then ask someone to pick out one card and memorise it. While this goes on, unobtrusively move the bottom card, after memorising it, and put it *under all those that were on top* of *the selected card*, which must then be returned to its old position. Close the pack and shuffle it a little. After this, pass the pack to someone else to turn up card by card, then, when the selected card appears, call out " Stop ! That is the chosen card." It should be the one following the *original bottom card*.

In shuffling there is not a lot of risk of separating this bottom card and the one which has been chosen, but do not worry if they should get parted. Little mistakes like this always bring forth more applause when finally the trick is completed successfully.

THE MAGIC TOUCH

THIS trick is so simple that anyone can do it, but it will impress an audience if the young magician includes it in his show. Ask someone to produce an ordinary sheet of paper, and with ruler and pencil to divide it into nine equal parts—this can be quite easily done by drawing two lines across and two down.

Then call for the name of an animal and write this in the top left-hand corner, or, better still, get someone else to do it so that it cannot be said that the paper has been tampered with. Follow this with the name of a bird written in the next space, continuing in this way, with animal and bird alternately, until all the spaces are filled. Request an-

other member of the audience to tear the sheet into its nine divisions along the pencilled lines, and then announce that you are going to show, that the magic touch is so sensitive that while you are blindfold, it can pick out the birds from the animals ; and proceed to do just that.

If you try this out, you will discover that the explanation is absurdly easy. By arranging the names alternately and starting with an animal, there are only four divisions for the birds, and they all have *one* straight edge (the outside of the sheet of paper) and three torn sides, which provide the clue. But do be careful not to give the whole trick away by feeling the edges too obviously.

JOHN CHINAMAN MADE OF PEANUTS

HERE is a quaint John Chinaman doll made from peanuts. Eleven peanuts of different sizes are threaded together with strong cotton, as shown in the first picture, the face being drawn in ink and the eyes given a slanting line to make them look like a Chinaman's.

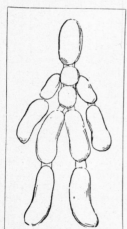

The nuts strung together

Three pieces of black wool should be plaited together to form the pigtail which can be stuck, or fixed with cotton, to the top of the head. To dress this doll, make a little pair of trousers with two square pieces of bright-coloured material; hem each piece on one side, and join halfway at the back ; then join the two together and fasten to the doll at the top of the legs, letting the feet show.

The smock is made in the shape of a little sack, simply drawn in at the neck. Two very wide sleeves are next made, each one like a small bag, sewn on the smock quite close to the neck.

The hat looks very nice made out of two round pieces of cardboard covered with silk, and joined together with a little silk cord overstitched all round. It is kept in place with a coloured glass-headed pin stuck right through the head of the doll.

The black lines seen on the smock can either be made by putting a little braid round the bottom and at the edge of the sleeves, or by working some fancy stitching. Lastly, paint in the shoes with a little black paint or Indian ink.

John Chinaman

THE GOLD RUSH GAME

THIS is a treasure hunt which is good fun where there are lots of players and plenty of room. It is most successful out of doors, though it can be played in a house which affords a big variety of good hiding-places.

Into separate little envelopes put slips of paper, on some of which the word gold is written, the others being left blank ; or, to save using envelopes, the slips could be folded. Use plenty of slips, for a lot will be needed if the game is to go with a swing. Hide them all beforehand.

Then send the players off to hunt for gold —that is, the slips or envelopes—and tell them to collect as many as they can in a given time, but *not* to open them. This is done at the end, when each of the slips marked gold counts £100, and the winner is the one who has amassed the largest fortune.

If there are many players, it is easier to arrange them in teams of six or eight, with one as captain who organises his team's " gold rush," and, at the finish, collects and adds up the " money " found by them.

SCHOOL LESSONS

Simple Learning Made Easy For Very Little People

WRITING—THE TWINS GIVE A PARTY

THE twins came down to breakfast one morning with very long faces. Mother had told them that she and Daddy were going away, and that for two whole weeks they were going to stay with their Grandmother.

They loved going to Grandmother, but they had not been on their very own before. After breakfast Daddy had a surprise packet for each of them. In the packets were some sheets of notepaper and stamped envelopes, all addressed to Mother and Daddy. Mother said they could write story-letters while they were away. John and Jennifer cheered up, and felt very much better.

They promised not to ask Granny anything, but try to find the words they wanted, and write them so plainly that even if they did make one or two spelling mistakes the words would be so beautifully written that Mother and Daddy would be able to find out what the word was meant to be. This they did.

While Mother and Daddy were away John and Jennifer planned to have a party when they came home, just to celebrate. They told Granny about it and she promised to help. They played a game pretending that Granny was deaf. All the things they wanted to have at the party they wrote down (beautifully written and properly spelled), for Granny to read. They thought of all the things that Mother and Daddy liked best. They hunted through picture books and catalogues, looked at advertisements and in shop windows, to find how to spell the words they wanted. Some of the words they remembered from writing the lists for their café.

John wrote a list for Granny, and Jennifer wrote one to send to Mother and Daddy, so that they knew what they were going to have.

This was the list:

Tea. Coffee. Milk. Sugar. Bread. Butter. Jam. Paste. Fruit Cake. Chocolate sandwich. Trifle. Jellies. Ice cream.

Just before Mother and Daddy came home the twins sent them an invitation to the party. Granny wrote it out for them. John copied one for Daddy, and Jennifer copied one for Mother, all in their very best writing:

John and Jennifer would like you to come to a tea-party when you come home.

Mother and Daddy were delighted, and answered the invitation by the very next post, saying they would like to come to the tea-party very much indeed.

READING · WRITING · ARITHMETIC · MUSIC · DRAWING · FRENCH

NUMBERS—ALL ABOUT 12

When John and Jennifer were tiny they loved to sit on Daddy's knee and listen to his watch. He used to take it out of his pocket and hold it close to their ears for them to hear it ticking.

Now that they were older they wanted to learn how to tell the time. First they had a talk with Mother about 12. They remembered that 12 was one ten and two more, that there were 12 months in a year, 12 pennies in a shilling, and now they learned that there were 12 hours on a clock.

Daddy made them a big, round, wooden clock with a large and a small hand. The clock was painted blue, and the hands were white. Round the clock were little holes.

Daddy also had some wooden figures with little pegs at the back, which fitted into the holes.

The first " time " the twins learned was 12 o'clock. That was an easy one, they both agreed, as the two hands were one on top of the other. They found a wooden 1

and a 2, put them up on the top of the clock, and put the hands over them. Then Mother showed them where to put the other figures so that their clock looked like this.

Six o'clock was the next they learned, as that was bed-time, and the big hand stayed straight up on 12 and the little hand went straight down to the bottom of the clock on to 6.

Then Mother taught them a rhyme and they found the right time for each line.

7 o'clock, get up and dress,
Say our little prayer, " God bless."

8 o'clock is breakfast time,
Milk and porridge, both are fine.

9 o'clock, a game with Mummy,
In the garden, warm and sunny.

10 o'clock, sit down to table,
Work as hard as we are able.

11 o'clock, our milk we drink;
The nicest time of all we think.

12 o'clock is time for play,
So we put our work away.

1 o'clock, sit down to dinner,
Eat it up and not grow thinner.

2 o'clock, we have our rest,
Like a birdie in its nest.

3 o'clock, we take a walk
In the park, and have a talk.

4 o'clock, go home again;
Earlier, if it starts to rain.

5 o'clock is time for tea;
Daddy's coming, there's his key!

6 o'clock, good-nights are said;
Off we go, upstairs to bed.

John and Jennifer had always kept a weather chart, marking whether the days were sunny or wet, windy or foggy, and they knew the days of the week. Now they knew there were twelve months in the year, and they wanted to learn their names, so Daddy bought them one of those " roller " calendars, and every day the twins used to turn the little rollers round to show one day more, and the new months. They soon learned the names of the twelve months, and Mother taught them the pretty old song which begins:

January brings the snow,
Makes our feet and fingers glow.

John and Jennifer liked this song, but they wanted to make a calendar for themselves. They called it the Twelve Months of the Year, and with Mother's help they made it up like this :

January has 31 days.
The first day is the beginning of a New Year.

February has 28 days.
The fourteenth day is the birds' wedding day.

March has 31 days,
The eighth day is Daddy's birthday.

April has 30 days.
Primroses grow in April.

May has 31 days.
The first is May Day, when the May Queen is crowned.

June has 30 days.
The sixth day is our own birthday.

July has 31 days.
The tenth is Mother's birthday.

August has 31 days.
On the first we go to the seaside.

September has 30 days.
On the first Sunday we have our Harvest Festival.

October has 31 days.
The thirty-first is Granny's birthday.

November has 30 days.
The fifth is Guy Fawkes day.

December has 31 days.
The twenty-fifth is Christmas Day,
The best day of the whole year.

READING—LETTERS THAT COME TOGETHER

MOTHER said John and Jennifer must learn some sounds that we call double sounds—that is, when two letters work together.

The first thing to learn, said Mother, is that when two vowels come together the first one usually says its name. You remember each letter had a name as well as being able to say its own sound.

There is EA as in:

sea	bean
bead	near
meat	seal

There is OA as in:

boat	road
coat	toad
foal	moan

There is AI as in:

sail	nail
pail	pain
tail	mail

and AY as in:

day	clay
play	may
hay	bay

" Then we have the House of ER," said Mother.

" Whatever is that? " said John.

" Well," said Mother, " all these say ER, when they come together. So we say they live together in this House of ER, just to help us to remember them.

er
ir
ur

We find them in words like:

her	fir	fur
hunger	bird	turn
mother	sir	nurse

" Next we have to remember the lazy letter E, which, when it comes at the end of the word, makes the working letter in the word say its name, while it says nothing at all. Words like:

cake	lake	name
like	hike	mile
joke	poke	pole
rude	mule	June

" Also we have two lots of twins just like you—OO and EE. We call OO the Crying Twins because they make a sad sound, as in:

book	good	food
cook	moon	noon
hook	hoop	pool

and the Laughing Twins, because they make a happy sound, as in:

seed	been	green
peep	deed	heed
seem	feed	reel

" That is all I think you need remember," said Mother, " except that there are a few words in which these letters don't play fair and say what they should. Don't worry about them. I will tell you what they say when you come to them, and you will soon learn these words."

One wet morning Mother said they could get all their story books and hunt through them, and see how many words they could find with the same letters in them. "Word families," she called them.

John and Jennifer thought this a good idea, and on a sheet of paper Mother ruled off "houses" for each family, and the twins had to put all the words they found in the right houses, like this:

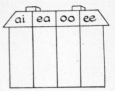

MUSIC—CONTRASTS AND MOODS

No doubt you sometimes switch off radio music and say, "I don't like that!" But do you ever ask yourself, "Why don't I like that music?"

If you had had only bread and butter for breakfast, only bread and butter for dinner, only bread and butter for tea, you would not want any more bread and butter before going to bed! Not because bread and butter is a bad thing, but because you would have had too much of the same sort of diet. Listening to music is like eating meals: if we are to enjoy it we need variety.

Make up your mind to sample all the different kinds of music. At the seaside we often hear military bands—and what fun they are! The players in red or blue uniforms, the conductor with a coloured sash round his waist, the silvery shine of the instruments, and the cheerful tunes echoing across the water. You sit back in a deck chair, gaze at the sky, and think there is nothing more pleasant in the world. We all love out-of-doors music.

So did some of the great composers. Handel wrote pieces (the Water Music) to be played on the river, and pieces (the Music for the Royal Fireworks) to be played in the park on a day of national rejoicing; Mozart and Haydn wrote many pieces to be played on summer evenings in warm, flower-scented Austrian gardens. For music of this sort wind instruments were particularly used because they are (or can be) loud instruments which can make themselves heard in the open air.

On a winter's evening we stay at home. We still want, sometimes, to have music. We sing or play pieces for one, two, or three performers. What a change is this type of music after the military band music!

We go to the concert hall. We hear an orchestra of seventy or eighty players. Perhaps somewhere else we hear a choir of a hundred singers. Again, if we are lucky, we may hear a choir and an orchestra together.

There is music for all sorts of times and places: music for all moods, grave and gay. We need never tire of listening to music. When we have had enough of one kind of music we can change to another. Just as all work and no play, or all play and no work is bad, so all serious music and no light music, or all light music and no serious music is bad. For if we stick to the same thing always we have no contrast.

Contrast is one of the most important words to apply to music. The first contrast we notice is between quick and slow. A piece which you would enjoy hearing is the overture to be played before Shakespeare's Midsummer Night's Dream. The composer, Felix Mendelssohn, wrote this because he enjoyed reading Shakespeare's play, and because he felt that he could translate some of the beauty of the play into music.

The first notes are very slow. They are four-beat notes (a semibreve or taa-aa-aa-aa). they say, and we are carried into the woods where the fairies live. We stop and listen. The sign above the note is called a pause, and tells us to wait for even longer than the note itself tells us. Composers put pauses over very important notes. Mendelssohn's slow notes keep us wondering what is coming next. Very high, because high notes are bright, we hear a quaver patter The fairies have come out and are dancing quicker than can any mortals. The fast notes sound all the faster coming after the very slow notes.

The first music of the overture is very, very soft, because it is about fairies. But in Shakespeare's woods it is not only fairies we see. There are the country folk, loud and boisterous. So, in contrast to the quiet music, Mendelssohn writes loud tunes which we cannot mistake.

The contrasts do not finish here. The fairy music is given only to the higher stringed instruments (violins and violas): the rustic dance belongs to the strings (all of them, with cellos and basses) and to the wind. The first four notes (the " going into the woods " notes) are different again. They are given to members of the woodwind family.

The fairies have their music in a minor scale: the mortals have their music in a major scale. Sometimes the music is serious, sometimes it is funny. Once or twice we hear a donkey. " Hee-haw," he says, with one high note and one low note.

When we listen to this famous overture —and the composer was only 17 when he wrote it—we listen especially to these effects, and as we notice each one we seem to see a different picture arising before our eyes.

There are many pieces, or sets of pieces, which have helpful titles, titles which tell us what kind of music to expect. Lullabies are soft, marches loud, jigs fast, solemn melodies slow. Aubades tell of the morning, nocturnes of the evening. One wonderful warm June afternoon is described in The Faun's Afternoon, by the French composer Debussy. You might find this piece a little difficult to follow, but these you will enjoy: Tame Bears and Wild Bears (from Elgar's Wand of Youth suite No. 2); The Little Chickens (from Pictures From an Exhibition, by Moussorgsky); the Roman Carnival overture by Berlioz; and the pieces in Ravel's Mother Goose suite.

We should look at such titles (there are many more), and try to make up our minds how we would ourselves describe such scenes in music—with high notes or low notes, with quick notes or slow notes, with this instrument or that. Then we can listen to what the composer has done, feeling that we know something about his work.

The more we know about contrast in music the better musicians we become. A bad choir is one which sings loud all the time. No piece of music is loud from beginning to end. This is important to remember when we are singing or playing.

Remember that a composer tells us what he wants us to do. He measures out the length of notes, he shows whether they are high or low. Further, he tells us when we are to sing (or play) soft and when loud. He tells us about this by writing in his music certain letters and signs. Here are a few of the most important. Look for them in any music which you may have in your house.

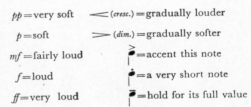

pp = very soft	$\prec$ (cresc.) = gradually louder
p = soft	$\succ$ (dim.) = gradually softer
mf = fairly loud	$\overset{>}{\bullet}$ = accent this note
f = loud	$\bullet$ = a very short note
ff = very loud	$\bullet$ = hold for its full value

ART—DRAWING WITH PEN AND INK

Most people at one time or another make little pen drawings in the margins of writing paper, on the cover of a writing pad, or on odd scraps of paper. Sometimes these sketches prove to be interesting patterns with thin and thick strokes, and some parts filled in solid. " Doodles " is a name given to the drawings done when we are not thinking what we are doing.

There is a kind of drawing which only pen and ink can produce. It is quite different from pencil drawing, and has more of a *line* look about it, and a richness in the ink line.

A good thing to draw with pen and ink is a large seashell with its spiral curves and patterned surfaces. Try to draw one on a sheet of smooth surfaced paper over which the pen will move easily without ploughing up the surface. Make the drawing fairly large, and place it well on the paper.

Try to sense the wonderful corkscrew-like curves of the shell, and express what you feel about them with pen lines. Notice the way in which the spots, jig-saw shapes, or lines of pattern come, and the effect they produce, and how well they "belong" to the shell. Where there are solid dark patterns these should be made in the drawing by putting the lines very close together; but, of course, you are creating a pen-and-ink shell on paper, and the finished drawing should look like that.

If you look at the illustrations in an old herbal or book of seashells you will find that they are really fine little pictures, each beautifully designed to give information about the subject, and at the same time to make pages of pleasing appearance.

The artist who made the drawings looked carefully at each subject, found out all he could about it, and then made a lovely pattern drawing of what he had felt and noticed.

It is surprising what a lot you know about plants which you often see but of which you seldom take particular notice. You have pictures stored up in your mind and can draw a seashell, a leaf, or a fruit

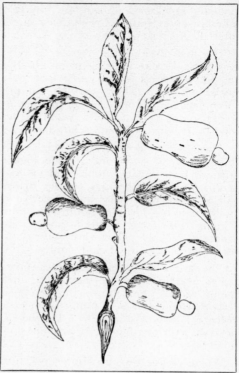

A CASHEW NUT PLANT

at will from these pictures in the store-house of your memory. The more you look at all the wonderful works of Nature the more you will notice and the greater will be your store of memory pictures; and you will tend to remember most the things you discovered yourself and which impressed you.

The artist who made the drawing of the creeping crowfoot had noticed the hairi-ness of the leaves and stalks near the root, and the way the plant extends by sending out runners which in turn send down roots to make new plants. He noticed the shiny gold petals of the flowers as well as the triangular pattern made by the leaves and the thin, wiry stalks of the flowers. He may have had a plant to look at when he made the drawing for the engraving shown in the illustration, for he was not merely copying, but drawing what he noticed and felt about the plant.

The drawing of the cashew nut was made by a West African entirely from memory, and it shows how much the memory can store and what a good sense of the pattern of the plant he had in his

THE CREEPING CROWFOOT

mind. The original drawing is 22 inches long and has a fine big feeling about it.

To make your drawing you need an ordinary writing pen with a fairly fine nib, a bottle of indian ink, and some paper with a smooth surface, an "ivory" quality paper writing pad, detail paper, or smooth thin cardboard are all suitable. Dip your pen in the ink, but avoid getting it over-loaded, and try it out on a piece of scrap paper of the kind you intend to use for your drawing. See what kind of lines you can make freely and easily. Long flowing lines and short ones, thick ones and fine ones, and try crossing some to make darks or shading in your drawing.

Next decide on what you are going to draw and the size of your drawing, and choose your paper accordingly. It is

A SEASHELL

better to work on a large scale, otherwise you tend to become niggly and cramped in your drawing. Suppose it is a twig of horse chestnut you are going to draw—the one with the sticky buds which open out in May into large hand-like leaves and tall spires of blossom. Notice the way they tend to open and the little horseshoe pattern marks on the twig where last year's leaves grew. Even the little horseshoe nails can be seen if you look care-fully. Observe how the twig gets thinner and thinner towards the end and after each little twig branches off. Feel the hard woodiness of the twig and the soft tender little hands of the opening leaves, and, when you have looked well at them and can see the pattern of your drawing in your mind's eye, draw direct and freely with your pen.

FRENCH—ON THE WAY TO PARIS

HERE the story tells how the party travel from Calais to their hotel in Paris. We must remember that the first line under each picture is the French ; the second line gives the English word for the French word above it ; and the third line shows how we make up the words in our own language.

Nous sommes à Calais.
We are at Calais.
We are at Calais.

Le bateau s'arrête.
The boat itself stops.
The boat stops.

Nous courons vers le bord.
We run to the edge.
We run to the side.

Bébé dit: " Regardez ces bonshommes ! "
Baby says: " Look at those queer fellows ! "
Baby says: " Look at those funny men ! "

Ils ressemblent à des poupées.
They resemble to some dolls.
They look like dolls.

Ce sont les gendarmes.
They are the men-at-arms.
They are " gendarmes."

Nous voulons quitter le bateau.
We wish to quit the boat.
We want to get off the boat.

Les marins baissent le passerelle.
The sailors lower the gangway.
The sailors let down the gangway.

Il est presque une heure.
It is nearly one hour.
It is nearly one o'clock.

Nous allons à la douane.
We go to the custom house.
We go to the custom house.

Tout le monde cherche ses bagages.
Everybody seeks their baggage.
Everybody looks for their luggage.

Il y a le temps de déjeuner.
There is the time for to lunch.
There is time for lunch.

Papa nous dit de rester prés de lui.
Papa us tells of to stay near of to him.
Papa tells us to keep by him.

Nous avons du lait et des gâteaux.
We have some milk and some cakes.
We have milk and cakes.

Papa regarde sa montre.
Papa looks at his watch.
Papa looks at his watch.

Il faut se dépêcher.
It is necessary oneself to hurry.
We must hurry.

Le train nous attend.
The train us awaits.
The train is waiting for us.

Nous montons pour chercher des places.
We mount for to seek some places.
We get in to look for seats.

Le train est complet.
The train is complete.
The train is full.

Enfin nous nous asseyons.
At last we ourselves seat.
At last we are seated.

Maman est très fatiguée.
Mamma is very tired.
Mamma is very tired.

Un garçon me prête un livre.
A boy to me lends a book.
A boy lends me a book.

Je dis: " Merci bien."
I say : " Thank you well."
I say: " Thank you very much."

Je regarde le livre.
I look at the book.
I look at the book.

Je le montre à Jeannette.
I it show to Jenny.
I show it to Jenny.

Nous sommes quatre heures dans le train
We are four hours in the train.
We are in the train four hours.

Enfin nous voilà arrivés à Paris.
At last we there are arrived at Paris.
At last we are in Paris.

Nous allons en taxi à l'hôtel.
We go in taxi to the hotel.
We drive to our hotel.

The Story of the Boundless Universe and All Its Wondrous Worlds

Sea scorpions of the Silurian Age

THE WORLD IN THE SILURIAN AGE

WHAT is known as the Silurian Period in the development of life and the building of the foundations of Britain, is illustrated in these pages of our Picture Geology. The lower picture on page 1010 gives a section of the Silurian limestone rocks, in which the petrified remains of the chief forms of life of that time are shown; our artist shows them very much as they are found at the present day, but of course much enlarged. In the upper picture on page 1010 is shown an ideal scene on the seashore—an impression of what the coasts of Britain were like millions of years ago.

In those Silurian times there was very little of Britain, probably no more than a few volcanic islands where North Wales now stands, and a mountainous mass studded with volcanoes in the north of Scotland and the Hebrides—the islands which appear to be absolutely the oldest part of Britain.

All the rest of our country was under the sea, most of it very deep. Around the barren coasts—for there were no trees or flowers, only mosses and ferns—strange forms of life multiplied enormously. Trilobites, which we saw in the preceding Cambrian Age, still predominated in the Silurian Period. But in the meantime the small shrimp-like type of *crustaceans*, the phyllopods, had increased enormously, and

some of this crustacean family developed into great creatures resembling lobsters. These phyllopods were destined to become lords of these early seas, and the soft-bodied molluscs—creatures like the whelk, winkle, oyster, or mussel, of which there were vast numbers—found it best to keep within their shells, when the pterygotus, the great lobster-like crustacean, was about. • Some of the fossils of these primeval lobsters have been found, showing that they reached a length of seven feet.

It is easy to understand that many of the smaller trilobites began to have a hard time with such armed monsters to contend with, but some of these persecuted creatures, in the course of some millions of years of struggling for existence, deviated from the general form of trilobites.

Active movements were essential to their safety, and while they retained the broad and hard-cased trilobite-like head, they acquired active and slender bodies. Moreover they increased their flexibility by gradually dispensing with the three-lobed shell of their bodies, which they had most inconveniently to shed periodically in order to grow, and they acquired permanent bony plates which expanded as they grew. Gradually, too, some of them developed a gristly centre of cartilage,

ASTRONOMY · GEOLOGY · GEOGRAPHY · CHEMISTRY · PHYSICS · LIFE

LIFE AND REMAINS OF THE SILURIAN AGE

A VIEW OF THE WORLD IN THE SILURIAN AGE, WITH A SECTION THROUGH THE SEA AND THE SEA-BED, SHOWING THE FIRST FISHES IN THE SEA, AND OTHER SEA CREATURES IN THE MUD

A SECTION THROUGH THE ROCKS OF THE SILURIAN AGE, SHOWING THE FOSSILS (GREATLY ENLARGED) IN THE ROCKY STRATA

extending through the middle of their soft bodies from head to tail. This was divided into numbers of joints, with a nerve running through the whole straight from the brain, which enabled these creatures to move instantly, twisting and turning in every direction with the greatest speed, so that nothing could catch them. Equipped with all these advantages they began to flourish exceedingly.

THE FIRST BACKBONED CREATURES MAKE THEIR APPEARANCE IN THE WORLD

In this period came into existence the first fishes, queer-looking little creatures. This was a stupendous event, and a great step upward in animal development, for it was the beginning of the backbone in life, so that the Silurian Age is chiefly to be remembered for the birth of the Vertebrata—backboned animals—and fishes.

From this time creatures with backbones were able to develop enormously, while those without backbones had to give place to them, and generally fell behind, becoming small and short-lived.

There was an immense amount of the lower forms of life, but nearly all, as far as is known, was in the sea. Some, like those queer animals called crinoids and cystideans, grew stalks and spent all or most of their lives attached to a rock. Others founded colonies and built up round themselves habitations of lime, which we now know as coral. Some of this coral lime, mixed with the lime of other fossils, is found today in the shape of miles and miles of solid limestone rock.

Careful measurement has shown that Silurian rock at least 26,000 feet thick still exists, and forms part of the foundations of Britain.

Most of the Silurian rock consists of limestone, other portions are composed of pebbles and petrified mud, or of sand compressed and hardened into sandstone.

THE LIMESTONE THAT WAS MADE AT THE BOTTOM OF THE SEA

These sandstone types of rocks had their origin in river mouths, sandy beaches, and coastal areas, while the limestone represents areas that were once the bottom of a deep sea.

The Silurian rocks come to the surface over a large part of Britain; and will be found just beneath the mould, sand, or made-up ground, over the areas shown on the map which appeared on page 886. Their depths will vary, as a rule, between a few inches and two or three feet, except along river banks and the bottom of valleys and similar places where rainwashings have collected from the hills.

Water-formed Silurian rocks are found not only at the surface over the greater part of Wales, Southern Scotland, and the Cumbrian district, shown in the map, but also deep down over probably the whole of England, for they have been found thousands of feet down in borings at Rochester in Kent, at Ware near London, below the Mendip Hills, and elsewhere.

Geologists divide these layers of rocks into Upper and Lower Silurian. The lower, commonly called Ordovician, now generally exhibits an earlier and simpler type of life. Their immense depth of 26,000 feet represents only what is left of the rocks formed during the long Silurian Age. How much more was laid down in this great sea that covered most of our country we cannot tell; we know only that much was subsequently worn away by the elements, and entered into the composition of the succeeding rocks.

SIXTY MILLION YEARS REQUIRED TO BUILD UP THE SILURIAN ROCKS

Existing Silurian rocks may have been formed in six million years, but it is more probable that they required a period approaching sixty million years. It is much easier to calculate the least time of a geological age than the whole time. It might be possible to estimate the minimum time it took to build a high wall knowing the number of successive layers of bricks, knowing also the rate of which the bricklayers built, but if several layers were subsequently removed from the top by wind and rain, and the rest very much bent and twisted, calculation of the time actually taken would be out of the question.

In the same way the entire existing strata of sedimentary rocks beneath the surface of our land may indicate a minimum length of time of some forty or fifty million years; yet in view of disturbing circumstances the time actually taken was probably many hundreds of millions of years. Indeed, other means of calculation —such as the time necessary for certain radio-active substances to change from one element into another, the progressive saltness of the sea—indicate that many more than fifty million years have passed since the first sedimentary foundations of Britain were laid.

BALBOA AND HIS MEN MARCH INTO THE WILD TERRITORIES OF CENTRAL AMERICA, WHERE THEY
START THE FIRST EUROPEAN COLONY

The Story of Immortal Folk Whose Work Will Never Die

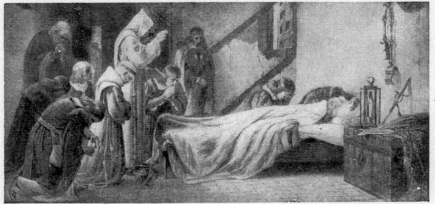

The Death of Columbus

THE DISCOVERERS OF AMERICA

IT is a remarkable thing that our knowledge of America is only a little over 400 years old. A continent exceeding the combined area of Europe and Africa is a happy accident of the map. Europe knew less about America in the fifteenth century than about the North and South Poles in the tenth.

We knew the Poles were there whether we reached or did not reach them, but the site of America was regarded as empty space. Columbus was in peril of being burned at the stake, not for saying that America existed but that land of any sort might exist where America proved to be.

Believing the world to be much smaller than it actually is, he imagined Asia to extend so far round the Earth as to thrust its eastern frontier out parallel to the western frontier of Europe. Therefore, said he, it is but a few days' sail distant.

Columbus, who gave civilisation its fourth continent, died in the belief that there were only three. America was as unthinkable to him as Australia. He sought only to find India, and to his dying day he thought he had found it.

We expect the unexpected in regard to gold mines and diamond fields. We rejoice, but do not marvel, when one is revealed in a reef of rock which breaks a farmer's heart. Another yields its treasure among the pebbles of a cabbage-patch without exciting more comment than, " What luck ! " Even our own little island, so well surveyed, revealed a coalfield under the Kentish orchards when engineers sank a shaft for the Channel Tunnel.

But a continent unknown ! A continent possessing treasure so rare, novel and revolutionary ! There was the potato, the greatest addition to food since wheat was first cultivated. There was maize to feed cattle and keep them alive through the winter. There was cotton to clothe three-parts of the world. There was quinine to preserve millions of lives from the fatal effects of malaria. There was tobacco to found a new world-wide industry. There was rubber, to give us the bicycle, the motor-car, the airship and the thousand trades depending now upon vulcanite and other rubber products. There were underground seas of oil waiting to furnish man with a new fuel to drive his ships, his cars, his aeroplanes, his ploughs, his lighting plant, his fire-engines. All these and more, new, undreamed-of powers for human advancement, lay locked up in the land awaiting to be discovered.

EXPLORERS · INVENTORS · WRITERS · ARTISTS · SCIENTISTS

In a reverie one might imagine that America *thought* and tried, with unheard voice, to call the Old World to her.

Every year America sent messages to Europe, but no one could read her language. She sent out her seeds and birds by wind and waves. Some landed and germinated; some alighted and nested, all unheeded. She uprooted her fine trees and urged them down her rivers where they took the sea, crossed, reached the Orkneys, and for centuries formed the only fuel for the island winters. The logs were used and no man was the wiser.

EARLY MESSAGES FROM AMERICA THAT NOBODY COULD READ

Long after Columbus old Sir Martin Frobisher, sailing for Queen Elizabeth, puckered his brow as he saw those sea-fed fires. But he made no guess. He thought the habits of the islanders " very rude and beastlie," jotted that down, forgot the ocean-brought trees, and went his way.

Pines from a northern clime sailed, like unmanned ships, from out of the west to the Azores; wood carved with tools not of iron came in by the same strange way, and nobody formed a theory. And, one day, Life, as if seeking reinforcements, sent out Death. Two men rose up from the sea to an Azores beach, to tell a story without words.

Form and features spoke for them where still, cold tongues could not. The men were not natives of Europe. That alone was clear. Nothing could be added, for these strangers from the waters were dead.

Then said the islanders, " Out to the west, Somewhere there is a Something."

Columbus, when he reviewed this evidence, put it more definitely: " It is a country which is fertile. It is a country which is inhabited. It is a country whose people have skill and art. It is India !"

WERE THE CHINESE THE FIRST DISCOVERERS OF AMERICA ?

And all this mystery is rendered still more romantic by marvels whose story has to be studied before we finally set sail with Columbus. The continent which seemed clamouring for a place on the map, had already been found and lost. It was already colonised in parts.

Chinese records state that early in the Christian era bold sons of the Celestial Empire pushed out across the ocean in their junks and visited a great land in the east. If that claim be valid, the Chinese may have been the first finders of America, for such a landing can only have been on the Pacific coast of that continent whose eastern shore Columbus found after sailing across the Atlantic.

The truth can never be known. Features of Peruvian life and manners are thought to have had a Chinese origin. The colonising of ocean sites by Polynesian islanders suggests that these men cannot have failed to find a continent where they adventured so stoutly for islets. Whatever their origin, people of high ability were in America before Europe knew of the land. Those original inhabitants knew as little of the rest of the world as the world knew of them. There was no more conscious communication between them and ourselves than between the Earth and Mars.

At last, however, a link seemed about to be forged between the Old World and the New. It was just as accidental as the dream visions which led Columbus to his goal. The tide began to set from east to west 500 years before the time of Columbus. As a return for her sea-borne gifts Europe sent America living men—by chance rather than of set purpose.

THE HARDY NORSEMEN WHO CARRIED THE VIKING FLAG INTO THE NEW WORLD

It was a Viking, Bjarne Herjulfsson of Iceland, who, as far as we know, first arrived from Europe. While out to harvest the sea, in 986, he was blown north and west, but instead of ships to plunder he found a continent. He did not realise it. What he did realise was that the land he saw was not the Greenland with which he was familiar. So, when a favouring gale carried him home again, he told his tale and all men wondered.

Had there been a way to the Moon those hardy Vikings would have colonised in the skies. Naturally, they returned to seek by design what Herjulfsson had found by misadventure. Herjulfsson sold his little ship to Leif the Lucky, and a second time that timber sea-bird breasted the uncharted seas and approached the coast of North America.

Leif found his object. He touched the coast of Labrador, explored south as far as Massachusetts, and then went home to report progress. That was in the year 1000. Six years later a true colonising expedition, led by Thorfinn Karlsefne, an expedition of 160 men and women, with

THE QUEEN WHO GAVE HER JEWELS

WHEN ALL ELSE HAS FAILED, THE QUEEN OF SPAIN GIVES HER JEWELS TO HELP COLUMBUS

COLUMBUS MEETS QUEEN ISABELLA OF SPAIN

cattle and all that was needed for life in the wilds, carried the Viking flag ashore.

A rich and varied civilisation flourished in Mexico and Peru at the time, but Incas and Vikings never met: neither knew that the other existed.

Three years the party of Thorfinn Karlsefne stayed in North America, without pleasure or profit. Natives, whom the Vikings called scraelings, made constant war on them and so disgusted the sea rovers that at last they hauled out their ships and returned to Iceland. The first European attempt to colonise a New World had failed, but the story was written down in the literature of learned Iceland, and there it is to this day, telling how the hardy Norsemen dwelt awhile in a land which it afterwards became an offence against religion even to imagine.

COLUMBUS HEARS OF THE THRILLING FEATS OF THE VIKINGS

But modern research suggests that those great voyages in little ships were not wasted. We know from the writings of Columbus that he visited Iceland, and the story runs that he first obtained his positive conviction of the existence of land in the west from the records of the thrilling feats of Herjulfsson, Leif, and Karlsefne.

Five centuries passed, a period of dismal ignorance. Rome and learning had fallen long before. Knowledge was in the keeping of the Arabs and they were broken by the Crusaders. It was shut up, too, in Constantinople, and in isolated monasteries. Learning slumbered for a thousand years. The Sleeping Beauty was not awakened by a fairy prince but by an ogre. The Turk appeared in Constantinople, and Learning fled before him. All that could be saved of written knowledge came into Western Europe when those cloistered scholars hurried from the city on the Bosphorus.

GALLANT COLUMBUS AND HIS FIGHT FOR HIS GREAT CHANCE

Printing and valuable things to print came together. All that had been known and guessed about geography came, and at Genoa, about 1446, in a humble woolcomber's home, Christopher Columbus was born to turn the result into golden treasure. Never was there more clearly a man with a mission. Columbus took to the sea as naturally as a swan to a river, and he was able to say in 1501, " These

40 years past I have been familiar with every place to which men sail today."

He had been down to the west coast of Africa; he had been all round the Mediterranean; he had been to Iceland.

A bold, courageous seaman, he was also deeply studious. All the books of travel available he read; all the maps and charts in existence he conned. It became a certainty to his mind that God had destined him to sail out to the West, to find India there, to reap its riches for a king, and to gather heathen souls into his Church.

How could he give effect to his dream of reaching India? Who would provide ships and men? Genoa could not. Portugal, after long disappointment and delay, failed him. Ferdinand and Isabella of Spain kept him seven weary years, while they fought out their wars with the Moors in Spain, before they would say yea or nay. He sent an offer to Henry the Seventh to carry out his project for England; he offered the same terms to France, and to Genoa again. Poor Columbus spent his time following the Court from place to place, seeking favour, and disputing with learned commissions set up to examine his scheme.

WHAT THEY THOUGHT OF THE PEOPLE AT THE OTHER SIDE OF THE WORLD

The scholars were more deadly than the Moors. Instead of discussing geography they sought to prove that Columbus was denying the teaching of the Bible. If there were people on the other side of the world they must be upside down; and to make matters worse such people, so far away, could not have been born sons of Adam, since it was impossible for them to have crossed the intervening ocean.

Columbus was often much nearer a bonfire of his bones than he was near India before the rulers of Spain at last gave him three little ships and sent him sailing, on August 3, 1492, from Palos in Andalusia. The entire venture, ships, stores, wages, cost just over £10,000. No continent was ever gained more cheaply.

The voyage is for ever memorable, not only from its results, but from its conditions. Few of the 120 men who formed the crews were volunteers. The majority had been forced into the ships by the king's orders, and one of the three vessels was obtained by lawful violence.

The friends of the crews wept on shore; the men themselves wept on board.

WEARY AND WORN WITH PLEADING AGAINST HIS DETRACTORS, COLUMBUS SITS IN DESPAIR AT THE
COUNCIL OF SALAMANCA — FROM THE PAINTING BY PROFESSOR N. BARABINO

To all they seemed doomed to death in some hideous form by agencies not of a natural kind. The first trouble was a deliberate disabling of one of the rudders, and this, with the vain attempt to get a substitute ship, caused three weeks' delay at the Canary Islands.

When the crews were not openly mutinous they were abjectly terrified. The variation of the compass caused a creepy horror in the pilots; calms seemed to threaten fixity of position, in which the ships would rot and the men perish; and favouring winds suggested that they always blew in one direction, and so would forbid return.

Had they known the thoughts of their admiral, the crews would have been still more dismayed. Estimating the Earth at one-third its actual size, he had quite miscalculated the duration of the voyage. The crew had his imaginary figures of the distance, and the facts were daily proving him to have erred, so he kept two records of the voyage. One showed the crew what he wished them to believe was the number of miles covered, the other was the true record known only to himself.

HOW COLUMBUS LOOKED FOR INDIA AND FOUND AMERICA

Days grew into weeks, weeks into months, and still he steered his westward way. "The West," he argued, "is like the pointed end of a pear. All this time I am sailing up-hill, and at the top of the hill of waters lies the Earthly Paradise."

The sight of birds cheered the mariners, but the discovery of that great tract of weeds called the Sargasso Sea, its long strands clinging to the ships like the arms of gigantic sirens, renewed all their fears. They cleared the danger and went to the opposite extreme, seeing land in every cloud, to be the more cast down when no land was reached.

Down and down sank all but the hopes of the inspired Columbus, and the men fell to mutiny in earnest. Once more fortune smiled, however, and land-signs came into view. Flocks of song-birds and a duck and a heron were seen ; fresh vegetation, a cluster of berries, a reed, a board, a carved staff—these were the evidences of life which saved Columbus from death at the hands of his crew.

As was fitting, his were the eyes first to behold sure proofs of human life. It was as if a light arose from the sea as he stood at night staring into the dark. With the earliest peep of dawn a gun was fired from one of the ships, and on the morning of Friday, October 12, 1492, Columbus, in splendid armour, with flags flying and his men in brave array, stepped ashore in the New World, knelt and kissed the ground, praised and blessed God for His mercy and guidance, and took possession in the name of the King and Queen of Spain.

HOW THEY SENT THE HERO HOME IN CHAINS

Never doubting that he had reached his beloved India, Columbus called the islands he had reached the West Indies, and the people Indians. The natives worshipped him and his men as creatures come from Heaven in great birds whose white wings opened and closed as the sailors raised or lowered the sails.

Watling Island is thought to have been the scene of the first landing. From there Columbus explored Cuba, Haiti, and other thickly populated islands ; left a fort and a little colony on Haiti, and returned to Spain with evidences of the wealth of his discovery, to be received with almost royal honours.

Three more voyages Columbus made, twice touching the mainland of America. Rivalry and jealousy caused him to be disgraced and sent home in chains. Popular indignation caused his chains to be struck off, but in the bitterness of his disgrace the poor hero retained them in his keeping and desired that they should be buried with him in his coffin.

The noble man who had given a little country a great land, died at Valladolid on May 20, 1506. Deserted by his graceless king, he passed his closing days in poverty and dismal seclusion, unhonoured as the meanest sailor who had mutinied on the ships which first sailed to the golden west.

THE UNIMPORTANT MAN AFTER WHOM AMERICA WAS NAMED

But what was that land's name? India it could not possibly be; repeated expeditions made that more and more clear. The result was melancholy. The name passed away from Columbus.

A Florentine, Amerigo Vespucci, reached Spain as a naval contractor, helped to fill Columbus's ships with stores, and so found it easy to form an expedition which, following in the wake of the

THE TWO DISCOVERIES OF AMERICA

HOW THE VIKINGS WENT TO AMERICA A THOUSAND YEARS AGO

THE FIRST LANDING OF COLUMBUS IN AMERICA

discoverer, explored the coast of Venezuela. The stories he wrote of that and of doubtful voyages which he claimed to have made gave Vespucci an exaggerated fame. He was, however, the first to proclaim the so-called India a New World.

The upshot was that when a title had to be found for the New World Vespucci's Christian name was employed, and so for all time the continent remains America, and not Columbia.

The task of filling in the new map now proceeded rapidly. Giovanni, or John, Cabot, a Genoese who had settled in England in 1490, was furnished with an expedition by Henry the Seventh, and in 1497 re-discovered the North American mainland, to which the Vikings had been. His son, Sebastian, extended the work, and as governor of the Merchant Adventurers began the search for a north-east passage to Russia. Vincent Pinzon, one of Columbus's captains, crossed the equator and discovered Brazil, whither three months later came the Portuguese Cabral, blown west to America when seeking to sail east to India.

THE SPANISH ADVENTURER WHO CLAIMED THE PACIFIC

Adventurers flocked west in everincreasing numbers. Romance was still mixed with fact, and Juan Ponce de Leon, sailing to find a fabled abode of eternal youth, founded Florida in 1513. Following that, Vasco Nuñez de Balboa, a Spanish adventurer of the loftiest type, reached the isthmus of Darien, and, hearing from natives in 1513 that a great sheet of water lay westward, proceeded in haste to test the story.

There, climbing a tree in a dense forest, he looked out and beheld the boundless Pacific Ocean, and rushing down, flung himself into it and claimed the ocean and all its contents for Spain.

Other names which come into our chapter include Juan de Grijalva, who first heard of the wealth and civilisation of Mexico and set Hernando Cortes to work upon a marvellous career of conquest; while Francisco Pizarro gained Peru by deeds as colossal and cruel. Francisco de Orellana made a splendid march right down the river Amazon; Hernando de Soto conquered the land between the Gulf of Mexico and the Ohio, reached Arkansas and died on the scene of his conquest.

The French took a hand in the contest for territory and knowledge, and between 1533 and 1543, Jacques Cartier made three splendid voyages to the north-west, and found and explored the St. Lawrence up to where Montreal now stands. Our noble-spirited Sir Humphrey Gilbert, a man of the true Elizabethan type, took possession of Newfoundland, our first North American colony, in 1583, to go down to death when his little 10-ton ship, the Squirrel, was swallowed by the sea on her homeward way.

THE BRAVE HENRY HUDSON AND THE HEROIC JOHN SMITH

Equally sad was the fate—which remains to be told elsewhere—of Henry Hudson who, beginning his voyages in quest of "the spicery isles" by way of the dim north-west, touched Nova Zembla, sailed into the Hudson River, and finally entered the great Hudson Bay, where death took him.

And a Smith was there, too—Captain John Smith, of whom we read among the Empire Men. After adventures in Europe which read like a stage-play, John Smith joined an expedition in 1605 to colonise the land known as Virginia.

Magellan and Drake are linked with America. Drake, indeed, blown south for days, cleared the mainland and proved that the New World does not stretch on to the South Pole.

Other names which cannot be left out of the records are those of Sir Thomas Cavendish, the third man round the world; Samuel Champlain, intrepid explorer and governor of Canada when all Canada was French; and Pedro Teixeira, systematic searcher of the luxuriant Amazon wilderness.

PERHAPS THE HAPPIEST ACCIDENT OF THE MAP OF THE WORLD

The whole wonder was founded, as we see, on inspired ignorance and fortunate miscalculation, transformed by heroism and genius into one of the grandest of revelations. A continent appeared where a familiar country's coast was sought. Seventeen million square miles of land and an ocean exceeding in area Columbus's estimate for the entire world were found in the position where it was death to argue that land could be.

In four centuries America has become a giant among nations. Nevertheless, she began her career as perhaps the happiest accident of the map of the world.

PROUD CORTES AND THE CABOTS

CORTES MARCHES ON TO THE CONQUEST OF MEXICO

JOHN AND SEBASTIAN CABOT LEAVE BRISTOL ON THEIR FIRST VOYAGE OF DISCOVERY—FROM THE PAINTING
BY ERNEST BOARD

THE MEETING OF ROLAND AND OLIVER

"WE ARE BETRAYED AND OUTNUMBERED!" CRIED OLIVER TO ROLAND. "SOUND YOUR OLIFANT FOR
CHARLEMAGNE, AND PREPARE TO FIGHT DESPERATELY TILL HE COMES." See story on page 1025

The Great Stories of the World That Will Be Told for Ever

MILOSH RIDES WITH THE TSAR

THERE was once a Tsar called Doushan, who sent to King Michael of Ledyen asking for his daughter's hand in marriage.

The King replied:

" The Tsar shall have my daughter as soon as he likes to come to fetch her. Only in his procession he must not bring his nephews Voukashin and Petrashin, for they are quarrelsome fellows, and I will not have them in my Court."

When he got the message Tsar Doushan cried angrily:

" A curse upon my nephews, whose names are a scandal in a foreign country! When I return from the wedding they shall be hanged at their own castle gate."

One day the two brothers saw a gay company riding across the plain. All the finest gentlemen and the handsomest horses were there, with lances, pennons, and costly merchandise as a present to King Michael.

" Why have we not been invited to ride in the wedding procession? " asked Voukashin. " We are the Tsar's kinsmen, and the best knights in his army. There is some treachery."

Petrashin said: " The Tsar goes riding to a foreign country without a hero at his side. If there is treachery not one of those pretty courtiers will help him."

Their old mother spoke.

" Fetch your brother Milosh from his sheepfold in the hills. The Tsar has not seen him for many years, and no one will recognise him. Let him join the procession in disguise that your uncle may have a true heart at his side in time of need."

Milosh, the youngest, unlike his brothers, lived a simple life as the head of a band of shepherds. Nevertheless, he was brave and a good horseman. Petrashin gave him his own famous horse Koulash, while Voukashin dressed his brother in a fur cap and sheepskin cloak—the costume of a poor Bulgarian.

Milosh soon caught up the procession, and, joining the servants, asked if he might help them in return for his food.

All went well till toward noon Milosh was overcome by an old shepherd's habit and fell asleep. When Koulash no longer felt a firm grasp on the rein it stepped forward to the front of the procession, for as it belonged to a royal kinsman it was accustomed to go with the Tsar.

At this some would have clubbed the shabby stranger; but the Tsar laughed, and had him awakened, whereupon, covered with confusion, he wheeled round and joined the servants again.

When they were well advanced into the foreign land a herald came to meet them saying that King Michael's champion

IMAGINATION · CHIVALRY · LEGENDS . GOLDEN DEEDS · FAIRY TALES

challenged them to single combat, and unless one of the wedding party could overthrow him none of them should return home alive.

Now the fame of this champion was well known at the Tsar's court, and a silence fell on all the gay cavaliers. Doushan cried bitterly:

" Ah, if my nephews were here I should have no cause to be ashamed before these foreigners."

Then Milosh rode forward and said: " O Tsar, let me meet the champion."

The Tsar looked at his courtiers again, but no one spoke, so he said:

" Yes, Sir Sheepskin, go and do what you can for my honour."

Milosh went forward, and the challenger refused to meet such a fellow till Milosh taunted him into fight. Koulash wheeled and danced about him like lightning, while Milosh dealt such shrewd blows with his club that he sent the champion's sword spinning, and splintered his lance. Then, as he fled, Milosh galloped in pursuit, and just as his enemy gained Ledyen, flung a spear that pinned him to the city gates.

The Tsar gave Milosh many golden ducats, and said:

" You deserve to be ennobled, you brave beggar."

But presently King Michael sent another herald to say that the Tsar could not have his bride or his freedom unless one of his men could shoot an arrow through a ring and transfix an apple which hung twelve paces away. After that he must jump over three horses which had swords fixed to their saddles, point uppermost.

Milosh performed these feats, for no one else would or could.

Last of all he had to pick out the Princess from a bevy of beautiful maidens. None of the guests had ever seen the damsel; they only knew that she was extremely beautiful.

" It is impossible," said the Tsar.

" Not so," returned Milosh. " I can tell all my sheep apart, and I shall recognise the Princess from her likeness to her brother, whom I happened to see yester-eve on the ramparts."

Then, when all the tests were passed, the king was obliged to give up his daughter. But he did not give up his enmity, and sent an assassin after the wedding procession. Milosh was on the look-out, and discovered the ambush. He was now loaded with favours, and rode at the Tsar's left hand.

When they were back in their own country, and drew near the brothers' castle, Milosh turned to the Tsar, and said:

" My road lies yonder. Farewell, and Heaven bless you, Uncle! "

Then the Tsar understood, and bent his head with shame.

" May evil befall me," he cried, " if ever again I ill-use my kinsmen! "

THE MINSTREL QUEEN OF SPAIN

A LONG time ago the fierce Moors invaded Spain, defeated the Spaniards, and captured their king. The lovely Queen of Spain at once dressed herself in boy's clothes and went to the tent of the Moorish chieftain, and sang to him as he sat feasting with his companions.

" What a divine voice! " said the Moor. " Boy, you shall have a royal footstool! "

He forced the King of Spain down on the ground, and the singer put her feet softly on his neck. When the singing was done the Moor cried:

" Boy, you sing like an angel! Ask what you will, and I will grant it."

" Let me take this young king back to his people," said the singer.

Her request was granted, so she led the king into the northern mountains, and there they met the Spanish minister.

" Sire, you must marry again," he said. " Your queen has deserted you and joined our enemies."

A feast was held, and the cunning minister put his daughter next to the king, and she smiled on him. But the king turned away from her, and said to the singer: " Boy, sing me something merry."

And the singer sang:

Down the hills and along the plain,
Lute in hand, went the Queen of Spain,
Dressed in the clothes of a boy she went
And sang in the Moorish chieftain's tent.
He gave her a footstool fair and strong,
And she won the footstool with a song.

The King of Spain then recognised his wife. He took her tenderly in his arms, and had the cunning minister punished. In the end the Moors were defeated and driven out of Spain.

ROLAND FALLS AT RONCESVALLES

This is the story that the minstrel Taillefer chanted as he rode before the Norman troops at the Battle of Hastings.

MARSILE, the Saracen king of Saragossa, sat long in council with his emirs. Charlemagne had conquered every other part of Spain and forced the pagan kings to embrace Christianity; their own mountainous stronghold must fall in time. What was to be done?

A hopeless silence fell on the Saracens, but at last Blancandrin spoke.

He counselled Marsile to send an embassy to the Frankish Emperor with great gifts and hostages to ask for peace, and to promise that if Charlemagne would lead his army out of the land Marsile would speedily follow him to Aix, and there be baptised a Christian. Once the Frankish army had gone Marsile need not keep his vow; the hostages would be killed, but they would die for their king, and Blancandrin offered his own son to be one of them.

Marsile accepted this counsel, and sent Blancandrin to Charlemagne, with lions and bears, greyhounds, hawks, and dromedaries, and four hundred mules laden with silver, and in addition to these went a band of nobly-born boys as hostages.

The Emperor heard Marsile's message in amazement; after pondering it for a little he sent Blancandrin back, saying that he would send an ambassador with his reply.

Then, sitting beneath a pine tree, he debated whether this were a true message of peace or not. First spoke Roland, the Emperor's nephew and the hero of many a perilous adventure. He cried that Marsile was a traitor who had murdered two Franks who came to him with olive branches: it were better to lie in siege all their lives than leave him unpunished.

But Ganelon, Roland's stepfather, said that seven years' war was enough; and the old Duke of Neimes besought Charlemagne to make peace:

He who entreats your pity do not spurn.
Sinners were they that would to war return;
With hostages his faith he would secure;
Let this great war no longer now endure.

The Emperor, agreeing, asked whom he should send as ambassador to the Saracens. Roland begged for the dangerous errand, but his friend Oliver said the hero's temper was too hot for such delicate work. Oliver and the Duke of Neimes and Archbishop Turpin were denied the task by Charlemagne, who would not spare them.

Then Roland said that the best man for such a purpose was the shrewd Ganelon. The Franks instantly agreed, and Charlemagne approved the choice.

But, instead of being honoured, Ganelon was infuriated. His temples grew crimson as he cried to Roland, " Ah, I knew you hated me, and now you send me to my death! Well, I go, and I shall not return, but I will find some way of avenging this treachery yet! "

Roland laughed, and offered again to go instead, which angered his stepfather still more. A long-smouldering envy had flamed up into a passion of hatred for this idol of the army, this flawless knight. Ganelon flung himself away from the gathering, and set off sullenly. By the time he reached the Saracen camp he was ready even to turn traitor for revenge.

When Ganelon returned he brought full assurance of Marsile's good faith, and the Franks joyfully prepared to go home. The mighty army was ready to set off through the narrow defiles of the Pyrenees; it only remained to decide who should be the one to guard the rear.

The question was no sooner out of Charlemagne's mouth than Ganelon exclaimed that so important a charge must belong to the Emperor's nephew. Roland thanked him eagerly, and vowed that Charlemagne should not lose one sumpter-mule or stirrup strap through him.

Slowly the great army moved through mountains, and at last the advance-guard came out on the other side, and

Saw Gascony, their land and their seigneur's,
Their little maids and gentle wives and true.
There was not one that shed not tears for rue.

Last of all, the rearguard of twenty thousand picked men entered the narrow valley of Roncesvalles. With them were the famous Twelve Peers of France.

But presently a confused noise came to Oliver's ears. He rode to a little knoll and looked toward Spain. The whole countryside glittered with steel like a moonlit sea.

" We are betrayed and outnumbered! " he cried to Roland. " Sound your olifant for Charlemagne, and prepare to fight desperately till he comes."

But Roland refused to sound his horn for help. He would rather die than endure such shame.

Archbishop Turpin rode on to a little mound and preached his last sermon, clad in armour. He exhorted the Franks to repent of their sins; he gave them absolution, and the penance he appointed was to strike good blows.

The Franks rose from their knees and leapt into the saddle. Headed by Roland and shouting their famous battle cry of "Montjoie!" they charged the oncoming Saracens with vigour.

The battle which followed was savage and dreadful beyond words. Men who had hoped to see their homes in a little while were butchered and trampled in the narrow defiles. Their comrades, driven mad by the treachery, wrought fearful havoc in the ranks of the Saracens. Although they were outnumbered, although they lost half their men, such was the fury of the Franks that they forced the Saracens to retreat.

And now Marsile himself came up with a second army.

Roland looked round to see the earth strewn with his men, and the remnant bleeding and weary. He knew that all was lost. He would have sounded his olifant, but Oliver said:

"It is too late. If you had not been too proud to wind it at the outset these men would not have perished. Let us die too."

Then Turpin said: "Sound the olifant, and Charlemagne will come to find that we died faithfully, and he will give us Christian burial."

Roland sounded his horn three times, blowing with all his might. Far away Charlemagne heard the faint sound. He guessed the treachery. He had Ganelon bound. He called his captains and thundered back through the passes. But he came too late.

Marsile was now close at hand. Roland heaved a sigh for his slaughtered friends:

Lords and barons, may God to you be kind,
And all your souls redeem for Paradise!
And let you there mid holy flowers lie . . .
Barons of France, for me I've seen you die,
And no support, no warrant, could I find.
God be your aid, who never yet hath lied!
I must not fail now, brother by your side,
Save I be slain for sorrow shall I die:
Sir companion, let us again go strike!

Once more the Franks flung themselves into the battle. Before long Oliver was killed by a spear thrust through his backbone. Roland loved Oliver with all the ardour of his headlong nature, and when he saw his friend on his knees, with his helmet bowing to the dust, and his eyes veiled in blood, a rage came upon him which was terrifying to see. He felt his wounds and his weariness no more. He seemed to the Saracens like some supernatural being, angel or dragon, and he inspired the Franks afresh. They fought on, they performed prodigies, and when the pagans heard Charlemagne's horns from afar they turned and fled.

Roland had been surrounded. Suddenly his foes were gone. He stood with his mail hanging in tatters. He looked about him. No living Frank was left except the just-breathing Archbishop, who smiled at him and said, "The field is to us twain."

Then Roland's heart would have burst, and he felt the weakness of his wounds come upon him all at once. Yet he commanded his strength once more, and went about the field finding the bodies of their closest friends and bringing them to the Archbishop to be blessed. When he had laid down Oliver's body Roland swooned. Turpin tried to creep to a brook to bring him water, and died on the way.

When Roland came to his senses and found the last baron dead and the field his alone he tottered away to a little hill overlooking Spain. He tried to break his sword on the rocks, but he could not. Now he sat down with the sword behind him. He prayed to God for mercy on the sins of his comrades and on his own.

Over his arm his head bows down and slips,
He joins his hands: and so is life finished.

Charlemagne found him lying upon his sword, his face turned toward the enemy.

When Roland fell at Roncesvalles
  The last man on the field was he;
He stumbled to a little hill
  And laid him down beneath a tree.

On one side lay his lovely France
  He had not seen for seven years;
And thence, too late, the Franks would ride
  With swords as useless as their tears.

On one hand lay the land of Spain,
  The scowling rocks, the reddened sands;
And thence in treachery had come
  Mahound's black-faced, black-hearted bands.

When Charlemagne reached that silent field,
  And wandered there in direst pain,
He found the good knight Roland dead,
  And lo, his face was turned to Spain.

O grant us, Lord, to live and die
  As Roland lay upon that hill,
Not yearning for the land of ease,
  But fronting toward your foemen still.

THE PRINCESS WHO BECAME A GOOSE GIRL

A BEAUTIFUL Princess was to be married to a Prince she had never seen.

Preparations were made for the wedding, and the time came when the Princess had to bid farewell to her mother. The Queen was very sad at this parting, for the Prince's kingdom was so far away that she felt she might never see her daughter again.

As they were saying good-bye the Queen pricked her finger so that three drops of blood fell on to her handkerchief. Then, giving it to her daughter, she said :

"Carry this with you wherever you go, and no harm can ever happen to you."

The Princess thought this strange, but she obeyed, and soon set out with her maid to the land where the Prince lived. Before they had gone far the Princess began to feel very thirsty.

"Please fetch me some water from the brook," she said to the maid.

But the maid answered rudely : "I shall not."

The Princess made no reply, but alighted from her horse, drew the water for herself, and rode quietly on again. And the handkerchief said : "If your mother knew, it would break her heart."

By-and-by the Princess said again : "I am thirsty. Please fetch me some water."

But the maid answered : "You may fetch it yourself. I am not going to be your maid any longer."

THE PRINCESS BECAME A GOOSE GIRL

Again the Princess made no reply, but alighted from her horse and drew the water. And the handkerchief said once more : "If your mother knew, it would break her heart."

The Princess wept, and the handkerchief fell out into the brook.

Then the maid, who knew that the handkerchief could no longer protect her mistress, said : "Give me your dress, and take mine. We will change places. Take my horse and I will take your horse Falada. I will marry the Prince, and everyone must think that I am the Princess. If you refuse I will kill you."

The Princess was so terrified that to save her life she consented, and they rode on. Presently they came to the palace, and the maid was treated as the Princess, and the Princess as the maid. As the poor Princess stood, sad and alone in the yard, the King happened to look out of the window, and saw her.

"Do you want work ?" he inquired.

"Yes, please," answered the Princess.

"I want a girl to help my lad Kurdchen to mind the geese," said the King, "and if you would like to stay here you may be my little goose girl."

And so the Princess became a goose girl, and spent her days with Kurdchen.

Now, the wicked maid was frightened that the horse Falada might tell the King all that had happened, so she ordered his head to be cut off. But the Princess loved Falada, and she persuaded Kurdchen to hang its head over the kitchen door, and every day as she went out she would say to it : "Do you know who I am, Falada ?"

And the head would answer her : "You are the Princess. If your mother knew, it would break her heart."

One day the Princess let her golden hair down while Kurdchen was by. The lad was so struck with its beauty that he wanted to cut off a lock for himself. But the Princess refused, and this made him so angry that he ran to the King and told him that she was a witch.

When the King heard the story of the talking head that hung over the door, he wondered what it all meant. The next day he sent for her.

The Princess entered the palace and appeared before the King, who was so impressed with her beauty and grace that he asked : "Who are you ?"

"Alas ! I dare not say," she replied. "I have sworn to tell no one, and if I break my word I shall be killed."

Then the King said : "I am the king of all this land. No one shall hurt you. Tell me all and I will protect you."

The Princess burst into tears.

" I am the real Princess who was to marry your son, the Prince," she said. "But my maid took away my dress and my horse because she wished to marry him herself, and she threatened to kill me if I told anyone."

" Do not be afraid," said the King, who knew at once that this charming girl was the true Princess.

The King comforted her, had her dressed in royal robes, and sent for the Prince. She looked so beautiful and happy that the Prince immediately fell in love with her, and they were married that very day. A great feast was prepared, to which all the people of the Court were invited, and there was much rejoicing and merry-making because the true Princess had married the Prince.

The wicked maid was severely punished, as she well deserved, and banished from the country.

THE EGLANTINE AND THE MYOSOTE

IN the midst of the forest, near a rivulet that glided peacefully by, there grew among the moss an Eglantine.

It bore a single flower, the first in the year to bloom. This solitary blossom had for the first time unfolded its tender pink petals under the influence of the morning Sun, and they were lazily stretching themselves and smoothing out their creases in the fragrant summer breeze, while the satin calyx was still moist with dew. This Eglantine was so beautiful that the whole forest admired it.

At its feet, in the dark green moss, a pale Myosote, frail and delicate, stood looking at his little head reflected in the stream. Just out, he, too, was tasting the joys of life and admiring everything around him. Of all the neighbouring flowers the Eglantine especially took his fancy. He had only to raise himself a little on his stalk to catch sight of her, pink and white, amid the foliage. Of her he thought the livelong day, and of her he dreamed all through the night.

One evening the little Myosote fell to thinking how great would be the delight of being beloved by the beautiful Eglantine, of having her tender look fall fondly on

him, who was such a little insignificant thing, and he resolved that the very next day he would tell her of the hopes and fears that filled his heart.

So, on the next day, while dawn was painting the sky with wonderful colour, the little flower with the loving heart gathered courage, and timidly spoke of his love for his beautiful neighbour.

The Eglantine listened thoughtfully, and was moved.

" My dear little friend," she replied, " my answer is Yes. Let us love each other. I, too, feel affection for thee." And, bending over the poor little dazzled Myosote, she kissed him.

Alas ! their joy was not to last. A little dark-haired, black-eyed gipsy, clad in a ragged red dress and a grey apron, happened to be wandering along the bank of the streamlet. She stopped, plucked the Eglantine, fixed it on her frowsy hair, and ran off.

For the last time the little Myosote cast a despairing look at his best-beloved. A great quiver ran through his frame, and in bitter tones, sounding like the cry of a soul in distress, he called after her his sweet emblematic name, "Forget-me-not ! "

Nature's Wonderful Living Family in Earth and Air and Sea

Beavers building a dam

GNAWERS AND BURROWERS

THE Parable of the Talents applies with the same justice to the affairs of animals as to the affairs of men. Nature, like the man travelling into a far country, divided her gifts among her children, and chapter by chapter we see to what account those gifts have been turned.

The rodents were marked off from the rest of created things by a single four-fold talent. It consisted of four superb, live chisels, growing in the mouth, two in the upper jaw, two in the lower.

They have grinding teeth of course, teeth in the hinder part of the jaws; but the incisor teeth are the spear-head with which the rodents attacked their problems.

With four teeth they have achieved more than the man-like apes have compassed with four hands !

The gorilla has not put his talent to fruitful account. Like the sluggard in the parable, he has hidden it, not in the earth, but as unprofitably in the tree-tops. The rodent, however, fronting the world with those fine chisel-teeth, has gnawed his way to almost world-wide possessions.

In fact, the rodents are so many in species, so countless in numbers, as to form the greatest problem in the relations between man and the animal world. These thriving billions are more destructive of human fortunes than all the lions, tigers, elephants, wolves and wild dog forms. Statistics which are published from time to time show that damage costing millions of pounds every year is caused by the hordes of rats that infest our country. The mouse, far more numerous, causes almost as great a loss.

How, then, can such an order find favour in human sight? The answer is that rodents are old and civilisation new. They housed in the earth, and made homes in the trees before ever man built a house. They helped to prepare the world for our coming.

They were husbandmen and caretakers before our rise; and now they insist on sharing with us. We were the first invaders, theirs the territory taken. They have clung to their ancient homes, and, in return for our intrusion upon them, some have boarded our vessels and sailed with us wherever ship could sail, to colonise our dwellings, while we have colonised the land.

The account is not all one-sided. Squirrels, chinchilla, musquash, hare, and rabbit surrender life to clothe as many people as can buy furs, and there would be a marked deficiency in food supply if the flesh of rabbits and hares were no longer available.

It is true that squirrels take young birds in their nests, but we cannot keep down the wood-pigeons which pillage our fields.

PREHISTORIC LIFE · MAMMALS · BIRDS · REPTILES · FISHES · INSECTS

Now the young wood-pigeon is part of the natural food supply of squirrels.

The same little animals damage trees by nipping off the young branches as they bud forth. In common justice let us remember that the squirrel, and that other forester, the jay, gave us our woods. They bite down a growing tree's new limbs, but they planted the acorns and nuts from which our oaks and beeches mainly spring.

Moreover, the richest cornland in the world, the wonderful black loam of Manitoba, was prepared for cultivation by the labour of countless generations of rodents in mixing up decaying vegetation with the underlying soil. Similar land in Russia had a like origin.

It is impossible to view with resentment a Nature order which has the dainty squirrels at its head. Our little red British beauty has a multitude of cousins. First come peculiar little African animals, whose tails, furnished underneath with horny projections for use in climbing, cause them to be named squirrels.

THE SQUIRREL WITH ITS COAT OF BRILLIANT COLOURS

They are not squirrels, but little creatures that have grown up on squirrel-like lines; and as they must have a name, squirrels they are called, though science prefers to name them simply scale-tails. Some of them are mouse-sized, some are 14 inches long. The spiny squirrels of Abyssinia and elsewhere have thorny prickles among their fur, like the tenrecs of the Insectivore group.

Pleasanter to handle are the palm squirrels, which add insects to a general diet, and with delightful impudence enter human habitations. More formidable are the big species whose proportions—a full foot from the nose to the root of the long and bushy tail—entitle them to their description of giant squirrels. They belong to that forcing-house of animal life, the Indo-Malay countries, and one of the species has the distinction, rare among mammals, of a coat of brilliant colours during the courting season.

Our own ruddy gem, the common squirrel, ranging from Ireland to Japan, and from Italy in the south to Lapland in the north, has a slight change of colour, his foxy red coat of summer sobering down for winter by an admixture of greyish-white hairs. In the warmest part of its wide range the common squirrel does not hibernate.

In Britain and elsewhere, however, the squirrel has the daintiest nests in which to winter, snug and secure in a tree. So long as he is well conditioned he sleeps away the day and night. When hunger urges he awakes, pops down to one of his storehouses in the ground, extracts his nuts or acorns, re-charges his clamorous little stomach and goes back to bed.

THE GREY SQUIRREL THAT THRIVES IN THE LONDON PARKS

America has a red squirrel, redder than ours, called the chickari; but the common species there is the grey squirrel. By an astonishing freak of acclimatisation London knows more of this squirrel than of any other variety.

Early in the present century there was a surplus of squirrels born of a few introduced from the New World, so some were released in Regent's Park and Richmond Park. By every law of probability the little explorers ought soon to have been destroyed. But no, they have increased beyond all reckoning.

From Regent's Park they spread over a great part of Britain, banishing our gentler red squirrel from the woods and becoming such destructive pests that farmers everywhere wage war on them. For all their pretty ways they are wanton destroyers.

Their conquest is not by right of battle. Apparently it accords exactly with Darwin's theory of the struggle for existence. The grey seem more enterprising than the red, and observation suggests that they plunder the stores of the English species, leaving these to starve or retreat.

THE SQUIRREL ENGINEERS WHO BUILD THEIR HOUSES UNDERGROUND

Between 70 and 80 species of squirrels are known, and we must go below ground to find many of them. The chipmunks, common to old world and new, are ground squirrels, which store food in their subterranean homes, have additional supplies in secure places above ground, and sleep the best part of a five months' winter away, only coming out from time to time when a rise of temperature takes place.

Allied forms are the suslik of North-East Europe and Northern Asia, and its counterpart, the striped gopher of North America. Expert underground engineers, they feed on roots, grain, and fibres, occasionally on poultry and carrion.

They are as social as bees, and have admirable underground residences, and

PORTRAITS OF THE RODENT FAMILY

RED FLYING SQUIRREL   FOUR-BANDED CHIPMUNK   THE DORMOUSE

EUROPEAN SUSLIK   EUROPEAN HAMSTER

AMERICAN FLYING SQUIRREL   THE GREY SQUIRREL   THE BEAVER

HAIRY BAMBOO RAT   THE CANE RAT

EGYPTIAN JERBOA   THE MUSQUASH

PATAGONIAN CAVY

ENGLISH RABBITS

THE AGUTI

COYPUS

HAIRY-FOOTED JERBOA

THE VISCACHA

HARVEST MOUSE

THE WATER VOLE

SALT MARSH CAVY

THE HOUSE MOUSE

THE RED SQUIRREL

INDIAN BRUSH-TAIL PORCUPINE

NORWEGIAN LEMMING

GUINEA PIGS

THE CAPYBARA

THE BROWN RAT

THE BLACK RAT

THE CHINCHILLA

PRAIRIE MARMOT

GIANT SQUIRREL OF MALABAR

THE HARE

ALPINE MARMOT

CANADIAN TREE PORCUPINE

EUROPEAN CRESTED PORCUPINE

vigilant sentinels out in the open. But here the prairie marmots excel them, for these burrow to such an extent in the soil that their colonies are termed towns.

We think a man-made village of 100 acres a fair-sized place, but prairie-dogs, or barking squirrels, as they are sometimes called, add dwelling to dwelling until a site of 200 acres is one vast marmot city. Splendidly planned, with raised towers of earth as observation posts, a marmot town is a dreamland of organised ingenuity.

But what when civilisation wants the homes of prairie marmot or suslik ? In Southern Russia, especially in the region of the Don, the suslik takes one-quarter of the wheat crop. Suppression of susliks was made compulsory there as wolf-slaughter once was in England. In one year nearly eight million susliks were destroyed, and thirty million burrows were gassed with poison. On another occasion the people were organised like soldiers to fight these corn-devouring rodents.

THE FLYING SQUIRRELS AND THEIR WONDERFUL PARACHUTES

Fortunately no such charge can be levied against the common marmots of Europe. They keep to the Alps, the Pyrenees, and the Carpathians where everything grown is the bounty of Nature. It is well, for an Alpine marmot is an animal as much as 20 inches long not counting the tail—and it has an appetite to match its inches.

One of the marmots, the bobac, which extends no farther west than the eastern frontier of Germany, is not to be mentioned without a shudder. Plague, which has again and again swept like a slow fire over Europe and consumed half the population of England, came to us from a virus-bearing flea carried by the rat. But it originates with the bobac marmot.

Apparently the bobac is immune to the effects of the evil that it carries. Somehow, somewhere, the infected insects reach the rat and travel far and wide. The rat dies, and then only does the flea forsake it, to leap upon a human being and, with one bite, sow his blood with deadly bacilli.

We are still with the squirrels, and come now to the most interesting, those which got as far toward flying as the development of a parachute of hairy muscle extending from the fore limbs along the sides to rearward, then lost their way, so to speak, and contented themselves by remaining parachutists.

Many varieties of squirrels have worked out this method of so-called flight. Some of them measure only a few inches along the body; the more generously endowed—the Pteromys—have a body length of 12 inches and more; while one, the Eupetaurus cinereus, a native of India, clothed in a dense woolly coat, is 18 inches long.

THE MARVELLOUS WORK OF THE BEAVER IN BUILDING DAMS

All flying squirrels plane down from a height, flatten out and glide to a much lower point. Many of them cover 250 feet at one swoop.

Squirrels claim our warmest affections, but of all rodents the beaver commands our profoundest admiration for animal genius. As an engineer he has no peer save among men and the social insects.

His needs are modest, merely a burrow, or lodge, on land with an outlet from which he can enter water unseen; a constant supply, winter and summer, of twigs, bark, and juicy wood for his food. His plan for securing these privileges embodies the whole art of river engineering.

Some of the best paper is made in mills built near the little streams of Kent. The first printed edition of Shakespeare includes pages manufactured by this water of excellent properties. In order to convert petty trickles into good heads of water, the papermakers dam the streams at certain times, collecting unknown quantities and using known quantities at will.

That is exactly what the beaver does. With those superb gnawing teeth of his he bites through trees, cuts them into logs, pushes these into the water, fixes them, builds logs, branches, stones, mud, across the stream, and so makes his dam. He leaves open spaces at the summit as sluices to let excess of water escape.

He makes his dam bow-shaped, with the bow facing up-stream, so opposing the greatest possible resistance to the thrust of the water.

THE LITTLE ENGINEER OF THE WATER AND HOW HE BUILDS CANALS

Architects almost worship the man who made the first arch of masonry, but this humble rodent has been shaping the outline in water for millions of years!

As trees grow scarce by the river margin the beaver works inland and fells more. Lacking strength to push or pull his logs over dry land he digs canals, lets in water from the pool, and floats his logs down them. Or, still farther inland, he constructs a series of conducting channels to drain rainfall down to a main canal, and so still navigates his timbers to the river.

There is no perfection, even in the world of the beaver. Fate comes to his door as to ours. It is the mighty claws of the glutton which rip away his roof and expose him to the teeth of the ravenous flesh-eater. And man is there with the trap and snare for the beaver's life, with the implements that begin his conversion into gloves and other articles made of fur.

THE ENERGY OF THE DORMOUSE
AFTER HIS LONG SLEEP

The success of his engineering brings the flooding and destruction of our lands, so tighter and tighter grows the noose which necessity compels us to weave about him. The finest of animal geniuses is doomed. Life would be richer and more inspiring if we could preserve him.

This is the huge assembly of mouse-like animals. America has none of the dormice. These neat little creatures are confined to the Old World, and busy themselves at night as the squirrels do by day. They sleep soundly through the winter, but when on the move in summer nights their activity is unexcelled.

Dormice that have squirrel-like tails, tiny creatures that keep entirely to trees ; garden dormice that are said to share the pig and mongoose's defiance of snake-poison ; and dormice of distinctive markings peculiar to Africa lead us to India's speciality—the dormouse whose innocent-looking jacket hides spines as effective as the thorns of a rose.

A step farther and we reach the kingdom of little animals with hind legs shaped like those of kangaroos, the jumping mice and jerboas. Kangaroos always hop; these rodents walk in the ordinary way, but to hurry they are compelled to leap, using the hind legs as the kangaroos do.

THE ANIMALS ON THE FRONTIERS
OF THE MOUSE KINGDOM

These animals are on the frontiers of the mouse kingdom ; within the pale is a mighty group, true mice, rats, hamsters, lemmings, and so on. Even Australia, lacking other modern mammals, has rats among her natives, rats as much at home in the water as ours. Their gait is normal, but, in the Old World gerbils, a terrible plague to cultivation in India and elsewhere, we return to jumping rodents.

They lead us to the least specialised of all the family, the hamsters, an ancient type from whose ancestors all the big battalions are believed to descend. The hamster is general except in Australia, and everywhere it is famous for its underground architecture, its cosy home, its neat galleries, its huge storage chambers. Into these chambers go the fruit of men's labour, so hamsters are much persecuted. Like all rodents they make good great loss of life by equal power of reproduction.

Old World rats, like the Australian, have representatives devoted to existence in the water, though nesting, of course, on shore. Our water rats are the old British rats, for both the common black and common brown have come from overseas.

One water rat, a South American species, copies the otter in living on fish of its own catching. Ours is pretty mainly vegetarian, but destructive to the bark of trees and to river banks in which it makes its long tunnels.

Great havoc is wrought, however, by our short-tailed and long-tailed field mice, whose numbers rise periodically to amazing heights even in Great Britain.

HOW THE LEMMINGS MARCH IN THEIR MILLIONS TO DESTRUCTION

Similar tides in the affairs of lemmings lead to those great fatal migrations of which we read from time to time. Prosperity brings excessive population and threat of starvation for all, so millions of lemmings sally forth to seek an imagined land.

They march straight forward, over hill and dell, through gardens, farms, villages, into wells and pools to poison water and cause typhoid ; on and on, lessened by strokes of death from starvation, injury, disease, and a host of birds and animals preying on them ; on and on to the sea, then into the water to destruction.

Some few lemmings remain behind to repopulate the old haunts, and from these arise stocks which will in turn march to doom. It is sad and terrible, but if the dismal exodus did not occur lemmings would long ago have eaten Europe bare.

The musquash, now favoured among fur-wearers, is a musk rat capable of rapid multiplication, but it has so many enemies about its home by river and marsh, that it never outgrows supplies.

It is unnecessary to add to the story already told of them, except this : that the rat brings a dozen diseases to us in addition to plague, that it gnaws the feet and legs of live animals and birds, and is guilty of more attacks upon human beings than any other animal in the country. It is an atrocious pest, but engagingly clever, the nimblest-witted of all our foes.

Many species of rats and mice reward extended study : Black, brown, striped, bandico rats, mole rats, bamboo rats, sand rats, cane rats ; striped mice, harvest mice which construct globe-shaped nests on growing corn, dainty as fairy fancies ; rat-like gophers which burrow and use their pocket-like mouths as hods to carry away excavated material ; rats and mice resembling kangaroos ; and many so uncommon as to have no popular names.

Nearest to these is a hare built on jerboa lines called the jumping hare. Then we have the big coypu, a burrower and fine swimmer, familiar to us in shows as the giant rat, and the allied hutia couga, leading us to the porcupines.

THE GREAT PORCUPINE FAMILY AND THEIR WONDERFUL QUILLS

Common to west and east the porcupine attains its finest development in the Old World, where it follows the ordinary rule as to rodent food, but is known to eat flesh and carrion, and even to gnaw bones and tusks of dead elephants. Its splendid quills are weapons of defence ; they cannot be shot out. When attacked the porcupine erects his quills and charges backward, when the quills act as spears.

American porcupines, which have much shorter quills, are amazingly good climbers, and pass the greater part of their time in the trees, feeding on twigs and leaves. South American porcupines are so perfectly adapted to arboreal life that they are called tree porcupines.

Big porcupines, middle-sized porcupines, porcupines like prickly rats, have arisen in various parts of the world, and we find that a few steps lead us to their next-of-kin in such un-porcupine-like animals as the chinchillas, whose fur is so prized, and the viscachas which colonise like marmots.

And so on to the agutis, the pacas, and the cavies, from which last group all the guinea-pigs beloved of boys have been derived ; and away again to the maras, hare-like rodents over a foot high and nearly a yard long ; and the colossus of the order, the capybara or carpincho, a native of South American rivers.

A rodent curiosity, the pica, slightly different from the rest in the matter of teeth, leads us to the hares and rabbits. These have a useless pair of tiny teeth at the back of the functional teeth in the upper front jaw, and so link with the picas.

Fleetness and cunning are the distinguishing qualities of the hares, but the Scottish hare, blue in summer, turns white in winter to match its native snows, as do all its tribe in chilly latitudes, where Arctic hare is their name.

THE AMAZING STORY OF THE RABBIT AT THE OTHER SIDE OF THE WORLD

Born in the open fields at any time between January and November, the hare is a bold swimmer, a magnificent runner and unsurpassed for its power of quick turning and doubling. It is extremely destructive to growing crops.

Rabbits are little less serious in individual appetite but far more so in result, because they increase so rapidly. A few, taken to Australasia early last century, multiplied so incredibly that they became the foremost peril to the continent's agriculture. They were trapped, poisoned, slain by scores of millions every year ; but for long they sent land out of cultivation.

Wire fencing, industry, and the turning of a foe to account as food and fur, further reduced their havoc. In recent times, too, rabbits have been eliminated by the million by a disease called myxomatosis.

Domestication has done wonders with the rabbit. We have lengthened its skull and its ears to bring about the lop and half lop ; we have developed the Angora into fleece-bearing beyond all hope; we have produced so home-like a type that it is named the Belgian hare ; and have fixed breeds of chinchillas, silver-greys, and all manner of colours and sizes.

THE CHINESE EMPERORS AND THE SKIN OF THE SILVER-GREY RABBIT

Our old silver-grey breeds wild in warrens. For generations its skin was exported to China, where it rivalled the sea-otter in favour with the emperors.

And so with rodents as a whole. They were here before crowns and empires, they have withstood all assaults. Where civic life flags, they surge back triumphant, and even where it thrives they are there, in field, farm, and forest.

The March of Man from the Age of Barbarism to the United Nations

Figures of Greek horsemen from the Parthenon frieze

PYTHAGORAS MAKES A GUESS

IN the six centuries which went before the birth of Jesus in Palestine there was one country, and only one country, which prepared the human mind for that transcendent blessing.

This country was Greece. The more men think about the Greeks of that time, the more they are astonished. To some of them it even seems that life reached its great height in those centuries, and that, ever since, humanity has been going down hill. We need not believe that these men are right, but we must all admit that every nation in the world remains to the present hour a debtor of the ancient Greeks. That is a sufficiently memorable thought, and one not often remembered.

We have seen how Thales broke away from superstition and established a speculative habit of the mind, guessing at the origin of Nature ; and we have seen how Anaximander carried his movement farther still by going outside the world for the substance of which it is made. We are now going to read about a far greater man, one of the greatest men who have ever lived, and to see how his idea of searching for wisdom led him to take a step of tremendous importance, both in conduct and in politics.

This man was called Pythagoras. He was born in the island of Samos, about 580 years before the birth of Jesus ; and there is a story concerning the ruler of this island which helps us to understand the rude character of the times into which Pythagoras was born.

Polycrates, such was the ruler's name, lived as a tyrant, a merciless tyrant, and for many years flourished in wealth and happiness ; but presently his luck forsook him, everything went wrong, and Amasis, the King of Egypt, told him that he had evidently offended the gods and had better sacrifice to them something that was very dear to him. Accordingly, Polycrates threw into the sea a ring of which he was extravagantly fond. Some days afterward a fish was caught and taken to the palace; and in it the ring of Polycrates was discovered. On hearing of this, Amasis would have nothing to do with Polycrates, regarding him as a doomed man, and, sure enough, soon afterward the tyrant died in wretchedness of soul and body.

Rather than live under such a despot, Pythagoras had left his island home, and travelled about Greece, studying men and discussing the mysteries of Nature and the problems of politics with the chief people he encountered on these journeys. Up to this time clever people of eminence had been called sages; but Pythagoras did not like this word, which seemed to him immodest, and he invented another which has remained in use ever since.

The invention of a word is as interesting as the invention of a machine, and certainly the word invented by Pythagoras has had as great an effect on human history as many machines. For this word Philosopher, which means *a lover of wisdom, a seeker after truth*, turned the whole current of the mind in a different direction.

He taught that to arrive at truth we must not think of the obvious truth which presents itself to our human senses. For example, we say that a rose smells sweet; but there may be an intellect in the universe which has no sense of smell, and so to that intellect it would not be true that a rose has a sweet smell. He taught men to

RAPHAEL'S FINE PICTURE OF THE SPIRIT OF PHILOSOPHY

Men began to see that truth was not a secret knowledge possessed by priests, or a matter in which the sages were absolute masters ; but that it was something hidden from the eyes of all, something to be sought after, and hungered for, and loved.

Pythagoras took another step forward in guessing at the truth of Nature, a very wonderful step indeed, and we marvel when we think that so long ago there should have been a man on the Earth to take this extraordinary step.

conceive of a universal intellect, and to think of things they saw on the Earth only *as they were true to this Universal Mind*.

We know now, as facts, many things that Pythagoras did not know. We know, for instance, that the Sun does not rise, that the Earth is not still, that a door is not solid, and that all things are composed of the same material. We no longer trust our senses. We all know that there is one truth for the human mind, and another for the Universal Mind. But Pythagoras

This piece of Greek sculpture, two thousand years old, was found in the Appian Way outside Rome, and is believed to be by the sculptor Archelaus of Priene, whose name appears on it. It is in praise of Homer. At the bottom the great poet is seen sitting. Behind him are figures representing Time and the Earth. Myth and History offer a sacrifice before him, and Poetry, Tragedy, and Comedy hail him as a god. In the middle of the relief are seen Apollo with his lyre, the nine Muses, and their mother, and at the top Zeus sits enthroned. The relief was probably carved about 200 B.C., and some writers think the two figures behind Homer are representations of the Second Ptolemy and his queen. The historic interest of the sculpture is the proof it gives us that even at that time Homer was worshipped as a god-man.

arrived at this stupendous conception of truth by pure inspiration.

Since his day, philosophy has been a search for this universal truth—an effort of the mind to think itself out of its limiting humanity and into the region of spiritual *reality*. Not what is real to us interests philosophy, but only what is real to the Universal Mind.

Pythagoras was a scientist and a mathematician, he believed that all things were composed of *number*; and he perhaps foresaw the day when men were to invent the wonderful language of mathematics, and were by that language to arrive at new truths about the universe.

But the scientific work of Pythagoras is not so interesting to us as his moral and political work.

He took for his god, not the popular Dionysus, who was ready to encourage all folly and to forgive all stupid excesses, but the Olympian Apollo, who may be called the god of self-restraint. Pythagoras worshipped this god, drew about him disciples who saw the beauty of a life of self-restraint, and founded a great monastic establishment in Crotona, a Greek colony in the South of Italy. So far as we know, this was the beginning of all those great monasteries in Asia and Europe which have played so great a part in the history of the world.

THE HARD MASTER WHO FORBADE HIS DISCIPLES TO SPEAK

Pythagoras was a severe master. His disciples were not allowed to speak for some years. They were obliged to learn by heart the works of Homer and Hesiod. They were encouraged to exercise their bodies and to cultivate music. Not one hour was devoted to idleness. The disciples were taught not to fight against temptation, but to make temptation impossible by attending to wholesome matters. They were always at work. They rose and lay down, ate their meals, and did their labour, all by rule. The great object of their lives was to free their souls from the tyranny of their senses, and to establish an ever deepening communion with the universal and invisible reality.

Now, the views of Pythagoras led him to entertain a certain feeling of contempt for mankind. He could not help observing some form of stupidity wherever he looked, and decided that the multitude ought to be ruled by an aristocracy.

Aristocracy means *the rule of the best*. Pythagoras did not think of aristocracy as a set of fashionable people, but as a body of virtuous and educated people. He conceived of a State as a number of human beings whose existence was governed by the most virtuous and wise among them, and governed in the interests of virtue and wisdom. He set himself to train, by severe moral discipline, a body of men fit to rule over their fellow creatures. His idea of "the best" has never been surpassed; but he left out of his account a feeling of compassion for the unwise and the stupid which could save his system from ruin.

THE FIRST GREAT MAN TO SEE OUR KINSHIP WITH THE ANIMALS

We shall see later that this idea of Pythagoras came into action among a people destined to reach the noblest height of political greatness; but it was an idea which those of his day would not accept, and it is believed by some people that Pythagoras was killed during an attack of the democratic party on his monastery.

One other teaching distinguishes Pythagoras. He was the first great man who made human beings feel not only consideration for animals, but that they had kith and kin among them. He taught that the soul never dies, that it is for ever passing from one body into another, and that life is a long experience in many different forms. This doctrine was not known in Egypt before his time.

We may say of Pythagoras that he is of the company of the greatest of the children of men. Not only did he bring the idea of philosophy into existence, and not only did he lift the human mind beyond the limitations of our human senses, but he taught that to reach our highest and to be our best, we must submit both our bodies and our minds to a severe discipline. He was a mighty prophet of *moral earnestness*.

GREEK ART AT THE HEIGHT OF ITS ACHIEVEMENT

Because of Pythagoras, Greek art reached the supreme heights of achievement. If we look into the faces of Greek gods, goddesses, and women, as their sculptors created them, we see that the characteristic which distinguishes them all is that of seriousness and self-restraint. There is no note of flippancy in Greek art. Serenity was its aim, and dignity its spirit.

Plain Answers to the Questions of the Children of the World

WHY DO I DREAM?

THE brain has many parts, and some parts of it may be asleep while another part is awake and active. That is what happens when we dream.

Most of the brain, especially the highest part of it, is asleep in a dream, but parts of it are awake, and these, unguided by the highest powers of the mind, work on the materials of past experience, especially recent happenings. Perhaps only the very deepest sleep is entirely free from dreams, and it seems certain that most of us have dreams of which we remember nothing when we wake.

The more vague and shadowy and the more easily forgotten a dream is, the fewer are the parts of the brain that have been awake; but when we have long and complete dreams, very clear, and very clearly remembered, then it is probable that more of the brain has been awake. The fewer dreams we have, the better it is, for that means that our sleep has been more complete; and if we are to have dreams, it is best to have the kind which are scarcely remembered. *No dream has any meaning about the future.*

By far the worst kind of dream is a nightmare—a dream which seems very real, and is horrible or frightening. When nightmares occur often they should be attended to. In some people they are due to heart disease, which prevents the supply of blood to the brain from being smoothly and evenly maintained. But, as a rule, a nightmare has its origin in the stomach, and it is disagreeable because it is aroused by disagreeable sensations there.

By far the most common of all these causes is indigestion, and everyone who is liable to nightmares should be very careful about what he eats before going to bed. On no account should such a person take anything like a heavy meal less than three hours before going to bed. Besides the unpleasantness of nightmares, we should remember that they mean that the sleeper is not getting sleep of the best quality, and his waking hours will suffer accordingly.

Sometimes we seem to do quite impossible things when we dream, and are never surprised at doing them, and the reason is that in a dream the very highest part of our brain, the part which has to do with our knowledge of ourselves, with judgment, and with the power of distinguishing between what is real and what is only fancied, is asleep, and so unable to do its work. When we are awake we may often build "castles in the air," or imagine ourselves doing all sorts of wonderful things; but the highest part of the brain remains active, so that all the time we know we are only imagining these things.

SUN · MOON · STARS · FIRE · WIND · WATER · LIFE · MIND · SLEEP

Why Does Furniture Make a Noise at Night ?

Perhaps we cannot be quite certain that furniture cracks so much more at night than in the daytime.

For one thing, there are other noises going on in the daytime ; for another, it is known that when we lie awake at night in the dark, our hearing is more acute than it usually is in the daytime. Still, when all this is allowed for, it is no doubt true that furniture does make strange noises at night, and that is not difficult to understand if we remember that the air has been warmed up, more or less, during the day, and then cools down again during the night.

The general rule, which is true of wood as it is of most other things, is that things expand as they are heated and shrink as they are cooled. Thus, furniture is liable to shrink more or less at night as it cools, and we can understand how different parts may suddenly get adjusted to each other, and so start the waves in the air which make us say that the furniture is cracking.

The question of moisture may play a part, too, because as air cools it is apt to deposit the moisture which it could hold in itself when it was hotter, and that moisture is apt to affect the state of whatever object it is deposited upon.

Why Have we Two Eyes ?

Sometimes we may have noticed that people, in pouring milk or putting a lump of sugar into a tea-cup, have made a mistake, and put the milk and sugar in the saucer. That is what is very likely to happen to anyone who uses only one eye.

The two eyes do not look at anything from exactly the same place, but from rather different "points of view," as we say. The brain takes these two points of view and sees from both of them together; so that it is very much helped in judging distance by the difference between the two images of a thing seen by the two eyes.

It is because we have two eyes that we see things in their relation in front of or behind each other. An ordinary photograph looks flat, because, so to say, the camera only saw it with one eye. But if we take two photographs of a thing, from two points of view corresponding to the distance between the two eyes, and then put the two photographs side by side at the right distance, and look at them with both eyes, through the simple little instrument called a stereoscope, or "solid see-er." then we see the view as if it were solid. We see it as we should have seen the thing itself if we had looked at it with our own two eyes.

How Does the Stone get in the Plum ?

A plum is the last stage of a long series of changes that happen in the flower of the cherry tree or the plum tree. After these flowers have been fertilised—which means made fertile, or capable of producing something—they begin to change. If we look on, we may think that the flower is dying. The beautiful petals fall off, not because any harm has come to the flower, but because the petals are no longer wanted.

Then a little hard thing with a tough skin appears, and that is really the fruit. But at this stage it consists of hardly more than the stone and the skin covering it. But there is a layer of very active cells which lie between the stone and the skin, and they produce the flesh of the fruit, for which we prize it. Birds prize it, too, and so they eat the fruit, and in so doing carry the stone away with them. If it is fortunate, it falls upon suitable ground, and begins to grow, or to germinate, as we say. The living interior of the stone, which contains the seed of the young plant, begins to grow and passes through the shell, and so a new tree begins to form. It was for this that the flowers were made.

Where Does Pumice-Stone Come From ?

We think of pumice-stone as merely something that rubs our skin so hard that it will take out ink-stains, but it has a wonderful history. The word is really from a Latin word which means foam, and we can see for ourselves that this stone is very light and spongy, so that it is almost like foam. It is spongy and full of spaces because it was formed under the influence of intense heat, and the spaces in it were filled with gas when it was made.

Pumice-stone is really volcanic rock, formed deep in the Earth and thrown out upon the surface from the crater of a volcano. It has a particular value for our knowledge of the Earth in that its composition tells us something of the deeper part of the Earth's crust.

Why is a Snowflake Lighter than a Raindrop ?

A snowflake is made of ice-crystals—that is to say, of solid water. Now, it is a most important and peculiar fact about water that ice is lighter than liquid water, even though it is colder. The general rule, of course, is that things get heavier as they get cooler and lighter as they get hotter, as heat expands them and cold contracts them. But at just near its freezing-point water does not obey this rule; it *expands* as it gets cooler and freezes. That is why it sometimes bursts pipes in winter if they are unprotected from the frost.

So a snowflake is made of water in a lighter state than the water in a raindrop, and yet another reason why the snowflake is lighter is that there is a great deal of air in among the ice-crystals. This makes the whole thing lighter, just as the air in the bones of a bird makes them lighter and therefore assists flight.

Why is it Hotter at the Equator than in England ?

We know that the Equator is the name given to the great line that we imagine to run round the middle of the Earth. Of course, there is no *real* line, except on maps and globes. The belts, or zones, of the Earth on both sides of the Equator are called the tropic zones, and are the hottest parts of the Earth's surface. The reason is that, no matter whether it is summer or winter, farther north or farther south, in the temperate zones—in one of which England is—the tropic zones are always very directly exposed to the Sun's rays, which strike down more vertically. For the Sun rises very high up into the top of the sky in the tropical regions, and so it is always very hot there. But it is too hot for human life at its best, and the greatest achievements of man with hand or brain have been done on one side or other of the tropical region.

WHAT IS THE BLUE RIBAND OF THE ATLANTIC?

THE term blue riband, or ribbon, is applied to certain high distinctions ; the winner of the Derby, for instance, is said to gain the blue riband of the turf, and the blue riband of the law is the Lord Chancellorship. It has its origin in the dark blue ribbon of the Most Noble Order of the Garter, Britain's most ancient Order of Knighthood.

By the same token, the blue riband of the Atlantic is held by the ship which has made the fastest crossing.

The two points between which the journey is timed are Bishop Rock, off the Scilly Islands, and the Ambrose lightship near New York. The present record of 3 days 10 hours 40 minutes was set up in 1952 by the American liner S.S. United States.

When the Italian liner Rex broke the record in 1933, she arrived in Genoa flying a long blue streamer, but this practice has not been carried out by other ships who broke the record.

S.S UNITED STATES, HOLDER OF THE BLUE RIBAND OF THE ATLANTIC

Can a Fly Hear?

The more we study the senses of different animals, the more do we learn that the sense of hearing ranks high in the scale, and comes late in the history of the progress of life; and thus we find that various creatures, whose powers of touch and of smell and of vision are marvellous, seem to be almost, or entirely, deaf.

There are a few insects which can hear, but the greater number, including flies, cannot hear at all. Every imaginable kind of sound has been tried, and insects, with the exception of very few, take no notice whatever. Lord Avebury thought that perhaps insects might respond to sounds of so high a pitch that our ears cannot hear them, but he could not get them to take any notice.

The highest string of a violin has been scraped an inch away from bees engaged in pillaging flowers, and they have taken no notice whatever. The senses of insects, including flies, are so wonderful, and in some respects so superior to our own, that it is immensely interesting to find that nearly all insects are perfectly deaf.

Why do we not Laugh when we Tickle Ourselves?

This is an exceedingly interesting question, because we cannot think about it without discovering a most important fact about our minds and the way in which they are made for use, for safety, and for the purposes of living. If we do not have this mighty key to mind and body, we shall never understand why it is that the same thing should make us laugh and squirm when someone else does it, and have no effect at all when we do it ourselves. The whole point and purpose of the feeling in our skins, and of what happens—such as laughing and squirming—when this feeling is aroused in particular ways, is that it gives us information about what is not ourselves, and leads us to protect ourselves.

Our minds have so much power over the way in which our bodies reply to things that when we know the cause of the feeling to be ourselves, and therefore nothing we need concern ourselves about, the body feels no inclination to behave as it does at all other times. The results of tickling are what is called a reflex action, and we learn from this case that a reflex action is a reply to the outside world.

If it is sought to call forth the reply by what we know not to be really the outside world—as when we tickle ourselves—then the body does not trouble. This shows how reflex actions are controlled by and adjusted to the needs of the body.

Why is it that the Sea does not Freeze?

Sea-water, like any other kind of water, can freeze, and it does freeze if the conditions are right; but there are some good reasons why the sea does not freeze nearly so easily as a pond or lake, or even a river. It is not the salt in sea-water that makes the difference so much as the depth and constant motion of sea-water. Until the whole depth of a quantity of water has been cooled down it cannot begin to freeze, for until it has all cooled, the warmer water, being lighter, must always come to the top. Therefore, when water is very deep, it is very difficult to freeze, and thus the great depth of the sea, is one of the chief reasons against its freezing.

But the sea is also in constant movement under the influence of tides and winds and currents. The motion of water interferes very much with its freezing, though not nearly so much as the depth.

But in the coldest parts of the Earth's surface the sea does freeze, as we find in polar regions. The same seems to be the case on our near and wonderful neighbour, the planet Mars, for we can see through our telescopes what looks like the ice or snow-caps at each of its Poles.

Why does Starch Stiffen Our Clothes?

Starch is a very curious chemical compound, with its own way of behaving. As a matter of fact, like the proteins—white of egg, and so on—it consists of molecules so big that we can scarcely say that it really dissolves, certainly not as sugar or salt, which have small molecules, dissolve. But it forms a sort of solution with water, and when the water evaporates the starch is left behind.

Starch is called one of the substances that are not at all volatile—that is, able to fly off into the air. The big molecules of the starch, left behind in the clothing, form a sort of stiff layer by all holding together. We know how water affects this when we see how our collar gets limp if we perspire.

Why does Oil help the Wheels to go Round ?

It all depends upon where the oil is put. If it be on the ground, then, though the wheel will go round when it is driven, it will not grip, and we find that the motor-car, for instance, does not go on. But there is a very useful and, indeed, all-important place where oil does make the wheel go round more easily, and also makes it last far longer. That place is the axle, on which the wheel turns.

Here there is rubbing, or friction, for the wheel turns and the thing which supports it is still. The friction means that there is wear and tear and the making of heat. These things have to come from somewhere, and they come from the power of the motion of the wheel. This means that the wheel has to move more slowly, for it has lost part of its power of motion.

When we use oil we get a very smooth layer between the wheel and the axle, and that lessens the friction, and so saves the power in the wheel. Nowadays it has been found that if tiny little steel balls are used, and kept properly oiled, they save still more friction, and these ball-bearings, as they are called, are now used in all sorts of machines where it is important for wheels to run smoothly and wear long and well.

If we think of oil as made of a vast number of smooth balls, far too small to see, we shall understand that oil itself makes a kind of ball-bearing.

Does Air Dissolve in Water ?

Certainly air dissolves in water, and the pleasant taste and sparkle of nice drinking water are due to the air dissolved in it. If we are in some part of the country where we are not sure about the water, and fear there may be dangerous microbes in it, perhaps we boil it in order to kill them. When we boil it, we drive out the air which was dissolved in it, and if we keep up the boiling for some time, we do this very completely. As it cools, the water dissolves a little more air in it again, but we shall still find it very flat and dull to drink. The thing to do is to pour it a long distance through the air from one vessel to another a few times, and then it will become sparkling and pleasant again, When we go on boiling the water we use for making tea or coffee, we spoil the beverage, because we drive out the air

dissolved in the water. The water riches: in air will, of course, be that in a shallow running stream, and that is the kind of water which was praised long ago as the best for making tea with. If air did not dissolve in water, no life of any kind could exist in water.

If the Earth is a Ball, why does an Earthquake Shake only Part of it ?

Scientists who study this subject inform us that we really need two words for what happens in what we call earthquakes, and this question suggests exactly the point they make. We should really speak of *earth-quakes*, and of *earth-shakes*. In an earth-shake, the whole Earth is shaken as it rolls through space, and this must happen because the Earth is a ball, and we cannot shake part of a ball without shaking the whole of it.

But if the ball is a very big one, as the Earth is, and if it is made of a great many different parts, including a crust of many layers, it is quite possible that we might have a disturbance somewhere that shook one of these layers against another, without shaking the ball as a whole; and that is the kind of disturbance that we shou'd call an earth-quake, and not an earth-shake.

Do Animals Think ?

The answer to this question depends entirely on what we mean by thinking. We should not say *think* when we mean *feel*, and we should not use the word Thoughts to mean feeling. To think is really to put one thing and another together in our minds, so as to make a link between them, and when the two things are linked together like this, that is a thought. To feel that you want your dinner is not to think, but to say to yourself "I am hungry " is a thought, because you have put together in your mind your idea of yourself, and the idea you have of the feeling we call hunger.

So, if we use the word properly, the answer must be that animals can scarcely think at all, but that some of the higher animals—such as dogs—do, beyond a doubt, act sometimes in a way which can only possibly mean that they have somehow " put two and two together," and to do that is to think. The answer, then, is that some animals are capable, in a very small degree, of doing what we call thinking.

Does a Rock Breathe ?

At first sight, this seems to be rather an absurd question, because we always associate breathing with living creatures, and rocks are certainly not alive in the ordinary sense of the word. It really rather depends on what we mean by the word breathe. Rocks do not have lungs; they do not take in oxygen, then give out carbon dioxide as we do; but if by breathe we simply mean take in oxygen, then the answer to the question is Yes.

Long ages ago, the rocks took in huge amounts of oxygen when they were being formed. It is reckoned that there is enough oxygen contained in a layer of rocks a few feet deep to equal the amount of oxygen in the air above them.

This process of the in-take of oxygen from the air by rocks still goes on in some degree, and it helps in part to explain why many kinds of rocks crumble and break down and wear away from year to year, especially when we take the wearing action of rain and wind into account as well.

What makes the Sea Roar ?

Roaring is a kind of sound, and though sound is something that can travel in all kinds of matter, it is usually, as we know it, a wave in the air, because, as a rule, our ears are not pressed up against any solid thing, and so all sounds that reach them must reach them through the air.

This is true when we hear the sea roaring, though a swimmer, when he goes head first through a wave may hear a roaring coming through the water when he is below the surface. Everywhere the surface of the water is in contact with the air, and if the water moves at all violently it may start in the air those kinds of waves which our ears can hear and which we call sound.

These waves are of the kind that are not very numerous in each second, and so they make sounds of low pitch which we call roaring. Sometimes, when a wave breaks, a great volume of water may fall upon the rest of the water, and so make a sound which is more like an explosion than a roar.

Tennyson wrote once about what he called " the scream of the maddened beach "; and it is very interesting to notice that we do hear on the beach sounds which are much more like a scream than a roar, though the sea itself never screams. It is the beach, and not the water directly, that makes the scream, and the kind of scream will depend on the kind of beach. Soft sand will not scream, but, where there are pebbles of certain kinds, as the waves move up and down they rub the pebbles against each other, and that produces air-waves of a quicker rate, which may be likened to a scream.

Why do the Hills look Blue at a Distance ?

The blueness of the sky is due partly to reflection of the blue rays of sunlight from dust particles in the air, and partly, as Lord Rayleigh showed, to the blue colour of the nitrogen gas in the air.

Now, if we look through a layer of anything that is coloured at something beyond it, the layer will contribute its own colour to the colour we see. The blueness of the air, however, is a very faint blue, and we do not usually notice the blueness it contributes to anything near. But when we look at distant hills we are looking through such a thick layer of air that it gives them a blue tinge. But the actual colour which we see depends upon many other things, as, for instance, the colour of the hills themselves, and the time of day—which decides the angle at which the sunlight falls upon the hills, and also affects the colour of the sunlight. That is enough to explain why the colour of hills changes from moment to moment.

What is the Cause of a Quicksand ?

Quick is really an extremely old word which means living, or moving. These words, living and moving, meant practically the same thing long ago.

A quicksand is a bank of sand in water; perhaps in the sea, or a lake, or a river, or we may even meet a quicksand when we dig in the earth. The sand moves with the water which is around or in it, and thus a person or a boat that is caught in such a sand may be gradually drawn down into it, as the water and some of the sand sinks.

The famous Goodwin Sands, once an island, may be quite firm and dry in parts for some hours, but when covered by the sea they shift and become quicksands. In this state they are terribly dangerous to vessels that get caught upon them. The weight of the moving sand is tremendous and irresistible. We must not think of it as sticky. It is the weight and the movement of it that give it its terrible power.

The Story of the Beautiful Things in the Treasure-House of the World

Christ in the Manger, by Hugo van der Goes

THE ARTISTS OF FLANDERS

ONE of the most delightful chapters in the history of medieval Europe is that telling of the interest taken by royal and other rich people in the arts of architecture, sculpture, and painting.

There are in the museums of Europe, as well as in many private collections, treasures of these early days in the form of illuminated missals, Bibles, Books of the Psalms, and other devotional volumes done by artists at the order of men who could afford to pay them for their labours. The English, Flemish, and French manuscripts are foremost in artistic merit. Some good examples in colour were reproduced on page 489 of this book.

France was particularly fortunate in her rulers in the 14th century. Charles the Fifth and his son, the Duc du Berry, showed an intense enthusiasm for matters of art and scholarship ; and to execute their commissions Flemish artists came to Paris and established, with the French painters, a kind of school there.

To this period belong a charming array of illuminated manuscripts containing miniatures, initials, border designs which preserve, to this day, their wonderful quality. Outstanding among these is the rich and exquisite Book of Hours of the Duc du Berry, illuminated by Pol de Limbourg and his brothers.

A few years later a French artist, the famous Fouquet, some of whose small illuminated books are in the British Museum, painted about forty miniatures for a Book of Hours for Etienne Chevalier. Both these manuscript volumes are in the museum at Chantilly.

Beautiful work was being done in the meantime by the English illuminators, the best belonging to an earlier period than that of the Hours of the Duc du Berry. Generally speaking, the fourteenth and early fifteenth centuries saw the end of the finest of the illuminators both in England and France.

The invention of the printing press naturally caused the death of this fascinating branch of the arts, and one of the reasons why the lovely books shown in the British Museum and other collections are so dear to us is that they belong to a period whose activities can never recur. Painting and sculpture and architecture advance and decline and advance again; the day of illuminated manuscripts is for ever passed.

Flemish art, one aspect of which showed in the decoration of these rare volumes, was the outcome of the same Gothic move-

PICTURES · STATUES · CARVINGS · BUILDINGS · IVORIES · CRAFTS

ment which had stirred the Sienese to paint their mystical saints and Madonnas.

Although we have been accustomed to look on Italy as the first home of men of genius in painting, we must not forget that at the same period the Low Countries were producing artists who rivalled them.

It would seem that the Venetians were destined to achieve an immediate immortality ; the Flemish artists are still, after five hundred years, labouring for their just renown. There are certain critics who place the early Flemish before the Italians, others who give them a different judgment. For ourselves, we have learned the story of Italian painting, and that in itself is an immeasurable benefit, for, apart from other considerations, it gives us a standard to work by. Then we must remember that artists were a travelling community, and many of the Florentines and Venetians had seen the Flemish at work and been influenced by them, just as the Low Countries had been moved by the art of Italy, so that the two great schools of Renaissance art were in practice more akin than one would think.

But perhaps we ought to realise most of all that racial temperament separates the Italian from the Flemish to such an extent that their work ought to be more contrasted than compared.

THE VIGOUR OF THE FLEMINGS AND THE IMAGINATION OF THE VENETIANS

The Flemish, impregnable in their domain of strength and truth, never had the soaring imagination of the Italians. In the art of the southern country there is always the idealistic strain ; you never know when genius is going to take wing and fly above your head. In the Flemish, uninteresting, every-day events and persons are made superbly great ; genius sits firmly on a bench by the wall and is very content with things as they are.

Then, too, there was the difference caused by climate and town life. Venetian painters lived, riotously happy, in a city that was caught in a silver mesh between a radiant sky and a radiant sea. The Flemish, breathing their colder air, were more ascetic, more moved by fixed thoughts, of a more frugal and commercial habit of life. They were a race of weavers, and had a passionate love of textures of silk and cloth.

When we think of their greatest expressions of art we think of men and women heavily clothed, generally in dark material, from whose rich gloom emerged a face and hands. There is no need for laborious composition. The person is the picture, and it contains something immeasurably great because it is the essence of humanity, the humanity that labours and contrives and is fixed to the soil.

The picture may merely be a man—a merchant—and a woman, his wife; but they are still and timeless and eternal, like the Pharaohs of Egypt who sit, carved in stone, looking out across the level sands.

TWO BROTHERS WHO STARTLED THE WORLD BY THEIR WORK

The first men who stamped the school of Flanders with this peculiar quality were the van Eycks, two brothers, painters in Bruges. Hubert, the elder, who lived from 1366 to 1426, took the greater share in a piece of work which had a tremendous effect on the artists of the day. This was an altar piece called The Adoration of the Lamb, painted for a church in Ghent. The various panels, the work of Hubert van Eyck, show in themselves the whole difference between the religious paintings of Flanders and Italy. The composition may not be so triumphant as much of that marking the southern schools, but the technique and character of the work showed the brother-artists to be without peers in that realm of painting.

Tradition gives the invention of oil painting to the van Eycks. The medium was most probably discovered before their day, but they perfected its use and learned many secrets of treatment and clear colour which artists for hundreds of years have envied.

There is something statuesque and superb in Hubert van Eyck's angels and saints; they are reposeful, quiet people, the women grave and sweet, the draperies painted in the sonorous tones that mark the Flemish school. The share of Jan van Eyck (1387—1440) in this work is uncertain, but as he was above all a portrait painter it is probable that the pictures of the donors, in this splendid altar piece, are his.

THE MAN WHO WAS THE GREATEST PORTRAIT PAINTER IN EUROPE

Jan van Eyck, indeed, stands out as the greatest portrait painter of Europe, and the chief glory of the Flemish school. When he painted saints and Madonnas he showed quite clearly that he was

FAMOUS PICTURES OF THE FLEMINGS

THE VIRGIN AND CHILD
BY VAN DER WEYDEN

THE ADORATION OF THE SHEPHERD
BY VAN DER GOES

THE VIRGIN AND CHILD
BY QUENTIN MATSYS

THE ADORATION OF THE LAMB—BY HUBERT VAN EYCK

JOHN ARNOLFINI AND HIS WIFE
BY JAN VAN EYCK

SAINT CECILIA—BY VAN DER
GOES

BISHOP GARDINER
BY QUENTIN MATSYS

PRINCESS ELIZABETH OF AUSTRIA—BY FRANCOIS
CLOUET

HANS MEMLING'S PICTURE OF THE VIRGIN
AND CHILD

THE ADORATION OF THE CHILD—BY GERARD DAVID

M VAN NEWENHOVEN—BY HANS MEMLING   PORTRAIT OF A MAN—BY THIERRY BOUTS

HANS MEMLING'S PICTURE OF THE ADORATION, IN THE HOSPITAL, BRUGES

bored; when he made portraits of ordinary men and women his power rose to a superb height.

But he was a portrait painter pure and simple. He has nothing to do with idealism, or philosophy. He did not show in a person's face the significance of the character, as Leonardo da Vinci did ; he was content with the face as it was, mirroring the thoughts and impulses which, up to that point of living, had stamped it. To this genius of insight he added genius of technique, and the result is a series of portraits which now, 600 years later, hold us enthralled.

Of the many wonderful pictures painted by Jan van Eyck three portrait groups stand out: The Merchant and His Wife, in the National Gallery—one of the chief glories of that collection—the picture of Canon van de Paelen at Bruges, and the portrait of the artist's wife. In the National Gallery are two other pictures, each described as " Portrait of a man."

THE PAINTERS WHO PUT SADNESS IN THEIR PICTURES

Roger van der Weyden, who was born in 1400, was also an artist of Bruges; and though he shared their skill in technique he was of a different cast from the van Eycks. He was a visionary and a mystic with a strange love for sad subjects and tragic places. The Descent from the Cross, in the Escurial, is a picture of beautiful sorrow. Philip le Bon, of the house of Valois, whom he painted, may have had some very happy hours, but van der Weyden saw only the grey ones, and drew the prince with a face of pathetic endurance—as of a man who had to work very hard and was over-anxious about his next half-crown.

Thierry, or Dierick, Bouts (1410–75), a man of Haarlem, who followed the van Eycks and later worked under van der Weyden, was another artist who had a leaning toward painting unhappy-looking people. But in his case it is not because he is filled, like van der Weyden, with the northern mysticism which saw the glory of suffering as greater than the happiness of the saints, but because he had a passion for drawing the brutal side of life. He could not bear to gloss over or idealise any subject, and his treatment of colour matched his crude vigour of drawing.

A little graciousness and gentleness, and a sense of beauty in composition,

might have made of Bouts a great artist. His best pictures are the Meeting of Abraham and Melchisedec, in Munich, and the Judgment of the Emperor Otto, in Brussels. Examples of his paintings in the National Gallery include The Entombment, and two Madonnas.

The Flemish school rose to great heights in the latter half of the fifteenth century. Among a number of less important names three or four stand out—Memling, van der Goes, Gerard David, Quentin Matsys.

ALL THE FEELING OF MEDIEVAL EUROPE IN ONE MAN'S PICTURES

Memling, who lived from about 1430 to 1494, sometimes called the Raphael of Flemish art, is one of the most famous names in the early story of the Low Countries. He was a portrait painter second only to Jan van Eyck, and though he fell short of the mastery of delineation which was van Eyck's peculiar genius, he added a touch of imagination and romance that the other lacked.

Memling painted a number of beautiful religious pictures and portraits. There is all the feeling of medieval Europe in his painting, The Arrival of St. Ursula at Cologne, in the hospital of Bruges, and it is also a piece of perfect composition.

Memling was not really sensitive to sacred subjects—only van der Weyden, in this group of Flemish artists, was naturally a religious painter—but he rendered them with a kind of exquisite gentleness added to his strength of workmanship. The pictures of Christ being nailed to the Cross, and Christ being put into the tomb are wonderful examples of his skill. To get the essence of Memling's genius we should study his portraits.

Those of Barbara de Vlanderbergh and Martin van Newenhoven are the kind of pictures to which, as to Jan van Eyck's, we return again and again, captivated by their poise, their calm and serene dignity.

Some of Memling's pictures are in the National Gallery; they include Saint John the Baptist and Saint Lawrence, and the Duke of Cleves.

ONE OF THE LOVABLE QUALITIES IN THE PICTURES OF FLEMISH WOMEN

Hugo van der Goes (about 1435 to 1482) was another painter of beautiful religious subjects. In his picture of Saint Magdalen and Saint Margaret we have a composition in which solemn and gracious figures stand out before a background of

The Story of the Marvellous Plants that Cover the Earth

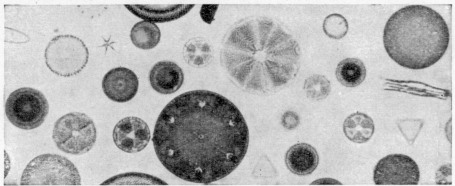

A highly-magnified group of the flinty coverings of diatoms, tiny one-celled plants

PLANTS IN THEIR HOMES

PLANTS have such great powers of spreading over land and sea that we cannot wonder that there is no vacant corner anywhere.

Many of the scattered seeds come to nothing, for some fall on stony ground, others are choked, and others are devoured; but the plant makes up for these risks by producing countless seeds that are not needed. As Tennyson wrote of Nature: " Of fifty seeds she often brings but one to bear "; and he afterwards thought he should have written " myriad " instead of " fifty."

Linnaeus, whom we call the Father of Botany, calculated that if an *annual* plant—dying within the year—produced only two seeds, and if the seedlings next year grew up into plants, producing two seeds each, and so on, there would be in twenty years *a million plants*. But this calculation started from a very slow rate of multiplication—only two seeds at a time; whereas in a single season the number of seeds produced, say, by an average radish, is 10,000; by a shepherd's purse, 64,000; by a tobacco plant, 360,000; by a flaxweed, 730,000.

Natures prodigality is stressed by the fact that a single flower of one of the orchids may have 1,756,440 seeds in its seed-box. Another of the orchids is said to produce 74 million seeds from the plant considered as a whole.

Thus, we see that the plant can often afford to lose many of its seeds. Or, to put it in another way, those plants have succeeded well which have a safe margin of seeds in proportion to their chances of failure. The flaxweed, with about three-quarters of a million seeds in a year, would cover the whole land surface of the Earth in three years. This does not happen because the chances of death are so great, and because many haunts are quite impossible for this kind of plant.

In connection with the power of spreading that many plants have, a practical point of great importance is the invasion of a country by weeds.

What usually happens is that man introduces a strange plant into a new country, where it runs riot. It may find many empty niches to fill, and it may be free from the competition that kept it within bounds at home. Thus, the nettle, the shepherd's purse, and the greater plantain have followed man wherever he has gone. One of our leading botanists has told us that the least common of our three nettles is reported to have been brought to Britain by the Romans, and it still grows only round some of the villages of the south coast of England.

BOTANY & ITS WONDERS · FLOWERS · TREES · HOW THINGS GROW

Another tells us that Roman soldiers brought the seed with them and sowed it at Romney for their own use—to rub and chafe their limbs, when, through extreme cold, they were stiff and benumbed. A North American kind of feverfew has, in our time, established itself round many east coast fishing villages in Britain, and has become, in some places, more abundant than the native species.

HOW THE PLANTS GO OUT INTO THE WORLD AND SEEK NEW KINGDOMS

This sort of thing is continually happening, and sometimes, as with the prickly pear in Australia, the invasion is a calamity. It is very striking to read that 550 kinds of plants have been introduced into New Zealand, which has a native flora of 750 species; and the newcomers often tend to oust the natives on grazed, cultivated, and cleared ground.

Darwin called attention to the case of the cardoon thistle, which was introduced from Spain to La Plata, where it soon spread over enormous tracts of country, ousting other plants. Another botanist gives an example of a native plant of Mexico which was introduced into Ceylon as a garden plant in 1828, and has spread all over the island, taking up waste land to the exclusion of other plants. Whereas the cardoon thistle is spread by the wind which wafts the down everywhere, the Mexican plant is spread by birds which eat its pulpy fruits.

While plants have this great power of spreading, and are always, so to speak, looking out for new kingdoms to conquer, the other great fact is that certain kinds of plants are found living together in certain places. The conditions of life are very different in different places, and each haunt has its own type of plant life or vegetation. Many kinds of plants are so well suited for particular surroundings that if the seeds are sown somewhere else they do not sprout, or if they sprout the seedlings do not flourish. Many run riot for a year, and then vanish.

THE RICH AND BEAUTIFUL SEAWEED AND ITS GRACEFUL FORMS

If we ask what are the great haunts of life for animals the answer must be—the shore of the sea, the open sea, the deep sea, the fresh waters, the dry land, and the air. Let us first inquire how this general grouping applies to plants; and then we can pass to the different kinds of plant-associations found on dry land.

There is a rich and beautiful vegetation of seaweed in the shallow waters near the shore, extending up between the tide-marks. Fastened to rocks and stones and big shells, and also to other seaweeds, there are hundreds of different kinds of graceful forms, from minute growths to great pennons many yards long. If there is a sloping shore the seaweeds extend down and down till there is not enough light to allow them to flourish. All of them have the green pigment called chlorophyll, which enables them to utilise the sunlight as a source of power; but in the brown and red seaweeds the green is veiled by other colours. It is believed by some botanists that the brown seaweeds can make more of the light than the green ones can, and that the red ones can do with scantier light than the brown ones. In any case, the green ones are usually highest up, and the red ones lowest down.

Seaweeds absorb air, water, and salts by the general surface of their fronds; they have no roots in the true sense, only holdfasts or anchors; they are very pliable so that they are not readily broken by the waves, and they often have gas reservoirs, as we see in the common bladder-wrack, which buoy them up.

PLANTS OF THE SEA AS COUNTLESS AS THE STARS IN THE SKY

Often among the seaweeds grows the sea-grass, a true flowering plant. In localities where it flourishes its fragments form an important part of the vegetable sea-dust which is wafted down the slope, and is the chief food of many animals living on the shore area.

The plants of the open sea, away from the shore, are mostly very minute, but they are countless. There may be more in a bucket of water than we can see of stars on a clear night. They are sometimes so multitudinous that the water has a distinct plant-smell. Most of them are microscopic seaweeds, such as diatoms, but they form what was once described as floating sea-meadows. They sometimes make the surface waters like a vegetable soup, so numerous are they; and they form the main food supply of those open-sea animals that are vegetarians.

HOW A PLANT RISES IN THE WORLD

THE AQUATIC FROGBIT, WITH TWO WINTER BUDS LYING AT THE BOTTOM OF A POND

THE BUD OF A WATER FROGBIT IN SUCCESSIVE STAGES OF DEVELOPMENT

The aquatic frogbit, which spreads along the surface of ponds, multiplies by buds which drop and lie on the bottom while the seeds develop. In spring the buds rise to the surface.

The great drifting beds of Sargasso weed in the Atlantic Ocean are impressive, and have an animal population of their own; but the seaweeds composing them have mostly been torn by storms and currents from distant shores. As is so often the case, the more prominent things like the Sargasso banks are not nearly so important as the small things, and especially we must remember the invisible bacteria of the Open Sea, which play a great part in the constant circulation of matter.

As for the Deep Sea, there are no plants at home there, for, apart from luminescent animals, it is a world of darkness. There do not seem to be even bacteria in the great abysses, so that there can be no rotting. Of course, there are the remains of surface plants like diatoms, which have died or have been killed in the Open Sea, and have sunk slowly down to the great depths—a contribution to the scanty rations there.

THE FLOATING MEADOWS ON THE WATER OF A LAKE

In the open waters of a lake there are often "floating meadows" of very tiny plants, such as diatoms, desmids, and blue-green algae.

These are devoured by small crustaceans, and these, again, by freshwater fishes, often with several transformations between. It is in this way that the world is kept going. At certain times, especially in spring, the multiplication of tiny water plants may be so prolific that the water comes to look like living soap.

But there are plants of higher degree which also float quite freely. Thus, near the shore in sheltered nooks, the surface of the water is often covered with duckweed. What look like leaves are flattened shoots, very buoyant and difficult to wet. On the underside are delicate white roots, used in absorbing water, and on the edge of some of the discs there are very small flowers. There is another kind of duckweed (*Wolffia arrhiza*) which has still smaller flowers and no roots. This must be the smallest flowering plant in Britain.

Another unattached plant, widely distributed in tarns and lakes, is the bladderwort with beautiful golden flowers that are lifted out of the water on rather long stalks about midsummer. It has no roots, and the long floating stems are beset with small traps—apparently transformed leaf-tips—which catch many tiny water animals. Duckweed, bladderwort, and frogbit form store-buds in late summer, which sink to the bottom, remain as if asleep through the winter, and float up again, in spring, to the surface, where they start new plants. This is their way of multiplying—by detaching buds; but all produce seeds.

THE FLOWERING PLANTS OF THE LAKE AND HOW THEY GROW

But only a few of the flowering plants of a lake are unattached. The great majority are rooted on the floor and have their leaves on or near the surface. The water-lily is a good example. It is a perennial, rooted in the mud, with a long-buoyant shoot, and with broad leaves floating on the surface, as is also true of the beautiful flowers. The little openings (stomata), which allow of exchange of gases with the atmosphere, and also regulate the giving-off of water-vapour from the plant, are in ordinary leaves chiefly or exclusively on the under-surface; but in the water-lily they are all on the upper surface. This is a kind of special fitness that explains itself, for little openings would not be of any use on a surface which is continually washed with water.

The pond weeds, with their glossy leaves, are very common freshwater plants, and it is interesting to find that, while some kinds have leaves that float and leaves that live below the water, there are others whose leaves are all submerged, only the flowers coming to the top. There are other submerged freshwater plants, such as the gritty stoneworts and water nymph, found in lakes with much lime in the water, which may cover the floor for large areas and extend a hundred feet down. But the stoneworts are plants of low degree, not far removed from algae.

THE HOMES OF THE LAND PLANTS AND THEIR TENANTS

In similar freshwater basins we find similar plants, and they have certain characters in common. They have taken to the water from the land, and many of them have slipped down a little on the ladder of evolution. Their roots are less important than those of land plants, and they may be absent altogether; they are thin-skinned, for they often absorb by their whole surface; they are lightly built, for they are supported by the water; they often have spaces full of air which

THE LIFE-STORY OF A FAMILIAR MOSS

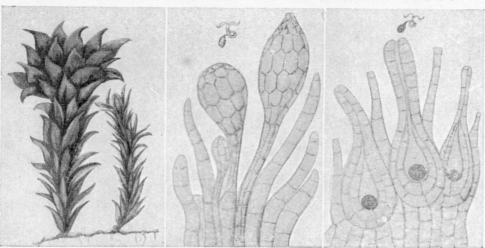

1. These pictures show the life-story of hair moss, which has its male and female parts on separate plants. Here, on the left, is a male plant, magnified, and on the right a female plant.

2. Here we see the male organs highly magnified. These break and release small spores, which are curved spirally and are able, by means of tiny threads called cilia, to move in water.

3. The spore enters the flask-shaped female organ, here shown highly magnified, and works its way down the neck to the egg-cell at the bottom, which it will fertilise.

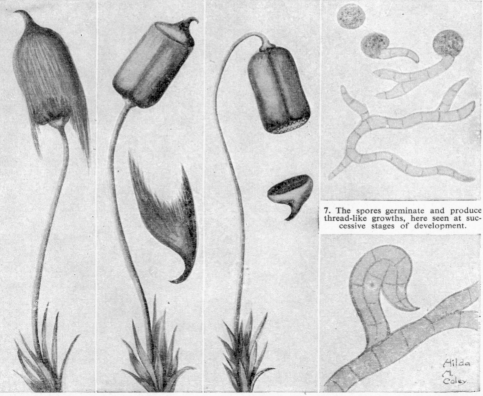

7. The spores germinate and produce thread-like growths, here seen at successive stages of development.

4. The union of the two cells results in the formation of a long-stalked capsule, shown here very greatly enlarged, containing spores.

5. When not yet ripe the capsule is green and is covered by a brown, hairy cover, which later becomes detached, revealing a lid beneath.

6. When the capsule ripens the lid is cast off and teeth are seen, closing up tiny openings; but in dry weather these shrivel, and the spores escape.

8. A bud forms on the thread, as shown here, and develops into a perfect moss plant, either male or female, like those in the first picture, and the life-story is repeated. All our pictures are magnified.

make them buoyant. In these and many other ways they are suited to their home.

It may seem absurd to speak of plants in the air, yet we have to remember that there are many perched plants which live off the ground altogether, on the stems and branches of other plants.

Many of the orchids do not touch earth at all, and they must get water from the rain or by condensing the vapour in the moist atmosphere. The pitcher plants grow on trees, and as they cannot get the usual salts from the soil we can understand why they capture insects as food.

It must also be noted that many bacteria spend part of their life floating in the air; and perhaps it is not far-fetched to remind ourselves of the air journeys of spores and pollen-grains and wind-swept seeds.

The homes of the land-plants are very varied, and each has tenants in some measure suited to the particular conditions.

Communities whose members have a good deal in common are called Plant Associations. Thus there are associations suited for the bog, the marsh, the moor, the high mountains, the desert, the forest country, the sea-shore, the barren-grounds of the Far North, the sand-dunes, and so on. This does not mean that the desert plants of one dry and parched land need be the same as those in another, two thousand miles away; what is meant is that the vegetation in the two arid regions will show similar fitnesses or adaptations to the peculiar conditions of life. The Alpine plants of Mont Blanc may be very different from those of Mount Everest, but they are sure to show some similarities of appearance. And, of course, there are many instances of closely related

THE BEAUTIFUL YUCCA PLANT, A NATIVE OF AMERICA WHICH HAS COME TO ENGLAND

plants, such as the groundsels, occurring in similar places far apart.

Let us take some examples of different vegetations. One of the poorest is that of the tundra, as we call the barren-grounds to the north of Europe and Asia.

The deeper parts of the soil there remain permanently frozen, and it is hard for any plant to make a living, so that there is in the worst places little beyond mosses and lichens. It is the same sort of scanty vegetation that we see on the tops of the mountains that are not snow-covered.

On more favourable ground in the Far North, there may be dwarf willows and hardy grasses, and sometimes bulbous plants like tulips which make the desert blossom like the rose in the short springtime.

Gradually the tundra passes into moorland, with grasses and sedges, cranberries, and crowberries, willows and birches. There is probably much heather, which succeeds so well because it has entered into partnership with a fungus. In wet places there may be great stretches of bog-moss, which, along with the other bog-plants, forms accumulations of peat so useful to mankind as fuel.

Where the ground is less water-logged, and where the water is less sour than in the peat-bog, there is a wealth of cotton-grass with its white flags, the fragrant bog-myrtle, the beautiful Grass of Parnasus, and the delicate bog-pimpernel. Where the earthworms have been able to make more than a little soil, and where there is some drainage, we reach what may be called pasture-land.

On another line is the *steppe-country*, such as the North American prairies. The prevalent plants are suited to survive a long summer drought, and it is not often that there are trees. Where the soil is better and the dry season less severe and prolonged, the steppe may give place to meadow-lands with a rich grassy vegetation. The long parallel leaves of the grass make it possible for the plants to live in dense crowds without hopelessly over-shadowing one another. The artificial vegetation of corn-fields is plainly due to man's imitation of the natural pampas of South America or the grassy plains in certain parts of Australia.

On another line are the natural forests, great societies of trees whose extension is limited by conditions of temperature. For there cannot be forests where the average temperature in the growing and leafing season of the year falls below 46 degrees Fahrenheit. But the variety of forests is a long story in itself ; there are pine-forests and tropical forests ; there are palm-groves and jungles, and much more; and besides the trees there is the ground-vegetation of shade-loving plants.

THE TRANSFORMATION SCENES IN THE LIFE OF PLANTS

We may pass through many different vegetations in a day's walk, for we may begin with a sort of desert-country on the sand-dunes, and pass into meadow-land; we go on to climb the lower slopes of the mountain through the forest zone and then get into upland pasture like steppe-land ; we skirt the bogs and tramp through the heather-covered moor ; we climb to the top and find ourselves in a tundra with nothing but lichens and moss.

It is interesting to discover near at home the miniature kinds of vegetation that in some parts of the world spread over enormous tracts of country. Thus, where the sand has been swept from the shore on to the inland flats, and has smothered many of the plants, there is a hint of the great desert. The rich meadow is a little savannah, and an untended copse, thick with brambles and honeysuckle, is an image of the jungle. Another point is that one vegetation frequently gives place to another, for all things flow. As the tree-stumps often show, the area of the peat-bog may once have been occupied by a forest. The peat-bog itself may become a meadow and the heather-covered moor may come to be covered with grass.

It must be understood that each of the great kinds of vegetations can be divided again into smaller associations. Thus, in an upland moor, the botanist would distinguish several zones marked by distinctive plants. There is a Bog Moss Association, a Cotton Grass Association, a Sedge Association, a Bilberry Association, and a Heather Association. In that order they correspond to a gradually decreasing amount of soil-water.

HOW PLANTS SOLVE THE DROUGHT PROBLEM IN DRY PLACES

The most interesting question in regard to the various haunts and homes of plants is how the difficulties or peculiarities of the situation are met and overcome. This is the study of fitness or adaptation. Let us take, as an example, those plants that live in very dry places, or in places where there is a long dry season. The problem is to make the most of a limited water-supply, and there are various solutions. One is to reduce the leaf area ; a cactus, for instance, may dispense with leaves altogether, and form a big globular green stem. Another solution is to have juicy tissues, as in a stonecrop on the wall or an onion in the dry sandy soil. The juicy interior means a capacity for storing water.

Another way in which plants solve the water problem is to have very deep-going roots, or roots with a very large number of rootlets, for this increases the chances of getting at more of the soil-water. Still another solution is to have a thickened outer skin which will prevent too much evaporation of water, and if this is varnished over with wax, as in some glistening leaves, so much the better. A woolly surface solves the problem in such plants as edelweiss.

THE REMARKABLE POWER OF THE EUCALYPTUS OF AUSTRALIA

They say that the fragrant oils produced by plants like lavender and rosemary also serve as heat-screens. And how remarkable is the adaptation in the eucalyptus or blue gum trees of Australia, where the leaves do not expose a flat surface to the sky, but hang down with only their edge turned up.

What is true of plants living in dry conditions is true of plants living in wet conditions ; they are rich in fitnesses, but these fitnesses are, of course, different in each case. This is a very interesting inquiry ; but there is one still more interesting, though far more difficult, and that is *how these fitnesses have been established.*

CARDINAL WOLSEY PASSES OUT OF HISTORY

THE PROUD CARDINAL

THE FALLEN WOLSEY ARRIVES AT LEICESTER ABBEY TO SPEND HIS CLOSING DAYS—FROM THE PAINTING
BY R. WESTALL, R.A.

The Story of the Peoples of All Nations and Their Homelands

Queen Elizabeth receives the French Ambassador after the massacre of St. Bartholomew's Eve

THE TIMES OF THE TUDORS

As we mount the steps leading to the chapel of Henry the Seventh in Westminster Abbey we seem to pass into a new England. The decorations of the chapel, particularly those on the beautiful gates, form a link between the old and the new. The dragon of the last king of the old Britons takes us back to the beginning of our history.

The lilies of France and the lions of England remind us of the long struggles of the two countries. The crown on a bush recalls the story of Henry's hasty coronation on the battlefield of Bosworth, where the cruel Richard died in the thick of the fight, and his crown was found hanging on a hawthorn-tree. The Tudor roses are everywhere, formed of red and white roses, the badges of the two parties in the long civil wars.

When you have admired the roof, the windows, the carved stalls, you will turn to the large tomb within a screen, planned by Henry himself, in which he and his wife both rest. Elizabeth, sister of the little boys Richard had murdered in the Tower, was the first to be buried in her husband's splendid new chapel. The figures on the black marble tomb are both portraits.

A fine portrait, too, is that of Henry's mother Margaret Beaufort, in the south aisle of the chapel. As you look at her calm, thoughtful old face, her delicate hands raised in prayer, think of her as one who loved and helped the poor, as the friend of Caxton the printer, as the founder of colleges at Cambridge. Of her the famous words were said : " Everyone who knew her, loved her, and everything that she said or did became her."

Henry was very grasping about money; he needed it badly, and made people angry and discontented by the way he forced it from them. He had a hard task to set England straight and to keep it at peace. He saw that nothing could improve if fresh wars were undertaken. So he tried to keep Scotland and Spain quiet by marrying his children into their royal families. He little thought how far-reaching the results of these marriages would be. His daughter Margaret, named after her grandmother, was married to James the Fourth of Scotland, and his eldest son was married to a Spanish princess, Catherine of Aragon.

To understand how great a change came about in the world in the times of the Tudors, we must go back to the beginning of our country's story, when the nation was still young. No one then knew anything about the shores of the other side of the sea which lay round about them. Then, as time went on, glimpses

THE FIVE CONTINENTS & 100 NATIONS & RACES THAT INHABIT THEM

THE PAGEANTRY OF TUDOR ENGLAND

HENRY THE EIGHTH EMBARKS AT DOVER FOR THE FIELD OF THE CLOTH OF GOLD—FROM THE PAINTING BY HOLBEIN

A QUAINT OLD PICTURE OF THE FIELD OF THE CLOTH OF GOLD IN 1520

THE DOOM OF THE GREAT ARMADA

A THRILLING SCENE ON AN ENGLISH SHIP IN ACTION AGAINST THE ARMADA

THE DOOM OF THE SPANISH ARMADA—FROM THE PAINTING BY ALBERT GOODWIN IN THE
MANCHESTER ART GALLERY

of the empire beyond, of which they formed a part, came to the Britons when conquered by the Romans. The Saxons and Danes, from the other side of the North Sea, handed on in their new home the tales of the wild motherland they had left.

THE STREAM OF SOLDIERS, SAILORS, AND SCHOLARS THAT CAME INTO ENGLAND

The coming of the Normans brought a never-ending stream of soldiers and traders, teachers and scholars, constantly crossing and recrossing the Channel. The views gained through them of the continent beyond were ever made larger and clearer as the Crusaders pressed on to the East, armies spread all over France, and trade steadily increased. All this time England was slowly learning more and more about the Earth.

There were wise men throughout the centuries, who understood that the Earth is not really flat. One of them had even found out how to measure its size and weight. Others, who were adventurous, sailed into the Unknown and came back with strange tales of what they had seen, and Columbus and later navigators showed a New World to the Old World. The excitement of this new wonder, the longing to know more about it, and to share in the riches and glory of the discoveries, spread all over the times of the Tudors in the fifteenth and sixteenth centuries.

Men's minds were still further awakened in these days by the opportunity that came to them to study, in the beautiful old Greek language, the learning that had been hidden away and neglected for long years. There was a new learning to delight scholars, as well as a new world to astonish the people. There was a new form of religion, too. It began with Wycliffe and his translated Bible, and many men, dissatisfied with the old religion, sought to create a new form of worship.

THE BLACK CLOUD THAT HANGS OVER THE TIMES OF THE TUDORS

Presently people had to do more than think—they had to act. We who live in this twentieth century, when everyone is free to worship God as he thinks right, find it hard to understand that only four centuries ago Englishmen believed they were pleasing God by putting people to death if they refused to agree with them. The sadness of the religious struggles in those days hangs like a black cloud over the times of the Tudors.

Catherine of Aragon's bridegroom, Arthur, died before his father, and the Pope was asked to say that it would be right for her to marry her brother-in-law who became Henry the Eighth.

When Henry became tired of Catherine, he wanted the Pope to say that she was not really his wife, because she had been his brother's wife first. This the Pope refused to say, and at last Henry made up his mind not to consider the Pope as the head of the Church any longer, but made Parliament declare himself the head, so that he could do as he liked. But Wolsey was against his marrying Anne Boleyn, as the king wanted to do (and as he eventually did), and Henry, in anger, took Wolsey's high office from him, so that he died in sorrow and disgrace. Shakespeare has written of him in a great play, and has reminded us that some of Wolsey's last words are said to have been these : " Had I but served my God as diligently as I have served my king, He would not have given me over in my grey hairs."

THE HORRIBLE STORY OF HENRY THE EIGHTH AND HIS WIVES

Henry's married life was more disgraceful than that of any other English king ; King Bluebeard he really was. He had six wives in succession. First was Catherine of Aragon, whom he got rid of by divorce. She lived for some years afterward, a saddened woman, and died a natural death. Then came Anne Boleyn, his second wife. She was the mother of Queen Elizabeth, but Henry grew tired of her and had her beheaded. Jane Seymour, his third wife and mother of Edward the Sixth, died a natural death. Anne of Cleves, his fourth wife, was divorced quickly, because Henry—who had not seen her before he married her—found she was too plain for him. Catherine Howard, the fifth wife, he beheaded because, like Anne Boleyn, she had had a lover before Henry married her. Last of all came Catherine Parr, the sixth wife of this man, and she was fortunate enough to outlive the callous king.

After Wolsey, Thomas Cromwell was the next favourite, and for ten years helped Henry to sweep away the old freedom of the country. People were made to pay taxes as the king and Cromwell chose ; these two made what laws they pleased, and imprisoned anyone they wished ;

GREAT FIGURES OF THE TUDOR AGE

FRANCIS BACON

LORD BURGHLEY

WILLIAM SHAKESPEARE

EARL OF ESSEX

SIR WALTER RALEIGH

SIR FRANCIS DRAKE

QUEEN ELIZABETH, BY ZUCCHERO

EARL OF LEICESTER

MARY QUEEN OF SCOTS

THOMAS CRANMER

ANNE BOLEYN

HOLBEIN'S FAMOUS PORTRAIT OF HENRY THE EIGHTH

THE BOY KING, EDWARD THE SIXTH—BY HOLBEIN

QUEEN ELIZABETH SIGNS THE DEATH WARRANT
OF MARY QUEEN OF SCOTS—BY JULIUS SCHRADER

THE LAST HOURS OF QUEEN ELIZABETH—FROM
THE PAINTING BY PAUL DELAROCHE

QUEEN ELIZABETH MAKES MERRY WHILE
RALEIGH LANGUISHES IN THE TOWER

THE FOUNDATION OF ST. PAUL'S SCHOOL BY
KING HENRY THE EIGHTH

The painting of The Foundation of St. Paul's School is by W. F. Yeames, and is reproduced by courtesy of the Gresham Committee

LINKS WITH TUDOR ENGLAND

THE MOOT HALL, ALDEBURGH

THE MARKET HOUSE, LEDBURY

CARVED HOUSE,
WARWICK

OLD HOUSES, HIGH STREET,
TONBRIDGE

THE ENTRANCE TO
ST. BARTHOLOMEW'S, LONDON

A TUDOR COTTAGE NEAR CROWBOROUGH

A TUDOR HOUSE AT HEREFORD

THE COURTYARD OF MORETON OLD HALL,
CHESHIRE

ANNE HATHAWAY'S COTTAGE,
STRATFORD-ON-AVON

GREAT CRESSINGHAM PRIORY IN NORFOLK

LAYER MARNEY HALL IN ESSEX   HORHAM HALL IN ESSEX

THE MOATED GEDDING HALL IN SUFFOLK

WOLSEY'S GATEWAY
AT IPSWICH

A GATEWAY OF HAMPTON
COURT PALACE

GAWSWORTH HALL IN CHESHIRE

HOUSES AT CHIDDINGSTONE
IN KENT

A HOTEL AT MAYFIELD
IN SUSSEX

One Thousand Poems of All Times and All Countries

ELIHU

Here is a whole tale of mother love told by an American author, Alice Cary (1820–1871). A boy who had run away to sea remained, in the thought of his mother, a little boy even until he came back so old that she did not know him.

O SAILOR, tell me, tell me true,
    Is my little lad—my Elihu—
A-sailing in your ship ?
The sailor's eyes were dimmed with dew.
" Your little lad? Your Elihu? "
   He said with trembling lip;
   " What little lad—what ship? "

WHAT little lad?—as if there could be
    Another such a one as he !
" What little lad, do you say?
Why, Elihu, that took to the sea
The moment I put him off my knee.
   It was just the other day
   The Grey Swan sailed away."

THE other day? The sailor's eyes
    Stood wide open with surprise.
   " The other day?—the Swan? "
His heart began in his throat to rise.
" Ay, ay, sir; here in the cupboard lies
   The jacket he had on."
   " And so your lad is gone,

" GONE with the Swan. And did she stand
With her anchor clutching hold of the sand
For a month, and never stir?"
" Why, to be sure! I've seen from the land,
Like a lover kissing his lady's hand,
   The wild sea kissing her—
   A sight to remember, sir."

" BUT, my good mother, do you know
    All this was twenty years ago?
I stood on the Grey Swan's deck,

And to that lad I saw you throw—
Taking it off, as it might be so—
   The kerchief from your neck."
   " Ay, and he'll bring it back."

" AND did the little lawless lad,
    That has made you sick and made you sad,
Sail with the Grey Swan's crew? "
" Lawless! The man is going mad;
The best boy ever mother had;
   Be sure, he sailed with the crew—
   What would you have him do? "

" AND he has never written line,
    Nor sent you word, nor made you sign,
To say he was alive? "
" Hold, if 'twas wrong, the wrong is mine;
Besides, he may be in the brine;
   And could he write from the grave?
   Tut, man, what would you have? "

" GONE twenty years ! A long, long cruise;
    'Twas wicked thus your love to abuse;
But if the lad still live,
And come back home, think you you can
Forgive him? " " Miserable man !
   You're as mad as the sea; you rave !
   What have I to forgive? "

THE sailor twitched his shirt so blue,
    And from within his bosom drew
   The kerchief. She was wild :
" My God !—my Father !—is it true?
My little lad—my Elihu !
And is it?—is it?—is it you?
   My blessed boy—my child—
   My dead—my living child ! "

POEMS · SONGS · BALLADS · VERSES AND RHYMES WITH MUSIC

THE BLIND BOY

Colley Cibber was a famous actor and writer of comedies who lived from 1671 to 1757. He was also Poet Laureate. These verses, which have been long familiar in the children's books of several generations, were written by him.

O SAY, what is that thing called light
    Which I must ne'er enjoy;
What are the blessings of the sight?
    O, tell your poor blind boy!

You talk of wondrous things you see,
    You say the sun shines bright;
I feel him warm, but how can he,
    Or make it day or night?

My day or night myself I make
    Whene'er I sleep or play;
And could I ever keep awake
    With me 'twere always day.

With heavy sighs I often hear
    You mourn my hapless woe;
But sure with patience I can bear
    A loss I ne'er can know.

Then let not what I cannot have
    My cheer of mind destroy;
Whilst thus I sing I am a king,
    Although a poor blind boy.

PITTYPAT AND TIPPYTOE

We shall read in these pages many of Eugene Field's charming poems of child-life, but none more charming than this description of Pittypat and Tippytoe.

ALL day long they come and go—
    Pittypat and Tippytoe;
Footprints up and down the hall,
    Playthings scattered on the floor,
Finger-marks along the wall,
    Tell-tale smudges on the door—
By these presents you shall know
Pittypat and Tippytoe.

How they riot at their play!
And a dozen times a day
    In they troop, demanding bread—
    Only buttered bread will do;
And that butter must be spread
    Inches thick with sugar, too!
And I never can say: " No,
Pittypat and Tippytoe! "

Sometimes there are griefs to soothe,
Sometimes ruffled brows to smooth;
    For (I much regret to say)
    Tippytoe and Pittypat
Sometimes interrupt their play
    With an internecine spat;
Fie, for shame! to quarrel so—
Pittypat and Tippytoe.

Oh, the thousand worrying things
Every day recurrent brings!
    Hands to scrub and hair to brush,
    Search for playthings gone amiss;
Many a wee complaint to hush,
    Many a little bump to kiss;
Life seems one vain, fleeting show
To Pittypat and Tippytoe!

And when day is at an end
There are little duds to mend:
    Little frocks are strangely torn,
    Little shoes great holes reveal;
Little hose, but one day worn,
    Rudely yawn at toe and heel!
Who but *you* could work such woe,
Pittypat and Tippytoe?

But when comes this thought to me:
" Some there are that childless be,"
    Stealing to their little beds,
    With a love I cannot speak.
Tenderly I stroke their heads,
    Fondly kiss each velvet cheek.
God help those who do not know
A Pittypat and Tippytoe!

On the floor and down the hall,
Rudely smutched upon the wall
    There are proofs in every kind
    Of the havoc they have wrought;
And upon my heart you'd find
    Just such trademarks, if you sought.
Oh, how glad I am 'tis so,
Pittypat and Tippytoe!

THE HAPPY TREE

This striking poem, gemlike in its workmanship, was written by Gerald Gould, a distinguished essayist and poet who died in 1936.

THERE was a bright and happy tree;
    The wind with music laced its boughs:
Thither across the houseless sea
    Came singing birds to house.

Men grudged the tree its happy eyes,
    Its happy dawns of eager sound;
So all that crown and tower of leaves
    They levelled with the ground.

They made an upright of the stem,
    A cross-piece of a bough they made:
No shadow of their deed on them
    The fallen branches laid.

But blithely, since the year was young,
    When they a fitting hill did find,
There on the happy tree they hung
    The Saviour of mankind.

THE LITTLE GRANDCHILDREN OF EUGENE FIELD GAZE ON HIS MONUMENT IN CHICAGO

BEFORE BATTLE

Charles Dibdin was a celebrated song-writer who lived from 1745 to 1814. He was chiefly famous for his songs of the sea, such as "Poor Jack" and "Tom Bowling." The following has the ring of victory in its vigorous and confident verse.

THE signal to engage shall be
    A whistle and a hollo;
Be one and all but firm, like me,
    And conquest soon will follow!
You, Gunnel, keep your helm in hand—
    Thus, thus, boys! steady, steady,
Till right ahead you see the land—
    Then, soon as we are ready,
      The signal to engage shall be
      A whistle and a hollo;
    Be one and all but firm, like me,
      And conquest soon will follow!

Keep, boys, a good look out, d'ye hear?
    'Tis for Old England's honour;
Just as you brought your lower tier
    Broadside to bear upon her.
      The signal to engage shall be
      A whistle and a hollo ;
    Be one and all but firm, like me,
      And conquest soon will follow!

All hands, then, lads, the ship to clear,
    Load all your guns and mortars;
Silent as death th' attack prepare,
    And, when you're all at quarters
      The signal to engage shall be
      A whistle and a hollo;
    Be one and all but firm, like me,
      And conquest soon will follow!

O WERT THOU IN THE CAULD BLAST

This exquisitely tender song, which has been set to music by Mendelssohn, was written in a few minutes by Robert Burns. He asked a lady at whose house he had called to play him a favourite Scottish air, and wrote these words to it.

O WERT thou in the cauld blast
    On yonder lea, on yonder lea,
My plaidie to the angry airt,
    I'd shelter thee, I'd shelter thee.
Or did misfortune's bitter storms
    Around thee blaw, around thee blaw,
Thy bield should be my bosom,
    To share it a', to share it a'.

Or were I in the wildest waste,
    Sae black and bare, sae black and
      bare,
The desert were a paradise
    If thou wert there, if thou wert there.
Or were I a monarch of the globe,
    Wi' thee to reign, wi' thee to reign,
The brightest jewel in my crown
    Wad be my queen, wad be my queen.

THERE IS AN AWFUL QUIET IN THE AIR

As an example of the serious and impersonal verse of Hartley Coleridge we take this sonnet on Prayer.

THERE is an awful quiet in the air,
    And the sad earth, with moist, im-
      ploring eye,
Looks wide and wakeful at the pondering
    sky,
Like Patience slow subsiding to Despair.
But see, the blue smoke as a voiceless
    prayer,
Sole mistress of a secret sacrifice,
Unfolds its tardy wreaths, and multiplies
Its soft chameleon breathings in the rare,
Capacious ether—so it fades away,
And nought is seen beneath the pendent
    blue,
The undistinguishable waste of day.
So have I dreamed!—Oh, may the dream
    be true!—
That praying souls are purged from mortal
    hue,
And grow as pure as He to whom they pray.

THE UPRIGHT LIFE

This is the idea of a perfect life according to Thomas Campion, the Elizabethan song-writer, and the writing has a grace which suits the wisdom of the man who is pictured.

THE man of life upright,
    Whose guiltless heart is free
From all dishonest deeds
    Or thought of vanity;

The man whose silent days
    In harmless joys are spent,
Whom hopes cannot delude
    Nor sorrow discontent:

That man needs neither towers
    Nor armour for defence,
Nor secret vaults to fly
    From thunder's violence.

He only can behold
    With unaffrighted eyes
The horrors of the deep
    And terrors of the skies.

Thus, scorning all the cares
    That fate or fortune brings,
He makes the heaven his book,
    His wisdom heavenly things;

Good thoughts his only friends,
    His wealth a well-spent age,
The Earth his sober inn
    And quiet pilgrimage.

THE HORNÉD OWL

In this poem Barry Cornwall gives us a more sympathetic and friendly description of the bird of night than poets, as a rule, are inclined to devote to the owl. His poem also reminds us that, although we may be apt to consider the owl a lonely bird, we are wrong in thinking so, for there is a companionship of the night as of the day.

IN the hollow tree in the old grey tower
    The spectral owl doth dwell;
Dull, hated, despised in the sunshine hour;
    But at dusk he's abroad and well:
Not a bird of the forest e'er mates with him;
    All mock him outright by day;
But at night, when the woods grow still and dim,
    The boldest will shrink away.
Oh, when the night falls and roosts the fowl,
Then, then is the reign of the hornéd owl!

And the owl hath a bride who is fond and bold,
    And loveth the wood's deep gloom:
And with eyes like the shine of the moonshine cold
    She awaiteth her ghostly groom!
Not a feather she moves, not a carol she sings,
    As she waits in her tree so still;
But when her heart heareth his flapping wings
    She hoots out her welcome shrill!
Oh, when the moon shines, and dogs do howl,
Then, then is the joy of the hornéd owl!

Mourn not for the owl nor his gloomy plight,
    The owl hath his share of good:
If a prisoner he be in the broad daylight,
    He is lord in the dark green wood!
Nor lonely the bird nor his ghostly mate;
    They are each unto each a pride—
Thrice fonder, perhaps, since a strange, dark fate
    Hath rent them from all beside!
So when the night falls, and dogs do howl,
Sing ho! for the reign of the hornéd owl!
We know not alway who are kings by day,
But the king of the night is the bold brown owl.

A GRACEFUL STORY OF LIFE

Jean Ingelow, the graceful English poetess, was the author of this plaintive little summary of a human life.

SWEET is childhood; childhood's over,
    Kiss and part.
Sweet youth; but youth's a rover—
    So's my heart.
Sweet is rest; but all by showing
    Toil is nigh.
We must go. Alas! the going.
    Say " Good-bye."

LORD OF ALL BEING

This lovely hymn of adoration and appeal for guidance is the noble close to Oliver Wendell Holmes's book " The Professor at the Breakfast Table." Dr. Holmes introduces it as a hymn " to the Source of the light we all need to lead us, and the warmth which alone can make us all brothers."

LORD of all being, throned afar,
    Thy glory flames from sun and star;
Centre and soul of every sphere,
    Yet to each loving heart how near!

Sun of our life, Thy quickening ray
Sheds on our path the glow of day;
Star of our hope, Thy softened light
Cheers the long watches of the night.

Our midnight is Thy smile withdrawn;
Our noontide is Thy gracious dawn;
Our rainbow arch Thy mercy's sign;
All, save the clouds of sin, are Thine.

Lord of all life, below, above,
Whose light is life, whose warmth is love,
Before Thy ever-blazing throne
We ask no lustre of our own.

Grant us Thy truth to make us free
And kindling hearts that burn for Thee,
Till all Thy living altars claim
One holy light, one heavenly flame.

FREEDOM OF THE MIND

This sonnet is from the pen of William Lloyd Garrison, the founder of the American Anti-Slavery Society, and the central figure in the movement that cleared from the good name of the American Republic its last reproach. Garrison was imprisoned for his defence of human freedom. Now his statue stands on the place where once he was mobbed.

HIGH walls and huge the body may confine,
And iron grates obstruct the prisoner's gaze,
And massive bolts may baffle his design,
And vigilant keepers watch his devious ways;
Yet scorns the immortal mind this base control!
No chains can bind it, and no cell enclose;
Swifter than light it flies from Pole to Pole,
And, in a flash, from earth to heaven it goes!
It leaps from mount to mount—from vale to vale;
It wanders, plucking honeyed fruits and flowers;
It visits home, to hear the fireside tale
Or in sweet converse pass the joyous hours.
'Tis up before the sun, roaming afar,
And, in its watches, wearies every star!

LITTLE VERSES FOR VERY LITTLE PEOPLE

WHAT BOBBIE WOULD LIKE

I'D like to be a farmer,
  With lots of stacks and mows,
And fowls and pigs, and carts and gigs,
  And four-and-twenty cows.
I'd drive them all to market
  On summer mornings fine;
" Oh, come and buy," I'd stand and cry,
  " Buy, buy, good masters mine! "
But if they would not buy them
  It would not give me pain;
I'd simply say: " Fair sirs, good-day! "
  And drive them home again.

I wish I were a farmer,
  With lots of lambs and sheep,
I'd run and play with them all day
  Until we went to sleep.
I'd take the wool to market
  On summer mornings fine—
" Oh, come and buy," I'd stand and cry,
  " Buy, buy, good masters mine! "
But if they would not buy my wool
  It would not cause me pain,
I'd come and say: " Dear sheep, good-day,
  Here is your wool again."

And if they could not put it on
  I'd put it on myself;
And all the rest, when I was drest,
  I'd lay upon the shelf.
For when the winter days come round,
  And all the world is cold,
I know full well my wool will sell
  For all its weight in gold.
And so I'll be a farmer,
  Right happy in my lot,
And he who cares may buy my wares,
  And other folk need not!

  Frederic E. Weatherly

THE FLY-AWAY HORSE

OH, a wonderful horse is the Fly-Away
  Horse,
Perhaps you have seen him before;
Perhaps while you slept his shadow has
  swept
  Through the moonlight that floats on
  the floor.
For it's only at night, when the stars
  twinkle bright,
That the Fly-Away Horse, with a neigh
And a pull at his rein and a toss of his
  mane,
  Is up on his heels and away!
    The moon in the sky,
    As he gallopeth by,
  Cries: " Oh ! what a marvellous
  sight! "

And the stars in dismay
  Hide their faces away
In the lap of old Grandmother Night.
It is yonder, out yonder, the Fly-Away
  Horse
Speedeth ever and ever away—
Over meadows and lanes, over moun-
  tains and plains,
  Over streamlets that sing at their play;
And over the sea like a ghost sweepeth he,
  While the ships they go sailing below,
And he speedeth so fast that the men at
  the mast
  Adjudge him some portent of woe.
    " What ho there! " they cry,
    As he flourishes by
  With a whisk of his beautiful tail;
    And the fish in the sea
    Are as scared as can be,
  From the nautilus up to the whale!

And the Fly-Away Horse seeks those far-
  away lands
You little folk dream of at night—
Where candy-trees grow, and honey
  brooks flow,
  And corn-fields with popcorn are white;
And the beasts in the wood are ever so
  good
  To children who visit them there—
What glory astride of a lion to ride,
  Or to wrestle around with a bear!
    The monkeys, they say:
    " Come on, let us play,"
  And they frisk in the coconut trees;
    While the parrots that cling
    To the pea-nut vines sing
  Or converse with comparative ease!

Off! scamper to bed—you shall ride him
  tonight,
For, as soon as you've fallen asleep,
With a jubilant neigh he will bear you
  away
  Over forest and hillside and deep!
But tell us, my dear, all you see and you
  hear
In those beautiful lands over there,
Where the Fly-Away Horse wings his
  far-away course
With the wee one consigned to his care.
    Then grandma will cry
    In amazement: " Oh, my! "
  And she'll think it could never be so;
    And only we two
    Shall know it is true—
  You and I, little precious, shall know.

  Eugene Field

1095

THE OLD WOMAN TOSSED IN A BASKET

THERE was an old
woman tossed up
in a basket

Seventeen times as
high as the moon.

Where she was going
I couldn't but ask
it,

For in her hand she
carried a broom.

OLD woman, old
woman, old
woman, quoth I,

Where are you going
to up so high?

*To brush the cobwebs
off the sky!*

May I go with you?

Ay, by-and-by.

The Story of Where Power Comes From, What It Does, & How It Works

THE STORY OF ELECTRIC LIGHT

Many of us, particularly if we live in towns, do not fully appreciate how large a part electric light plays in our everyday life. Hundreds of years ago light in a house came from oil lamps or candles. These were expensive and poor people could not afford much light, so they had to make the maximum use of daylight. In winter, when the days were short, their working activities were considerably cut down.

What a different story it is today ! Electric light is very cheap and it is used not only in the homes, but for street lighting, advertising signs, and for flood-lighting buildings.

The electric lamp must be looked upon as a tiny machine which turns electricity into light, and it must be specially regarded as being still in the growing stage. The incandescent lamps of today give eight times as much brightness for a given amount of electricity as the early lamps of 1880. Even more efficient is the discharge lamp which has no filament. This lamp gives about three times as much light as a modern filament lamp.

The electric arc, the first real type of electric lamp, is the only artificial light which in any way compares in grandeur with that king of lights, the Sun. It was discovered by an Englishman, Sir Humphry Davy, in the early part of the nineteenth century, and, although it has now been largely replaced by the little glass bulbs so familiar in our own homes, it is still used wherever very powerful light is required, and so intense is the heat of its flame that huge electric arcs are used in industry as electric furnaces.

Sir Humphry Davy began by discovering the most powerful light the world had known ; he later invented perhaps the feeblest—the miner's safety-lamp, which has saved many thousands of lives. He invented the arc lamp through finding that if two pieces of carbon are joined to the poles of a powerful battery, and are brought together, intense heat is produced which turns some of the solid carbon into gas. This gas acts as a conductor of electricity, and if the pieces of carbon are drawn slightly apart the current will continue to flow across this gaseous path, emitting an enormously powerful light, due to the burning particles of carbon.

With a huge battery of 2000 cells Davy produced an arc flame four inches long. It later became known that such a high voltage as this battery gave is not wise ; about 50 volts is sufficient to produce an arc, and the amount of light given is made to depend on the current that is supplied to it.

ELECTRICITY · WIRELESS · OIL · GAS · MOTORS · ENGINES · SHIPS

Arc lamps of up to one thousand million candle-power are used in the big searchlights of naval vessels. The rays from a flame arc, or " high intensity " arc, which in the ordinary way would spread outward in all directions, are concentrated in a searchlight beam by means of parabolic reflectors, and so will carry for miles.

LAMPS OF ENORMOUS POWER IN THE MODERN CINEMA

A high intensity arc lamp is used largely in the powerful projectors or magic-lanterns of the cinema. Here, a tiny picture the size of a postage stamp has to be magnified to the size of a theatre screen, perhaps 1500 square feet in area, and lamps of enormous power are required, using electrical power of ten or fifteen horse-power. The heat of such an arc is so intense that if the celluloid film were to stop running for an instant it would burst into flame, and special devices have to be used in every theatre in order to make such an accident impossible.

The light of the electric arc is blue compared with that of the incandescent lamp, but if a central hole running through the length of the rods is packed with a core of certain chemicals the colour of the arc flame can be made yellow or pinkish. Such rods are used generally in the studios where moving pictures are photographed. If the arc be burned in an enclosed glass vessel it quickly burns up all the oxygen in the air of the vessel, and then becomes very violet owing to the presence of the nitrogen which is left, air being a mixture of the two gases.

THE AMERICAN ENGINEER WHO INVENTED THE CARBON LAMP

The electric lamps in our homes are very different from the arc lamps, and have a history all their own. They date back to 1841, when an American engineer named Starr invented a lamp which produced light by sending an electric current through a very fine piece of carbon which became so hot that it grew incandescent. We know that all materials offer more or less resistance to the passage of an electric current. The thinner or smaller the material the greater is the resistance offered, and in the second half of the nineteenth century two master minds—those of Edison and Swan—were engaged, unknown to each other, at the same time, in producing a fine wire of carbon which

would glow brilliantly with the heat produced in it when an electric current passed through it. These very fine carbon wires were known as filaments, and Edison first made his of little strips of burned or *carbonised* bamboo, while Swan used a thread of cotton chemically treated.

Lamps made in this way, known as carbon filament lamps, held the field for more than twenty years, from 1880 until 1904. The threads of cotton or shreds of bamboo were placed in a small glass bulb from which the air was exhausted, and, turned into a charred wire, they became so strongly heated when a current passed through the lamp that they glowed with a brilliant white light. So successful were they that they became used on a large scale, and the era of the electric light began in earnest.

THE LAMP THAT ASTONISHED THE WORLD BY ITS BRIGHTNESS

The price of electricity was such that it was rather a luxury to have a house fitted with electric light, but the wonderful convenience of being able to flood a room with light by touching a switch was fascinating. Matches, gas, the smell of oil lamps, became things of the past. The electric tram and train had hardly been thought of, the value of the electric furnace was undiscovered, electric stoves and heating appliances were unguessed ; the carbon lamps of Edison and Swan made the first real demand for big quantities of electricity, and paved the way for its use in the thousand-and-one forms in which we know it today.

The next development was a lamp invented by the German scientist Nernst in 1897 which had an element in the form of a rod of oxides. This lamp was not a great success.

In the meantime the chemists had been busy and it had been found that a metal called tungsten could withstand enormous heat, and glow with a very brilliant white light. In 1906 a drawn wire of tungsten was made by the famous General Electric Company in their experimental laboratories in Schenectady ; and when sealed into the little glass bulb, with an electric current passing through, the wire gave a much purer white light, and gave more light for a given amount of electricity.

This important discovery revolutionised not only electric lighting, but the whole of electrical enterprise, for lighting now became so cheap that electricity was before long in great demand.

The success and importance of the tungsten lamp was that it gave four times the light of the old carbon lamps for the same number of units of electricity. This meant that electric lighting would in future cost only a quarter of what it had cost before, and with this discovery elec-

First of all a crude ore dug from the mines, called wolframite, is crushed in the mills. It is then mixed with soda-ash and roasted in a furnace. Various chemical processes are employed, and a yellow powder called oxide of tungsten is produced. This yellow oxide is baked in another furnace at a temperature ten times hotter than boiling water, and afterward

Buckingham Palace floodlighted with nearly 200 Osram electric lamps, each of 1000 candle-power.

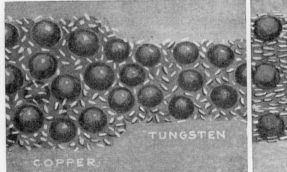
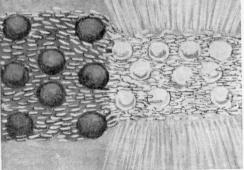

These picture-diagrams show why we can light our towns with electricity. On the left we see the tiny electrons and big molecules of the thick copper wire and the thin tungsten filament within the lamp before the electric current flows. The switching on of the current sends through the wires myriads of new electrons which collide with the molecules so forcibly that heat is produced. Owing to its extreme thinness, the filament gives less space for the electrons to move in, and the greater resistance to their passage produces a fierce heat causing the filament to glow as in the right-hand picture.

THE SECRET OF THE ELECTRIC LAMP

tricity became the cheapest substitute for sunshine, instead of the dearest.

The making of one of the little bulbs that light a house is a scientific operation requiring great skill, and fortunes have been spent in working out a hundred problems which had to be solved before they could be made on a really commercial scale. At the present time tens of millions of them are turned out every year in factories all over the world.

it is turned into tungsten metal, again in the form of a powder, by treatment with hydrogen gas.

The powder is weighed out into little lots, and pressed into "slugs" by a hydraulic press. The slugs, each one the size of a fountain pen, are raised to an intense heat, and beaten with rapidly-moving hammers. This operation is called "swagoning," and the effect is to beat out the tiny crystals of tungsten into long ones, which makes the material much more pliable.

The heated slugs are forced through a diamond in which a tiny hole has been drilled, and the metal is squirted out into one long filament. A length of this black filament is sealed into the glass bulb, and now comes the important operation of getting rid of the air in the bulb.

Every electric bulb is a little vacuum chamber, containing only one ten-millionth part of the amount of air that it could hold. The really high vacuum achieved in the modern lamp is obtained with the help of a little bit of phosphorus, which " cleans up " the tiny traces of gas that cling to the inside of the bulb and to the various parts.

Another advance in the electric light was the introduction of a very small quantity of certain gases into the bulbs, the result of which is a lamp giving twice as bright a light as before. The gases used for these so-called half-watt lamps are argon and nitrogen ; they are known as inert gases. The name half-watt simply means that for every candle-power of light half a watt of electricity is used.

THE MAGIC THAT MAKES A CITY LIKE ALADDIN'S CAVE

The ease with which electric light is controlled has led to its being used for many ingenious purposes. The most familiar is, of course, the advertisement sign. The great city has become an Aladdin's cave with a thousand flashing colours which race away and blink the night out. These lamps are switched off and on with amazing speed by quite simple automatic switches, and by lighting them up in the correct order all kinds of magic effects are produced, such as that of a motor-car with rapidly revolving wheels, and so on.

Almost every boy has a pocket-lamp today, and each flash of his lamp is a reminder of the long process of converting the wolfram ore into tiny filaments. There is perhaps no better example than the flash-lamp of the stupendous progress of electricity—the little battery discovered by Volta linked up with the metal filament lamp, burning in a globe the size of a pea from which all but a ten-millionth part of its air has been extracted by the lamp-maker's wonderful pumps.

So rapidly does progress take place in the vast research laboratories of the big electrical concerns, that no man can foresee what sort of light we shall be using a few years hence. Incandescent lamps depend on the white heat of a filament ; half-watt lamps, which a few years ago could be made only of twenty candle-power, are now made with spiral filaments of such immense candle-power that the days of the arc lamp are numbered!

BILLIONS OF COLLISIONS WHICH GIVE RISE TO A WONDERFUL COLD LIGHT

But a *cold* light has now been discovered, a beautiful shadowless light caused by violently agitating in a vacuum bulb the molecules of a gas such as neon or carbon dioxide with the ions and atoms of a metallic vapour. Traces of mercury and gas are introduced into the bulb which has just a plain metal plate or electrode at each end to which the electricity supply is connected. The current decomposes some of the molecules of the gas, and their collisions with the atoms of the mercury vapour, which take place billions of times a second, give rise to a wonderful light which is two and a half times as economical as that of the half-watt lamp.

These remarkable lamps are a development of the gaseous type now familiar to us in shop signs and advertisements—long tubes filled with the rare gas neon, or a mixture of neon and another gas which glow with light of various colours when a current at about 1000 volts is passed through them.

THE ASTONISHING NEW LIGHTS THAT ALLOW FOR SAFE DRIVING

Such lamps are already illuminating arterial roads, for in their astonishing light a motor-car can travel with safety as fast as in the daylight.

The lamps with sodium gas inside give a yellow light and those with mercury a blue light. A further development is the fluorescent lamp or tube, which can be made to give light of various colours. The lamp does not cast any shadows and can be built into a ceiling in louvres. This type of lamp is much used in factories and offices and indeed in some homes.

There we have the lighting of to-day. But what of tomorrow? With the coming of the atomic age there will also come a new source of lighting, perhaps to make the electric lighting of today appear as out-of-date to our successors as the candle does to most of us.

Imperishable Thoughts of Men Enshrined in the Books of the World

Shylock and the Merchants on the Bridge in Venice   From the painting by Sir John Gilbert

SHAKESPEARE AT HIS HEIGHT

No one has ever explained satisfactorily why it was that between the years 1600 and 1608—or his thirty-sixth and forty-fourth year—Shakespeare's outlook on life became so serious. In those years his mind grew deeper, broader, and more sombre, and he gathered into his character the qualities that made him supremely great.

He had been a bright and masterly poet, a fervent patriot, a wonderful observer and delineator of life, a delightful humorist, a happy trickster with playful fancy, but now he became a deep student of the passions that move men to do such deeds as stir our hearts to mingled admiration, abhorrence, and pity. All his greatest tragedies belong to this stern and lofty period, and his style of writing changed, growing in beauty and power as it had to express more profound feeling and more exalted thought.

Julius Caesar, Hamlet, Othello, Macbeth, King Lear, and Antony and Cleopatra were all written at this time, and they carry the British drama to its highest tide-mark. In these plays Shakespeare pictures men striving like demi-gods with fate, a prey to ambitions, weaknesses, self-deception; overthrown, yet remaining noble in their fall.

The Roman plays were based, with frank quotations, quite openly, on Plutarch's Lives and the British plays (Macbeth and Lear) on Holinshed's Chronicles; for Shakespeare took his materials from wherever he could find them, tales of all kinds being at that time common property. But he transformed whatever he took; he built up the old materials into a noble structure gloriously new.

Julius Caesar, in which Brutus and not Caesar is the hero, though he is a regal figure, shows how an honest manliness may, by subtlety, be worked on and warped till it is led into deeds that it would naturally abhor. The play is the story of a plot to mislead the upright, simple-minded Brutus to throw the cloak of his honesty over a group of conspirators. The plot works, but it ends in tragic disaster, and all the conspirators are its victims, as Caesar was their victim.

Caesar himself, far more clear-sighted than Brutus, in a moment sums up the conspirators as they really are; but Brutus never finds them out. When, passing along the street, Caesar gives a single glance at Cassius, the arch-conspirator, he says to his friend Antony:

Let me have men about me that are fat;
Sleek-headed men, and such as sleep o' nights.
Yon Cassius has a lean and hungry look;
He thinks too much; such men are dangerous.

ROMANCE · HISTORIES · DRAMAS · ESSAYS · WORLD CLASSICS

ANTONY: Fear him not, Caesar, he's not dangerous;
He is a noble Roman, and well given.

CAESAR : Would he were fatter ! But I fear him
not ;
Yet if my name were liable to fear,
I do not know the man I should avoid
So soon as that spare Cassius. He reads much;
He is a great observer, and he looks
Quite through the deeds of men; he loves no
plays,
As thou dost, Antony; he hears no music;
Seldom he smiles; and smiles in such a sort
As if he mocked himself, and scorned his spirit,
That could be moved to smile at anything.
Such men as he be never at heart's ease,
While they behold a greater than themselves,
And therefore are they very dangerous.

There we watch Caesar, the man of the
world, reading character through and
through at a glance, while plain, honest
Brutus has scarcely a glimmer of suspicion.
Indeed, right at the end of the play, when
Caesar is dead, the plot has actually failed,
and Brutus, himself a fugitive, deceived,
defeated, hopeless, is about to die, he still
is blind to the deception practised on him,
and holds all men as honest as himself.

Farewell to you—and you—and you, Volumnius;
Strato, thou hast been all this while asleep—
Farewell to thee too, Strato. Countrymen,
My heart doth joy that yet, in all my life,
I found no man but he was true to me.

After that supreme, though fondly simple,
trust in other men, well might Mark Antony
say of the noble Brutus

This was the noblest Roman of them all.
All the conspirators save only he
Did that they did in envy of great Caesar;
He only in a general honest thought
And common good to all made one of them.
His life was gentle; and the elements
So mixed in him that Nature might stand up
And say to all the world, 'This was a man!'

The contrast between plain but blunder-
ing honesty and the subtle skill of quicker
minds is made with amazing delicacy and
power in the speeches of Brutus and
Antony to the Roman mob after the
murder of Caesar, when Antony, gradually,
by scarcely perceptible degrees, turns the
Roman populace from a desire to give
Brutus " a statue with his ancestors,"
and rouses in them a frenzied wish to burn
his house and tear him to pieces.

It is in scenes like this that Shakespeare's
new power of making the dead live, with
all their passions and weakness aflame, is
expressed as a reality that startles us when
we first see or read it, and yet never fades
in our memory.

Hamlet, by far the most frequently
played of all the classical tragedies, is a
profound study of the irresolute mind.

The reflective tone of the play has caused
it to be more quoted, in brief sayings, than
any other, to the almost infinite enrich-
ment of English speech. This being so, it
is fitting that a speech should be included
in the play that is made up of sententious
advice, and that Polonius, who has reached
the period of garrulous old age, should be
the speaker, and should unload his wisdom
on his son in the form of a " few precepts."
They may be called the commandments of
the worldly wise.

Give thy thoughts no tongue,
Nor any unproportioned thought his act.
Be thou familiar but by no means vulgar.
The friends thou hast, and their adoption tried,
Grapple them to thy soul with hoops of steel;
But do not dull thy palm with entertainment
Of each new-hatched, unfledged comrade. Be-
ware
Of entrance to a quarrel; but, being in,
Bear it that the opposéd may beware of thee.
Give every man thine ear, but few thy voice,
Take each man's censure, but reserve thy judg-
ment.
Costly thy habit as thy purse can buy,
But not expressed in fancy; rich not gaudy;
For the apparel oft proclaims the man,
And they in France of the best rank and station
Are most select and generous, chief in that.
Neither a borrower nor a lender be;
For loan oft loseth both itself and friend,
And borrowing dulls the edge of husbandry.
This above all—To thine own self be true,
And it must follow, as the night the day,
Thou canst not then be false to any man.

In Othello, Shakespeare traced the
effects of jealousy acting on a noble but
impetuous Oriental nature. The character
of Iago seems to be an attempt to paint
the complete villain without a redeeming
quality, the careless Cassio and simple
Othello acting as foils to show up the
picture.

There is no greater triumph of literary
skill in the world's books than the way in
which Shakespeare keeps the sympathy of
the reader or the playgoer with Othello,
even when he is putting out the light of
life in Desdemona, the most purely beautiful of all the women whom the great poet
created. We are made to feel that this is no
vulgar violence, but a high defence of the
sweet cause of purity.

In Othello pathos is carried to an intensity perhaps only once again touched in
our literature. It broods over the play.
We feel its beginnings when Othello is

A SCENE FROM "AS YOU LIKE IT": ROSALIND GIVES ORLANDO A CHAIN AFTER THE WRESTLING MATCH — FROM THE PAINTING BY HAROLD SPEED

A SCENE FROM "AS YOU LIKE IT": ROSALIND AND CELIA IN THE FOREST OF ARDEN — FROM THE PAINTING BY SIR J. E. MILLAIS

A SCENE FROM "HAMLET" SHOWING OPHELIA AND THE GUILTY KING AND QUEEN OF DENMARK—FROM THE PAINTING BY HENRIETTA RAE IN THE POSSESSION OF THE CORPORATION OF LIVERPOOL

SIR JOHN FALSTAFF, IN SEARCH OF RECRUITS, COMES UPON FEEBLE, THE WOMAN'S TAILOR—"WILT THOU MAKE AS MANY HOLES IN AN ENEMY'S BATTLE AS IN A WOMAN'S PETTICOAT?"

KING LEAR RENOUNCES HIS DAUGHTER CORDELIA IN FAVOUR OF HER SISTERS — FROM THE PAINTING
BY FORD MADOX BROWN

FALSTAFF REVIEWS HIS RAGGED FOLLOWERS — A SCENE FROM "HENRY THE FOURTH," PAINTED BY
SIR JOHN GILBERT

MALVOLIO AND THE COUNTESS IN "TWELFTH NIGHT"— FROM THE PAINTING BY DANIEL MACLISE

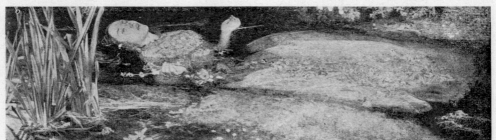

THE DEATH OF OPHELIA IN "HAMLET"— FROM THE PAINTING BY SIR J. E. MILLAIS

CORDELIA APPEALS TO HER FATHER, KING LEAR — FROM THE PAINTING BY FORD MADOX BROWN

called upon to defend before the "potent, grave and reverend signiors " of Venice his love for Desdemona and her love for him. Though he is successful there is a feeling that an unkindly fate is impending; and that his later exclamation " If it were now to die 'twere now to be most happy," will come true. Yet all the pitifulness of the play is a noble sensation, upholding the ancient idea of the purifying power of pity. The poignancy of it all surges up in Othello's speech before he, as he thinks, executes justice on Desdemona :

It is the cause, it is the cause, my soul!
Let me not name it to you, you chaste stars!
It is the cause! Yet I'll not shed her blood,
Nor scar that whiter skin of hers than snow,
And smooth as monumental alabaster.
Yet she must die, else she'll betray more men.
Put out the light; and then put out the light.
If I quench thee, thou flaming minister,
I can again thy former light restore
Should I repent me; but once put out thy light,
Thou cunning'st pattern of excelling nature,
I know not where is that Promethean heat
That can thy light relume. When I have
    plucked the rose
I cannot give it vital growth again.

Othello is the best example of how tragedy may be terrible without being brutal or vulgar. Incidentally it gives, in Cassio, the most effective stage picture of waste of life and character through drink.

In Macbeth, Shakespeare makes his fullest use of the supernatural. It was a powerful dramatic resource in the days when witchcraft was firmly believed in, even by intelligent people; and today his supernatural devices remain impressive. He used omens in Caesar, a stately ghost in Hamlet, apparitions in Richard the Third, and all these devices in Macbeth; while his lighter plays, like A Midsummer Night's Dream and The Tempest, are steeped in fanciful magic. The witches, or weird sisters, meet us in the opening scene of Macbeth, and the veil between the real and supernatural worlds is thin throughout the play. Yet the supernatural is always secondary. It does not control the fates of men, it only foreshadows, accompanies, and assists. The limits of its power are clearly drawn by one of the witches in Macbeth, who is pursuing a seafarer with her malevolence :

Though his bark cannot be lost,
Yet it shall be tempest-tossed.

Macbeth shows the demoralising effect of ambition, both on stronger and weaker natures, when it becomes a dominating passion. No play by Shakespeare is cast in a more romantic mould.

The tainted but hesitating Macbeth, and the masterful Lady Macbeth, are at last equally demoralised and broken up by their treacherous sin, the murder of their king while he was their guest, till the life which seemed glorious to them, as king and queen in the murdered Duncan's stead, is so empty that it it summed up in Macbeth's words of terrible hopelessness :

Tomorrow, and tomorrow, and tomorrow,
Creeps in this petty pace from day to day,
To the last syllable of recorded time;
And all our yesterdays have lighted fools
The way to dusty death. Out, out, brief candle!
Life's but a walking shadow, a poor player
That struts and frets his hour upon the stage
And then is heard no more. It is a tale
Told by an idiot, full of sound and fury.
Signifying nothing.

When read as the despairing words of a disillusioned bad man, all this is profoundly moral—as all Shakespeare's plays are if they are rightly read.

King Lear is the play that competes with Othello in poignancy and pathos. It is a study of ingratitude, so agonisingly pitiful that many think it can never be acted perfectly ; it would be too full of anguish to do and to see. Whether it has been acted perfectly cannot well be decided, for acting is not capable of transmission. We can only judge it by the records left by our fathers, whose tastes may not have been like our own. Everyone of us must agree with the touching words of Lear's faithful friend Kent, as Lear is dying:

Vex not his ghost! O! let him pass; he hates
    him
That would upon the rack of this rough world
Stretch him out longer.

Here we have but glanced momentarily at a few of the mighty tragedies that have placed Shakespeare on a pedestal apart as the supreme poet of the modern world. But the great period of his life when Shakespeare wrote of

            exultations, agonies,
And love, and man's unconquerable mind,

passed away, and in his later years he sailed his bark into quieter waters, and approached his too early end apparently in a spirit of serenity.

The three plays which best illustrate this period of Shakespeare's quiet eventide, when he had become a wealthy man, as wealth was then counted, and probably lived mostly in retirement at his native

Stratford, are Cymbeline, A Winter's Tale, and The Tempest. The tone of all three is peaceful, and the endings tell of reconciliation and forgiveness. It is no mere fancy that Shakespeare was looking forward to his final rest, and perhaps even foresaw something of his own fame. The feeling expressed in the song in Cymbeline is echoed more faintly again and again.

Fear no more the heat o' the sun,
  Nor the furious winter's rages;
Thou art worldly task hast done
  Home art gone, and ta'en thy wages.
          *   *   *
Fear no more the frown of the great,
  Thou art past the tyrant's stroke;
Care no more to clothe and eat;
  To thee the reed is as the oak.
          *   *   *
Fear no more the lightning flash,
  Nor the all-dreaded thunder-stone;
Fear not slander, censure rash;
  Thou hast finished joy and moan.
          *   *   *
Quiet consummation have;
And renownéd be thy grave.

But the most significant of Shakespeare's later plays is The Tempest, which may be accepted as his deliberate farewell to the stage, though probably he could not stand entirely aloof, even though he had pictured himself as the magician resigning his wand.

HOW SHAKESPEARE PASSED TO HIS EVERLASTING FAME

Into this play he poured afresh samples of the kinds of verse in which he had taken his dearest early delight. He creates new sprites, after the fashion of Puck in A Midsummer Night's Dream, to sing new dainty songs, such as Ariel's seaside air :

Come unto these yellow sands,
  And then take hands;
Curtsied when you have, and kissed—
  The wild waves whist;
Foot it featly here and there;
  And, sweet sprites, the burden bear.

The last line is an invitation to the sprites to join in the chorus. Or, again, there is the companion song, to lure the shipwrecked Ferdinand to the place where he will meet the fair Miranda.

Full fathom five thy father lies;
  Of his bones are coral made;
Those are pearls that were his eyes;
  Nothing of him that doth fade
But doth suffer a sea change
  Into something rich and strange.
Sea nymphs hourly ring his knell.
Hark! Now I hear them—ding-dong bell.

What exultant merriment there is in the song of the tricksy Ariel when he has been promised perfect freedom by the enchanter Prospero who is giving up his magic powers.

Where the bee sucks, there suck I;
  In a cowslip's bell I lie;
There I couch when owls do cry.
  On the bat's back I do fly
After summer merrily:
  Merrily, merrily, shall I live now
  Under the blossom that hangs on the bough.

The graver passages of sublime thought that were never very far away from Shakespeare's pen are again brought into his closing play, as when, having entertained Ferdinand, the shipwrecked prince, with some magic visions, he brings down the curtain with the words :

Our revels now are ended. These our actors,
As I foretold you, were all spirits and
Are melted into air, into thin air;
And, like the baseless fabric of this vision,
The cloud-capped towers, the gorgeous palaces,
The solemn temples, the great globe itself,
Yea, all which it inherit, shall dissolve
And, like this insubstantial pageant faded,
Leave not a rack behind. We are such stuff
As dreams are made on, and our little life
Is rounded with a sleep.

Perhaps most striking is the Epilogue that ends the play. After Prospero has renounced his " so potent art," as Shakespeare was renouncing his, and has determined to break his magic staff and " bury it certain fathoms in the earth," he tells his hearers, now his charms are all o'er-thrown, what his aim has been. It was *to please*. And he marks the ending of his project by the confession:

                    Now I want
Spirits to enforce, art to enchant;
And my ending is despair
Unless I be relieved by prayer,
Which pierces so that it assaults
Mercy itself, and frees all faults.

We refuse to give up the fancy that that is how " the gentle Shakespeare," as his contemporaries called him, once a poor player who strutted and fretted his hour upon the stage, and then the most sweet and gracious as well as solemn and powerful of all poets, made his adieu to his audiences and his readers, and passed on to everlasting fame.

He was in his own person as elusive as his Ariel or his Puck. By far the larger part of what we know of him is arrived at by inference from his writings, but this we know, that the Shakespeare who is before us in the printed book, whatever the man who walked the earth may have been, is " all mankind's epitome."

The Great Words that Stir the Hearts and Minds of All Mankind

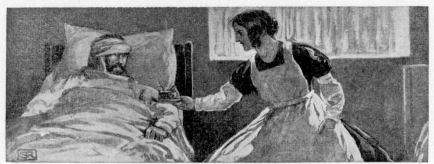

Sister Dora, the cheerful nurse who made her patient want to get well

FAITH

FAITH is a word which will be born again. Its day is by no means done. Quite possibly it may govern your own day—may lead you to a far happier world.

To understand this suggestion, you must drive out of your mind the idea that faith means saying Yes to something you cannot understand. Faith has nothing to do with surrender of the intelligence. It is not a cold-blooded thing, but the most hot-blooded of all passionate things. It means, feeling that something which you cannot prove is truer than anything else in the world is true ; and it also means *acting on that belief.*

Suppose you said to a boy, " A thick coat keeps out the cold " ; and he replied to you, " Yes, I believe in that " ; and one bitter cold day you found him with his overcoat on his arm, freezing to death. You would say he had not acted on his faith. But suppose somebody said to you, " It is a far better thing to lay down your life for the poor and the sorrowful than to seek riches for yourself," and you went out from a comfortable home to work among the lepers, giving up everything to minister to those unhappy people ; would it not be said of you that your faith was real, because you had acted on it ? David Livingstone acted on this faith. So did Sister Dora, the cheerful nurse of Walsall, whose story we tell on page 6824.

This is the very first thing we must all learn about faith. There is no real faith without action. Faith means acting on what we believe.

There are some things in life which we can prove to be true ; but there are many things in our daily life which nobody can prove to be true. It is in the region of these things that faith is a power, and a most tremendous power.

No child can prove to the complete satisfaction of a cynic that its mother loves it ; the cynic would say : " Her love is selfish ; she would not love you if it did not give her pleasure ; it is not you, but herself, that she loves." The child, however, does not need to prove that the mother's love is real. The child acts on the faith that the love of its mother is real, and so makes its life both happy and beautiful. All the joy of life depends on faith.

No manufacturer can prove that the merchant who buys from him is honest. He may say : " I have dealt with him for twenty years, and he has never failed to keep his word " ; but how can he *prove* that one day this honest merchant will not yield to the temptation of dishonesty?

All civilised life depends on faith. We are paid our wages in bits of paper worth nothing at all ; but the tradesman has faith in British Credit and gives us food in exchange for that paper ; and we eat that

DISCOVERY · WILL · HONOUR · HOPE · RIGHTEOUSNESS · REASON

food in the faith that it is honest food and will not poison us.

We could not get along without faith. Wipe faith out of existence and we should be plunged into savagery, each man fighting like an animal for all he could get. The great banks of our cities, and the great insurance offices, and the great docks and warehouses—all these are monuments of faith. Civilisation is threaded together at every turn by the confidence one man feels in another, and all men feel in the State, and one nation feels in another. War comes when nations break faith. Faith is essential both to the business and to the security of human life.

Now that we see how big a thing is faith, and also how commonplace a thing, a thing of every day, let us look at it in another aspect. All of us, whatever we choose to think about it, are living on a planet which belongs to an immense universe. How we came here, how the universe began, and how it all hangs together, nobody can tell. We can theorise about it, make good shots and bad shots ; but we can never prove our theories. And so it is that every person on the Earth takes the universe on faith.

THE IMPASSIONED FAITH OF THE MAN WHO BELIEVES IN GOD

One person says the universe is a machine, without intelligence and without purpose. Another person says, " Because it is so beautiful and so majestic, I believe the universe to be the creation of a great Power whom I call God." Now observe the difference in these two faiths in conduct. Few men who believe the universe is a machine dare act upon that faith, for to act on it would be to live selfishly, to live brutally, to live badly. But a man who believes in God, and who acts on that faith, seeks moral perfection in just the same way as a painter or a sculptor or an architect seeks beauty. His faith is impassioned. He believes not only in the reasonableness of virtue, but in the power of love. He bears all the trials of life with a good courage, and, as for death, he says it is but the gateway into eternal life.

History is full of the stories of men who have lived this life of faith—lived it up to the very moment of death. Socrates died with a smile and a jest for the sake of truth, and would not make his escape from prison, so sure was his faith. Latimer and Ridley died in the flames for their faith with many other courageous martyrs. Sir Thomas More had his jest on the scaffold, and the jest was only a proof of the confidence with which he went to God.

Science, too, has had its noble army of martyrs: glorious men of genius who died rather than deny the truth of their reasons. To believe in a thing is to be uplifted beyond the reach of all fear. To believe in God is to regard death as a friend.

THE GREAT POWER OF FAITH A BIG FACT IN HISTORY

Such, then, is the power of faith over conduct. It is evidently, obviously, a very big thing. Nobody can deny that ; it is a fact of history. The most beautiful lives in the long chronicle of humanity have been governed by faith in God and devotion to mankind. But there is yet another aspect of faith.

Jesus used this word in a very striking way. He did not use it as so many of the churches use it. He did not use it only to make men see what a difference true belief could make in the conduct of their daily lives. He used it in the sense of a power which they all possessed and might use if they would. He declared that faith was such a terrific power that if a man said to a mountain, and believed it would happen, " Be thou removed and cast into the depths of the sea," the mountain would obey. No man, of course, could believe that a mountain would obey his command ; and so no mountain will ever vanish out of sight at a man's word. But Jesus used this phrase to make men realise what a tremendous thing faith is— what a *power;* believe that a mountain will obey you, and it will obey you ; believe the impossible, and it will become the possible. Jesus told his disciples to believe that their prayers would come true, and they would come true. It is told of Him that in one place he visited he could heal no sick because they had no faith in Him.

THE GREAT PART THE POWER OF THE SOUL MAY PLAY ON EARTH

It seems as if men are now thinking about faith as Jesus thought about it. They are not thinking of it as agreement with a set of words, but as action on the part of the mind, as a power over life. Doctors tell invalids to think they are well. Teachers of all kinds are telling their pupils to assure themselves that they are getting on and will conquer their difficulties. It is generally agreed that, while despairing thoughts are bad, hopeful and confident thoughts are good and helpful.

Perhaps we may see this power applied once more by the soul to its destiny, and on a much greater scale than has ever yet been attempted. Many say "I believe in God," but few, very few, know the passionate joy of such a faith. Really to believe in God, really to love Him, really to believe in reunion after death, is to live at the radiant centre of the universe, to which no darkness ever comes, and to possess a power over all the circumstances of life which is unconquerable. True faith means peace in the heart, joy in the mind, and power in the soul—a tremendous power.

No one can say how great a part this power of the soul may play on the Earth; but already there are signs that it will make a vast difference both in the health of a nation and in its wealth. People see that it is bad for them to dwell upon ills, to take a depressing view of life, to hug their diseases and to nurse their complaints. Also, they begin to see that peace between

FAITH, FROM THE PAINTING BY FREDERICK J. SHIELDS

masters and men, and peace between nations, can best be won by friendly conferences in which suspicion is banished and confidence is sought as the cure of misunderstanding. All this will make a difference to the fortunes of humanity. Jesus, we may say, is still proclaiming to the world, "According to your faith be it unto you." Faith is our birthright and our destiny.

But this great thing is greater than national prosperity and international peace; it is nothing less than knowledge of God and the exercise of divine power. Faith at its greatest is a passionate belief in love as the law of the universe, and a belief so passionate, so unquestioning and intense, that it drives the soul to action. Pascal said, "How far it is from knowing God to loving Him!" There seems to be a moment in which certain souls can pass from saying they believe, to believing with all their force ; and that moment changes their whole lives.

Enough for us at the present to tell ourselves that faith is an action of the soul, not a belief or an opinion, and to keep our faith in the power of love and goodness always in a state of growth.

THE BOY WHO WAS HIDDEN FROM PHARAOH

THE CHILD MOSES, HIDDEN BY HIS MOTHER AMONG THE BULRUSHES TO SAVE HIM FROM EGYPTIAN VENGEANCE, IS DISCOVERED BY PHARAOH'S DAUGHTER, WHO BRINGS HIM UP IN HER PALACE

The Story of the Most Beautiful Book in the World

Moses adrift on the waters

THE RISE OF MOSES

WHILE the Israelites grew rich and happy among the Egyptians the older rulers and princes died one after another, until a king reigned over Egypt who knew nothing at all about Joseph.

This mighty Pharaoh, sitting on his throne and listening to the complaints of his Egyptian counsellors, came to consider the foreign Israelites first a nuisance and then a danger to his kingdom. For while the Egyptians were somewhat indolent, the Israelites were hard-working, and took a pleasure in both making and saving money for the sake of their children. You can imagine how bitter it made the easy-going Egyptians to see these foreigners growing richer and more numerous every year.

Perhaps the Israelites grew a little proud in their wealth. Certain it is that the Egyptians grew to hate and fear them. So Pharaoh, listening to those who said that in a war the Israelites would surely fight with the enemies of Egypt, set himself to break the spirit of these proud foreigners. By a word of command the great Pharaoh made the whole host of these prosperous Israelites the slaves of his will. They were driven from their homes and merchandise, formed into gangs, and marched away, under task-masters who lashed them with whips, to make bricks for Pharaoh's new cities. The happy Israelite, laughing and happy in the midst of his wife and children, became a flogged and bleeding slave toiling under a burning sun, without wages and without hope.

But such was the quiet endurance of these Israelites that even as slaves, and in the midst of a life so hard and cruel and hopeless, they grew in numbers, and showed a cheerful face to their oppressors. Pharaoh, seeing how they still increased, gave the cruel order that every boy born to an Israelite should be instantly strangled. The people ordered to do this refused, and instead the boy children were thrown into the Nile. How many a poor Israelitish mother must have tried to hide her baby from the cruel Egyptians.

Among these mothers was a woman named Jochebed, who had a little baby boy. For over three months she managed to conceal him, and then, fearing that the spies would discover her secret, she set about a very original plan of saving him. She made a little ark or cradle of papyrus, coated it with pitch, and put her baby carefully within; then she placed this baby's boat among the bulrushes of the Nile, and set her daughter Miriam to watch.

GREAT FIGURES OF THE OLD TESTAMENT . THE LIFE OF JESUS

The sister Miriam, standing under the blazing sun and shading her dark eyes to watch the blue water of the Nile, beheld a company of noble Egyptian ladies approaching the river, and knew that the chief of these noble ladies was the Princess of Egypt, the daughter of the mighty Pharaoh. The princess, walking beside the river, espied the ark floating on the water, and bade one of her maidens fetch it. The order was obeyed, and the ladies crowded round the princess as the ark was presented to her.

When the covering was raised, the baby opened its eyes and burst into tears. This touched the princess to the heart, and, though she knew the baby to be an Israelite, she determined to rear him and keep him at her side. While they were all bending over the baby and admiring him, Miriam approached, and, hearing what the princess said, asked whether she should go and fetch a nurse to rear the baby. The princess said Yes, and off went Miriam to fetch her mother, who rejoiced to know that once again she would nurse her boy.

HOW THE CHILD MOSES GREW UP IN THE PALACE OF PHARAOH

Pharaoh's daughter called the baby Moses, which means *saved from water*, and took the greatest pains with his education.

The little Israelite was trained by the wisest of the Egyptian teachers, and grew up in Pharaoh's palace amid all the luxury and learning of a great court.

But, although he grew up exactly like an Egyptian, he remained deep in his heart an Israelite, and his blood burned like fire in his veins whenever he saw the cruelties under which his people groaned. One day, when he was a grown man, the sight of an Israelite being flogged by a taskmaster so worked upon the mind of Moses that, thinking himself unobserved, he went forward and slew the taskmaster. Some time after this he sought to persuade two quarrelling Israelites to " make it up "; but instead of doing this they turned on him, and taunted him with having murdered an Egyptian. Moses was frightened at this, and, thinking that if the murder was discovered he would certainly be killed, he fled away and took service with Jethro, the chief of the Hebrew people in Midian.

In this pleasant country Moses dwelt for many years. It must have seemed to him that his strange and romantic life had now settled down to peace and quiet domestic happiness. He married one of Jethro's daughters, and tended his father-in-law's flocks, dwelling much among the vast, silent spaces of Nature, where God's peace seemed to rest.

HOW MOSES PONDERED OVER THE SUFFERINGS OF HIS PEOPLE

But Moses could never forget the awful sights he had seen in Egypt. Again and again the vision rose before his eyes of gangs of almost naked Israelites making bricks under a burning sun while the lashes of the taskmaster's whips hissed through the air and tore at the flesh of their straining bodies. The injustice and cruelty of it embittered his thoughts; the hopelessness of ever altering it made him sad.

It happened that one day as he was watching Jethro's flocks close by a mountain he saw a bush on fire, and, going toward it, he observed to his amazement that although the fire blazed all round and through the bush it was not consumed.

He went nearer, and then a Voice called to him out of the midst of the fire. Moses, so frightened that he knew not what to say, answered the Voice which called him by name; and the Voice bade him take off his shoes, for the ground on which he stood was holy. Then did the shepherd realise that he was in the presence of God, and, taking off his shoes and covering his eyes with his hand, he waited in great fear.

THE VISION THAT CAME TO MOSES FROM THE BURNING BUSH

The voice of God in the bush said:

I have surely seen the affliction of my people which are in Egypt, and have heard their cry by reason of their taskmasters; for I know their sorrows . . . Come now, therefore, and I will send thee unto Pharaoh, that thou mayest bring forth my people, the children of Israel, out of Egypt.

But Moses was afraid, and sought to escape from this duty. God constrained him, and Moses asked what he should say to the children of Israel when it was demanded of him: " What is the name of thy God? "

Then God said words which have a wonderful meaning for us, a greater meaning than they could ever have had for Moses:

Thus shalt thou say unto the children of Israel, I AM hath sent me unto you.

Think for a moment what those two words mean. *I AM!* They teach us

MOSES BEFORE PHARAOH AND THE PEOPLE

MOSES SPEAKS TO PHARAOH

MOSES SPEAKS TO THE PEOPLE

that to God there is no yesterday and no tomorrow, but that with Him everything *IS*. He *IS*. Backward for ever and ever, and forward for ever and ever, the eyes of God look in one eternal gaze, and lo ! everything *IS*. It is all eternity, it is all everlastingness, it is one divine and beautiful present. Our cares and trials, which sometimes seem to us so hard to bear, are less than the tick of a clock in the vast eternity to which God has called us to enjoy with Him.

So Moses was at last persuaded, and God told him that his brother Aaron should go with him to stand before Pharaoh; and that, although Pharaoh would refuse to let the Israelites go, yet in the end, by the might of God's hand, Pharaoh should be bound, and the Israelites go free.

Moses, although reluctantly, accepted the duty laid upon him, and forsook his flocks and herds, and gave up the quiet peace of his life, and in his old age went forward on the greatest and most momentous journey that ever fell to the lot of mortal man.

AND THE LORD SENT THUNDER AND HAIL

When Moses knew that it was the will of God that he should go back to Egypt and deliver his oppressed nation from the terrible slavery of Pharaoh, he no longer hesitated and argued with himself, but set out, with his family and with Aaron his brother, for the land where the Israelites toiled. Here the two brothers gathered the people together and declared to them the will of God. Imagine the joy of these once rich and prosperous and happy people, who had been degraded by Pharaoh to the meanest slavery, when they heard that the God of Abraham and Isaac cared for them, and had sent Moses to deliver them out of the hand of Pharaoh and give them a country of their own.

Moses went forward again, strong in the gratitude of his people, and stood before the mighty King of Egypt.

Pharaoh listened to the Hebrew's words with a sneer. The God of the Hebrews was nothing to him. He despised the people and their God.

To show Moses how little he cared for his strong words, Pharaoh gave orders that the straw which hitherto had been provided for the Hebrews at their brickmaking should be gathered by themselves, and yet that the taskmaster should see that the number of bricks made each day was the same. Under this new tyranny the spirit of the Israelites broke, and their hearts grew furious against Moses and his brother Aaron.

" What have you done but add to our burdens ? " they cried bitterly.

Moses bade them have patience. He said that Pharaoh had refused to believe the words of God ; now he should know what this God of Israel could do. Moses calmly and quietly set himself in this strange land against the tyrant king, sure in the knowledge that God would deliver His people.

Moses stood before Pharaoh and showed him by marvellous deeds that he did indeed speak for the invisible God, to whom nothing is impossible. But Pharaoh laughed, thinking that Moses and Aaron were but clever magicians. Then Moses warned him that God would certainly send signs to Pharaoh—signs many and terrible of His wrath and indignation. But Pharaoh only laughed, and would not let the people of Israel go free.

The warning of Moses came true. Egypt was smitten by the displeasure of God. Ten plagues fell upon the land.

The waters became red like blood.

A multitude of frogs spread themselves, and died in vast heaps, so that the air stank.

The dust became a heaving, creeping swarm of lice, which settled upon man and beast.

Flies rose up in the air and descended upon the houses, entering in at doors and windows and blackening all the glory of man's art.

THE PLAGUES THAT FELL UPON EGYPT

A GREAT PLAGUE OF LOCUSTS FELL UPON THE LAND

THE DEATH OF PHARAOH'S FIRST-BORN

A fearful disease broke out among the cattle of the Egyptians, so that they died.

The people of Pharaoh were afflicted with boils and blisters, corrupting their bodies and destroying their peace.

Thunder rolled, the heavens opened, and a storm of pitiless hail beat upon the crops, broke even the branches of great trees, and made desolate the whole land.

Locusts, greater in size than had ever been before, so numerous that they darkened all the land, marched like an invincible army across the country, destroying everything over which they passed.

Darkness, blacker than blackest night—a thick darkness, a darkness which might be felt—descended out of heaven and steeped the land of Egypt in its gloom.

Last of all, and more terrible than all, the Angel of the Lord passed through the land of Egypt and smote the eldest child of all the Egyptians, from the first-born of Pharaoh on his throne unto the first-born of the captive that was in the dungeon.

Then Pharaoh rose up in the night, he and all his servants, and all the Egyptians ; and there was a great cry in Egypt, for there was not a house where there was not one dead.

THE CHILDREN OF ISRAEL BEGIN THEIR WONDERFUL MARCH TO FREEDOM

Now the mourning and broken-hearted Egyptians were eager for the Israelites to go, and they cried to Pharaoh that he should send the slaves away ; and Pharaoh ordered Moses and Aaron to gather the Israelites together and to depart immediately.

So at last the people were delivered out of tyranny, and were free again. With great rejoicing they came together in a mighty host, and, with Moses and Aaron to guide them, set out on the march to the land of Canaan.

Now, to avoid a nation that might have afflicted them again, they went, not by a straight route to the Promised Land, but by a great curve, and it is that curve of the Israelites which remains for all ages as one of the most wonderful marches in the story of mankind.

Their first adventure occurred at the Red Sea. God had led His people so far in a wonderful way. By day a pillar of cloud went before the marching host, and by night a pillar of fire.

It came to pass that as they drew near the banks of the Red Sea, rejoicing in their deliverance, and delighting greatly in the prospect of a new country where they would be free and happy and pros-perous, suddenly a noise from behind broke upon them.

Turning about, the Israelites beheld the chariots and horsemen of Pharaoh approaching them in battle array. In an instant the host of Israel was thrown into confusion.

THE CHARIOTS OF PHARAOH PURSUE THE ISRAELITES TO BRING THEM BACK

First the people called upon Moses to save them, and then they bitterly upbraided him for delivering them out of slavery only that they should fall at the point of the sword. But Moses quieted the terrors of these foolish and ungrateful pilgrims, whose courage and manhood, we must always remember, had been broken by years of the most oppressive tyranny. He bade them trust in God, and remember the plagues which had afflicted Pharaoh and all his people. Then God spoke and said, " Speak unto the children of Israel that they go forward."

The pillar of cloud stood between the Israelites and Pharaoh's host, and Moses, going forward, stretched out his hand over the sea, and a great wind arose which blew all the night and divided the waters. So the children of Israel went into the midst of the sea upon the dry ground ; and the waters were a wall unto them on their right hand and on their left hand.

THE ISRAELITES CROSS THE RED SEA AND PHARAOH'S HOSTS ARE DROWNED

But when Pharaoh's host entered the sea in pursuit of the Israelites the wheels of the chariots stuck fast in the sand ; a frightful confusion broke out among them, and in the midst of that host of plunging horses and shouting soldiers the walls of water fell with deafening clamours, and the host of Pharaoh perished in the sea.

The Israelites, standing on the farther bank in the young light of an Eastern morning, when they beheld this miracle, and realised that now at last they were free, broke into songs of thanksgiving ; and Miriam took a timbrel in her hand, and all the women went out after her with timbrels and with dances, singing:

Sound the loud timbrel o'er Egypt's
    dark sea,
Jehovah hath triumphed, His people
    are free,

a song that has been set to music and is sung more than 3000 years after the event it commemorates.

The Interests and Pleasures of Life for All Indoors and Out

HOW TO PLAY CHESS

THE game of chess dates back to very ancient times, although no one knows who first invented it.

It is played on the same board as draughts. This contains 64 squares, arranged in eight rows of eight, and alternate squares are black and white. There are 32 men, 16 being black and 16 white. Each set consists of a king and queen, two bishops, two knights, and two castles, or rooks, and eight pawns.

The players sit facing one another, with the board between them, so placed that there is a white square in the right-hand bottom corner. Each player arranges his men as shown in the diagram, as follows : On the row of squares nearest to him—that is, the back row—the more important men are placed in this order, white starting from his left, black from his right : rook, knight, bishop, queen, king, bishop, knight, rook. On the next row the eight pawns are placed in adjoining squares across the board. White moves first.

Unlike the men in draughts, the different kinds of chess-men move in different ways. The king moves one square at a time in any direction, forward, backward, sideways, or diagonally. The queen moves any number of squares in a straight line in any direction. The rook or castle moves any number of squares in a straight line, but only in a direction parallel with the edges of the board.

The bishop moves any number of squares diagonally, so that it remains throughout the game on the same colour square as that on which it started. The knight moves two squares, neither more nor less, each time, the move being across one square diagonally and then on to the next one parallel, or vice versa. The result is that a knight at each move always passes on to a different colour square from the one it was on. Pawns move one square forward, but never backward. For their first move, however, they may move either one or two squares, at the option of the player.

Though in ordinary moving they always go straight forward, they only capture other men diagonally. If a pawn succeeds in crossing the board to the farthest row of squares it may be exchanged for a queen or any piece that the player may desire except a king. The knight can pass over a man, but all other men move over only unoccupied squares.

The object of the game is not to take pieces, but to checkmate the king—that is, to place it in such a position that if it were another piece it would be captured.

The best defence is to attack your foe, and whenever you attack his king you must say " Check," and he must put his king out of check—either move it or interpose another piece between it and the attacking piece.

The fewer men that are captured and removed during a game the more interesting the game will prove. If the king is in check, and cannot be put out of check, then the game is lost by the player whose king is thus checkmated. If, however, the king is in such a position that, while it is not in

CRAFTS · GAMES · NEEDLEWORK · PUZZLES · SCIENCE EXPERIMENTS

check, it cannot be moved without placing it in check, and no other move by any other piece is possible, then this is called stalemate, and the game is drawn. The game is also drawn if the force remaining on the board is unable to give checkmate.

Once in a game each player is allowed to "castle" —that is, if the move will be an advantage, he may move the rook to the square next the king and place the king on the other side of the rook. This, however, may only be done when no pieces intervene, when the king is not in check, when neither king nor rook has been previously moved, and when the king does not cross a square commanded by an opposing piece.

Any opponent's piece, except the king, may be taken when it is in the line of an attacking piece. Thus, if a rook is somewhere on a diagonal line with nothing between it and a bishop or queen, the bishop or queen may be placed on the square of the rook and the rook taken.

HOW TO SET THE CHESS-MEN

The most curious method of capture is that known as taking "en passant." When one side—say, black—has a pawn well advanced, so that it is in the fourth row from the farthest side, and an adjacent white pawn that has not moved at all is advanced two squares, as it can be on the first move, the player of black may take it off the board and plant his own pawn diagonally, as if the white had moved only one square.

When a player has lost all but the king, he may insist on his opponent winning in fifty moves; otherwise the game is drawn. If a player repeats the same line of play again and again his opponent may demand that the game be limited to fifty moves more on each side; and if neither checkmates the game is drawn.

Chess was a favourite game of the Vikings, and ability to play chess was regarded as one of the necessary accomplishments of the knights of chivalry. The game as we play it now dates from the sixteenth century.

A GOOD GAME WITH THE ATLAS

IT is always difficult to remember the outlines of the different countries and islands shown in the atlas, and to keep on drawing the maps again and again, in order to fix them in our mind, is dull work; but there is a way of learning the shapes of the countries so that they are not easily forgotten.

Take the atlas and, copying or tracing the outlines of certain countries and islands on paper, look at them carefully and try to think what familiar objects they are like. Then alongside each country draw the object which it resembles, keeping very closely to the outline of the map.

It is astonishing, with a little ingenuity and a few lines, how many of the countries and islands and seas can be quickly turned into pictures of things with which everyone is familiar. Italy, for example, is remarkably like a riding-boot; Lake Erie is like a whale; Corsica has the form of a hand, and so on.

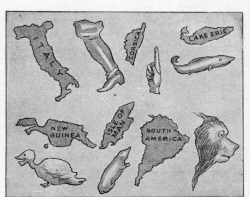

THE MAPS MADE INTO PICTURES

Having drawn a map of a certain country, and with a few touches changed it into a bird or animal or fish, the general outline will always be remembered, and if the object made has some connection with the country it will be even more helpful.

This game of making picture maps may be used as a round game for a party of any number. Half a dozen countries or islands or seas are mentioned, and their names are taken down by the competitors. Then atlases are opened, and the outlines of the countries are drawn by each player on pieces of paper, room being left at the side for the duplicate outline changed into an animal or some other object. When all the maps are drawn, a certain time is allowed for the pictures to be made, and the maker of the best picture is the winner.

The great temptation to be guarded against is that of varying the shape too much.

CAKE MAKING, BAKING, AND DECORATING

WHETHER it is a birthday cake, a Christmas cake, or one to celebrate big brother's captaincy of his school eleven, here are a few hints to help you to take your share in making it.

One of the most important things in making a cake is to be sure that the oven is heated to the temperature given in the recipe before the cake is put in; for if the oven is too low, the cake may sink in the middle, become too dry, or have too sugary a crust, while if the oven is too hot, it may have tunnels in it, rise unevenly, and be burnt outside and heavy inside.

A good way to begin is by baking, in a little tin for a dolls' tea party, a portion of a cake mixture made by a grown-up, preparing the tin as for a big cake, as follows: Cut a band of grease-proof paper, broad enough to come well above the tip of the tin, and long enough to lap over itself when placed inside. Cut half-inch slits at half-inch intervals diagonally all the way round. Fit this band of paper inside the tin with the cut part resting flat on the bottom, then lay a round of paper, cut to fit the bottom, flat over this, and brush all over inside with a pastry brush or a clean feather dipped in tasteless cooking oil or melted salt-free shortening.

Fill the tin just two-thirds full and make a slight depression in the middle of the cake mixture, so that it will rise evenly. Opening and shutting an oven door before a cake has set properly can spoil it completely, so ask a grown-up cook to say how soon you can peep into the oven to see if it is ready to come out. When you are older you will learn how to make and bake a cake from start to finish. This is how you should set about it then.

Collect utensils and ingredients and set the oven to the correct heat. Sift the flour on to the weighing machine, and then from the weighing machine to the mixing bowl, adding first, baking powder and spices, if the recipe includes these. The double sifting is worth the trouble, for it lightens the flour by letting in air. The sugar may also need sifting to remove lumps. Experienced cooks find it easy to beat the shortening and sugar to a cream first, but beginners would be wise to rub the fat in, using this Foundation Cake recipe:

Cut half a pound of butter, margarine, or dripping, into one pound of self-raising flour

A novel decoration for a cake—a posy of real flowers on a paper doily. Bind the stems together with a damp rag, and wrap them in silver paper. The posy will then keep fresh without spoiling the cake top.

with a pair of blunt-pointed kitchen scissors, then rub it in with the fingers till fat and flour together look like very fine breadcrumbs. Add half a pound of granulated or castor sugar and mix well. Break two eggs into a separate bowl and beat them together with three or four tablespoonfuls of either fresh or sour milk. Add this liquid, and any kind of flavouring preferred, to the dry mixture, and stir till the cake dough is moist but firm and leaves the sides of the mixing bowl clean. Finally turn this mixture into a lined, greased tin, and bake in a moderate oven at 360° to 370° F. for one and a half hours if the tin is deep and round; or for a shorter period if it is large and shallow.

When ready to come out of the oven a cake shrinks slightly away from the tin all round. Test by inserting a warmed skewer or knife, and if this comes out clean, without any underdone dough sticking to it, the cake is cooked. Use a good thick oven-cloth to lift the hot tin out of the oven, and allow the cake a minute to begin to cool in the tin; then, placing a sieve or stand above it, turn the cake out on to the stand with a quick firm twist of the hands.

To make this foundation cake mixture into a Fruit Cake, mix a teacupful of dried fruits in with the cake dough prior to adding the eggs and milk. These fruits could be stoned raisins or dates, sultanas or currants, previously cleaned by rubbing in a little flour in a cloth or, of course, a mixture of all four. For a Seed Cake allow one ounce of caraway seeds to the dough. A Chocolate Cake can be made by dissolving in the milk three tablespoonfuls of sweetened, grated chocolate, and beating this in with the eggs as soon as the chocolate has melted sufficiently. Use a double saucepan for this.

Any of these mixtures can be cooked as little Buns for a change. To make these, two-thirds fill small paper baking cases, or well-greased patty tins, and cook in a rather hotter oven for about a quarter of an hour. If a Rock Bun is preferred, put a little less milk when mixing, and pile in rough heaps, not too close together, allowing room for spreading, on a greased and floured baking tin. Put in the hottest part of the oven so that the buns will rise quickly, otherwise they will run into one another.

Rainbow Cake is always a favourite, and friends will think how clever you are if you give them this for tea, yet it is very easily made from the foundation recipe with the addition of vegetable colourings. Portion the mixed dough equally into as many bowls as you have colours. Add the colour drop by drop very sparingly and work lightly in, so that the mixture is just tinted all over, and not made too dark. A drop or two of the flavouring which goes with the colour, like almond or vanilla essence with the plain mixture, lemon with yellow colouring, raspberry or strawberry with pink, can be added at the same time, but again be very careful not to put too much. To get the rainbow effect, spoon each colour separately into the tin.

A true sponge-cake mixture has neither butter nor baking powder in it. All its light texture comes from not less than half an hour's beating of the eggs, which is boring and tiring for beginners, but here is a Two-minute Sponge which is not difficult to make. Beat together three new-laid eggs. Sift into a basin a heaped cupful of flour, add a level cupful of castor sugar and a pinch of salt, and mix lightly. Then make a well in the centre, pour in a tablespoonful of melted butter and the eggs, and beat all together for two minutes. If the eggs are small, a little milk may be needed to make the mixture the right consistency— it should drop but not run from the spoon. Lightly fold in two teaspoonfuls of baking powder, and divide equally into two greased and floured sandwich tins. Bake in a quick oven for about a quarter of an hour or twenty minutes, and when cold put together with jam between, and sift castor sugar over the top.

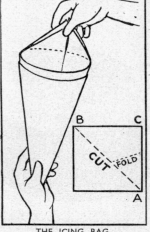

THE ICING BAG

This sponge mixture makes a delicious layer birthday cake. Make twice the quantity and use four shallower and wider sandwich tins for baking. When cold, turn one sponge upside down and spread with tangerine butter icing ; put another sponge on top, and spread this with apricot jam mixed with chopped almonds ; place the third sponge on this and spread with more butter icing. If the sponges have not risen evenly, level them with a sharp knife first. To make the tangerine butter icing, beat three ounces of butter and six ounces of sieved icing sugar to a cream, add the strained juice of one small tangerine or half a small orange, and some crystallized tangerine, or orange slices, cut up small. When the fillings have been put in, the top and sides of the cake can be iced. To do this, put the cake on a board or an upturned plate, with paper surrounding it and on the floor, in case of spills. Cream two ounces of butter or margarine with four ounces of icing sugar sieved until quite free from lumps. Then add the remaining four ounces of sieved icing sugar, and mix all together with about three tablespoonfuls of boiling water. Work round and round with a wooden spoon till the mixture resembles thick cream. This quantity should be sufficient to cover a cake made from the foundation recipe given on the previous page.

Directly the icing is mixed pour it over the middle of the cake. It will trickle down from the top over the sides ; then, with a palette knife or any flexible, blunt-pointed knife dipped in boiling water, smooth the icing round the sides of the cake, scooping up any that has run on to the board and working it into the icing on the sides. Leave the iced cake (protected from flies and dust) to set before preparing an additional few ounces of icing for piping or decorating the cake by using an icing bag.

An icing syringe can be bought, but the bag is quite as good, and saves trouble, for the syringe must be washed and carefully dried after use, while a fresh bag can be made for each occasion. To make one, take a sheet of strong greaseproof paper 14 inches square, and cut this diagonally as shown by the dotted line in the illustration.

Take the triangle point marked A in the inset sketch and fold it in the centre at the point marked fold. Twist the point of the paper marked B round to form a cone, and fold back the upper end of the cone along the dotted line, fixing it with a paper clip. The icing bag is now ready to use, though for really good work an icing nozzle must be inserted in the tip. There are dozens of different shaped nozzles for professional cooks to choose from, but first an amateur need only buy three—a nozzle, size two or three, for icing names or greetings, a ribbon nozzle for making borders or scrolls, and a rose nozzle for flower decorations.

Never have the bag more than two-thirds full, and to get the icing mixture through the nozzle press gently downwards. Lift the bag sharply at the end of each stroke of a letter, or after forcing out a rose, and wipe it free from sugar when necessary with a cloth just moistened with hot water.

Left-over icing used to stuff dates and served with biscuits, makes a change from the cooked " afters " given on page 1247.

THE MYSTERIOUS MOVING PLATE

This is a little magical joke to be played on friends during dinner or supper.

Start the fun by asking the company : Did you ever try to mesmerise a plate? Naturally they laugh at the idea; but assure them that it can be done, and proceed to prove it. Taking a clean plate, breathe on it back and front, and make " mesmeric " passes over it. Of course, the mesmerism is imaginary, but pretend to be quite serious about it.

Place the plate in front, and, keeping the hands away from it, say gravely: " Plate, are you mesmerised? " To everyone's astonishment one side of the plate lifts itself half an inch or so, and then sinks down again. Now remark, " We have got on all right so far. Now, plate, perhaps you will answer a few questions. First, show us how you say Yes." The plate rises and sinks again three times. "And how do you say No? " This time it rises once only. " And if I ask you something

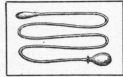
The Magic Plate-lifter

you don't know, what do you do then? " The plate rises and falls twice.

The secret lies in the use of a little appliance which may be bought at a toy-shop. It is a thin rubber tube, two to six feet in length, with an air-ball the shape and size of a small pear at one end, and a tiny bag of thin rubber at the other. The bag, when not inflated, is quite soft and flat, and in this condition it is laid upon the table, beneath the cloth, opposite the seat of the performer, with the tube and the air-ball hanging down in front of him. When the ball is pressed the little bag at the opposite end swells up to the size of a bean, and so raises the plate. When the pressure is relaxed it sinks again.

A tumbler or salt-cellar may be used instead of the plate. Of course the pretended mesmeric business may be left out and the plate allowed to begin its antics without attention being called to it beforehand.

A FILTER THAT IS SIMPLE TO MAKE

Sometimes, particularly when camping in out-of-the-way places, it is wise to filter drinking water, and there is a very simple form of filter that can be made with hardly any trouble, and which can be carried around easily if necessary.

Take an ordinary garden flowerpot about eight or nine inches in diameter at the top and, after thoroughly washing it, stop the hole with a piece of sponge, which must not fit too tightly. Then put in a layer of charcoal, about two inches deep, and above this a layer of clean sand, with a layer of

clean, coarse gravel three inches thick on top of the sand.

The filter is now quite ready for use. Fix it up over a vessel of some kind, and let the water which is to be filtered run through the various layers in the flower-pot slowly so as not to disarrange them, for if this happens the filter would be useless. Of course, from time to time the filter wants cleaning out, and then the flower-pot must be emptied, and after being thoroughly scrubbed and rinsed, must be filled as before with fresh and clean charcoal, sand, and gravel.

HOW TO MAKE A BOTTLE BLOW OUT A CANDLE

It may seem wonderful, but an apparently empty bottle may be made to blow out a candle. The trick is really an interesting scientific experiment, showing how compressed air, directly the pressure which confines it is removed, tends to assume the normal density of the atmosphere.

Take an ordinary bottle, such as those in which vinegar is sold, and, seeing that it is empty and dry, place the ball of the thumb over the mouth with just a small opening uncovered. Then, placing the mouth to this, blow steadily into the bottle.

The Flame Going Out

The result is that the air in the bottle is compressed, and care must be taken not to let any of this escape by instantly closing the whole gap with the ball of the thumb (which is already pressed over part of the opening) as soon as the lips are taken away.

Now turn the bottle upside down, and, placing its mouth against the flame of a lighted candle, remove so much of the hand as will make a small opening.

The result is that the compressed air, directly the pressure is removed, rushes out and blows upon the flame. It is well to use a small candle or nightlight, for the pressure may not be sufficient to extinguish the flame of a large candle. If this trick is being done in front of spectators, it is more impressive if they do not see the blowing into the bottle.

This part of the performance can be done outside the room, and the bottle can be brought in with the thumb over the opening till the moment when the air must be released. This should be done in such a way as not to attract notice.

LITTLE PROBLEMS FOR ODD MOMENTS

THESE problems are continued from page 998, and their answers, together with more questions, will be found on page 1248.

72. How Many Marbles?

" How many marbles have you? " asked Fred's mother, and he replied, " If you add one-quarter to one-third of the number, you will have ten more than half of the number."

How many marbles had Fred?

73. How Much had Each?

James and Harry had equal sums of money. When James had spent half of his, and Harry had spent two-thirds of his, James had 3s. 4d. more than Harry.

How much money had each at first?

74. What is the Word?

There is a word of six letters, the meaning of which is made exactly opposite by changing the places of the two middle letters.

What is the word?

75. How Fast did the Train Go?

A train passed through a station at its proper time, and continued running at a uniform speed until it passed a station 40 miles away, when it was 2 minutes late. If it had run at 50 miles an hour it would have been 10 minutes late.

At what speed did it actually travel?

76. How Long did Brown Take?

Hodge and Jenkins were cutting the hedge at one side of the railway, while Brown was cutting it at the other side. Brown found that to cut the same length of hedge he took exactly twice as long as Hodge and Jenkins.

The next week all three worked together on the same side, and found that they finished a piece equal in length to last week's work in two days.

How long did Brown take when he worked on the hedge alone?

77. How Long to Fill the Tank?

A water-tank is filled from a pipe that can fill it in two hours, but there is a hole in the bottom which could, if it were full, empty it in ten hours. The pipe starts running when the cistern is empty.

How long will the tank take to fill?

78. What Time was It?

The clock on the church tower takes the same time to make three strokes as the town-hall clock takes to make two strokes. " As I came home," said Jones, " they began to strike the hour at the same instant, and the last stroke of the church clock came exactly at the last stroke but two of the town clock."

What time was it?

THE ANSWERS TO THE PROBLEMS ON PAGE 998

65. The three nephews received portions represented by 8, 7, and 6, or 21 in all, of which George received $\frac{8}{21}$, John $\frac{7}{21}$, and Charles $\frac{6}{21}$. The sum of £420 divided by 21 is £20, so that George got £160, John £140, and Charles £120.

66. If tea sold at 3s. a pound, yielded 20 per cent. profit upon the cost price, the cost price of the mixed tea must have been 2s. 6d. a pound, because 6d.—the difference between 2s. 6d. and 3s.—is 20 per cent. of 2s. 6d. The problem is, therefore, to find what proportion of tea at 2s. a pound, and tea at 2s. 8d. a pound, will give a tea at 2s. 6d. a pound; 2s. a pound is 6d. *below* 2s. 6d.; 2s. 8d. a pound is 2d. *above* 2s. 6d. So that 2 pounds of 2s. tea cost 12d. below the cost of the mixture; 6 pounds of 2s. 8d. tea cost 12d. above the mixture. Hence, 2 pounds of 2s. tea and 6 pounds of 2s. 8d. tea cost the same as the mixture. The grocer therefore mixes them in this proportion, which is the same as 4 ounces of cheap tea with 12 ounces of dearer in every pound.

67. The lowest number that will divide by four, five, or six is 60, so that the woman must have bought 60 or a multiple of sixty of each. If she bought 60 of each she would pay 1s. 3d. for the 4 a penny, 1s. for the 5 a penny, and 10d. for the 6 a penny, or 3s. 1d. for the whole 180 windfall apples. If she sold them all at 5 a penny she would get 3s., and thus lose a penny. As she actually lost fourpence she must have purchased 4 times 60—that is, 240 of each.

68. The 45 is divided up into 5, 8, 12 and 20 which exactly meets the conditions set forth in the problem. By multiplying 5 by 2 the answer is 10, then, adding 2 to 8 also makes 10; the same result is obtained by subtracting 2 from 12, and by dividing 20 by 2. Jennifer was therefore quite as clever as Bob.

69. The third boy was right. When the ninth man went in, the eighth man was still batting, and the eighth, ninth, and tenth men had to go out.

70. Harry began at the end and found that 3 is the only figure which, when multiplied into 215, gives 4 in the second figure, so that the third figure in the

quotient was 3. As the first figure in the quotient is 1, the line below the dividend is 215.

$$215) \times 7 \times 95 (1 \times 3$$
$$2\ 1\ 5$$

$$\times 5 \times 9$$
$$\times 5 \times 5$$

$$6\ 4\ 5$$
$$6\ 4\ 5$$

The first figure in the dividend must be a 3, because when 2 is subtracted from it something remains. This gives the first remainder as 15×9. Obviously the middle figure in the quotient must be 7, and the second multiple in the sum must therefore be 1505. The figure below the 0 is 6, so that the figure above it must also be 6, and the middle figure in the dividend must be 1. Thus, the entire sum is now like this :

$$215)37195(173$$
$$215$$

$$1569$$
$$1505$$

$$645$$
$$645$$

71. Three dozen pencils and 5 dozen pens would be the same price as 13 dozen pencils. Three dozen pens and 5 dozen pencils are the same price as 11 dozen pencils. The difference in price between 13 dozen pencils and 11 dozen pencils was 6s., so that the two dozen pencils cost 6s., or one pencil cost 3d., and a pen cost 6d., or twice the price of a pencil. The sum may be proved. Three dozen pencils at 3s. a dozen and 5 dozen pens at 6s. a dozen come to 39s. ; 3 dozen pens at 6s. and 5 dozen pencils at 3s. would have cost 33s., and the difference is 6s.

Simple Learning Made Easy for Very Little People

NUMBERS—POUNDS, SHILLINGS, PENCE

JOHN and Jennifer learned quite a lot about money when they played with their café. They had learned how to price the things they sold, and how to give change.

They also knew all the things that made 6d. They had learned how to write down 1d, 2d, 3d, and so on, in the games they had played with their bus tickets.

One day Granny came to tea, and gave the twins a new shilling each. They knew that 12 pennies made 1s, and Daddy lent them 12 real pennies each to go into their cashbox at the café. They counted them, and found they had 24 pennies altogether, which made up their 2s.

The following evening Mother told them how to write 1s, and they took their pennies, and found out all the ways in which they could add them up:

$$\left.\begin{array}{l} 6d + 6d \\ 9d + 3d \\ 7d + 5d \\ 8d + 4d \\ 10d + 2d \\ 11d + 1d \\ 12d + 0d \end{array}\right\} \text{ each equals 1s}$$

Then they put their pennies into three piles, and found that:

$$4d + 4d + 4d = 1s$$
$$3d + 3d + 6d = 1s$$
$$6d + 4d + 2d = 1s$$

Next Mother showed them how to write out bills, like this:

2 glasses of orangeade	4d
2 cakes	4d
	8d

1 glass of milk at 3d	=3d
6 biscuits at 1d each	=6d
1 ice cream cornet at 3d	=3d
	1s

Then John and Jennifer learned how to give change. They had their 12 pennies, and when the bill came to 8d they counted out the 8 pennies, and found they had 4 pennies left, so they learned that they had to give 4d change.

Soon after this the twins became so interested in money that they decided to have a bank. They told Daddy about it and he promised to buy them some cardboard money, so that they could have plenty. He also showed them how to make some " pretend " notes.

They made some £1 notes by cutting oblong pieces of light green paper, and some 10s notes by cutting oblong pieces of light brown paper, and writing on them like this:

£1 One pound

10s Ten shillings

READING · WRITING · ARITHMETIC · MUSIC · DRAWING · FRENCH

When Daddy bought the cardboard coins he bought a lovely big wooden box with divisions in it, which was just right to keep separate all the different kinds of coins.

John and Jennifer knew their Mother and Daddy had cheque books, so they asked Mother to sew together some pieces of white paper in the shape of cheque books, and they each had one.

They called their bank The Bank of London, and took it in turns to be Bank Manager and customer. In the first bank they had:

One	£1 note
Two	10s notes
Twenty	shillings
Ten	sixpences
Sixty	pennies

Here is a page from their cheque books:

THE BANK OF LONDON

Date............

Please Pay ....

The Sum of ....

£ _____ s. _____ d. _____ Signed............

Each day they counted up their money to see what they had drawn out and what they had left in the bank. They spent some of the money playing in their café, and often found they had some left, if they had drawn out too much. This they paid back into the bank, adding it to what was already there.

READING—MORE ABOUT WORD FAMILIES

MOTHER said it would help John and Jennifer with their spelling if they made up some little rhymes and stories, using the words in their " families."

Mother wrote the rhymes on cards, and the twins read with her. First there was the little e family:

John is   he
Jennifer is   she
Together they are we
And mother is   me

Then we come to the letters we call the Laughing Twins, ee:

In our garden we have a
     see - saw,
And a fat white donkey who says
     hee - haw.

Jennifer, John, and Daddy
All sat under a   tree,
Mother came and counted them,
One, two,   three.

John and Jennifer had four feet,
They ran together down the street,
Mother and Daddy they did meet,
Daddy gave them both a sweet.

" We must not forget the Crying Twins oo," said John, and Jennifer said, " I've made up a rhyme about them! "

I like to go to the kitchen and   cook,
I have a little cookery   book,
It hangs on the wall on its own little hook.

John liked Jennifer's rhyme so much that he also made up one:

I love the stars, I love the moon,
I love to sit in the sun at noon,
And eat an ice with a silver spoon.

Here we have some of the ea family:

Down by the   sea,
I took my   tea;
With a shell to my ear,
The sea I could hear.

Jack Sprat could eat no fat,
His wife could eat no   lean,
And so between them both,
They kept the platter   clean.

" There is oa as well," said Mother:

It is cold in the   boat,
So I took my winter coat.

Sitting by a puddle in the road,
After the rain, I saw a tiny toad.

We also have the ai family with their different sounds:

I love to feel the wind in my hair
When I stand up on the garden chair.

A little speckled garden snail
Went round and round a wooden pail
In a paper boat with a leaf for a sail.

Next comes ay:

I feel so gay
On a sunny day
And in the hay
I like to play.

" We must make some rhymes for the family of er," said Mother:

I like snow in winter,
I like sun in summer,
I like sausages for dinner,
And bread and milk for supper.

A little brown bird,
Sat on a fir,
Singing, " I like you, Sir."

I had sixpence in my purse,
I bought a baby doll to nurse.

Now for some lazy e words:

I dropped my cake,
In the lake.

Jennifer ran a mile,
John climbed a stile,
Daddy came along and said,
" Smile, smile, smile."

Three little mice
Ate an ice
And a bag of rice
They found it nice.

What a joke—
A pig in a poke !

WRITING—BIG AND SMALL LETTERS

JOHN and Jennifer found the small letters much easier to write neatly than the big letters, particularly when they wanted to write something very big, such as a new poster or a price list for their cinema show. So Mother bought a box of big wooden letters and showed the twins how to use them.

One way was to draw a line with a ruler across the paper, place the letters on the line, draw round them while holding them very still, and then fill in with either paint or crayon. Here is a notice they did:

THIS SHOP CLOSES
AT 6 P.M.

Another way was to draw round the letters on some coloured papers from the packet Daddy had bought, then cut the letters out very carefully, and stick them on the poster, like this:

WE SELL ICES

The little odd bits of coloured paper they cut up into shapes, and made a pattern round the edge to make the poster gay.

While they had been staying at Granny's she had been very interested in their reading and writing, and she promised that when she came to stay for a week-end she would bring a surprise with her, something that she thought would help them. John and Jennifer did wish that week-end would hurry up!

At last it came, and when they met Granny at the station she was carrying a big, flat parcel. When they got home and opened it, they found that Granny had drawn them a lovely picture of big and small letters. It was framed so that it could hang up in their bedroom, where they could always see how to make beautiful letters.

Aa Bb Cc Dd Ee
Ff Gg Hh Ii Jj Kk
Ll Mm Nn Oo Pp
Qq Rr Ss Tt Uu
Vv Ww Xx Yy Zz

MUSIC—TONES AND SEMI-TONES

You need a cricket pitch, so you go into the field, measure out 22 yards, make holes for the wickets, and mark lines where the batsmen are to stand.

Then you discover a hole (which you should have noticed, but somehow missed!) in the middle of the pitch. That will not do at all. You have to try another part of the field and mark out a new pitch.

Here is the beginning of a melody, an old nursery tune, My Three Hens:

This is a melody which can be played on the white notes of the piano, and because the chief note is C we say that it is in the key of C (major). Look at that part of the keyboard on which we might play this melody:

If you have a piano, play the notes. Now sing them, taking care to give each note its proper value. The tune placed on those notes is rather low. If you have a high voice you will find yourself growling. We have—as in the cricket field—put the pitch in the wrong place.

We can, again like the cricket pitch, find a new place which is more convenient. We can, for instance, choose the note G, call that *doh* and put the whole melody into a brighter register. If we write out the melody, with G as the starting note, we find:

Thus a melody can be moved about without losing its shape or its character.

Here is the rest of My Three Hens in the first key of C:

Draw five lines, put on them a G clef, and put that part of the melody into the key of G.

My Three Hens is a very economical tune. It uses only five notes—**drmfs**. We had better look at the remaining notes of the scale to see how they fit into G major:

That phrase shows us all the notes of the scale. Now let us suppose we want it to start on G. We write it out, as before, five notes higher:

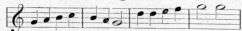

If we play those notes exactly as they are written the melody will sound incorrect. We must look a little closer. From (t-d¹) is a *semitone*. (If we look at the keyboard we will see that there is no note, not even a black one, between B and C.)

But from is a *tone*.

This is serious, for unless we can reduce this to a semitone we cannot put our melody into the key of G. And this is where the black keys on the piano begin to show their usefulness. Between F and G is a black key; its name is F♯ (*sharp*). From F♯ to G is a *semitone*, and by bringing it into the scale which begins on G we can have all the tones and semitones arranged in the correct order, as shown here:

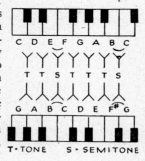

This picture puts opposite to each other those parts of the keyboard which produce the scales of C major and G major, and we can see in each case exactly which notes we should play. We also see that whenever we are dealing with the key of G we are going to meet one note which *does not belong to the key of C.* The note is F♯. Therefore a piece of music in the key of G major is shown: which we play throughout any piece which has this in the key signature.

Now we can go back to the opening of Unto Us a Boy is Born and write it correctly in the key of G. On the treble stave it will appear:

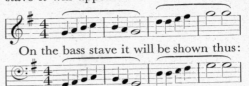

On the bass stave it will be shown thus:

There is one other point which we might learn here. Sometimes a composer feels (if he is in the key of G) that he would like to vary his melody by including a white key F. If he does he puts this sign in the music: ♮. This sign is called a *natural.*

ART—MAKING A PICTURE BOOK

W E all like to look at books with pictures on their pages. Even in the days before printing was discovered the people who wrote books used to make pictures on many of the pages of writing—illustrations, as they are often called.

In those days the people who wrote books and painted pictures in them often painted on the walls too. In the British Museum are some fine early books, and fragments of the walls of the old Palace of Westminster, with early wall paintings still showing on their surfaces. These wall pictures are about the trials of Job, and each one has some beautifully written wording underneath it.

In cases close to these fragments you can see many books which were written and painted about the same time as the wall paintings. They are shown with the pages open, and you can see how well the pictures and writing go together.

Have you ever thought what splendid books you could make if you used your handwriting and your small pictures in this way? If you have not, it is well worth trying. Your books will differ from those in the Museum because those were all made by grown-ups who spent many years of their lives making them.

Your books will be much simpler, but they can be very lovely and about so many things. For instance, you could make drawings of your pet animals on one page (or part of a page) and write about them and their interesting ways on the rest of the open page. Look at the illustration of a black cat, Jetty, drawn by a girl of six with a B (soft) pencil.

THIS IS JETTY

You can make pictures of places or things you saw on a holiday and write about them; or your pictures could be of subjects you have been doing at school. These would include scenes from history, discoveries in science and biology, or settings for plays. Whatever your subject, the important thing will be the way in which you plan your page. You will need to make the whole of the open page look lovely, and to do this you will have to make the pictures and the handwriting look as though they belonged to each other. In a way it is like making a good pattern of your picture and your writing on the open page of your book. You will need to leave a little space, or margin, round both pictures and writing; and, of course, keep your work quite clean.

Choose a book with plain paper (unruled) for this purpose, and the cover can be printed with patterns made from potato-cuts, or painted with writing patterns.

The pictures for your books can be made in quite a number of materials, including pencil, crayon, pen and ink, as in the illustration The Cliff; water colour or powder colour; or they can be printed from potato or lino-cut blocks on which you have cut your picture.

For subjects such as the barks of trees you would need to make rubbings on thin paper with cobbler's heelball or soft crayon, and mount these on the pages of your book, leaving margins all round. It is a good idea to draw a frame of lines on your paper first and mount your rubbings inside the frame. Artists who work in water colours often mount their pictures in this way, and fill in between the lines with a grey or light colour which goes well with the pictures.

Your rubbings, potato- and lino-cuts, or similar illustrations for your books, should be placed face downwards on some old newspaper and the backs evenly covered with paste. This can be spread with a brush and worked from the middle of the paper outwards until it is covered evenly. Then lift up your rubbing and fit it into its line frame in your book, cover it with a piece of scrap paper, and, again working from the middle, press outward with your hands.

For making your picture with a pencil use a soft (B) grade with a thick wood handle. You can also do your writing in pencil, and so make the two halves of the open page look well together. Pencil is apt to rub easily, and the way to prevent this happening is to spray your page with a sprayer and fixatif, which you can buy from an artists' materials shop.

Colour, too, can be used with pencil if you wish. If you do use pencil, start off with a clear idea of where your drawing will be and what it will be like on the paper. Thus you will avoid alterations. It is better to put in a correct line by the side of a less correct one rather than rub out and make a messy pencil drawing.

Crayons can be obtained in many colours, and may be used to make thin or thick lines or to fill in shapes with solid colour. Used lightly in places, they give the effect of paler colours. Other colours can be made by going over one colour with another.

You have already done some drawing with pen and ink and know something about its lovely qualities. It is the method which the early book writers used, and if you make your picture and your writing with pen and ink you are likely to make a good pattern of your page. Ordinary writing ink, indian ink, or sepia ink are all good to use; and you can also get white

The Cliff

Cliff set in a silver blue sea,
Shining with summer sun
At thy feet the wavelets play
And roll and frisk and run

Cliff hidden in swaying mist
Wet with the grey green tide
Washed with the mud of the ocean swell
While ships sail by your side

Cliff hiding in stormy dark
The furious waters beneath
Splashing your hard white face of chalk
With the help of the wind from the deep

Cliff in a clear Spring morning,
With a larks song overhead
And the sea below now blue and clear
Causing no one dread

THE CLIFF

PAINTING IS SUCH FUN!

ink which can be used on grey or coloured papers. Whichever ink you use you must know what you are going to draw or write before you start, for a good pen drawing should look as though it had been made in that way without alterations or scratchings out. Your pictures could have little pen-drawn borders or frames round them which may ·be made of simple zig-zag, straight, or wavy lines, or small flower or leaf shapes. The kind of frame or border needed will depend on the picture inside it, and you must try to feel just what is right for each picture and page. A Christmas subject picture could have a frame made of tiny sprigs of fir tree, or stars, or frost patterns drawn quite simply with the pen. A very famous old book, called the Book of Kells, has all kinds of tiny animals and birds drawn in between the rows of writing; they are coloured and look very fine on the open page with the coloured pictures opposite.

Water colours or powder colours would

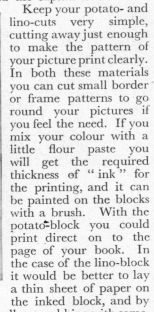

ILLUMINATED LETTERING IN THE BOOK OF KELLS

be best for some kinds of subjects, as, for instance, a gaily decorated street, flowers, or butterflies. You can use some colours in the writing, too, especially for ornamentation round the capital letters.

Keep your potato- and lino-cuts very simple, cutting away just enough to make the pattern of your picture print clearly. In both these materials you can cut small border or frame patterns to go round your pictures if you feel the need. If you mix your colour with a little flour paste you will get the required thickness of " ink " for the printing, and it can be painted on the blocks with a brush. With the potato-block you could print direct on to the page of your book. In the case of the lino-block it would be better to lay a thin sheet of paper on the inked block, and by pressure with a roller or rubbing with something like an old toothbrush handle take a print and afterwards stick it in the book.

A simple way to use picture and writing is to write and illustrate a letter.

FRENCH—AT THE HOTEL

HERE we learn how our travelling party spent their first evening at the hotel in Paris. The first line under each picture is the French ; the second line gives the English word for the French word above it ; the third line shows how we make up the words in our own language.

Nous sommes à l'hôtel.
We are at the hotel.
We get to the hotel.

Le gérant nous salue.
The manager us salutes.
The manager greets us.

La bonne nous montre nos chambres.
The maid us shows our rooms.
The maid shows us our rooms.

Nous lui demandons son nom.
We of her demand her name.
We ask her her name.

Elle répond : " Annette."
She replies : " Annette."
She answers : " Annette."

Bébé a bien sommeil.
Baby has much sleep.
Baby is very sleepy.

Maman dit : " Embrassez-moi, bébé."
Mamma says : " Embrace me, baby."
Mamma says : " Kiss me, baby."

Bientôt nous entendons un petit cri.
Soon we hear a little cry.
Soon we hear a little cry.

Jeannette court à la porte.
Jenny runs to the door.
Jenny runs to the door.

Une petite fille est là.
A little girl is there.
A little girl is standing there.

Jeannette la conduit à maman.
Jenny her conducts to Mamma.
Jenny leads her to Mamma.

Elle pleure.
She is crying.
She is crying.

Maman la console.
Mamma her comforts.
Mamma comforts her.

Elle a perdu sa bonne.
She has lost her nurse.
She has lost her nurse.

Nous lui montrons de drôles d'images.
We to her show some droll of pictures.
We show her some funny pictures.

Quelqu'un frappe à la porte.
Someone knocks at the door.
Someone knocks at the door.

Maman crie : " Entrez ! "
Mamma cries : " Enter ! "
Mamma calls out : " Come in! "

La porte s'ouvre.
The door itself opens.
The door opens.

Une jeune femme entre.
A young woman enters.
A young woman comes in.

C'est la bonne de la petite fille.
It is the nurse of the little girl.
It is the little girl's nurse.

La bonne tend les bras.
The nurse tenders the arms.
The nurse holds out her arms.

La petite fille court à elle.
The little girl runs to her.
The little girl runs to her.

Nous crions tous : " Bonsoir ! "
We cry all : " Good-evening ! "
We all call out : " Good-night ! "

A fish of the Devonian Age

THE WORLD IN THE DEVONIAN AGE

WE now come to that long period of the Earth's history when fishes were the highest and dominant form of life.

This geological period is known as the Devonian, because it was in Devonshire that its chief rock, the Old Red Sandstone was found in exceptional abundance and was first seen to represent a great era in the development of life. It is, however, found in many other parts of Britain, as our accompanying map shows, and it spreads also over vast tracts of North America, Africa, Northern Europe, and elsewhere.

We saw in looking at the Silurian Age how the descendants of the trilobites, in order to save themselves from the increasing numbers and size of their enemies, had by constant effort and exercise acquired rapidity and flexibility of movement, and so transformed their bodies as to become fishes. Small and strange-looking little creatures they were in Silurian times, but a great change took place during the millions of years when the Silurian Age was gradually changing into the Devonian.

Vast numbers of lobster-like creatures, called eurypterids, of which the pterygotus was one of the most formidable, had developed enormously and infested the seas and great lakes. But by their activity the little fishes ultimately outstripped and

escaped these enemies, and the fact that their bodies were not encased in a restricting shell, but grew round a central backbone, enabled them to develop into giant creatures over thirty feet long.

Their bodies—more particularly their heads and more vital parts—were protected by bony plates, some small and some large, like coats of mail, which grew with the fish and conformed to each type's mode of life. Some lived their lives one way, and some another, but their instincts ever impelled them to adapt themselves more and more to their surroundings, and so they ever improved and became more wonderful. For the Great Giver of this abundant life gave, too, the wonderful power of adaptation and development.

In the course of this long Devonian Age, which lasted many millions of years, the fishes multiplied enormously, and by their efforts to adapt themselves they acquired new characters, such as fins, better suited to their movements than the paddles of the pterichthys. They developed, also, powerful teeth which were far more efficacious for all purposes than the great claws of the pterygotus or the tentacles of the octopus, and which, later on, set in powerful jaws, were to become the most powerful weapons in the animal kingdom.

ASTRONOMY · GEOLOGY · GEOGRAPHY · CHEMISTRY · PHYSICS · LIFE

THE BUILDING OF BRITAIN—DEVONIAN AGE

THE DARK GREY AREAS ON THE MAP REPRESENT THE DISTRICTS WHERE THE DEVONIAN OR OLD
RED SANDSTONE ROCKS COME TO THE SURFACE

LIFE AND REMAINS OF THE DEVONIAN AGE

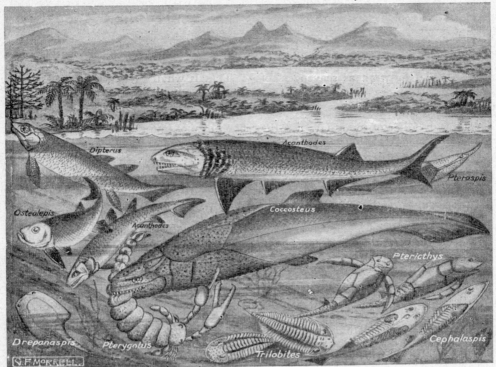

Here we see the surface of the Earth as it probably appeared in the Devonian Age when fishes were the highest form of life. In the water are some of the fishes and crustaceans which then abounded.

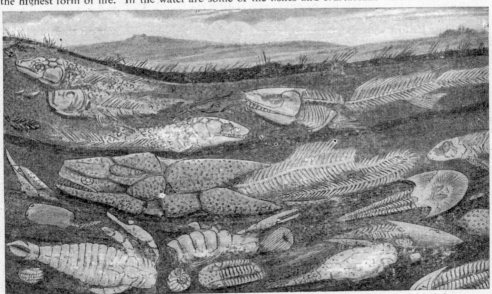

This picture shows a section through the sandstone rock of the Devonian Age, containing an accumulation of fossil remains of the life of that time. The fossils are chiefly fishes, mingled with Trilobites and other crustaceans. The big fish in the centre is a Coccosteus, and above is a Dipterus.

THE LAND AND THE RIVERS OF BRITAIN IN THE AGE OF THE OLD RED SANDSTONE

Great sharks with frilled gills and rows of terrible teeth also developed, feeding on the dead and surplus creatures of those densely populated waters. These acanthodians, as they are called, some of them quite small, have descendants to this day carrying on their work as scavengers of the open sea.

THE QUEER AND TERRIBLE REPTILES ON THE EARTH IN THOSE DAYS

Another monster of those days was the berry-boned fish, or coccosteus, varying in size from one to 25 feet long. Others, known as the terrible fish and the titan fish, developed into a much higher type than the sharks, and acquired lungs, so that they could breathe air and leave the water or live in the sand when stranded by the tides. It is probably through these terrible creatures, with their rough, bony armour and reptilian-looking head, eyes, and teeth, that man has ascended from the first life forms. The coccosteus has gone, and only its form remains in these Old Red Sandstone rocks; but its direct descendants are the amphibians and reptiles, creatures resembling newts and crocodiles. Already, in Devonian times, the dipterus—shown in our picture with its head out of the water making for dry land—had advanced a few steps farther in the ascent of life toward the amphibian type. This fish not only had lungs as well as gills, but its fins were beginning to take the form of limbs, which to its descendants in the next great geological Age (the Carboniferous) became tiny arms and legs—four limbs in all. These, after many millions of years, developed into the limbs of the higher animals.

THE GIANT TREES THAT GREW IN THE LONG AGO

There are lung fishes now existing in Australia, South America, and Africa which are the direct descendants of the dipterus, and have changed but little from their far-distant ancestors.

The vegetation chiefly consisted of mosses, almost the first of land plants, but in Devonian times they became great trees somewhat like the monkey-puzzle in appearance. These great moss trees are called Lepidodendrons. Ferns also flourished, growing tall like palms, and forming forests, and the sort of reed called calamite grew in profusion. These forms of vegetation are shown in the upper picture on page 1135.

There have been found traces of pine trees, but, so far as is known, there were no flowers. The kind of plant life that existed then indicates a very moist atmosphere, much cloud, heavy torrential rain, and very little direct sunshine.

That is what we should expect in this early age of our Earth, and other facts point the same way. The lower picture on page 1135 gives us some idea of how the creatures of those far-off days are now found fossilised, although they are shown unduly crowded in our small space and, of course, on a much enlarged scale in proportion to the thickness of the rock strata. This strata reaches enormous thickness, from 4000 feet in Scotland to 10,000 in South Wales.

The accompanying map shows where this Old Red Sandstone or Devonian Rock is at or near the surface; but this rock is not always red—only when impregnated very much with iron. Sometimes it is yellowish or grey; sometimes large quantities of lime are present, derived from the limy skeletons of little coral creatures, and the rock then becomes limestone. But it is generally red sandstone, and it extends under the whole of Southern England from Devonshire to Essex.

THE GREAT LAKE THAT REACHED FROM SCOTLAND TO NORWAY

If any of our homes is within one of the dark shaded areas shown on the map, the Devonian rocks, in which are found the fossil remains of these creatures of possibly fifty to a hundred million years ago, may be found at or close to the surface, often beneath the garden mould, or under the sand and mud when near a river.

If our homes are in the Devon or Cornwall area we know that in those far-off times the land about us was formed at the bottom of the sea, out of the sand formed from the worn-down rocks of the preceding Silurian and Cambrian and still earlier times. This great Devonian sea covered the whole of Europe south of Belgium, while most of Northern Europe was land. But this land contained some great freshwater lakes, probably three, comparable with the great Canadian lakes. It is believed that one of them extended from the North of Scotland to Norway across what is now the North Sea, that another extended across Central Scotland and Northern Ireland, while the third covered the South Wales area and Herefordshire

The Story of Immortal Folk Whose Work Will Never Die

William Carey

Henry Martin

Bishop Selwyn

Bishop Hannington

Robert Morrison

Hans Egede

Bishop Patteson

John Williams

Robert Moffat

James Chalmers

FAMOUS MISSIONARIES

THERE are many battles where no gun is fired, and many heroes who do not wear khaki, for Peace, as Milton once said, has victories no less renowned than War. Among the world's great heroes stand out the names of many brave men and women who have gone out to teach the Bible to peoples of distant lands, and to carry the blessings of Christianity into uncivilised countries. Let us look at some of these brave missionaries.

One of the most famous of them was Hans Egede, a young Norwegian pastor of the Moravian Brothers, who sailed from Bergen, in Norway, in 1721, to live among the Eskimos in the frozen North. He landed on the inhospitable shores of Greenland, and soon found how difficult it was to teach people so gloomy and superstitious. For many years he had to endure great hardships with little encouragement. But he held on, and at one time, when the Eskimos were plague-smitten, he made his house their hospital, and tenderly nursed them, an act of mercy which won their gratitude.

Egede was a man of simple faith, and with great humility did his work at a time when there were few missionaries anywhere, and none at all in the Arctic regions. As quite an aged man he returned home to Copenhagen, bringing his wife's remains for burial among her own people.

Another early missionary was David Brainerd, a Yale student, who preached to the North American Indians in the colonies of New England. Brainerd was born so long ago as 1718, and, his parents dying while he was yet a boy, he began life an orphan and with delicate health. As he grew up he took to farming, but in the end he resolved to take the Gospel to the Red Indians, who were then much more numerous than now.

The hardship of travel, the sleeping in the open air, and the scanty food, soon began to tell on his weak constitution. The language, too, was difficult, and he had to work very patiently at it, riding twenty miles through the dark forests to his instructor.

The story of his work among the Indians is one of truest heroism, for he had to work for many years without a glimpse of success. At last the revival came, thousands of the men of the forests came flocking to Brainerd, so that the heart of this humble servant of God was filled with gratitude. He was an old-fashioned saint, and his journals are a treasure of sweet musings.

But it is to William Carey, the learned cobbler, who translated the Scriptures into

EXPLORERS · INVENTORS · WRITERS · ARTISTS · SCIENTISTS

Bengali, that we owe the organisation of missionary work throughout the world and enterprise in the churches of our English-speaking lands.

Carey was a country boy, born in the village of Paulerspury, near Northampton, and his father, who was parish clerk and schoolmaster, taught his son thoroughly and well. William liked books, and was also fond of gardening. Picking up a little Greek and Latin while working as a shoemaker, he became a Baptist minister on £16 a year, and to add to his income still made and mended shoes, and also did a little teaching.

CAREY THE COBBLER, WHO BECAME THE FATHER OF MODERN MISSIONS

One of the outstanding events in all missionary history is a famous sermon preached by Carey at a meeting of ministers at Nottingham, in June, 1792; it led to the formation of the Baptist Missionary Society, the first organisation of its kind.

Then came his call to India as a missionary for Bengal. He had difficulty in getting there because of the opposition of officials, but at last he arrived at Calcutta, and found himself and his family homeless, friendless, and with scarcely any money. He tried to earn something by planting indigo, and at once gave himself up to the translation of the New Testament into Bengali, becoming so proficient in that language that he was appointed one of the tutors in Fort William College. Largely through his efforts the government passed a law forbidding the burning of widows, and during his forty years of splendid Christian labour, he earned the position of distinction which he holds in the history of missionary enterprise. A domed tomb of solid stone in the cemetery at Calcutta marks his resting-place.

ONE OF THE NOBLE SAINTS OF THE MISSIONARY CALENDAR

Another noted missionary to the people of India was Henry Martyn, the Cambridge student, who travelled also in Persia. He was a Cornish boy of Truro, but was so weak in body that it seemed impossible that he would make any mark in the world, or live to find himself famous. But at St. John's College, Cambridge, he showed great aptitude for study, and it was during a vacation spent in Wales that his heart responded to the call to enter the mission field. While at the university he became fast friends with another deeply religious student, Henry Kirke White, the Nottingham poet. After his father's death, Martyn had to make some provision for his sisters, so he went out to India as a chaplain under the Board of the East India Company. On the voyage out he preached to the crew, and spent much time in learning Hindustani. After a short stay at the Cape he reached Madras on April 22, 1806.

In his Indian work he met with great opposition, not so much from the natives as from the English officials, but he persistently laboured on, translating the Bible with his faithful teacher. He also turned his eyes towards Persia, translated the New Testament into Persian, travelling in that country that he might get to know and understand the people.

When, in a time of plague and fever, he passed away at Tokat, in 1812, Lord Macaulay wrote his epitaph; and he is counted as one of the saints of the missionary calendar.

THE MISSIONARY WHO LIVED LIKE A CHINAMAN AND WORE A PIGTAIL

Robert Morrison, like Carey, was a shoemaker, and it was he who translated the Bible into Chinese. As a youth he learned his father's trade at Morpeth, but before going abroad he became a medical student at St. Bartholomew's Hospital, and found a young Chinaman who taught him his language, and also showed him the sort of people to whom he was going to preach.

Arriving in China, he let his hair grow, wore a pigtail, and tried to live like a Chinaman, until his health failed. His great work was the translation of the Bible; but he also gave the English Prayer-book to these people in their own tongue. He was of great service to the British Government in difficulties which arose with the Chinese. Before he died in 1834, Morrison had finished his great dictionary of the Chinese language in six quarto volumes, and today all Christian workers in China use the Bible he left behind.

John Williams, known everywhere as the Martyr of Erromanga, was a young blacksmith. It was in City Road, London, that he swung the hammer at the forge. One Sunday in 1814 a good woman took him to Moorfields Tabernacle, and this led to his becoming a missionary.

He had little education, but was quick-witted, and impressed people with his honesty; he had also the knack of sticking to a thing, otherwise he would never have mastered the language of Tahiti, in the Society Islands, where he first went to preach. He taught the natives handicraft, and they watched him build his house and his mission ship with scarcely any tools. Perhaps his most difficult task was to make a pair of smith's bellows of goat skins, and when he had done, the rats ate his work before morning!

In his boat, with mat sails, he made dangerous voyages from time to time, thousands of natives bidding him farewell with songs of sorrow. Six times Williams was nearly drowned, the sea waves dashing his vessel on the rocks. He was spared, however, to evangelise these South Sea Islands, and translated the New Testament into Raratongan. He came home, after many years, to plead the cause of the natives in England, and, returning in 1839, he landed with three companions on the shore at Erromanga. But the natives there were hostile. A big savage struck Williams on the head, killing him, and a shower of arrows followed. In a few moments "the rippling water was red with the blood of the noblest man that has ever gone to those far-off isles of the South Sea, laden with blessing for the ignorant and the outcast."

Captain Allen Gardiner, who took Christianity to the wild Patagonians, had his first taste of the sea in war-time. Later he bought a Bible at a second-hand shop, and the reading of it changed his whole life. He went out to Africa after many dangerous adventures, preaching to Din-

WILLIAM CAREY, WHOSE ZEAL FOR FOREIGN MISSIONS GREW AS HE MENDED SHOES IN HIS LITTLE SHOP

gan, the Zulu chief, over whom he exerted a good influence. After a time he sailed for Brazil and worked among the Indians of Chile. Several times he nearly lost his life, but, nothing daunted, he resolved to visit Tierra del Fuego, and landed among the Patagonians with a few brave companions. He found these people very degraded, as Darwin had described them, but with infinite patience and faith he tried to bring light to their dark hearts.

The closing days of this brave life make a pathetic story. With food supplies from England long overdue, Gardiner and his little band found themselves at the point of starvation. In vain they searched for food in this desolate, barren country, and one by one they lay down to die on the beach, looking hopefully out to sea for the help that, alas, arrived too late.

It was a month later when the supply ship anchored by the silent shores of Tierra del Fuego. All was still in that dreary region as the ship's boat pushed its way to the beach. There lay the faithful martyrs, and the captain cried like a child at the sight.

Allen Gardiner, the last to perish, had fallen by the launch that had once contained their provisions, too weak to climb back again. Scattered on the beach were the papers on which he had scribbled in pencil the story of their sufferings. Written on the rocks were the words: "My soul, wait thou only upon God, for my expectation is from Him," painted there by him as he lay, racked with pain, waiting for death.

Robert Moffat was a young gardener, who became the pioneer missionary of South Africa. He was born at Ormiston, in East Lothian, on the shortest day of 1795, and his early days were divided between his Latin grammar, the blacksmith's hammer, and his fiddle. Afterward he became an under-gardener in Cheshire. Seeing a placard of a missionary meeting, he attended, and this so influenced him that he offered himself as a missionary.

He sailed for the Cape in 1816, and his first work was with the farmers and the poor Hottentots, who were little better than their slaves. He then founded mission stations in Namaqualand, and worked among the Bechuanas at Lattakoo. In 1873, as a tall, white-bearded old man, he was invited by Dean Stanley to speak in Westminster Abbey, and a great crowd listened with reverence to his thrilling story of work in South Africa.

His later work was at Kuruman, where his daughter married Livingstone, and at last, with his faithful wife, he returned home, and died full of years and public honours in August, 1883, the veteran apostle of the mission field.

THE BISHOP WHO LEAPT OVER A BUSH AND SOMERSAULTED INTO A RIVER

We read elsewhere of David Livingstone, the Scottish weaver boy whose heart was buried in Africa. We are not likely to forget his honoured name, and on the floor of Westminster Abbey, where the sunshine falls through the stained windows, we find his grave—though his heart is buried in the land he loved so well.

We read elsewhere of Bishop Crowther, the black slave boy who became a bishop. There have been few histories of the mission field equal in interest to the life of this black bishop. He was a marvellous example of what a Negro may be and do in the service of God and man.

Bishop Selwyn, the athletic student who worked so successfully in New Zealand, was born in Church Row, Hampstead, in 1809. After some preparatory schooling at Ealing, the boy was sent to Eton, where he made friends with many who in later years became great men. His school friend was Mr. Gladstone. Selwyn was first in all the sports. It was said of his good nature that "he always took the labouring oar in everything." He could dive like none other, and in the grounds was "Selwyn's bush" over which he leapt and turned a somersault into the river on the other side. In due time he became a curate at Windsor, and then Bishop of New Zealand.

BISHOP SELWYN'S DEATH, AND HIS INFLUENCE OVER AN ETON BOY

The Maoris were not yet settled to English rule, and in the conflicts that often occurred, the personal influence of Bishop Selwyn counted for much. The Maoris trusted him, and he was peacemaker often at great risk to himself. "I am your mediator," he used to say to them. "I have eaten your food, slept in your houses, talked with you, prayed with you; let us dwell together with one faith, one love, and one Lord." He travelled through the country, and once, after visiting an island, he brought two little girls back with him, arrayed in garments made by himself out of an old quilt.

Afterwards he came home and became Bishop of Lichfield, where he worked hard, and at last he lay a-dying. Calling some children to his bedside, he said softly : "I wish you were little robins so that you might sit on my finger." A little later he whispered in the Maori language: "It is light," and, smiling, passed to the land of everlasting day.

Bishop Patteson, an Eton boy who was martyred in Melanesia, was a Devonshire lad, fond of books and of a game of cricket. A sermon by Bishop Selwyn inspired him to work among the islands of Melanesia. Here for years he laboured, specially caring for the native lads, whom he loved and trained as teachers, on Norfolk Island.

THE BRAVE BISHOP PATTESON WHO DIED A MARTYR IN MELANESIA

A man of great courage, Patteson used to swim through the surf at great personal risk. He tried to protect the natives from being kidnapped by white men, but one day, when he had landed alone among a crowd of infuriated cannibals, he was killed, and his body, with five wounds and five sprays of palms on his breast, was floated out to the ship. A beautifully carved pulpit to his memory stands in Exeter Cathedral.

Bishop Hannington, the merry schoolboy who died for the faith in Africa, was such a cheerful youth that at school they called him "Mad Jim," and all through

JOHN G. PATON AMONG THE SAVAGES
OF THE PACIFIC ISLANDS

HANS EGEDE, UNABLE TO OBTAIN A PASSAGE,
WATCHES A SHIP DEPARTING FOR THE NORTH

ALLEN GARDINER, WHO TOOK A PARTY OF MISSIONARIES TO TIERRA DEL FUEGO, LIES DOWN TO DIE
BY HIS BOAT AFTER ALL HIS COMRADES HAVE PERISHED FROM HUNGER

his life this happy-heartedness never left him. He landed at Zanzibar in 1882, and travelled up the country, through dense forests, through perils from robbers and wild animals, and eventually reached Ujiji, near the spot where Stanley had said good-bye to Livingstone some years before. Wherever he met the chiefs he preached to them, and after reaching the Victoria Nyanza he turned homewards, and was back in England after a year's absence. But he soon went out again to Uganda, and in 1885 was captured by a treacherous chief and shot with his own gun.

James Chalmers is often spoken of as Tamate, the name by which he was known in New Guinea. When he first landed a native called out : " What fellow name belong you ? " " Chalmers," was the answer. " Tamate, Tamate," the native shouted as he ran back to his companions.

HOW JAMES CHALMERS MET HIS FATE AMONG THE CANNIBALS

This is how he came to go to New Guinea. His father, who gave him sixpence for learning the 23rd Psalm, was a stonemason in Argyllshire, and sent the boy to Sunday-school, where he heard from his teachers of the need of help in Fiji.

He determined to answer the appeal, and in due time started for Samoa and Raratonga with a brave wife who shared his trials. His work among the cannibals was rendered more difficult by the alcohol which Europeans took to them. But he loved the savages, though he often stood in great peril when dealing with strange chiefs, who tried to rob him and threatened his life with their clubs and spears.

Tamate, however, unarmed, lived to be an old man. Then one day, hearing of trouble among the natives on Goaribari Island, he went up the Fly River and in his fearless way walked among them, seeking to make them quiet and peaceful; but they knocked him down and killed him, and afterward feasted upon his body.

John G. Paton, a Dumfries laddie, became the Apostle of the New Hebrides. He won his title of honour by living among the natives of these islands until his hair was white, gaining their friendship by his patience and helpfulness, and teaching them how the love of God could make the very worst of men good.

He left Glasgow as a young man, and the chief of the Island of Tanna told him the fever would soon kill him; but his life was mercifully spared, not only from disease, but from the clubs of these cannibals; for he was not afraid to stand between quarrelling tribes; and on one occasion his house, with all his books and medicines, was burned to the ground.

THE NOBLE SACRIFICE OF FATHER DAMIEN IN THE SOUTH SEAS

One of the noblest of all chapters in the annals of foreign missions is the story of Father Damien. Two brothers in Belgium were in the same college. The elder brother was soon to become a missionary to the South Sea Islands. His eyes used to sparkle whenever he spoke of the work that waited for him across the sea.

One day, however, he was taken seriously ill, and was carried to his bed. Fever wasted him. He fretted and grew pale and melancholy. His younger brother came to his bedside and said softly, " Would it make you happier if I took your place as a missionary ? " The eyes of the sick man lighted up for a moment, and he pressed his brother's hands, smiling. Then the younger brother wrote to the authorities begging that he might go in place of his sick brother.

So Joseph Damien, bubbling over with the excitement of a boy, started out for the South Sea Islands and became a missionary. He worked nobly and well till he was 33. Then, while he was working among the people, he one day heard the bishop say that he had no one to send to the poor lepers in Molokai, and that these stricken creatures were abandoned to this most dreadful disease.

Joseph Damien begged the bishop to send him out, and his offer was accepted.

THE HEROIC WORK OF THE BELGIAN PRIEST AMONG THE LEPERS

Here was a far greater sacrifice than going from Belgium to the savages. The lepers lived all by themselves separated from healthy people, shunned by all mankind. They were outcasts. The misery of their bodies made them evil in their souls. Their hovels were like pigsties; they lived no better than beasts.

But Father Damien came to these outcasts with the simple message that God loved them; and his cheerful face, his caressing voice, his loving eyes, and his living faith, changed them from beasts to men, and presently from men to children of God.

For sixteen years this devoted man lived among the lepers. He built them a church, he built them better houses, he gave them a proper water supply, he nursed them, he dressed their wounds, he comforted them when dying, and he dug their graves.

And people in the great world outside heard of this lonely priest toiling among the lepers. People wrote to him, sent him cases of comforts for his people, and some went out to see him and help him. It is good to know that England honoured this Belgian priest, and helped him. One day the warning came. He happened to spill some boiling water, which splashed upon his foot. He was surprised to find that it did not hurt him. He went to a doctor. "Have I got leprosy?" he asked. "I hate to tell you," said the doctor; "but, yes, you are a leper." From that moment Father Damien talked not of "my brethren," but of "we lepers."

"SEND ME OUT TO THE LEPERS," SAID FATHER DAMIEN, AS THE BISHOP PLEADED FOR THE OUTCASTS

He was perfectly happy. He said that if he could be cured by forsaking the island he would not desert the lepers. So he worked on as a leper, with death creeping swiftly and fiercely through his body.

When he was carried to his bed he thanked God for all the blessings and comforts he received. Two priests and Sisters of Charity knelt by him.

"When you go to heaven, Father," said one of the priests, "will you, like Elijah, leave me your mantle?"

"Why, what would you do with it?"

asked Father Damien; and then he added slowly: "*It is full of leprosy.*"

Soon afterward, in 1889, the soul of Father Damien was released from pain. His life had been one long golden deed.

In 1859 Mary Slessor, a little girl of eleven, was working at a machine in a Dundee textile factory. In 1915 she died on a hill-top in the remote Calabar country of West Africa. Between those events lay one of the most romantic stories in modern missions.

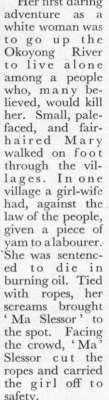

Her first daring adventure as a white woman was to go up the Okoyong River to live alone among a people who, many believed, would kill her. Small, pale-faced, and fair-haired Mary walked on foot through the villages. In one village a girl-wife had, against the law of the people, given a piece of yam to a labourer. She was sentenced to die in burning oil. Tied with ropes, her screams brought 'Ma Slessor' to the spot. Facing the crowd, 'Ma' Slessor cut the ropes and carried the girl off to safety.

All through the Calabar country Mary Slessor's fearlessness was known. Seeing a living fowl speared through on a stick, she knew the witch doctor was at work on a sick man. Standing by his side, she laughed at the powder, bones, seeds, and egg-shells which he said the doctor had taken from his back. That night two women were killed to appease the evil spirit. But Mary patiently cleaned the sore and bandaged it daily until it was healed, to the astonishment of the village. Her big fights against the drink trade, against carrying arms, and her insistence that quarrels be settled by discussion made this little woman who walked bare-footed through the African jungles a real peace-maker in Africa.

Four tired Chinese Miao tribesmen walked into the mission at Jowtong in Central China in July, 1904. They were greeted by Sam Pollard, a young Cornish-man. " Can we see Jesus? " asked their leader. To answer them Sam Pollard set off on foot into the Miao country, risking his life, for foreigners were hated in those days in China.

One night in the Miao country Pollard was awakened by the barking of dogs. Flashes of light shot past the windows, and into his bedroom rushed a crowd of men carrying swords, spears, and torches.

" What do you want? " cried Pollard.

" We want you! " replied the leader. Knowing he was going to his death, Pollard, in the confusion, jumped into a stream and ran for his life, down the bed of the stream. Felled by a club from behind, Pollard was dragged from the water and lashed to a tree.

" Thumbs up," cried the brigand chief. " Little fingers down." The chief was counting the votes of life and death. Thumbs up meant life, and thumbs won.

THE MISSIONARY IN WHOM THE TRIBESMEN HAD " SEEN JESUS "

Pollard's bravery won a place for Christianity among those hill tribesmen ; and ten years later, in 1915, the same unselfish care for others cost Pollard his life. He died nursing Chinese in a typhoid epidemic. At his funeral sixteen stalwart Miao carried him to his grave on a hill-top. Twelve hundred people stood round among the wild rhododendron ; they knew that in Pollard they had " seen Jesus."

Sitting in the shade of a tree on a hot Indian day were two men. One was a shrivelled man dressed in the simple cloth of an Indian villager—Mahatma Gandhi. The other was a tall, bearded man with deep-set eyes—Charlie Andrews. They were friends as close as ever a Briton and an Indian have been.

From 1904 to his death in 1940 Charlie Andrews was " the man India loved." He often dressed in Indian style and sat cross-legged in Indian homes. He more than anyone saw into the soul of India. In one cholera epidemic Charlie

Andrews helped to bury the dead—an act no Englishman had ever done before. Wherever there was a flood or famine, Charlie Andrews was sure to appear, looking after the children or distributing rice. Coming home one evening he met an Indian outcast villager struggling with a huge bundle of firewood. Charlie Andrews at once lifted the bundle on to his strong shoulders, while the man walked in amazement by his side.

CHRIST'S FAITHFUL APOSTLE AND FRIEND OF THE POOR

When plague broke out in one village, Charlie Andrews arranged some empty houses as a hospital and nursed four Indians back to life. Wherever there was need Charlie Andrews was found, and his life service to India made England better understood than ever before, but, above all, India saw Christ in him. He lies buried in Calcutta, with this inscription on his grave: " Christ's Faithful Apostle, Friend of the Poor."

A laughing boy used to sail a small yacht down the estuary of the Essex Blackwater in the 1930's, and his skill as a seaman made him an ideal missionary for the Gilbert Islands in the Pacific. There, in 1942, the Japanese found him teaching in the school in the island of Beru. He refused to leave his post when he had the chance to reach safety, sending home to Britain the message, " I stay until I am pushed out."

His cheerful courage and gay laughter mystified the Japanese commander, who tried to trick him one day by placing a Union Jack in front of his house, hoping he would step on it. Instead, Alfred Sadd picked it up in his arms and kissed it.

THE BRAVE YOUNG MAN WHO SAW THE FUNNY SIDE OF THINGS

Taken away to the island of Tarawa, Alfred Sadd was put to forced labour on the air-strip, working in the hot sun with twenty other Britishers. His gaiety and his gift of seeing " the funny side of things " never forsook him. He sang hymns and cracked jokes as he worked. Even on the morning he was led out to die with his comrades his face was cheerful and his spirit undismayed.

Now there is a memorial cross over the spot, with the inscription, " Standing unarmed to their posts they matched brutality with gallantry and met death with fortitude."

The Great Stories of the World That Will Be Told for Ever

PUSS IN BOOTS

A MILLER had three sons, and on his death-bed he left his mill to the eldest, his ass to the next, and his cat to the youngest.

The youngest son was at first disappointed with his share of his father's property, but the cat said to him: " My dear master, buy me a pair of boots and a sack, and I will soon show that I am more useful than a mill or an ass."

So the youngest son spent all his money in buying his cat a handsome pair of boots and a sack.

The cat put on the boots, and then slung the sack on his shoulder, and went to a warren. There he opened the sack, put some bran in it, and lay down as if he were dead. A rabbit smelled the bran and ran into the sack. The cat at once caught the rabbit and killed it, and took it to the king, and said: " Sire, the noble Marquess of Carabas desires me to bring you this rabbit. Boiled with onions, you will find it makes an excellent dish."

" Rabbit? " said the king. " How delightful! My cook can never catch any. Pray thank your noble master for me."

The next morning the cat caught two partridges, and brought them to the king as a present from the Marquess of Carabas. The king was so pleased that he at once called for his royal carriage to take him and his daughter, the princess, on a visit to the neighbour who had so kindly sent him such fine gifts.

The cat hastened back to the youngest son, and said to him: " Come with me at once and I will show you a place in the river where you can have a good bathe."

The cat took him to a spot where the royal carriage was about to pass, and told him to undress, and hide his clothes under a stone, and get into the water. He had just entered the river when the king and the princess drove by.

" Help! Help! " shouted the cat.

" What's the matter? " said the king.

" Some thieves have stolen the clothes of the noble Marquess of Carabas," said the cat. " My master is in the water, and I am afraid he will get the cramp."

The king ordered his attendants to run to the palace and bring the finest suit of clothes they could find, and they returned with a gorgeous suit which the king had had made when he was courting.

The youngest son put it on, and he looked so handsome in it that the princess immediately fell in love with him. The king was so touched that he whispered to his daughter: " That's just how I looked twenty years ago when I went courting."

The cat was delighted at the success of his scheme, and, running on in front of the royal carriage, he came to some wheatfields and meadows, and said to the peasants there: " The king is coming, and unless you tell him that these wheatfields and meadows belong to the noble

IMAGINATION · CHIVALRY · LEGENDS · GOLDEN DEEDS · FAIRY TALES

Marquess of Carabas, you will be chopped into the finest mincemeat."

So when the king passed by and asked them to whom the wheatfields and meadows belonged, they said: "To the noble Marquess of Carabas."

"Dear me!" said the king to the youngest son. "You have a fine estate!"

The youngest son smiled in a bewildered way, and the king said in a whisper to the princess: "I was just as bewildered when I went courting."

The cat still ran on in front of the royal carriage, and passed through a forest, and came to a magnificent palace. In the palace lived an ogre, to whom the wheatfields and the meadows really belonged, and the cat at once called upon the ogre, and said to him:

"My dear ogre, what wonderful tales everybody tells about you! Is it true that you can change yourself into any shape that you please?"

"It is quite true," said the ogre. And he at once changed himself into a lion.

"That's nothing," said the cat. "Anybody can puff himself up into something bigger than he really is. But it is only the wise who can make themselves appear smaller than they indeed are. Can you turn yourself into a mouse, for instance?"

"It's just as easy," said the ogre.

He then changed himself into a mouse, and the cat pounced on him and gobbled him up, and ran down and opened the gate just as the royal carriage arrived.

"Welcome, sire, to the palace of the Marquess of Carabas," said the cat.

"Dear me!" said the king to the youngest son. "What a fine palace! Kindly help the princess to alight."

The youngest son shyly offered his arm to the princess, and the king then said to her in a whisper: "I was just as shy when I went courting."

In the meanwhile the cat whisked into the kitchen and ordered a grand lunch, and got all the choicest wines out of the cellar, and by the time the king and the princess and the youngest son were seated at table the repast was ready.

After making a very enjoyable meal the king turned to the youngest son, and said: "You are as bashful as I was when I went courting. But I can see you are as deeply in love with the princess as she is with you. Why not propose to her?"

The youngest son then asked the princess to be his wife, and she consented, and in a short time they were married in great state. The cat came to the marriage feast in a new pair of boots with crimson leather tops set with two rows of diamonds.

THE LUCK OF SIMPLE JACK

SIMPLE JACK was the best silk weaver in Spitalfields, but he had not the least idea of the value of money. If he went out with plenty of silver in his pocket he was sure to pay whatever the seller asked for any article; and, as the people all knew his weak points, Simple Jack was swindled whenever he went out to buy. He was just as silly if he wanted to sell, for then he would take whatever price was offered for his goods, no matter how absurdly low that price might be. So his wife used to do all the buying and selling that they needed.

But one day Simple Jack resolved to go a-marketing himself. He took a bundle of fine silks and sold them to a merchant for forty pounds. Then, seeing a man with a donkey, he said:

"That donkey would be useful to me. Will you take forty pounds for it?"

Of course the man readily sold it at this high price. But Simple Jack found that the donkey was very obstinate, and would not go the way he wanted.

"What will you give me for this beast?" he said to a costermonger.

"It would be dear at ten shillings," said the artful costermonger.

Simple Jack took the ten shillings, and with the money he bought a sack of new potatoes. But the sack was very heavy, and Jack soon tired of his new bargain. So he exchanged it at a fish shop for a mackerel.

His wife was very angry when he told her how he had spent the forty pounds. But, in cutting the fish open, she found in it a pearl of remarkable beauty.

"Why, this must be worth thousands of pounds!" she cried.

"There you are, my dear!" said Simple Jack merrily. "I spent a beggarly forty pounds in buying a fish containing a rich jewel, and yet you say that I have no idea of the value of money."

UP THE ENCHANTED MOUNTAIN

ALTHOUGH everything in old Japan was so small and delicate there was once a Japanese giant called Visu. He was a woodman, and he lived on a plain with his wife and family in simple comfort.

Visu had the good fortune to be the first person who set eyes on Fujiyama, that most lovely of mountains, whose praise fills half Japanese literature, and whose beauty has travelled all over the world in Japanese pictures.

Visu did not presume to go scrambling about on those magical slopes, but he found his work all the pleasanter for having such a sight to look upon.

One day a Buddhist priest came by, and after some talk asked Visu if he said his prayers regularly. The giant replied: " No; and neither would you if you had a wife and family to keep! "

The priest was offended; he told Visu that after he died the gods would surely

TWO LADIES WERE SITTING ON THE GRASS PLAYING

Where it lived before it came to its present site no one knows, but every good Japanese child believes that it ran under the earth for three hundred miles, and suddenly thrust up its head on the plain.

The noise of its approach wakened poor Visu, who thought it was the end of the world. But when he saw the glorious fire-crowned mountain he quite forgave the damage it had done to his crockery.

send his soul into the body of a spider or a slug unless he attended to his religious duties. Visu was cowed at once, and promised to be devout henceforth.

Now, giants are a notoriously stupid race, and Visu was no exception to the rule. Instead of taking Work and Prayer for his watchword, he gave up his whole time to religious forms and ceremonies. If he was not reciting texts he was sitting lost in meditation. Rust gathered on his axe; his crops rotted ungathered; his garden was choked with weeds; his children went hungry.

At last the long patience of his gentle wife gave way, and she reproached him for neglecting his duties.

Visu's indignation was great. He could not even say his prayers in peace! He could not do anything right! She was a worldly-minded woman, and he would have nothing more to do with her. So saying, Visu stalked out of the house, and strode off to the mountain to sulk.

The crest of Fujiyama was clothed in snow, which glittered like opals against the blue sky. Lower down were clusters of trees, and grass thickly scattered with coloured flowers.

"Here I shall get some peace," thought Visu, climbing at leisure.

Presently he saw bright garments through the leaves. He approached cautiously. Two ladies were seated on the grass playing *Go*, a Japanese game more difficult than our European chess. By the jewelled ornaments in their hair, the rich material of their dresses, and the elegance of their hands, he could see that they were people of high rank. They were also very beautiful; it was a joy to look at their pensive faces and graceful movements.

Visu was now quite accustomed to do nothing, and he sat down to watch behind a screen of leaves. Neither of the ladies spoke; and Visu, too, soon became absorbed in the game, which seemed endless. At length one of the damsels made a false move. In his excitement Visu cried out: "Wrong!"

At his cry a queer thing happened. Instead of the great ladies there were only two foxes, which ran off into the undergrowth.

Visu felt dizzy and frightened. He tried to rise, but he was so stiff that it was long before he could get to his feet. Then, as he tottered painfully down the mountain, he passed a little pool, and the reflection of a white-haired old man looked back at him from the clear waters. He understood now that he had been enchanted, but he hoped that still he might meet his dear ones, though changed by time.

Alas! he could not see his hut. As he stood gazing about him a girl passed by with her pitcher. He called to her and said: "Maiden, will you guide me to Visu's house?"

She stared at him. "There is no such thing. I think there is no such person. Grannie tells a fairy story about a man called Visu who disappeared three hundred years ago; but it is only a tale."

For a moment the old giant stood still, stricken by the thought that the wife and children whom he had so ill-used were dead. Then, feeling that he would follow them very soon, he gave his last message to the world:

"Maiden," he murmured, "pray, but work too!"

THE LAND OF GREAT DELIGHT

A LONG time ago Elidorus, a boy of twelve years of age, was punished by his schoolmaster, and he ran away and hid in a cave by the river, and there he remained without food for two days. Two little men then appeared, and said: "Follow us and we will take you to the Land of Great Delight."

And Elidorus followed them through a dark passage down the earth out into a rich and beautiful country. But there was no sun or moon or star there, only a strange twilight falling from a strange sky.

The two wee men led Elidorus to their King, and their King made Elidorus the companion to his eldest son. All the people of the Twilight Land were very small, but they were very handsome, and they had long golden hair that fell over their shoulders. The King of the Twilight Land allowed Elidorus to go back through the dark passage and visit his mother, and one day Elidorus was telling her what a rich country he lived in, and she bade him bring her some of its treasures.

So the next time Elidorus played with the son of the King he stole a golden ball and ran with it to his mother's house.

The two wee men, however, pursued him, and they tripped him up just as he got indoors, seized the golden ball from his hand, and departed.

Elidorus was very sorry that he had stolen the golden ball, and he wanted to beg the King's pardon; but the passage in the cave by the river-side was closed, and was never again opened to him.

LEGENDS OF TOWN AND COUNTRY

THE MAN IN THE MOON

ONE Sunday morning an old man went to a forest and cut a fagot of firewood, which he put on his shoulder, and then began to trudge home. But while he was on the way an angel came and said to him:

"Do you know this is Sunday on Earth, when all men rest from labour?"

"Sunday on Earth, or Monday in Heaven," said the old man, "it's all the same to me."

"Then," said the angel, "as you do not keep Sunday on Earth you shall live in a Moon-day in Heaven, and there you shall stay and carry your fagot until the Day of Judgment."

And the old man rose up to the Moon, and there, on a clear night, you can still see a great shadow, as of a man carrying a bundle of sticks on his shoulder. It is said that

> The man in the moon
> Came down too soon,
> And asked his way to Norwich;

but there is no news of his ever having arrived at that great and famous city.

ST. KEYNE'S WELL

CORNWALL, of all the counties of England, is the one most rich in folk-lore and legend. The names of many saintly men and women who brought the Gospel to the pagans who dwelt there still linger in the villages. Many, too, are associated with holy wells, and the following is the story of St. Keyne's Well.

St. Brechan, the ancient Welsh king who built the town of Brecknock, had twenty-four children, and fifteen of them became saints, like their royal father.

Chief among them was a maiden of entrancing beauty whose name was Keyne. She wandered about England, preaching to the pagans and converting them, and her name is preserved in the village of Keynsham, in Somerset, and in St. Keyne's Well, in Cornwall. The well is near the spot where she died, and it is said that before she died she planted about it four trees—a willow, an oak, an elm, and an ash—and blessed the water. And because the well was blessed by the saintly maiden the water is reputed to have a strange virtue.

Newly-married couples often come to drink from the well, for this is the legend.

If the bridegroom is the first to taste the water he henceforward obtains the mastery over his wife. If, on the other hand, the bride is able to drink first she ever afterward obtains in all things the mastery over her husband.

THE CHEST OF CALLER PIT

CALLER PIT is a watery hollow lying near Southwood, in Norfolk, and there was an old saying that an iron chest filled with gold lay at the bottom of it.

So one hot summer, when the water had been dried up, two Southwood men dug deep down in the pit, and there, sure enough, they found the chest. It was very heavy, but they managed to raise it up, and one of the men joyfully cried, as he clutched the iron ring at the top of the chest: "We've got it now, and the Spirit of the Pit can't take it away."

A thick, black smoke at once arose from Caller Pit, and out of the black smoke came a great black hand, which seized the chest. The two men clung with all their strength to the iron ring, but in vain. The black hand wrenched the chest away, and all that was left them was the iron ring. This ring is now fixed to the door of Southwood Church, but, though Caller Pit is often dry, nobody has ever again found the chest of gold there.

THE BIDDENDEN MAIDS

ON Easter Sunday, for many years, a thousand cakes were given away to persons attending service in the church of the picturesque little village of Biddenden, in Kent. On each of the cakes there was stamped a rough, antique picture of two women joined together at the shoulders and hips.

These are the Biddenden Maids, and their names are Elizabeth and Mary Chulkhurst. They were born in Biddenden in the year 1100, and for thirty-four years they lived joined together in the manner shown on the cakes. When one of them died her sister's sorrow was great, and she said: "Together we came, and together we must go."

And she passed away six hours after her sister, leaving to the churchwardens of Biddenden twenty acres of land, on the condition that the income should be spent in giving away cakes every Easter in commemoration of the sad event.

LITTLE PRINCE HORN

ONE day, as King Murry of Suddene was riding near the shore, he perceived sails in a certain well-hidden bay.

He spurred to the place with his two followers. There were fifteen ships, filled with Saracens, who were swarming ashore like ants. They immediately attacked and killed the three Christians.

Then the invaders spread over the land. They burned churches and tortured people to make them give up their faith; and those who yielded became slaves.

Queen Godchild managed to escape into the woods, where she lived for many years in a cave, secretly worshipping the Christian God, and praying for her only son, who might be alive or dead.

Prince Horn was only twelve years old when the Saracens caught him and his twelve playmates. They were dragged before the pagan leader. He was so struck by Horn's beauty and courageous bearing that he could not bring himself to give the death sentence. Yet these thirteen boys would grow up to avenge their fathers' deaths if they were spared. So they were put into a mastless boat, which was towed out to sea and abandoned. All the children began to weep and wail except Horn. He managed to get his little craft into the grip of a current which carried them swiftly away.

Horn took the part of a leader. He comforted his companions; he shamed and exhorted them. At length the night began to pale, and in the light of dawn they saw land before them.

Now some of the lads took heart, especially Horn's favourite friend, Athulf, and they got the boat ashore. Then the sea-sodden children began to walk inland.

They were presently met by a little party of horsemen. Their leader stopped and asked who the invaders were.

Horn answered: " Sir, pagans have killed our fathers and set us adrift in a boat. We do not know where we are."

Horn was too proud to boast of his royal descent, since he had no kingdom.

The stranger replied: " You are the prettiest invaders I ever saw. I am King Ailmar of Westernesse, and I will take you to my Court. My steward shall train you to be good pages and esquires, for I think you are of gentle birth."

So it was done, and Horn became the King's own page and attendant.

Ailmar had one daughter, Rymenhild, who loved the noble youth and thought she was dying of it. She sent for Horn to tell him the cause of her death; but when he replied, sighing, that he loved her also, she immediately recovered. However, Horn reminded her that a princess could not marry a penniless page.

While they were talking together they were overheard by Fykenhild, one of Horn's twelve companions, a jealous traitor.

He hastened to Ailmar and told him that the foundling page was wooing his daughter. Ailmar, in his rage, would have hanged the youth but for certain feats of courage he had performed in battle for the king. Therefore the sentence was banishment. Horn went, vowing to return.

His pride was stung, and he set himself to make a name which should shine brighter than Ailmar's crown. Far and wide he wandered for seven years, doing great deeds. He helped King Thurston of Ireland to win back his kingdom.

And meanwhile Rymenhild's heart was breaking. No news came. She thought Horn must be dead, and her father told her she must marry King Modi of Keynes. She sent out a messenger, and he at last met Horn, who bade him tell the Princess that he would return. But one day, as Rymenhild walked on the seashore, she found her messenger's dead body washed up on the sand.

The wedding day came. Rymenhild would not repeat the wedding vows or accept the ring, yet she was carried off to Modi's castle. While he feasted some poor beggars gained admittance to the hall.

A little later a postern was unbarred and a party of armed men stole in. It was Horn and his Irish friends. Modi and his men were slain after a short fight in the torch-lit hall, and Rymenhild was saved.

But Horn would not wed her yet. First he would have a kingdom to offer her : she should not marry him till Ailmar acknowledged him a worthy bridegroom.

Horn returned to Suddene with a company of Irish knights and soldiers. The land groaned under the Saracen tyranny, and it was not long before the usurpers were overthrown. Horn's mother came, weeping and laughing, from her cave, and Athulf's father shook off his chains.

Then, with a battered shield and a rich crown, Horn went to claim his bride.

Nature's Wonderful Living Family in Earth and Air and Sea

A herd of Bison on a Reserve in Canada

THE GREAT CATTLE FAMILY

WHEN this chapter was first written an appeal was being issued by learned men to all travellers in far, strange lands, to seek out new foods, new fibres, and new drugs—for anything indeed which might help to increase the common possessions of mankind.

For long the voice of Nature, felt rather than heard, cried to men as science now cries, inciting them to draw upon the resources of the animal world for their own betterment. The response to that voice was the first triumph of mind over matter, the victory of a feeble upright mammal over brutes fierce enough to rend and devour him, swift enough to outrun him, strong enough to crush him.

Man's first idea of conquering his fellow mammals may have been suggested to him by certain of the animals themselves, dogs and cats who formed the habit of accompanying him—at a respectful distance—hoping for discarded scraps from the chase.

The greatest task of all had yet to be faced. Men had to grapple with the most powerful order on Earth—the mammals with hoofs, and many of them with formidable horns. Early, unknown men did it. They mastered the elephant, the camel, the horse; they tamed the goat, the pig, and cattle.

How the conquest began we can only guess. Today when we read how, after thousands of years of domestication, a bull gores a man to death, or spreads panic through a town in which it breaks loose; how a horse sometimes attacks its groom; how an elephant tramples down a village and kills all upon whom it can lay its trunk; when we read of commonplace events such as these, we imagine what was the nature of the contest when first misty-minded savages decreed the captivity of the giants of the Earth.

We must omit here any consideration of the greatest wonders flowing from that old conquest, and limit ourselves to the story of the cattle. With these began man's first advance beyond the crudest savagery. Going naked into the wilds with his dog he captured the parents of man's future herds, and brought back to his family food, drink, raiment, power; flesh, milk, leather, and strength to bear burdens and to haul loads.

The cow is worshipped as a sacred animal in India; all civilisation owes it gratitude as the foundation of human progress. At one bound the first tamers of cattle passed from a condition of wandering savagery to the possession of property. No longer, after that, need men, women,

PREHISTORIC LIFE · MAMMALS · BIRDS · REPTILES · FISHES · INSECTS

and children creep like wolves in the tracks of wild beasts to secure food. They domesticated the giants and formed homes around their pastures. The law of property came into being, and a rude anticipation of the Tenth Commandment, " Thou shalt not covet thy neighbour's ox," must have been among the first of laws on which man built up his earliest moral code.

In other ways the results were of immediate importance. No longer did the illness of a mother involve the death of her baby. Milk from the cow took the place of nourishment which the stricken parent was unable to furnish.

The slaughter of babies is one of the oldest crimes known to man. It has been practised in all ages, in all societies, and is a scourge today among tribes which do not possess cattle. The loss of cattle in France, Belgium, and the Balkans, was one of the disastrous consequences of the two World Wars. In Russia the extinction of the herds was one of the chief factors in a famine of almost unparalleled horror.

THE LITTLE MEN WITH FLINT TOOLS WHO FIRST MASTERED CATTLE

At a blow, food for babies and invalids vanished, with meat for the robust and leather for the boots and shoes of all. Death from starvation and cold was the necessary consequence of the passing of Russia's cattle. Other countries were saved from dangers as terrible by the effort of many nations in sending cows and oxen to replace those which had been destroyed during the wars.

These facts help us to realise how very different human history must have proved had not the old twilight savages risked life and limb to win service from the order of animals which includes the last of Earth's surviving giants.

The cattle-tamers ceased to be homeless wanderers. Each man could, if he would, become what is now an impossible political dream, the owner of " three acres and a cow "; and with the first of dairies came a new food, so that babies and invalids need no longer perish for lack of proper nourishment.

Our ancestors in Europe had not far to go in quest of their cattle. The towering aurochs roamed the grassy plains and browsed in the thick forests. With the aurochs all domestic herds began.

They were here before man—their bones in the soil prove that. The little men with flint tools must have been their first masters in Britain. The Celts, who came later, had them in domestication when the Romans arrived. The Romans brought their own breeds, descended from the same source, and, later, Anglo-Saxons introduced their own results of long ages of breeding from the aurochs.

Wild cattle still existed in Eastern Europe, few but precious relics, until the war, and then, we fear, unless unsuspected groups had previously managed to establish themselves in remote mountains, valleys, or far forests, the last vanished. They, however, were not aurochs, but bison.

THE CATTLE THAT ROAMED THE GREAT FORESTS WHERE CITIES NOW STAND

We have so-called wild cattle in Great Britain, the nearest approach to a pure descent from the aurochs now to be found, but they are not like their colossal forefathers. Centuries ago, when cattle roamed the land in semi-wildness, the blood of all the three strains already named became mixed, and we got a generalised type of animal as the result.

They frequented the great forests by which London and other centres of population were surrounded, and when the forests were cleared, and land enclosed for private ownership, these animals were shut up within walls and fences in parks. It does honour to certain of our old families that these animals have been so long preserved.

The best known today is the Chillingham herd, white with curly hair, with red above the muzzles and the inside of the ears. They have many characteristics of the ancient free stock, an invincible and shy wildness, resentment of intrusion, and the habit of feeding by night and hiding by day.

THE CATTLE THAT WERE HIDDEN DOWN A MINE FOR SAFETY

Many corresponding herds have been dispersed, but we know with what loving care the survivors have been guarded by the fact that once, during an outbreak of foot-and-mouth disease, the Duke of Hamilton had his herd all taken down his Lanarkshire coal mines, and safely tended there until the danger was gone.

In ancient days our forefathers used the ox as a beast of burden. All work on the land was done by cattle. It cost sixpence for a man and his oxen to plough an acre of land and a penny an acre for women to

THE CATTLE OF A THOUSAND HILLS

THE AMERICAN BISON, THE WANDERER OVER THE OPEN SPACES OF NORTH AMERICA

THE EUROPEAN BISON, DWELLING IN THE FORESTS

The photographs on these pages are by the Canadian Pacific Railway, Messrs. Gambier Bolton, W. P. Dando, and others.

THE HANDSOME GAYAL AT HOME IN THE HILLS OF INDIA

THE WILD ENGLISH BULL

THE GAUR OF SOUTH-EASTERN ASIA

THE YAK AT HOME IN THE MOUNTAINS OF TIBET

THE BANTIN, OR JAVAN OX

THE MYSORE COW

HIGHLAND

DEVON

LONGHORN

JERSEY

SHORTHORN

ABERDEEN-ANGUS

KERRY

HEREFORD

EIGHT BREEDS OF BRITISH CATTLE

The March of Man from the Age of Barbarism to the United Nations

The Death of Socrates

THE MARVELLOUS MAN OF GREECE

To look back to the past only to laugh at it is almost as foolish as looking back to it only to admire.

In the comic papers you will find stupid people making game of all antiquity, and in serious papers you will find clever people exalting the past, particularly the past of Greece, as the supreme hour of human existence. But both these extreme attitudes of mind are wrong.

Fortunately for those of us who take a more reasonable view of this matter, Greece has given us a great master of reasonableness, whose life is our authority for what we assert to be a wiser frame of mind. We look back to past ages with sympathy and with criticism. We look back to distinguish what was good and helpful in times past from what was bad and dangerous.

This great master of reasonableness was Socrates. He was born some 470 years before the coming of Jesus, and his early manhood was passed at the time when the glory of Athens was at its highest. He was poor and ugly—so ugly that some people could not help laughing at him. As for his poverty, he wore only one garment, and never went to the needless expense of sandals.

We may imagine, then, what the *quality* of Socrates was, when we think of such a comic-looking, barefoot old soldier attract-ing universal attention in Athens at a time of her greatest glory. And we see how real and lasting was that quality when we know that it is said of him that *his name is one of the most conspicuous in the whole history of thought and civilisation.*

Those who first hear of this wonderful man at once feel a consuming desire to get all his books from the library, so that they may fill their minds with such extra-ordinary wisdom. He lived at the time of Pericles, and was greater than Pericles. Since his day there have been many mighty men of action from Alexander to Napoleon, but the glory of all of them fades away in the glory of Socrates. Since his day, too, there have been many luminous teachers of wisdom, men of marvellous genius and prodigious know-ledge; yet we still say that the name of Socrates is among the most conspicuous in the whole history of thought and civilisation.

But when we hasten to the library to buy the works of this greatest of the kings of men, it is to receive the staggering infor-mation that such works have no existence. What then, are we reading of some legendary hero, some mythical superman? Was there ever a real Socrates? There was, indeed, such a man as Socrates; and it was just his *reality* which made it un-

MIGHTY EPOCHS OF THE WORLD & MAN'S WONDERFUL ADVENTURES

THE IMMORTAL MAN OF ATHENS WHOSE WORDS DREW ALL MEN UNTO HIM—SOCRATES
This glorious piece of sculpture, worthy of its great subject, is

necessary for him to write books or to bequeath to posterity a written record of his life. How real he was we will now go on to discover.

We have seen how early thinkers in Greece studied nature and how there came to birth with Pythagoras the beautiful idea of philosophy—the search for knowledge, the passion for truth, the faith of the mind in its power to unravel, disentangle, and comprehend the supreme riddles of human existence. And this philosophy went hand in hand with a strict moral discipline.

Between the time of Pythagoras and Socrates there was a great deal more guessing at the mystery of Nature and not so much carefulness as to conduct. A race of men came into existence not only contemptuous of superstition and priestcraft, but contemptuous of moral teaching. They thought they knew everything. They had no modesty, no sense of humour. They strutted about the cities of Greece selling their " wisdom " to all who were ready to pay for being startled. They laughed at the gods and goddesses of Homer, laughed at the theories of old thinkers, but forgot to laugh at themselves. The universe? It could be explained. Philosophy? They were its final voice.

Now imagine the danger of this sort of stupidity to the future of civilisation. A

TALKING ON HIS ENDLESS THEME OF ETERNAL JUSTICE AND EVERLASTING LIFE
by Harry Bates, and the photograph of it is by F. Hollyer

young man of intelligence found himself confronted by a choice between superstition and cynicism. Either he must believe in contemptible gods and goddesses, and take part in religious ceremonies which filled him with angry disdain, or he must laugh at faith, tell himself he understood how the world was made, and live with no moral enthusiasm in his heart.

Remember, Greece was preparing the whole future of civilisation, the whole future of our modern world. There was no other nation at that time in her place. She alone held in her hands a blessing for posterity. In all we now think and do

there is something Greek, and it is impossible for us to imagine modern civilisation without these Grecian roots. Think, then, of the peril to us of that crisis in the life of Athenian culture.

Now we can ask ourselves how Socrates, so poor and so ugly, did this mighty work for the whole world?

He did it, in the first place, simply by being real. He was by nature a very honest man, and he soon saw that it is necessary for a man to be honest in his private thoughts as well as in his transactions with other men.

This was the first thing Socrates did for Greece, and for us; he made honesty seem a splendid thing and all humbug a contemptible thing. The second thing he did was also in the region of honesty; he never used a word which he had not carefully reflected on for its meaning, and never professed a belief of whose truth he had not assured himself by honest thinking.

PUSHING HIS WAY THROUGH WORDS TO THE THINGS BEHIND

Thus equipped, he haunted the crowded streets of Athens and talked to men about their souls. He did not talk of their souls as one who knew all there is to know, or as one who wanted to found a new school of philosophy or establish a new religion. On the contrary, he was often laughing when he spoke, and most of his utterances were in the nature of a jest.

He made men see that most of the explanations of the universe were ludicrous, and that behind even those which sounded plausible the mighty fact of the universe remained. He was for ever pushing his way through words to the things words are supposed to represent. He saw that it is possible for men so to blind their eyes with words that they never see the things those words stand for—the facts behind the words. We may often read an article on science which seems to explain in perfect detail exactly how the world has come to be what it is; but we go out into the garden a few minutes afterwards and see the Moon rising above the trees, feel the breath of evening on our face, see the colours of the flowers, and hear the last song of a thrush in the calm distance, and of the answer in our own heart to all loveliness, both physical and spiritual; *we feel convinced that science has not yet explained reality.*

THE MESSAGE OF SOCRATES TO THE AGES COMING AFTER HIM

This was the spirit of Socrates. He kept his eye on the real world. No words satisfied him. No formula could make an end of his wonder and his mystery.

What was it that Socrates had to say? His message may be summed up in not many words. He would argue like this :

The universe will never contract to the dimensions of any formula of the human mind. It will always escape through your net of guesswork, for behind everything you see with your eyes is a reality which is invisible.

If you would form some notion of this invisible reality, look within. You are not flesh and blood; you are not hands and feet; you are not eyes and ears; you are Spirit. Your real life is the inward reality which says *I*. Then, if you would be wise, you will concentrate all your care on this inward reality which is You.

You must care for your soul. You must defend it against the illusions of your senses and the illusions of words—your own words, the words of others. You must make it honest. You must never say anything which you do not feel to be perfectly true, and you must never do anything you do not feel to be perfectly right. You must be careful, too, not to desire things which only minister to the pleasure of your body, for your body will die; you must be careful to desire only those things which enrich your soul, invisible things, the great virtues.

To run after wealth, fame, and power is very illogical. Your business is to walk quietly and contentedly with truth, beauty, and goodness. Constantly examine your own soul, and you will find that what I tell you is truth. Understand, however, that I, too, am a seeker of truth; for no man knows all there is to know.

THE ENORMOUS INFLUENCE OF SOCRATES ON THE MIND OF MAN

He brought to birth, in one of the most critical hours of human existence, the spirit of *scepticism*—but a creative scepticism, a scepticism which insisted on the one solid reality of the moral life. He led men to look within, and to search there for the truth that was real. He made them critics, but chiefly critics of themselves. He did away with blind idolatry, both in religion and philosophy; he did away with all dogmatism and all slavish credulity; he did away with every form of intellectual vanity, every form of intellectual or moral hypocrisy, and he set the mind of man on the road of a most scrupulous honesty, bidding it travel to the unknown with all humility but with an unconquerable courage.

No man ever went to a martyr's death for truth more nobly than Socrates went to his. The bigots of his day charged him with " corrupting youth " and introducing new divinities in place of those recognised by the State, and he was condemned to drink a cup of hemlock. He remained in prison when he might have escaped; he died when he might have lived, and he died with the gentlest of wise jests on his smiling lips, though also with a majesty of confidence and a glory of tranquillity which were like a revelation of the divine.

Chinese tappers with pails of latex on the Dunlop rubber estate

THE REMARKABLE STORY OF RUBBER

NOT once, nor twice, but many times small things have changed the world. We see it in the ravages of the boll-weevil, which, by the havoc it wrought in American cotton plantations, threatened to slow down Lancashire mills. On the other hand it may be that another insect, a wood-boring beetle, did the world a good turn when it began to attack a tree and caused the tree to give out a juice to heal its wounds; for, as far as we know, motor-cars and bicycles might not have developed without the rubber from this juice, or latex; and we might not have found a substance for making cables under the sea.

In all these things a vital part is played by one of the most wonderful materials in the world—natural rubber. It was the latex containing rubber which perhaps first astonished man in the wild forests of Mexico and the Amazon when it oozed from numerous trees, vines, and shrubs to heal the wounds in the bark caused by the wood-boring beetle, and protected the tree by becoming solid and imprisoning the insect as we find a fly imprisoned sometimes in amber.

The story of rubber before the first Europeans went to the New World is lost in the mists of time. Probably the first men from the West to be astonished by the sight of it were the crew of Columbus, who, late in the fifteenth century, found the natives of Haiti playing with solid balls which bounced up into the air. They were made of the gum of a tree. In 1615 the Spaniards were known to use the crude gum to wax their canvas cloaks so that they would resist water; and La Condamine, who in 1731 was sent on a scientific expedition to the Equator by the Paris Academy, sent back samples of a blackish resinous mass called *caoutchouc*, which is rubber, and reported that the natives of Peru and Brazil covered linen with this material and wore rubber shoes.

It was not till nearly 200 years after the Spaniards used it that people began to pay much attention to this remarkable stuff which was working wonders among these natives of America—the "Red Indians", as their discoverers imagined them to be, so that they first named this stuff india rubber, after them. Certainly in the meantime, rubber had found a use, however, and one to which children still put it, for Joseph Priestley, the famous chemist, mentioned in 1770 that it was useful for rubbing lead pencil marks off paper, and that a little cube of it could be got for three shillings!

INDUSTRIES · HOW THINGS ARE MADE · WHERE THEY COME FROM

Even at this price artists were glad to have it, but that was practically the only use known for it: and it was not till some 20 years later that the first attempts were made to use rubber in industry. Then Samuel Peal invented a process for covering cloth with rubber dissolved in turpentine. For waterproofing garments it was smelly and sticky, but the idea led to attempts by other people, and in 1823 Charles Macintosh, a thoughtful Scotsman, made the first waterproof coats called macintoshes after his name.

Thus began one branch of a very big industry, which started to develop after 1836 when Thomas Hancock of London found that rubber, cut into small strips and kneaded under the influence of heat, became plastic, and could be cut into any desired shape.

Now, the natural rubber was very sensitive to changes of temperature; it became stiff and hard when cold, and soft and sticky when hot, so that a waterproof which was stiff in cold weather and sticky on a damp, warm day, or beneath the Sun's rays, was very uncomfortable.

THE GREAT DISCOVERY OF THE PROCESS OF VULCANISING RUBBER

Inventors were still hard at work and seeking to overcome this when Charles Goodyear in America made a discovery which may be looked back upon as the greatest step in the development of the rubber industry.

This was the notable discovery, in 1839, of *vulcanisation*—the discovery that by heating powdered sulphur with rubber, the rubber lost its sticky character and became elastic, pliable, and pleasant to the touch over a wide range of temperature. Goodyear had been working at his discovery for years, suffering bitter poverty and the jeers of his fellow men, but he ultimately conquered.

While others then proceeded to new discoveries by varying his method, Goodyear, and Thomas Hancock in England, found that by adding more sulphur than first used, and heating the mixture at a higher temperature for some hours, a hard substance like ebony could be produced. This was called ebonite or vulcanite, and is used today to make many things such as combs, pipe-stems, electrical goods, and so on.

It was this vulcanised rubber which first made cycling possible. There had been cycles long before—hobby-horses, bone-shakers, and other things of the same style. The rubber tyre gave them new form, new life and dignity. But, as those who rode the velocipedes, or the first " safeties," of a century and more ago discovered, the first rubber tyres were small and solid. How they jolted and jarred along the stony highways, carrying the rider home with his teeth aching and his wrists almost shattered! Motorcars could never have been run at high speed with tyres of this sort.

JOHN DUNLOP'S GRAND IDEA OF MAKING AN AIR CUSHION TO RIDE ON

Now, though in 1845 Robert William Thomson had taken out a patent for an air-filled tyre, nothing came of it. Happily, in 1888, John Dunlop, a Scottish veterinary surgeon in Belfast, thought out afresh the grand idea of making an air cushion for a bicycle tyre. He was a long time working at it, and at first he fitted one on a block of wood and trundled it about his yard. It answered well enough, so he made and fitted a tyre of this sort to his own bicycle, then put one on his son's machine, enabling him to win a race for which he had entered.

The principle of this first Dunlop tyre was the same as that which makes our motor-car or bicycle run so delightfully today. The inner tube is made of comparatively soft, thin rubber. The cover which fits over this is stout and hard, to protect the inner tube from injury. It is the tube beneath the cover, filled with air, which has worked the marvel. The wheels of a bicycle or a motor-car actually run on compressed air.

THE BIG DEMAND FOR RUBBER THAT GREW UP EVERYWHERE

The invention of John Dunlop was taken up by a keen man of business, Mr. Harvey Du Cros. Today the invention has gone all over the Earth, and there are in the United States enough tyred motor-vehicles to allow every person in the country to be riding at the same time.

In every country there are cycles, motor-cars, and aeroplanes using these wonderful tyres. They are used even on great lorries which carry several tons. On pages 1409 to 1412 we see how the stout covers which stand up to such hard work on motor-cars are made.

The new discoveries caused a big demand for rubber, and this has steadily

ONE OF THE GREAT PNEUMATIC TYRES THAT HAVE MADE THE FLYING AGE POSSIBLE

increased so that now rubber is grown in most tropical countries. Once, when the American native wanted rubber, he gashed the tree with a hatchet; he got plenty of rubber, but insect and fungus pests got into the wound, and the tree died. Now, trees are cut (called tapping) by special knives which make a cut just deep enough for the latex to flow out. Tapping is started well up the tree, and is made lower and lower week by week, so that when the lowest cut has been made those at the top have healed and can be opened again.

THE SEED THAT CAME FROM THE WEST TO START A GREAT INDUSTRY IN THE EAST

One of the great romances of the rubber industry concerns the introduction of the South American rubber plant into British territories in the East—an enterprise to which we are indebted to several far-seeing civil servants, and in particular to Sir Joseph Hooker, Director of the Royal Botanic Gardens at Kew.

In the Amazon jungles grows a plant called Hevea which yields the finest rubber. In 1873 seed from this plant was obtained from Brazil and as a result several plants were raised at Kew and sent to India. Owing to the climate these plants failed, and the experiment, made two years later, of sending seed direct from Brazil to India was even less successful, for no plant was raised.

Sir Joseph Hooker decided to try again and engaged a young coffee planter, Henry (later Sir Henry) Wickham, to collect the seed.

SEVEN THOUSAND YOUNG RUBBER PLANTS IN KEW

Wickham, one of the great pioneers of the rubber industry, went about his task with enthusiasm and collected 70,000 seeds near a place called Boim, on high land in the central valley of the Amazon. Legend has it that the seed was smuggled out of Brazil. The truth is that although he encountered much difficulty Wickham managed to charter a special ship and with the willing co-operation of the Brazilian authorities he sailed home with the precious collection of what he called "exceedingly delicate botanical specimens," reaching Kew on June 14, 1876.

The orchid and propagating houses at Kew had been specially prepared for him, and the Hevea seeds were planted. They throve so well that "a fortnight after-ward," Wickham says, "the glass-houses afforded a pretty sight—tier upon tier of young Hevea plants, 7000 odd of them." The young plants were shipped off to India, Ceylon, and Singapore, and today thousands on thousands of splendid trees have sprung from them.

On the plantations, and indirectly in the rubber workshops of the world, hundreds of thousands of people must owe their livelihood to the juice oozing out of these precious trees.

Manufactured rubber has now a thousand uses, entering in some form nearly every trade, occupation, and sport. They range from a child's ball and the football bladder to rubber floors and even rubber roads. Rubber is used in the making of certain kinds of paper and also to produce the wonderfully soft cushioning material called latex foam. It is found in paints, varnishes, adhesives, and even in some kinds of cement.

A PROBLEM FOR THE ALLIES WHEN SUPPLIES WERE CUT OFF

In 1910 nearly all the world's rubber came from Brazil and Africa, Brazil producing 41,000 tons and Africa 21,000; only 8000 tons were cultivated on plantations. By 1915 nearly 160,000 tons were grown, of which only 50,000 came from Brazil, Mexico, and Africa. By 1921 something like 1,700,000 acres of trees were yielding more than 300,000 tons. Today, the plantations produce over 1,700,000 tons of rubber each year.

The use of rubber leapt up tremendously during the First World War. Then, with the war finished, rubber in such quantity was no longer wanted, but still large areas of the world were yielding more and more rubber, and its value fell.

With the outbreak of the Second World War, however, there was again a great demand for the commodity. When the Japanese hordes overran Malaya and other rubber-producing areas in 1941 the Allies were faced with a very serious problem. However, production was speeded up in Ceylon, Africa, South America, and elsewhere, and in the meantime clever scientists evolved various synthetic substitutes which enabled the small production of rubber to go a very long way.

With a return to more normal conditions rubber production rose again ; and there still remain endless possibilities for its further use.

PICTURE-STORY OF RUBBER

Rubber is a substance obtained from the milky juices, known as latex, which are present in many kinds of tropical and sub-tropical plants. More than 95 per cent of the world's rubber is produced in South-East Asia's nine million acres, nearly half of them in Malaya. Here is a typical Malayan plantation.

The most important rubber-producing tree, the Hevea Brasiliensis, came from the Amazon Valley of South America. It will grow in most places with a hot, moist climate. Here we see the nursery ground being prepared for seedlings.

HOW THE RUBBER TREES ARE GROWN

When big enough, the young trees are transplanted to the place where they are to mature. Here we see workers hoeing between the trees.

Here is a row of healthy young trees, which are planted in avenues with approximately 100 trees to the acre. They grow to between 60 and 100 feet.

The trees are first tapped five years or so after planting, the average annual yield of each tree being about eight pounds. Here a worker is tapping a tree in a 15-year-old plantation.

TAPPING THE TREES TO GET THE LATEX

The tree is tapped in the early morning, when the latex flows more freely, by cutting off a fifteenth-of-an-inch thick sliver of bark. Every other day a new cut is made immediately below the last.

The latex flows into cups placed below the end of the cut, first in drops and then in a slow, continuous flow. Here latex is seen running into a cup from a spiral cut made in the trunk of the tree.

The latex is allowed to flow for four hours, during which time each tree yields about a cupful of liquid. It is then collected by workers who empty the cups into pails and carry them, as seen here, to waiting lorries.

It is essential that the latex reaches the plantation factory without delay, so, as the workers bring their pails, the liquid is emptied into tanks on lorries which speed the precious fluid to the factory.

FORMING LIQUID RUBBER INTO SHEETS

At the rubber factory the latex is poured into great tanks and acid is added. After having been stirred and skimmed, the latex changes into a spongy mass known as coagulum.

The coagulum is then passed between a series of rollers, as seen here. At the same time the rubber is sprayed with water to wash out impurities. From the rollers, one of which is usually ribbed, the rubber emerges in sheets about one-eighth-of-an-inch thick.

THE RUBBER IS READY FOR EXPORT

The sheets of rubber are then hung on racks in a smoke house to dry; this process takes some 48 hours or more. The smoke turns the sheets an amber colour.

Here the sheets are seen being wheeled from the smoke house. Each sheet is carefully inspected before being taken to a press to be made into bales for export.

Each bale weighs 250 pounds, and to ensure its arrival in good condition it is wrapped in rubber sheets before shipment. A pronged instrument fastens the rubber wrappings together and the bale is then addressed by stencilling, as seen here.

HOW CRÊPE RUBBER IS MADE

The coagulum is rolled into long sheets by passing through special machines which force out the water.

Crêpe sheets are air-dried to give the white appearance. The sheets are examined and any imperfections cut out.

Lengths of crêpe are heated on steam-heated tables until they are slightly sticky. Then a number of lengths are placed one on top of another, as seen here, until the required thickness is obtained. They are passed through heavy rollers which press the sheets together, emerging as thick sheets ready for cutting into stout crêpe rubber soles for shoes.

Some of the pictures in these pages are Crown copyright; others are by courtesy of the British Rubber Development Board

Plain Answers to the Questions of the Children of the World

WHAT MAKES THE KETTLE BOIL?

WE must know what it is that forms the bubbles when water boils. They are bubbles of water. If you hold a cold plate over boiling water you will find drops of wet water form upon it, though you can see no water passing upward between the surface of the boiling water and the plate.

The truth is that, though we always think of water as something that is liquid and wet, just as we think of air as something that is always a gas, we have no right to do so.

Water happens to be usually fluid, but we all know that when it is cold it becomes solid, ice being simply solid water; and we must now learn that, when it is hot enough, water becomes a gas just like air. Indeed, the air contains a quantity of gaseous water, or water-vapour, as it is known, and when we find the weather close and muggy, as we say, it is usually because there is more of this water-vapour in the air than we like. When water boils, then, the bubbles are bubbles of water-vapour, and if this vapour strikes a cold surface like a cold plate, it becomes liquid or wet again.

One of the things that decides whether anything shall be solid or liquid, or a gas, is heat; and so, of course, the simple answer to the question, What makes the water boil? is *heat*. We apply heat to water and it begins to turn into gas, which makes the bubbles.

If we go on boiling the water, of course we boil it all away as gas, until there is none left. In an ordinary way water always begins to boil when it is at a certain *temperature*, or hotness, and this is called the boiling-point of water. It is not possible in an ordinary way to have wet water any hotter than this point, no matter how much heat you apply to it.

We said "in an ordinary way," because water can be made to boil without being nearly as hot as boiling water usually is. One of the things that decides the boiling-point is the pressure of the air, at the bottom of which we live. If you take water up to the top of a high mountain, where the pressure of air is much less because there is not so much air above you, and if you heat the water, it begins to boil when it is nothing like so hot as it needs to be made before it will boil at the bottom of the mountain. *On the mountain there is less pressure of air squeezing the water, and so it can more easily expand into bubbles of gas.* So, if you put an egg in the water at the top of the mountain, you may boil and boil as long as you please, but you will never boil the egg hard, simply because you can never make the water hot enough to make the egg hard.

SUN · MOON · STARS · FIRE · WIND · WATER · LIFE · MIND · SLEEP

How does a Mussel Build its Shell?

The protecting shell of a mussel is built by a special part of its body called the mantle, and, especially the edge of the mantle. The surface cells at the edge of the mantle have the power of separating the carbonate of lime from the blood of the mollusc, and when the lime is thrown out to the surface it hardens, and takes the form of a shell.

As the mussel grows its mantle grows, too, and the ever widening edge deposits more and more lime as it expands. Any spine, scallop, or irregularity of the shell corresponds with some irregularity of the margin of the mantle. Usually the shell can be divided into three layers, each made of thin plates running in different directions, and the inmost layer usually shines with rainbow colours, and is known as mother-of-pearl. The lime in the mussel's blood was originally in limy rocks, dissolved by rain and rivers, and washed down into the sea.

The mussel is one of the molluscs, and all the molluscs have shells made in the same way out of limy material, though some are microscopic and some weigh hundreds of pounds. The two shells of the bivalve mollusc known as the giant clam sometimes weigh more than 500 pounds.

Is Night Air Bad for us?

There is a general belief that night air is dangerous for us to breathe; but this is nonsense. Night air is purer than day air. Fewer fires and furnaces are burning at night, and so the air in cities contains less carbon dioxide. Also, as there is less traffic, there is less dust in the air at night. We know exactly how the old belief as to night air arose, and the history of it is very interesting.

It was noticed that people who exposed themselves to the night air in certain parts of the world were very apt to get a serious disease which was supposed to be due to the quality of the air. So long ago this disease was called *malaria*, which simply means *bad air*. But we have discovered that malaria is due to the bite of a certain kind of insect which carries the microbes of the disease, and this insect is a kind of mosquito. It only bites at night. There are no mosquitoes of this kind in Britain, and there is no malaria in this country except in the case of people who have brought it from abroad; but they cannot give it to other people, since the mosquito that carries the disease does not exist here.

So far, then, as Britain is concerned, night air is purer and better than day air, and there is nothing to be said against it. Thousands of people are killed by night air even in Britain, but it is the foul night air which they have made in their own bedrooms, and have not allowed to escape. This weakens their bodies in such a way that the microbes of consumption can enter and destroy them.

What causes Cramp?

Cramp is really a spasm or contraction of one or more muscles in a limb, or in the body. It may be very painful, or may be present along with numbness. We have, perhaps, often felt a sudden pain in playing some game or other when we are seized with cramp in a muscle, and this pain has, perhaps, passed off after a little vigorous rubbing. It may also be caused by over-exertion and severe cold, and is often due to some complicated change occurring in the muscle itself.

A sharp rubbing over the surface of the muscle will usually put it right; but if we should be seized with cramp when swimming, it is very dangerous, because we must get to land before the cramp can be treated, and the fact that we have been seized with cramp might prevent us doing so. This is one of the reasons why it is dangerous to stay too long in the water, or to go beyond our depth.

What Makes an Arrow Fly?

The motion of the arrow through the air is a kind of power, and that, like all other power, has to come from somewhere. It was not in the arrow when it was put in the bow; but when the cord was released and pushed the arrow forward the arrow got its power of motion.

The power, then, came from the stretching of the bow; for if the bow were not stretched it would not drive the arrow; and so, if we trace the power backward, we find it came from the strong muscles of the archer who bent the bow. But the question for us is: What happens in the bow when it is stretched? All we can say is that when the cord and the bow are bent out of their normal shape by being stretched, they carry in themselves, ready to act, the power they have got from the muscles of the archer.

Is it a Sign of Rain when the Smoke Blows down the Chimney ?

It may or may not be. If we think about this question for ourselves, we shall see that no one could answer simply Yes or No to it, for so many different things come into it. The travelling of smoke up a chimney and of wind down it are complicated matters.

We may be sure that when the wind blows down the chimney the air is not still, and wind very often brings rain, for wind is moving air, and this air may be full of moisture, which is apt to fall as rain.

But though wind and rain often go together, so that rain is more likely to fall when the smoke is blown down the chimney, yet there are winds which are usually dry, and bring no rain with them. Different chimneys smoke with different winds, and some smoke with all winds, and some with none ; so, plainly, it is impossible to answer this question, except in a general way.

Why can we Hear Better when we Shut our Eyes ?

This question is partly true and partly not true, according to what we mean by hearing, or, rather, according to what it is that we are listening to. If we are listening to music, which requires our attention, and our enjoyment of which depends upon our putting together in our mind what we have just heard with what we are actually hearing at the moment, and also with what we expect to hear a little later, then the fewer things our brain is doing at the time, the better ; and we certainly enjoy the music more with our eyes closed, or with them just fixed vacantly upon nothing.

The only exception to this is when we are listening to music and at the same time reading the score. In such a case the shapes of the phrases, and so on, as they are seen by the eye on a page, help the ear to understand and enjoy the shapes of them as they are heard.

But it is very different when we are, for instance, listening to a tiresome lecture in a stuffy room on a sleepy afternoon. Instead of hearing better when we close our eyes, we shall soon find that we are not hearing at all ! The brain must be more or less awake in order to hear, and where it might otherwise sleep, light pouring into the eyes will help to keep it awake. If we make experiments with bright lights and sharp sounds, we find that either of them helps us to feel the other more intensely if they are going on at the same time.

How can Sound come into a Room through a Wall ?

When a sound wave, travelling in the air, reaches a wall, it communicates itself to the wall, which is thrown into waves of exactly the same shape and number in each second, but of rather smaller size, for a little power is lost in transferring the waves.

The waves travel on through the new medium, as it is called, and then are conveyed by it to the air on the other side of it, just as the head of a drum, when beaten, shakes the air next to it into waves. In this second transference back to air again a certain amount of power is lost, and so the sound is a good deal weakened in passing through the wall.

Of course, the extent of this weakening will depend on the thickness and on the material and structure of the wall. If we have materials like wool or sawdust or heavy curtain-hangings, which vibrate very badly, they will absorb most of the sound wave, and it will become faint.

Could the Sky Fall Down ?

The sky could not fall down because there is really no such thing as what we call the sky. It often appears to us as if we lived inside a great bowl turned upside down ; the Sun, the Moon, and the stars seem to be fixed in that bowl and to be moved round as it moves. In all ages men have had this idea, and we refer to it in such a phrase as " the heavenly sphere."

But when the movements of the heavenly bodies were more carefully studied, it was supposed that there were more spheres than one at different distances from us. In our cloudy climate we cannot get so clear an idea of the sky in the form of a great sphere as it appears to men in other parts of the world.

If the sky were made like a great dome we should indeed wonder what keeps it up. But what we see is only light reflected from the air and the dust in the air of our own Earth. The blue looks very far away, but from forty to sixty miles, at the very outside, is the greatest distance from which the light is reflected by the air and dust to our eyes ; and it is the effect of this reflection that we call the sky.

Why Can We Hear the Scratching of a Pin at the Other End of a Pole?

Sound is made of waves in matter, waves of a certain kind and rate which our ears can hear. Any kind of matter may be thrown into these waves, and so may convey sound. The thing that conveys the sound, and in which the waves are, is called the medium, which really means the *thing in between*.

By far the commonest medium for sound in our case is the air. In the case of fishes, of course, it is the water. But many solid things convey sound-waves extremely well, and when we scratch one end of a long pole with a pin the matter of which the pole is made is thrown into a series of waves, that go on as long as the pin continues to move, and that we can readily hear through our ear, or perhaps even by merely putting our end of the pole against the side of our head or against our teeth; but the ear is best because it contains special arrangements for conveying sound-waves to the real ear inside our head much better than the bones of the skull do.

We have all heard stories of how Red Indians can hear sounds at great distances by putting their ears to the ground, and this shows us that the Earth may convey sound-waves—that is to say, waves which our ears can feel and appreciate as sounds —just as well as air, or water, or a pole.

Why do Our Eyes Sparkle when We are Merry?

People are not at all agreed as to what really happens when they say that some-one's eyes are " sparkling." We all know that something happens in the eyes of people when they are delighted, and we know that it looks as if they shone, or something shone through them or from their surface. But if we watch very carefully, whenever our friends give us a chance, we shall find that there is more to notice than we thought.

Probably it is not the eye at all, in itself, but the eyelid that makes the difference. When we express merriment, the chances are very great that, whatever things look like, the effect is really obtained by the moving of some muscle or other.

In this case, people who have watched carefully declare that the eyelids make little, quick, lively movements, which attract the attention to the eye. Every time the eyelid falls it brushes a fresh tear over the eyeball, so that the surface of it is kept supplied with an unusual amount of fluid, and glistens for just the same reason that it glistens when we cry. But it is the eyelid that makes the difference, and this really causes the sparkling.

Does it Take More Power to Stop a Train than to Start it?

We might extend this question by asking why it takes more power to stop the train the faster it is going. We find, indeed, that the power required to stop the train depends on the mass of the train, and on its speed. The greater these are, the greater is the power in the train, and the greater will be the power that is required to stop it, for this must be exactly equal to the power in the train.

When a train is at rest, the power required to start it depends simply on the weight, or, to use the best word, the mass, of the train. We all know that it takes more effort to move a heavy thing than a light one. We know, too, that it is one matter to let a heavy thing rest on the foot, and another matter to let it fall on the foot ; and the greater the height it falls from the more it hurts. That is because the greater the height the faster it is moving when it strikes the foot.

Such a case teaches us that movement adds power to anything ; and that is so, for movement is itself a form of power. More than that, the greater the weight of the moving mass, the greater is the power required to move it, and therefore the greater is the power required to stop it.

Is it Bad to Sleep with the Moon Shining on Us?

It is not bad to sleep with the Moon shining on us, but it is very bad to believe nonsense. Every night the Moon shines, millions of animals sleep with it shining on them, and if anyone fancies that it is bad for human beings to sleep out of doors, whether the Moon is shining or not, he makes a great mistake.

All notions of this kind are really remnants of the old astrology, which ascribed all sorts of influences to the heavenly bodies, and thought that lunacy —the word comes from the Latin *luna*, meaning the Moon—was caused by the Moon. Moonlight is only reflected sunlight, and, though it is very feeble in proportion to its brilliance, it has its value, just as sunlight has.

Are We Healthier than Our Ancestors ?

Certainly we are far healthier. The death-rate has been falling all over the British Isles for many years.

We know at what ages our ancestors commonly died—even those who had most wealth and knowledge. We know that, long ago, the children of our kings and queens died at much the same rate as the children of the slums do nowadays. We know that hideous diseases once raged in Britain but are now unknown, or very rare here. Last century, for instance, typhus fever was very common, and now it hardly causes ten deaths in the whole of Britain in a year, though the disease is still sadly common on the Continent.

Nothing is more stupid than to talk of the " good old days," as if everyone had been happy, and wise, and strong, long ago. The more we learn of those " good old days," the more we learn how bad they were, and how much better off we are.

Why is Our Right Hand Stronger than Our Left ?

It is quite certain that the difference in *strength* between our hands is not natural, in the sense of being a thing decided from our birth, but is the result of the different treatment that our two hands have received since.

Difference in *skill* is another matter. There is a simple instrument, meant to be squeezed in the hand, which measures the strength of the grip of the two hands, and it shows that the right hand is considerably stronger in right-handed people and the left hand in left-handed people. So that we should really have added to our question the words " if we are right-handed." These differences between the hands do not exist if we use the two hands equally. Some children are very carefully looked after, to see that they become what is called *ambidextrous*, using both hands alike, and their hands are equally strong.

We see, then, that it makes a great deal of difference to our muscles how much they are exercised. There is no doubt that the difference in the strength of the two hands depends on the size of the muscles, for a tape measure put round the two forearms, or even a pair of gloves put on, will often show the difference that use or exercise has made.

It is true of every part and every power of our bodies that they can be improved by use. On the other hand, it is no less certain that, for every part and power of the body or the mind of everyone, there is a limit which, if we are wise and careful, we may reach, but cannot pass.

How Can Thin Iron Ropes and Rods Support a Suspension Bridge ?

In the first place, it very much depends upon the kind of iron. No one could trust very much to a suspension bridge made of any ordinary kind of iron. But if we dissolve certain things like carbon or tungsten in molten iron, the iron when it cools is a different kind of metal, which we call steel. Steel is vastly stronger than iron, and special steels are used in making such structures as a suspension bridge.

Why steel, or iron containing tungsten, vanadium, or carbon is so much stronger than mere iron by itself was something of a mystery until a few years ago, when scientists succeeded in taking photographs with X-rays which showed the actual arrangement of the atoms in the tiny crystals of which the mass of metal is composed. These crystal-pattern photographs brought about immense progress in the making of steels and other alloys. Today they can be made stronger than ever before, so that their great tensile strength, as it is called, makes it possible for comparatively thin wires to support enormous weights.

Which Side of the Cloud is the Thunder On ?

Thunder is the noise, an irregular wave in the air. Its cause is the very sudden heating of the air, high up above our heads, by the quick passage of electricity through it from cloud to cloud, or from a cloud to the Earth. Air offers great resistance to the passage of electricity through it, and when anything resists the passage of electricity that thing becomes hot. If it becomes hot, it expands suddenly, and so it starts the air wave we call thunder. A sound—and the same is true of a light made at any place—spreads out, if it can, quite equally in every direction.

So the sound of the thunder spreads upward from the clouds, and sideways through the air and through the clouds themselves. The part we hear is the part that reaches our ears, part of the wave that spreads downward from the place where the electricity passed and started it.

Does a Hen Know that Chickens will Come Out of Her Eggs?

One of the greatest of facts in the animal world is what is called instinct, and the mighty difference between our minds and those of the lower animals is that in us instinct has become largely changed into a much more wonderful thing which we call intelligence. One of the most important facts about an instinct is that the animal goes through the action without knowing what its purpose is, and what will come of it. If an animal could foresee the consequences of its acts, then it would be a reasoning and intelligent being, worthy to rank beside ourselves.

This is true of all instincts, that the action is done because something within the creature impels it to perform that action, but with no knowledge of its use and purpose. Thus, when a baby instinctively sucks from a bottle it does not know that the object of doing so is to supply itself with material and power for its life.

It may possibly be that in some cases an animal of the highest type, such as a dog, may notice, after a number of times, that certain consequences follow upon its instinctive actions, and so it may get to know what will happen, just as we do after a time when we exercise our instincts.

But it is very unlikely that the hen, whether it be the first time or the twentieth time that she sits, has any idea except simply that things like eggs are very good to sit on. This is true, even though she is glad to see the chickens when they come.

What Makes a Watch Go?

The great law about power and energy, to which we so often have to refer, gives us the answer to this question. The spring of a watch is a piece of tightly coiled steel which tries hard to become uncoiled. This effort by the spring to become uncoiled and free is due to the very springy nature of the steel of which the spring is made. As long as it has the power to uncoil itself, it can be made to drive the wheels of the watch. After a time the watch stops, because the spring has freed itself and has no more power. It has spent itself in moving the hands of the watch and in overcoming the friction of the little cog wheels and their spindles in the bearings.

As no power can come from nothing, every clock or watch that is driven by a spring must, sooner or later, have fresh power put into it from without.

The power was put into the spring when the watch was wound up. We coiled up the spring tightly again by using the force of our muscles, force obtained from food, which in its turn, obtained the force from the Sun. So the Sun really drives the watch! When we wind a watch, we feel that we are pressing against something; and the first turn needs little effort, but the last turns need more. What we are doing is simply coiling a steel spring tightly. It is made to uncoil itself in a regular way with the help of what is called a balance wheel, which gives to the wheels of the watch *at a regular rate* the power we have stored up in the spring.

Why does a Stick Make a Noise when Swung in the Air?

All kinds of noises, however different from each other, and all kinds of musical notes, high or low, full or thin, are really of the same nature in the chief respect that they all consist of waves of a certain kind, produced in the air as a rule, though they may be produced also in solids or in liquids. These sound waves are of a special kind, and consist of a swinging to and fro of the tiny particles of whatever medium is carrying the sound—air, or water, or rock, and so on.

If air were not elastic it could not carry such waves, for the parts of the air pushed forward by anything would not swing back again, and so there would be no sound waves produced. Therefore, if we want to interfere with the travelling of sound, we use wood, or cotton-wool, or sawdust, and these things, not being very elastic, damp down the sound waves.

Not until we know what sound is can we hope to understand the answer to this question, but when we have learned the main facts about sound, the answer is easy. Thus, elastic air is disturbed when a stick is swung through it, for countless millions of atoms of the gases that make up the air are quickly moved aside to make room for the stick.

They strike the atoms next them, and, being elastic, they rebound. The atoms struck do the same, and for a little while all the atoms of the air are swinging backward or forward, and that motion makes the sound wave which we hear as a humming noise.

A STUDY OF A CHILD, IN THE BASLE MUSEUM

GEORGE GISZE (BERLIN MUSEUM)

BONIFACE AUERBACH, IN THE BASLE MUSEUM

SIR THOMAS GODSALVE AND HIS SON JOHN (DRESDEN GALLERY)

PORTRAIT OF A YOUNG MAN
(VIENNA GALLERY)

HOLBEIN'S PORTRAIT OF HIMSELF, IN THE
BASLE MUSEUM

ROBERT CHESEMAN, FALCONER TO KING HENRY THE EIGHTH, IN THE HAGUE GALLERY

THE MADONNA OF THE BURGOMASTER MEYER (DRESDEN GALLERY)

the artist thinking, learning, experimenting, working in one medium and another, and succeeding in imprinting with his pencil the thought and adventures of the soul whereon he was for ever embarking.

He seems to spend some time of every day in the far land of the spirit. Hence we get the genius that created The Knight and Death, Melancholy, The Repose in Egypt, The Mills, The Adoration of the Magi, and The Four Evangelists—this last the greatest contribution Germany has made to the world's art.

And this man, whose thoughts and imaginations carry him to such a height, is at the same time a very faithful portrait painter. We can see this in the picture of his father in the National Gallery, and in such portraits as the famous Jerome Holzschuher, belonging to Berlin Museum, and The Young Girl in the same collection; in the portrait of Oswolt Krell, The Artist, and A Man, in Munich.

Dürer's most beautiful painting is The Adoration of the Magi, now in the Uffizi, Florence. There is something very delightful in the delicate gradation of tone; the composition, as in all Dürer's work, is faultless. His great masterpiece, The Four Evangelists, in Munich, has a simple grandeur that is almost unrivalled in painting. Were it not for the rather German heads, we should think that a group of Greek statuary had taken to itself colour and pictorial rendering.

DÜRER'S LINES AS FLEXIBLE AS THE STRANDS OF A SPIDER'S WEB

Nuremberg was famous for its wood carving, and perhaps that is why the art of engraving and woodcutting is Dürer's greatest expression of genius. He may be challenged by other painters of other countries, but in his engravings he stands alone. He was a master of line; his heaviest lines are flexible as the strands of a spider's web. His engravings are charged with a wealth of minute detail, and these fit so harmoniously into their place that the picture gives an impression of largeness, of grandeur. Not a buckle, a link of a chain, a nail, not one fold in a garment or one leaf on a branch escaped him. Dürer is an undying reproach and shame to those artists who think they can gain largeness by " scamping " drawing.

When we look at these engravings and cuts we see Dürer working in this way because of his intense love for the medium. Outside influences may have caused him to excel in painting, but he was at home by himself in his engraving.

There is little to stir the heart in the wonderful scenes which he drew on wood and metal. One cannot be sorry for the Melancholy, or the Knight whom Death accompanies; rather one's brain responds to the artist's thought and behind the work one can see the thinker, the man who is engrossed in the problem of life and death, in the eternal why? of human questioning.

HANS HOLBEIN THE ELDER AND HANS HOLBEIN THE GREAT

Hans Holbein, who lived from 1497–1543, was Dürer's companion in greatness, but a man of a very different stamp. He had not the rock-ruggedness of Dürer, and he had a grace which was lacking in the older artist; more, where Dürer was for ever searching and analysing, probing into human destiny, Holbein was a very accomplished looker-on at life and fate.

Holbein began painting at Augsburg under his father, who is only memorable because of his son; but soon left him to travel and work in various towns of Europe. He employed himself in many ways, from working at illuminated manuscripts to painting house fronts. At one time he was in the service of German merchants at the Steelyard in Thames Street, London. Later he became artist to Henry the Eighth, and some of his nobles, his portaits of the king and of Sir Thomas More being among the most famous in the world.

The National Gallery has a masterpiece Holbein painted a year or so before he became attached to the English Court. It is a portrait group, known as The Ambassadors. The portrait of the Duchess of Milan is in the same collection.

THE ONLY GREAT IDEALIST GERMAN ART HAS EVER KNOWN

All Holbein's portraits have his peculiar personal quality. He is very German in the thoroughness of his attention to detail, as we can see from the numerous " properties " in a portrait like that of the Merchant Gisze, belonging to Berlin Museum; he is distinctly un-German—a little French, perhaps—in his elegance. He read the very inmost soul of all the people he was painting, and showed in his canvases their coarseness and greed and

meanness, their virtues and lovable-
nesses, and these qualities he invested with
a curious dignity and nobility that was
Holbein's, not the sitter's.

Holbein's strength was that he picked
out the essentials in his work. All the
details of his portrait groups are chosen,
not to fill up spaces, but to cast a light
on the surroundings, the nationality, the
character of the persons painted. This
artist, who was such a gifted observer, had
seen a great deal of Flemish and Italian
art; and when his innate genius most
shows itself is in his power of making his
own the best of what he sees, and walking
away from the rest.

The pictures he saw made him more
certain of his own instinct—that two or
three colours used in the right way produce
a greater effect than a rainbow-plenty;
that restraint and economy with light gave

A number of Holbein's pictures other
than portraits are in existence—notably
his famous group in Darmstadt Castle,
where the Virgin and Child are painted
as guests in the Burgomaster's family.
Another drawing of the wife of this
burgomaster is in the Basle Museum, and
makes us understand people who say that,
great as Holbein was with his brush, he
was greater with his pencil. In another
person's hands the drawing would be a
sketch; in Holbein's it is a finished study.
There is another of these lovely drawings,
in red chalk, in Windsor Castle.

Holbein's genius was really divided
between his portraits and his engravings.
The fame of his engraving work he shares
with Dürer; as portrait painter he stands
isolated in his country's story.

After Holbein came a few lesser men
who for the most part imitated Italian art,

SAINT GEORGE AND THE DRAGON, AND A KNIGHT AND A LADY—TWO DRAWINGS BY ALBERT DÜRER

to a dark-toned picture a greater sense of
clarity than was possible in a painting
which was all high tones and radiance.

To such a pitch did Holbein carry his
efforts toward strength and restraint that
in his finest portraits it seems the light
and the colour are not laid on with a brush,
but live inside the people painted, are part
of their physical and mental being.

and killed what there was in themselves of
native worth. Then the religious wars
swept over Germany, wiping out culture
and art; and it would appear that from
the submersion the country has never since
recovered. A number of artists there have
been, but they only climbed the flanks of
the mountain on whose peak Dürer and
Holbein lived and do still live.

OURSELVES

The Wonderful House We Live In, and Our Place in the World

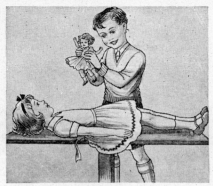

The first picture shows a child balanced on a see-saw looking at a doll ; the second shows
how more blood goes to her brain and her head sinks when she thinks or works out a sum

THE HEART AND WHAT IT DOES

WE find in the bodies of all the higher animals a wonderful pump, which we call the heart. It is of different kinds in different orders of animals, but in all main points the heart of all the animals that have red blood is one and the same.

We know that it beats during life, for we can feel it beating in ourselves if we have been running very hard, or if we are frightened; and if we pick up a kitten or a bird we can feel its heart beating under our fingers. It is a most astonishing thing that, though as much as this was known for thousands of years, it was not until the seventeenth century that men discovered what the heart really does and how the blood moves. Here we consider what it was that William Harvey discovered about the tireless working of the heart.

The microscope in Harvey's time was not powerful enough to enable him to see the tiny channels by which the blood passes between the large vessels that leave the heart and the large vessels that go back to the heart. He died in 1657, and four years later a great Italian, the fortunate possessor of a new and more powerful microscope, was able to discern in the lungs of the frog the tiny vessels

Harvey had to die without seeing, though they completed the proof of his discovery.

These little vessels are so small that they are almost like hairs, and so they are called *capillaries*, from the Latin word for the hair of the head. The large vessels which leave the heart are called arteries, and those which carry the blood back to it are called veins.

The circulation of the blood, discovered by William Harvey, is a central fact of the body's working; and we must learn to understand it. Let us begin by looking at the heart itself.

The heart is really a pump. Its walls are made of muscle, and it is certainly the most important of all the muscles in the body. Day and night it ceaselessly beats so long as we are alive. If it stops or falters for only a short time, we faint and fall to the ground. Its work is harder in human beings than in any other living creature, for the part of the body which always most urgently needs blood is the brain, and in us, as we stand erect, the brain is above the heart instead of in front of it, so that the blood has to be pumped upward by the heart. Also, the heart has to beat so strongly as to send the blood down our legs with such force

BODY, MIND, AND SOUL · CITIZENSHIP · ECONOMICS · GOVERNMENT

that it will come up them again through the veins. It is the warm blood that keeps the feet warm, as they produce very little heat for themselves.

The heart lies in the upper half of the body, which we call the chest, and the chest is bounded by the long, thin bones we call ribs. Some people have a curious way of thinking that the chest is only the front of the body; but, of course, the chest is in the whole of the upper half of the trunk, and has a back as well as a front. The organs it contains it are very simple to remember—a lung on each side and the heart between them.

We usually think of the heart as on the left side of the body, but actually, about one-third of it lies on the right side and two-thirds on the left. If you put your hand on the front of your chest—it is best to use your right hand—then with the tips of your fingers you can usually feel your heart beating, especially if you have been running hard, or are frightened or angry. You feel something coming up and bumping against your fingers about eighty times a minute. From seventy to eighty is the rate in grown-up people; it is rather slower in men than in women. But if you happen to be a small child your heart beats much more quickly, and in a new-born baby it beats about twice every second. When we are feverish it beats more quickly.

Where the Heart is

If you put the fingers of one hand on your wrist you will feel something beating there, too. This is called the pulse.

If, while you have one hand placed on your heart you put the thumb of the other on the wrist of the first hand, you will find that the number of beats in both cases is the same; but you will also notice that the beat at the wrist always comes a very short time after the beat of the heart. It is the beating of the heart that makes the pulse, for it means that the heart is sending a wave of blood through the arteries, and as the blood takes a little time to travel the beat at the wrist must be a little later than the beat at the heart itself.

We usually call the pulse at the wrist *the* pulse, but every time the heart beats it sends the blood through all the arteries, and there are several other places where we can notice a pulse. You may find for yourself one pulse which we have all noticed, though perhaps we did not know what it meant. If you cross your legs and watch the crossed foot, you will see that it gives a little jerk up and down. If at the same time you feel the pulse at your wrist, you will find that the two rates are the same, but your foot always jerks a little later than the wrist pulse.

That little kick is due to the fact that the great artery of the leg runs down the middle of the back of the knee in a beautifully protected fashion; and when you cross your legs you press the artery against the hard bone of the other knee, so that every time the artery swells with the pulse of blood in it the leg gives a jerk.

Now let us consider the veins themselves. These are tubes very like the arteries, but much thinner, for the pressure of blood inside them is not nearly so high as in the arteries. Many of the veins lie on the surface of the body just under the skin, so that we can see them.

As we have said, the blood in them is running back to the heart. There is no pulse in the veins, because, before the blood has reached them, it has had to pass through the tiny tubes which are the communication between arteries and veins, and there the pulse gets less noticeable, so that the blood flows upward quite evenly through the veins.

The time may come to any one of us when there is an accident to ourselves or to someone else. An artery or a vein is cut, and the person bleeds. Now, the blood is very precious, and no one can afford to lose it. Therefore, our duty is to stop bleeding whenever we see it. It may happen to anyone who has a little bravery and a little knowledge to save a life in this way. Here are the rules.

The first does not depend on any knowledge of the circulation, and is as simple as can be. Let us suppose a stone has been thrown, and someone's face has been cut. There is a handkerchief at hand, of course, and when that is dabbed on and taken away you can usually see some point where the blood is oozing out. Press the handkerchief firmly on that point with your finger, and keep it there. Once your finger is put on, there is no danger, and everyone has time to think. A doctor can be brought or the wounded person can go to a doctor; but the first rule is to keep pressing on the point from which the blood is oozing.

The other rules depend on our knowledge of the circulation of the blood. Let us take a common instance. There are quite large veins on the surface of the leg and sometimes they get stretched and swollen and weak. One of them may even give way altogether, and the blood may begin to ooze through the skin. Where there is no help at hand, a person may bleed to death in consequence of this little accident. Of course, anyone who knew the rule about pressing firmly on the bleeding point, and who kept his head, would always save himself, but then some people do not learn these little rules. They are so busy learning names of kings, or battles, that they have not much time to learn how to save lives.

But when that rule has been followed, what else can be done? What we do will depend on our knowledge of the circulation. The blood in this broken vein in the leg is flowing up toward the heart. Therefore, we must apply pressure, let us say, with a handkerchief *below* the bleeding point.

Veins have valves in them, which are so arranged as to prevent the blood from flowing back through them; but it is sometimes necessary to apply the pressure both above and below the bleeding point, for sometimes the valves give way Also,

the valves in our veins are not arranged in the best way for a creature walking erect; they are arranged in the way that would be best for a creature walking on all its four limbs. That is very interesting.

But now let us suppose that there has been an accident, and someone is bleeding in a different way. Let us suppose that the blood is brighter, and that instead of oozing out, it comes in jets or spurts. This means that an artery is bleeding, and though in any case we press firmly on the bleeding point, the next thing to be done is different, for the blood is coming from the centre, and not going back toward it, so we must apply our bandage above the bleeding point, on the side nearest the heart.

Now let us look at the heart, and see exactly how it does its work. What we call the circulation of the blood is really two circulations, and the two circles meet in the heart. There is, of course, only one continuous stream, but as the blood passes along this stream it really goes through two circles, one large and one small. There is the circulation through the lungs, the use of which we know, and there is the circulation through the body, the use of which we also know. The heart, then, is really two pumps. It has a left side and a right; the left side gets the pure blood from the lungs and sends it to the body; the right side gets the impure blood from the body and sends it to the lungs.

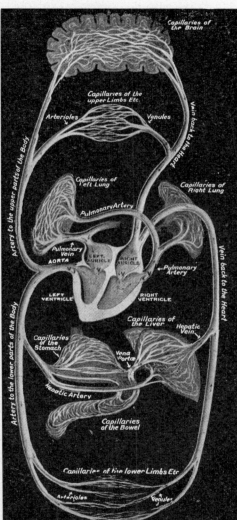

HOW THE BLOOD CIRCULATES. THIS DIAGRAM SHOWS OUR ORGANS AS SEEN FROM THE BACK

The two sides are made on the same principle, and each consists of two chambers. The upper one, which is the smaller, is called an *auricle*. It receives the blood, and then drives it into the lower chamber, which is much larger and stronger. The auricle has only thin walls, for its work is not hard—it has only to send the blood a very short distance through the valves.

But the *ventricles*, as the larger chambers on each side are called, are different. The right ventricle has to send the impure blood, which the right auricle has received from the body, to the lungs, and as this needs a good deal of force, the right ventricle has a fairly thick muscular coat. But the left ventricle has to send its blood through the entire body —brain and toes and all, and so its walls are exceedingly thick and its power is tremendous. It is much the bulkiest part of the heart, and the tip of the heart, which you feel when you put your finger on your chest, is the tip of the left ventricle.

THE WAY IN WHICH A DROP OF BLOOD FLOWS THROUGH YOUR VEINS

Let us imagine that we could watch it, and let us take a drop of pure blood that has entered the left auricle. The auricle squeezes it, like a fist squeezing something in it, and drives it into the left ventricle. When the ventricle is stretched and full, it replies by squeezing in the same way, and drives the blood through the largest artery in the body, called the aorta, so that it goes to nourish every part.

Perhaps the drop of blood we are watching stays in the aorta until the openings of many of the first branches of it are passed, and runs down the branch which goes to the left leg, nourishes the life of the cells at the base of a toe-nail, and then begins its journey back through the veins.

But now, of course, it is dark and impure. It does not go straight to the lungs, for the force with which it was sent from the heart is now nearly exhausted; it goes back to the heart itself and so completes the larger circle of the circulation. It passes up in a great vein which opens into the right auricle. When the auricle is full it contracts, and beats and sends the blood into the right ventricle. This contracts in its turn, and sends the blood to the lungs. It comes back from the lungs, pure and bright, by vessels which open into the left auricle—and that is where we began.

We must not suppose that all the purifying of the blood is done in the lungs. Many waste matters are filtered out of it as it passes through the skin and the kidneys; also, as it passes through the body, it gets fresh food material, so that the blood which comes back to the right auricle from the body is in some respects better than the blood which left the left ventricle. Only it is much worse in respect of its gases, and that is why it has to be sent to the lungs.

THE LITTLE NERVE CELLS THAT START THE HEART'S BEAT

In asking ourselves how and why the heart is made to beat, we must think of it as a great muscle, very complicated, and very different from any other muscle in the body; but still a muscle. Now, muscles are not masters, but servants; they are made of living cells, which contract; but they never contract of themselves. Every kind of muscular tissue in the body is the servant of nerves, and does what it is told. It contracts only when a nerve orders it to do so.

We find in the heart a large number of nerve cells, and it is these that really start the heart's beat. They are very sensitive, and quickly affected by almost every possible influence. Heat affects them very much, and the heart beats more quickly when we are hot; then all sorts of strange things in the blood affect them, such as alcohol. Some make the heart beat more quickly, some more slowly, and smoking may occasionally make it beat irregularly.

The nervous government of the heart and its beating is very wonderful. After all, the whole of the body really exists for the sake of the brain, and if the brain could not control the heart, things would soon go wrong. For instance, the work required to send enough blood to the brain when we are standing upright is harder than when we are lying flat. It is therefore necessary that the heart should beat more forcibly when we stand or sit than when we lie, and so it does—by the brain giving orders.

THE TWO SETS OF NERVES THAT RUN FROM THE BRAIN TO THE HEART

So we find that two sets of nerves run from the brain to the heart. For convenience we may call them two nerves. These control the nerve cells that belong to the heart itself When an order is sent down through one of these nerves the heart beats more strongly and quickly; when an order is sent down through the other, it beats less strongly and less quickly. From moment to moment, throughout the whole of our lives, the brain is thus able to control the beating of the heart. We know the exact position of the cells that do this work.

There is another important fact about the circulation which teaches us how marvellously the brain controls the body. If we examine the wall of an artery we find it beautifully and wonderfully made.

It has a firm outer coat and a smooth inner coat; and between these two there are a great number of elastic fibres, so that the artery can be stretched when the heart sends a pulse of blood through it, and can then spring back to its former size. But there is also a great quantity of muscular tissue in the wall of every artery. Every fibre of this muscular tissue in the arteries of the body is governed by nerves, and acts on the orders which nerves send; and all these nerves spring from, and carry messages from, a small group of cells in the brain lying quite close to the cells that govern the heart.

HOW THE BRAIN REGULATES THE SUPPLY OF BLOOD TO THE BODY

Now, the extent to which the muscular tissue of an artery is contracted decides its size, and this decides the quantity of blood that will go to the part of the body which the artery supplies; there is not a single part of the body that has not its supply of blood regulated by the brain. When we examine it further we find that, as in the case of the heart, there are two sets of nerves—one to carry messages ordering the blood-vessels to contract, the other to carry messages to relax.

In almost every part of the body these changes are going on as they are needed. Usually a message is sent by the part of the body in question up to the brain— perhaps a message for more blood, and perhaps a message for less blood. When we go out on a very cold day, the nose needs a large quantity of blood in order to warm the cold air that passes through it on its way to the lungs. It sends a message to the brain, and the blood-vessels in the lining of the nose are all ordered to relax, so that large quantities of warm blood rush quickly through the nose, and warm the air we breathe. Sometimes the message may be of a different kind, and perhaps it may be impossible to see its use. For instance, in the act of blushing, a message is sent from the brain to the arteries which supply the face and neck, so that they become relaxed, and a flood of blood surges through the skin.

What we must remember is that, though the body is a machine, it is a living machine commanded by life. Hardly anything is more wonderful than the circulation of the blood with its power of adapting itself to every need of the body.

AN EXPERIMENT TO PROVE WHAT IT IS THAT HAPPENS WHEN WE THINK

When we think, the brain requires more blood. Suppose we take a child and lay her flat on a delicately balanced table, and place her so that the table lies quite flat and not tilted up at either end. Then, when we have got this right, let us give her a difficult sum to do in her head. No sooner has she begun to work it out than the end of the table where her head is begins to fall. The reason is that the blood has become heavier and weighs down that end of the table.

There is another thing we must clearly understand about the circulation. We have got the idea of the blood streaming round in a system of closed tubes; but if the walls of the tubes let nothing through them the circulation would be of no use, and we have already learned that they let gases through. The arteries themselves are too thick for this, and so are the veins. It is the tiny tubes, or capillaries, consisting of only a single layer of very thin cells, that allow gases to pass in and out of the blood.

THE WASTE OF THE BODY THAT GOES AWAY THROUGH LITTLE TUBES

That is what happens in the lungs. But throughout all the rest of the body, while carbon dioxide is passing inward through the capillaries from the tissues, all sorts of food supplies are soaking out through the walls of the capillaries into the tissues for them to live on, while all sorts of poisonous things which the tissues have been making soak back into the capillaries, and are carried through the veins to the heart. But the opposite happens when the blood visits the kidneys, for thousands of capillaries in the kidneys are specially arranged close to little tubes lined with special cells that have the power of picking out all these waste products from the blood, and so getting rid of them.

FOOD FROM THE GREAT DESERT SPACES

LUTHER BURBANK SHOWS TO SOME FRIENDS THE SPINELESS CACTUS HE HAS CULTIVATED, THUS GIVING TO
THE WORLD A NEW AND VALUABLE CATTLE FOOD

The Story of the Marvellous Plants that Cover the Earth

The crab-apple and what it has become

HOW PLANTS CAME TO BE

WE look out on the world around us, with its myriads of flowering plants; its pine forests and groves of coco-palms; its club-mosses, ferns, and horsetails; its mosses and liverworts ; its toadstools, moulds, and microbes; its seaweeds and simple single-celled diatoms ; and its quaint double-plants, the lichens ; and we are bound to ask how the world of things has come to be as it is.

The first part of the answer we have seen. It is very likely that the first plants were free-swimmers in a universal or almost universal sea.

Then fixed seaweeds arose in shallow water ; and from the seaweeds, more or less directly, as the dry land rose out of the water, there emerged land plants. From simple forms there also arose the ancient ferns, with mosses on a side-track ; and from the great fern alliance there were derived conifers and cycads and, eventually, the ordinary flowering plants which gladden our eyes today.

There has been a gradual ascent, the simpler plants giving rise to the more complex. The present is the child of the past, and the parent of the future. This is what is meant by saying that the plant world of today has *evolved* from a simpler plant world of the day before yesterday, so to speak ; that again from a simpler

vegetation of a million years ago ; and so on backward and backward, till we come to the mist of life's beginnings, in regard to which we know almost nothing.

But on the top of the first question comes a second. If the present-day flora evolved from an older and simpler flora, how did it do it ? What are the factors at work in evolution?

Everyone knows the crab-apple by the wayside, with its very beautiful flowers and its very sour fruit. Now, it seems that this wild apple is the ancestor of all the cultivated apples of the orchard, just as the wild rock dove is the ancestor of all the domesticated pigeons in the dove-cot. It is not that good soil and comfortable shelter directly changed the crab-apple into a golden pippin ; it is rather that the crab-apple, under cultivation, has produced promising new departures or novelties that man has fostered and established as races of cultivated apples. Man did not change a wolf into a domestic dog in some magical way by taming and teaching ; it is probable that he took advantage of docile and kindly wolf-cubs to which more or less captive wolves had given birth.

But, to be honest, we must confess that we do not know how our ancestors were able to domesticate so many useful animals, or to cultivate so many useful plants. The gleam of light we have on these achievements is just this—that living creatures are very changeful, not so much in themselves as in their offspring, and these new departures, or novelties, or freaks, or sports, or variations—what a lot of names they have !—are the raw material out of which have been sifted new races. In wild Nature the sifting is what we call the Struggle for Existence; but when man came upon the stage, he became the maker and holder of the sieve.

THE BIG FAMILY OF THE WILD CABBAGE OF THE SEASHORE

The wild cabbage of the seashore sported, and he gave food and shelter to those sports that seemed to him promising. More sports followed, and he sifted again. So we have cabbages and cauliflowers, Brussels sprouts, and more besides—all evolved from the wild cabbage.

In some cases, like the apple, the cabbage, and the wheat, we are reasonably certain of the wild ancestors of our cultivated plants ; but in most cases the origin and history of our garden flowers, fruits, and vegetables remain obscure. We may know in a general way where they came from, but we cannot tell the precise story. It was not till lately that the wild wheat was discovered. Most of the important cultivations began very long ago, and the clue has been lost.

But this does not matter very much as far as concerns the general question— how things came to be as they are. For the process of change continues briskly still, and we have only to visit a flower-show to see how many novelties are always being produced.

THE RACE OF ORANGE TREES WITH SEEDLESS FRUITS

The orange growers and marmalade makers decide that it would be a good thing to have a seedless orange, and after a few years of patient care they have what they want. How is it done? Those orange trees which showed a tendency to produce fruit with few seeds were selected ; cuttings were taken which grew into trees, and again there was a sifting out of those which showed fewest seeds in their fruit. The process was then continued until there arose a race of orange trees with delicious seedless fruits. In wild Nature this race would im-

mediately perish just because there are no seeds ; but man propagates the orange trees by cuttings, and under his shield the race prospers. In other cases, like wheat, man separates the seed of individual good plants, and cultivates these till he has large numbers ; or, again, he may dust the pollen from one good plant on to the pistil of another which is equally promising in another direction.

In our own day there are many botanical magicians in progressive countries all over the world. They would be the last to allow the word magician to be used about them, for what they always do, like other practical evolutionists, is simply to take advantage of promising novelties that Nature puts into their hands and to breed from them.

Of course, there must be a keen eye to detect their first appearance. The novelty of promise is bred from, and sheltered from the possibility of being crossed by commonplace relatives ; similar forms are paired together so that the new race becomes *inbred*, as we say ; " rogues " and " throwbacks " and other undesirables are got rid of, and so a new race is started.

THE FREAK OF NATURE THAT GAVE US THE STONELESS PLUM

A world-famous American cultivator, Luther Burbank, reared the stoneless plum. In the centre of the juicy fruit there is, as usual, a kernel or seed, but it is naked. By some freak, which naturalists call a *mutation*, trees showed fruits in which the hard stone was suppressed. just as sometimes cats may have kittens without tails ; and Burbank encouraged this new departure. *He fixed a freak.*

Another success was a cross between the bramble and the raspberry, which yielded the Phenomenal berry. This is so fixed and stable that it breeds true from seed, whereas some of the bramble-crosses can only be propagated by cuttings and layers. Another good thing was the " primus " berry, a cross between the Californian dewberry and the Siberian raspberry ; it is a good new creation.

The work of Burbank has consisted in setting apart and fostering promising novelties which appeared in Nature's fountain of change, or else in crossing one promising plant with another and then sifting the results of the crossing. It sounds simple, but Professor De Vries, the Dutch botanist who has particularly

TRANSFORMATIONS OF THE PLANT WORLD

THE EVENING PRIMROSE AND THREE OF THE MANY NEW SPECIES PROFESSOR HUGO DE VRIES OBTAINED FROM IT

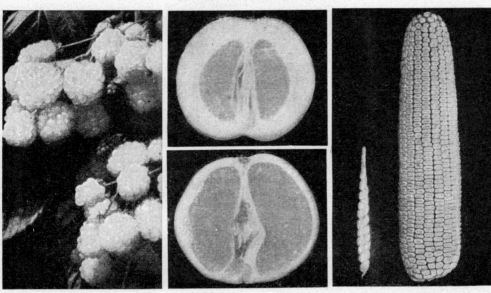

THE WHITE BLACKBERRIES LUTHER BURBANK MADE

HOW LUTHER BURBANK CHANGED THE ORANGE PEEL

WILD MAIZE AND THE CULTIVATED VARIETY

THE WILD CABBAGE AND THE BRUSSELS SPROUT MAN HAS CULTIVATED FROM IT

THE WEAKLY WILD CARROT AND THE HEALTHY CULTIVATED CARROT

studied these changes, calls attention to the amount of work that was often necessary to produce a new race of superlative excellence. Forty thousand blackberry and raspberry hybrids were produced and grown until the fruit matured, and then from all these, a single variety was chosen as best. It is now known under the name of Paradox.

The professor tells us what happened to the others ; it is very interesting :

All the others were uprooted with their crop of ripening berries, heaped up into a pile twelve feet wide, fourteen feet high, and twenty-two feet long, and burned. Nothing remains of that expensive and lengthy experiment, except the one parent-plant of the new variety.

Similar selections have produced the famous plums, the brambles and the blackberries, the Shasta daisy, the peach-almond, the improved blueberries, the hybrid lilies, and the many other valuable fruits and garden flowers that have made the fame of Burbank.

Of course, it must be understood that Luther Burbank is only one of the many evolutionist gardeners who are working hand in hand with Nature in establishing *new creations*.

THE EVENING PRIMROSE AND ITS WONDERFUL OFFSPRING

What is true of plants under cultivation is also true of plants in natural conditions, though it must be admitted that some plants are very stable, as if they had attained to a finely-balanced constitution. It is very likely that Professor De Vries is right in his suggestion that in the history of plants as a whole, and in the history of particular kinds of plants, there are periods of changefulness which alternate with periods of stability. It is very probable, for instance, that a marked change of climate might, in many plants at once, " pull the trigger " of the changefulness which is part of the secret of every living creature.

In a potato-field near Amsterdam, Professor De Vries found an escaped stock of evening primrose, belonging to the kind known to botanists as a native of North America.

The escaped stock was remarkably variable. Almost all its parts varied as if swayed by a restless internal tide.

From this stock De Vries obtained half a dozen or more distinct varieties—*new species in the making*. What was striking about many of the novelties was their separateness from the parent forms—as if they had leaped from one kind to another

suddenly; and a second striking feature was that the new departures bred true; that is to say, they produced offspring like themselves. So De Vries was led to the very important conclusion that "new varieties are produced from existing forms by sudden leaps."

PLANTS THAT CHANGED SUDDENLY FROM THE LIKENESS OF THEIR PARENTS

Darwin thought that the most important changes from generation to generation in living creatures were small changes—a little more of this and a little less of that. From a continuous crop of these little changes, which might be called *fluctuations*, a big change may be brought about in a long time, if the little changes are accumulated from generation to generation, and if the sifting process continues in the same direction.

But the conclusion of De Vries is rather that changes of a striking kind sometimes come about abruptly. Some of the new evening primroses which the Dutch botanist reared from his changeful stock were very different from their parents. Some had few branches instead of many; some had small flowers instead of many; some had quite different leaves. It is certain that very considerable changes may suddenly crop up from generation to generation, and it is likely that many of our cultivated plants arose in this sudden way. Evolution may *leap* as well as creep, for there is no longer any doubt that novel characters may suddenly appear in great perfection, and not linked to their parents by half-way stages.

THE CURIOUS THING THAT HAPPENED IN THE APOTHECARY'S GARDEN

Another striking feature is that when a novelty of this sort comes, it usually comes to stay. It takes grip and reappears generation after generation. In other words, it is very hereditary. Thus, the oak-leaved variety of the greater celandine seems to have appeared suddenly in 1590 in an apothecary's garden in Heidelberg, and it has been breeding true ever since. Its main peculiarity is in having much-cut-up leaves, and this peculiarity is constant whether the plant is multiplied by cuttings or by seeds. Weeping willows and copper beeches illustrate the same kind of sudden change, and the abrupt origin of the new is occasionally seen in the simplest plants of all—the bacteria.

The Story of the Peoples of All Nations and Their Homelands

The soldiers mock Charles the First at his trial

THE TIMES OF THE STUARTS

So secure did James Stuart of Scotland feel about his succession to the English crown that his journey south was a sort of pleasure excursion, taking three or four weeks. A few lords attended him, and they ambled along day after day, through the heart of the quiet country, in the pleasant spring weather, being entertained at fine houses on the southward way to London, his new capital.

Three centuries had passed since the old Hammer of the Scots, Edward the First, had ardently desired that the north and south kingdoms should be united under one ruler, three centuries of constant war. Yet, in spite of all this fighting and killing, the desired union of the crowns did not come about on the battlefield, but peacefully and by request of Parliament, when James the Sixth of Scotland was crowned James the First of England in the old coronation chair, over the old block of stone that the Scots had so hated to lose, within a few feet of Edward's resting-place in the Abbey. For another hundred years the two countries had their own Parliaments and governments; but under the last of the Stuarts the union became complete.

Sir Walter Raleigh shall lead us into the Stuart times, the times when England began to spread beyond her old sea boundary, for he was one of the first to understand the real use of the discoveries of Columbus and Elizabeth's sea captains. James set his heart on finding gold and treasures that could be brought over in ships. What really was needed was for English people to go over the ocean and make new homes in the New World, and found States to be governed by the same laws as at home. Then the settlers, or colonists, must cultivate their new estates and grow food, not only for themselves, but for other parts of the world. It took many years for the nations on the east of the Atlantic to realise the wonderful extent and use of the lands on the west, and nearly all the sixteenth century passed away before they seriously put in claims to share in them.

The first settlers from any country had hard times to bear, and much failure. It was Sir Walter Raleigh who named England's first colony after Queen Elizabeth, Virginia; and James gave it a charter. By this time Spain, Portugal, Holland, France, all had dominions on each side of the Atlantic, and very soon struggles and fights about the new lands arose, which led to nearly two centuries of war among the five greater nations of Europe.

This spreading out of empire across the ocean led to another cause of war. When the ocean became a pathway to

THE FIVE CONTINENTS & 100 NATIONS & RACES THAT INHABIT THEM

the New World, instead of a boundary to the Old, each nation wished to be mistress of the seas, and to have the greatest number of ships upon them, manned by the most daring sailors. They wanted to protect their countrymen as they passed to and fro, whether they were bringing home rich treasures or carrying goods for other countries.

Up to the Second World War, the British had more shipping than any other nation, and had spread out over the world more than any other people. We find the first step toward this great expansion in the days of the Stuarts.

THE BEGINNING OF THE FIGHT BETWEEN THE KING AND THE PEOPLE

James Stuart had even stronger ideas about the rights of kings than the Tudors; he believed not only that as a king he could rule and do as he liked, but that because he was a king he could do no wrong. This ridiculous idea, which he passed on to his sons, caused great trouble in England; and freedom had once more to be fought for.

There is an echo from the early days of James's reign that we hear every year in our streets, which reminds us how real and bitter was the struggle three hundred years ago. We all learn to know the words of the old jingling rhyme :

" Please to remember
The fifth of November,
Gunpowder, treason and plot."

Year by year an ugly Guy Fawkes is carried round the town to be burned in a bonfire at night. This old custom has been kept up in memory of the horror felt when Guy and his friends tried to blow up the king and Parliament by hidden barrels of gunpowder in the cellars under the House of Lords.

THE LITTLE BOAT THAT CARRIED THE PILGRIMS TO AMERICA

Soon after this a new plan was tried in Ireland to bring it into line with the rest of the kingdom. The owners of the land in Ulster were declared to have lost their rights to it by rebelling against England, and were driven out. English and Scottish settlers obtained these lands, and, being thrifty and industrious, they and their descendants have made the north-east corner of Ireland the most prosperous part of the country.

The bitter intolerance of King James was not only seen in his determination to rule in public affairs as if by right Divine, but to regard all opposition as presumption to be severely punished, but it extended to religion. He even declared that he would make his subjects conform to his views of religion or he would "harry them out of the land." And that is what he did to many who were possessed of the most sterling manhood in the nation.

The Puritans of his day were men whom no danger could daunt and no force could bend. Freedom to worship God as their consciences dictated was what they claimed and would have, if not in England, then elsewhere. These were the men who, under pressure from this vain weakling, left their native land and founded the nation that in course of time was to become the mighty American Republic.

Little did James guess how his intolerance would be over-ruled for the world's lasting good. A group of God-fearing men, pledged to find freedom, had withdrawn from the persecutions that James abetted, and had settled at Leyden in Holland, which then was a land of refuge for the oppressed. From thence, in 1620, they set out in a little ship, the Speedwell, to cross the Atlantic and make a home for themselves in the Western world.

THE KING'S MESSENGER BATTERING IN VAIN AT THE DOORS OF PARLIAMENT

At Southampton they met a sister ship, the Mayflower, and the two tiny vessels went down the Channel together to Plymouth. There the Speedwell, which had sprung a leak, stopped, and eventually returned to London with a few of the voyagers, while the rest crossed the stormy Atlantic in the foulest of weather.

That amazing voyage, under the buffetings of the autumn storms, was one of the greatest turning points in the history of mankind. The granite boulder on which the feet of these immortal Pilgrim Fathers first trod when they reached the American shore is still to be seen carefully railed round in front of the Pilgrim Hall in the town of Plymouth in the New World; and the American nation feels it an honour to be descended from that determined, God-fearing band of men and women who left all in the Old World that they might have the freedom denied them at home.

When he died it was his second son, Charles the First, who succeeded him. As soon as Charles began his reign, he showed that he believed even more

THE TROUBLED DAYS OF CHARLES THE FIRST

HENRIETTA MARIA, THE FRENCH WIFE OF CHARLES THE FIRST, WHO URGED ON THE KING
IN HIS FOLLY, HIDES IN A BARN FROM CROMWELL'S MEN

THE CAPTIVE KING CHARLES, WHILE WAITING FOR HIS TRIAL, IS ALLOWED TO SEE HIS CHILDREN
WITH CROMWELL'S SOLDIERS LOOKING ON

strongly than his father that, being a king, he could do no wrong, and was thus above all law. Englishmen had been fighting for hundreds of years to make it certain that the sovereign of the country should rule by law, and Charles's doings roused the nation into steadfast resistance.

Imagine, for instance, this scene. Charles was angry at some remarks made in the House of Commons, and sent his messenger to summon the members to his presence to be rebuked. A great patriot, Eliot, sprang to his feet, and in blazing anger defended the right of free speech in the House. As he spoke the doors were locked, and the king's messenger battered vainly outside, and all the time, amid growing tumult and noise, loud cries of "Aye, aye!" supported Eliot in his claims for English liberty. He finished with words never forgotten :

"None have gone about to break Parliaments but in the end Parliaments have broken them."

BRAVE JOHN HAMPDEN WHO REFUSED TO PAY THE KING'S TAX

Eliot died in prison because he refused to take back his words, and Charles dissolved Parliament and ruled without one for nearly twelve years. During this time he trampled more and more heavily on the liberties of the country, and many people joined the Mayflower emigrants across the sea.

One of the most unjust things Charles did to exasperate the people was to force money from them in ways not allowed by law. John Hampden, a country gentleman (of whom we read on page 526) refused to pay, and went to law with the king about it. The judges decided against him, to their great disgrace; but the resistance of the brave man roused the nation to a still deeper sense of their danger. The growing anger of the people was like the mutterings of a storm, ever getting nearer and louder.

When Parliament was called together again at last, a great leader was found in Pym, who had the splendid gift of being able to speak so well that he could persuade men to do as he wished. The storm was getting louder. Now imagine the king bursting one day into the House of Commons in a rage, demanding that Pym and his friends should be given up to him! That was the burst of the storm. The country rose and armed men to fight—the Parliament and the nation against the king and the nobles.

At first Charles had the best of it. The brave Hampden was killed at one of the first battles, and for a time the Civil War raged, as in the times of the Roses, up and down our fair homeland.

THE COUNTRY GENTLEMAN WHO LEFT HIS FARM TO LEAD THE PEOPLE

Oliver Cromwell, a plain country gentleman in Parliament, now became a brilliant soldier, and raised a model army, one of the finest armies ever seen. He trained and disciplined his men, and fired them with an intense desire to fight for freedom in religion and government. "Trust in God, and keep your powder dry," was his famous advice to them one day when crossing a river. They were able to meet the soldiers of Charles, long used to arms; and later their leader could say with pride, "Truly they never were beaten at all." These brave soldiers were known as the Ironsides.

It was they who turned the tide against Charles. He had to flee from Oxford, and at last fell into the hands of his enemies. His soldiers surrendered or fled; his possessions were captured; he was the poorest, saddest man in the country. He was kept some time at various castles, one being Carisbrooke Castle in the Isle of Wight, where we can still see the green on which he played bowls, and the window from which he tried to escape. A little later he was brought to London.

WHY CROMWELL'S NAME IS NOT LOVED IN IRELAND

Between Charing Cross and Westminster lies a very wide road; the statue of Charles on horseback stands at the Charing Cross end of it. At the other end, included in the present Houses of Parliament, is the famous Westminster Hall built by William Rufus. To this hall, every day for a week, Charles was brought, to be tried for taking away the liberties of the people. He was condemned to death. Halfway down the broad road is the Banqueting Hall of the Palace of Whitehall; outside one of the windows he was beheaded in the sight of his people. His dignity and charm made many people pity him.

For eleven years there was no king in England. It became a free State, in which the power of government rested with the people—a Commonwealth. Both the Parliament and the Army were strong forces

THE PITY AND THE PATHOS OF IT ALL

THE ROYALIST—BY JOHN PETTIE

CHARLES ABOUT TO DIE

THE PURITAN—BY JOHN PETTIE

THE LAST WALK OF CHARLES THE FIRST, FROM ST. JAMES'S PALACE TO WHITEHALL
The window through which the King walked on to the scaffold is still to be seen opposite the Horse Guards

THE BURIAL OF CHARLES STUART AT WINDSOR—FROM THE PICTURE BY ERNEST CROFTS, R.A., NOW
IN BRISTOL ART GALLERY

in these years; but the man who really ruled the country was Oliver Cromwell, the Protector. He was a very strong and determined man, and did his best to make England great by setting things in order at home, and by extending her power abroad. The poet Milton was one of his secretaries.

After the death of Charles both Ireland and Scotland declared for his son, and Cromwell went to Ireland to put down rebellion there. So harsh and cruel were the measures he used, so terrible were the sufferings of the people, that to this day Cromwell's name is hated in Ireland, and the memories of the bitter struggle have never died out.

THE DAY WHEN CHARLES STUART'S SON HID HIMSELF IN A TREE

Charles' son tried to become king after his father's death, but Cromwell was too strong for him, and he was defeated at Worcester. The prince had to cut off his hair and dress in a servant's clothes to escape being taken by Cromwell's men. For six weeks Prince Charles wandered about in great danger, and had many near escapes. One day he hid himself in an oak tree, and actually heard the soldiers talking about how soon they would catch him as they hunted about below him. But he escaped across the Channel, to wait in France for safer times to come.

Some of the greatest names of the Commonwealth are held in remembrance by a plain stone close to the tomb of Henry the Seventh, in Westminster Abbey, but their bodies are no longer there. There was Cromwell himself, with his friends, Ireton, his son-in-law, and Bradshaw, who was not afraid to say these bold words when Cromwell in great anger sent away the Long Parliament : " You mistake, sir, if you think the Parliament dissolved. No power on Earth can dissolve the Parliament but itself ; be sure of that."

THE GREAT OLIVER PASSES OUT IN A GREAT STORM

In the midst of a terrible storm, on the day that Cromwell considered his great day—for he had won two battles on that date—the noble spirit of the Protector passed away from the Earth. He was worn out in mind and body, so hard had been the task to guide the country through these troubled times.

His son Richard was a poor creature, and ruled the country in name only for a few weeks. One April he sat on the throne of England; in May he wandered homeless, his trunk filled with congratulations from the monarchs of Europe. He came home at last to live in lodgings, and lived to be an old man.

There is a story told of a great pageant in which Queen Anne was the central figure. In the throng was an old man wearing the plain dress of a country farmer, and somebody, wondering how such a sight impressed a simple countryman, asked him: "Have you ever seen such a sight before?" "Never since I sat in her chair," said the old man. It was Cromwell's son, who had been all but king himself, and was now forgotten.

Among the men who attracted great public notice during the Commonwealth period was Admiral Blake, the first seaman to have the honour of a grand funeral in Westminster Abbey. Blake fought at sea with great success against the sturdy Dutch, and against the Spaniards, and he also cleared the Mediterranean of pirates so that English trade could spread overseas with safety.

THE STUARTS COME BACK WITH A WORTHLESS KING

With Blake served General Monck, who in Cromwell's later days became the most trusted soldier, and he it was who, after the great Protector's death, took the leading part in bringing back from the continent Charles's pleasure-loving son to rule as Charles the Second.

There had been many troubles during the Commonwealth ; the Puritan party, to which Cromwell and his friends belonged, had been often overbearing and very disagreeable, and the people, forgetting what they had suffered from the Stuarts, hailed the change with joy, thinking all would now go well.

The Puritans, hating pleasure-loving ways and smart clothes, dressed themselves plainly, and cut their hair short. One of the greatest of the Puritans, John Bunyan, spent years in prison during Charles's reign, for his religious opinions While shut up away from his wife and little blind child, he wrote what has been called the most widely-read book in the English language next to the Bible—the Pilgrim's Progress.

King Charles's sympathies were all against the Puritans ; he was a man of loose character. He went as far as he

CROMWELL RIDES THROUGH YORK—FROM THE PAINTING BY ERNEST CROFTS. R.A.

dared in trying to take away rights and liberties from the country, but openly said that he would do nothing that would "send him again on his travels." A very important Act, called the Habeas Corpus Act, was passed in this reign by which no Englishman could ever be kept in prison indefinitely without a trial.

In these times there occurred a great plague, a terrible disease which carried off thousands of men, women, and children. People fell ill so suddenly, and died so quickly, that no one felt safe. It was a wonderful thing that in the year after this plague smote London there broke out the Great Fire, destroying any traces of the plague that might be left behind. The fire spread all over the centre of the city, from the Tower to the Temple Church, in 1666. The tall Monument near London Bridge marks the spot where it broke out. A writer who saw it describes the stones of old St. Paul's Cathedral rattling down and the molten lead running along the streets in a stream, the very pavements glowing with fiery heat. Four hundred streets, over thirteen thousand dwelling houses, and nearly a hundred churches were destroyed. The king and his brother did what they could to stop the progress of the flames by blowing up houses with gunpowder, so making a gap which the fire could not cross. Dreadful as it all was, it really was best for London, for when the Great Fire had swept away the streets in which there had been so

THE COWARD KING JAMES THE FIRST THREATENS TO DRIVE THE PURITANS OUT OF THE LAND

much sickness and misery, a new and healthier city was built, largely through the efforts of Sir Christopher Wren.

England was brought very low about the time of the plague and the fire. All that Elizabeth and Cromwell had tried to do toward making it a power in Europe seemed to be undone by Charles the Second in his dealings with foreign countries. He received a great deal of money from the powerful King of France, Louis the Fourteenth, by promising to help him to secure part of the Netherlands; he even sold him the town of Dunkirk, near Calais, which Cromwell took because it commanded the Channel.

Can you imagine the feelings of the country about this, and also when the war was so mismanaged that the Dutch sailed up the Thames itself and burned our ships in the Medway? After this, for a time, it was the turn of the Dutch to sail proudly up and down the Channel. Presently it was felt that France was getting too strong, and must not be allowed to encroach so much on Holland, and at last peace was made for a while.

All through the times of the Stuarts trade was growing. We have seen how the Flemish weavers in wool helped to establish this trade; and more than once religious persecution in their own country sent away numbers of industrious men with their looms to set up in England, to our great profit. French silk weavers, too, sought refuge here, and started their

HOURS OF DECISION FOR CROMWELL

OLIVER CROMWELL LEAVES PARLIAMENT, ANGERED BECAUSE ITS MEMBERS HAD DISPUTED HIS AUTHORITY

CROMWELL ALONE WITH HIS THOUGHTS AFTER HE HAD REFUSED TO BECOME KING

From the painting by J. Schex, in the Walker Art Gallery, Liverpool

beautiful work, chiefly in the East End of London. We read of Queen Elizabeth being delighted with a great novelty as a present—a pair of woven silk stockings.

In Stuart times, frames for knitting were set up in the towns of Leicester and Nottingham, where now there are thousands of workers in the mills. The linen and calico trades began to employ workers, though most of the cotton brought from abroad was used to make candle-wicks.

In this seventeenth century coal began to be used in houses, chiefly in London, as it could easily come by water from Newcastle. People began to use it also instead of wood to obtain heat for smelting iron. It was feared that before long all the forests would be cut down, for it took two loads of wood to make one load of charcoal, and two loads of charcoal to make one ton of iron.

Birmingham started to be a manufacturing town in that century ; ships were built on a large scale, and at the end of the century England had twice as many ships as at the time of the Armada.

JAMES THE SECOND LOSES HIS THRONE TO WILLIAM OF ORANGE

When Charles the Second died, his sailor brother became king as James the Second. He took money from the French king, as Charles the Second had done, and there were many struggles and tumults, both with the people and the bishops, about the things James did contrary to law, which interfered with the rights of the people. As we look at his heavy face we can understand his want of tact, and his failure in governing his people. In a short time they could stand him no longer, and William of Orange, who had married his eldest daughter Mary, was invited from Holland to take his place.

James's wife, Mary of Modena, fled to France with her baby boy under her cloak, under cover of night, when her husband lost his throne. When the baby grew up his friends called him James the Third, but those who were against him called him the Old Pretender because he claimed to be king. Both he and his son after him, called the Young Pretender, or Bonnie Prince Charlie, made many attempts to get back the throne James had lost, but they failed every time.

A very important Act was passed at the beginning of William and Mary's reign, to make quite clear for the future what power the sovereign of the country should possess. The old principles that we have seen fought for over and over again since the time of John came up once more—that Parliament must make and unmake laws ; that Parliament must settle what taxes are to be paid ; that speech in Parliament must be free.

THE LONG STRUGGLE FOR MASTERY BETWEEN ENGLAND AND FRANCE

The French helped James to make a last stand in Ireland, where William gained the battle of the Boyne, and for nearly ten years fighting went on with France. The Scots were against William for some time, but gave in when they saw it was useless to try to get James or his son back. Mary's sister, Anne, became queen next, and a great war broke out during the same year with France. The old king, Louis the Fourteenth, who had driven out the silk weavers, had bribed Charles the Second and his brother, had helped James the Second and fought William the Third, now wished that his grandson, the King of Spain, should succeed to the French throne ; but, as this would have given too much power in Europe to one man, England, Holland, and most of the German princes united to prevent it.

"Patience will conquer all things," was the Duke of Marlborough's favourite motto, and the victories of this time for which he is famous are among the greatest in our history. They secured that the two crowns of France and Spain should not be united, and that the Stuart Pretender should not be helped any more. England also obtained the right of sending one ship a year to the South Seas.

ENGLAND AND SCOTLAND ARE UNITED AS ONE NATION

In the midst of the war the final union of England and Scotland was completed, to the great gain of both countries ; and the name was henceforth Great Britain. The Scottish National Church and the old Scottish laws were left untouched ; the Parliaments were united, and trade was thrown open. The meeting of the first British Parliament was a grand affair. Each Scottish lord was led to his place by two English lords, and Queen Anne, in her fine robes, made a speech of welcome.

Thus was the white cross of St. Andrew, on a blue ground, added to the red cross of St. George, on a white ground. But the Union Jack was not yet complete.

GREAT SIGHTS OF LONDON

IN THE HEART OF THE CITY : THE ROYAL EXCHANGE IN THE BACKGROUND

LONDON BRIDGE, WITH THE DOME OF ST. PAUL'S HIGH ABOVE THE SURROUNDINGS

THE BRITISH MUSEUM

THE ADMIRALTY ARCH

LONDON UNIVERSITY

HYDE PARK CORNER

ST. THOMAS'S HOSPITAL, FACING THE HOUSES OF PARLIAMENT

SOUTHWARK CATHEDRAL—SAINT SAVIOUR'S CHURCH

NEW SCOTLAND YARD   NUMBER TEN DOWNING STREET   THE TOWER OF LONDON

BUCKINGHAM PALACE   THE ADMIRALTY

TRAFALGAR SQUARE AND THE NELSON COLUMN

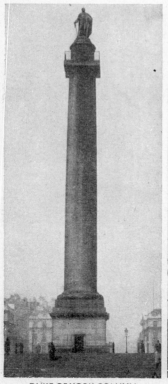

DUKE OF YORK COLUMN   CLEOPATRA'S NEEDLE   THE MONUMENT

THE THAMES EMBANKMENT

THE THAMES BELOW THE TOWER BRIDGE

THE COUNTRY IN LONDON—A CORNER OF KENSINGTON GARDENS

THE LIBRARY, LINCOLN'S INN

THE MARBLE ARCH

INIGO JONES'S WATER GATE, ADELPHI

WHISTLER'S REACH AT CHEYNE WALK, CHELSEA

WATERLOO BRIDGE SEEN FROM VICTORIA EMBANKMENT

THE HOUSES OF PARLIAMENT AND WESTMINSTER BRIDGE

BLACKFRIARS BRIDGE, WITH THE DOME OF ST. PAUL'S TOWERING ABOVE THE CITY ROOFS

THE BYRON STATUE, NEAR
HYDE PARK

DUKE OF WELLINGTON'S STATUE,
HYDE PARK CORNER

CAPTAIN SCOTT MEMORIAL,
WATERLOO PLACE

W. T. STEAD MEMORIAL
ON THE EMBANKMENT

JOHN WESLEY'S STATUE
IN CITY ROAD

THE GRIFFIN AT
TEMPLE BAR

FRANCIS BACON'S STATUE,
GRAY'S INN

THE ALBERT MEMORIAL
IN KENSINGTON GARDENS

MILTON'S STATUE IN
CRIPPLEGATE CHURCHYARD

One Thousand Poems of All Times and All Countries

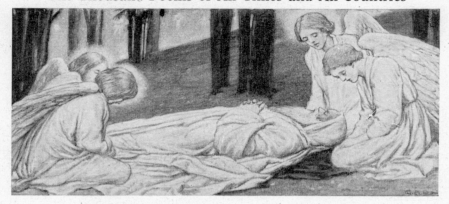

THE BURIAL OF MOSES

Cecil Frances Alexander, who wrote this poem of the burial of Moses, was the wife of Dr. Alexander, Archbishop of Armagh. The poem, so stately in imagination yet simple in wording, will live with Mrs. Alexander's exquisite hymns, such as There is a green hill far away, and Once in royal David's city. Born in 1818, this gentle poet died in 1895.

By Nebo's lonely mountain,
  On this side Jordan's wave,
In a vale in the land of Moab
  There lies a lonely grave.
And no man knows that sepulchre,
  And no man saw it e'er,
For the angels of God upturned the sod
  And laid the dead man there.

That was the grandest funeral
  That ever passed on earth,
But no man heard the trampling,
  Or saw the train go forth—
Noiselessly as the daylight
  Comes back when night is done,
And the crimson streak on ocean's cheek
  Grows into the great sun.

Noiselessly as the Springtime
  Her crown of verdure weaves,
And all the trees on all the hills
  Open their thousand leaves,
So, without sound of music,
  Or voice of them that wept,
Silently down from the mountain's crown
  The great procession swept.

Perchance the bald old eagle
  On grey Beth-peor's height
Out of his lonely eyrie
  Looked on the wondrous sight;
Perchance the lion, stalking,
  Still shuns that hallowed spot,
For beast and bird have seen and heard
  That which man knoweth not.

This was the truest warrior
  That ever buckled sword;
This the most gifted poet
  That ever breathed a word;
And never earth's philosopher
  Traced, with his golden pen,
On the deathless page truths half so sage
  As he wrote down for men.

And has he not high honour,
  The hillside for a pall,
To lie in state while angels wait
  With stars for tapers tall,
And the dark rock-pines, like tossing
  plumes,
  Over his bier to wave,
And God's own hand, in that lonely land,
  To lay him in the grave?

In that strange grave without a name,
  Whence his uncoffined clay
Shall break again, O wondrous thought!
  Before the Judgment Day,
And stand with glory wrapt around
  On the hill he never trod,
And speak of his strife that won our life
  With the incarnate Son of God.

O lonely grave in Moab's land!
  O dark Beth-peor's hill!
Speak to these curious hearts of ours,
  And teach them to be still.
God hath His mysteries of grace,
  Ways that we cannot tell;
He hides them deep, like the hidden sleep
  Of him He loved so well.

POEMS · SONGS · BALLADS · VERSES AND RHYMES WITH MUSIC

THE MORNING OF THE BIRTH OF CHRIST

Early on Christmas Day in 1629 John Milton, a student at Cambridge, 21 years old, sat down to commemorate in verse the birth of Our Lord, and offer his poem as a sacred tribute, comparable with the gifts brought to Bethlehem from afar. His purpose is expressed in the opening lines.

SAY, Heavenly Muse, shall not thy sacred vein
  Afford a present to the Infant God?
Hast thou no verse, no hymn, or solemn strain
    To welcome Him to this His new abode
    Now while the heaven, by the Sun's team untrod,
Hath took no print of the approaching light,
And all the spangled host keep watch in squadrons bright?

See how from far upon the eastern road
    The star-led wizards haste with odours sweet!
Oh run! prevent them with thy humble ode,
    And lay it lowly at His blessed feet;
    Have thou the honour first thy Lord to greet,
And join thy voice unto the Angel Quire,
From out his secret altar touched with hallowed fire.

Then follows the tributary ode which the young poet presented, so establishing his right to be regarded as one of the very great masters of musical English verse.

IT was the winter wild
    While the heaven-born child
All meanly wrapt in the rude manger lies;
    Nature, in awe to Him,
    Had doffed her gaudy trim,
With her great Master so to sympathise;
It was no season then for her
To wanton with the Sun, her lusty paramour.

No war or battle's sound
    Was heard the world around;
The idle spear and shield were high up-hung;
    The hooked chariot stood
    Unstained with hostile blood;
The trumpet spake not to the arméd throng;
And kings sat still with awful eye,
As if they surely knew their sovran Lord was by.

But peaceful was the night
    Wherein the Prince of Light
His reign of peace upon the earth began.

The winds, with wonder whist,
    Smoothly the waters kissed,
Whispering new joys to the mild ocean,
Who now hath quite forgot to rave,
While birds of calm sit brooding on the charméd wave.

The stars, with deep amaze,
    Stand fixed in steadfast gaze
Bending one way their precious influence,
    And will not take their flight
    For all the morning light,
Or Lucifer, that often warned them thence;
But in their glimmering orbs did glow
Until their Lord Himself bespake and bid them go.

The shepherds on the lawn,
    Or ere the point of dawn,
Sat simply chatting in a rustic row;
    Full little thought they than
    That the mighty Pan
Was kindly come to live with them below:
Perhaps their loves, or else their sheep,
Was all that did their silly thoughts so busy keep.

When such music sweet
    Their hearts and ears did greet
As never was by mortal finger strook,
    Divinely-warbled voice
    Answering the stringéd noise,
As all their souls in blissful rapture took
The air, such pleasure loth to lose,
With thousand echoes still prolongs each heavenly close.

Such music (as 'tis said)
    Before was never made
But when of old the Sons of Morning sung,
    While the Creator great
    His constellations set,
And the well-balanced World on hinges hung,
And cast the dark foundations deep,
And bid the weltering waves their oozy channel keep.

Ring out, ye crystal spheres!
    Once bless our human ears,
If ye have power to touch our senses so;
    And let your silver chime
    Move in melodious time,
And let the bass of heaven's deep organ blow;

And with your ninefold harmony
Make up full consort to the angelic sym-
    phony.

For if such holy song
Enwrap our fancy long
Time will run back and fetch the Age
    of Gold;
And speckled Vanity
Will sicken soon and die,
And leprous Sin will melt from earthly
    mould;
And Hell itself will pass away,
And leave her dolorous mansions to the
    peering day.

Yea, Truth and Justice then
Will down return to men,
Orbed in a rainbow; and, like glories
    wearing,
Mercy will sit between,
Throned in celestial sheen,
With radiant feet the tissued clouds
    down steering;
And Heaven, as at some festival,
Will open wide the gates of her high
    palace hall.

But see! the Virgin blest
Hath laid her Babe to rest.
Time is our tedious song should here
    have ending:
Heaven's youngest teeméd star
Hath fixed her polished car,
Her sleeping Lord with handmaid lamp
    attending;
And all about the courtly stable
Bright-harnessed Angels sit in order ser-
    viceable.

SEVEN TIMES ONE

Jean Ingelow, who was born in 1820, at Boston, Lincoln
shire, and died in London on July 20, 1897, had charming
gifts of melody and sentiment that placed her among the
most popular of poetesses. She wrote delightfully about
childhood, including her own earliest recollections. Her
power of interpreting children is shown in these lovely
birthday verses, which express the pride and the fancies
of a seven-year-old. Miss Ingelow's poems and stories
are published by Messrs. Longmans, Green & Co.

THERE's no dew left on the daisies and
    clover,
    There's no rain left in heaven;
I've said my " seven times " over and over,
    Seven times one are seven.

I am old, so old, I can write a letter;
    My birthday lessons are done;
The lambs play always, they know no
    better—
    They are only one times one.

O moon! in the night I have seen you
    sailing
    And shining so round and low;
You were bright, ah, bright! but your
    light is sailing—
    You are nothing now but a bow.

You moon, have you done something
    wrong in heaven
    That God has hidden your face ?
I hope, if you have, you will soon be for-
    given,
    And shine again in your place.

O velvet bee, you're a dusty fellow,
    You've powdered your legs with gold!
O brave marsh marybuds, rich and yellow,
    Give me your money to hold.

O columbine, open your golden wrapper,
    Where two twin turtle-doves dwell;
O cuckoo-pint, toll me the purple clapper
    That hangs in your clear, green bell.

And show me your nest with the young
    ones in it;
    I will not steal them away;
I am old, you may trust me, linnet, linnet—
    I am seven times one today.

THE SHEPHERD'S COT

William Shenstone, the author of this artless little poem,
was born in 1714 and died in 1763. He was a pleasant
writer, but is not among the notable poets of England.

MY banks they are furnished with bees,
    Whose murmur invites one to sleep;
My grottoes are shaded with trees,
    And my hills are white over with sheep.
I seldom have met with a loss,
    Such health do my fountains bestow,
My fountains all bordered with moss,
    Where the harebells and violets blow.

Not a pine in the grove is there seen
    But with tendrils of woodbine is bound;
Not a beech's more beautiful green
    But a sweetbriar entwines it around.
Not my fields in the prime of the year
    More charms than my cattle unfold;
Not a brook that is limpid and clear
    But it glitters with fishes of gold.

I have found out a gift for my fair,
    I have found where the wood-pigeons
    breed;
But let me such plunder forbear,
    She will say 'twas a barbarous deed;
For he ne'er could be true, she averred,
    Who would rob a poor bird of its young;
And I loved her the more when I heard
    Such tenderness fall from her tongue.

LITTLE VERSES FOR VERY LITTLE PEOPLE

THE BURIAL OF THE LINNET

FOUND in the garden, dead in his
    beauty—
O that a linnet should die in the spring!
Bury him, comrades, in pitiful duty,
    Muffle the dinner-bell, solemnly ring.

Bury him kindly up in the corner;
    Bird, beast, and goldfish are sepulchred
    there.
Bid the black kitten march as chief
    mourner,
    Waving her tail like a plume in the air.

Bury him nobly, next to the donkey;
    Fetch the old banner and wave it about.
Bury him deeply—think of the monkey,
    Shallow his grave, and the dogs get
    him out.

Bury him softly, white wool around him;
    Kiss his poor feathers—the first kiss
    and last.
Tell his poor widow kind friends have
    found him;
    Plant his poor grave with whatever
    grows fast.

Farewell, sweet singer, dead in thy beauty!
    Silent through summer, though other
    birds sing.
Bury him, comrades, in pitiful duty,
    Muffle the dinner-bell, mournfully ring.
                Juliana Horatia Orr-Ewing

ALL THE CHILDREN

I SUPPOSE if all the children
    Who have lived through the ages
    long
Were collected and inspected
    They would make a wondrous throng.
Oh, the babble of the Babel!
    Oh, the flutter and the fuss!
To begin with Cain and Abel,
    And to finish up with us.

Think of all the men and women
    Who are now and who have been—
Every nation since creation
    That this world of ours has seen,
And of all of them not any
    But was once a baby small;
While of children, oh, how many
    Have not grown up at all!

Some have never laughed or spoken,
    Never used their rosy feet;
Some have even flown to heaven
    Ere they knew that earth was sweet;
And indeed, I wonder whether,

If we reckon every birth
And bring such a flock together,
    There is room for them on earth,

Who will wash their smiling faces?
    Who their saucy ears will box?
Who will dress them and caress them?
    Who will darn their little socks?
Where are arms enough to hold them?
    Hands to pat each shining head?
Who will praise them? Who will scold
    them?
    Who will pack them off to bed?

Little happy Christian children,
    Little savage children too,
In all stages, of all ages,
    That our planet ever knew;
Little princes and princesses,
    Little beggars, wan and faint,
Some in very handsome dresses,
    Naked some, bedaubed with paint.

Only think of the confusion
    Such a motley crowd would make,
And the clatter of their chatter
    And the things that they would break!
Oh, the babble of the Babel!
    Oh, the flutter and the fuss!
To begin with Cain and Abel,
    And to finish up with us.

JESUS BIDS US SHINE

These lines by Susan Warner (known as Elizabeth
Wetherell) are often attributed to Emily H. Miller

JESUS bids us shine
    With a pure, clear light,
Like a little candle
    Burning in the night;
In this world of darkness
    So we must shine—
You in your small corner,
    And I in mine.

Jesus bids us shine
    First of all for Him;
Well He sees and knows it
    If our light is dim,
He looks down from heaven
    To see us shine—
You in your small corner,
    And I in mine.

Jesus bids us shine,
    Then, for all around;
Many kinds of darkness
    In the world abound;
Sin and want and sorrow;
    So we must shine—
You in your small corner,
    And I in mine.

The Story of Where Power Comes From, What It Does, & How It Works

The greatest heat men can make is in the electric furnace, which generates 4000 degrees Centigrade ; the hottest coal gas flame is 1500 degrees, and the surface of the Sun 6000

ELECTRIC HEATING

THE highest temperature that man can produce for industrial purposes is that of the electric arc furnace. There are a very large number of electric furnaces in the world producing millions of tons of steel every year. The clean and easily controllable heat which electricity produces has been applied to many industries, and also to a great number of interesting experiments.

The farmer is already looking to the furnace to supply him with fertiliser for his crops, for natural compounds of nitrogen are today not enough to keep pace with the ever-growing needs of agriculture, and the supplies of nitrogen obtainable from the air seem almost endless.

Thus from the arc lamp of Sir Humphry Davy, used for so many years as a source of light, there has come the huge electric furnace of industry—a lamp of millions on millions of candle-power, in the flame of which the bonds which unite Nature's simple elements break down as if smitten by a fairy spell.

If we dip a finger into very hot water we are conscious of a sharp pain, and get some idea of what temperature means. We know more or less what the tempera-

ture of boiling water feels like—it is a hundred degrees on the Centigrade scale (°C). But it is very difficult to understand even dimly the extraordinary heat of the electric furnace, which can be 4000 degrees Centigrade !

The temperature of the hottest part of a coal gas flame, as used to light an incandescent gas mantle, is about 1500°C. The electric arc is nearly three times as hot. With its heat the chemist has been able to melt substances never melted before, and to produce many remarkable chemical effects.

Just as the alchemist of old attempted to use chemical science for turning base or cheap metals into gold, so for many years the new power offered by the electric furnace tempted a new kind of alchemist to try his skill at making diamonds. Certainly the new alchemist met with more success, for he succeeded in making diamonds as genuine and as real as those dug from the mines. But despite all efforts the artificial diamond has never been made of larger size than a mere speck of matter.

Diamonds are nothing more than crystals of carbon. If a chemist wants to make crystals of any substance he

ELECTRICITY · WIRELESS · OIL · GAS · MOTORS · ENGINES · SHIPS

dissolves that substance in water or some other liquid, and lets the solution evaporate. As the water evaporates little crystals of the substance begin to appear on the side of the vessel.

The artificial diamond is made in almost the same way. The French chemist Moissan knew that carbon would dissolve in molten iron, and that if the molten iron was made very hot—as by an electric furnace—the quantity of carbon that will dissolve in the iron becomes much greater.

When the molten iron containing the carbon had reached a temperature of 4000 degrees Moissan plunged his crucible into cold water, and the sudden cooling at once formed a solid outer layer of iron, within which the yet molten iron eventually became solid, too.

HOW MEN TRIED TO COAX THE CARBON TO BECOME A DIAMOND

Now on becoming solid the molten iron would expand in the ordinary way. Imagine the molten mass imprisoned within the outer wall of iron and we can understand how enormous pressure was produced—pressure which caused the crystals of carbon—tiny diamonds—to be formed, just as crystals of salt are given up on drying a solution of salt and water.

Moissan took the solid lump of metal from his crucible, dissolved away the iron, and found as many as fifteen diamonds in a single ingot. The rarest gem in Nature had been made in the laboratory !

How, from that time on, men fought with the black, worthless carbon and tried to coax it to grow into its beautiful sister substance, the diamond, we can well understand. But the artificial gem remains obdurate. It defies all attempts to make it except in useless little specks.

HOW WATER HELPS CREATE A GAS WHICH BURNS WITH INTENSE HEAT

The electric furnace uses very big quantities of electricity, but its simplicity and ease of working place it far above the ordinary furnace for many purposes. The production of steel from cold pig-iron or iron scrap requires about a thousand kilowatt hours for each ton. That means the use of a million watts for one hour, for a kilowatt is a thousand watts.

The huge furnaces used may turn out as much as 180 tons of high-grade steel a day, and steel is only one of the things the electric furnace is used for. Another great industry is the making of calcium carbide, a grey substance which, when moistened with water, gives off acetylene gas. This gas, on account of its intense heat when burned with oxygen, is used on a big scale for acetylene welding.

Although this important substance had been made by a German chemist named Wöhler as long ago as 1862, it was not until the day of the electric furnace that it could be made on a useful scale, and Moissan and a Canadian named Willson made the discovery almost simultaneously in 1892. Lime and carbon are mixed together and are heated in the furnace, when calcium carbide is produced, together with monoxide of carbon, a gas which easily escapes.

Calcium carbide is tremendously important because it is a sort of half-way substance used in the preparation of cyanamide, from which the farmer obtains large quantities of fertiliser. A hundred thousand tons of calcium carbide have been made every year for this purpose at Odde in Norway.

THE PROCESS THAT WILL BRING THE FUTURE UNTOLD WEALTH

We next come to a process which depends on the electric furnace, and which will mean untold wealth to future generations—the process of obtaining large supplies of nitrogen from the air.

In the intense heat of an arc flame the nitrogen and oxygen of the air combine to form a gas known as nitric oxide. The chemist can do with this gas what he cannot do with nitrogen alone ; by allowing lime to absorb the gas he can turn it into nitrate of lime, and it is this substance which is made and sold for agricultural purposes.

An arc flame is formed between powerful electrodes, and by means of an electric magnet the flame is repelled, so that a long sheet of flame of tremendous heat plays between the walls of the furnace. As the arc flame conveys the current from one pole to the other, it is itself a magnet, so that it can be easily deflected this way or that by another magnet. This blinding flame is called an electric sun, and it is probably the nearest thing to the actual Sun that has been produced by man.

Through this flaming sun the air is driven, causing the formation of nitric oxide which is passed through " towers "

THE GREATEST HEAT THAT MEN CAN MAKE

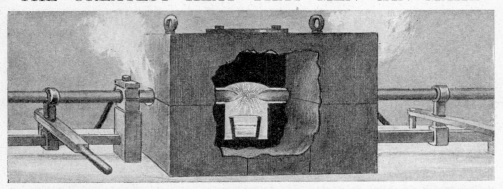

In the electric furnace man has discovered a means of generating the greatest heat known on Earth. In the Moissan arc furnace a temperature of nearly 4000 degrees Centigrade is obtained—a temperature, that is to say, two-thirds that of the surface of the Sun. Electric furnaces are constructed on two principles, which we see in the Moissan and Héroult types, shown here. In the Moissan type, in the top picture, the substance to be melted is placed in a chamber lined with some stubborn material and is exposed to the heat generated by the electric arc. In the Héroult type, shown below, the substance is placed under a carbon pole and is heated by the current that flashes across to it from the pole. The substance is, in fact, melted by its own resistance to the passage of the current. Electric furnaces are rapidly supplanting the old blast furnaces. They produce purer products.

filled with milk of lime, where the so-called Norwegian saltpetre is manu-factured.

The welding of large masses of steel is accomplished with the help of the electric current. Here again the hot flame of the arc is used.

THE MOLTEN METAL THAT ADHERES LIKE GLUE

The arc is struck between the article to be welded and a rod. The rod is connected to one pole of an electrical generator (dynamo), and the article to the other. The welding rod is made of special metal and melts in the arc. The molten metal from it adheres like a glue and can be used to join two pieces of steel. Steel components are built up by welding to replace castings, because they are often lighter and cheaper. This method is used in building steam boilers, in welding the joints of rails, and in many engineering repair jobs.

Electric welding is gradually replacing the riveting of the big steel plates of which ships, bridges, and modern steel structures are built. Several ships are now afloat which have been electrically welded throughout, and the ringing taps of the riveters' hammers are gradually dying out in the shipyards.

There is a terrific glare from such an intense welding flame, and the operator has to have eyes and head protected by a dark glass screen. The ultra-violet rays produced by the light would otherwise act harmfully upon him.

METALS THAT RESIST ELECTRIC CURRENT BUT STILL GET HOT

We have seen in another part of this book how an electric current makes metals hot. Certain metals offer great resistance to a current, and get very hot in consequence. This fact is made use of in certain kinds of welding. The current is passed through two bars of metal which are pressed together end to end ; when the metal is hot enough the bars are " jumped " together, and become one piece. Twenty-two horse-power is needed for one minute to join two bars of iron an inch in diameter.

Another type of furnace is known as the induction furnace. An intense electric current is induced in the ore or steel in the crucible by means of current passed through a coil of wire wound on the outside. The current induced in the crucible causes its contents to become white-hot. Induction furnaces are now used on a large scale in many industries. One interesting use is for melting high-grade steel which is to be used in the manufacture of tools. Another is the heating of steel bars before forging.

Many small electric furnaces are used in industry, just large enough to take a small crucible, and heated by a red-hot resistance wire through which the current is passed. These are similar in principle to the electric cookers used in the kitchens of modern homes.

Larger furnaces are made and some have continuous belt conveyors passing through them. The material to be heated is placed on these belts and passes through the furnace. Many types of articles are treated in this way, pottery—the making of which is described in a section beginning on page 301—being a good example.

For hardening tools, too, small furnaces are used in many modern factories—little baths of salts, fused or liquefied by the heat generated by the current, into which the tools can be dipped.

CURRENT WHICH CHANGES ITS DIRECTION 100 MILLION TIMES A SECOND

Although not actually generating such high temperatures, a new type of electric heating, of which we are likely to hear a great deal, must be mentioned. This is high frequency or electronic heating, in which alternating current changes its direction as much as 100 million times a second. These high frequency currents are made in generators which are very similar to radio transmitters, hence this method of heating is sometimes called " radio-frequency heating."

There are two main types : (1) induction heating, which is similar in principle to the induction furnace and is used, among other things, for the mass production of small soldered articles ; (2) dielectric heating, which is used for the heating on non-conductors of electricity, such as wood and plastics. It is used for the glueing of furniture and in the manufacture of plywood.

There are, of course, many other applications of electric heating, such as the de-freezing of aircraft wings and floor-warming, which owing to lack of space have not been mentioned in this chapter.

Imperishable Thoughts of Men Enshrined in the Books of the World

The Two Brothers save their Sister—A scene from Milton's Comus

MILTON THE GREAT

AFTER the death of Shakespeare in 1616, English literature showed a serious decline for forty or fifty years, and only one name stands out brightly. John Milton's fame as a poet is second only to the fame of Shakespeare.

He was born in 1608, in Bread Street, Cheapside, where was an entrance to the Mermaid Tavern, in which the play-writers of the period kept each other merry with their frolicsome wit. So it is not at all improbable that John Milton, as a boy of eight, may have seen William Shakespeare walk down to the Mermaid to meet his dramatist friends there, when he was up in the City for a cheerful visit, after spending time more heavily in the rural solitudes of Warwickshire.

Whether the boy of six to eight, at the comfortable scrivener's house in Bread Street, saw Shakespeare go by at the age of 50 to 52 or not, it is certain that later he knew Shakespeare's writings well, while he was quite young, for at 22 he wrote:

What needs my Shakespeare for his honoured bones,
The labour of an age in pilèd stones?
Or that his hallowed reliques should be hid
Under a stary-pointing pyramid?
Dear son of memory, great heir of fame,
What need'st thou such weak witness of thy name?
Thou in our wonder and astonishment
Hast built thyself a livelong monument.

Though over sixty years separated the writing of Shakespeare's chief works and the publication of Milton's greatest poem, we see that the two poets were comparatively near in time. Indeed, Milton's earliest poem, the hymn, " Let us with a gladsome mind," was written within seven years of Shakespeare's death.

John Milton was born and trained to be a poet, and from his boyhood thought of himself as " a dedicated spirit," to use Wordsworth's description of his own boyish relation to poetry.

Milton's father was a cultured man and a great lover of music. He had enough fortune to retire quietly into the country in his later years. The boy John went to St. Paul's School, not far from Bread Street, and from there to Cambridge, where he studied seven years, and gained a high reputation as a scholar and a poet.

Then, for nearly six years, he lived chiefly in the country with his father; but when he was 29 set out on his travels through France, Switzerland, and Italy, where his fame as a poet had gone before him, the more so because he had written poems in Latin and Italian, languages of which he was a master. He returned home in his thirty-first year, to take part in his country's struggle, which he regarded as a fight for freedom against the autocratic rule of Charles Stuart.

Up to this time Milton had justified his own belief that he had in poetry a talent

ROMANCE · HISTORIES · DRAMAS · ESSAYS · WORLD CLASSICS

which it was death to hide. He had written peoms in his student days, and others in his days of studious leisure, that, if he had written no more, would have preserved his name while English literature lasts, for he had written on some great themes with a scholarly grace and sweetness that were then unequalled, and have never been surpassed.

WHEN MILTON WAS ARRESTED AND HIS WRITINGS BURNED

But now followed a period of twenty years in which, from a poetical point of view, Milton's life is almost a blank. The poet became a politician, and, except for a few sonnets, mostly personal, wrote only in prose. Some of his prose writings are interesting, as, for instance, his Tractate on Education, for he now became temporarily a schoolmaster; and his magnificently eloquent plea, Areopagitica, for unlicensed printing ; but generally his outpourings—sometimes in Latin—were too fiercely controversial, and were unworthy of Milton's position in the world of letters. For the last ten of these twenty years Milton was Latin Secretary to the Council of State, that is, he wrote in Latin the dispatches forwarded by the Commonwealth Government to foreign countries.

Then came the Restoration, and Milton, as an official of the Republican Government, and one who in his writings had defended strongly the execution of Charles the First, was in great personal danger. He was arrested, and his writings were burned.

Exactly how he escaped has never been explained in a fully trustworthy manner. Perhaps the fact that for eight years he had been blind excited pity. Perhaps his distinction as the living Englishman best known on the Continent since Cromwell's death had a restraining effect. The traditional story is that in the days when the Royalists were being persecuted he saved the life of Sir William Davenant, the Cavalier poet, and that Sir William and his friends saved his life in return.

THE ACHIEVEMENT BY WHICH MILTON STANDS ALONE IN FAME

Anyway, he was forgiven, lived in quietness fourteen years longer, and wrote the great poem which he had been planning all his life, the supreme epic in the English tongue, an amazing achievement that placed him alone on a pinnacle of fame with no competitor near. Milton will always be known first as the conceiver and architect of Paradise Lost; but in other poems, which we must now glance at, he earned the right to wear immortal bays.

All Milton's poems have a religious tone. He began as a boy with a paraphrase of the 136th Psalm; he ended with a Biblical play, Samson Agonistes, published 48 years later. Between, he wrote as if he were conscious always that he was watched by his "great Task-Master's eye," and he himself declared that his life had been " untouched from all profligacy and vice."

It is splendid to think that this was so, for never was there a more glorious beginning to a poet's poetical life. Milton made such a beginning when, on Christmas morning in 1629, he himself having come of age on December 8, 1629, he sat through the night writing his Ode on Christ's Nativity. Never has there been a more touching dedication of God-given gifts to God. This fine Ode embraces the most gorgeous poetical hymn ever cast in the mould of the English tongue, a revelation in harmonious words. On page 1224 we give the stanzas referring to the music which, according to the Biblical account, heralded the birth of Jesus. Music in any form always stirred the soul of Milton.

THE FIVE POEMS MILTON WROTE AFTER A STAY IN THE COUNTRY

Among Milton's early poems was another on music, descriptive of his exaltation of spirit at a sacred concert and showing his early mastery of verse of varied rhythm. And he had begun to use the sonnet form, both in English and Italian, a form that he handled with fine effect.

His stay in the country at his father's home in Buckinghamshire produced five poems framed in a classical mould with many references to the poetic figures of ancient literature. These were L'Allegro, picturing the scenes of a day from morn till eve in a spirit of cheerfulness, and Il Penseroso, picturing the scenes of a night from eve till morn, with an appropriate pensiveness. The titles mean, literally, the cheerful one and the pensive one. In the morning he brings us waking into the strains of music, and tones his thought to such a scene as King's College Chapel, at Cambridge or Westminster Abbey.

But let my due feet never fail
To walk the studious cloister's pale,
And love the high embowéd roof,
With antique pillars massy-proof,
And storied windows richly dight,
Casting a dim religious light.

DID MILTON SEE SHAKESPEARE PASS BY?

IT IS POSSIBLE THAT YOUNG JOHN MILTON STOOD AT HIS FATHER'S SHOP DOOR IN BREAD STREET AND
SAW WILLIAM SHAKESPEARE PASS BY

There let the pealing organ blow
To the full-voiced quire below,
In service high and anthems clear,
As may with sweetness, through mine ear,
Dissolve me into ecstasies,
And bring all Heaven before mine eyes.

One of Milton's friends at this time was Henry Lawes, the music-master of the Chapel Royal and a popular composer, and for him Milton wrote songs for a Masque called Arcades, the masque then being the most popular form of fashionable entertainment. This was followed, in 1634, by the writing of the whole of a Masque, Comus, for a fine amateur theatrical production at Ludlow Castle, and Comus is the one Masque that remains from a once showy fashion a permanent part of English literature. All the others are faded curiosities. Comus is written round the idea that modesty, chastity, virtue, are self-protective against evil. The play shows the adventures of a maiden in an enchanted wood, and her rescue by a watchful good Spirit.

Mortals that would follow me,
Love Virtue; she alone is free.
She can teach ye how to climb
Higher than the sphery chime;
Or, if Virtue feeble were,
Heaven itself would stoop to her.

Or, in greater detail and poetic beauty, the same thought is expressed—

Some say no evil thing that walks by night,
In fog or fire, by lake or moorish fen,
Blue meagre hag, or stubborn unlaid ghost
That breaks his magic chains at curfew time,
No goblin, or swart fairy of the mine,
Hath hurtful power o'er true virginity.

*   *   *

So dear to Heaven is saintly Chastity
That, when a soul is found sincerely so,
A thousand liveried angels lackey her,
Driving far off each thing of sin and guilt.

Lycidas, the last of the poems written by Milton in his years of youthful leisure, is a lament for the drowning of one of his companions at Cambridge, Edward King. A volume of poems by various college friends expressed their sorrow. All but one of the poems were undistinguished. That one, however, by its music and haunting charm, has set the standard for lofty English classical rhyme.

Listen to the cadences of this gentle dirge, not the first memorial poem the poet had written.

Yet once more, O ye laurels, and once more
Ye myrtles brown, with ivy never sere,
I come to pluck your berries, harsh and crude,
And with forcéd fingers rude
Shatter your leaves before the mellowing year.
Bitter constraint and sad occasion dear
Compels me to disturb your season due;
For Lycidas is dead, dead ere his prime,
Young Lycidas, and hath not left his peer.
Who would not sing for Lycidas? He knew
Himself to sing, and build the lofty rhyme.
He must not float upon his watery bier
Unwept, and welter to the parching wind
Without the meed of some melodious tear.

John Milton and Edward King, as friends, often spent their time at Cambridge together; and this is how the survivor expressed it in the poetical imagery of the period.

For we were nursed upon the self-same hill,
Fed the same flock, by fountain, shade, and rill;
Together both, ere the high lawns appeared
Under the opening eyelids of the Morn,
We drove afield, and both together heard
What time the grey-fly winds her sultry horn,
Battening our flocks with the fresh dews of night,
Oft till the star that rose at evening bright
Towards Heaven's descent had sloped his westering wheel.

Here is a passage that tells of Milton's observation of the flowers that surrounded his country home, and which he calls on to decorate his friend's grave.

Ye valleys low, where the mild whispers use
Of shades, and wanton winds, and gushing brooks,
On whose fresh lap the swart star sparely looks,
Throw hither all your quaint enamelled eyes,
That on the green turf suck the honeyed showers,
And purple all the ground with vernal flowers.
Bring the rathe primrose that forsaken dies,
The tufted crow-toe and pale jessamine,
The white pink, and the pansy freaked with jet,
The glowing violet,
The musk-rose and the well-attiréd woodbine,
With cowslips wan that hang the pensive head,
And every flower that sad embroidery wears.
Bid amaranthus all his beauty shed,
And daffadillies fill their cups with tears,
To strew the laureate hearse where Lycid lies.
For so, to interpose a little ease,
Let our frail thoughts dally with vain surmise.
Ay me! whilst thee the shores and sounding seas
Wash far away. . . . . .

With Lycidas Milton said farewell to his earlier style. " Tomorrow to fresh woods and pastures new " was his closing line. He laid aside the pastoral pipe, on which he had played a lovely tune, but he little foresaw what long years would pass before he again made poetry the chief outlet for his creative energies, or how experience of a sterner world would deepen the tone of his verse to a mighty organ note that would reverberate for ever down the ages.

The Great Words that Stir the Hearts and Minds of All Mankind

---

From Everlasting to Everlasting

Lord, thou hast been our dwelling-place in all generations.

Before the mountains were brought forth, or ever thou hadst formed the earth and the world, even from everlasting to everlasting, thou art God.

Thou turnest man to destruction ; and sayest, Return, ye children of men.

For a thousand years in thy sight are but as yesterday when it is past, and as a watch in the night.   Psalm 90

ETERNITY

THERE is an odd little story in an old book somewhere. It says that far away in the west of the world is a mighty granite rock, a mile high, a mile wide, and a mile deep. Once every hundred years a little bird comes to the rock and sharpens its beak on the granite, and when the birds have worn the rock away that will be one day in Eternity.

Perhaps from a piece of imagination like that the mind can begin to think what Eternity means. It is a word that stirs the mind to solemn thought.

There have been many civilisations. Thousands of years ago men felt that they had at last reached the topmost peak of existence, and that the end of life was near at hand.

There was a wonderful civilisation in Egypt, another in Crete, another in Babylon, another in Greece. But these civilisations passed away, and men found themselves still scaling the difficult mountains of existence whose peaks are even now still lost in the sky.

Now, in all these vanished civilisations, it is possible for us to mark the moment in which they approached their full greatness, and the moment in which they began their descent to extinction. We can say definitely, from the statues and architecture and pottery of these vanished civilisations, that *original genius* was the mark of their full greatness, and mere *copying* was the mark of their decline.

What is the difference between original genius and mere copying? It is a thing of feeling. The original genius feels enthusiastically; the copyist feels coldly or tepidly. To the one beauty is a possession; to the other it is an art. To the one life is a most glorious opportunity for adventure; to the other it is a difficult business, calling above all things for prudence.

It would seem that in the greatest periods of human life words have played an enormous part. There comes a time in the life of a nation when a word sounds like a trumpet-call, rousing the national spirit from torpor, urging the nation's soul to creative work.

Then the ring of the word passes away, dies on the air, and the mere copyist comes along, using that same mighty word, but without enthusiasm, without really meaning it, without feeling that it is a word that can inspire mankind.

It is a part of patriotism, a part of religion, to keep the true meaning of great words alive. We serve our country, we serve civilisation, we even serve God, when we stand between the mere copyist and a word which has meant passion and enthusiasm in times past. We can do great things for mankind merely by setting our faces against the use of grand words

DISCOVERY · WILL · HONOUR · HOPE · RIGHTEOUSNESS · REASON

in a slovenly manner; for so we bring home to the minds of unthinking people that there are tremendous meanings behind these words; and when they come to think about the meanings they begin to feel the greatness of life, they become ashamed of littleness.

WHAT WE MISS BY CARELESSLY USING GREAT WORDS

One thing is certain: if we want our British civilisation to hold its own in the world, we must *mean* every word in which it has expressed itself hitherto, and be on our guard against using these words without thinking of the things they stand for, the ideas they symbolise.

We see the danger of using great words carelessly by reflection on the word Eternity. At one time in our past this word suddenly lifted up the English mind from grovelling in the dust and set it building beautiful cathedrals, and making lovely poetry and living in the sunshine of gladness. Now we use this word chiefly in ballads, and a tenor warbles to sad-faced people in a concert-room about the eternity of his love for some very sensible lady who will have nothing to do with him. This sublime word has come to be a convenient wind-up for second-rate poetry, it has fallen to the copyist, it has lost its meaning. We use it, but do not feel it.

What is the result? We live only between the two points of birth and death. We lose the sense of grandeur. We scurry through existence. We miss the steadiest thought that can direct the human mind. We behave as if our lives had no more dignity or purpose than a cork tossed to and fro by the waves.

WHERE WAS TIME WHEN THERE WAS NEITHER SUN NOR MOON?

But consider the truth of existence. Eternity is an idea forced upon the philosopher. No man who uses his brain can think without the background of this idea. Eternity is not a dream, or a word for the sentimentalist; it is not a mad idea outside the power of our understanding; it is a first condition of rational thinking. What does it mean?

We cannot think of time without thinking of watches and clocks. Once there were no such things. Yet time existed before watches and clocks. Those people who lived before clocks, or before the invention of the sun-dial, measured time by days and weeks. The Sun rose, the Sun set. There was morning, and there was night. The Moon also waxed and waned. Moreover, there was a time of sowing and a time of reaping. There was a time when the Sun was at its hottest, and a time when snow covered the Earth. Men measured time by all these things.

But where was time when there was yet neither Sun nor Moon? How could time be measured when there was no planet to turn its face to the Sun? Think of space with no stellar universe. It is possible to think of that; possible, because science goes back to the creation of that universe. Space filled with ether, but with no suns and no planets—think of that, and then ask yourself, *Where was time?*

THE WONDERFUL CIVILISATIONS OF THE PAST THAT HAVE DISAPPEARED

To ask that question brings us to the thought of Eternity. For the word means *that which exists outside all the relations of time.* Think away watches and clocks, think away days and nights, think away months and years, and the idea of Eternity will creep into your mind and knock for entrance at the door of your imagination. Time was born; it came into existence, like an apple on a tree, or a bud on a rose bush; but before time there was the existence into which it was born, and that existence we call Eternity.

Now see the value of this word. Time is the child of Eternity. We are here on this Earth for a few years. We are the children of time. But if time is our mother, Eternity is the mother of time, and therefore we belong not only to time, but also to Eternity.

It is the same with our planet. At one period men thought the Earth was the centre of the universe, that the Sun was created to light it by day and the Moon by night. There came a period when they discovered that our Earth was not the centre of the universe, that it was indeed only an insignificant part of a universe inconceivably large and magnificent; and many people were sorrowful because of this discovery. But what does it matter whether our planet is big or little, so long as it is a part of the universe? *Big! Little!* What are those words doing in a universe which is infinite? They are merely human terms. They have no meaning outside the human mind. Our Earth is as much a part of the infinite universe as the greatest planet.

So, too, with our human time. It exists only in our minds, it is made for us only by the movement of our planet through space. We measure those movements of the Earth by our watches and our calendars, but they have no meaning for the Eternity in which we exist, as our planet exists in space. We are a part of Eternity. We can think away our human time, but we cannot think ourselves out of Eternity.

THE EVERLASTING REALITY BEHIND ALL THE CHANGES OF TIME

It was this realisation which gave such power to the thought of Plato. He saw that days and nights are in the nature of an illusion, and that Eternity has neither beginning nor end. He taught men to say of God, not that *He was* or that *He will be*, but only that *He is*. He encouraged them to dwell with the thought of this everlasting reality, so that they might never be deceived by the illusions of time. Just as Moses spoke of God as *I AM* —a marvellous inspiration in those days— so Plato spoke of *He is*. God is the everlasting Reality behind all changes of time and all forms of visible creations.

The value of this idea now becomes plainer to us. The thought of Eternity puts us in the way of searching for the only happiness which endures. It prevents us from taking the things of time at their face value. We look at all those temptations and we say to ourselves, " What is their real value? Time, we know, is only a convenience of the human mind; it has no meaning for the Eternal Reality; therefore these things of time cannot be worth buying."

THE REGION OF REALITY IN WHICH OUR WHOLE WELFARE LIES

Then we proceed to search for things which have nothing to do with time, things with what philosophers call an *absolute value*—a value independent of time and circumstance. And we find that the only absolute values are spiritual things; not eating and drinking, but self-denial and compassion; not laying up riches and wearing fine clothes, but wisdom and understanding—a consecrated life of devotion and love.

So we come to a condition of mind which renders us proof against all the deceptions of our senses, and all the adversities of fortune. We no longer feel that we are like so many rabbits bolting out of the darkness of birth and back again into the darkness of death. We no longer think that our one purpose on Earth is to have " a good time." We no longer forget man's difficult past, no longer refuse our aid to his nobler future. We see that all the vanished civilisations of time past came to naught because they ceased to think of life as part of Eternity. We see that our peace, our happiness, our prosperity, lie solely in the invisible region of moral values—the region, not of illusion, but of reality. We come to realise in fact how true are the words of Robert South, that homely yet humorous preacher and writer of the seventeenth century: " Certainly the highest and dearest concerns of a temporal life are infinitely less valuable than those of an' eternal : and consequently ought, without any demur at all, to be sacrificed to them, whenever they come in competition."

THE VASTNESS OF THE GULF BETWEEN TIME AND ETERNITY

And, finally, we live gladly and enthusiastically because our spirits no longer pine as prisoners in bodies that grow weak, old, and dead, but are for ever breathing eternal air and strengthening their divine powers in the everlasting kingdom of wisdom, virtue, and loveliness.

> Why shrinks the soul
> Back on herself, and startles at destruction?
> 'Tis the divinity that stirs within us;
> 'Tis Heaven itself that points out a hereafter
> And intimates eternity to man.

Here is a little incident which will help us to see the vast difference between a man to whom Eternity is a fact and the man to whom time is a fact. We were once walking through a fashionable street in a great European city when we saw two young men, very flashily dressed, who were laughing at a little old man they had just passed. We overtook this old man, so shabby, so simple, so modest, so out of place in that street, and recognised in him the greatest and wisest of living historians.

Think of the thoughts that filled the capacious brain of this great historian, think of their range, their dignity, their grandeur, their everlasting wisdom; and then think of the silliness in the brains of the two young swaggerers who laughed at him. They were looking for their values in time; he in Eternity.

ON THE WAY TO THE PROMISED LAND

THE WORSHIP OF THE GOLDEN CALF

THE GATE OF THE CAMP

THE HANDS OF MOSES HELD UP IN BATTLE

MOSES SEES THE PROMISED LAND

The Story of the Most Beautiful Book in the World

Aaron is chosen as the Great High Priest

THE GREAT MARCH IN THE DESERT

Never in all the story of the world has been a march so romantic, so wonderful, so full of meaning for the rest of mankind, as the march of the Israelites under the leadership of Moses.

Think of the spectacle! Through the wild country on the farther side of the Red Sea went a whole nation. Husbands and wives, fathers and mothers, brothers and sisters, boys and girls, and babies in their mothers' arms. For an immense distance stretched this extraordinary caravan, this multitude of humanity. And remember that this nation trekking across the wilderness had been weakened almost to dust and ashes by slavery, their manhood flogged out of them by the whips of Pharaoh's taskmasters.

For centuries they had toiled on the red dust of Egypt, under the pitiless glare of the Egyptian sun, despised, scorned by the people over them, hopeless of any change in their condition, powerless to strike a blow in defence. It sounded like an idle tale in their ears that once in the days of Joseph they had been a free and mighty people in the land of Egypt.

Tyranny destroys men. The tyranny of the sword destroys their body; the tyranny of the word destroys their reason.

Remember, then, that this huge caravan was a poor and draggled host of querulous slaves, whose backs were still raw with the whips of their tyrants, and whose souls were still cowed and shameful with the fear of their despots.

For three rainless days this ragged multitude streamed across the desert, now elated by their escape from slavery, now plunged into despair at the unending waste of land always before them. We can surely hear with the ears of our imagination the groans of the old and the murmurings of the young as Moses marched steadily forward in this burning and waterless land. After all, many must have thought it better to make bricks for Pharaoh than to die of thirst in a wilderness.

The air of that long-silent desert must have been continuously loud with the increasing murmurs of the Hebrews; and when at last water did appear, and the people rushed forward with a wild excitement to drink, lo! it was so bitter that they murmured against their leader.

Moses must have realised to the full at the waters of Marah—which means *bitterness*—the terrible difficulties of his task. It is often hard for a king or a statesman to keep a prosperous people happy; but

GREAT FIGURES OF THE OLD TESTAMENT · THE LIFE OF JESUS

Moses was alone with a horde of miserable slaves in a strange and desolate country.

Guided by God, this truly great and far-seeing captain took a tree that grew near the bitter waters, and threw it into their midst. The waters immediately became good to drink. Then the thirsty people drank, and went forward refreshed till they came to a place of much water and many palm trees, where they rested and were glad.

Once again they plunged into the desert, and soon hunger drove them into more murmuring against Moses and Aaron. " Would to God," they cried, " we had died by the hand of the Lord in Egypt, when we sat by the flesh-pots, and when we did eat bread to the full; for ye have brought us forth into this wilderness to kill the whole assembly with hunger."

Some took up stones to kill Moses, but he rebuked them, and drew water for them from a rock. But while they drank, resting themselves in this place, which is called Rephidim, a warlike body of a tribe called the Amalekites appeared in the distance. For the first time the Israelites found their way seriously disputed by an enemy.

HOW JOSHUA FOUGHT THE AMALEKITES TO THE GOING DOWN OF THE SUN

Then Moses called to his side a warlike young man called Joshua, and bade him go out with a picked body of the Israelites to meet the Amalekites; and while Joshua did his bidding Moses went up with Aaron and Hur to the top of the hill, and we read:

It came to pass when Moses held up his hand that Israel prevailed; and when he let down his hand, Amalek prevailed. But Moses' hands were heavy; and they took a stone and put it under him, and he sat thereon; and Aaron and Hur stayed up his hands, and his hands were steady until the going down of the Sun. And Joshua discomfited Amalek and his people with the edge of the sword.

Moses received at Rephidim a visit from his father-in-law Jethro, who had heard the wonderful news of the march from Egypt. Seeing how Moses was overburdened by the work of leadership, and how he had to sit in judgment in any little dispute between these quarrelsome people, Jethro said to Moses: " Thou wilt surely wear away. This thing is too heavy for thee; thou art not able to perform it thyself."

And this wise old man bade Moses to provide out of all the people, " able men,

such as fear God, men of truth, hating covetousness; and place such over them, to be rulers of thousands, and rulers of hundreds, rulers of fifties, and rulers of tens; and let them judge the people at all seasons; and it shall be that every great matter they shall bring unto thee, but every small matter they shall judge."

WHAT GREW OUT OF JETHRO'S TALK WITH MOSES

This wonderful talk of Jethro with Moses, in the 18th chapter of Exodus, is the earliest account we have of a *social reform*. It might be called the beginning of politics.

Politics is the science in which men study how they should arrange the laws of a nation so that people may grow in virtue, prosperity, and happiness. No politician, it is quite certain, ever had so difficult a task as Moses, and this conversation of Moses with Jethro interests us exceedingly because the first step in social reform was made in those far-off days and has been followed and developed by almost every nation since.

The great march was continued. The mighty caravan, flushed by their victory over the Amalekites, and dreaming of Palestine, pushed across the desert and halted in the shadow of Sinai. Here occurred the chief events in the history of the whole race. Moses was called by God into the mountain, and there, in the midst of a great cloud, received the ten commands of God which are the foundation of all law and all honour to this day.

The old statesman, writing down those commandments for the Israelites on tables of stone, little guessed, perhaps, that he was writing words which would be translated into every language under the Sun, and would guide the conscience of all humanity to the end of time.

THE MAKING OF THE GOLDEN CALF AND THE BREAKING OF THE TABLES OF STONE

These laws commanded obedience to the worship of the One God, who made Heaven and Earth; they forbade the making of images and the taking of God's name in vain; they enjoined resting from work one day in the week, and honouring parents; they forbade murder, stealing, impurity, and lying; and they closed with a law which Jesus was to show in a more clear and beautiful light—the law which forbade men to wish *in the heart* for things that did not belong to them.

MOSES COMES DOWN FROM THE MOUNTAIN WITH THE TABLES OF STONE

These great laws, which seem so simple and right to us, were not so simple to the Israelites, and when Moses descended from the mountain he found that his people had disobeyed the chief of them by persuading Aaron to make them an image of the golden calf worshipped in Egypt as a symbol of God.

So wrath and indignant was Moses that he threw down the tables of stone, hurled the golden calf into a fire, and killed the guilty makers of the idol. Then he returned to the mountain, and learned still more of God's laws for humanity.

For more than a year the Israelites were encamped in the shadow of Mount Sinai, and there they built their movable temple, its Holy of Holies containing an oblong chest called the Ark of the Covenant, wherein reposed the two tables of stone. Here the sons of Aaron were chosen as priests, and Aaron himself became the great High Priest of the nation. The feasts of the Hebrews were instituted at this place, and worship was celebrated in a manner to remind the Israelites of God's great mercy and kindness.

When at last the mighty host moved on once more toward Canaan, the Israelites again broke into murmurings and complaints concerning the shortness of food. Food was given to them in abundance, and they ate of it so greedily that many died and were buried in a place called The Graves of Lust. Thus warned they proceeded on their way, and pre-

made known to Moses that he would punish the people, and that, save Joshua and Caleb, none of that generation should enter the Promised Land. He bade them return once more to the wilderness, and when some of them disobeyed this command, and went forward, a company of Canaanites and Amalekites fell upon them and smote them back.

In the wilderness fresh trouble arose. A conspiracy came to light. Three important men, Korah, Dathan, and Abiram,

PICKING UP QUAILS IN THE DESERT

sently Moses was near enough to the Promised Land to send forward his spies. These men returned with two tales: First, that the land was rich, fruitful, and altogether desirable; and, second, that it was occupied by mighty people who would fight for it.

So the Israelites were first eager to push on, and then so fearful of fighting that they broke out into violent murmurings against Moses and Aaron. Then God

with the support of many others, charged Moses and Aaron with taking too much upon themselves. The rebellion was put down, but Moses and Aaron began to despair of ever making a great people of these Israelites.

For many years, wearisome and fretful, the Israelites remained in the wilderness, and here Aaron died. The death of this great and noble leader staggered the Israelites, and for thirty days they

THE DEATH OF AARON

MOSES AND JOSHUA IN THE TABERNACLE

mourned him, feeling that something of their past had perished. Yet a few days after their mourning, coming into a barren waste of land, they once more murmured against God, and were the same bitter, suspicious, and quarrelsome people as before. Then from the rocks came little fiery serpents, which stung them so that many died ; but when they repented Moses was commanded by God to make a bronze serpent and to fix it on a pole, and all who looked on it were healed.

And now it seemed as if the Israelites had learned their lesson. Across their line of march lay many cities, and against these people, who refused to let them pass, they went up stout-heartedly in battle under the captaincy of Joshua, trusting in God.

Battle after battle ended in victory for the Israelites, city after city fell before them, and they went forward, no longer a rabble of beaten and grumbling slaves, but a terrible people, manly, brave, and resolute.

THE FALSE PROPHET BALAAM RIDES ON HIS ASS TO MEET ISRAEL

They had now reached the frontier of a territory occupied by the Moabites. The King of the Moabites, whose name was Balak, became so fearful of the Israelites, whose victories were spreading terror throughout the country, that he sought to stay their progress by magic. He sent to a famous prophet named Balaam, and begged him to come and put a curse upon these invading Israelites. But Balaam found that God would not put a curse in his mouth. However, Balak sent to him again, and with such tempting offers, that at last Balaam consented to come; but he protested that he could only utter whatsoever words God put in his mouth.

The Bible tells us that as Balaam rode upon his ass the angel of God stood in his way, and the ass saw it and stopped, and Balaam smote it. Again the angel appeared, and the ass, starting to one side, crushed Balaam's foot against a wall. Balaam struck it again, and suddenly the ass spoke in human language, and the eyes of Balaam saw the angel, who warned Balaam that he should speak only those words which God put into his mouth.

So Balaam went forward, and was received by King Balak with great honour. He was taken on to a high hill overlooking the host of Israelites, and seven altars were erected there, and a bullock and a ram were sacrificed on each altar. But Balaam refused to lay a curse upon the Israelites. Instead, gazing upon the tents of Israel, the spirit of God came upon him, and he cried: "How goodly are thy tents, O Jacob, and thy tabernacles, O Israel !"

BALAAM TEMPTS THE ISRAELITES TO GREAT WICKEDNESS

But when the spirit passed away from him Balaam loitered among the Midianites with evil thoughts. He could not bring himself to curse Israel, but he greatly longed for Balak's reward ; and he tempted the Israelites to join an evil feast that they might enter into the wickedness of all about them. Alas, great bodies of the Israelites flocked to this feast and rioted with the Midianites, utterly forgetting the laws of God given for their own happiness and advancement.

They fell into the vilest sins, and the anger of God descended on them. Plague broke out among them; they perished in great numbers, and Moses hanged the chiefs of the people. But the Midianites were to suffer too. The faithful of Israel were massed by Phinehas, who had been a sort of Cromwell among the wicked ones, and he went up against the Midianites, destroyed their cities and their chiefs, took captive their women and children, and slew Balaam.

MOSES VIEWS THE PROMISED LAND FROM MOUNT NEBO, AND DIES

This great fight put the Israelites in possession of valuable land, and here the tribes of Reuben and Gad, and half the fighting tribe of Manasseh, settled down to occupy the country.

And now it came upon the aged Moses that the day of his death was at hand. The veteran law-giver, whose life had begun so romantically in the palace of Pharaoh, who had spent all the vigour of his manhood in the wilderness with these unruly people, knew that he was to die, knew that he would never enter the Promised Land to whose frontier he had so bravely brought his people.

There is something deeply pathetic to us in the ascent of this noble old man to the top of the mountain of Nebo, from whose windy peaks his fading eyes could behold the goodly land. He looked upon it all; and he appointed Joshua as his successor; he declared to the Israelites the majesty of God; and, trusting that he had done his duty, he fell asleep.

The Interests and Pleasures of Life for All Indoors and Out

MAKING A TOBOGGAN

A TOBOGGAN is a kind of simple sledge or sleigh that affords boundless delight and healthy exercise to children who live in lands where deep snow is more common than it is in our British winter.

But even in Britain a toboggan can be a source of immense pleasure when by chance we have one of the old-fashioned Christmas-card sort of winters, with its heavy snow-drifts and soft, clean snow lying several inches thick in the meadows and lanes, but particularly on the steep slopes, for it is there that boys and girls can use the toboggan.

There are two kinds of toboggans. One is made with runners like a sleigh; the other sort is only a piece of board curved up in front. Those with runners are the better kind and one of these is described here. The flat variety is good when the snow is quite soft; but as it soon hardens with sliding the runner toboggan is more useful.

THE TOBOGGAN

To make a toboggan, first get two pieces of board about four feet long, six inches wide, and one inch thick. These must be cut to form the two sides.

Now get some more wood and cut it into lengths of twenty inches. This wood should not be more than half an inch thick. As each piece is cut it should be nailed to the long pieces in the way shown in the picture. The piece in front may be a little narrower than the others as it is fixed to the turned-up part. By looking carefully at the picture two pairs of nails on the side will be seen. These nails hold in position two pieces of wood stretching from side to side so as to strengthen the toboggan.

Every boy and girl in Norway, Switzerland, and Canada, has a toboggan. A merry party goes to where there is a long, steep slope covered with snow. Then, one after another, the children sit upon their toboggans, and, starting at the top of the slope, let them slide right down to the bottom, guiding the toboggans meantime by touching the snow occasionally with their feet.

When the toboggans stop at the bottom, the children walk up the slope again, dragging their toboggans with them. Then they repeat the sliding down, and climb up again, and so on, until it is time for them to go home.

Sometimes the toboggans are made into a long file. One boy, generally the eldest, goes first. He sits on his toboggan and then another boy gets his toboggan and puts it close behind the first. He stretches out his legs so that the leader can hold his ankles. All the others do the same in turn till there is a string of children on toboggans. From a little distance the long line looks like a big black snake. When all are ready, the first boy shouts to the others to hold tight, and then he lifts up his feet and away they all go. The long line winds to right and left down the slope, and sometimes it goes faster than a train.

If any let go and fall off they are left behind in a moment, for the toboggan train goes at such a rate that it cannot be stopped easily.

CRAFTS · GAMES . NEEDLEWORK · PUZZLES · SCIENCE EXPERIMENTS

THE MYSTERIOUS JACOB'S LADDER

A VERY old puzzle, which is easily made, is that known as the Jacob's ladder. It consists of an ingenious arrangement of little pieces of wood and tape, so fastened together that by holding the top piece of wood and alternately inverting it and bringing it back to its original position, another of the pieces of wood is apparently constantly falling from the top to the bottom.

To make one of these clever little toys, first of all get some suitable wood from which to cut the pieces.

Then decide how many steps the Jacob's ladder shall have, and although it may consist of any number, great or small, a good number is ten. More than this becomes rather unmanageable.

The pieces of wood must all be of exactly the same size—say, $3\frac{1}{2}$ inches by 2 inches; and when they are cut out with a fretsaw they should be nicely smoothed, and the top and bottom angles rounded slightly by rubbing with sandpaper.

Ordinary white or pink or black tape rather less than half an inch wide is used for joining the pieces of wood, and the method of fitting them to the wood is shown in picture 1. Each piece of wood has three tapes, and all the tapes should be of the same length—about 5 inches—so that the ends pass round with enough length to glue down on the wood as seen in the picture.

There is a centre tape and side tapes for each piece of wood, and the arrangement is the same in each case, however many steps the Jacob's ladder may have. The centre tape a on the board A is fastened on the far side of the board B at b. The side tapes c_1 c_2 on A are fastened on the other side of B at d_1 d_2, while the middle tape e on the board B passes on to the board C, and is fastened at f, and so on through the entire length of the ladder.

HOW TO FIX THE TAPES AND WORK THE LADDER

When all the tapes have been glued, and left to set thoroughly, hold the top board A as in picture 2, and B seems to fall to the bottom; then invert A, and again the board next to it seems to fall to the bottom. A is returned to its original position, and the board drops again, and so on without end.

The whole thing is a clever optical illusion. This toy is said to have been invented in Japan many hundreds, if not thousands, of years ago, and hundreds of thousands of Jacob's ladders were formerly sent from Japan for sale in Europe and America.

MEASURING THE HEIGHT OF A TREE

THERE is a very simple way of measuring the height of a tree which it is impossible to measure by climbing or in any direct way. Suppose, for instance, it is required to find out the height of the apple tree, A B, in the picture. First of all go to where the tree is standing and measure a distance of, say, 30 feet from it, in a straight line, marking the spot that is 30 feet from the tree. Then take a stick, C D, of any convenient length—a fairly straight branch of a tree will do—and stand this upright in the ground at the marked spot. Suppose that the stick used is 4 feet in height above the ground. Now walk farther away from the tree in the same straight line as when measuring off the distance of 30 feet, until a point E is reached, where, from ground level, the top of the stick and the top of the tree are seen in the same straight line—that is, the top of the stick just covers the highest part of the tree. There are now two imaginary triangles, as shown in the picture, and the proportion of the side C D to the side C E, in the smaller triangle C D E, is exactly the same as the proportion of the side B A to the side B E, in the larger triangle B A E. It is clear from this that every schoolboy or schoolgirl can work out the height of the tree. Suppose that the line C E is 6 feet. It is known that the stick is 4 feet high and length B E 36 feet. From these measurements the simple proportion sun.. 6 is to 4 as 36 is to B A is obtained. Multiply 36 by 4, making 144, and divide by 6, which gives 24 feet as the height of the tree. The height of church steeples and other buildings can be measured in this way.

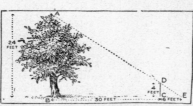

AN EASY WAY OF MEASURING A TREE

BAKED, BOILED, AND BATTER PUDDINGS

Puddings give scope for all sorts of experiments and, with these standard recipes as a guide, many new ways with old favourites can be contrived.

MILK or Cereal Puddings are delicious if properly made, and the secret is to cook them slowly and well. Allow one and a half ounces of sago, tapioca, rice, pearl barley, or other cereal for every pint of milk, and sweeten this with an ounce or more of sugar mixed with a small saltspoonful of salt. Golden syrup or honey can be used for sweetening if it is added after the cereal has been cooked and started cooling. Honey loses value when cooked, and treacle usually curdles the milk, so that the appearance, though not the actual food value, of a pudding is spoiled.

To bake a Milk Pudding big enough for eight people put three ounces of cereal into a greased pie dish, add the sugar and a quart of milk, and cook in a very slow oven for about two and a half hours. A smaller pudding cooked like this often becomes dry, and for this reason it is a good idea to cook one-pint milk puddings slowly in the top of a double boiler with the lid tightly on. Afterwards the pudding can be poured into a pie dish, sprinkled with a dessertspoonful of castor sugar, and browned beneath the grill.

A cold Cereal Cream tastes and looks very different from an ordinary milk pudding if the sugar for it is first seasoned by putting the finely-pared rind of an orange or lemon into the screw-stoppered sugar jar for two days. This will give the pudding a delicate orange or lemon flavour. Then tint the mixture pink with a spot of cochineal, and add a cupful of any chopped mixed dried fruits as it is turned into the serving dish to cool. A Chocolate Cream is made in the same way, but with the addition of two to three tablespoonfuls of powdered sweet chocolate for every pint of milk.

To make a Batter Pudding to go with roast beef, sift four ounces of flour into a basin with a pinch of salt. Gradually beat in an egg mixed with half a pint of milk. Beat egg, milk, and flour together ceaselessly for 15 minutes. Leave it to rest for an hour or longer, then beat it again; pour the mixture into a shallow well-oiled tin, bake for 20 to 30 minutes in a really hot oven, and use immediately it is cooked. The same pudding makes a good sweet, served with butter and

Make sure the water keeps boiling or the pudding will be heavy. Fill up with boiling water from the kettle as needed.

sugar, or with warmed jam; or it can be made into Pancakes. For these, pour a dessertspoonful at a time into a slightly-oiled hot frying pan, allow it to spread thinly over the pan, and cook quickly till lightly browned, then toss or turn neatly with a palette knife to brown the other side.

A quarter of a pound of finely-chopped suet or fat, and a pinch of salt, rubbed into eight ounces of self-raising flour and mixed to a very stiff dough with a little milk, sour milk, or water, is a simple basic recipe for Dumplings, or Dough Boys as they are called, to serve with stews. Divide the dough into small balls, roll in a little flour, drop into boiling meat stock, and boil quickly for 15 to 20 minutes. For sweet dumplings mix in four ounces of sugar and some dried fruit before adding the milk. Another way is to leave out the fruit and to make separate dumplings by wrapping the dough round pared and cored apples stuffed with dates, or round large plums. Drop into boiling water and cook a little longer than plain dumplings.

This same recipe will serve as a standard one for Boiled and Steamed Puddings, but mix it with a well-beaten egg, for extra lightness and goodness, and a little milk, first adding to the liquid whatever flavouring is preferred. Some varieties which can be made from this mixture are : Orange or Lemon, using the grated rind and the juice of one fruit and a tablespoonful of orange or lemon marmalade, instead of milk; Pineapple, when chopped pineapple chunks are added to the dry ingredients, and the juice takes the place of the milk; Date, with four ounces of chopped, stoned dates and a little nutmeg added before moistening.

When mixed, turn into a well-greased pudding basin, cover with greased paper, tie down with a pudding cloth, and stand in a saucepan of boiling water with the lid lightly on and boil for three hours ; or put into a steamer to steam for at least half as long again. Any of these varieties can be made into a Roly-Poly. For this, take a well-floured clean cloth, roll it round the pudding mixture, and tie it tightly at both ends, allowing room for the pudding to rise.

For a change from suety steamed or boiled puddings, try a cake mixture lightened with a couple of tablespoonfuls of toasted breadcrumbs. Puddings of this kind are nice served with custard sauce. See page 1369.

LITTLE PROBLEMS FOR ODD MOMENTS

*T*HESE problems are continued from page 1124, and their answers, together with more questions, will be found on page 1370.

79. How Long to Cycle a Mile?

In a cycle race of one mile, A can give B 15 seconds start, and B can give C 176 yards start. A beats C by one minute when he gives no start.

How long would each of them take to ride a mile?

80. How Many Nuts had Each?

Jane said to her sister, " I have five times as many nuts as you have." The sister replied, " Yes, you have 24 more than I have."

How many nuts had each?

81. How Many Passengers?

" I will take you for ninepence each," said the boatman at the ferry. " Will you take two more and make it eightpence each?" asked a passenger. " Yes," answered the boatman; " I shall make sixpence more if I do."

How many passengers were taken altogether by the boatman?

82. How Much for a Horse and a Cow?

" I once sold nine good horses and seven cows for £300," said Farmer Giles. " I suppose you got more for each horse than you did for each cow?" asked his friend. " Yes, I got double," replied the farmer.

What was the price of the animals?

83. What did the Pencils Cost?

A shopkeeper sold pencils at 4½d. each or three for a shilling. One day he saw his assistant sell one pencil to a customer, and he said, " Why did you not sell the lady three pencils?" " Because," said the assistant, " you have the same profit on one as you have on three."

What did the pencils cost the shopkeeper?

84. When were they Married?

" My father is 47 years old today," said Mary to Joe, " and my mother is just 38. When they were married my father was exactly half as old again as my mother. Now can you tell me how long my father and mother have been married?"

85. How Much did the Grocer Lose?

Said the grocer, " One of my customers has failed, and I have lost a good customer. I used to sell him tea at 60 per cent. profit on cost price. He is going to pay 12s. 6d. in the pound."

How much did the grocer lose?

86. What was its Price?

" During sale week," said the draper to a customer, " we will allow 20 per cent. off the prices marked on the goods, but next week, after the sale is over, we will allow only 5 per cent. discount." After the sale was over the lady bought something, and paid for it 3s. more than the sale price.

What was the marked price?

87. How Far is it to the Station?

If I walk to the railway station at three miles an hour, I shall be 15 minutes too late for my train; but if I cycle to the station at 10 miles an hour, I shall be 27 minutes too soon.

How far off is the station?

88. How Many Persons Were They?

" This party," said the host, represents father, mother, uncle, aunt, sister, brother, nephew, niece, and two cousins."

What was the fewest number that could be in the party?

THE ANSWERS TO THE PROBLEMS ON PAGE 1124

72. One-quarter added to one-third is seven-twelfths, and the difference between seven-twelfths and half, which is six-twelfths, is one-twelfth of the whole. But Fred said that this difference was ten marbles, so that the total number of marbles must have been 120, or twelve times ten marbles. The answer can be proved by adding one-quarter and one-third, which make 70, and this number is ten more than half the number of marbles.

73. The difference between one-half and two-thirds is one-sixth. Thus, one-sixth was equal to 3s. 4d., so that James and Harry had 20s. each to begin with. Now prove the sum. When James had spent half of 20s. he had 10s. left ; when Harry had spent two-thirds of 20s. he had one-third of 20s.—that is, 6s. 8d.—left. The difference between 10s. and 6s. 8d. is 3s. 4d., so the answer of 20s. is correct.

74. The word " united," which is " untied " with the two middle letters changed.

75. To go 40 miles, at 50 miles an hour, the train took four-fifths of an hour, or 48 minutes. This was 10 minutes too much, so the time allowed for the distance was 38 minutes. But the train was really only 2 minutes late, and therefore took 40 minutes to do the 40 miles. Its actual speed was 60 miles an hour.

76. Brown took six days to do the work alone. Since he takes twice as long as Hodge and Jenkins to do the same work, it is clear that when they all work together he would do half the amount which the other two do—that is, one-third of the total. Therefore, as he does one-third in two days, he could do the whole hedge when working alone without Hodge and Jenkins in six days.

77. If the inflow would fill the tank in 2 hours, it would make the tank half full in 1 hour. If the leak would empty the tank in 10 hours, it would in 1 hour allow one-tenth of the capacity of the tank to escape. The net result of the running in and of the leakage would be that four-tenths of the tank capacity would run in in an hour, and the tank would be filled in 2½ hours.

78. If the church clock struck 3 in the same time as the town-hall clock struck 2, the interval between the strokes of the town-hall clock must have been twice as long as the intervals between the strokes of the church clock. Thus, the clocks would strike together at all alternate strokes. As they struck 1 together, the church clock would strike 3 when the town-hall clock 2 ; the town-hall clock would then have only one more stroke to make to tell the hour. Then the church clock would strike 5 as the town-hall clock struck 3, and the town-hall clock would have two more strokes to make to tell the hour. Thus the time was 5 o'clock.

THE BOOMERANG AND HOW TO MAKE IT

IT is simple to make a boomerang of cardboard that when flung out into space will travel for a certain distance and then return again.

Boomerangs can be made of various shapes, but the simplest and most familiar is that shown in the first picture. Take an ordinary postcard of medium thickness, and first draw the boomerang carefully to the proportions shown in the picture.

Then, having drawn it, lay the card on a flat piece of wood or strawboard, resting on an even surface, and, with a sharp penknife cut it out clearly and neatly. No jagged edges must be left or the boomerang will not work. Do not cut it out with scissors, for that causes the card to curl, and a cardboard boomerang must be quite flat.

THREE BOOMERANGS AND HOW TO THROW THEM

Another very good shape for a boomerang is shown in the second picture, and here again first draw the outline on a postcard, and, after making sure that the curve and the proportions are quite accurate, cut the weapon out with a sharp penknife.

A more complicated form of boomerang is that shown in the third picture. Here be watchful that there are no jagged surfaces in the angles where the arms join one another.

It will be noticed that in the case of all three shapes the ends are carefully rounded. This is important or the boomerang will not work properly. It may sail through the air swiftly and well, but it will not come back.

The method of throwing each of these cardboard boomerangs is the same, and the picture on this page showing how the first shape is driven into space will explain how to act in each case. The boomerang is placed on some flat surface, such as a book with one end projecting slightly over the edge, and then it is flicked off sharply with a pencil. As it sails off into the air it will whirl round and round, and after going some distance, will describe a curve and come back again.

Any failure of the boomerang to return to its thrower will be due to faulty shaping or cutting out, or to too heavy cardboard.

In its native home, Australia, the true boomerang, made of hardwood, is thrown by hand and with amazing skill, a twist of the wrist giving it the necessary skew. But toy boomerangs of cardboard are too light for this, and the required spin has to be given by the sharpness of the flick with the pencil.

TWO SIMPLE LIFTING TRICKS

THERE are many simple lifting tricks which seem easy to do, but prove almost impossible when tried out. Here are two.

Sit upon a chair and place the right hand flat upon the middle of the head, as shown in the first picture. Then invite any friends who may be present to take it in turn to raise the hand by simply lifting it off, They may use both hands, but must lift steadily and not jerk or pull sideways.

Unless they are exceedingly strong they will be quite unable to move the hand, provided it is kept pressed firmly and squarely down upon the head. The task set seems simple enough, but there will be great astonishment when it is found that no one can do it.

In the other trick ask someone to stand

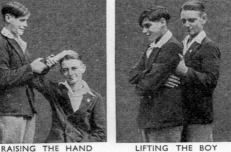

RAISING THE HAND   LIFTING THE BOY

at the back and, putting his arms under your armpits, lift you up. This will be quite easy. Now say that, by a simple trick, you will prevent him from lifting you off the ground. He will be sceptical, but the truth of the words can soon be proved.

When he gets his hands and arms in position for lifting as before, place your right hand under his left wrist, and push upward, as in the second picture. Your friend will then be unable to lift you from the ground, unless, of course, he is very strong indeed, and you are very light.

The reason for the difficulty is that your centre of gravity is changed, and much more force is needed to raise you under the new conditions.

THE MYSTERIOUS PURSE

THE conjurer borrows a sixpence. Taking a piece of paper about four inches square, he lays this on the table, puts the coin in the centre, and folds down the sides over it. There is "no deception" so far; the coin is honestly wrapped in the paper. Picking up the little packet, he asks someone to blow upon it, or does so himself. When he again opens the paper, the sixpence has disappeared, and the owner probably begins to wish he had not lent it. But again the wizard folds the paper. Once more he blows upon it, and once more unfolds it. The sixpence has come back, and the owner of the coin looks quite cheerful again.

But the simple-looking bit of paper is not so simple as it looks. In fact, it is a "trick" paper, specially arranged for the purpose.

The young conjurer may like to prepare such a paper for himself. If so, this is the way:

Take a half-sheet of ordinary notepaper and fold it in two. Then, with a sharp needle, make four little holes through both thicknesses of the paper, two inches apart, so as to form a square, as shown in the first picture. Then cut apart the two portions of the paper, and fold down the edges of one of them towards the centre, using the needle-marks as guides. The paper thus folded will form a sort of little pocket, or envelope, as in picture 2. Paste or gum this in the centre of the other paper, exactly between the needle-marks. The two together will now look on the one side like picture 3, but on the other side like a plain piece of paper.

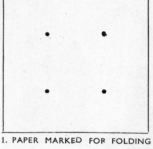

1. PAPER MARKED FOR FOLDING

2. THE FOLDED PURSE

It is the plain side which, in performing the trick, is shown to the company, care being taken, by the way, not to have a light behind it, which would give away the secret. Then lay the paper, with this side uppermost, on the table. Having placed the coin on the paper, fold down the edges over it, again using the needle-marks as guides, so as to make the folding correspond exactly with that of the pocket on the other side. The paper will now in reality form two such little pockets, back to back. In offering the paper to be blown upon, turn it over so that it is the empty side which is opened next time. When it is blown upon for the second time, again turn it over so as to bring the side in which the sixpence was placed uppermost.

Do not of course let the company see the paper being reversed. To do this in proper conjuring style, hold it in the first instance clipped between the first and second fingers of the right hand. In offering it to be blown upon, push it upwards with the thumb and clip its outer edge between the thumb and forefinger, when it will have performed an imperceptible somersault. The turn over should be made with the arm in motion, when the greater movement will conceal the less important from the spectators.

The sixpence is brought back again by a repetition of the process. Of course it is not necessary to use a sixpence. A penny or half-penny, or a bone counter, may be substituted, according to the effect it is wished to produce. Further, the paper may be used not only to vanish, but to change one thing into another. For instance, in order to change a sixpence into a farthing, just place a farthing beforehand in the pocket on the reverse or trick side of the paper.

The same paper may be used more than once, but it will show by the creases that it has been previously folded, and the effect is scarcely so good as with a freshly prepared piece of paper.

The method described is the simplest form of the trick. It may be improved upon considerably by using three pieces of paper instead of one. One of these must be rather smaller, and the other larger, than the trick paper. The smallest we will call number one, the trick paper number two, and the largest paper number three. The first and last are mere plain pieces of paper, but there must be an exact duplicate of number one, and this must be placed there beforehand, in the pocket of number two. When working the trick show, in a careless sort of way, both sides of number one before wrapping the coin in it. Place this paper, with the coin in it, in number two, and then this latter in number three, first, however, turning it over. The trick is now done. Coming to number two, it is the empty duplicate of number one that is found inside. Hand this to someone else to open. Numbers one and three being plain paper, no one will suspect number two.

3. THE BACK OF THE PAPER PREPARED FOR USE

Simple Learning Made Easy for Very Little People

READING—MORE RHYMES AND STORIES

ANOTHER thing to remember, Mother told John and Jennifer, is that always after a Q comes a U. Let us see how many words we can think of:

Queen	Quill	Quilt	Quake
Quart	Quack	Quick	Quince
Quality	Quantity	Quagga	Queue

"There are some words that have ew," said Mother. "in which they sound like the Crying Twins." Such as:

Knew	Few	Stew	Mew
Grew	Flew	Blew	View

and two more, ue, which sound just the same:

Blue	Flue	Due	Rue
Clue	Sue	True	Cue

Mother said that they must also learn about two letters which go together to make one sound, th, as in the word *the*. Sometimes they come at the beginning of a word, sometimes in the middle, and sometimes at the end:

Tom Thumb and Tom Thin
Went out together,
They both liked the rain
And thundery weather.
" I think this is fun,"
Said little Tom Thumb.
Tom Thin said, " Be quick,
The fog's getting thick;
And thirty-three thrushes
Are thirsty and thankful."

Then Mother told them about the Sneezing Sounds, whose letters were ch:

Charlie had a chill;
The chill was on his chest.

Three cheers for a Chinaman,
He chatters in the breeze,
He bought a chalk-white cat
Who ate cherries, chocs, and cheese.

" Next," said Mother, " we have the Hush Sounds."

They knew the rhyme Hush-a-bye Baby, On the Tree Top, and Mother made up another Hush story for them:

Along the road went a flock of sheep and behind them came the shepherd and his son, Jack, and a sheep-dog called Dash. Dash ran up and down to keep the sheep in the right road. As they went along they came to a shop, and the sheep ran in. Dash was after them like a shot, and drove them out.

By and by they got to Farmer Sharp's gate, and Dash and the shepherd drove them, one by one, into the fold. The cows were in the cow-shed, and Dash went into his kennel. The shepherd went in to supper, and Jack cried out, " Good-night! Good old Dash! "

" Bow-wow, bow-wow," said Dash.

Jack took off his shoes and had a good wash, and went in to his supper. They had fish from a hot dish.

Dash stayed out to mind the sheep in the fold, and the cows in the cow-shed, and the tools in the tool-shed, and the hens in the hen-coop, and the pigs in the sty.

READING · WRITING · ARITHMETIC · MUSIC · DRAWING · FRENCH

NUMBERS—USING THE SCALES

When Mother took the twins shopping they always hoped that she would go to the grocers. They loved to watch the coffee, the barley, and the oatmeal being weighed, as well as all the different kinds of sugar—lump, white, and brown sugar. How they wanted to help!

One day when they were coming home Mother said, " Why don't you add another counter to your café and have a grocer's shop? I have a small set of scales that you can have."

John and Jennifer were so excited at the idea that they could hardly wait to get home and have their dinner. Mother said they couldn't have real things to play with in their shop, as that would be wasteful; they would have to think of things which would do instead.

For brown sugar, they had sand; for lump they collected acorns and chestnuts; they made sweets of different shapes and sizes out of clay—round ones for bull's eyes; round flat ones for butter pats; square ones for toffees; little round flat ones for fruit drops. When they were made they let them dry and harden, then they painted them the proper colours.

Another way they made sweets was out of papier mâché, and when they were dry they wrapped them in coloured Cellophane, and pieces of gold and silver paper they had saved from their own sweets. As a special treat Mother gave them some haricot beans to weigh.

When it was all ready they paid a special visit to the grocer's to find out how much all the things were, and when they got home they made out a price list. Then something very sad happened; Mother could not find the little weights which belonged to the small set of scales. They hunted everywhere, but could not find them. So Mother made some little bags out of ticking, embroidered the weights on the outside, filled them with sand, and sewed them up.

John and Jennifer weighed these weight bags and found that two $\frac{1}{2}$ lbs made 1 lb, four $\frac{1}{4}$ lbs made 1 lb, and sixteen 1 ozs made 1 lb. Then they tried to weigh the goods in their grocer's shop.

WRITING—THE POETRY BOOKS

After practising hard at making beautiful letters, the twins learned to write some easy poems. They had already written Nursery Rhymes, and now they were going to make their own poetry books.

Mother reminded them that rhymes and poems are written in little lines, and often have the same sound at the end of each line—" sounds like music," said John. First of all they chose some poems that are called Nursery Rhymes, but were not the usual ones. Mother read to them, and the twins chose the ones they liked best.

Mother said they must always remember that:

> Every rhyme we write in a line,
> Begins with a capital every time.

Daddy bought them a book of poems, and the twins copied the short ones they liked. They each copied their favourites.

Then Mother and the twins set to work to make some new rhymes. Mother helped them by saying one line, and the twins made up the next line. Here is one they made up:

> Susan was a little grey cat,
> She ate a lot, and grew quite fat.

John and Jennifer grew quite clever at making up these little rhymes, and loved their poetry books.

Mother loved poetry, too, and read it so often that one day the twins decided to make up a poem themselves.

First of all they thought what the poem was to be about; then they made up the rhymes, and Mother wrote them down. They often changed their minds, and altered the rhymes, but at last the poems were finished, and copied out into their poetry books.

The twins were so pleased that Daddy gave them each a clean sheet of paper, and they wrote the poems again in their very best writing as a birthday present for Mother. Here is John's poem:

The Panda

Percy the Panda lived at the Zoo,
Mabel the monkey lived there too.
With a big balloon they had great fun,
They played in the gardens in the sun.
Percy liked strawberries, nuts, and jam;
Mabel liked coconuts, peas, and ham!

Jennifer's poem was about Mother:

My Mother

My Mother is a lady,
She is very fair and tall.
Of everybody in the world,
I love her best of all.

Daddy saw the poems and thought they were very good. He said he wanted one too, so John and Jennifer each wrote one for him. John wrote:

My Daddy

My Daddy gets up early,
He goes to catch a train,
He goes right up to London,
In sunshine or in rain.

Jennifer wrote about the cinema Daddy had made:

Our Cinema

My Daddy made a cinema,
He made it out of wood,
He painted it bright yellow,
And it looked very good.

ART—MAKING A PICTURE MAP

In Hereford Cathedral there is a wonderful old map which shows the Earth round and flat like a penny, as people imagined it to be when the map was drawn about the year 1300, before America was discovered or the Earth was known to be round like a ball.

Although the map is inaccurate it does give a pictorial idea of the world as it was then thought to be. All the important rivers, mountains, and cities are shown, and pictures of buildings and things for which they were famous. It was drawn by a learned man who knew a great deal about the subject of this picture map.

How much of the district in which you live can you imagine in this way? Try to make a picture map of it. Perhaps you will need to take a walk round to refresh your memory, and notice the appearance and position of railways, streets, lanes, buildings, bridges, open spaces, gardens, and trees. See if there is a river, canal, stream, a lake or pond, or a hill, cliffs, or quarry in your area.

Try to get a picture of it all in your mind. Your own home could occupy the centre of the picture, or perhaps your school, or your village green or market square.

When you have the idea clearly in your mind get a large piece of paper (or a large blank wall, if you can find it) on which to make your drawing. Put the main lines in first, and the general pattern of it all, and make sure of the important things before adding details. You can use chalk, charcoal, or pencil, and complete it in powder colour or chalks.

If there is a field in your picture map it would be enough to draw a few of the animals in it large, and this also applies to a lake or pond, when only a small number of birds floating or fishes swimming need be shown.

Houses and other buildings can be drawn in the way which best shows what they look like from the road. A building like a stadium or the Oval cricket ground would be best drawn as you imagine seeing it from above.

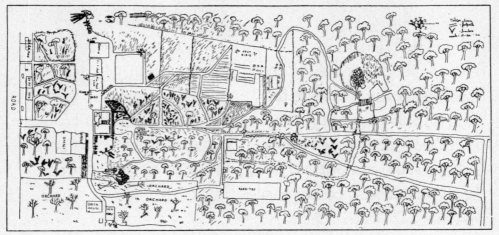

PICTURE MAP OF A COUNTRY GARDEN, DRAWN BY A BOY

If some important person lived in the place of your map, he or she might be included in it. Similarly, a picture of any great event might form a part.

You will want to colour your map and have some kind of a finishing border or frame round it, and for this the previous chapter will have given you some ideas. Sometimes there is a coat of arms or crest belonging to your district, and the addition of its pattern and colour to the border would look well. The names of roads and streets or persons can be written on the map in clear handwriting.

If you wanted to make a picture map of your own house and garden you could use your average stride as a standard measurement in finding the main proportions. That is what was done by the boy who made the map of a country garden which is shown in the illustration. The original drawing is about a yard long.

MUSIC—MUSICAL ARITHMETIC

THE minuet of Mozart's day (his symphonies and those of Haydn have as their third movement a minuet, a dance in 3/4 time) goes with dignity. In the movement of the music we can feel the leisurely rhythm of the Court dance of two centuries ago.

After Mozart, Beethoven. His third movements are usually called scherzi, and, although they have the same time-signature, they go much faster than any of the minuets of Mozart.

Next you may hear such a movement as Rimsky-Korsakov's Flight of the Bumble Bee. So fast does this go that we wonder how the clarinet player manages to play all his notes. The nearer we come to our own time the faster seems the pace of music.

This progress towards speed is shown in the very names of the notes (though some have fallen out of use). The man who played the organ with his clenched fist could only play a note now and then. When he played a note he held it for a considerable time. The note he most often played was called the " long."

A note of less value which came early into written music was the breve. Breve means brief or short. We sometimes, but not very often, meet the breve in hymn tunes. It looked like ⊨ . As the speed of musical performance increased the breve gave way to the semibreve (half a breve), quite familiar to us as the longest note which we employ. The semibreve is shown thus: ○.

When minims were introduced it was thought that the end of the craze for rapidity had been reached, for minim means the least. Two minims took the time of one semibreve, and a semibreve was but half a breve. With these note values music managed quite happily for a long time. Here is the beginning of an ancient melody written mostly in minims and semibreves:

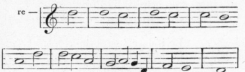

This is the opening of the Agincourt Song, written to commemorate the battle. It is in the old *re-re* scale. Sing the melody and feel how dignified it is with all its white notes. Two bars from the end we meet some black notes—crochets. They are still faster than minims and one minim can hold two crotchets.

When violins became popular they were able to show a further turn of speed. They took the place of the viol. The viol, very sweet sounding, had six strings. The violin had four, so that, with less to worry about, the player could manage faster tunes.

So we meet the quaver. Two quavers to a crotchet. After the quaver the semiquaver. Quicker and quicker.

We know what crotchet and quaver look like. Here is the semiquaver and if we meet four all together (which we do, as four semiquavers take the same time as one crotchet) we see.

There for the moment we may stop. There are notes even shorter than the semiquaver but we are not likely to meet them just yet.

We should accustom ourselves to seeing combinations of these notes as we are likely to meet them. Here are a few ways in which we might meet semibreves, minims, crotchets, quavers, and semiquavers in 4/4 time:

Rhythm is one of the most fascinating things in the world. In music the rhythmic value of the notes tells us a great deal before we even begin to play or to sing. We may look at three melodic openings. Each is different and each uses a different set of notes. The first is an old psalm tune from the sixteenth century:

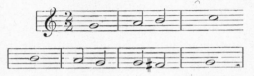

Semibreves and minims make this solemn and well suited to the singing of a large congregation. Because it was meant to be sung by many people the speed was deliberate.

We may see a melody by Bach in crotchets and quavers. What key is this melody written in? This is not too fast and not too slow. It was written to be played by his own children:

And last, a phrase with quicker notes:

The sign is a quaver *rest* which means that we are to be quiet for the length of a quaver. We shall have more to find out about rests. Notice how the quavers and semiquavers give the feeling of wave movement. And this is music

Underneath the notes are the French rhythm names, syllables by which you may easily remember the note values.

Clap the rhythm shown above. The pattern is slow at first, but then it gathers momentum.

about waves. It is the phrase on which Mendelssohn based the opening of his beautiful overture The Hebrides, sometimes called Fingal's Cave, and it is a wonderful tone-picture of the lovely scenery of the Scottish islands.

FRENCH—THE FIRST DAY IN PARIS

First line : French.   Second line : English word.   Third line : As we say it in English.

C'est notre premier jour à Paris.
This is our   first   day at Paris.
It is our first day in Paris.

La bonne tire de côté les rideaux.
The nurse draws at side the curtains.
The nurse draws aside the curtains.

Nous faisons vite notre toilette.
We   make quickly our   toilet.
We dress quickly.

Nous avons du café au   lait et des petits pains.
We   have some coffee with the milk and some little breads.
We have coffee and rolls.

Nous nous éveillons de bonne heure.
We ourselves awake   at good hour.
We awake early.

Elle dit : " Le jour est superbe."
She says : " The day is   superb."
She says: " It is a beautiful day."

Puis nous descendons à maman.
Then we   descend to Mamma.
Then we go down   to Mamma.

Nous avons bientôt   fini.
We   have   soon   finished.
Soon we have finished.

Nous voulons aller   nous   promener.
We   wish   to go ourselves to promenade.
We want to go for a walk.

Nous rencontrons une petite fille.
We   encounter   a   little   girl.
We meet a little girl.

Nous disons tous : " Bonjour! "
We   say   all : " Good day ! "
We all say: " Good morning! "

Elle dit : " Puis-je vous accompagner ? "
She says : " May I   you to accompany ? "
She says: " May I go with you ? "

Nous courons chercher nos chapeaux.
We   run   to fetch   our   hats.
We run to get our hats.

C'est notre petite amie de la   veille.
This is our   little friend of the last evening.
It is our little friend of last night.

Nous disons que nous allons nous   promener.
We   say   that we   go ourselves to promenade.
We say we are going for a walk.

Maman répond :   " Oui, certainement."
Mamma responds : " Yes,   certainly."
Mamma replies: " Yes, certainly."

Nous marchons vers les boulevards.
We   march   toward the boulevards.
We go toward the boulevards.

Le nom de notre petite amie est Julie.
The name of our   little friend is Julia.
Our little friend's name is Julia.

Il est presque l'heure du déjeuner.
It is nearly the hour of the lunch.
It is nearly lunch-time.

Ils ressemblent aux parcs de Londres.
They resemble   to the parks of London.
They are like our London parks.

Elle a une belle. Nous faisons une bonne partie.
She has a ball.   We   make   a good   game.
She has a ball.   We have a good game.

Nous devons   aller   chez nous.
We   must   to go to the house of us.
We must go home.

The Story of the Boundless Universe and All its Wondrous Worlds

One of the seven hundred kinds of fishes that lived in the Carboniferous Age

THE CARBONIFEROUS AGE

THE Carboniferous rocks are found all over the world, sometimes in small patches and sometimes in huge areas. In England, France, and Germany there are usually small areas of this rock, while in Russia, China, and North America there are sheets of rock, spreading over thousands of square miles.

There are two main types of rock in the Carboniferous system—the limestone built up in the sea by various coral-forming animals, and the sandstone and shale rock formed in shallow lakes and lagoons. Rocks of both types are found in Britain.

In South Wales and the adjacent areas of England there is limestone of marine origin 500 feet thick, and this limestone extends northward in the Pennine Chain, and increases in thickness to 4000 feet. In Scotland, on the other hand, the Carboniferous rock consists chiefly of sandstone and shale, with a few thin layers of limestone here and there. Through both kinds of rock there run seams of iron and coal, and therefore the rock of the Carboniferous age is of inestimable value to the welfare of mankind.

The changing nature and decreasing depth of the rock as we go northward from England to Scotland show that at the time this rock was formed the Carboni-ferous areas of England were deep under the sea, while the same rocks in Scotland were under comparatively shallow water, partly in the form of inland marshes, lakes, and lagoons. During this age about half of Scotland, and almost all Ireland, was under the sea, but the Irish Sea and a great part of Wales were land surface. There was a large island that might be said to represent Scotland, another large island that might be considered as a united England and Ireland, and several other islands of smaller size.

The animal life of the Carboniferous Age was various. In the rock laid down under the sea we find especially crinoids, corals, foraminifera, and brachiopods; and great masses of the limestone are composed of the skeletons of these creatures. Trilobites were rare, but there were many crustacean ostracods, and more than 700 kinds of fishes have been found. The fishes were mostly sharks, and most of them had flat-crowned teeth adapted for crushing the shells of the creatures on which they lived.

In rocks formed in the marshes and lagoons over the land are found numerous small fishes, crustaceans and molluscs.

Among land animals are found cockroaches, crickets, beetles, locusts, mayflies, and dragonflies ; even bugs and walking-

ASTRONOMY · GEOLOGY · GEOGRAPHY · CHEMISTRY · PHYSICS · LIFE

COAL Areas of the
Carboniferous Period:
other CARBONIFEROUS STRATA
tinted as:
PERMIAN STRATA shown as:

G. F. MORRELL

This map shows the Carboniferous strata in light grey, with the coal-fields a darker grey. The Permian strata are shown striped. There are Carboniferous patches in various parts of Scotland and England. The Permian rock is rarer; but a long strip runs between Sunderland and Nottingham. It will be seen that where there are patches of Carboniferous rocks are the industrial cities of England. It is, indeed, to the forests of the Carboniferous Age that England owes her commercial prosperity.

LIFE & REMAINS OF THE CARBONIFEROUS AGE

THE LUXURIANT VEGETATION OF THE CARBONIFEROUS AGE—FERNS, MOSSES, HORSETAILS, AND SOME OF THE ANIMAL LIFE OF THE PERIOD, INCLUDING AN ARCHEGOSAURUS AND A FISH

A CUTTING THROUGH PERMIAN, CARBONIFEROUS, AND DEVONIAN STRATA. IN THE CARBONIFEROUS STRATUM ARE SEEN FOSSILS AND STUMPS AND BRANCHES OF TREES IN A COAL SEAM

stick insects. But, so far, there were neither flies nor moths, neither butterflies nor bees. The wings of one curious beetle-like insect measured seven inches across. Scorpions were plentiful, some of gigantic size, and there were a few crustaceans of the crab and lobster family, and many species of millipedes and spiders.

THE JUNGLES AND FORESTS OF THE ARCTIC REGIONS

But perhaps the most interesting fossils found in the Carboniferous rocks are the Labyrinthodonts, so-called because of the peculiar structure of their teeth. They were the first amphibians, and in the British Isles 26 species have been identified. They had heads covered with bony plates, long bodies, and weak limbs, and they varied in length from a few inches to seven or eight feet. Probably most of them lived in rivers, feeding on fishes and crustaceans, but a few apparently lived chiefly on trees.

Plant life was very abundant in the Carboniferous Age, and there were forests extending over a considerable part of the Earth; but there were no flowering plants. We find remains of the great forests particularly in Britain, Germany, China, and North America. In North America alone there were at one time more than 200,000 square miles of marshy forest land. Even in the Arctic regions—Melville Island, Baffin Bay, and Spitsbergen—remains of jungles and forests are found.

The vegetation of the age was not only very extensive but luxuriant and rank, and some geologists and botanists think that the atmosphere was then much richer in carbon dioxide and also much warmer than now. There is no proof, however, that there was more carbon dioxide, and those who have made an examination of fossil plants find no modifications in their structure which point that way. But the climate must certainly have been mild and moist, and very similar everywhere to account for such uniformity.

THE HUMBLE CLUB-MOSSES THAT GREW INTO TREES SIXTY FEET HIGH

These Carboniferous forests and jungles, it must be understood, were not like the forests and jungles of today. They consisted almost entirely of giant ferns, giant mosses, and giant horse-tails, with a few yews and cycads here and there. The humble club-mosses which today creep upon the ground were represented by trees growing 50 or 60 feet high; ferns grew into trees almost equally high; while there were dense thickets of enormous horsetails known as Calamites.

This luxuriant vegetation, which flourished so many years ago, has been of the greatest importance to modern man, and without it modern civilisation and industry could not have been; for most of the coal in use today is formed from its decayed and compressed remains, now found in the Carboniferous rock, in layers a few inches or a few yards thick. Some of it seems to have been formed in the place where a forest flourished, and some seems to have been formed out of drift wood.

In coal we sometimes find leaves and spores and stems of the trees of that bygone age, and when we burn coal we are really burning the trees of these ancient forests and setting free the energy of the sun stored for millions of years in their wood.

THE REPTILES AND AMPHIBIANS IN THE ROCKS OF THE PERMIAN AGE

Our cities are lit, our machinery driven, by the energy of the sunlight that beat down in those days on these old jungles of club-mosses and ferns. There were no men then; there were not even birds or mammals; but for thousands or millions of years these forests grew and decayed, and gradually became the coal which has meant so much to humanity. It is largely because these forests grew in Britain that Britain is now one of the foremost countries in the world; and owing to its coal seams the Carboniferous rock may be called the most important of all rocks.

Overlying the Carboniferous rocks is a layer known as Permian, which belongs partly to the Palaeozoic and partly to the Mesozoic Periods. These rocks are found in Somerset and Devon, in the Midlands, in the north-west of England, and in Scotland. They consist sometimes of red sandstone and sometimes of limestone and dolomite.

The animal life of this period is found chiefly in the limestone rock. It very much resembles the animal life of the Carboniferous Age, but most forms of life are much less plentiful. Amphibian life, is, however, more abundant, and reptiles have been found. The plant life of the Permian Age is also comparatively scanty, and most of the plants found are found also in the Carboniferous rocks.

The Story of Immortal Folk Whose Work Will Never Die

Ben Jonson   James Hogg   Lady Nairne   Andrew Cherry   Charles Dibdin   Charles Mackay

Thomas Campbell   James Thomson   Thomas Haynes Bayly   David Garrick   Edward Fitzball   Henry Russell

WRITERS OF FAMOUS SONGS

A FAMOUS man once said that he would rather make the songs of a country than make its laws. He meant that songs had such a hold on the people that, if they were good songs, they were better worth considering as a moral power than the laws which are made for us by Parliament.

That was going just a little too far, but there is a great deal of truth in the saying. Songs really have a great influence. Many of us know Home, Sweet Home, or The Last Rose of Summer, or Auld Lang Syne, or Rule Britannia, before we know much about the laws of our country. And we get not only ideas and principles from songs, but even powerful persuasions to action.

The world's most popular writer of songs was Robert Burns, but he wrote so many, and yet is so much more than a song writer, that he must have his place elsewhere, and so we give here the first place to the writer of a single song—Rouget de Lisle, who produced the famous and inspiring French Marseillaise. This was prohibited by the Bourbons and under the First and Second Empires, though sung in times of revolution, and did not again become the French national song until the outbreak of the Franco-Prussian war in 1870. But we shall know the tremendous effect it once had if we read any story of the French Revolution. Carlyle says:

"The sound of it will make the blood tingle in men's veins; and whole armies and assemblages will sing it with eyes weeping and burning, with hearts defiant of Death, Despot, and Devil." One republican general declared that it was worth an addition of a thousand men to his ranks; and there was a great German poet who said that it had caused the death of fifty thousand of his countrymen.

The author of this grand martial song, Rouget de Lisle, was a captain of engineers at Strasbourg just before the French Revolution broke out in all its fury. He was an all-round man; poet, dramatist, violinist, and singer; and he wrote the song in a mood of excitement and inspiration one night in April, 1792. A picture representing the scene appears on page 651. To its strains the soldiers from Marseilles entered Paris, and marched to the attack on the Tuileries.

It was because of this connection with Marseilles that the song was called the Marseillaise. De Lisle got a pension from Louis the Eighteenth on account of the song; and we can see a monument erected to his memory in the town of Choisy-le-Roi, where he died in 1836.

A song which has made so much history as the Marseillaise should have a history of its own, and our expectation is not dis-

EXPLORERS · INVENTORS · WRITERS · ARTISTS · SCIENTISTS

appointed. De Lisle came of old Royalist stock, and his mother was for King and Queen to the end. When she heard this new melody surging like an angry sea across the land, and learned that a man named De Lisle had written it, she asked her son, "What do people mean by associating our name with this revolutionary song the brigands sing?"

But De Lisle himself was actually condemned in those stormy days as a Royalist. In peril of death from Republican fanatics, he fled for safety to the Jura mountains. On the way, while escape and capture were but even chances, and every sign had to be examined to see if it meant sympathy or danger, he heard a melody being roared in the distance by a multitude of excited people.

Unable to recognise the chorus, he asked a passer-by, "What is it that they sing?" and the answer came, "They sing the Marseillaise Hymn." So he knew he must flee faster and farther, for where his song was sung, his head was in danger. So he fled, in peril from both sides! Long he lived in poverty and obscurity before at last a pension came to him.

A STIRRING NATIONAL SONG WRITTEN BY THE POET OF NATURE

We have nothing even nearly resembling the Marseillaise among our own songs. God Save the Queen, an anthem of which the origin and authorship are uncertain, is almost tame by comparison with the fiery French strain.

But we have Rule, Britannia, a grand song which Robert Southey, the poet, said would be the battle-hymn of England so long as England maintained her political power. It is a pity we should not be able to say with absolute certainty to whom we owe this stirring piece. The difficulty arises in this way. Rule, Britannia, appeared first in a sort of stage-play, written in 1740 to commemorate the accession of George the First. The authors of the play were James Thomson the poet, and David Mallet; and unfortunately they did not put their names to the parts of the play that each had written. Thomson died in 1748, before Rule, Britannia, became very popular; so he had no special reason for claiming it for himself.

But experts who have looked into the matter generally give him the honour, and we may safely follow them. "Jemmy" Thomson, as they familiarly called

him, was not a great poet, but lovers of Nature and the open air still like to read his book on the Seasons. He took life so easily—so indolently, we should say—that, as the story goes, he could often be seen standing in his garden at Richmond, Surrey, eating the ripe side of peaches off the trees, with his hands in his pockets!

THOMAS CAMPBELL AND HIS FAMOUS SONGS OF WAR

After him we may mention his brother Scot, Thomas Campbell, considered a great poet in his day. He was a Glasgow man, born in 1777, and he wrote his once popular Pleasures of Hope when he was only 21. His reputation is not nearly so great as it was, but we shall never forget his war-songs, such as Hohenlinden, and the magnificent Battle of the Baltic, describing incidents connected with Nelson's historic fight at Copenhagen in 1801. It was Campbell, too, who sang of The Exile of Erin, and made Ye Mariners of England immortal. The last-named was written in imitation of an old seventeenth-century song bearing the same name. It is perhaps his best war poem.

While we are thinking of this song, let us think of some more sea songs known to us. The man who wrote the greatest number of sea songs was Charles Dibdin. Everybody has heard his Tom Bowling and if we don't often hear his Poor Jack or I Sailed from the Downs in the Nancy, or 'Twas in the good ship Rover, and other old-time favourites from his pen, we are probably hearing much less entertaining and breezy things.

THE WRITER OF SEA SONGS WHO KNEW LITTLE OF SAILORS OR THE SEA

Dibdin had very little personal acquaintance with either sailors or the sea; but up to his time the British tar had not received much attention in song, and, as Dibdin had a great liking for the plain, manly, honest, patriotic character of the British tar, he resolved to make verses about him. His songs had a real practical effect, for they moved to heroic deeds thousands of English sailors, besides warming their hearts in hours of merriment, and lightening their dreary hours when prisoners in the hands of the enemy. Poor Dibdin had rather a hard life, but the Government, in his later days, gave him a pension for his sea songs. He died in 1814, at the age of 69, and was buried at Camden Town.

SALLY IN HER ALLEY

A GLIMPSE OF A YOUNG LONDONER AND HIS SWEETHEART ON HOLIDAY GIVES HENRY CAREY THE IDEA
FOR HIS FAMOUS SONG, "SALLY IN OUR ALLEY"

We think of David Garrick chiefly as a great actor, but it was David Garrick who wrote the grand patriotic song, Hearts of Oak. He wrote it under the inspiration of that wonderful year of military victories, 1759, of which it makes mention—the year of Quiberon and Quebec and Minden. We know all about Garrick, but we know very little about the man who gave us that other familiar sea song, Ben Bolt. His name was Thomas Dunn English. He was born an American, a life-long friend of Edgar Allan Poe, the author of The Raven, and he lived till 1902.

Then we ought to mention Andrew Cherry, who wrote The Bay of Biscay, and also the best song that we have about the " dear little Shamrock of Ireland."

A SONG THAT WAS REPEATED TILL THE SINGER COULD SING NO MORE

Cherry was the son of a Limerick bookseller. He took to the stage, and appeared at Drury Lane Theatre in 1802, ten years before his death. Nor must we forget Samuel J. Arnold, who wrote The Death of Nelson, a national song of years gone by. Arnold was very fond of sea subjects, and wrote another once popular song, Speed On, My Bark, Speed On. He was the son of Dr. Arnold, the composer.

The Death of Nelson appeared in an opera produced in London not very long after the admiral's death. Braham, the great tenor, who once sold pencils in the street, had written the music, and it was he who sang it first. The enthusiasm was tremendous. Nelson had been the nation's hero, and this song about him had to be repeated again and again, until Braham was in a state of collapse.

Among the sea songs we must not forget Rocked in the Cradle of the Deep. It was written by Mrs. Willard, an American, but we should probably never have heard of it had not a clergyman, Joseph Knight, made for it the fine tune that we know so well.

THE SONG WHICH IS KNOWN WHEREVER ENGLISH SOLDIERS AND SAILORS GO

There are not so many songs about soldiers as about sailors, perhaps because there is less romance about life on land than about life at sea. But we have The British Grenadiers, a song about which we know nothing more than this, that the words date from about 1690, and that the tune comes down from the sixteenth century. And then we have the favourite,

The Girl I Left Behind Me, which may be regarded as the property of both soldiers and sailors. It has been played for a century or more when a man-of-war weighs anchor, and when a regiment quits a town in which it has been quartered; consequently it has been made known wherever English soldiers and sailors go.

In the days of the Crimean War our people sang Cheer, Boys, Cheer, by Charles Mackay, with music by Henry Russell; but no song in wartime has been so popular as It's a Long Way to Tipperary, sung universally through the two World Wars.

Henry Russell was a popular song and story entertainer for many years, and he wrote many songs, both words and music, of his own. Many will know A Life on the Ocean Wave, and his setting of Dickens's verses about The Ivy Green. He was a very realistic singer, and moved his audiences strongly. Once he sang a song which he had written about a Newfoundland dog that had bravely leapt overboard from a vessel and saved a drowning child. At the end of the song, a man in the gallery called out: " Mr. Russell, if that dog is yours, I'll give you a sovereign for a pup." Clark Russell, Henry Russell's son, gave us many stirring sea stories.

SAD SONGS OUR GRANDMOTHERS USED TO SING

Then there was Thomas Haynes Bayly. We do not know his songs so well as our grandfathers and grandmothers used to know them. They all knew The Mistletoe Bough, She Wore a Wreath of Roses, Oh, No! We Never Mention Her, and I'll Hang My Harp on a Willow Tree. Bayly was born in the old town of Bath in 1797. and died in 1839, after years of misfortune. His father was a solicitor, and he wanted his son to become a solicitor; but the youth took a great dislike to the law. The father then tried him with the Church, but he did not like that either; so at last he joined the ranks of those who looked to literature for a living. There is a fine old flavour about his songs, something like what we should experience, perhaps, if we opened an old bureau and turned over the letters of our great-grandmothers.

Andrew Lang said that turning over Bayly's songs is " like listening, in the sad mellow evening, to the strains of a barrel organ, faint and sweet, and far away "; and so it is.

Famous songs have often been made

about real people. There is Annie Laurie, for instance. Few of us probably think of Annie Laurie as having existed in real life; but she did. If we go to Dumfries today we may see her " last will and testament " in one of the institutions there. The song begins " Maxwelton braes are bonnie," and Maxwelton is near Glencairn. Well, Annie Laurie was born at Maxwelton, in December, 1682, and today she lies at rest in the picturesque churchyard at Glencairn, a village which is within a few miles of her birth-place.

THE STORY OF ANNIE LAURIE AND HER SWEETHEART

Now, this Annie Laurie had a sweetheart, William Douglas of Kirkcudbright, and it was he who made the original of the song about her. But his lines were not very refined, and so they were recast about seventy years ago by Lady John Scott, a member of the great Buccleuch family, who died in 1900. She had no idea that her version of the old song would become popular, but she printed it for a bazaar on behalf of the widows and orphans of soldiers who had been killed in the Crimea, and it was soon sung everywhere.

Then there is My Pretty Jane, a song which the great tenor Sims Reeves made immortal by his splendid rendering of it. This song was written by Edward Fitzball, a farmer's son, who used to wander about the lanes of Burwell, a little village some eleven miles from Cambridge. Near one of these lanes " a farmer did dwell," as the song says. He had a daughter, and she was the " Pretty Jane." Jane had a bewitching manner, and Fitzball fell madly in love with her.

A FAMOUS SONG THAT WAS WRITTEN BY A FARMER'S SON IN TEN MINUTES

One day he sat down in his father's fields, when the bloom was on the rye, and wrote this song in ten minutes. Later he gave the words to Sir Henry Bishop, the man who composed the tune for Home, Sweet Home, and Bishop produced the melody which has since gone round the world. It is sad to have to add that " My Pretty Jane " died of consumption in the height of her youth and beauty.

The Lass of Richmond Hill, too, was a real heroine, the daughter of a King's Bench solicitor, who had a place called Hill House, in Richmond, Yorkshire. Her name was Frances l'Anson. She married Leonard MacNally, an Irish

barrister, who wrote the song about her.

Still another real heroine was Henry Carey's Sally In Our Alley. Sally was a London girl who had gone out one holiday with her sweetheart. Carey happened to notice the pair, and the song was the result of his study of them. His friends roared at the idea of making a song on such a subject, and they made Carey very unhappy by calling him the " alley poet." But he lived to see his song make its way into the very best society, and even to hear of its being sung in the royal palace. Other songs universally known set to airs so old that their origin has not been traced are the ballad The Bailiff's Daughter of Islington, and Ben Jonson's exquisite Drink To Me Only With Thine Eyes.

THE PATHETIC SONG THAT WAS NAMED AFTER A SHEPHERD

When we come to think of women songwriters, it is curious to reflect that many of them were Scottish; still more curious to note that two of them, at least, wanted to hide what they had done. There was, first, Lady Anne Lindsay, who wrote the fine ballad of Auld Robin Gray, for which Mr. Leeves, a Somerset clergyman, made such an exquisite tune. She was one of a family who had long been known for their literary and artistic gifts. Her father was the Earl of Balcarres, and she was born in 1750. Her mother, who was very severe, used to shut her children into dark closets or give them only bread and water when they did anything wrong.

One day the young people decided to rebel and run away. They did run away, but the old shepherd of the place stopped them and brought them back to be punished. Now, the shepherd's name was Robin Gray, and it was this incident that made Lady Anne take his name for her pathetic song.

The song soon became popular, but she had not put her name to it, and people began to ask about the authorship. Indeed, a learned Edinburgh society offered twenty guineas for the name of the writer. This strikes us as very curious nowadays, when we find everybody rather proud of being able to write. But we must remember that people were not so proud of writing a hundred years ago. We all know how Scott wrote the Waverley novels secretly. People occupying a high station in life thought it undignified to write for print. What Lady Anne said about it was this. She declared she had a dread of writing anything " because of the shyness it created in those who could write nothing." In other words, she did not want to make people who could not write uncomfortable in her presence.

Another lady writer of Scottish songs held the same view. This was Lady Nairne, the author of that most pathetic song The Land o' the Leal, and Caller Herrin'. Lady Nairne sent her songs to the publisher under the name of Mrs. Bogan, and when she went to see him she went disguised.

She is best known now by The Land o' the Leal, which was written to console a dear married friend who had lost her firstborn child. Lady Nairne belonged to an old family that had fought and bled for the Stuarts, so it was no wonder that she made many fine songs about the Jacobites and the miserable cause which ended at Culloden.

James Hogg, better known as " The Ettrick Shepherd," another song-writer of that time, was one of the most wonderful natural geniuses Scotland ever produced. He had little more than six months' schooling, and he was a man before he could write down the letters of the alphabet ; yet he gave us such songs as Flora Macdonald's Lament and When The Kye Comes Hame. He was a real shepherd, and lived all his days near that Yarrow of which Wordsworth has written so tenderly and finely.

TOM MOORE OF IRELAND AND THE BEAUTIFUL SONGS HE WROTE

Of writers of Irish songs which have become famous there are quite a number. Perhaps there is nothing more popular than Tom Moore's Last Rose of Summer, though Robin Adair, the writer of which we do not know, runs it pretty close. Moore was a perfect master of song-writing, and his Irish Melodies included many songs that were once greatly popular. Some, such as The Minstrel Boy to the War has Gone and The Harp that once thro' Tara's Halls, are still widely known, and are often heard on the concert platform. Moore is, without question, one of the greatest of our song-writers. His sentiments are so beautifully expressed that they appeal not only to the Irish nation, but to the whole Anglo-Saxon race.

Many authors have reaped small reward for the songs which millions have sung, but Moore was one of the happy few who have derived both praise and profit from their inspired labours. He dined one night with Lord Byron at the old villa on the Thames-side at Twickenham, and conversation between the two poets turned on Fame. While they sat talking the question over, a boatful of people glided by. They were singing one of Moore's Irish Melodies.

Byron jumped up, and, placing his hand on Moore's shoulder, said, " There; that is Fame! " Such moments of satisfaction are not common, and Moore composed many a song in times of sadness which has since charmed the entire English-speaking race.

THE SONG THAT STIRS THE IRISHMAN ALL THE WORLD OVER

The Wearin' o' the Green is always in great request at Irish patriotic gatherings. Both the Irish exile and the Irish patriot find their sentiments reflected in it, and its vein of melancholy appeals to them. There are many versions, but the favourite one is that by Boucicault, the actor.

We know all about Kathleen Mavourneen, the beautiful song written by an Irish lady, Mrs. Crawford, and set to music by Mr. F. N. Crouch, who had sung as a choir-boy in Westminster Abbey. Crouch got just £5 for his music, the same as Milton got for Paradise Lost ; but when the copyright was sold some years ago it realised the substantial sum of £600.

It was the music of Michael William Balfe that made the song of Killarney, written by Mr. E. Falconer, known in all English-speaking lands. If Balfe had composed nothing but this song and the opera of The Bohemian Girl, his name would have been handed down to posterity.

THE MELODY WHICH CAME STRAIGHT FROM THE HEART OF ITS COMPOSER

Let us turn again to English songs, to note two which are favourites wherever our mother tongue is spoken. Sullivan's Lost Chord has its own little story. The melody came straight from the heart of its composer. Sullivan had once tried to provide a musical setting to Adelaide Proctor's little poem, but had not satisfied himself, and so put aside his work.

One night he sat watching by the bedside of his dying brother, and in the stillness of his vigil the poem came back to his mind, and music seemed to come unsought to match it. As he read and re-read the lines the melody and its fine harmonies started into being in his mind, and almost

THIS WAS FAME, SAID LORD BYRON

The harp that once through Tara's halls
   The soul of music shed,
Now hangs as mute on Tara's walls
   As if that soul were fled.

So sleeps the pride of former days,
   So glory's thrill is o'er,
And hearts that once beat high for praise
   Now feel that pulse no more.

WHILE TOM MOORE WAS BYRON'S GUEST AT TWICKENHAM, A BOATLOAD OF PEOPLE PASSED BY
SINGING ONE OF MOORE'S IRISH MELODIES. "THERE; THAT IS FAME!" SAID BYRON.

mechanically he wrote down the result. He gained £10,000 profit from the sale of his sweet song.

Sir Arthur Sullivan was one of the musical benefactors of the nineteenth and twentieth centuries. The Gilbert and Sullivan series of operas gave the world a clue to British taste in light, gay, tuneful music, beauty without triviality, sound and colour without crash and discord.

THE AMERICAN SCHOOLMASTER'S SON WHO WROTE HOME, SWEET HOME

A song that was immensely popular with our grandparents was Home, Sweet Home. It is still a song which can transport an English-speaking exile back for a few moments to the dear familiar scenes of his home. An American wrote it. He was John Howard Payne, son of a New York schoolmaster.

The Paynes were of English descent, but the author of our song was born in New York in 1791. He scorned law and commerce to seek favour on the stage, and, having failed as an actor, wrote for it. Much of his time was spent in England and France, and it was for a play produced in London and called Clari, the Maid of Milan, that he wrote the song that is his one masterpiece.

Payne himself received no great profit from his work, and he was often in need of assistance before he died in 1852, nearly 30 years after his song was first sung in public. He was ever a rover. He wrote his song for a London audience while he was staying in Paris; and he died in Tunis, where its sentiment must have been specially significant to himself.

The music of the song is, of course, one of its chief charms. This was composed by our Sir Henry Bishop, who is said to have borrowed the melody from a Sicilian air. The truth is that Bishop, editing a volume of national airs some years before, had invented one to serve for Sicily, for which none existed, and that same tune he adapted later for Home, Sweet Home.

THE OLD FOLKS AT HOME, A SAD SONG OF A NEGRO SLAVE

Another American who plucked at the world's heart-strings with a song about Home was Stephen Collins Foster, who wrote The Old Folks at Home. Like most of Stephen Foster's popular ballads it was a song written about Negroes. As well as bringing tears to the eyes of millions, it may well have aroused their indignation against one of the worst abominations of slavery. For the character in the song is obviously a poor Negro slave who has been torn from his family and " sold down the river."

Stephen Foster was born in Pittsburg in 1826, the son of a merchant of Irish descent. He wrote his first song when he was only 13, and became a professional song writer when he was about 20. He wrote both words and music of most of the songs that made him famous. He died in 1864.

But the most popular song in the English-speaking world is a Scottish ballad, Auld Lang Syne, and it is ever-green because it extols human friendship. We all ascribe it to Burns, but he only gave a modernised form to a song that was centuries old. He saw the beauty and pathos of the thought, and, preserving the mould and some of the substance, he filled in the gaps with the pure gold of his genius. We owe thanks for the original to an earlier author whom we do not know.

Coming to a later time, an extraordinarily prolific writer of songs was Frederic Weatherly, who died in 1929. He was a barrister and K.C., but in the course of more than fifty years he wrote the words of scores of songs, many of them being so happily set to music that they are popular favourites in the home and concert hall, and will still have their appeal for generations to come.

THE SONG THAT CAUGHT THE FANCY OF A HARD-PRESSED ARMY

It was Weatherly who gave us such familiar songs as The Old Brigade, The Children's Home, The Star of Bethlehem, The Holy City, Up from Somerset, Nirvana, Stonecracker John, At Santa Barbara, Friend o' Mine, When You Come Home, Danny Boy, and Roses of Picardy.

The most remarkable war-time song, as we have said, is It's a Long Way to Tipperary, which will always be associated with 1914. Yet this very ordinary music-hall chorus was written and composed by Jack Judge and Harry Williams about two years before the war began. It caught the fancy of a hard-pressed army and helped weary men to march along the roads between Mons and the Marne. It echoed round the Empire, and millions of copies of it were sold.

In the succeeding years dozens of war songs had their little day, some of them being unworthy sentiment set to trivial tunes; but when they are forgotten Tipperary will still be a hallowed memory of voices that sing no more.

About the time that Tipperary was written the world was beginning to listen with surprise and amusement to songs with a syncopated rhythm which had been borrowed from the music of the American Negroes. This rhythm was at first called ragtime, and it developed into the familiar jazz. One of the first ragtime songs, which became instantly popular and is still sometimes revived, was Alexander's Ragtime Band. It was written by a Russian-born American, Irving Berlin.

But sentimental ballads of the older tradition remained as popular as ever and another of the most prolific writers of these, who began writing in our parents' young days and whose songs are still well-beloved was Edward Teschemacher. He wrote the words of those old favourites : Because; Until; I Know a Lovely Garden; and Tommy Lad. Altogether he wrote over 1000 songs.

Carrie Jacobs-Bond, who was born in the United States in 1862 and died in 1946, began writing verses, and music for them, as a pastime. Later she earned her living as a song-writer, and she will always be remembered for When You Come to the End of a Perfect Day.

A lovely song of a more literary kind, for it is really a beautiful poem set to music, is Joyce Kilmer's Trees. Joyce Kilmer was a young poet who lost his life in the First World War when he was only 31. This exquisite poem will be found on another page (see Poetry Index).

Another poet who gave us a song which has become almost a second National Anthem, was Arthur Christopher Benson, who wrote Land of Hope and Glory, which Sir Edgar Elgar set to impressive music. Arthur Benson was born in 1862 and died

JOHN HOWARD PAYNE, A WANDERER FROM HOME, SITS DOWN TO WRITE HOME, SWEET HOME

in 1925. He was the son of an Archbishop of Canterbury, and he was educated at Eton College where, after his schooldays, he served as a master from 1885 to 1903. He wrote biographies and essays as well as poems, but it is this noble song of his native land that has won him a permanent place in British hearts. We can read Land of Hope and Glory on page 98.

Another stirring patriotic song which is still a great favourite is Drake's Drum. It was written by Sir Henry Newbolt who was born in 1862 and died in 1938. Henry Newbolt loved to write about the sea and the deeds of British seamen, and it was a volume of his verse, Admirals All, which made his reputation in 1897.

One of the leading British composers of recent times gave us that delightful song, Down in the Forest Something Stirred. He was Sir Landon Ronald, who was born in 1873 and died in 1938, and who wrote more than 200 other songs. He was at one time Principal of the Guildhall School of Music.

Honours and rewards are for the few of those who cheer our hearts, make our homes tuneful, our solitude melodious; but for the gifts of a great number we can only offer our indebtedness in a general thanksgiving, as to half-divine birds that have come into life in the guise of men and women making songs for humanity.

Blest be the song that brightens
The blind man's gloom, exalts the veteran's
    mirth.

So sings Wordsworth, for himself and for us all. Somewhere there is a song for everyone, for every mood, for every thought, for every emotion, for joy and exultation, for sorrow and suffering, for duty and sacrifice, and for consolation in the hour of death; but it has been given to only the very few to say the things our hearts would sing.

THE MAGIC HORSE OF SHIRAZ

THE HORSE ROSE WITH THE PRINCE INTO THE AIR

The Great Stories of the World That Will Be Told For Ever

THE ENCHANTED HORSE

As the Shah of Persia was keeping the Feast of the New Year in the city of Shiraz an Indian magician came to his Court leading a very ugly horse. It looked more like wood than a living creature, and the Shah could hardly help laughing when he saw it.

"Laugh as you will, sire," said the magician. "I think you will be glad to pay a great price for my horse when you know what it can do. If your brave young son Prince Frouz will deign to mount it, and turn the peg in the saddle, he will be able to test its power."

"Well, let me see what it can do," said the Prince.

He sprang on the horse, and, without waiting to learn how to manage it, turned the peg in the saddle. The strange animal at once rose with him into the air with the swiftness of an arrow, and carried him out of sight.

At first he was delighted at the speed with which he rushed through the air. He did not grow uneasy until he tried to turn the horse back to Shiraz, and found that it would not obey the rein.

"I suppose," he said, "I must twist the peg the other way."

He did so, and, to his alarm, the horse leaped up higher into the sky, and began to travel as fast as lightning.

Prince Frouz did not lose his wits, and, after examining the saddle, he found another smaller peg. He gave this a wrench, and the horse then stopped and carried him downward, and he alighted on the roof of a strange palace.

It was now night, and everybody was in bed. Prince Frouz crept downstairs, and came into a splendid hall. There he saw a lovely young lady sleeping on a sofa, with ten women reposing around her. Going up to the sofa, he awoke the lady, and, asking her pardon, told her the story of his wonderful adventure.

"And now," he said, "may I ask, sweet lady, who you are and where I am?"

"You are in the palace of the Princess of Bengal," said the lady kindly, "and I am the Princess."

She then called her women and bade them set out a repast for Prince Frouz, and conducted him to a royal bedchamber.

The Prince slept soundly, and rose up fresh and gay of heart, and the Princess sent for him and begged him to tell her again the story of his wonderful adventure. They remained together all day long, and fell in love with one another.

At break of day next morning, before anyone else was awake, the Princess climbed to the terraced roof of the palace and found the Prince waiting for her, and

IMAGINATION · CHIVALRY · LEGENDS · GOLDEN DEEDS · FAIRY TALES

they both mounted the enchanted horse and set out for Persia, where they intended to get married. The Prince now knew how to manage the horse, and in a short time he arrived with the Princess at a castle a little way from Shiraz.

Leaving his sweetheart there to array herself in richest attire for the wedding, he went to his father, the Shah, to tell him of her coming. Unhappily, he left the enchanted horse at the castle instead of taking it with him. While he was telling his father the story of his wonderful adventure the Indian magician heard what he said. He ran to the castle, fetched the enchanted horse with all speed, and exclaimed to the Princess :

" The Shah wishes to see you at once, and Prince Frouz has asked me to fetch you. Mount with me on the horse, and we shall reach Shiraz in a moment."

The Princess got up beside the magician, and he at once turned the horse's head away from Shiraz, and carried her off to Cashmere. They descended in a road near the chief town of that country, just as the Sultan was riding by.

" Save me! " cried the Princess. " Save me from this wicked man! "

The Sultan of Cashmere was amazed at her loveliness, and with one stroke of his sword he slew her enemy, and then led her kindly into the stateliest room in his palace, and commanded a hundred slaves to wait upon her.

" I have escaped from one snare," she said to herself, " and fallen into another."

So she had. The Sultan was wildly in love with her, and instead of taking her back to Prince Frouz he arranged to marry her himself.

But the Princess was as subtle as she was beautiful, and she frightened him away by pretending that she was mad. He sent his wisest doctors to cure her, and she rushed upon them, raging like a madwoman, and they, too, fled in terror.

One day a strange physician came to the Sultan, and promised to take the madness away from the Princess.

" You see, sire," he said, " the lady has been bewitched by an enchanted horse. Let me place her again on the horse, and I will cure her."

The Sultan was delighted, and the strange physician was immediately taken to the Princess. " Do you not know me, dearest ? " he whispered.

It was Prince Frouz, who had been wandering in disguise all over the world in search of her.

He placed her upon the enchanted horse, and sprang beside her, and in less than an hour he brought her to Shiraz, where they were happily married.

THE WANDERING JEW

THE story is told that, as our Lord was carrying the Cross up to Calvary, He stayed for a moment to rest by the house of a shoemaker, but the shoemaker drove our Lord away, saying: " Go on! You shall not rest here."

And our Lord took up the cross, and said, " I am going to My rest, and you must wander until I return."

So the shoemaker was turned into the Wandering Jew, who will never find rest until our Lord comes again on Earth at the Day of Judgment. The mark of a red cross appeared on his forehead, and he left his wife and children and followed our Lord to Calvary, and then he turned away from Jerusalem, and began his long, strange pilgrimage.

On and on he went, a barefooted, tall old man, with his hair hanging about his shoulders and a black bandage round his forehead to conceal the red cross.

And on and on he still goes at the same striding pace, over mountains and across deserts, and down all the long, white roads of the world. But a little rest is sometimes allowed to him. If he happens to be passing by a Christian church on Sunday morning, just as the service is beginning, he can enter and listen.

A weaver once in Bohemia, whose name was Kokot, was trying to discover some treasure which his grandfather had hidden in the royal palace. And as he was vainly, but still hopefully, digging the Wandering Jew passed by.

" Your grandfather was burying the treasure the last time I came by here," said the Wandering Jew, " and I think he was burying it beneath that wall there."

Kokot at once dug beneath the wall, and there he found the treasure. But before he could thank the Wandering Jew the strange pilgrim had passed out of sight.

A BOY WHO BROKE THE WINGS OF THE WIND

Thousands of years ago, when men carved histories on stones and worshipped gods with birds' heads, Assyrian children were told this story of Adapa.

ONE day a boy was fishing on a calm sea when the South Wind came swooping along and snapped his mast with a burst of laughter. The sails fell into the water, the boat turned on her side; Adapa had much ado to get ashore.

As he stood looking at the wreckage of his vessel the South Wind came whistling and laughing round his ears.

"Ah, demon!" shouted Adapa. "If I could only see you I'd break your wings."

Suddenly the South Wind made herself visible. She was a huge monster, half-woman, half-bird, but Adapa, nothing daunted, leapt, caught her, and broke her wings in his fury.

She made herself invisible again, but he could hear her wailing and flapping her broken wings as she rolled on the shore.

The days passed. Anu, king of the Assyrian gods, sat in his golden halls with the windows wide open, yet the South Wind had not returned to her master. Ships were becalmed, the crops drooped, but still the South Wind did not blow summer clouds over the parching land.

At last Anu sent a messenger after the truant, and he brought her back in a sorry plight. Anu's wrath flamed like a sunset.

"Summon hither the man who so ill-used my servant," he commanded.

Adapa was awakened from sleep by a bright light, and beheld a radiant being who hovered near his couch.

"Anu bids you come to his judgment bar," said the messenger, "because you have broken the wings of the South Wind."

The story does not say what instructions he gave Adapa about finding his way to the Heavenly Halls. Perhaps he was to follow the Moon-track on the sea, or find a chariot waiting for him on the mountain.

As soon as the vision vanished Adapa awakened his father, and said: "Alas, Ea, my father, our happiness is over! Never again shall we lower the net, or break bread, or walk in the shade of the trees together! For I have angered the gods and am summoned to judgment."

Ea mastered his sorrow and replied: "Go into their presence clad in mourning garments and humility. Lay aside your own fiery nature. Seek their forgiveness with earnest words. If you win the gods' pardon return to me quickly. Above all, do not eat or drink the heavenly food lest you forget the Earth."

Adapa set out, and by some strange means found his way to the golden halls that stand on the clouds. Two winged giants kept the gates; he saluted them reverently, and they let him through.

The splendour of the place itself was outshone by the glory of the Immortals who sat there, clothed in starlight. Anu, the king, burned brighter than the Sun. Adapa knelt and veiled his eyes.

Anu spoke in tremendous tones: "How have you dared to harm my servant?"

Adapa replied in a humble but unfaltering voice: "O King! I have come to crave forgiveness. South Wind wrecked my ship, and in my hot anger I laid hands on her, forgetting whose servant she is. Deeply do I repent my wrath."

The assembled gods murmured: "Truly the little mortal is sorry for his fault."

Anu mused a moment, and said: "You are forgiven. But you must not go back to Earth and tell men what you have seen. You shall dwell with us for ever. Let the youth taste the wine of Immortality, and give him the divine bread."

But as the heavenly cup-bearer stepped forward Adapa threw himself on the ground before Anu.

"O Great One," he cried, "be not angry with the least of your creatures! Be patient with your foolish servant, and pardon me that I do not taste your wine or take your gift."

Anu's voice rolled round the golden rafters like thunder: "You refuse my wine! Do you think I offer you the poisoned draught of death? Evil-minded pygmy, I offer you a seat at the table of the gods!"

"As you are the Father of Truth, pardon me!" prayed Adapa. "I understand your bounty, of which I am not worthy. But I promised my father that if I could win your forgiveness I would return to him quickly."

The anger was gone from Anu's voice as he replied: "If you return to Earth you return to toil, sickness, age, and death. It is man's lot. Yet, if you choose, you shall go in peace."

Adapa thanked him and went his way.

Thus did a boy refuse godhead and obey his father, rejecting eternal ease to take up the human joys and manful sorrows that are our common lot on Earth.

THE BINDING OF THE MONSTER

As Odin, king of the gods, sat on his watch-tower in the skies he could see everything, even the dwarfs on the Earth. Thus he discovered, hidden in a forest cave, three monsters. One was a mighty wolf called Fenris, the next a piebald giantess called Hel, and the third a huge snake.

Odin feared that these creatures would do harm to the puny Earth-folk, so, stepping down from his cloudy palace, he bribed them to go. Hel was to rule a kingdom under the ground, the serpent was to be king of the sea, and Fenris was to return with Odin.

The gods meant to make him gentle by kindness ; and surely to dwell in the Heavenly Halls, caressed by gods and goddesses, was a goodly fate. But Fenris only grew more savage and cunning, and bigger, as time went on. His brother, the snake, had now grown so huge that he encircled the whole world under the sea. Who could tell what Fenris would become ?

The gods saw that he must be bound.

He was now so immense that none of them could overpower him, and they had to resort to trickery. One day they said :

" Come, Fenris, you are proud of your strength ; see if you can snap this chain."

Fenris let them fasten it about him, and broke free in a moment. They tried a stronger one, with no more success. The gods pretended to laugh with the exultant wolf, but their minds were troubled. And with cause, for Fenris was now as big as a horse, and as vicious as evil itself.

Then Odin sent to the dwarfs, the magic-workers, and asked them to make him an unbreakable chain. This took some time, for its ingredients were difficult to procure. They were the spittle of birds, the sound of a cat's footstep, the roots of a mountain, the longings of a bear, a woman's beard, and the voice of fishes. But at length it was done, and seemed to be nothing more than a silken twist.

Its very slenderness made Fenris suspicious when the gods proposed that he should test his strength with the new bond.

" I will let you bind me," said the monster, " if one of you puts his right hand in my mouth."

Every one of the Immortals felt his heart stand still. Each one knew that he ought to do this thing for the sake of the rest. But the northern gods were warriors, and who could bear to lose his sword hand ?

Before Fenris could mark their hesitation, Tyr, the battle god, stepped forward with a tranquil look. The wolf took the god's wrist between his dreadful fangs, and the magical cord was wound about him.

" Now Fenris, break free !" cried Tyr.

The monster strained his vast sinews in vain. His giant bones would crack before that gossamer thread. Then, wishing that it had been his head, Fenris bit through Tyr's wrist. The giant's sword arm swung to his side, useless.

But Evil had been fettered, and Tyr did not count the price too high.

THE WEDDING FEAST

A FATHER one day asked his two daughters: "What is the sweetest thing in the world ?"

"Sugar," said the older girl.

" Salt," said his younger daughter.

Her father thought she was mocking him, but she held to her opinion. So, much enraged, he pushed her out of the house, saying: "As you hold that salt is sweeter than sugar you had better find another home where the cooking is more to your taste !"

It was a beautiful summer night, and as the pretty maiden sat singing merrily in the forest around her father's cottage a young prince, who had lost himself while hunting deer, heard her voice, and came to ask her the way. Then, struck by her beauty and gaiety, he fell in love with her, and took her home to his beautiful palace and married her.

The bride invited her father to the wedding banquet, without telling him that she was his daughter. All the dishes were prepared without salt, and the guests began to murmur.

" Ah," said the bride's father "salt is truly the sweetest thing in the world ! But when my daughter said so I turned her out of my house. If only I could see her again and tell her how sorry I am !"

Drawing the bridal veil from her face, the happy girl went up to her father and kissed him. And properly salted dishes of fish, flesh, and fowl were then brought in, and all the guests were very happy.

THE BROWN BULL OF ULSTER

THERE was once a farmer of Ulster who went to a fair while his wife lay grievously ill at home. There were tournaments and races.

"Ah!" cried the farmer. "My wife could outstrip everyone, even the horses. She runs like the wind."

The king overheard and commanded: "Bring her here."

"Alas, sir," replied the peasant, "she lies on her bed in great suffering."

But the king ordered his men to fetch the woman, and vowed that unless she could fulfil her husband's boast the farmer should be hacked to pieces.

of the province, so that they lay as helpless as dying women for days together.

Long afterward there was a queen in Connacht, called Maev, who had set her heart on possessing a certain brown bull, the finest in Ireland, which belonged to an Ulsterman. As he would not sell it she determined to take it by force. One day her spies told her the Ulstermen were stricken with their strange sickness.

"This," cried the queen, "is the hour for my foray!" and she summoned her men and allies with promise of pillage.

On the day before they set out there suddenly appeared before Maev's chariot

A VISIONARY MAIDEN APPEARED

The sick woman made a mighty effort, and gathered all her strength, and ran the race. She outstripped everyone, even the horses, for there was fairy blood in her.

But at the goal she fell to the ground, uttering a terrible cry. With her last breath she prayed that from time to time, unto the ninth generation, the men of Ulster should be stricken down with the weakness that she now endured.

Then her kindred took her back to the Invisible World. From that day a mysterious malady was wont to visit the men

a visionary maiden clad in green, weaving with a shuttle of gold.

"I am the prophetess from the Fairy Mound of Croghan," said the maiden. "I weave the stuff of battle. I see thy host all ruby-red. I see a man of small stature, but the hero's light is on his brow; I see a modest young stripling, but in battle a dragon; he is like unto Cuchulain of Murthemny."

The vision disappeared, but Maev laughed, thinking, "There is not an arm in Ulster strong enough to lift a sword."

Cuchulain, guarding the southern passes of Ulster, soon heard the rumours of an approaching army. He and his adopted father, Sualtam, were untouched by the malady, for Cuchulain's own father was thought to be one of those Invisible People whose castles stood unseen on the Irish hills, and who sometimes gave their love of friendship to mortals.

Sualtam hastened to warn the folk of Ulster, and Cuchulain tarried to guard the pass. First he went into the forest, and, standing on one foot and using one hand, he cut an oak sapling and twisted it into a circular withy. He cut a message on it, putting Maev's host under *geis* not to advance till one of them could do the like. A *geis* was a bond, or solemn obligation : to break *geis* brought great misfortune. He hung the withy on a pillarstone in the way, and it delayed the host for a day and a night.

By such tricks and devices Cuchulain sought to gain time till the men of Ulster should recover. He also wheeled about the host doing severe damage with his sling. No one knew whence the whistling stone would fly.

There seemed to be a band of deathdealing scouts about them. Nearly every day Cuchulain would spring out on small groups and kill three or four men with sword or spear. Those who escaped brought back tales of how he seemed to swell to giant stature and smoke like a dragon when his battle frenzy was upon him. The army was seized by a superstitious terror ; Maev herself was cowed when his stone slew a pet bird that was perching on her shoulder.

The Brown Bull strayed, and fell into Maev's hands. Nevertheless she did not return satisfied. Her men pillaged the countryside, though they could not advance into the heart of the province, and Cuchulain continued to slay some of them every day.

At last she made a compact with him that if he would cease to harry her host she would send only one man at a time against him at the ford of the Dee. There, one after the other, Cuchulain slew the chief men of the raiders, fighting in the midst of the river. He never slept except leaning on his spear. At length his weariness became so great that he was ready to take any rest, even if it were the rest of the grave.

Then a tall warrior, clad in green and carrying two spears, came toward him, and said : " Sleep, Cuchulain ; for three days I will hold the ford in thy stead."

Cuchulain guessed that this was his father from the Invisible World, and he fell upon the grass and slept.

While Cuchulain slumbered the raiders were amazed to find a little band of a hundred and fifty boys riding down upon them with battle cries. The curse only fell on grown men, and these boys had ridden out to do their fathers' work and aid their old comrade Cuchulain. Every one of them perished.

Cuchulain awoke, and returned to the fray infuriated by the slaughter of the boy warriors.

At last Maev forced Ferdia to challenge him. Cuchulain and Ferdia had been companions in boyhood ; only a little while ago they shared their bed and lessonbooks. Cuchulain was loth to strike his friend, but Ferdia compelled him to fight.

The encounter lasted for four days, ending in friendship each evening. At last, after a sharp contest in which he nearly lost his life, Cuchulain gave Ferdia a death blow. He bore the body to the shore, and fell down in a swoon, caring for nothing now that he had slain the friend of his boyhood.

So the raiders poured across the ford into Ulster.

All this time the Ulstermen lay in a stupor. Sualtam rode from place to place crying, "The men of Ulster are being slain, the women carried away captive, the kine driven off ! "

None heeded him. In the king's house, also, he was met by glazed eyes and dull ears. At length, in despair, he mounted his horse to ride away. The horse reared violently, and the sharp rim of the shield on his back severed his neck, so that he died, still continuing to cry, " The men of Ulster are being slain, the women carried away captive, the kine driven off ! "

At last the cry pierced the fogs of enchantment. The newly-awakened king called upon his warriors; they started up, they snatched their armour from the wall. Soon the Earth rumbled under their war chariots, and Ulster's deliverance began.

As for the Brown Bull, unguarded in the confusion, it fought another, and then, intoxicated by victory, it galloped, bellowing, about the plains till it fell dead.

Nature's Wonderful Living Family in Earth and Air and Sea

THE SHEEP AND THE GOATS

ONE of the new wonders of the world was the discovery of radium in the Belgian Congo. To civilisation radium is worth many times the price of the purest diamonds, though to the poor savages in whose midst the discovery was made radium is as useless a mystery as a deposit of grand pianos or old manuscripts.

When we put on a coat made of wool and stitched together with cotton we have there the product of two simple, natural marvels whose discovery has meant ten thousand times more to mankind than the revelation of radium.

The little hairs that form around the fruit of the cotton plant acquire a natural twist as they grow. The sheep is clothed with multitudes of wool · fibres which are furnished with scales, tending to make the fibres curl and cling one to another. Thanks to this natural twist of the cotton we can spin it into threads and form materials to clothe three-fourths of the population of the world. The structure of wool makes it possible to weave it into cloth and a thousand other things.

From these two simple secrets of Nature have grown up the English cotton and woollen industries, the richest ever dreamed by man. In cotton we keep a man cool and comfortable at the Equator. In wool we keep him warm at the Poles. The man who tamed the first sheep,

then, prepared the way for all the conquests which bodily warmth helps a man to achieve. He prepared clothing to enable Madame Curie to withstand the cold of the frigid old shed in which she wrested radium from its ore. It is well that we should understand, as early man probably did not, Nature's greatest gift.

As Robinson Crusoe clad himself in the skin of the goats whose flesh he ate, so early men wrapped themselves in the woolly hides of the sheep they killed. Every time a human being needed new raiment a sheep had to die. Supposing that rule had continued, and each of us wanted one warm garment; if we killed all of our flocks in The United Kingdom we should have but some 20 million skins to clothe a population of some 50 millions.

Even Australia has only about 100 million sheep, of whom some 10 to 15 millions are slaughtered annually for food. That little trick of the woollen fibre has done away with the need to kill the sheep for its covering.

We harvest our wool as we gather the fruit of our orchards.

Australia keeps the greater number of her sheep alive for the sake of their wool, the production of which in a recent year exceeded a total of over 1000 million pounds. In our own small way at home we have a little gold mine in sheep. The

PREHISTORIC LIFE · MAMMALS · BIRDS · REPTILES · FISHES · INSECTS

breeders live by the sale of the animals; the shepherds by tending them. They fertilise the land on which they feed. The farmer pays his rent with the price of his wool; the man without sheep who takes in other farmers' sheep as winter boarders pays *his* rent with the help of the money thus gained.

PERHAPS THE GOOSE THAT LAID THE GOLDEN EGGS WAS A SHEEP

The wool reaches Yorkshire and there builds up such wealth that some of the towns in that county are said to be, for their size, the richest in the world. The cloth passes to the tailors and other traders, and even when they have used all they want we have a quantity left over for export to countries abroad that brings us in scores of millions of pounds every year.

It is impossible to guess where or by whom the first sheep were tamed. We should raise a monument to the man if we but knew; and another to the man who first discovered how to secure the wool and keep the sheep alive. Perhaps, after all, the goose of the fable was a sheep, and the golden eggs a fleece!

But we must not forget that the modern fleece is the result of scientific breeding. Wild sheep are hairy, not woolly. There may be a woolly undercoat for some, but in general the coat resembles the goat's in being short hair, though with that precious tendency to curl and fall together.

For long ages man has kept the breeds in which the tendency to wool has been constantly developed, so that at last he has fixed types as securely in fleeces as he has in pippins and pears. Yet the force of Nature is restrained, not destroyed. Neglected flocks, or flocks which become poor through various causes, lose their luxuriant woolly overalls and drift back to hair. The St. Kilda sheep is said to grow yearly more hairy.

THE BIG HORNED RAM WHICH LEAPT FOUR FEET INTO THE AIR

Nor is that the only instinctive process against which we have to guard. There are others more rapid and sensational which we have never bred out of sheep.

Rams are at times as fiercely combative as rhinoceroses. The writer was one of half a dozen people scattered like reeds by a big horned beauty which leapt four feet into the air and came, a true battering-ram, at us from its pen. Another has been seen to knock a bullock fairly over.

Their love of playing King of the Castle is but battle-lore bred in lambs—a rehearsal of the combats they may fight in high places when age and anger prompt them to serious contests.

The most mysterious impulse is also the most tragic—that is, the amicable follow-my-leader feeling which leads to self-slaughter. We all know the habit. A little flock is being ferried from Gravesend to the other side of the Thames. As the steamer nears the landing-stage a big athletic ram seeks to quit the ship too soon. The shepherd puts up his crook to bar the way; but the ram clears it at a bound, and reaches the gangway. The shepherd withdraws the obstacle and gives the remainder free passage. But every one of them leaps at the same spot, and to the same height, over nothing !

That would be splendid if all had leapt to imitate their leader in springing over a chasm or in eluding a lurking wolf; but here it is merely a foolish loss of energy. It is instinct in its dotage.

TWO THOUSAND SHEEP THAT FOLLOWED THEIR LEADER OVER A PRECIPICE

Follow that a step further to Grenoble, where 2000 sheep, a few years ago, were being brought down for the winter from their mountain pasture at Treney d'Oisans. A dog frightened the leading ram, which jumped down a precipice. The whole flock tried to follow. The shepherd interposed; but a resistless torrent of life surged round him and overbore him, and 2000 sheep plunged down to death, carrying their shepherd with them. That was the same instinct, instinct become stark madness.

Another point equally interesting, but less known, is the ability of the hardy hill breeds of sheep to endure privation. One winter when tremendous snowstorms overspread the country, and long after town damages had been made good, woeful stories of missing sheep appeared in the papers. Twenty-eight days passed and then a little flock was dug out of the snow, alive, at Axe Edge, near Buxton. Higher Teesdale sheep came to light out of 15 feet of snow after much the same period. Time slipped away, and each week brought more wonders, until after six weeks men thought the tale was ended.

Even then, a shepherd near Belford, in Northumberland, retained his faith in the endurance of his favourites, and one

THE GREAT SHEEP AND GOAT FAMILY

THE ABYSSINIAN MANED SHEEP WITH ITS MAGNIFICENT CURLING HORNS

THE FAT-TAILED SHEEP WITH ITS TAIL WEIGHING MANY POUNDS

ONE-HORNED SHEEP

TWO-HORNED INDIAN SHEEP

LONG-TAILED GORAL

LEICESTER SHEARLING RAM

THE MUSK OX   AN ARGALI IN THE ROCKY MOUNTAINS

WENSLEYDALE RAM

A BLACKFACE SHEEP AND HER BABY LAMB

THE TAHR

THE HAUSA SHEEP

MERINO RAM

HAMPSHIRE RAM

SUFFOLK RAM   ROCKY MOUNTAIN GOATS AT HOME   DORSET HORNED RAM

A GOAT AND HER FAMILY OF PRETTY LITTLE KIDS

THE MOUFLON

THE IBEX

THE TAKIN

FOUR-HORNED SHEEP

THE CHAMOIS

DOMESTIC GOAT   THE MARKHOR   WALLACHIAN SHEEP

THE BARBARY SHEEP   THE BHARAL SHEEP

day he found his last lost ewe alive beneath the snow that had buried her no less than 48 days earlier.

Even that record was later eclipsed. A little Black-faced Scottie was rescued on a farm at Westgate, in Durham, after no fewer than 54 days of starvation in a snowdrift—eight weeks all but two days !

This must not mislead us into believing it not important to feed sheep. These poor animals were able to defy death because their conditions were ideal for them. The sheep were fat; they could not move head or foot, and so were prevented from making any exertion to exhaust energy; their temperature was high and constant; they lived indolently upon the great reserves of fat stored within their bodies.

Hibernation, the fasting winter sleep of animals, must have begun in some such way as this, when our Ice Age was here; when animals advanced northward as the ice retreated in summer, and turned southward as it returned in winter.

Many must have been snowbound on the way south. Many must have fasted and survived; many must have perished. The successful migrants would transmit their powers of resistance to their descendants, and true winter-fasts would slowly come within the powers of creatures whose existence depended upon their survival of winter imprisonment.

SHEEP AS BIG AS DONKEYS WHOSE HORNS WERE USED AS FOX-HOLES

It is almost certain that in course of time, if the conditions recurred frequently, skilled breeders might evolve a race of hibernating sheep from the hardy strain of hill breeds that weathered the tremendous snowstorms we have just referred to.

Flockmasters have no need of such sheep, so they will not make the attempt. They go on from year to year improving flesh and fleeces from existing stocks. Probably the wilds have nothing better to give them than the breeds they already possess, for sheep breeding is as ancient as the oldest Bible days.

From what stock our breeds come we do not know. There are several wild species, creatures of the mountains all of them, though not of the steeper heights to which the goats resort. Bighorns we call the first famous members of the family, found in America and Asia. In North America the bighorns are called Rocky Mountain sheep, but they range far from the mountains from which they take their name. They are big, active animals, the males over 40 inches at the shoulder, and with horns 40 inches long. The coat is hairy with a soft woolly under-fur. Light brown, in its wider habitat, the bighorn is white, or yellowish, in Alaska, and black in the Cassiar and Stikine Mountains, white again in Kamchatka, and brownish-grey in Siberia.

A still finer wild sheep is the Argali of Central and North-Eastern Asia, animals as big as donkeys, with noble curving horns of such size that little mountain foxes and other animals use them as homes when they become detached.

MARCO POLO THE FIRST TO DISCOVER AND DESCRIBE THE ARGALI SHEEP

Various local races of the Argali are found in various areas, and it gives all lovers of Marco Polo a thrill to find that he was the first European to discover and describe them. That was in 1273. Exactly 600 years later a European scientist first saw the old Venetian's animal, and named it Marco Polo's sheep. Not till then was Marco Polo's story believed.

The Asiatic Urial, or Shapo, is among the most timid of wild sheep; yet, when men hide, or are absent, it will pop down from its rocky home and enjoy a browse with domesticated sheep. Which does it covet, the good pasture or the companionship? Men have no time to learn, for it is gone like the wind at their approach.

Noting the existence of the old red or Gmelin's sheep in Asia, we pass to the famous European Mouflon, now confined to Corsica and Sardinia. The rams carry horns as much as 38 inches in length; they stand nearly 30 inches high at the shoulder, are powerfully but neatly built, and very wild and wary.

THE CLEVER FIGHTING WAYS OF THE MOUFLON SHEEP

No human soldier trained to modern war was ever more astute in his methods than the Mouflons. Not only do they take cover in the scantiest bushes, but they hide in the shadow of a bush; and, a fact which is most important of all, the sentinel ram takes his place at a point where several currents of air from different quarters come together, so that the scent of an enemy may be detected from any direction. In the use of the nose the Mouflon is a master detective.

From such sheep as those mentioned we must have derived our breeds, but it is certain that could the early fathers of the wild flocks see their descendants they would not recognise them as kindred.

We have evolved so many kinds that it is difficult to group them; but it is not inaccurate to tabulate them as Mountain breeds, Long-wooled breeds, and Short-wooled breeds. Experts may subdivide this grouping into eight or more lesser brigades, but ours will serve.

The Long-wools give us nine pedigree stocks—Leicester, Border Leicester, Lincoln, Kent or Romney Marsh, Cotswold, Wensleydale, South Devon, Devon Longwool, the Roscommon—and a half-bred Border Leicester-Cheviot type.

HOW ONE BREED OF SHEEP HAS BEEN USED TO IMPROVE OTHERS

The Leicester is one of the most important of our foundation sheep, and typifies the progress of all. In little more than a century and a half it has been improved from a gaunt, coarse sheep of heavy inferior wool into such quality of flesh and fleece that it has been associated with several other varieties for their betterment.

The Border Leicester is simply Leicester characteristics combined with the hardihood of sheep that thrive in the north. Supreme size is attained by the ancient Cotswolds and their rivals the Lincolns. The Lincolns, denizens of the fens and alluvial land, once competed with the Leicesters, but it was Leicester blood that made them famous.

The Romneys also owe a debt to the Leicesters, but are themselves ancient and famous for their resistance of foot-rot and an independence of spirit which causes them to keep apart and so avoid overcrowding of pasture. Ireland has only one native sheep, the Roscommon, which turns sparse hillside herbage into good mutton and wool.

EXCELLENCE OF SOUTHDOWN MUTTON DUE TO A DIET OF SNAILS

The Short-wools give us nearly a dozen classes : Southdown, Shropshire, Suffolk, Hampshire Down, Oxford Down, Dorset Down, Dorset Horned, Ryeland, and the Western or Wiltshire Horned. Sweet-scented breezes playing over sheep-trimmed downs sing to the mind at the very names of some of these breeds.

Here the Southdowns are the Leicesters of the party ; famous not for size but for their mutton and the excellent quality of their wool. They began their career as a breed of fame at the same time as the Leicesters, and have relations in many of our distinguished breeds.

One point of interest is that the peculiar excellence of Southdown mutton arises from the multitude of microscopic snails they eat. Snails teem on the herbage of the Downs, and snails and grass go together to stay a Southdown appetite. The Shropshire Down and Dorset Horned flocks give us the earliest lambs; the Shropshires put on flesh and wool at express speed. They are very popular abroad, and an analysis of the destinations of those exported in recent years shows that the emigrants went to no fewer than 23 different countries.

Life is anxious and arduous for the mountain sheep, yet our domestic breeds live in conditions nearest those which wild sheep enjoy, so we need not be surprised that the mountain breeds are the most numerous of our family, 17 varieties —Black-faced Mountain or Heath, Scotch Blackface, Lonk, Rough Fell, Swaledale, Derbyshire, Gritstone, Limestone, Penistone, Cheviot, Welsh Mountain, Radnor, Herdwick, Exmoor Horned or Porlock, Dartmoor, Kerry Hill, and Clun Forest.

MOUNTAIN SHEEP AS UNCHALLENGED OWNERS OF THEIR HILLS

These animals do wonders in surroundings which would be impossible to cattle, not only as regards perilous climbing, but the paucity and poor quality of food available. Yet their flesh is esteemed for its quality, and their wool, though of less value than other breeds, is abundant and admirable for coarser manufactures.

Nature is mindful of their conditions, and not so many lambs are born to mountain sheep as to breeds in more favoured pastures. Their hardihood is attested by the feats of endurance already cited in favour of the hill breeds; and there is this to be added, that if attempts at improvement are made by the introduction of other sheep into mountain flocks, stern winters soon find out the alien strain and the mountaineers remain unchallenged owners of their hills.

There is a sheep for every place and a place for every breed of sheep. For proof of this consider what happened when kindly English farmers sent sheep to replace those which the Serbians lost in the First World War. They sent Wensleydales for rough pastures, Cheviots for the herbage clothing the foothills, and Herdwicks to adventure into the high, bleak mountains of the unfortunate land.

There is a fascinating story about the Herdwicks—that they descend from 40 sheep which swam to land from a Spanish Armada ship cast ashore at Drigg. The facts, however, are even more romantic. If historians of the breed have told their story aright, the Herdwicks are Vikings, descendants of sheep carried centuries ago by the hardy Norsemen to the Isle of Man, and taken thence when they added Cumberland to their dazzling gains.

Passing to foreign breeds we note the hairy long-legged sheep of Guinea; the gnu-like Hausa sheep with their curious spiral horns; a black and white hairy Zulu sheep which produces wool in England; the fierce Hunia sheep of India, of which the rams are kept for fighting, as bulls are in Spain; and also the unicorn sheep of Nepal. The two horns of the unicorn sheep grow together into one stout back-curving horn, and the growth of this appendage is often so excessive that it has to be cut at the tip to prevent it from growing into the back of the ram. For a contrast we have the Wallachian sheep, whose long horns,

SHEEP IN NEW ZEALAND COMING DOWN FROM THE HILLS TO WATER

twisted like corkscrews, branch fantastically out to right and left.

Another freakish growth is the tail of the fat-tailed sheep, many pounds in weight, and often supported, to prevent injury, by a board, with sometimes even a little wheeled-trolley attached.

Having mentioned an Abyssinian sheep which has a mane, and a goat-like sheep of Tibet called the Bharal, we close our list with the Udad or Barbary sheep, the sole surviving wild sheep of Africa, and a master tactician in the art of eluding pursuit in its arid hilly home.

The sheep are so nearly allied to the goats that only the scientist can say positively where the line is to be drawn. Goats always take the highest part of a range. Male goats have an unpleasant odour; sheep have not. Goats may have beards, but sheep never have them.

Where sheep are lacking goats serve many people for milk, cheese, flesh, and clothing. Their fault is that they are terribly destructive. They eat practically anything, including trees, vines and shrubs. It is said that in old times goats were responsible for the desert conditions existing around the Mediterranean.

Tur are the closest goat allies of the sheep. Their home is in the Caucasus. They are at home near snows but not in the highest ranges. The Spanish wild goat of the Pyrenees are their nearest kindred in the goat family, but the common wild goat, over a yard high and with wonderful horns curving in a noble sweep over 50 inches long, range from Europe into Asia. They are superb climbers, making dizzy leaps with perfect accuracy. They are able, in case they slip and topple over, to use their horns to save their lives.

THE BEST STOCKS OF GOATS ARISE FROM FOREIGN BLENDS

Goat-keeping is probably as ancient as sheep-keeping, but in England the more docile wool-bearer has become first favourite. Goat's milk grows in favour, however, for the animal is little subject to tuberculosis. Children love the animal when it is used as a steed for little carriages, and cottagers who have gardens, or access to waste land, find the animal a useful source of income.

There are many breeds of goats, but as the practice of rearing these animals in Great Britain is limited, we may content ourselves with a hurried glance. The English goat is horned, and may be white, black, grey, or brown. The Irish is white or black and white, sometimes reddish, and the hair is long and shaggy.

Our best stocks arise from foreign blends. The most favoured alien is the hornless Toggenburg from St. Gallen, in Switzerland, with the Saanen, another Swiss, as next in esteem. Nubian goats have also improved our stocks, and with the Swiss and the British give us the chief of the goat glories we boast.

Passing on again we reach another wild tribe, the agile Ibexes, common to the Alps, to Arabia, and Abyssinia, and widespread in Asia. I stands for Ibex, says the alphabet rhyme, and we may note that A stands for all its homes.

THE GOAT FAMOUS FOR ITS CLIMBING POWERS AND DASHING COURAGE

Its splendid horns, scimitar-shaped and marked by bold cross ridges, its fine climbing and dashing courage, make the Ibex famous among all who frequent mountains. They make him too famous in fact, for in Europe he is almost extinct, thanks to the horrid zest of " sportsmen." The noble Markhor, 43 inches at the shoulder is preserved for the present from a like fate by the fact that its home is in the far mountains of India, Kashmir, and Afghanistan. Its blood is thought to run in some domesticated breeds of goats.

Tahrs, goat-like animals of the Himalayas; the Gorals, which link goats with antelopes and with the Serows, lead us to the Takin, an animal which, long defying capture in its mountain jungles of bamboo and rhododendrons, has at last been brought within the pale and exhibited during recent years in London.

There too, in stable and paddock, munches the weird-looking musk ox. Indeed the Zoo has had a number of these strange-looking creatures. They used to be placed by naturalists as a connecting-link between sheep and cattle, but now they are classed with the Takin, Serow, Goral, and Rocky Mountain goat.

Creatures of the Arctic circle, musk oxen are of ancient type, and in colder epochs roamed freely over Europe, even extending to England. But they hate men and wander far from their haunts. Even in captivity they are morose and dangerous if we enter premises that they regard as their own.

THE LEAPING FEATS OF THE DARING AND GRACEFUL CHAMOIS

The Rocky Mountain goat already named is the clumsiest in build of all the goat clan, but in spite of its stocky limbs it is a fine climber. When pressed by hunger it will descend to the lowlands, but its home is in the heights, and it seems now as sure to survive man's coming as the closely-guarded bison.

The same remark, let us hope, may now be applied to the delightful Chamois, the lissom leaping beauties that seem the very embodiment of Alpine life. They have been much persecuted, but their range is not limited to the Alps. They are in the Pyrenees, the Carpathians, Caucasus, Apennines, and in the Taurus range in Asia Minor.

Also, they are in New Zealand! A few were taken there some years ago and there thrived splendidly. There is nothing more thrilling in Nature than the sight of a Chamois glissading down a snowy slope, to bound afresh up a new height and land like some incredible bird with all four dainty hoofs gathered together upon a pinnacle no bigger than a man's hand.

For daring, adroitness, and grace the Chamois is the little king of his order, an order superbly fitted for hill and valley, and to make rough places seem plain and the crooked straight.

The March of Man from the Age of Barbarism to the United Nations

Plato and Aristotle as they appear on the walls of the Vatican

HOW TWO MEN DIVIDED HUMANITY

WHILE the kings of the East were increasing the number of their slaves, enriching with gaudy splendours their barbaric palaces, and planning farther and bolder invasions of foreign territory for the sole purpose of adding to what they called their glory, the people of little Athens were thinking of Socrates.

Among these people was a man named Plato, and among the disciples of Plato there was a young man who came from the court of Macedon, Aristotle by name.

Plato had listened to Socrates, had loved him, and had understood what lay behind his jests and his irony; but he was quite a different man from Socrates himself. He was handsome, aristocratic, rich, princely in manner and behaviour, an artistic man who loved beautiful things, a poet who found a keen and delightful pleasure in the skilful use of words.

Aristotle, when he first attached himself to Plato, was a dandy, and many people thought he was more interested in clothes and jewellery than in knowledge, imagining that his attendance at the lectures of Plato was merely a pose.

But these two men, the master and the disciple, were the two greatest men living on the Earth at that time, and what they said and what they taught changed the world more powerfully than all the battles of Oriental kings and all the gorgeous ceremonial of Oriental priests.

Because of them history was to take a new turn, and even at this present day there is no country in the civilised world which is not what it is because of Plato and Aristotle. Indeed, it has been said that every man on Earth who uses his brain is either a follower of Plato or of Aristotle.

Therefore, we may well overlook all the stupid battles and tyrannies of the world at this period, and keep our attention fixed on little Athens, which was altering human history for all time and giving mankind an entirely new conception of existence.

Plato developed the teaching of Socrates. He taught men that the senses can never give them a true notion of reality. He made them realise that in all they can see with human eyes there is an invisible truth which no words can define. He brought home to men the thought of a divinity in the universe, the feeling of a divinity in their own souls, and encouraged them to dwell on this thought and make it the centre of their lives by meditation, wonder, and adoration.

Aristotle listened to Plato for many years. He did not disagree with him on the central truth of his teaching. He, too,

MIGHTY EPOCHS OF THE WORLD & MAN'S WONDERFUL ADVENTURES

believed in God; he, too, was ready to confess that behind all shapes and forms there is a divine reality. But he came to think that men might better approach to some knowledge of this reality by observation and experiment than by meditation or worship.

THE TWO MEN WHO DIVIDED THE WORLD INTO TWO CAMPS

There were other ways in which these two men were at variance; but here we have the centre of their difference—a difference destined to divide the whole world into two camps. Plato's influence passed into religion, and, after the death of Jesus, saved Christianity from becoming a mere sect of the Jewish Church. The influence of Aristotle, after having inspired the religion of the Arabs, and after having helped to shape the early Christian Church, passed out of all religious keeping and became the inspiration of modern science.

We see what was happening to the mind of man at this great crisis in his progress by thinking of what would happen in our own home if we decided to give ourselves up to a life of meditation on invisible things, such as Justice, Beauty, Freedom, and Truth, while our brother decided that he would devote himself entirely to collecting birds' eggs, catching butterflies, observing the habits of bees, and dissecting the bodies of bats, moles, and mice.

Plato felt that it was foolish to think we could understand the *mystery* of a thing by cutting it open and looking inside. He did not say that we could find out nothing by examination; he said that the only thing of supreme interest could not be discovered by such methods. Aristotle, on the other hand, distrusted the imagination, and came to teach that it was only by examination and experiment that men could find out the truth which was useful to human life.

THE PHILOSOPHER WHO BLAZED A PATH FOR THE HUMAN MIND

Now, Aristotle was the braver of the two, and the greater original genius. For in those days philosophers scorned the idea of turning knowledge to purely human use, and as for studying animals, as for asking questions about fishes from sailors, or about birds from hunters—such an idea seemed to them vulgar and contemptible. But Aristotle, behind all his dandyism, was a man of the very highest courage, and he cared nothing for what philosophers might

say of him. He set to work and classified all the animals of the Earth, and many of the plants, and laid the foundations of all physical science for all time.

Even though his observations were sometimes untrustworthy, and his inferences far-fetched and fantastic, he at least had the curiosity of mind and the desire to know the truth upon which all science is based. He was not content with current theories and explanations; he was ever questioning, examining, and inquiring. His scientific methods were perhaps faulty and lacking in precision, but his scientific ardour was altogether admirable and his classification of animals and plants may be regarded as the beginning of systematic zoology and biology, and marks an epoch in the development of both sciences. He was a great scientific pioneer blazing a path through the jungles of ignorance.

Plato was one of the greatest writers in the world, and, as long as men read at all, his works—in spite of many errors—will remain among the masterpieces of the human mind. But, original as were many of his speculations, the roots of all of them can be traced back to the philosophers who were before him, so that, vast and immortal as were his achievements, we do not feel that he blazed a path for the human mind in quite the same way as Aristotle did.

THE UNIVERSE CAN BE EXPLAINED IN THE LANGUAGE OF MATHEMATICS

We see that this is true when we come to our own time; for all the Platonists of any consequence in these days practise the method of Aristotle in searching for truth. They believe in observation and experiment. They are searching for a higher truth than Aristotle aimed at, but they no longer ignore the marvellous discoveries of physical science. They still exalt Imagination; but they no longer distrust or despise Reason.

One of the great changes wrought by Aristotle soon showed itself in the Greek world. A little less than three hundred years before the birth of Jesus there was born at Syracuse a man named Archimedes, who has been called " the greatest mathematician and engineer of antiquity." Notice that word *engineer*. Plato used the language of mathematics to prove that man was divine. He said in effect: " Here is a wonderful speech which man

PLATO WITH HIS PUPILS IN THE GOLDEN DAYS OF ATHENS

himself has invented. It has come out of man's mind. And it is the only speech in all the world by which we can understand the universe: indeed, it *is* the language of the universe. No one can explain the universe in the language of common speech; but it can be explained in the language of geometry."

Archimedes, on the other hand, turned this invention of mathematics to the service of invention itself. He used mathematics, not to find his way about the stars, but to bring into existence things which had never existed before.

He used mathematics to make wonderful machines, and he used his knowledge of natural laws to produce results which looked like miracles.

FREEING THE MIND FROM THE TYRANNY OF PRIEST AND MAGICIAN

Greek genius was liberating the human mind from two powerful despotisms—the despotism of the priest, and the despotism of the magic-worker. Plato set men thinking of a Divinity that was pure Wisdom, Beauty, and Virtue; Aristotle and Archimedes set them thinking of a power in the human mind infinitely greater than anything possessed by the magician.

But, this work accomplished, the history of the human mind was swept suddenly into a new channel. We are about to turn our eyes away from Greece, and to direct them for the rest of our journey to a quarter of the world from which, hitherto, wisdom had never come. We must turn our eyes from the brilliant, originating, but already ageing East, to the dark, savage, and youthful West—from the glorious palaces of Pharaohs, from the mighty cities of Babylon, from the sublime art and genius of Greece, from all that is splendid and stately and civilised, to all that is barbarous, mis-shapen, and savage.

CIVILISATION TO THE GREEKS WAS A THING OF THE SOUL

It is as if God had tried the East in his balance, and found it, in spite of all its glory and slow-accumulated wisdom, useless for His great purposes. A new power is to arise on Earth, the mightiest yet in all the history of mankind—the power of Rome. Yet, that power is not long to reign over the destinies of mankind; and we shall see that with its fall, which remains one of the chief events in human history, the sons of Greece became again a beacon on the forward path of humanity.

Let us, then, before we turn the page, take a last look at this wonderful city of Athens, in which Socrates had walked barefooted, Plato had talked to his disciples, and Aristotle had pored over books in his home.

What is it that strikes us most in the buildings of this immortal city and in the many statues which dignify its temples and gardens? We answer at once *an absence of all vulgar display.*

This loveliness of Athens is the loveliness of the first real civilisation. It aims not to overawe, not to startle, not to strike the eye at all; only to satisfy the soul with a sense of rightness. Civilisation to the Greeks was a thing of the soul.

Look long at the simplicity of their majestic buildings and at the divine serenity of their sculptures, for their like is never to be seen again. Imperial Rome was to strike out in a path of grandeur, and when men realised that this grandeur was vulgar, they could only return to *copying* the Greeks. But as we look at Athens we are looking at an original conception of beauty—the fine effort of the soul to express its first sense of the divine. Never had the world seen any such beauty as Athens gave it, and all future efforts to express our human sense of divine loveliness will be inspired by the Greek's idea of restraint, repose, and simplicity.

MORAL CHARACTER THE FOUNDATION OF HUMAN LIFE

If Greece had not fallen before the sword of Rome it is possible that the inventive work of Archimedes might have saved her from destruction and paved the way to an immense empire of political power. But perhaps there was something lacking in Greek character which made such an event impossible. Physical science was only tottering on infant feet when Rome threw Athens to the ground, and it was in Rome itself that physical science was to learn to walk among men as a power full of promise for human life.

Let us remind ourselves that the beautiful cities of Greece were undrained, that the average Greek person was uneducated, and that even among the greatest of their teachers sin held an undisputed sway. Brilliance of intellect is not enough. All the foundation of human life is moral character. All that was good in Greece has never died; all that was bad lies buried under the ruins of her vanished greatness.

The Story of the Things We See About Us Every Day

The paper mills by the Thames where The Children's Encyclopedia paper is made

A PIECE OF PAPER

*T*AKE *care of the thing you hold in your hand : it is more precious than gold. Civilisation must fall to bits if paper goes.*

It is the bridge between barbarism and learning, between anarchy and government, tyranny and liberty. Without it we should lose the inspiration that stirs the hearts of men and leads them to do great things. Let us think what paper means.

These pages were written in the great Reading Room of the British Museum, where all round the room thousands of dead men still speak to the world, still influence men, still make people laugh and cry by the books they have written. On the shelf close by are books by Plato and Aristotle and Caesar, and on another shelf are books by Tennyson and Wordsworth and Shakespeare and Goethe. All these writers have gone ; some of them died more than two thousand years ago. yet there they are, still talking, still telling us what they wrought and thought when they walked the Earth.

At first men painted or carved pictures and signs on bones and wood and bark and stone ; then they made bricks of clay and stamped inscriptions on them ; then they carved their hieroglyphics on the walls of temples. The Egyptians were probably the first people to invent a kind of paper, and the word papyrus was the name of the

bulrush from which they made it. It is probable that the ark in which the little Moses was placed by the river's brink was made of this bulrush.

The papyrus paper was very primitive, and was not paper in the modern sense. The white pith of the papyrus was cut into long strips, which were laid side by side, with shorter strips across them, and then all the strips were cemented together with Nile mud or some other sticky substance, and beaten into thin sheets like paper. Even this paper served a very useful purpose, for many most interesting papyrus rolls have been found. One about five thousand years old tells of the reign of King Assa, and others contain writings of Homer and Plato and Demosthenes, and a long-lost work of Aristotle.

We really owe our modern paper to the ingenious Chinese. Originally the Chinese wrote on bamboo boards, or on a tissue of silk, but in the first century of the Christian era, or perhaps before, a clever Chinese succeeded in making paper of bark and hemp and rags, and even of old fishing-nets.

We do not know when the first piece of real paper was made, but there is an extraordinary story of the oldest paper documents which have come to light. It carries us away to the ruins of the Chinese Wall which stretch across the desert sands

INDUSTRIES · HOW THINGS ARE MADE · WHERE THEY COME FROM

of Turkestan. They were explored by Sir Aurel Stein, who went out for the British Museum to trace the lost cities under Asian sands. Here and there along the ancient wall stand the ruins of old watch-towers, and in a heap of rubbish in one of these towers Dr. Stein and his workers made a wonderful discovery.

They found wooden tablets with Chinese inscriptions, a strip of silk paper with writing on it, and bundles of letters on actual paper, made from bark and rags. The letters were in an unknown tongue, but when the language had been translated there was evidence which convinced Dr. Stein that these three kinds of writing were deposited in the tower about the same time, and the date is fixed by the writing on the wooden tablets, which are dated in *the actual year of the birth of Christ*. Here in this ruined tower, with the sands of time blowing all about it, three civilisations seem to have met, and the first three kinds of writing materials lay side by side.

These letters are the oldest pieces of paper known. The oldest paper document known before went back to about a hundred years after Christ; these take us back, perhaps, a century earlier.

WHAT EUROPE LEARNED FROM CHINESE CAPTIVES

The paper the Chinese made in those days was made chiefly from the bark of the mulberry tree—the tree that silkworms feed on, so that to the same tree we owe both silk and paper. In that first century, however, China was little known, and for about seven hundred years Europeans learned nothing about paper. It was only by an accident that papermaking found its way to Europe, and it was an accident of war. It happened in this way. In 751 A.D. the Arab governor of Samarkand, a city in Central Asia, captured some Chinese paper-makers, who were with a Chinese army invading his capital. These men instructed the Arabs, and the Arabs, in their career of conquest, introduced the invention into Europe.

In the history of the world many great wars have been waged and many great victories won, yet we may doubt whether any war had ever a more momentous effect on history than this little raid ending in the capture of the paper-makers.

Now, what was the secret of the Chinese paper? They mashed up the bark of the mulberry, so that the woody fibres were broken up and pulled apart. The tiny fibres were then allowed to sink through the water on a grating, where they formed a kind of tangled felt-work which could be compressed together into a thin sheet. Roughly speaking, that is the principle on which the Chinese made paper, and, though paper-making has been improved and elaborated century after century, the principle remains the same, and all modern paper consists of a deposit of vegetable fibres. Not only wood but any vegetable fibre can be used, and about four hundred different kinds of woody fibre have been tried at one time and another, though the fibres now chiefly in use are cotton, linen, straw, wood, and esparto grass.

THE WONDERFUL THING THE SUN MAKES IN THE GREEN LEAVES

Vegetable fibre consists of a substance called cellulose, and, even apart from its uses in paper-making, cellulose is a very interesting natural product. No man has ever succeeded in manufacturing it. It is manufactured in green leaves by the Sun, and were there no green leaves of plants there could be no white leaves of paper. Chemically speaking, it is a carbohydrate—that is to say, it is composed of the hard, black substance carbon and the gases hydrogen and oxygen, and it very closely resembles starch and sugar. In fact, the Sun and the green leaf first make starch, then turn the starch into sugar, and then turn the sugar into cellulose; and these three substances are the most extraordinary simple substances in the world. For starch and sugar are the source of all animal life and energy, and cellulose, in the form of paper with a little ink on it, is the source of most of the intellectual progress of mankind.

THE AMAZING POWER IN THE WORLD OF STARCH AND CELLULOSE

If a chemist were asked what is the most important elementary substance in the world he would probably answer Starch, because starch is the material out of which all flesh is made, and the chief fuel of the fire of life, which gives energy to all living creatures. And if he were asked what is the next most important elementary substance in the world he would probably say Cellulose, because cellulose, with ink on it, is the most important fuel in the furnace of the mind and the soul of man.

THE MACHINE THAT TURNS TREES INTO PULP

The bulk of the world's paper supply is now made from wood pulp, and here we see a great pile of logs stacked at a pulp mill in Newfoundland, waiting to be ground into pulp. The paper of this book was made from similar logs.

To show in one picture the whole of the actual machinery which turns wood logs into pulp would be impossible, but we give here a photograph of a model of the machinery concentrated into a small space. At the top is the water-tank, with the acid tower below, and the block bin and trough below that. This model shows the apparatus for the chemical, or sulphite, process, which makes the best and strongest pulp, and also the apparatus for the mechanical process.

Every time we write on a sheet of paper we should feel a sense of the wonder of the world, and the strange way in which different and distant things come together and work together. Think! Where did this leaf of paper come from? It certainly was made by the Sun in some green plant lying at first in the green leaf in the form of starch, and then flowing as a solution of sugar in the sap. Perhaps it was made of esparto grass from some Spanish or African meadow; perhaps it was made of trees of a Canadian forest. And we read on it words in ink, made chiefly of galls—the galls produced on oak-leaves by the poisonous secretion of a little insect.

THE FIRST PLACE IN EUROPE WHERE PAPER WAS MADE

The Sun, the plants, and the insects are all working to a far-off end! Out of black carbon and two colourless gases is made the white paper, and by arranging on the paper some streaks of lampblack, or a bitter substance produced by an insect, we can make the most potent instrument of intercourse, of truth and lies, of life and death, that the world contains.

Now to return to our paper-making. Paper was brought from China to Samarkand on the point of an Arab sword, and by the same conquering sword it was carried to Europe. Toledo, in Spain, was the first place in Europe to practise the art. That was in the eleventh century. In the thirteenth century the art reached Italy, and in the fourteenth it arrived in Germany, but not till the fifteenth century did it reach England, and not till the eighteenth was paper made in England in any great quantities or with any great skill. At first, European paper was made almost entirely of rags, and, even still, rags are largely used, but now the main raw material is wood, and some publications, such as this book, have their own forests. It makes one's brain reel to think of mighty forests turned into sheets of white paper covered with the thoughts we write.

THE LITTLE INSECT THAT SHOWED MAN HOW TO MAKE PAPER

Thousands of years before man discovered how to utilise wood in this way (thousands of years before the Chinese paper-maker), a little insect, really the first paper-maker, had been making a paper nest out of wood. The wasp's nest is really a wood-paper, for it is made of paper manufactured from decayed wood, and it was this nest that suggested the modern methods of making paper from wood-pulp. When Solomon advised the sluggard to go to the ant, he might also have advised the paper-maker to go to the wasp, but no one thought of going to the wasp till 1765, when a priest of Ratisbon, named Schaffer, began to experiment with wasps' nests and sawdust and wood shavings, and succeeded in making excellent wood-paper. His experiments were continued by a Dutchman named Koops, and by a Saxon weaver called Keller, who in 1844 made considerable quantities of paper from wood-pulp. The first manufacturers of paper from wood-pulp ground the wood into sawdust; but some chemical processes for making pulp were invented, and these have proved so successful that now wood is the chief material in paper-making. In 1873 only twelve thousand tons of wood were used in England for paper; in 1900 a million tons were used; but in our own time the annual production of wood-pulp for all the world's paper needs is more than 20 million tons.

THE VAST FORESTS WHICH ARE CONVERTED INTO PAPER EVERY YEAR

Whole forests must be converted into pulp, and England has only three million acres of forest-land. So we are compelled to look elsewhere for our supplies of wood-pulp, and vast quantities come to us from the colossal forest-lands of Canada, Newfoundland, and the United States, which together provide the bulk of the world's wood-pulp needs. The Scandinavian countries and Finland also have a very large output of wood-pulp, much of which comes to us.

The area that could be covered by all the paper in the world must be enormous. One ton of pulp will make over three acres of paper, and one hundred and eighty tons of wood-pulp will make a square mile of paper. So one year's production from 20 million tons of wood-pulp would cover more than 110,000 square miles—enough to make a path more than four miles wide right round the Earth!

The life and industry of a nation might well be judged from its consumption of paper. It is the best measure of a nation's mental energy, and if any lack of starch is a danger to its physical energy, so a lack of paper endangers its intellectual energy and its moral power.

PICTURE-STORY OF PAPER

1.   In the mechanical process of turning wood into pulp all the original ingredients of the wood are ground up together, the fibre, resins, gums, and so on, but in the chemical process the foreign bodies are removed, and only the fibre is left. The pulp is made where the trees grow, and is then baled and sent to England, where it is stacked at the mill.

2.   The pulp is broken up and mixed with water, and then, after the impurities have been drained out with the dirty water, the pulp is placed in these bleaching tanks, where chemicals are added to make the paper white.

3. Here is the actual machine, about 200 feet long, which makes the paper out of the pulp. The material enters the machine as a thin watery fluid, and by a series of delicate and complex operations the composition is drained of its water, and the fibres felted together to form over a ton of paper an hour. Several machines are working at the same time.

KNITTING THE FIBRES TO MAKE PAPER

4. A closer view of part of the great paper-making machine seen in the last picture shows water being sprayed on the pulp to keep the froth down before it flows on to the wire on which the paper is formed.

5. The principle of paper-making, whether wood-pulp, esparto grass, or rags are used, is that the fibre of the material shall be made to knit together to form a continuous sheet, and in this part of the machinery flowing water is carrying the fibres so that they will form a network and become paper.

FIVE MILES OF PAPER IN ONE ROLL

6. Here we see the paper passing between a maze of rollers which press and dry it, and give it a calendered surface, that is they make the surface perfectly smooth and equal, and give it a glaze which enables it to receive clear impressions of pictures like those on this page. Various degrees of smoothness can thus be produced.

7. The paper is now finished, and comes off the machine in a roll five miles long. All that is required is to cut it into the widths required for use, and here the paper is rushing through a machine which cuts it as it travels.

Plain Answers to the Questions of the Children of the World

Fluorescent lighting in a drawing office

WHAT IS FLUORESCENT LIGHTING?

THE best light is, of course, sunlight, but man has now made a light for our homes very similar to that of the Sun. This is a form of what is known as fluorescent lighting, and it is rapidly replacing the electric bulb with its filament, and the incandescent gas mantle, in our factories, shops, and homes.

A beautifully-diffused light, casting little or no shadow, fluorescent light is excellent for our eyesight and is much cheaper than its predecessors. In establishing a standard for its economic use the Illumination Engineering Society has measured and worked out, with the aid of the photo-electric cell, or "electric eye," just how much light is best for children at their school desks, for draughtsmen in their offices, for all kinds of industrial workers in the factories, and so on. This is how this lovely fluorescent light is produced.

When some broken-up oyster shells and some sulphur are ground together and heated, a substance—calcium sulphide—is produced which has a very extraordinary property. If stood in a bright light for a minute or two, and then taken into the dark, calcium sulphide glows with a brilliant bluish-violet glow—a form of phosphorescence. Men experimenting with other phosphorescent substances discovered later that zinc sulphide will glow with a beautiful green colour if excited first by X-rays, or radio-active substances, or cathode rays.

Other sulphides may be made to glow red, yellow, pink, and even white. Here lies the secret of the fluorescent lamps. The light is produced, not from the glow of an incandescent filament or wire, but from the white glow of a fluorescent substance inside the glass tube of the lamp which is *excited* by the discharge of high tension electricity passing between two metal electrodes, one at each end. Certain gases can be made to glow similarly, carbon dioxide with a whiteness very closely imitating daylight.

When an electric current is passed through a glass tube containing a trace of some inert gas, the gas becomes split up into its atoms, or *ionised*; the electrically excited ionised gas emits ultra-violet rays, which are invisible in themselves, but are absorbed by the fluorescent substance with which the inside of the tube is coated. Fluorescence really means taking in light of one colour or wave-length and giving back light of another colour or longer

SUN · MOON · STARS · FIRE · WIND · WATER · LIFE · MIND · SLEEP

wave-length. The ultra-violet light is taken by the coating in the tube, and given out again as a visible light of great brilliance and softness. So it is that by choosing the right kind of material, the tube can be made to give out light almost identical with that of the Sun.

Another advantage of the fluorescent lamp is that it gives out only a quarter of the heat that is given out by the tungsten filament lamps in our homes. Consequently four times as much of the electric energy that is supplied to the lamp is turned into *light*, so that the cost of illumination is very much less, though the lamps are rather more costly to instal than their predecessors.

Why Do Some Street Lamps Give a Greenish Light?

Like the white fluorescent lamps used for indoor lighting, the greenish lamps used today for lighting our roads give an illumination that is practically free from shadow, and this is a great aid for safe driving. These lamps are operated by passing a moderately high tension electric current through a mixture of mercury and sodium vapour. Mercury vapour gives an unpleasant green light, which is quite unsuitable for general illumination, while sodium vapour glows with an intense yellowish orange light. By using the two in combination a less displeasing light has been obtained. By mixing the vapour of certain other metals, such as zinc or cadmium or both, the light given can be made very closely to resemble daylight, and as time goes on, these mercury zinc lamps are likely to replace those giving a coloured light.

Is There a Whiter Light Than That of the Sun?

If two rods of carbon, each rod joined to one pole of an electric battery, be touched together and then brought slightly apart, an intensely white and brilliant " arc " flame burns between the two rods; and we have seen elsewhere that these arc lamps were used for many years for outdoor illumination, as they each gave a thousand candle-power of light. Immensely powerful arcs, giving many millions of candle-power, may be used in searchlights; very powerful ones are used in cinematograph projectors. But the electric arc may one day be a forgotten thing, except for electric furnaces.

What is destined largely to take its place is the high-pressure mercury vapour lamp, a tiny flame of mercury burning in a little tube made of quartz, but giving light of such tremendous brightness that it is actually whiter than the light of the Sun. These lamps are known by the initials " h.p.m.v.," and while we shall not use them in our homes, they will play a great part in our future entertainment.

Mercury is turned into vapour with the little quartz tube or bulb, and instead of using a partial vacuum in the tube, the vapour is actually excited by the current under pressure. The light is intensely white, and with the right conditions gives a perfect imitation of sunlight, or an even whiter light still! But, we may ask, " What can be whiter than the light of the Sun? "

Scientists measure the whiteness of a light by comparing it with the light given by a black body that is raised to the necessary temperature to match it. The temperature is measured on the absolute, or Kelvin, scale, starting with the absolute zero as o, so that freezing point becomes 273° Kelvin; the boiling point of water as 373° Kelvin. The gas-filled bulbs burning in our homes have a " colour temperature," as it is called, of about 2900° Kelvin, the electric arc of 3600° Kelvin, and daylight of 5400° Kelvin. The new h.p.m.v. lamps are capable of giving us light of 10,000° Kelvin; hence we may say that their whiteness is almost double that of the Sun.

What was the Ring of Polycrates?

One of the best known stories of Herodotus concerns Polycrates, an exceedingly rich and powerful tyrant of the island of Samos. Above all things Polycrates was famous for his amazing good fortune; so much so that his ally, Amasis of Egypt, began to fear that such unbroken prosperity would excite the envy of the gods. Accordingly he wrote to Polycrates advising him to throw away one of his most valued possessions, in order that he might thus inflict an injury on himself; and, acting on his ally's advice, the tyrant cast a splendid ring into the sea. But a few days later the ring was found inside a fish which a fisherman had presented to Polycrates, so that his amazing luck was still unbroken. Hearing this, Amasis broke off the alliance, and it was not long before Polycrates was captured by his enemies and put to death.

Does a Sound go on For Ever?

There is a true sense in which everything goes on for ever, and there is an equally true sense in which nothing goes on for ever.

Nothing is destroyed, and nothing is without everlasting consequences. But it is no less true that nothing goes on for ever *as it was*; for everything changes, and that is what the word evolution means —that everything always changes in an orderly way, though nothing is ever lost or destroyed.

No sound lasts for ever as a sound. It dies away and is heard no more. We may be watching it by scientific instruments, which are more delicate than our ears, but after a time they will certainly record the fact that the sound is no more. The waves that made it have been smoothed away.

But all waves, of whatever kind, are made by power, and contain the power that made them; and, because no power is ever lost, this has to be accounted for when sound ceases. We could trace it in the movement of particles of air, and of other things ; if we knew enough we could trace the doings of this power in our own ears, and we could also show that a certain amount of heat was produced. The sound ceases, it is true, but its effects do not ; they go on for ever.

Why Must we Cut the Claws of Caged Birds?

Such things as bristles, hair, teeth, claws, and nails behave differently in various animals, according to the kind of use they are likely to be put to. The rule, on the whole, is that when any of these things are liable to be used constantly in such a fashion as to rub them away, they keep on growing continuously throughout the life of the animal.

Our own teeth do not grow continuously, but the teeth of animals often do so. For instance, a hare may die of starvation because it has lost one of its teeth, and the tooth in the other jaw, opposite it, having nothing to rub against, grows and grows, and at last forces the poor creature's mouth open and so kills it by starvation. Claws and teeth follow the same rules in many ways, for they belong to the same class. A bird's claws are meant to be constantly used. When we keep birds captive, and feed them without work on their part, the claws go on growing, because they are no longer worn away by use and the friction, or rubbing down which that involves, so they need to be cut.

What Makes a Knot in a Piece of Wood?

We know that knots are very common in woods of certain kinds, and in specimens which are good and show no signs of disease. Therefore, knots are natural to these woods, and must have some purpose. The wood that makes them is extremely hard, as we know well in carpentering, and this hardness is explained when we learn that knots are, as a rule, simply hard places where branches are coming off from a larger stem. At such a place extra strength is naturally required.

In many trees such as beech, and elm, and cedar, there are knots found at the surface of the woody part of the stem, and these have really been formed in the bark. They begin their existence meaning to be buds, but have come to nothing.

These baby buds, as they might be called, stop their development and, being pressed upon by the parts around them, they become very firm and hard.

Why Does Damp Air Often Make Us Ill?

Damp air is often cold air, and the cold has usually been blamed for making us ill, though many facts prove that it is not blameworthy at all. There is one great difference between damp air and dry air, which accounts for the fact that people usually feel at their best in dry air, while many feel at their worst in damp air.

Water is always leaving our bodies by many channels, such as the skin and the breath. When the air is dry, this journey of water is readily made, but when the air is damp it already contains a quantity of water, and so does not easily take up more, and the passage of water from our bodies is, to a certain extent, checked.

If life is to go on, enough fresh water must always be supplied to the living body, no matter whether it be a man or an animal or a plant. When the passage of water is slowed, as it is in damp air, then the processes of our lives are checked, and our bodies are apt to get choked up with things which would otherwise have been burned up and got rid of. This seems to be the real key to the effect of damp air upon rheumatism.

Why Cannot we Break an Egg if we Hold it Lengthways?

It is not exactly true that we cannot break an egg held lengthways, but certainly it is much more difficult to break the shell when we apply pressure to it at the two ends.

The answer depends upon the shape of the shell. It might partly be that the shell is made thicker at the ends, or it might be that the shell is made of threads or fibres running in a particular direction; but that is not the explanation here.

We may think of the egg-shell as made up of arches. Now, when an arch is narrow and high, it is much stronger, other things being the same, than if it is very wide and flat.

The more upright and narrow an arch is, the more directly does the mass of it resist any pressure from above. In fact, if an arch is narrow enough, it is almost the same as a straight pillar, or column, which directly resists the weight of anything upon it. On the other hand, if the legs of an arch are wide apart, they cannot possibly resist so well, but will be apt to be forced away from each other more easily, and then the arch will break.

Now, we may look upon the egg, when we press it from side to side, as made of two wide, and therefore weak, arches. When we press, we are pressing only against the thickness of the shell, and that resists us little. But when we press the ends, we are met by narrower arches, and we are pressing not so much against the mere thickness of the shell from outside to inside as against the length of it from end to end of the egg.

What is the Difference Between Hard Water and Soft?

The difference between these two kinds of water is that the hard water contains certain salts not found in soft water. These salts are almost always salts of lime, which the water has picked up from the earth as it passes through it. Hard water is very good to drink, as a rule, but the objection to it is that it interferes with the use of soap, and is not good for washing purposes. When soap is used with hard water a chemical change occurs, so that the soap is turned into something which does not dissolve in water; whereas soap used with soft water produces something which dissolves in water, and forms a good lather.

Is It Possible to See the Smallest Things?

The smallest of all things that have ever been discovered are tiny particles of negative electricity called electrons; all matter is made up of electrons revolving round a central mass of positive electricity called the proton. Electrons and a proton compose the atom, but an atom, which is the smallest bit of any substance that can take part in any chemical change, is far too tiny to be seen. A group of atoms forms a molecule, which is the smallest thing that can exist in the free state; but no one can see a molecule. What, then, are the smallest things that we can see?

The microscope will magnify and enable us to see things so small that a hundred thousand of them lying side by side within the space of an inch would be separately visible. But if we use photography instead of our eyes, we can now see things a hundred times smaller still.

In order to see an object as a separate thing, it must not be smaller than half the length of the wave of light by which we are seeing it, and that sets a limit to what we can see with a microscope. But something new has enabled us to photograph objects a hundred times smaller than the smallest object we can see with a microscope made with glass lenses. The lenses of a microscope bend the rays of light and focus a magnified image that the eye can see. But by using magnets instead of lenses we can focus "rays" of electrons and make them form an image which, though invisible to us, can be photographed on a sensitive plate.

This new wonder instrument, called the electron microscope, has revealed an astonishing new world of tiny things. It has shown already that tiny cells, only visible formerly with the most powerful microscope with glass lenses, and thought to be just simple cells, are built-up of myriads of tinier parts, infinitely small, yet having the most wonderful and perfect structure.

Thus, we can see in electron-microscope photographs things which will remain for all time invisible to our eyes. Whether these minute things are yet the smallest in Nature, no one can tell. Perhaps some new discovery will enable us to see, in a photographic print, the image of the electron itself, only to find that it, too, is composed of things yet tinier.

The Story of the Beautiful Things in the Treasure-House of the World

The Forge of Vulcan, by Velasquez

THE SPANIARDS AND THEIR PICTURES

WHEN Ferdinand and Isabella drove the Moors out of Spain they set back by centuries the civilisation of the country.

Instead of planting in the rich soil of Moorish culture, they allowed the land to become desert. The wider the possessions of Spain grew, the more her soul was shrunken. She was too busy wielding the sword to learn the delicate art of holding the brush. The beautiful warmth of the Gothic movement passed her by, and it was not till the sixteenth century that she was stirred to real activity in art.

Her early painters were cold, monkish men. There was Morales (1509-1586), who never seemed to tire of painting his sad-faced Madonnas and Saints. After him came Domenico Theotocopuli, a Cretan, known as El Greco. He lived from 1545 to 1614, and worked at Toledo.

El Greco seemed sorry to be alive at all, and tried to explain all about it in his pictures. They were queer, distorted religious subjects, not pleasantly out of drawing like the saints of the Sienese school which appear to have been painted by happy children dreaming of the heavenly land; rather are they the work of a man whom some inward sorrow kept from seeing the lovely and the fair either in men and women or angels.

But El Greco is one of those artists of whom people will think more and more because of what he was trying to express.

He was a pupil of Titian's, and during his student days capable of painting pictures which were taken for his master's. When he came to Toledo to paint, about the age of 30, his work entirely changed. From the sweetness of Titian's sane and gracious light and colouring he turned to a sourness and a wilful ugliness. His lights and shades became harsh and exaggerated, like those of the realists in the decadent years of Italian art. It was as if he dared not do otherwise, and had a horror of drawing faces that smiled naturally.

His last work is extraordinarily distorted and queer. That he was capable of composition, movement, and energy is quite plain from his picture of Christ driving out the traders from the Temple, in the National Gallery. Some of his portraits have a fine dignity. His masterpiece is the Burial of the Conde de Orgaz, at Toledo.

El Greco was a voice crying in the wilderness, preparing for the beauty to come; a figure in the shadows, peering for the dawn. That beauty and that day-spring was presently to make a sudden glory of Spain.

PICTURES · STATUES · CARVINGS · BUILDINGS · IVORIES · CRAFTS

In the meantime, Ribera was painting some of his striking pictures—pictures where colour had become a bleached and angry light, and shadows looked as if they had been dug with a spade out of a black pit ; where men's muscles seemed ready to crack, and scarcely a face but was expressive of a violent emotion or pleated with the lines of age. From El Greco's sacred gloom we thus step into the fierce and artificial light of Ribera's realism.

WHAT IS MISSING IN THE GREAT SPANISH PICTURES

Ribera, who lived from 1588 to 1656, was a mixture of Spanish and Italian realism; he had a considerable effect on the Seville school of painting, and also on the men who came after. Italian realism, we know, started with Caravaggio, the Neapolitan artist. We remember how angry this man had got with painters who were content with imitating the best in others, and he went to a sorry extreme of brutality in trying to show that it is better at all costs to imitate oneself. Ribera had sat at the feet of Caravaggio a long time; he carried on his work, and for about two hundred years the spirit of his pictures acted and reacted on European art.

There was something in the Spanish country and character that made an excellent soil for Ribera to work in. The Spaniards, as a race, are unimaginative and a little cruel. These qualities showed themselves in the times of the Inquisition, and persist even to this day in the mean national sport of bull-fighting.

The Spaniards believed only what they saw; the pictures of this school are thus void of the spiritual beauty of imagination. You are never allowed to guess, in looking at their work, that something is hiding behind the picture ; you never feel the soft rain, and the scent of the roses in the background ; you do not guess that the woman painted has just stopped saying something you want to hear, and presently will go on with her song and her sorrow.

THE GREAT MISTAKE THE REALIST ARTISTS MAKE

Nor was there any illusion in the physical country surrounding the people of Spain. Their eyes were trained to harsh lights and shadows. The sun takes away from their landscapes the dewy greens and gentle tones native to more northern countries.

Ribera made the great mistake of realists in thinking that in order to paint what he saw he must needs paint unpleasant things. It was necessary for a greater than he to show the beauty of actual objects to people.

But Ribera unconsciously prepared the way for the genius of Spain. He had turned people's eyes from the strange, distorted religious paintings of El Greco, and at times in his own work there is a hint of nobility, of lurking goodness.

Of the many artists who followed in Ribera's path the most memorable was Zurbaran. He lived from 1598 to 1662, and was a painter who devoted himself to studies of monks and saints. A famous picture of his was the kneeling Dominican in the National Gallery. The man is praying in a great fervour; and as one looks at the picture it seems that the inward radiance of the soul is stronger than the actual light falling on the uplifted face.

Another of Zurbaran's pictures showing this straining after effect and violent realistic treatment is the group of St. Bonaventura and St. Thomas Aquinas, in Berlin. The painting of St. Bruno and the Pope, in Seville, is a curious and interesting study of still, monkish men, their garments seeming to be the heavy casings of lifeless bodies; the faces, stamped by thought and suffering and ambition, are the only scraps of life in the picture.

THE GREATEST GENIUS OF TECHNIQUE THE WORLD HAS KNOWN

Don Diego de Silva y Velasquez, the great genius of Spain, emerged on to the tumult and activities of the realists like a great ship gliding over waves which unsteadied smaller craft. He lived from 1599 to 1660, and appeared from the beginning to be set apart for high deeds. Like Queen Elizabeth, he " could always count much on fortune." Poverty and disgrace, disappointment and loneliness never cross-starred his path. He was healthy and happy and sane; and he shook from him, as a dog would shake water from his coat, the influences which were weighing heavily on the Spanish artists of his day. He was unimaginative, and he believed in what he saw, being a true son of Spain; but what he saw was beauty incarnate.

In any art gallery of Europe where Velasquez's paintings are hung, we may see artists looking and peering and studying, sketching and copying, trying to read the secret of his unapproachable greatness

THREE FAMOUS PICTURES FROM SPAIN

THE PARASOL, BY GOYA

THE MADONNA AND CHILD, BY MURILLO,
IN THE PITTI GALLERY, FLORENCE

THE MADONNA AND ANGELS, BY MURILLO,
IN THE LOUVRE, PARIS

He is the mightiest genius of technique the world has ever known. His strength lay not in form, or in colour, but in revelation of light. He did not gloat over the human body as Michael Angelo did, but when he had to paint it he painted it flawlessly.

He was not seized with the passion for brilliant hues that marked the Venetian painters, partly because colour as colour in Venice does not exist in Spain, and partly because he was sensitive to something greater—light. Velasquez, like other Spaniards, loves neutral tints ; he is a master of greys. But El Greco's and Ribera's greys were cold and rocky; Velasquez's greys are silver and pearl, shining like the grey dew of dawn.

PORTRAITS THAT BRING SEVENTEENTH-CENTURY SPAIN TO LIFE AGAIN

It is probable that artists of many more generations will still strive to find how Velasquez got such radiance into his greys. Light seemed to hide in his palette and cling to his brush. He was not concerned with much preliminary drawing, but painted straight on to the canvas. Of his many imitators no one has come within speaking distance of his style; the secret of his genius is unassailable.

Velasquez became artist to Philip the Fourth of Spain. For forty years he was attached to the court, and during the latter part of this period became a kind of confidential secretary—" Gentleman of the Household." After the heavy routine of court life had swallowed his nights and days for some seven years he yielded to the persuasion of Rubens, who was then in Madrid, to escape for a holiday to Italy.

Velasquez contrived to let two summers roll by before he returned to his post. Twelve years later he visited Rome and Venice again. Save for these lulls his working life was given up to the Spanish monarch, to painting the series of portraits which have brought seventeenth-century Spain to life before our eyes today.

THE FAULT OF MANY PICTURES OF THE CRUCIFIXION

There were intervals, when he painted pictures of another kind, classical subjects like the Forge of Vulcan, or the famous Rokeby Venus, in the National Gallery; religious subjects like his Christ on the Cross, and the Madonna, in Madrid, and St. Bridget, in the National Gallery.

The Crucifixion painted by Velasquez is a noble and dignified study—as are,

indeed, all the artist's pictures—a study that makes one think profoundly without being tortured by the vulgar terrors which some painters worked into their pictures.

Whenever, in pictures of the Crucifixion, we see the painter showing the horror of physical pain and overlooking the agony of the soul, we know that that picture is poor art—bad taste, appealing to the senses and not the mind in a study of the most unearthly sorrow that ever befell a human spirit.

Velasquez's Madonna shows the same simple faith and understanding of the motherhood of Mary. She is a serious and beautiful woman lost in thought about the sturdy little baby boy on her lap.

It was for the great good fortune of people who live in a world unlikely to produce another man like Velasquez that the great Spaniard escaped two or three times to Italy. In those years he breathed a different air from the stifling atmosphere of the court, and he developed another activity. Save for those visits it is unlikely that he would have painted in his later years, when men are generally content to repeat their successes and imitate their own inspirations, two such masterpieces as The Tapestry Weavers, and The Maids of Honour. These two pictures alone would have set Velasquez on the heights of genius.

THE MAN WHO MIGHT HAVE BEEN THE GREATEST LANDSCAPE PAINTER

The Tapestry Weavers is a giant composition, a superb study of peasant women at work; its final greatness is in the amazing treatment of light. The light not only falls in a clean shaft behind the central archway, it plays hide and seek with the solid forms and properties of the workers in a way that no one save Velasquez has ever seen and painted.

The Maids of Honour is another triumph of lighted interiors. Radiance creeps softly into the room, resting on the little pathetic princess with her waiting women, and presently touches the older figures in the background, silhouettes the man in the open doorway beyond, and catches the face and brush of the painter himself whom, by an amusing conceit, he has actually put into the picture.

Velasquez's greatest work of a decorative nature is the Surrender of Breda; and there it seems that though he found an intense interest in painting the cavaliers, his happiest moments were when he

PICTURES BY THE SPANISH ARTISTS

SAINT BASIL, BY
EL GRECO

THE INFANTE PHILIPP PROSPER,
BY VELASQUEZ

THE ADORATION OF THE
SHEPHERDS, BY JOSE RIBERA

THE INFANT JESUS AND THE INFANT SAINT JOHN, BY MURILLO

THE MIRACLE OF SAINT HUGO,
BY FRANCISCO ZURBARAN

THE INFANT SAINT JOHN,
BY MURILLO

SAINT BRUNO AND POPE URBAN II,
BY FRANCISCO ZURBARAN

worked at the landscape in the background, and bathed it in a lovely glow. This picture alone makes one guess that had Velasquez lived in another age and in another country he would have been the world's greatest landscape painter.

His portrait work centres round the royal and aristocratic personages of Philip's court. There Velasquez is himself a prince among princes. All the hauteur and coldness of the Spanish king is painted by a man who knew that pride and personal dignity are true qualities of kingship. Cruel though Philip may have been, treacherous, we feel that in his hours of personal suffering he would present just the same unmoved face to the world.

A FACE THAT WAS DEAD BEFORE THE CANVAS WAS DRY

The pictures of the young Don Carlos and Maria Anna of Austria—in Madrid—show like characteristics. Poor great lady ! She is condemned to live for ever in the world's eyes a fantastic, pathetic figure burdened by an outrageous head-dress and clothed in so heavy a garment of silk and brocade and velvet that one wonders how she managed to move about.

Velasquez's incomparable touch rests on the soft and shining texture of her gown; it seems that its tissues are still brilliant and alive; in contrast, the face above the gown is cold and unhappy, and was already dead before the paint was dry. In these huge canvases of Velasquez's lies all the story of Spain.

Another master painter of Velasquez's day, and one, indeed, who owed much of his success to kindly help by the great man, was Murillo.

HOW MURILLO BRINGS ART TO THE LEVEL OF EVERYDAY LIFE

Murillo, a native of Seville, lived from 1617 to 1682. Although he could be realistic sometimes, Murillo was a painter who appeared strangely out of place among the Spaniards. If you look first at a picture of Velasquez's and then at one of Murillo's, it will seem that Velasquez is a cold aristocrat who really does not care in the least about the people he is painting, and that Murillo is a friend of the people, and likes to see children happy.

Murillo was not a genius like Velasquez, but he has a warmer heart. He is an artist we speak of affectionately—dear and gentle Murillo, we say, and forgive him for not being greater than he is. He saw the

world as a place which was nice, and might be nicer still if you made it so; and, therefore, why not pretend a little? Murillo was pretending in his happy way when he painted his religious pictures.

Perhaps he was weary of the canvases of El Greco, and Ribera, and Zurbaran, and determined that his Mary the Mother of Christ should be more lovable. We can see this feeling in the well-known Immaculate Conception in Madrid, and in many of the Madonnas which came from Murillo's brush. Perhaps, he was tired of angry and miserable men in pictures, and therefore, he painted his merry boys.

He must have been very happy drawing Boys eating Melons (Munich), and the Spanish Peasant Boy and the Boy Drinking, and, in another way, St. John and the Lamb, all three in the National Gallery. Not only in his subjects did he keep from ugly and austere people; he loved and pretended that colour and light were always gentle and caressing. He has his place in this way in humanising the art of Spain and bringing it more to the level of everyday people's lives.

CANVASES THAT GLOW WITH FINE PICTURES OF SPANISH FOLK

After the death of Murillo there was no Spanish painter of importance until Goya (1746–1828). He was a kind of miracle who descended on Spain a century after Murillo had painted his pleasant pictures. Velasquez and Goya have tremendously influenced the art of Europe. Goya drew a whole society of Spanish men and women, strong, warm, active. They glow and speak for ever on his canvases—people like the young women in the Lille Museum picture, the Ladies in the Balcony, in Madrid, and the Portrait of Dona Isabella, in the National Gallery.

From painting these portraits Goya ran sometimes to the limit of madness in working out his studies of an allegorical nature. Some of them are rather frightening, most a little disturbing. One feels that Goya is saying: " Look how powerful and satirical I can be! "; and he is saying the truth. His draughtsmanship was superb and masterly.

The world watches and waits. Spain's magnificent gift to art was Velasquez. The coming of Goya showed that her forces were not in any way spent. Who knows that any year may not see another equal genius arise in Spain?

The Wonderful House We Live In, and Our Place in the World

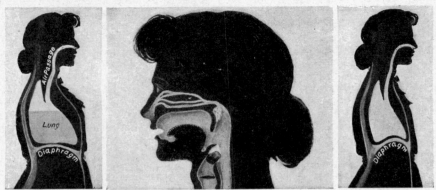

The middle diagram shows the air and food passages, with a lump of food lodged at the top of the windpipe. The side diagrams show how the diaphragm helps to fill and empty the lungs.

LIFE AND THE LUNGS

EVERY living thing must breathe, and now we come to study the lungs, the organs of breathing in ourselves and in all the higher animals. The real breathing or burning is done inside the living stuff called protoplasm, but the oxygen it needs is taken in by the lungs. These lie in the chest on a living floor of muscle which moves up and down as we breathe. The air enters the nose—or, when we breathe wrongly or in a hurry, by the mouth—and is there warmed, filtered, and moistened.

Then it passes through the voice-box into the tubes that lead into the substance of the lungs. So it reaches the air-cells, as they are called, and there it comes near the blood which the heart has pumped to the lungs to meet it. We breathe by sucking in the air, and if we are wise we are careful never to wear any tight clothing over out breathing muscles, but to allow them free play in their ceaseless work of sucking into our lungs the air which our blood carries to every part of the body.

We have already learned that everything must breathe, and that one of the reasons why the blood circulates in us and in all the other animals that have blood is to carry certain gases to and from the lungs. We have also learned that the real breathing is not in the lungs at all, but in the tissues of the body, where burning goes on. The scientific name for breathing is *respiration*, and real breathing is called *internal respiration*. We may say a word or two about it before we consider the lungs and how they should be used.

It has been found that there is a great difference between ordinary burning and the way in which living matter breathes. In ordinary burning, the oxygen just comes to the outside of the coal, or whatever it is that burns, and is then combined with it; but living matter does not burn in this way. It takes the oxygen brought to it by the blood right into itself, and probably does many wonderful things with it, producing all the time the changes which are life, before at last it gives out the oxygen combined with carbon to form carbon dioxide, and combined with hydrogen to form water. Thus we say that the breathing of living matter, or protoplasm, is inside its molecule, and as the word *intra* is Latin for *within*, the proper way of stating this it to say that the breathing of protoplasm is *intra-molecular*, or inside the molecules. It does not matter if you forget the scientific term so long as you remember the fact.

We have seen that the heart lies in the middle of the chest, and has one lung on

BODY, MIND, AND SOUL · CITIZENSHIP · ECONOMICS · GOVERNMENT

each side of it. We must now learn what makes the floor of the chest, for the lungs cannot be used without its help.

It is a flat sheet of muscle stretched across the middle of the body. There are a few openings in it, through which pass veins and arteries and nerves, but otherwise it is a complete partition between the upper and lower halves of the trunk. It has a rather curious name, which, however, is used for many other purposes; it is *diaphragm*, pronounced *di-a-fram*, and it is used for anything *stretched across*.

This diaphragm in our bodies has been described as flat, but really, it is dome-shaped. It is a living floor, for it is a muscle. When it contracts it becomes more nearly flat, for it presses downward. This, of course, means that everything beneath it is pressed upon, and as this muscle acts every time we breathe properly, you will notice that when you take a long breath the lower part of your body bulges forward. This is because the floor of the chest, which is also the roof of the lower part of the body, has moved downward and become flatter, so that the lower part of the trunk (the abdomen) is forced to bulge forward.

THE CHANNEL THROUGH WHICH THE AIR ENTERS INTO OUR BODIES

Upon this diaphragm, then, there rest the heart and the two lungs. The part of each lung that rests upon it is called its base; it is the widest and broadest part of the lung. If we look at the base of each lung and then follow it upward, we shall see that it becomes narrower and smaller, until at last it ends almost in a point which actually comes up near the neck behind the collar-bone. It is important to remember that the greatest bulk of the lung is its lower part, for there are two ways of breathing—one which fills the upper part of the lung with air and one which fills the lower part; and we see, of course, that it must be better to breathe in the way which fills the biggest and roomiest part of the lung. Now let us begin at the very beginning of the act of breathing, and see where the air goes.

There is a perfectly definite channel for the air from the outside world to the lungs, and if we are wise we always breathe by this channel. The opening of it is the nose. Now, this is very important, for it happens that we, unlike some animals, can also breathe through our mouths, and, though

there is no objection to doing this sometimes, we should know that the mouth is the opening of the canal that has to do with food, while the nose is the opening of the canal that has to do with air. Each opening is provided with suitable arrangements for its special purpose. The mouth has teeth and all the arrangements for tasting; the nose has little hairs for filtering the air, and it contains all the arrangements for smelling, as well as a wonderful lining or membrane which can be flooded with blood so as to warm the air before it enters our lungs.

THE WAY THE AIR IS FILTERED AS IT COMES INTO OUR LUNGS

But that is not all. If we trace out the passage of the air through the nose, we find that, instead of being straight and open, it is extraordinarily twisted and roundabout. This is a great advantage. For one thing, it compels the air to pass over a great surface which has warm blood beneath it, so that the air is warmed; and it means also, that a good deal of water vapour—water in the form of gas—can be added to the air if it does not already contain enough. That is good, for perfectly dry air is very irritating to our lungs, and dries them up in a very unhealthy way. Lastly, this long, twisted, in-and-out passage for the air makes a splendid filter. A large quantity of all the dirt in the air, and of any microbes that may be in it, is stopped by this filter, so that the air which is allowed to pass on to the lungs is not only warmed and moistened, but is greatly purified. Experiments have been made which show that when, by means of a tube passed into the mouth, we withdraw the air which has been through the nose filter and is on its way to the lungs; no microbes can be found in it—though it may have had hosts of microbes in it when it entered the nose. It follows, then, that it is the duty of everyone to breathe through the nose.

A MOST IMPORTANT THING IN LIFE IS TO BREATHE THROUGH THE NOSE

Now, the passage of air is easier through the mouth than through the nose, just because the mouth does not trouble to filter it; so that, if you keep your mouth open, air is sure to enter through it when you breathe. The rule, then, must be to keep the mouth shut. It should be opened when we have something to swallow or something to say.

HERE COMES EVERY BREATH YOU BREATHE

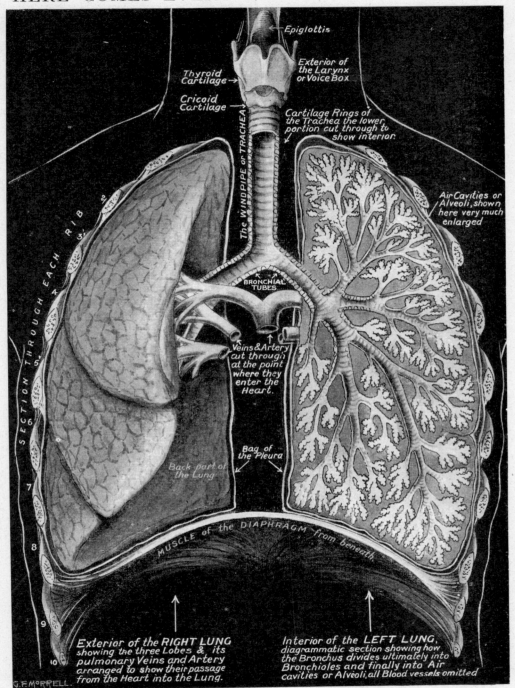

THE LUNGS, SHOWN AS THEY ARE AND ALSO IN SECTION

In this picture-diagram the front wall of the chest has been removed, so that the two lungs and their connections are seen. The windpipe is shown dividing into the two bronchial tubes, and a section through the left lung reveals the left bronchial tube dividing and finally ending in the air cells. The right lung, which is not shown in section, is seen to be divided into three parts, or lobes. The diaphragm is also represented, and the great lung artery and veins.

1319

There are few more important lessons for health than this lesson of breathing through the nose. Every child should be taught it, and the way to learn it is to learn to keep the mouth shut. All over Britain there are unfortunate children who are not as tall and heavy as they should be for their age, who suffer from frequent colds and sore throats, and so on, simply because they have something the matter with their noses which prevents them from breathing properly.

WHAT IT IS THAT HAPPENS WHEN WE HAVE A CHOKING FIT

After passing through the nose filter, the air streams into the throat at the back of the mouth, and passes into the voice-box, the front of which you can feel in your neck. This voice-box has two folds of tissue stretched across it from each side, with a tiny chink between them. Every time we breathe in air, the brain sends an order through certain nerves to the muscles which govern these little vocal cords, and they swing widely apart, so as to leave a large space through which the air can pass without making any sound.

We all know what a choking fit is. What happens then is that something or other which has got into the voice-box has thrown this beautiful arrangement out of order, and the vocal cords, instead of separating to let us breathe, are thrown together so that the air can scarcely force its way between them. In doing this it sets them trembling and vibrating, and so makes little noises.

But, though we feel very miserable during a choking fit, we need not be afraid, for as soon as the brain finds it is getting too little oxygen in the blood brought to it, it *always* orders the vocal cords to relax, and in a moment we find that we can take a long, deep breath quite easily. Of course, this cannot save us in rare cases where a lump of food or something is actually stuck in the top of the voice-box, so that the air cannot get past it. This is the only serious kind of choking.

HOW WE MAY SAVE OURSELVES IN A CHOKING FIT

If we have all learned at school the simple things which really matter, no one need ever be killed in this way, so long as anyone else is present. Indeed, one could save oneself. The top of the voice-box is so near to the mouth, after all, that anyone can be saved by a forefinger quickly and boldly passed into the mouth so as to remove the obstacle.

Of course, little specks of food often find their way into the voice-box, but the result of that is to make us cough violently, which brings up a blast of air from the lungs, and blows the obstacle away.

It is a curious thing about the body that, of the two passages in the throat, one for the air and one for the food, the food passage lies behind. This means that everything we swallow has to be made to jump across the opening through the voice-box into the lungs. We find this very easy, because the act of swallowing is such a wonderful one, though most of us think little about it. It depends upon the beautifully balanced use of scores of nerves and muscles. If we laugh or try to talk just when we are swallowing, we throw this beautiful machinery out of order, and instead of everything passing safely over the opening that leads to the lungs, some of it is apt to get into the wrong passage.

THE TWO TUBES THROUGH WHICH OUR BREATH GOES TO THE LUNGS

After passing through the voice-box the air flows down the windpipe, a large round tube which you can readily feel in your neck. Just below the big part of the voice-box is a sort of ring, easily felt, which is really part of the voice-box itself, and below that you can feel the round tube running down into the chest. If you feel carefully with the tip of your finger you will find that this round tube is made of a number of little rings. This we usually call the windpipe, and its special name does not matter. After it has passed down some distance it divides into two tubes, one going to the right lung and the other to the left. Each of these in the substance of the lungs divides up again and again like a tree. These tubes are called the *bronchi*, a name which we can all remember, as when the tubes fall ill we call the trouble bronchitis. As they subdivide the branches get smaller and smaller, until at last they become quite tiny, and then we find that they end in a countless number of little buds, as we might call them, known as the air-cells.

These are not what we have learned to understand by the word cells, but little hollow spaces with very fine walls lined with living cells and containing air. With the first breath a baby draws, the lungs

PICTURE ATLAS

GREAT SIGHTS OF SCOTLAND

QUEEN'S VIEW AT LOCH TRUMMELL IN PERTHSHIRE

THE STILL WATERS OF LOCH INCH

HIGHLAND CATTLE NEAR BRAEMAR IN ABERDEENSHIRE

EDINBURGH CASTLE FROM PRINCES STREET GARDENS

GLASGOW UNIVERSITY ON GILMORE HILL

BALMORAL CASTLE, HIGHLAND HOME OF THE ROYAL FAMILY

THE NINETEENTH-CENTURY INVERNESS CASTLE

THE BRUCE STATUE
IN STIRLING

GOUROCK AND THE FIRTH OF CLYDE FROM GREENOCK, WITH THE
MEMORIAL TO FRENCH SEAMEN OF THE SECOND WORLD WAR

THE BURNS STATUE
IN ABERDEEN

AILSA CRAIG IN THE FIRTH OF CLYDE

THE GORGE AT GLENCOE

BEINN EIGHE NATURE RESERVE, IN ROSS-SHIRE

THE RIVER DEE NEAR BRAEMAR

BEN LOMOND LOOKS DOWN ON LOCH LOMOND

One Thousand Poems of All Times and All Countries

KING BRUCE AND THE SPIDER

Eliza Cook was a busy writer, both of prose and verse, who was born in 1818 and died in 1889. She was not in any sense a remarkable poet, and the following verses owe their interest as much to the legend they relate as to the manner of its telling. But the poem has a simple vigour and a direct appeal. The story has long been a favourite one to illustrate the wisdom of never giving in to failure.

KING BRUCE of Scotland flung himself
   down
  In a lonely mood to think;
'Tis true he was monarch and wore a
   crown,
  But his heart was beginning to sink.

For he had been trying to do a great deed
  To make his people glad;
He had tried, and tried, but couldn't
   succeed ;
  And so he became quite sad.

He flung himself down in low despair,
  As grieved as man could be;
And after a while as he pondered there,
  " I'll give it all up," said he.

Now just at that moment a spider dropped
  With its silken cobweb clue;
And the King in the midst of his thinking
   stopped
  To see what the spider would do.

'Twas a long way up to the ceiling dome,
  And it hung by a rope so fine
That how it could get to its cobweb home
  King Bruce could not define.

It soon began to cling and crawl
  Straight up with strong endeavour;
But down it came with a slippery sprawl,
  As near the ground as ever.

Up, up it ran, not a second it stayed
  To utter the least complaint,
Till it fell still lower, and there it laid,
  A little dizzy and faint.

Its head grew steady—again it went,
  And travelled a half-yard higher;
'Twas a delicate thread it had to tread,
  A road where its feet would tire.

Again it fell and swung below,
  But again it quickly mounted;
Till up and down, now fast, now slow,
  Nine brave attempts were counted.

" Sure," cried the King, " that foolish thing
  Will strive no more to climb;
When it toils so hard to reach and cling,
  And tumbles every time."

But up the insect went once more,
  Ah, me! 'tis an anxious minute;
He's only a foot from his cobweb door,
  Oh, say, will he lose or win it?

Steadily, steadily, inch by inch,
  Higher and higher he got;
And a bold little run at the very last pinch
  Put him into his native cot.

" Bravo, bravo! " the King cried out,
  " All honour to those who try ;
The spider up there defied despair,
  He conquered, and why shouldn't I ? "

And Bruce of Scotland braced his mind,
  And gossips tell the tale
That he tried once more as he tried before,
  And that time did not fail.

POEMS · SONGS · BALLADS · VERSES AND RHYMES WITH MUSIC

Pay goodly heed, all ye who read,
And beware of saying *I can't*.
'Tis a cowardly word, and apt to lead
To Idleness, Folly, and Want.

Whenever you find your heart despair
Of doing some goodly thing,
Con over this strain, try bravely again,
And remember the spider and king.

THE STORMY PETREL

The sea bird of this poem ranges the ocean, hardly ever coming to land. It is a small bird, and, save for a few white feathers on wings and tail, sooty black in colour. Sailors call it Mother Carey's Chicken, and partly because it is always busiest in stormy weather, partly because of its colour, look upon it as a bird of ill omen. The poem is by Barry Cornwall (Bryan Waller Procter).

A THOUSAND miles from land are we,
    Tossing about on the roaring sea;
From billow to bounding billow cast
Like fleecy snow on the stormy blast.
The sails are scattered abroad like weeds;
The strong masts shake like quivering
    reeds;
The mighty cables and iron chains,
The hull, which all earthly strength dis-
    dains—
They strain and they crack; and hearts
    like stone
Their natural hard, proud strength disown.

Up and down! Up and down!
From the base of the wave to the billow's
    crown,
And amidst the flashing and feathery foam
The stormy petrel finds a home—
A home, if such a place may be
For her who lives on the wide, wide sea,
On the scraggy ice, in the frozen air,
And only seeketh her rocky lair
To warm her young, and to teach them
    to spring
At once o'er the waves on their stormy
    wing.

O'er the deep! O'er the deep!
Where the whale, and the shark, and the
    swordfish sleep
Outflying the blast and the driving rain,
The petrel telleth her tale—in vain;
For the mariner curseth the warning bird
Which bringeth him news of a storm un-
    heard!
Ah, thus does the prophet of good or ill
Meet hate from the creatures he serveth
    still;
Yet he ne'er falters—so, petrel, spring
Once more o'er the waves on thy stormy
    wing!

THE PEOPLE'S ANTHEM

Ebenezer Elliott, the Sheffield "Corn Law Rhymer," wrote much verse that moved the hearts of the people of his day— he died in 1849—but this one poem, which thrills with a love of the great mass of men, was written for all ages.

WHEN wilt thou save the people?
    O God of mercy when?
Not kings and lords, but nations!
    Not thrones and crowns, but men!
Flowers of thy heart, O God, are they!
Let them not pass, like weeds, away,
Their heritage a sunless day!
            God save the people!

Shall crime bring crime for ever,
    Strength aiding still the strong?
Is it thy will, O Father,
    That man shall toil for wrong?
"No!" say thy mountains; "No!" thy
    skies;
"Man's clouded sun shall brightly rise,
And songs be heard instead of sighs."
            God save the people!

When wilt thou save the people?
    O God of mercy, when?
The people, Lord! the people!
    Not thrones and crowns, but men!
God save the people! thine are they;
Thy children, as thy angels fair:
Save them from bondage and despair!
            God save the people!

GOD SENDS LOVE TO YOU

There are few stories in the Old Testament more beautiful than that of Naaman and the little Jewish maid, which tells us how that young captive contrived to teach her master about the love of God. Dr. Henry Van Dyke, an American poet who died in 1933, wrote a beautiful play, "The House of Rimmon," which deals with this subject, and the little maid is therein made to sing the following beautiful song.

ABOVE the edge of dark appear the lances
    of the sun;
Along the mountain ridges clear his rosy
    heralds run;
The vapours down the valley go,
Like broken armies, dark and low.
Look up, my heart, from every hill
In folds of rose and daffodil
The sunrise banners flow.

Oh, fly away on silent wing, ye boding
    owls of night!
Oh, welcome, little birds that sing the
    coming-in of light!
For new, and new, and ever new,
The golden bud within the blue;
And every morning seems to say:
"There's something happy on the way,
And God sends love to you!"

MY LADY'S GARDEN

How does my la-dy's gar-den grow? How does my la-dy's gar-den grow? With sil-ver bells and coc-kle shells, And pret-ty maids all in a row.

A is an ARCHWAY
to Fairyland gay

B for the BUTTERFLIES
showing the way

C is the CASTLE
the queen reigns over

D is the DEW
that's brought from the clover

E the ELF-PAGES
surrounding her hall

F for the FAIRIES
that fly to her call

G for the GARLANDS
they weave for her hair

H for the HONEY
they bring to her there

I, INVITATIONS
she sends to a ball

J is the JOY
that they give to them all

K is the KELPIE
who reads hers with pride

L for the LIZARD
who offers a ride

a b c d e f g h i j k l m n o p q r s t u v w x y z

B FOR THE BUTTERFLIES SHOWING THE WAY

M is the MERMAID
who lives in the moat

N is the NUT-SHELL
she has for a boat

O is the OWL
keeping watch from the tower

P for the PERFUME
brought in by each flower

Q is the QUEEN
who is gracious and fair

R the RESPECT
that she gains everywhere

S is the SPIDER
(a bit in the way !)

T for the TUNES
when the band starts to play

U for the USE
that is made of each chance

V for the VIGOUR
displayed in the dance

W the WATCHMAN
who comes with a warning

X cannot stop,
for the day is near dawning

Y for their YAWNS
as they scamper from sight

Z is the end
of a beautiful night

Mary, Mary, quite contrary,
How does your garden grow?
With silver bells and cockle-shells
And columbines all in a row.

Little Jack Horner sat in a corner,
Eating a Christmas pie;
He put in his thumb and he took out
a plum,
And said, What a good
boy am I!

If bees stay at home
Rain will soon come.
If they fly away
Fine will be the day.

As I was going up Pippen Hill,
Pippen Hill was dirty;
There I met a pretty miss,
And she dropped me a curtsey.

Little miss, pretty miss,
Blessings light upon you!
Had I half-a-crown a day
I'd spend it all upon you.

How many miles to Babylon?
Threescore miles and ten.
Can I get there by candle-light?
Yes, and back again;
If your heels are nimble and light
You may get there by candle-light.

Peter, Peter, pumpkin-eater,
Had a wife and couldn't keep
her;
He put her in a pumpkin shell,
And there he kept her very well.

GREAT NATURE IS AN ARMY GAY

Richard Watson Gilder, who was born in 1844 and died in 1909, was the editor of The Century Magazine and a well-known poet. When he sang of Nature he sometimes struck a serious and almost a forbidding note, as in this fine example of his skill. The brisk idea of the opening lines is not maintained, and the reader soon begins to think that Nature's army, so far from being gay, is an appalling host of ants or locusts that mean to devour everything in their path, leaving not a shred behind—not even the poor author.

GREAT Nature is an army gay,
　　Resistless marching on its way;
I hear the bugles clear and sweet,
I hear the tread of million feet.
Across the plain I see it pour;
It tramples down the waving grass;
Within the echoing mountain pass
　　I hear a thousand canon roar.

It swarms within my garden gate;
　　My deepest well it drinketh dry.
It doth not rest; it doth not wait;
　　By night and day it sweepeth by.
Ceaseless it marches by my door;
It heeds me not, though I implore.
I know not whence it comes, nor where
It goes. For me it doth not care
Whether I starve, or eat, or sleep,
Or live, or die, or sing, or weep.
And now the banners all are bright,
Now torn and blackened by the fight.
Sometimes its laughter shakes the sky,
Sometimes the groans of those who die.
Still through the night and through the
　　livelong day
The infinite army marches on its remorse-
　　less way.

INCIDENT IN THE FRENCH CAMP

In this poem Robert Browning relates a real event which happened in Napoleon's war with Austria in 1809. The only difference between the poet's account of the incident and the actual episode is that the hero was a man.

YOU know we French stormed Ratisbon:
　　A mile or so away;
On a little mound Napoleon
　　Stood on our storming day;
With neck out-thrust, you fancy now,
　　Legs wide, arms locked behind,
As if to balance the prone brow
　　Oppressive with its mind.
Just as perhaps he mused "My plans
　　That soar to earth may fall
Let once my army leader, Lannes,
　　Waver at yonder wall,"
Out 'twixt the battery-smokes there flew
　　A rider, bound on bound,
Full galloping; nor bridle drew
　　Until he reached the mound.
Then off there flung in smiling joy,
　　And held himself erect.

By just his horse's mane, a boy;
　　You hardly could suspect—
So tight he kept his lips compressed
　　Scarce any blood came through—
You looked twice ere you saw his breast
　　Was all but shot in two.
"Well," cried he, "Emperor, by God's
　　grace
We've got you Ratisbon!
The Marshal's in the market-place,
　　And you'll be there anon
To see your flag-bird flap his vans
　　Where I, to heart's desire,
Perched him!" The chief's eye flashed;
　　his plans
Soared up again like fire.
The chief's eye flashed; but presently
　　Softened itself, as sheathes
A film the mother-eagle's eye
　　When her bruised eaglet breathes;
"You're wounded!" "Nay," his soldier's
　　pride
Touched to the quick, he said:
"I'm killed, Sire!" And his chief beside,
　　Smiling, the boy fell dead.

NOVEMBER IN ENGLAND

This poem is an excellent example of the half-serious, half-jocular spirit in which Thomas Hood could write when the mood seized him. The description suggests London rather than England, and it was most likely out of the fulness of his own experience of a London fog in the metropolis that the afflicted poet produced this bundle of negatives.

NO sun, no moon,
　　　　No morn, no noon,
No dawn, no dusk, no proper time of day;
　　No sky, no earthly view,
　　No distance looking blue,
No road, no street, no "t'other side the
　　way";
　　No end to any row,
　　No indications where the crescents go;
　　No top to any steeple,
No recognition of familiar people,
　　No courtesies for showing 'em,
　　No knowing 'em!
No travelling at all, no locomotion,
No inkling of the way—no notion,
　　"No go"—by land or ocean—
　　No mail, no post,
　　No news from any foreign coast;
No park, no ring, no afternoon gentility;
　　No company, no nobility;
No warmth, no cheerfulness, no healthful
　　ease,
　　No comfortable feel in any member,
No shade, no shine, no butterflies, no bees,
　　No fruits, no flowers, no leaves, no
　　　　birds—November!

FLYNN OF VIRGINIA

Bret Harte, the American poet, passed some of his early years among the Californian miners, and put their heroism and humour into verse that will remain a lasting memory of days and scenes that belong now to the past. In these verses he gives a miner's account of a deed of heroic self-sacrifice which the narrator cannot recall without tears.

DIDN'T know Flynn—
    Flynn of Virginia—
     Long as he's been 'yar?
    Look 'ee here, stranger,
Whar hev you been?

Here in this tunnel
He was my pardner,
That same Tom Flynn—
    Working together,
     In wind and weather,
Day out and in.

Didn't know Flynn!
    Well, that is queer.
Why, it's a sin.
To think of Tom Flynn—
    Tom, with his cheer,
    Tom, without fear—
Stranger, look 'yar!

Thar in the drift,
    Back to the wall,
He held the timbers
    Ready to fall;
Then in the darkness
    I heard him call:
" Run for your life, Jake!
Run for your wife's sake!
Don't wait for me."
And that was all
    Heard in the din,
    Heard of Tom Flynn—
Flynn of Virginia.

THE INDUSTRY OF ANIMALS

Thomas Miller (1807 to 1874) was a basket-maker during his early manhood, but he became a writer of stories and of verses, and was finally pensioned by the nation. Here is a rhyme for children showing his sympathy with animals.

THE lute-voice birds rise with the light,
    Their nestling young to feed,
Pursue their insects in their flight,
    Or pluck the feathery seed.

The golden-belted humming-bee
    Goes toiling hour by hour,
Over the moor and distant lea,
    Wherever grows a flower.

With weary journeys up and down
    He home his honey brings
From gardens in the distant town,
    And while he labours sings.

The long-tailed field-mouse to the wood
    Makes journeys many a score,
And in a granary piles his food
    And hoards his wintry store.

Within a hollow of the tree
    The nimble squirrel hides
His meat and nuts right cunningly,
    And for the cold provides.

His home the mole makes underground,
    With runs and chambers crossed,
And galleries circling round and round,
    In which you would be lost.

Although the swallow in her nest
    Displays such art and skill,
She has no tools save her white breast
    And small sharp-pointed bill.

There's not an insect crawls or flies
    But what has work to do,
And the same God their wants supplies
    Who watcheth over you.

No single thing did God create
    But He for it gave food,
And whether it be small or great
    " He saw that it was good."

A WISH

Samuel Rogers, who died in 1855, was a wealthy banker and the friend of many poets and literary men. He wrote a good deal of poetry, but not of a very high order. This is a pretty little poem in praise of the simple country life, and it is interesting to know that its author lived in a splendid mansion all his life. How true it is that we most admire those things which we have not got !

MINE be a cot beside a hill;
    A beehive's hum shall soothe my
      ear;
A willowy brook that turns a mill
    With many a fall shall linger near.

The swallow oft beneath my thatch
    Shall twitter from her clay-built nest;
Oft shall the pilgrim lift the latch
    And share my meal, a welcome guest.

Around my ivied porch shall spring
    Each fragrant flower that drinks the
      dew;
And Lucy, at her wheel, shall sing
    In russet gown and apron blue.

The village church among the trees,
    Where first our marriage vows were
      given,
With merry peals shall swell the breeze
    And point with taper spire to heaven.

The Story of Where Power Comes From, What It Does, & How It Works

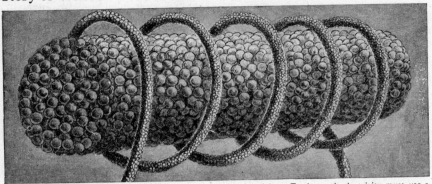

This picture illustrates the link between magnetism and electricity. To do work electricity must use a magnet, and by creating an electric current in a wire coiled round an iron bar the iron becomes a magnet.

THE MARVELS OF ELECTRICITY

MODERN civilisation may be said to be built on lodestone and amber—on a mineral ore found in the depths of the Earth, and on the gum that once oozed from a tree.

When Aladdin rubbed his magic lamp, he conjured up an imp. When Thales rubbed a piece of amber he conjured up much more than an imp—he conjured up a giant whose head is in the stars; and the little revolving figure cut out of lodestone that led the Chinese caravans across the trackless wastes of Tartary was to lead man across the deserts of barbarism to the sounding and shining cities of civilisation.

The lodestone and the amber were only the first hints of the giant forces lying ready for man to use, and the story of their growth and evolution from Thales to Clerk Maxwell, from Gilbert to Oersted and Faraday, from Franklin to Kelvin, Marconi and Hertz—from the sulphur ball of von Guericke to the electric furnaces and blazing electric lights of today, is one of the most amazing chapters of science.

The most astonishing thing, perhaps, is that a few seemingly small discoveries had such momentous consequences. The kick of a dead frog hanging from a nail seemed a small thing; but it led directly to the invention of the modern battery with the kick of ten thousand horses. When Hans Christian Oersted noticed that the magnetic needle moved if brought near the electric current, that also seemed quite a trivial matter; but it led to the invention of the dynamo—the mighty engine of force that lights all our cities.

We have seen that electricity is the expression of the power in all things, and that it is one of the ways in which the wonderful substance called ether is made manifest.

This ether fills all space; it is the mysterious medium which enables us to *convey* the effects of electricity. The light of an electric lamp is carried from the incandescent bulb to the surrounding space by vibrations set up in the ether. The heat of the electric iron or cooker is conveyed by means of ether waves of longer wave-length. The radiations which are sent out from the wireless aerial are conveyed by the ether—by a wave-motion set up in it of yet other wave-lengths.

Electricity can change its form and become light, heat, and power; it is the very essence of matter, and the metal of the dynamo or the electric motor is itself composed of countless myriads of particles of positive and negative electricity. Enormous power can be released by separating some of these particles, as we shall see later when atomic energy is explained. But before electricity could be of service to mankind men had to learn how to accumu-

ELECTRICITY · WIRELESS · OIL · GAS · MOTORS · ENGINES · SHIPS

late and store it, and the first step in this way was taken, as we have seen, by Professor Musschenbroek of Leyden in his invention of the Leyden jar. The principle of the Leyden jar is applied in all the static machines with revolving plates which we see in so many electrical laboratories. The second step, even greater, was made by Volta, who made the first electric battery out of discs of tin and silver, or copper. By this contrivance he was able to generate and accumulate a considerable current. Stronger batteries of the same type were afterwards invented by Bunsen, Leclanché, Daniell, and others, and it is batteries of this kind that we use for pocket electric lamps and electric bells.

A DYNAMO THAT CAN GENERATE THREE MILLION VOLTS

These were considerable steps, but not till Oersted's discovery of the relationship between magnetism and electricity was the power of electricity fully available to man. When once it was proved that electricity could produce magnetism and that magnetism could produce electricity, then, by a very simple device, we could change any form of mechanical power into electricity. The device by which this result is brought about is the dynamo.

We have seen that the first dynamo was a very simple machine, and that the electrical power it could generate was comparatively small. A great advance was made when electric magnets instead of ordinary steel magnets were used. Some of our modern dynamos generate currents of more than a hundred thousand volts. The current leaving the Canadian Power Station at Niagara Falls has a pressure of 220 thousand volts; and a transformer capable of generating three million volts has been built.

HOW NIAGARA LIGHTS UP THE STREETS OF A CITY

By means of dynamos tens of millions of horse-power are now generated from coal and water power, and there are still hundreds of millions of horse-power waiting to be utilised if we need them.

Significant of the change which has come about in the distribution of electric power is the huge network of overhead lines supported by the massive pylons scattered throughout the length and breadth of the country. In the dynamo, mechanical power is changed into electricity, but the electricity can be easily transformed into power again by the electric motor. The wires stretched between the pylons convey electricity at a tension of 133,000 volts, a voltage far too high to be used in any lamp or motor. But by using *transformers* wherever power is wanted, this high-tension current can be " broken down " to anything we want, 1000 volts for an electric locomotive, 440 volts for the factory motor, or 240 volts for the electric lamps, fires, fans, cookers, and other things used in our homes and offices. We can store the electricity in the accumulators of a ship, and drive and steer that ship by wireless signals sent from ashore a hundred miles away!

We are so used to electricity nowadays that we hardly realise what a large part it plays in everyday life; but if suddenly this convenient source of power were cut off most of our homes and buildings would be in darkness, and most of the machinery of civilisation would cease to work. Our electric lights, electric bells, telephones, telegraphs, wireless, motor-cars, and electric forges would all cease to work.

THE DISCOVERY OF THE HERTZIAN WAVES AND THEIR INFINITE POSSIBILITIES

In every branch of electricity the acutest minds of the world have been at work. Mathematicians, physicists, chemists, engineers, have all joined in experiments and researches. The ingenuity expended in explaining the theory of the new force, and in inventing batteries and dynamos and switches has been remarkable. Yet even now electricity is not full-grown. It is not quite correct to say that it is still in its infancy, for not even an infant Hercules could display such titanic force; but it is still growing, there seems no end to its development and applications. The discovery of the Hertzian waves alone, and of the electrons in the atom, opened up infinite new possibilities, while the photo-electric cell has brought about extraordinary changes in our daily work, and has given us television and the talking picture. No one can guess how big the giant will have become in another generation.

We now come to some of the marvellous applications of electricity with which we are all familiar—to the telegraph, and the telephone, and all the wonder of the wireless world, but first we will recall, in a series of pictures, what it is that we have learned already.

PICTURE-DIAGRAMS OF ELECTRICITY

We give in these pages a series of picture-diagrams simplifying the main principles of electricity and its applications, and illustrating the methods by which it is harnessed to the purposes of man.

The surfaces of some substances, such as vulcanite, become charged with electricity when rubbed on wool or silk and so acquire the power of attracting other substances. Here some children are shown attracting bits of paper with fountain pens which have been rubbed on their sleeves, and so have become electrified.

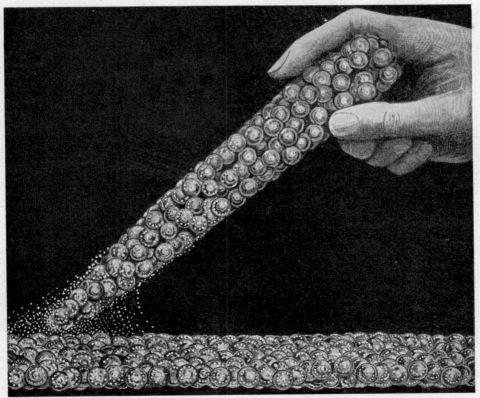

What really happens when we rub vulcanite on wool or silk is that the electrons—the tiny particles of the substances—transfer themselves from one substance to the other. The electricity obtained on the vulcanite enables it to attract light objects. Here our artist suggests the agitated electrons of an electrified stick of vulcanite.

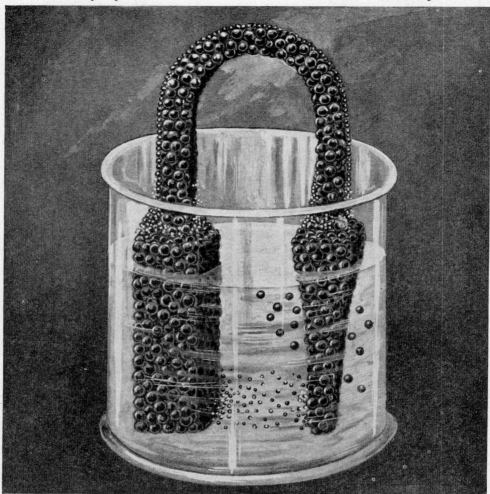

This picture shows the structure of a simple voltaic cell, which consists of two solids, copper and zinc, placed apart in an acid fluid capable of being broken up by an electric current. When the two solids are connected by a wire outside the liquid, a current flows from the zinc to the copper and then through the wire back to the zinc, making an electric circuit. The current is due to chemical action, the energy given out being furnished by the consumption of the zinc.

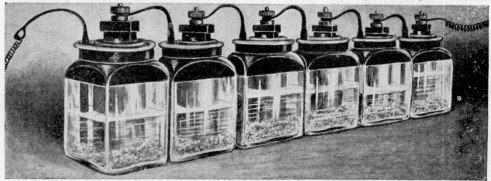

This picture shows six Leclanché cells coupled together by wires to make what is called a battery. By coupling these cells together their electric current can be increased in voltage by the number of the cells employed.

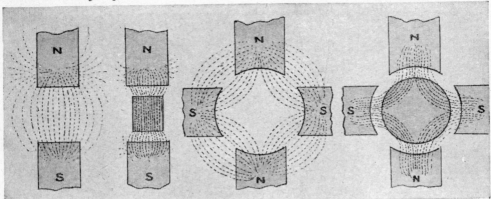

A magnet gives off " lines of force," and these diagrams suggest the lines of force passing from the poles of magnets. The first shows the lines as they pass with air between opposite poles ; the next with air and a piece of soft iron between them ; and the third as they pass when four magnets are used. A wheel going round in the centre of these four poles, as seen in the last diagram, picks up electricity by cutting through the lines of force, and this is the principle of the dynamo.

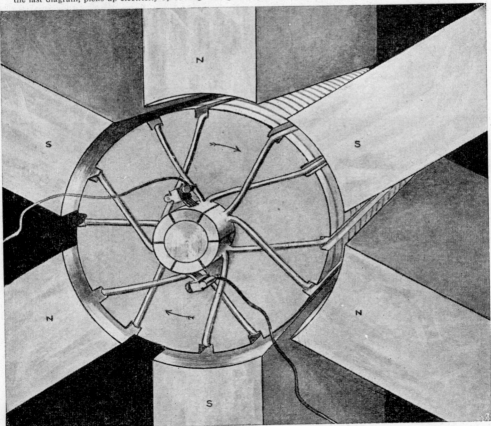

This diagram helps us to understand what happens in a dynamo as seen in the next picture. When a coil of wire is set revolving so as to cut through the lines of force passing from the magnets the coil picks up the magnetic force and generates an electric current. A dynamo consists of rings of copper wire wound on an iron core, which revolves between the fixed poles of magnets and so cuts through the lines of force. The core with the coils of wire drawn tightly over it is known as the armature of the dynamo, and here our artist suggests an armature between six magnetic poles. The ends of the coils of wire are brought to a number of metal strips arranged round a smaller drum called the commutator. Carbon brushes fixed to the dynamo press against this and pick up the current, which is carried off to the mains.

This picture shows a simple type of dynamo. To the right is seen the armature, between large and powerful magnets. Such an armature has an enormous number of coils, and as they fly through the invisible lines of magnetic force an electric current is created in them. The armature is driven round rapidly by the engine on the left.

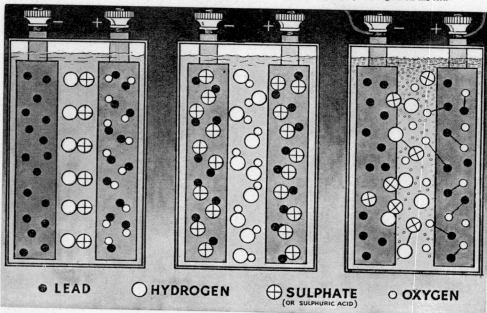

● LEAD   ○ HYDROGEN   ⊕ SULPHATE (OR SULPHURIC ACID)   ○ OXYGEN

These pictures show what happens in an accumulator. In each cell are seen two lead plates, one of them coated with lead oxide. If the accumulator is used as a battery, to light a lamp for example, the plates become coated with lead sulphate and the battery is exhausted. But if the current from the dynamo flows into the cell, the negative plate will be restored by chemical action to lead and the positive plate to lead oxide, sulphuric acid being set free. This process is called "charging." When the charge is complete, the accumulator is ready for use again as a battery. Lead accumulators are now being replaced to an increasing extent by cells containing plates of nickel and iron standing in a solution of caustic soda. They are much lighter and have many advantages.

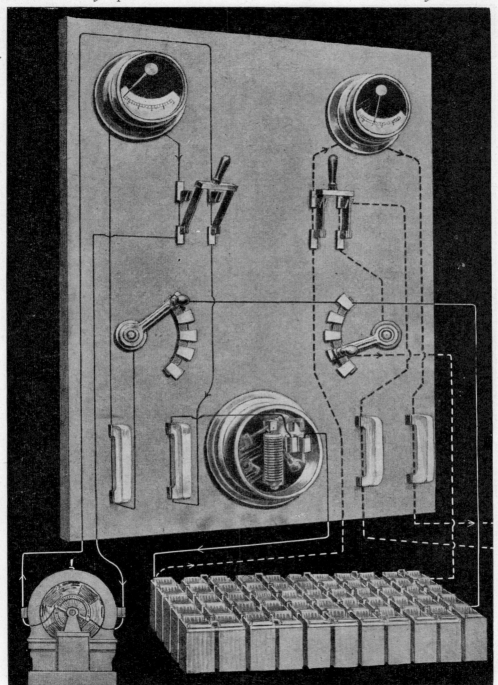

This picture-diagram shows the switchboard of a house which makes and stores its own electricity. The unbroken lines represent the circuit from the dynamo to the accumulator, and the dotted lines the circuit from the accumulator to the house. Beneath the two ampère-meters at the top of the board are the switches and variable resistances. At the bottom are four fuses and the cut-out, an automatic switch that will not complete the circuit unless the dynamo is revolving at or above a certain speed. This prevents voltage in the accumulator overcoming the weak current from a slowly moving dynamo.

THE MARVELS OF THE ELECTRIC HOUSE

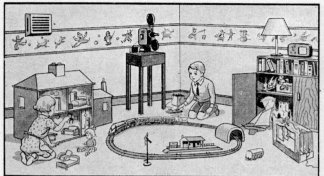

Here we see some of the many ways in which electricity may be used in the home. Apart from the various types of lighting, the playroom has a heater and air circulator, radio, and electric toys. In the bathroom are an electric razor and a towel airer, and water is heated by immersion apparatus in the cistern. The living-room has television and a radio-gramophone, the clock over the fire being worked from the mains. The hall, heated by an electric radiator, is being swept with a suction cleaner, and chiming tubes have replaced the front-door bell. In the kitchen are a kettle, refrigerator, cooker, toaster, coffee-pot, clock, ventilating fan, washing machine, drying cupboard, and flatiron—all electrical.

Imperishable Thoughts of Men Enshrined in the Books of the World

Milton meets Andrew Marvell, the poet. By George Boughton, R.A.

THE GREAT EPIC OF MILTON

THE twenty years that separated the early period of John Milton's poetic productiveness, when he was perfecting his mastery of what may be called academic, though delightful verse, and his resumption of his ambition to write an epic that the world " would not willingly let die," were lightened occasionally by sonnets, " alas too few," as Wordsworth lamented, and they were glorified by outbursts of the most gorgeous prose in the English tongue.

Milton himself felt that during this strenuous period, made noisy by argumentative conflict, he was neglecting his great gift of poetry, as can be seen in the touching sonnet on his blindness, which is partly an admission merging into an excuse for himself.

When I consider how my light is spent
Ere half my days, in this dark world and wide,
And that one talent, which is death to hide,
Lodged with me useless, though my soul more
  bent
To serve therewith my Maker, and present
My true account, lest He returning chide;
" Doth God exact day labour, light denied?"
I fondly ask. But patience, to prevent
That murmur, soon replied, " God doth not
  need
Either man's work or his own gifts. Who best
Bear His mild yoke they serve Him best. His
  state

Is kingly; thousands at his bidding speed
And post o'er land and ocean without rest;
They also serve who only stand and wait."

The argument addressed by Milton to the English Parliament in favour of unlicensed printing is much more than a magnificent example of the eloquence of English prose as it may be used by a great master of the tongue; it is the finest plea for freedom of speech and pen to be found in any literature, for the argument is based on the profound truth that right, if it is given an open chance of meeting wrong, is bound, in the end, to prevail.

The Areopagitica, so named from Areopagus in Athens, the open-air court where public questions were finally decided, includes a fine passage on books:

For books are not absolutely dead things, but do contain a potency of life in them to be as active as that soul was whose progeny they are. Nay, they do preserve as in a vial the purest efficacy and extraction of that living intellect that bred them.

Later in his petition the poet appeals to the English Parliament with a passionate patriotism that many feel who dare not express it openly; and then he passes on to the full height of his great argument in which lofty faith unites with the deepest wisdom:

Lords and Commons of England, consider what nation it is whereof ye are, and whereof ye are

ROMANCE · HISTORIES · DRAMAS · ESSAYS · WORLD CLASSICS

the governors—a nation not slow and dull, but of a quick, ingenious, and piercing spirit, acute to invent, subtle and sinewy to discourse, not beneath the reach of any point the highest that human capacity can soar to.

Is it nothing that the grave and frugal Transylvanian sends out yearly from as far as the mountainous borders of Russia, and beyond the Hercynian wilderness, not their youth, but their staid men, to learn our language and our theologic arts?

By all concurrence of signs, and by the general instinct of holy and devout men, God is decreeing to begin some new and great period in His Church, even to the reforming of Reformation itself. What does He, then, but reveal Himself to His servants, and as His manner is, first to His Englishmen?

Methinks I see in my mind, a noble and puissant nation rousing herself like a strong man after sleep, and shaking her invincible locks.

MILTON'S GREAT PICTURE OF THE MIGHTY YOUTH OF ENGLAND

Methinks I see her as an eagle mewing her mighty youth, and kindling her undazzled eyes at the full midday beam; purging and unscaling her long-abused sight at the fountain itself of heavenly radiance; while the whole noise of timorous and flocking birds, with those also that love the twilight, flutter about, amazed at what she means, and in their envious gabble would prognosticate a year of sects and schisms.

What should ye do, then? Should ye suppress all this flowery crop of knowledge and new light? Should ye set an oligarchy of twenty engrossers over it, to bring a famine upon our minds again, when we shall know nothing but what is measured to us by their bushel?

Believe it, Lords and Commons, they who counsel ye to such a suppressing do as good as bid ye suppress yourselves. If it be desired to know the immediate cause of all this free writing and free speaking, there cannot be assigned a truer than your own mild, and free, and humane government. It is the liberty, Lords and Commons, which your own valorous and happy counsels have purchased us, liberty, which is the nurse of all great wits.

Give me the liberty to know, to utter, and to argue freely according to conscience above all liberties. And though all the winds of doctrine were let loose to play upon the Earth, so Truth be in the field, we do injuriously by licensing and prohibiting to misdoubt her strength. Let her and Falsehood grapple.

Whoever knew Truth put to the worse in a free and open encounter? For who knows not that Truth is strong, next to the Almighty? She needs no policies, nor stratagems, nor licensing to make her victorious. Those are the shifts and defences that error uses against her power. Give her but room, and do not bind her when she sleeps.

THE POWER, PATHOS, AND BEAUTY MINGLED IN PARADISE LOST

It was not till he was over 50 that the poet reverted to the scheme of his youth and began to write, with the aid of friends who held the pen for him, the great Epic he had so long designed to "justify the ways of God to men."

Paradise Lost is a sheer effort of the imagination. It was literally created out of the mind of Milton. The materials in the Bible for a picture of the Fall of Man are but scanty, and little more could be gathered from ancient legendary story. Yet from this slender outline Milton built up, in twelve books or chapters, a poem of 10,565 lines. Most of the narrative is directly given by the poet, but in the middle part of the epic there is much recital of things past, and some foretelling of things to come, by angel visitants who supply Adam with knowledge and advice.

This has the appearance of padding out the story, and sometimes of argument rather than history or revelation; but in spite of these blemishes the effect of the whole poem is stupendous; and if the interest sometimes flags it is swiftly renewed, and rises again and again into crises of great intensity, in which power, pathos, and sheer beauty are mingled with a masterly intuition.

THE BLANK VERSE CONSTRUCTED WITH INFINITE VARIETY AND CHARM

The form of the poetic structure is blank verse, and it is managed with infinite variety and charm, dignity and grace being equally at the poet's command. Milton's wealth of classical learning brings many allusions into the poem from ancient literature and mythology, but Milton has such a sensitive ear for sounds that, even where he gives a list of names only, he can make them seem splendid in tone and touched with romance in the hearing of people who do not know enough to enjoy the full poetic flavour of his references. Whether judged by its plan, or style, or thought, Paradise Lost is one of mankind's supreme poems.

ITHURIEL AND ZEPHON SEARCHING THE GARDEN OF EDEN—A SCENE FROM PARADISE LOST

In his opening chapter the poet, after outlining his aim in writing the poem, pictures the overthrow in Heaven of the rebel angels, " who durst defy the Omnipotent to arms "; their rally in the nether world under Satan, and their determination to continue their rebellion. The portrait of " their dread commander," Satan, stands out as a triumph in description.

He, above the rest
In shape and gesture proudly eminent,
Stood like a tower.   His form had not yet lost
All its original brightness, nor appeared
Less than an archangel ruined, and the excess
Of glory obscured; as when the sun new risen
Looks through the horizontal misty air
Shorn of his beams, or, from behind the moon,
In dim eclipse, disastrous twilight steals
On half the nations, and with fear of change
Perplexes monarchs.   Darkened so, yet shone

Above them all the archangel.   But his face
Deep scars of thunder had intrenched, and care
Sat on his faded cheek, but under brows
Of dauntless courage and considerate pride,
Waiting revenge.

The effect of his oratory in rousing again his dispirited followers is mirrored in these magnificent lines:

He spake; and to confirm his words outflew
Millions of flaming swords, drawn from the thighs
Of mighty Cherubim.   The sudden blaze
Far round illumined Hell.   Highly they raged
Against the Highest, and fierce with grasped arms
Clashed on their sounding shields the din of war,
Hurling defiance toward the vault of Heaven.

The second chapter tells of their plot to destroy the human race, now, as they had heard, about to be created; and how Satan was sent out across the " dark, illimitable ocean " of space to pry on the newly-made Earth.

The third chapter, telling of Satan's journey, begins with an invocation to Light, and makes this pathetic reference to the poet's blindness:

Hail, holy Light, offspring of Heaven first born!

Bright effluence of bright essence uncreate!
Whose fountain who shall tell? Before the Sun,
Before the Heavens, thou wert, and at the voice
Of God, as with a mantle, didst invest
The rising World of waters dark and deep,
Won from the void and formless Infinite!

With the year
Seasons return; but not to me returns
Day, or the sweet approach of even or morn,
Or sight of vernal bloom, or summer's rose,
Or flocks, or herds, or human face divine;
But cloud instead, and ever-during dark
Surrounds me, from the cheerful ways of men
Cut off.

The fourth chapter describes Satan's arrival in Paradise, where he finds Adam and Eve, and at the sight of the gentle pair almost repents him of his terrible purpose. Here is Milton's description of Evening, most exquisite of pictures:

Now came still Evening on, and Twilight gray
Had in her sober livery all things clad;
Silence accompanied; for beast and bird,
They to their grassy couch, these to their nests
Were slunk, all but the wakeful nightingale.
She all night long her amorous descant sung.
Silence was pleased. Now glowed the firmament
With living sapphires; Hesperus, that led
The starry host, rode brightest, till the Moon,
Rising in clouded majesty, at length
Apparent queen, unveiled her peerless light,
And o'er the dark her silver mantle threw.

The temptation and fall of Eve and the decision of Adam to share her fate are traced in the remaining chapters with infinite tenderness, and the punishment, stern but not hopeless, is traced to the point where they are expelled from Paradise:

In either hand the hastening angel caught
Our lingering parents, and to the Eastern gate
Led them direct, and down the cliff as fast
To the subjected plain—then disappeared.
They, looking back, all the eastern side beheld
Of Paradise, so late their happy seat,
Waved over by that flaming brand, the gate
With dreadful faces thronged and fiery arms.
Some natural tears they dropped, but wiped
     them soon;

The world was all before them, where to choose
Their place of rest, and Providence their guide.
They, hand in hand, with wandering steps and
     slow,
Through Eden took their solitary way.

After writing his masterpiece, Milton, as a sequel, added Paradise Regained, portraying the final defeat of Satan through Our Lord's resistance of his temptations in the wilderness. His final work, in dramatic form, Samson Agonistes, published three years before his death in 1674, was not unlike a picture of Milton himself. He, too, was blind, and surrounded by triumphant enemies, but unconquerable.

The spirit in which Samson closes his life is that in which Milton waited for the end, and its expression reaches the bounds of beauty in the last speech of the play by Manoah, Samson's father.

Nothing is here for tears, nothing to wail
Or knock the breast, no weakness, no contempt,
Dispraise, or blame, nothing but well and fair,
And what may quiet us in a death so noble.

The finest and truest tribute ever paid to this great poet and sterling man was penned 128 years after his death by a fellow poet, William Wordsworth.

Milton! thou should'st be living at this hour;
England hath need of thee; she is a fen
Of stagnant waters; altar, sword, and pen,
Fireside, the heroic wealth of hall and bower
Have forfeited their ancient English dower
Of inward happiness. We are selfish men;
Oh! raise us up, return to us again;
And give us manners, virtue, freedom, power.
Thy soul was like a Star, and dwelt apart;
Thou hadst a voice whose sound was like the sea;
Pure as the naked heavens, majestic, free.
So didst thou travel on life's common way,
In cheerful godliness; and yet thy heart
The lowliest duties on herself did lay.

Some of the religious conceptions of this greatest of English religious poets are not now widely held by Christian people. Great as Milton was as a poet, a thinker, and a man, he belonged to his time, and some of its misconceptions of the Divine coloured his view. Probably, as time goes on, his idea of the ways of God to man will seem more and more strange, but he will remain always a great historical figure, a noble character, and a supreme poet, though he was fettered by a system of thought that is passing away.

The Great Words that Stir the Hearts and Minds of All Mankind

Cuthbert dreaming in the fields. From George Wetherbee's picture, by courtesy of Mr. S. B. Crook

VISION

It must have been early in the age-long story of human life that men invented a word meaning *sight*.

They could see things—the Sun ascending out of night's darkness, the bear coming toward them through the tremendous green tangle of the forest, the gaudy parrot screaming from the tops of the trees, the glittering snake coiled up in the grass, the metallic beetle sunning itself on a white stone.

Sight is not a simple thing, but it is a normal thing, one of those marvellous experiences of the human brain which come so often that we cease to regard them as miracles. Men must always have taken sight for granted, and when they invented a word for it, no doubt it was as simple a business as calling one animal by the name of bear and another by the name of wolf.

But later in this long story of human life another word was necessary to describe the things seen by the brain of men. At night, when there was no Sun to be seen, and when the eyes were closed, forms appeared to the brain of the sleeper, so vivid and so shining with reality that in the morning they were remembered. This was another kind of sight, and men gave it the name of vision.

Still later in the history of mankind came the thought that the eyes do not see all that is to be seen, that even those things which *are* clearly seen, like the Sun, a bear, or a tree, are not perhaps all that they seem to be to the physical eyes of mankind.

Then gradually men came to speak of sight and of vision as of two vastly different things, and presently the mighty truth flashed upon the soul of the most gifted men that there is one sight of the eye and another of the mind, one vision of the body and another of the soul.

Few words in common use are of more striking interest than this word *vision*. Indeed, it is difficult to think of any other word which so suddenly and so satisfactorily proves to us that we are indeed spiritual beings, quite different from the animals which surround us on every side and live entirely by instinct and the physical senses.

You remember the story of the blind beggar, blind from his birth, who saw the loveliness of Earth and sky for the first time when Jesus touched his sightless eyes with clay. It is said that this is one of the greatest of parables. The beggar was cured by means of something common, something he had walked upon all his

DISCOVERY · WILL · HONOUR · HOPE · RIGHTEOUSNESS · REASON

life, something that was there all the time, if only he had had the eyes to see it. So we, looking on the world with dull and unimaginative minds, fail to see in it the glorious revelation of divine power. The vision is there, but we do not see it.

In the same manner we are, all of us, using words without thinking what they mean, and so we miss, in the commonest and simplest of words, many a flash of inspiration which would light up for us the mystery of the universe. We think too much of big words, portentous words invented by the philosopher and the man of science; too little of simple words invented by the poet and the prophet.

Think of this word *vision*. You have eyes in your head and can see the physical world as clearly as the savage saw it; but you see it, with those same eyes, far differently from the way the savage saw it. For you, the Sun does not rise in the east, climb the heavens, and descend laboriously to the west. For you, this solid world of mountain ranges and tremendous oceans is not fixed and immovable. For you, the body of man is not the sudden work of some gigantic sculptor, or the tree a thing which was fashioned by some gigantic gardener. Education has given you another sight.

A PRIMROSE BY THE RIVER'S BRIM
A YELLOW PRIMROSE WAS TO HIM

Further, you know that other people do not see the world as you see it. You recall the story of the old woman who said to the painter Turner that she had never seen a sunrise like the sunrise in one of his pictures, and Turner's answer, " No, ma'am, perhaps not; but don't you wish you could ? " And you remember, too, the dullness of Peter Bell, to whom a primrose was a primrose and nothing more. And you remember, too, Wordsworth's wonderful line about the light that never was on sea or land, and his beautiful phrase about that *inward eye* which is the bliss of solitude; and also you remember how Tennyson strove to see in one little flower from a crannied wall the universal truth of God and man.

But you must go a step farther than even this; you must go as far as the word vision will take you—vision, meaning sight that is independent of eye and brain.

There is a phrase in the Book of Proverbs which journalists are fond of quoting when the political condition of their country appears to be critical with danger. They say, " Where there is no vision the people perish." This is perfectly true, but not many people stop to think what the words really mean. They use them as if they were saying, " Where there is no aspiration, the people perish." Vision, however, is a mightily different thing from aspiration. A traveller suddenly stricken down in the midst of the Arabian desert might aspire after water, but he would perish. A nation might aspire after idleness and luxury, as the degenerate Roman Empire did, but it would perish. A conqueror might aspire after empire, as Napoleon did, and yet perish.

MEN ARE NOT FETTERED AND IMPRISONED BY THEIR BODILY SENSES

No; vision does not mean aspiration. It does not even mean faith. It means a conviction of the soul that what it desires can be realised—a conviction so complete that the invisible future becomes visible to the spirit, so visible that it is as if the desirable is already the real.

A nation that believes so completely in the power of goodness that it has always before its eyes a perfect State, where justice and truth are the supreme powers of the commonwealth, will never perish. But a nation which merely thinks of trying goodness as a possible remedy, not quite certain whether it will really pay, not quite sure whether the remedy may not be worse than the disease, will surely perish.

You will see at once from this reflection that there is in man a transcendent power of vision—a power of seeing into the future. Such a thought drives out of the mind any shabby doubt that we are like the animals, fettered and imprisoned by our bodily senses. Repeat this word *vision* to yourself, with your eyes closed, thinking of men like Shakespeare and Abraham Lincoln, who saw far into humanity's future, and presently it will become to you as the clay with which Jesus opened the eyes of the blind beggar.

INVISIBLE HANDS AND EYES THAT NO MAN HAS SEEN

You will come to realise that *all* our physical appetites and senses have their spiritual counterparts. You will say to yourself, " Now I understand what Jesus meant when He said, *He that hath ears to hear, let him hear.*" You will almost jump with amazement at the sudden knowledge of your spiritual reality. You have ears that no one has ever seen, and they are the ears which hear the most majestic strains in the music of inspired composers, and the deepest meaning in the words of a great teacher. You have eyes that no one has ever seen, and they are the eyes which see the meaning in the look of a human face, the final loveliness of sunset or flower, and the path of your own spiritual progress. You have invisible hands, too, which can reach up to the heavens, a hunger and a thirst which can be satisfied only by right-doing.

THE GULF BETWEEN ANIMALS AND MAN, AND BETWEEN FOLLY AND WISDOM

A little thought, and how impossible it is to think of yourself as an animal. Who can suppose that any beast of the field ever conceived the idea which came to Isaiah of a Being yet to come who " shall not judge after the sight of his eyes, neither reprove after the hearing of his ears "; or saw this solid Earth as Shakespeare saw it, " an insubstantial pageant," the baseless fabric of a vision? Between animals and mankind there is a gulf which is wide as the universe of God. Even between men—the saint and the criminal, the wise man and the fool— there is a gulf so wide that they seem like creatures of two different worlds.

It is very easy to confuse oneself with long words, words which have been invented by philosophers struggling to articulate the most difficult of technical or abstract thoughts. But in those simple words which simple men easily uttered to express the sharpest and most real of their experiences we may often find a direct clue from darkness to light.

THE DIVINE FACULTIES WHICH TRANSCEND OUR PURELY ANIMAL FACULTIES

Language is a key to reality. Often we search it for a miraculous word which will open for us the door which promises us an entrance to knowledge, while all the time a simple word which can unlock that door in a moment is on the tip of our tongues. Be sure of this, that the earliest words of men are those which most quickly draw our attention to the remarkable facts of human experience. It was when the mind of man was fresh, and all experience came to him with keenness of edge, that he made words to express his feelings.

To think about such a word as *vision* is to think at once of our divine faculties, faculties which transcend our purely animal faculties and make us utterly different from all other creatures on the Earth. We really possess those things. We have words to express them. We *are* spirits. We perceive at once that the blind Milton saw farther into the mystery of existence than any man with telescope or microscope, and that the deaf Beethoven heard far more of the music of eternal life than any conductor of an orchestra straining his ears to detect a mistake on the part of his instrumentalists. We realise, without argument, that we have a spiritual existence as well as a physical existence, and that by far the greater part of our existence is spiritual, not physical—invisible, not visible.

But we should not be satisfied with this knowledge. We should say to ourselves, " If my physical senses can be improved by education, it is certain that my spiritual faculties can also be heightened and deepened by taking pains with them; and if my physical body has to be nourished with food, it is certain that my spiritual body should also be fed with that which will strengthen it and give it lordship over the other."

HOW EDUCATION INCREASES A MAN'S POWER TO ENJOY LIFE

Why is it that all men are not convinced that in very truth they are spirits, that even here and now by far the greater part of their lives is invisible and immaterial? How is it that Jesus had to say, " He that hath ears to hear, let him hear "? How is it that now we should have to say, " He that hath eyes to see, let him see "? The world grows old, and men are just as much in the dark now as they were thousands of years ago. How is that?

We see that some people remain stupid and dull all their lives, and that some people grow fat and unwieldy in body while their souls appear to have no existence at all, so like animals do they live, and move, and have their being. But we also see how many people grow bright and happy and more and more intelligent.

So it is with the spiritual faculties. Neglect them, and they atrophy, or sink into restless slumber. But feed them with thoughts which are true, good, and beautiful, and you will find that spiritual life is real and lasting.

THE ISRAELITES MARCH TO VICTORY

GIDEON CHOOSES THREE HUNDRED HEROES

THE SEVEN TRUMPETERS MARCH SEVEN TIMES ROUND JERICHO

The Story of the Most Beautiful Book in the World

Jephthah's daughter comes to meet her father.   By Jessie Macgregor, in the Walker Art Gallery

ISRAEL MARCHES FORWARD

THE story of the Israelites is now the story of Joshua. The name of this mighty captain who led the people into the Promised Land, whose victories gave them the possession of that beautiful country, is of great interest to us, because by his name was called the Saviour of mankind.

Jesus is the Greek form of the word Joshua. Our Saviour's name was Joshua; and looking back on the host of Israel, led from the wilderness by Joshua into the happy land of Palestine, we seem to see a foreshadowing of that mightier event in which we all take part—the march of humanity under the captaincy of that greater Joshua from the wilderness of trial into the Promised Land of our Heavenly Father's love.

Joshua fills the page of history directly Moses is carried to his unknown grave. As soon as the days of mourning for the Lawgiver were over, Joshua made his first great move forward. He crossed the River Jordan, and advanced against Jericho. Jericho was the key of Western Palestine, and without taking it Joshua could not possibly advance into Canaan. Yet the city, set in the midst of palms, was not only very beautiful, but was so walled about as to be almost impregnable. Joshua

was one day looking toward the city, and pondering his plan of attack, when a vision came to him of one with a sword in his hand who declared himself to be the prince of the army of Jehovah. From this heavenly visitor Joshua received instructions for the taking of Jericho:

Ye shall compass the city, all ye men of war, and go round about the city once. Thus shalt thou do six days.

And seven priests shall bear before the Ark seven trumpets of rams' horns : and the seventh day ye shall compass the city seven times, and the priests shall blow with the trumpets.

And it shall come to pass, that when they make a long blast with the rams' horn, and when ye hear the sound of the trumpet, all the people shall shout with a great shout; and the wall of the city shall fall down flat, and the people shall ascend up every man straight before him.

Thus was Israel taught to have faith in the purpose of God. The walls were to fall in a miraculous manner. And Joshua obeyed the vision.

The people of Jericho, who had heard of the warlike Israelites, must have been amazed as they looked down on the plain to see the Ark carried solemnly and silently round their city walls once every day for six days. Not a word came from the lips of the Israelites. But on the seventh day seven times did the Ark make the circuit of the walls, and as the people of Jericho

GREAT FIGURES OF THE OLD TESTAMENT · THE LIFE OF JESUS

looked and wondered the priests blew with their trumpets, and then, for the first time, did Israel speak—speak to the heavens in one victorious shout—and lo! the walls fell with a deafening clangour, and the army of Joshua swept forward and possessed the city.

From that moment the tide of victory rolled forward across the land. The wicked peoples of Canaan, living in idolatry, trembled at Joshua's advance. City after city fell before him. As the locusts had extended across the land of Egypt so the Israelites extended across the land of Canaan.

Nothing could stay their advance. Their very name was a terror in the ears of the Canaanites, and men questioned themselves as to this new God the Hebrews worshipped.

But there was living in Northern Palestine a mighty chief named Jabin, who had all the courage of the North, and had set himself to drive out these troublesome Israelites, who had only conquered the weaker peoples of the South. He gathered a vast army together and came marching down in strength and splendour against the advancing Israelites.

THE VICTORY OF JOSHUA WHICH GAVE ISRAEL NEW HEART

Joshua heard of their coming, and, swift to action, he massed his army, hurried forward like the wind, and, before Jabin suspected his approach, came down upon him and utterly demolished the Northern army. It was this feat of arms which practically decided the whole campaign of conquest. A long and dreary war of several years followed the defeat of Jabin, but from the moment of that defeat the fate of the country was sealed. The miserable and broken-spirited slaves of Pharaoh, who had hungered and starved in the deserts, who had threatened to murder Moses and Aaron, who had more than once abandoned God to worship images, had now become a nation, whose sword was terrible. They had at last a country of their own.

The long march was over. The hunger and thirsting was at an end. The old fear of Pharaoh's chariot wheels pursuing from behind, and the rattle of the Canaanite spears advancing from before, were forgotten. Proudly their young men looked upon a smiling country which was their own, and gladly sang their women the national songs of praise and thanksgiving.

But the old soldier Joshua, the son of Nun, gave himself up to no display of satisfaction. He knew that there still dwelt in this land people who hated the Israelites. True, they had conquered the country, and they occupied it, yet all about them lay people unsubdued, who, peaceful enough now, and fearful of these fighting Israelites, might await their hour and smite.

THE LAST SUMMONING OF THE PEOPLE BY THEIR GREAT CAPTAIN

Therefore, the last act of Joshua, when he found the invincible enemy Death marching upon his own brave heart, was to summon the people of Israel before him and to remind them of their destiny. "Fear the Lord," said the great soldier, "and serve Him in sincerity and in truth." And the people said they would serve the Lord, who had brought them out of Egypt: "God forbid that we should forsake the Lord to serve other gods; for the Lord our God, He it is that brought us out of the land of Egypt, from the house of bondage."

But Joshua was not convinced of this fickle people's sincerity. He raised a stone, and set it under an oak by the sanctuary, and said to the people, "Behold this stone shall be witness unto us; for it hath heard all the words of our Lord which He spake unto us; it shall be therefore a witness unto you, lest ye deny your God."

JOSHUA DIES AND ISRAEL INHABITS THE PROMISED LAND

Full well did the old warrior know the unstable heart of the Israelites, and, fearfully did he look into the mists of the future, lest they should forget God. But he had done his part. He had led this multitude across the Jordan, defeated kings, taken cities, and divided the land among the Israelites. Now it remained to him only to die with the name of God upon his lips.

So Joshua, the great soldier, died, and the people of Israel inhabited the land promised by God to Abraham and his seed for ever.

For a few years after the death of Joshua the people were brave, active, and God-fearing. Those who remembered Joshua kept his faith alive, but as the old men died the younger people thought it troublesome to be always on the watch for enemies, and they gave themselves more and more to the making of wealth. They were very happy, and lived very cheerfully ; their wives sang the old songs, and the children grew up among the vineyards and in the cities with all the comforts and delights of a powerful nation.

They were not actually wicked people, but they were careless, and so it happened that, in course of time, the one nation on the Earth worshipping One Invisible God, and living in cleanliness and righteousness, became like the heathen, even worshipping and bowing down to false images.

went with him, for she was held almost sacred by the now craven and repentant Israelites. So Deborah went with Barak, and Sisera's army was destroyed. Once more peace came to the land, but once again Israel relapsed into idolatry.

Deborah is the most heroic womanly figure in Jewish history. There are gentle figures like Rebecca and Ruth, and sad ones like Hagar, but only Deborah stands forth playing a heroic national part and succeeding in it finely.

In a part of history so far away that its figures are dim she is seen clearly, though in glimpses. Evidently she deeply im-

JEPHTHAH REPENTS HIS RASH VOW WHEN IT IS TOO LATE

But always there remained among the Israelites a sacred few who remembered God and obeyed His commandments.

Such was Deborah, the wife of a man named Lapidoth. She reminds us of our British Boadicea, or of the French Maid of Orleans, for she loved her people. It was this noble woman who roused Israel to remembrance of God when the Canaanites under Sisera came up against them with a vast army. She sent for an Israelite named Barak, and bade him summon an army to destroy Sisera ; but Barak said he would not fight unless Deborah herself

pressed herself on the national mind. She "judged Israel," we are told, and was regarded as a prophetess. She must have had great force of character to cause the Israelites of the North to answer to her call, though the people in other parts of Canaan shirked the combat with the hosts of Sisera.

That she was a poet too is shown by the song in which the victory was celebrated. It is almost the oldest of the Hebrew songs that have come down to us from the dim past. Such songs grew up around heroic figures, and at last were attributed to the chief actors in the scenes the songs described ; but one feels that in Deborah's song the woman herself is at the heart of it, fierce, excited, and inspiring, a woman who has broken some of the bonds of her sex in the East, as at intervals, through the centuries, other women were moved by a deep spiritual feeling.

GIDEON THE DELIVERER SENDS HOME 22,000 COWARDS AND KEEPS 300 HEROES

We wish we knew more of this warlike, poet-heroine Deborah, for the way she taunts the men who shirked the fight, and praised the brave, shows a nature born to rule. Parts of the song are harshly cruel, but it does not follow that Deborah was responsible for them. They are more likely to be additions made during the later centuries.

Then there came against the Israelites certain Arabian tribes known as the Midianites, who made tremendous havoc in the land, destroying cornfields and vineyards, sheep, oxen, and asses, and reducing Israel to poverty and want.

In this awful hour of national peril an Israelite named Gideon arose. He sent to all the tribes of Israel for warriors to fight against the mighty host of Midian, and 32,000 men flocked to him. But Gideon would not have so large an army lest they should say, " By our own arm we got the victory." So Gideon declared that any man who feared should return home, and 22,000 forsook the host of Israel. But even 10,000 was too great a number, and Gideon kept only 300. And when night was come he gave to each of his 300 a horn, a torch, and an earthen pitcher, and led them down from the mountain where they had encamped to the plain in which the host of Midian, seeming as numerous as the sand on the seashore, lay sleeping.

THE HOST OF MIDIAN IS SURPRISED AND FLIES BEFORE THE ISRAELITES

Then, at a signal from Gideon, the Israelites crashed together 300 pitchers, flashed into the air 300 torches, and blew with a loud blast 300 horns.

The host of Midian started from their sleep to hear a frightful shout and to see torches advancing against them on every side. Stricken by panic, they grasped their weapons, and in the confusion smote one against the other, and fled, beaten and discomfited, before the Israelites.

But yet again Israel sank into idolatry, and when Gideon was dead one of his sons, named Abimelech, made himself a king, and brought evil on the land. Then came the Philistines on one side, and the Ammonites on the other, and the news spread through Israel of the most terrible events.

A man named Jephthah, who was an Israelitish outlaw, was this time chosen as deliverer, and he saved Israel. But there is a sad incident in this strange outlaw's victory. Touched by what he felt to be the mercy of God in choosing him, a poor outlaw, to take up the sword of Joshua and Gideon, he vowed before the battle that if victory were his he would sacrifice to Jehovah whatsoever his eyes first beheld coming out of his house to welcome him ; and it came to pass after the battle that, as he returned to his home, his little daughter ran out to greet him.

Jephthah was utterly cast down, and told the child his vow. But, cruel as it was, she persuaded him to keep it, asking him to grant her two months to mourn alone in the mountain. At the end of that time the little maid returned to her father, who sacrificed her according to his vow.

JEPHTHAH CONQUERED AGAIN AND AGAIN AND BROUGHT PEACE TO THE LAND

Poor Jephthah's life was greatly troubled to its end, for some of the Israelites, jealous of his power, rose against him, and there was a long and troublesome war which disturbed all the country. But Jephthah conquered again and again, and after his death there was peace for some years, the judges ruling the land till the coming of the mighty Samson, at the hour when the Philistines were plaguing Israel on every side.

In reading these records of people's thoughts of God in the earlier ages of the world we must always remember that men's knowledge of what is Divine—that is, of the highest good—has always been progressive. Even the best of men did not at first see what was the noblest right, and the most pleasing in the sight of God.

Jephthah thought that faithfulness to his promise was the highest good, and he and his daughter were both ready to make any sacrifice to show their fidelity ; and that fidelity had a fine strain of nobleness in it. But, alas, they did not know that " the heart of the Eternal is most wonderfully kind," and that God has no pleasure in cruelty and human anguish. That conception of God came as a later revelation.

The Interests and Pleasures of Life for All Indoors and Out

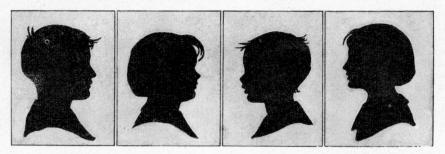

DRAWING AN OUTLINE PORTRAIT

IN the days of long ago, before photography was invented, our grandfathers and grandmothers used to have portraits of themselves taken sideways. They were what were known as silhouette portraits, and they were not taken with a camera, but were cut out of thin black paper.

The word silhouette comes from the name of Monsieur Etienne de Silhouette, a French Minister of Finance in 1759, who was thought to be very mean, and it was given to this kind of portrait because it consists of the mere outline of the head or figure, and is quite mean, or meagre, in detail.

A number of years ago men might often have been seen in the streets of London and other big cities who, for a small sum, would cut out a silhouette portrait of anyone who cared to stand before them for a few minutes.

But in still earlier days, when silhouette portraits were fashionable and popular, they used to be done in a more scientific way. The person whose portrait was to be taken sat sideways before a screen, with a light on a table on the other side of him, and in this way a clear shadow was thrown on the screen, giving a perfect portrait if the light and sitter were arranged properly.

Then the outline would be traced upon the screen, and from this it was, by mechanical means, transferred on a small scale to a sheet of special black paper, cut

MAKING A SILHOUETTE

out, and mounted on card. Many of these old silhouette portraits have come down to us.

The famous one of Edward Gibbon, the historian, was made not only of his face, but of his whole figure, and he considered it the best of all the portraits of himself that had ever been drawn. Another well-known silhouette portrait was of Robert Burns, the Scottish poet.

Now, with a little care, it is not difficult to make silhouette portraits of friends. It is not necessary to have an elaborate screen such as the old silhouette portrait makers used; all that is needed is to fasten a sheet of paper on a flat wall, put the sitter near it, with a good light of some kind on a table, placed in such a way as to throw the natural shadow of the sitter upon the paper. The silhouette must not be distorted, or a caricature rather than a portrait will result.

Then, with a pencil draw carefully round the outline of the shadow, and afterward cut it out. Use paper that is black on one side and white on the other, drawing the outline of the face on the white side and sticking the portrait down with the black side up; or draw the shadow-portrait on white paper, cut it out, and then, using it as a pattern, make a copy in black paper.

The picture on this page shows how a girl should sit to have her portrait taken in silhouette, and at the top of the page are some specimen silhouette pictures.

CRAFTS · GAMES · NEEDLEWORK · PUZZLES · SCIENCE EXPERIMENTS

TYING TWO PEOPLE TOGETHER

A VERY amusing and perplexing trick may be played at an evening party, in which the only apparatus needed is a piece of string, that should be divided into two parts, each about a yard in length. Two of the guests are asked to come forward, and the pieces of string are tied upon their wrists in the manner shown in the picture, so that they are fastened together. What they have to do is to release themselves from one another without untying the string from anyone's wrist.

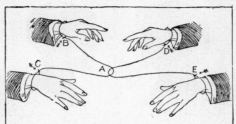

THE PRISONERS TIED TOGETHER

If the two who have been tied together in this way do not know the trick, they will either very soon give it up, or get themselves into a helpless tangle.

The secret is as follows. Take the string at point A, and, making a loop, pass it through the loop on the wrist at B in the direction of the arrow. Then pass it over the hand, and the prisoners will find that they are no longer bound together. Of course, the loop at A can be passed through the loop on the wrist at C and over that hand, and the result will be the same. Or, making the loop in the other string, it can be passed through the loops at D or E. The unravelling of this trick is not confined to the two persons tied together. When they have tried to free themselves and failed, or if they know the trick, the other members of the party may be invited to release them. By reversing the process, of course, prisoners may be joined up again. In trying this trick be careful to put the string at A through the loop of the wrists only in the direction pointed by the arrows, or failure will result.

KEEPING TORTOISES AS PETS

A TORTOISE needs less attention than any other pet that can be chosen. Indeed, during the winter a tortoise needs no attention at all, for it goes away into a corner of the garden, and sleeps under a pile of leaves until the coming of spring. It may be allowed to sleep for the winter in an outhouse, but it is not wise to take it into a warm place as it would be liable to wake up.

The best way to keep a tortoise is simply to put it in the garden and let it look after itself. It may go out of sight for days, or even weeks, but it will generally turn up again. It is supposed that tortoises are very stupid creatures, but they have been known to walk out of a flower-bed at the call of their owner, and although this is about the limit of their intelligence, it proves that they are responsive in some measure to attention.

When a tortoise is taken into the house, no difficulty will be found in persuading it to eat green food, such as lettuce, cabbage, and dandelion, and it may sometimes be tempted to take bread and milk.

TWO WAYS OF SPLICING A STICK

E VERY boy ought to know how to splice a stick or a pole, and as the method to be followed is quite simple, there is no reason why anyone need be unable to do this very useful work. By proper splicing, poles may be lengthened, broken sticks mended, and other pieces of wood extended to any length.

The simplest methods, though the result is not the best and strongest, is to make a straight splice as shown in the top picture. The two ends to be joined are cut to a sharp angle, and made to fit exactly upon one another. Then, in the case of a pole or a beam, the two portions are bolted together, while, if it is

THE TWO SPLICES

a stick or a thin pole, instead of bolting the pieces, glue or screw them to one another.

The best method of splicing, however, and by far the strongest, is that known as the bracing splice, which is rather more difficult.

Instead of there being a straight, slanting cut at the end of each portion, a kind of step is cut in each piece, the two portions being made to fit each other exactly, as shown in the bottom picture. They may be fastened together by having wire bound round, if the pole is a thick one, or by using glue if a stick is spliced. In splicing a new piece of wood to some article where the new wood needs shaping to match the old, the splicing should always be done first, and then the new portion can be worked to the required shape.

The great advantage of the second kind of splicing, especially in the case of a pole, is that a pulling strain on either end does not cause a weakness, the step preventing the two ends from coming apart. Of course, like everything else, splicing needs practice and, for this use an old broom handle.

SAUCES, SOUPS, AND SAVOURY SNACKS

WITH a good gravy or a perfect sauce the dullest meal can be made exciting.

To make thin liquid, such as milk or vegetable or meat stock, which forms the basis of all soups and sauces, four ingredients are needed. The most important of these is patience to stir and cook it slowly, the remaining three ingredients being one part of flour cooked in one part of fat and ten parts of seasoned liquid. These proportions are for making a thick sauce for coating fish, meat, or vegetables. For making a thin gravy or soup, double the amount of liquid should be used. If two parts of flour alone to 10 or 20 parts of liquid are used, the liquid would be thickened, but it would lack the lovely creamy softness which a good sauce should have.

When the flour and fat are cooked together it is called Roux. The usual English method of making this is to cook equal parts of flour and fat together in a saucepan over the fire, but a smoother, better tasting sauce results if roux is made the French way. Then for White Roux, mix the flour and fat together in a shallow fireproof dish, and put it in a low oven for at least half an hour, stirring occasionally with a fork so that it does not brown, but turns only a rich cream colour.

For Brown Roux, for gravy making, cook the flour and fat together in the same way but leave it till it turns brown. This will give the gravy a nice nutlike flavour, but because of long cooking, gravies made with brown roux need four ounces of flour to thicken ten ounces of liquid to a coating consistency. Roux made like this can be bottled and will keep a week or so if the bottle is dry and airtight. When mixing roux with liquid always add the liquid to the roux; if it is done the other way round the sauce will be lumpy. Stir in the liquid very slowly, away from the fire; mix thoroughly and cook in a double saucepan, stirring till the mixture thickens.

The quantity of seasoning needed for a sauce depends on the amount of seasoning already in the liquid used. For instance, with half milk and half liquid from cooked fish, which will have already been seasoned, about half a teaspoonful of salt for each quarter of a pint of milk should be right. A little pepper can be added.

To make gravy in the pan from which roast meat has been taken, as most cooks do, is rather a tricky job for a beginner. So to prepare half a pint of good Brown Gravy in which to hash up some thin slices of cold meat without spoiling the meat by reheating it, put the brown roux into the top of a double saucepan (or a bowl in a saucepan of boiling water will serve instead). Add a teaspoonful of a meat or vegetable extract and a very little gravy browning to half a pint of vegetable water or stock; taste to see if salt or pepper is needed and, if liked, add a drop or two of a savoury sauce. Mix this liquid with the roux as previously described, and bring to the boil.

For a Curry sauce or Mulligatawny soup, add Indian curry powder according to the directions given, and cook with the soup a few strips of sliced onion or chopped chives, and finally stir in a teaspoonful of mint and apple jelly and a teaspoonful of washed sultanas.

Cauliflower Cheese is very simply made by pouring a good thick white sauce over pieces of cooked cauliflower in a shallow dish, and sprinkling the top with grated cheese and breadcrumbs before browning it for a few minutes under a grill. Celery, carrots, beans, leeks, and Jerusalem artichokes can be turned into a complete meal in this way.

VARY THE SEASONINGS FOR SAUCES & SOUPS BY ADDING—

½ teaspoonful of anchovy essence to every ½ pint of sauce for serving with—

or as a savoury toast, or for sandwich spread.

To vegetable soups—

or mixed herbs chopped with—

so that their flavour does not all go into the chopping board. or

One egg hard boiled, shelled, and sliced, for every ½ pint of sauce

Then add a few specks of mustard and some grated cheese and serve with any vegetables

Supper Snacks can be contrived by coating vegetables, spread on hot buttered toast, with a thick white or gravy sauce, and decorating this with chopped parsley or chives, or anything else preferred which will give a contrasting touch of colour.

For Sweet Sauces, cornflour or custard powder, made as directed on the packet, or egg, can be used. To one egg allow half a pint of milk and one ounce of sugar, flavoured with two drops of vanilla essence or a piece of dried orange rind. Mix all these together away from the heat, and then cook as for a white sauce in a double saucepan, stirring all the time. For a Savoury Custard leave out the sugar, add one teaspoonful salt, and use onion-flavoured milk; and to make a thicker custard, two eggs would be needed for the half pint of liquid.

Now, after this rather dull cookery lesson, make the biscuits described on page 1492.

LITTLE PROBLEMS FOR ODD MOMENTS

THESE problems are continued from page 1248, and their answers, together with more questions, will be found on page 1494.

89. How Did the Engine-driver Do It?

The illustration on this page represents a railway line with a short loop line extending from one part of the main line to another part of the main line. In the middle of the loop line is a bridge under which a wagon can be pushed by the engine, but which is too low for the engine itself to pass through. On the left side of the loop line, near the lamp-post marked A, is a wagon marked B, and on the right side of the loop line, near the lamp-post marked C, is a wagon marked

90. How Many Miles per Day?

Hicks walked 117 miles, beginning on Sunday morning and finishing on Monday evening of the following week. He walked each day one mile farther than the previous day's journey.

How many miles did he walk each day?

91. How Many Men Were Lost?

Nine men, lost in the mountains, had food for five days. Next day they met other lost men without food, and it was found that the food divided among the entire company would last for three days only.

How many lost men were without food in the second party?

HOW DID THE DRIVER CHANGE THE WAGONS?

D. The engine-driver is told to take wagon B to the lamp-post C on the right side, and to take wagon D to the lamp-post A on the left side, leaving them at these points, and then to bring his engine back to the main line. The main line extends farther at each end than is seen in the picture.

How did he do his task?

92. How Many Passengers Were There?

A train puts down one-third of its passengers at its first stopping-place and takes up 24 new ones. At its second stopping-place it puts down half the number then in the train and takes 3 others. When the tickets were collected there were 62 passengers.

How many started in the train?

THE ANSWERS TO THE PROBLEMS ON PAGE 1248

79. It is evident that, to ride a mile, B takes 15 seconds longer than A, and C takes 60 seconds longer than A. Therefore C takes 45 seconds longer than B. Again, B can give C 176 yards, or a tenth of the distance—that is, C rides nine-tenths of a mile while B rides ten-tenths. Therefore, B's time and C's time for the whole mile are in the ratio of 9 to 10. Thus, to find the number of seconds B and C take to ride a mile we want two numbers which differ by 45, and which are in the ratio of 9 to 10. Evidently the numbers are 9 times 45 and 10 times 45—that is, 405 and 450 seconds. Therefore, A's time is 60 less than 450, or 390 seconds. Thus, the times are: A, 6½ minutes; B, 6¾ minutes; C, 7½ minutes.

80. Since Jane has five times as many nuts as her sister, and also has 24 more than her sister, 24 must be four times as many as her sister has. So the sister has 6 nuts, and Jane 30.

81. The boatman got 1s. 4d. from the two extra passengers, but as his total profit was only 6d. more by having the two extra passengers, the reduction of 1d. each to the other passengers must have come to 10d. altogether, so that there must have been ten passengers in the original number or 12 in all.

82. The price of one horse equalled the price of two cows, so that nine horses and seven cows would be the same price as 25 cows. If 25 cows fetched £300, each cow was worth £12, and each horse £24.

83. The profit of three pencils sold at 4d. each is the same as the profit of one pencil sold at 4¼d. Therefore, the profit of one at 4¼d. must have been three times the profit of one at 4d., and the difference

between 4d. and 4¼d. must have been equal to the profit of two at 4d. Thus, the profit of one at 4d. must have been ¼d., and the pencils cost 3¾d. each.

84. Mary's father and mother were married twenty years ago. The father is nine years older than his wife, and as he was half as old again as when they were married, nine must then have been half the age of Mary's mother. So that she was eighteen when she married, and as she is now thirty-eight it is clear that the wedding took place just twenty years ago.

85. Sixty per cent. of 12s. 6d. is 7s. 6d., so that for tea that cost the grocer 12s. 6d., he received 12s. 6d. plus 7s. 6d., which equals 20s. The bankrupt paid 12s. 6d. in the pound, so that the dividend was the grocer's cost price. He therefore lost nothing.

86. The difference between 5 per cent. and 20 per cent. is 15 per cent. The difference upon the article purchased was 3s., so we must find of what sum 3s. is 15 per cent. Three shillings is 15 per cent. of 20s., so that the price was 20s., reduced to 16s. during the sale, but only to 19s. after.

87. Three miles an hour is a mile in 20 minutes. Ten miles an hour is a mile in 6 minutes. Thus, it takes 14 minutes longer to walk than it does to cycle each mile. The difference between 15 minutes too late and 27 minutes too soon is 42 minutes, and dividing 42 by 14 we get 3, the station's distance.

88. There were four in the party. The father and mother were brother and sister, one having a son and the other a daughter. The children were cousins, therefore nephew and niece, and the father and mother were thus uncle and aunt.

CAN YOU READ THESE NAMES OF PLANTS?

Look at these fifteen sets of pictures carefully. By putting together the names of the objects in each set the names of fifteen British plants can be read. The correct solutions will be found on page 1494.

GAMES TO PLAY BY THE FIRE

No boy or girl need ever be dull on a dark night or a rainy day. There are hundreds of ways of spending a happy time indoors, and here are some games that are fun to play by the fireside. They not only pass the time pleasantly, but will help us to use our brains and to become quick and alert in thought.

BUZ

PLAYERS take it in turn to count up to 100, but instead of saying seven the word Buz must be used, and repeated at fourteen, twenty-one, and all the multiples of seven. If Bang be used also at every fifth interval, someone will be sure to pay forfeit.

RHYMES

THE player at one end of the row says, "I'm thinking of a word that rhymes with rip," or any word that may be chosen. Then each in turn tries to guess what the word is by asking a question, thus: "Is it something that sails on the sea?" If wrong, the thinker replies: "No; not a ship." Another perhaps asks: "Do we partly speak with it?" "No; not lip." "Can we do it with a rope?" cries a third. "Yes," answers the thinker; "the word is skip." Then the guesser chooses a word, and the game begins again.

RUSSIAN GOSSIP

THIS game will show how easily a story grows. No. 1 whispers to No. 2 a short sentence. No. 2 repeats it to No. 3, adding an adjective or an adverb. No. 3, in telling it to No. 4, adds another word, and when the story reaches the last player he, or she, repeats it aloud. It will be a surprise to find how the story has grown since starting from No. 1.

I LOVE MY LOVE

WHOEVER sits first in the row is A, and says: "I love my love with an A, because he is affable" (or anything beginning with the first letter of the alphabet). "He took me to Aden and gave me some apples. His name is Andrew, and he comes from Aberdeen." Of course, these last descriptions of my love may vary as the player wishes, just as the first can.. The next player uses words beginning with a B, and so on down to the last letter of the alphabet.

SPELLING BEE

THE first player begins with a word, which he does not tell, starting with A, the second player adds a letter, and all the other players do so in turn. The player ending a word drops out or pays forfeit.

Suppose the first player says T, the second R, the third E. Now comes the critical moment; if the fourth player says E, he finished a word—Tree. But if he is clever, he will say A, and then the fifth player may,

perhaps, say T. But he need not do so, as he can say S, leaving the next player to say U. Then the next might say R, and the next E, which would end the word Treasure. If the eighth player is clever, however, he will say I instead of E, so that the tenth player must make Treasuring or Treasuries.

The great point of the game is to keep a word up as long as possible; but, of course, all words must end sooner or later. No proper names are allowed, and it is best not to count words of three letters. The game should be played through from A to Z, the first word beginning with A, the second with B, and so on.

HOW, WHEN, AND WHERE?

ONE of the party must leave the room while the rest select a word to be guessed. The player is then called back, and begins the task of finding the word by asking each of the party the three questions: How do you like it? When do you like it? And where do you like it?

Supposing the word to be a simple name like tea or sugar, the answers will soon reveal it; but the game can be made more difficult by choosing a word with two meanings, such as pen or bank.

SIMON SAYS

SIMON stands up in front of the row and, with a finger or thumb held up, cries: "Simon says, turn up!" All the rest must immediately do as he does. Then he gives the order: "Simon says, turn down!" and each must point downwards. He watches carefully to see that no one disobeys.

If presently he gives an order, omitting the words "Simon says," anyone who obeys it must at once pay a forfeit. It is a trap that a player easily falls into, and great care must be taken not to do as Simon does unless the command begins "Simon says."

HIDE AND SEEK ON THE HEARTHRUG

ONE of the players is counted out to go and hide, but, without leaving the circle, thinks of some good place in which it may be supposed he or she is hiding. Having called Cuckoo! the others begin guessing one spot after another until the right one is hit upon, when the guesser hides in turn. In such a game the hiding-ground may be anywhere in the world, A street in Paris, or The top of Mont Blanc.

Each player takes it in turn to ask questions as to the whereabouts and nature of the hiding-place; but as the one who is answering may only say Yes or No, the seekers may have a long search. It is their business to question the hidden one so that his answers, Yes or No, give some idea of the place. For example, they will naturally ask whether it is far or near, high or low, and so on.

Simple Learning Made Easy for Very Little People

READING—NEW WORDS AND STORIES

THE next words John and Jennifer learned were those in which the letter U sounds like U in PUT. The pictures below give some of those words.

Sometimes their Mother would give them a little story with the words on loose cards; and in the story spaces were left and the twins had to find the missing words and put them in. Here these words are printed in capital letters.

One day little Tom BUSH went out for a walk, and by and by he came to the gate of a field.

Tom got over the gate, and was just going to cross the field when what do you think he saw? The farmer's big, fat BULL.

As Tom went up the hill he saw an old man with a truck FULL of coal, so he helped him to PUSH the truck up the hill.

PUSH, Tom, PUSH! Sad to say, some of the coal fell into the road, but Tom and the old man soon PUT it back again.

Here is a story with some WA words in it.

WALTER and Nelly WARD were two little twins like John and Jennifer, and when they were six years old their Daddy and Mummy gave them each a present. WALTER had a toy WATCH and

PUSS   BUSH   BULL   PULL   WATCH   WAND   WALL

SWAN   SWALLOW

Tom ran and ran till he came to a big BUSH, and he lay down under it out of sight. Under the BUSH what do you think he saw? A mother PUSS and her two little kittens. But the old BULL went on PULLING at the grass and eating it, and did not see Tom.

Tom PULLED the cats out from under the BUSH, and they all went home.

chain, and Nelly had a pretty book about a fairy and her WAND.

They took their WATCH and book, and went out for a WALK. They came to a low WALL by the side of a pond and sat on it.

As they sat they WATCHED the SWANS swimming on the lake, and they saw the SWAL-LOW flying in the WARM, sweet air.

READING · WRITING · ARITHMETIC · MUSIC · DRAWING · FRENCH

I WANT to go home now, said Nelly; so home they went. And that is all I have to tell of Little WALTER and Little Nell.

Sometimes, said Mother, we find words with O in them that sound like U. And she gave them rhymes to show what she meant:

To his mate said a DOVE
It is you that I LOVE.

Of prizes Lazy Sam has NONE
Because no lessons has he DONE.

For some cakes the twins have
COME,
I wonder if Mother will give
them SOME.

Here is a story about some monkeys in the forest:

Monkeys are very funny animals, and they like to do what they see men doing, if they can.

Once upon a time a man was walking in a forest in a very hot land; it was so hot that he lay down to rest. He had a large basket of red caps with him, which he was trying to sell, so he put on one of the caps and lay down to sleep.

When he woke up all the little red caps had gone! The basket was empty.

What shall I do? the poor man said to himself.

He looked every way, but no red cap could he see.

All at once he heard such a chatter, chatter, chatter, and he looked up. There, up in the trees overhead, were lots and lots of monkeys, each with a little red cap on its head.

Oh, dear! said the poor man, how shall I get my caps again?

Then he said to himself: I know what I will do.

He took off his cap and threw it down on the ground. And those funny little monkeys, who like to do what they see men do, took off their red caps and threw them down to the ground too!

The man picked them all up as quickly as he could and walked off; and the next time he lay down to rest he took care to cover up his basket, just in case there were any monkeys about.

NUMBERS—TAKING MEASUREMENTS

Measuring Liquids. Like most children, John and Jennifer liked playing with water. In the garden they had their own little pond which Daddy had made, and in the house they had a shallow bath enamelled blue and green inside, so that water in it looked just like the sea.

They collected large and small bottles and containers of all kinds, and soon found how many times a small bottle had to be filled to pour into a large bottle to fill it, and how many tablespoonfuls of water were needed to fill a small jar and a large jar.

One Christmas they had a present of a lovely set of real measures, a gill, a half-pint, a pint, a quart, and a gallon. What fun they had finding out how many times they had to empty a gill measure to fill a gallon one!

They also found out how much the lemonade bottles held, and how many glasses of lemonade they could make from each bottle in their café.

Measuring Solids. John and Jennifer were very fond of playing with bricks. They had bricks of all shapes and sizes, as well as painted tins, with the lids glued on, for building.

When Mother was shopping one day she bought three little wooden tubs, or bowls, of different sizes.

"Just like the three bears' bowls!" said John and Jennifer.

They had some sand and pretended it was porridge, and found that each bowl needed a different amount to fill it. Twelve spoonfuls for Father Bear's bowl, eight spoonfuls for Mother Bear's bowl, and only six spoonfuls for Baby Bear's bowl. When they had counted the spoonfuls, the twins wrote, 12, 8, and 6 on little pieces of paper and stuck them in the sand in the bowls.

Later Measuring. John and Jennifer were growing so tall that one day Daddy said he would see how tall they were, with his big measure. He found that John was 3 feet 2 inches and Jennifer was 3 feet 3 inches. Mother said she was not a bit surprised, as they were growing out of all their clothes!

She said it would be a good idea to keep a record of how much they grew in a month. So Daddy got a slat of wood 7 feet long, which he marked off in feet and inches, and fixed it up on their bedroom door.

John and Jennifer stood in front of it in turn, and with a slip of paper and a drawing-pin Daddy marked their heights. He measured Mother, and she was 5 feet 6 inches tall; and then John measured Daddy, who was so tall that he had to stand on a chair, and found that Daddy was 6 feet. Jennifer fetched her kitten and they measured him, and he was only 9 inches.

When they had been shopping with Mother the twins knew that she asked for 3 yards or 6 yards of material, and wanted to know why some lengths were called feet and inches, and some yards and inches. Mother explained this to them, and then made them something to help them to remember.

She got a board and on it she nailed some strips of tape-measure and printed some words. Then Mother found them a piece of string one yard long, and put a knot for the half yard; and they measured the chairs and the tables, the mats and the carpets—in fact they went about measuring everything !

WRITING—LETTERS TO GRANNY

ONE day John and Jennifer begged Mother to let them write with ink, and Mother said she would think about it and ask Daddy.

Two or three weeks went by, and nothing more was said, until at last a great day came—it was the twins' birthday. Now, although the twins had to share their birthday, and their party, they did not have to share their presents.

John and Jennifer were six years old, and they had a birthday cake with their names on it, and six candles. Everybody sang " Happy birthday " to them before the cake was cut. Mother and Daddy had lovely birthday presents for them: two beautiful writing desks, with writing paper and envelopes, pens and ink, and even stamps. Inside each desk was a present from Granny—a funny little doll standing on a little black mat, and round her neck hung a little rhyme:

Once I was a wishing bone,
Growing on a hen;
Now I am a little doll
Made to wipe your pen.

John's was dressed as a sailor doll, and Jennifer's as a nurse.

Mother showed them how to hold the pen (a thick one), and how to dip it into the ink very gently, so as not to scratch it on the bottom of the bottle, and spoil it; and how to write very carefully without making blots.

The next day, after the birthday party, Mother showed them how to start to write a proper grown-up letter. The address must be at the top, with the date just below. This is the letter that John wrote:

18 Butlers Lane
N.3
May 17, 1950

My dear Granny,
Thank you very much for the lovely penwiper you sent me on my birthday. I shall use it every day when I finish my writing, and keep my pen-nib clean.
Your loving
John

Jennifer also wrote a letter and enclosed it with John's. Here is her letter:

My dear Granny,
Thank you very much for the pretty penwiper you sent me. I want Mother to make me a nurse's apron and cap, just like the one my dolly has, for my dressing-up box.
Your loving
Jennifer

Very soon after this their Mother told them that she could not teach them any more about writing as it was now just a matter of practice.

However, as there was still a great deal they had to learn about reading and arithmetic she continued to give them lessons at home so that they would have a good start when they went to school.

MUSIC—THE MEANING OF DOTS

THERE is a lovely nursery song which runs :

Lav-en-der's blue dilly, dilly, Lav-en-der's green.

When I am king dilly, dilly, You shall be queen.

Learn to sing that before reading any further. If there are two of you in your house, sing it this way :

YOU : Lavender's blue, dilly, dilly, lavender's green.

BROTHER or SISTER : When I am king, dilly, dilly, you shall be queen.

If we sing it in that way we learn how music is divided into phrases. All the notes in the first four bars belong to one another, just as do the words in a sentence. In the fourth bar we stay awhile on a long note. Then the second phrase starts. Bars 5 and 6 are exactly the same as bars 1 and 2, and the remaining two bars bring us back to the key note. The key, we notice, is G major, and *doh*, therefore, is on the G line.

Phrases in music balance one another as do the lines in poetry. When we repeat part of one phrase the effect is as rhyme in poetry. This is interesting; but there is a really important reason why we should notice the length of musical phrases. At the end of a phrase we may, if singing, take breath. We should not take breath in the middle of a phrase. The composer helps us to see the phrases by putting over the notes phrase marks such as those shown above.

There is one other point about this little melody. Because it goes to a high note at the end of the first phrase it gives some feeling of excitement. The grown-up word for the most exciting moment in a melody—or a poem or a story or a picture—is climax.

The climax of the story of Cinderella is when the palace clock strikes twelve. What, we ask ourselves, is going to happen next ? Anxiously we wait for the rest of the story to unfold. When we arrive at the end of the fourth bar of " Lavender's blue " we find ourselves perched, as it were, on the top of a high hill. How are we coming down ? The composer shows us.

In the fourth bar we have a solitary note. It is an important note, the most important one in the whole song, and is emphasised by being held on. The note is a minim, a two-beat note. But it is a different sort of minim, for it has a dot. It is, we might say, a minim with a suitcase in his hand.

Now this music is in three-beat time: 1 2 3/1 2 3/, with the first beat in each bar sounding rather important. Each bar has three beats. The time signature tells that. Besides, we can count three crotchets in the first bar. And while we are talking about beats in the bar, look at the second bar. There we have one crotchet and four quavers. That gives us three beats, however, for we remember that two quavers take only the time of one crotchet.

How many beats must the minim with the dot (we call it the dotted minim) have ? It must have *three*.

From this we can reckon (we have another dotted minim at the end of the tune) that the dot makes the minim *half as long again*. That is, if we write ♩. we mean the note to last for the same length of time as  (two beats *plus* one = three). If we write the crotchet sounds as a separate note. We can, however, show that the crotchet is not to be sounded by writing ; this curved line (looking rather like a short phrase mark) is called a tie.

Sometimes we write and sometimes ; both mean that we must hold whatever sound is written for three beats. Dots do not only belong to minims. Anyone in the family of notes can have a dot if he needs one. The best thing we can do is to look at some more melodies.

Brahms, one of the great Viennese composers and one who wrote special music for his child friends, starts one of his songs :

Here we see two dotted crotchets, each being a crotchet plus half a crotchet

(a quaver). The other way of writing this pattern is shown underneath. It is not only important to recognise dotted notes on paper, but we must also see what effect they have on the music. Here we see that the holding-on of the note until after the next beat has started gives a beautiful swaying effect. This is what we want in lullaby music, such as this.

And now for a dotted quaver. Look at this :

This is the beginning of one of Dvorak's best-loved tunes. It is a Humoreske, which means a light-hearted piece. Change all the dotted quavers into ordinary quavers and notice how the music is spoiled. It is the dotted notes which here give grace and light.

We must remember that a dot is not only something in " theory "—it is one of the means by which music gains variety.

SING HIGH . . . SING LOW !

ART—FLOWERS DRAWN WITH PEN AND INK

Try to make a picture of flowers, using pen and ink for the drawing.

The picture should be a lovely pattern, and you can draw a frame round it, as if it were one of those gilt frames round a picture in an art gallery. Let us pretend that this vase of flowers is standing on a window ledge with the lace curtains pulled back, like the curtains at a theatre, to show the flowers. The lace curtains will be interesting things to draw with a pen, and so will the flowers, and it does not matter what kind of flowers are in the vase so long as the drawing gives some idea of their loveliness.

Try to imagine what you have noticed and enjoyed when looking at flowers — their variety of shapes and sizes, the fine delicate types of flowers as well as the large solid ones. Recall to mind the different sizes and shapes of leaves and the way in which the flowers show up against the leaves, like the little bells of lily-of-the-valley against the big spear-headed leaves.

The edges of leaves, too, are of many kinds. Some are smoothly curved while others are cut in most interesting shapes, called serrations, which may be sharply pointed or round lobed. Keeping a sense of pattern in mind, let your pen lines express this in your drawing.

Choose a fairly large piece of smooth-surface paper and get your pen and ink. Have your paper on a sloping desk or drawing-board, for you will find it more comfortable to work with a pen on a sloping surface than an upright one.

Then see that your pen nib is in good condition and have a piece of scrap paper at hand on which to try your pen before you actually do your picture. In that way you will discover how much ink your nib will hold without making a blot, and just how much to have in it to make a fine line. It will also show the kind of strokes and lines you can make with a pen.

Have a look at the paintings of flowers shown in Section 18. Two of the pictures were painted from imagination—one of a great vase of white lilies and the other with a vase of spring flowers standing on a mat with a V pattern on the border. They are both first efforts at flower pictures

Both these pictures have a good sense of pattern in the way the flowers are grouped together. The lilies are white and their background is yellow, and the picture has a wonderful feeling of the lightness of flowers as well as flower shapes. If ever you get the chance to see some tapestries woven about the year 1500 you will find that the flowers in them have the same sense of pattern. They have, however, a dark blue background which makes the flowers and leaves stand out in a wonderful way.

Flowers are such lovely things, and artists have always liked to draw them. They were painted on the walls of palaces and temples in Ancient Greece and Egypt. They were carved in stone in the cathedrals and churches of England, as well as worked in English embroidery. We enjoy seeing them in flower shows or in flower-shop windows, and most people like to pick them and arrange flowers in vases indoors. We feel the wonder of them, and want to express something of that wonder in poetry or art. Copying will not do this, for at best it would be secondhand, but if we express what we really feel about flowers we shall

enjoy doing so, and our drawings will be interesting.

Keep a look-out for the many different shapes of flowers. The circular kind like a daisy or a great big sunflower ; the tapering kind like a hyacinth, bluebell, or foxglove ; the cup-shaped like the tulip or buttercup ; the trumpet-shaped, the star-like, and many others.

Now turn to the making of your pen-picture of flowers. Try to visualise it big, and taking up most of the paper except for the frame. Put in the large shapes first, and draw them lightly with your pen. These shapes will include the frame, the curtains, the vase, and the window ledge. Mark where the larger flowers are to go, and the main stalks and leaves, and then draw the smaller flowers, buds, or slender stems. All the time try to feel the graceful curves of stems and petals as well as the way in which the leaves curve from the stalks.

When you have finished your large picture you could do another smaller one, suitable for a page in your book, described in Section 9. Blossom and berries and leaves would make good subjects for similar pictures.

THE OUTDOOR STUDIO

FRENCH—A TEA-PARTY IN PARIS

First line : French. Second line : English word. Third line : As we say it in English.

Nos cousins demeurent à Paris.
Our cousins live at Paris.
Our cousins live in Paris.

Nous allons les visiter avec maman.
We go them to visit with Mamma.
We are going with Mamma to visit them.

Nous désirons les revoir.
We desire them to see again.
We want to see them again.

Le commissionnaire appelle une voiture.
The commissionaire calls a cab.
The commissionaire calls a cab.

Jeannette dit: " Nos cousins, où demeurent-ils? "
Jenny says : " Our cousins, where live they? "
Jenny says: " Where do our cousins live? "

" Près d'ici," répond maman.
" Near here," replies Mamma.
" Close by," replies Mamma.

Nous sommes bientôt arrivés. Nos cousins et notre tante sont très heureux de nous voir.
We are soon arrived. Our cousins and our aunt are very happy us to see.
We are soon there.   Our cousins and our aunt are very pleased to see us.

Nos cousins nous montrent tous leurs joujoux.
Our cousins us show all their toys.
Our cousins show us all their toys.

Ils ont un grand chien.
They have a large dog.
They have a big dog.

Bébé croit que c'est notre chien nommé Prince.
Baby believes that this is our dog named Prince.
Baby thinks it is our dog Prince.

Il crie: " Mon toutou! "
He cries : " My bow-wow! "
He cries: " My bow-wow! "

Jeannette dit: " Comment l'appelez-vous? "
Jenny says : " How him call you? "
Jenny says: " What do you call him? "

Ils disent: " Son nom est Beau."
They say : " His name is Beautiful."
They say: " His name is Beau."

Jeannette tend son mouchoir.
Jenny tenders her handkerchief.
Jenny holds out her handkerchief.

Beau saute en l'air et il renverse la table à thé.
Beau jumps in the air and he upsets the table of tea.
Beau jumps up and upsets the tea-table.

La lait est répandu sur la robe de maman. Maman dit: " Cela n'est rien."
The milk is spilt upon the robe of Mamma. Mamma says : " That (not) is nothing."
The milk is spilt on Mamma's dress.   Mamma says: " It is no matter."

Notre tante crie: " Quel dommage!
Our aunt cries : " What damage!
Our aunt cries: " What a pity!

Je regrette! " Nous tirons la sonnette.
I regret! " We pull the bell.
I am sorry! "   We ring the bell.

La bonne entre pour enlever les tasses cassées. Nous avons joui de notre visite.
The maid enters for to take away the cups broken. We have enjoyed of our visit.
The maid comes in to take away the broken cups.   We have enjoyed our visit.

The Story of the Boundless Universe and All Its Wondrous Worlds

The Dinosaurs that roamed about the world in the Triassic Age

THE WORLD IN THE TRIASSIC AGE

So far we have been dealing with the rocks belonging to the oldest period of life on Earth—the period known as the Primary or Palaeozoic Period. Now, with the Triassic Age, we enter on a newer chapter of life, known as the Secondary or Mesozoic Period.

It is quite impossible, of course, to draw fixed lines in geology and biology, because both the rocks and the creatures and plants found embedded in them are the result of a slow, continuous process of evolution and development. The periods necessarily overlap and each period contains animals and plants common to ages before and after.

But about this time there seems to have been a marked and noticeable change both in the general character of the rocks and the general nature of life. From this point the crust of the Earth appears to have been more steady and stable, and the rocks somewhat different in their structure and disposition. In the Primary Period the crust of the Earth seems to have been subject to violent alterations and contortions, and its rocks are much more broken, twisted, crumpled, and displaced, than in the Secondary Period. In the Primary Age, again, the volcanoes were enormous and numerous, and seem to have been in a state of continual activity, pouring forth floods of lava which covered hundreds of square miles thousands of feet deep, while in the Secondary Period volcanoes were comparatively small and few, and were rarely in violent eruption.

With respect to animal and plant life, too, the Secondary Period seems to have been a new starting point. Old forms quickly vanished and new forms rapidly appeared. The trilobites passed away; the crinoids became more numerous; the giant ferns and horse-tails and mosses dwindled and were replaced by pine-trees and cycads; and the dicotyledons began to dominate the plant world.

The Triassic rocks, which are taken as the rocky boundary line of this new period of the Earth's geological and biological history, are to be found at or near the surface all over the world. Like the Carboniferous rocks they are of two kinds—one kind formed in lagoons and lakes, and another in deep seas.

The lagoon type consists of red sandstone and clays, with bands and layers here and there of salt and limestone. It is found in various parts of England, and also in the west and centre of Europe, and in the eastern states of North America. These rocks were formed of the mud of

ASTRONOMY · GEOLOGY · GEOGRAPHY · CHEMISTRY · PHYSICS · LIFE

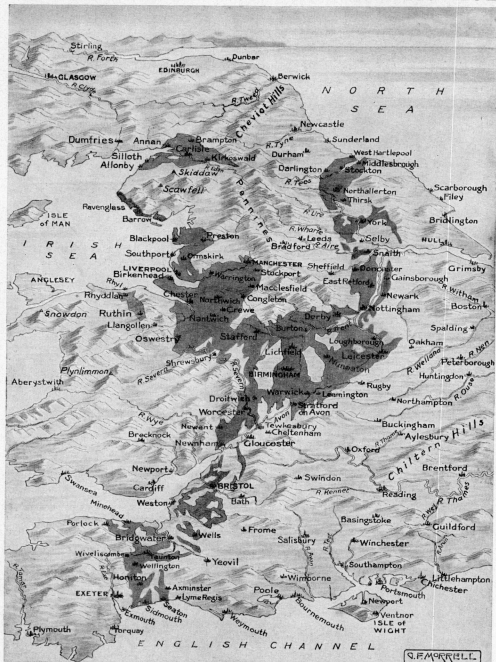

This map shows where the rocky deposits of the Triassic Age are exposed at the surface in England. The Triassic rocks form a broken patch taking in Leicester, Derby, Worcester, Birmingham, Crewe, Manchester, Chester ; and from this big patch three fragmentary arms extend north-east, north-west, and south-west. This Y-shaped system still shows the Y shape of the great salt sea that lay there in Triassic times. The Triassic rocks show the footprints and bones of dinosaurs and labyrinthodonts, and remains of fishes and plants. We find also marks of ripples and raindrops, showing that the sea was shallow in these places.

LIFE AND REMAINS OF THE TRIASSIC AGE

This picture-diagram shows a landscape of the Triassic Age and some of the strange, weird creatures then living. On land we see a reptile, munching a tree. Climbing from the water we see the early crocodile, while the long-nosed ichthyosaurus and the long-necked plesiosaurus are chasing fishes.

In this picture are seen fossil remains of the creatures shown above: the plesiosaurus, pelagosaurus, and ichthyosaurus. In the upper left-hand corner are the skull and footprints of a mastodonsaurus.

slowly-evaporating briny water, and are often marked with sun-cracks, ripples, raindrops, and the footprints of animals such as labyrinthodonts.

The deep sea type consists of great masses of limestone and dolomite sometimes thousands of feet thick, and is much more extensive. It is found in the Mediterranean basin, and stretches thence through the Carpathian Mountains and Southern Russia right into Asia and India. It is also found in Spitsbergen, Japan, North and South America, New Zealand, and South Africa. It contains sea creatures of many kinds.

WHEN THE MENDIP HILLS WERE ISLANDS IN THE SEA

In England and Scotland we have the lagoon type—red sandstone and clay. At the time this rock was formed from the wear and tear of the Palaeozoic rock, a great salt inland sea must have covered a considerable part of England, extending from Lancashire and Yorkshire to Devon. But the south-eastern counties, Cornwall, Wales, and most of Scotland stood above the briny water. In many places the great salt sea must have been studded with islands, and no doubt among those islands appeared the Mendips, the Quantocks, and Charnwood Forest.

This great inland Dead Sea has proved of great importance to modern England, for from its brine was deposited the rock-salt beds of Cheshire and Droitwich. In places the sea must have been very deep, for beds of salt are found 90 or 100 feet thick. Hundreds of thousands of tons of salt are produced every year by English mines, and the supply is believed to be almost inexhaustible.

Scotland, as we have seen, was mostly above water in these days, and very little Triassic sandstone is to be found except on the west coast, and round the Moray Firth.

THE PLAINS OF ENGLAND AS A BROAD LAGOON

The plant life of the Triassic Age does not seem to have been nearly so rank and luxuriant as the plants of the Carboniferous Age when the great coal forests of fern trees and club mosses flourished; but in New Zealand and Australia, and in some other parts of the world, there is coal made from Triassic forests. There were still ferns, cypresses, and other cone-bearing trees, but the most abundant and characteristic

trees of the age were cycads, plants like great ferns in appearance, but with tufty tops, and related not to ferns but to pines.

All the flat plainland of England was under water at Triassic times, but we can picture the shores of the great lagoon fringed with cycads and cypresses, the haunt of dinosaurs and labyrinthodonts.

Animal life in and around the salt lagoon was apparently not very plentiful. Probably the water was too salt to be suitable for most amphibians and fishes, and the general land conditions were not favourable for land animals. Still, bones of reptiles and labyrinthodonts have been found, and also large numbers of footprints. Skeletons of fishes and shells and wing-cases of insects, have also been discovered.

The Triassic rock near Elgin is specially rich in fossils, and there have been found reptiles, lizards and crocodiles, as well as a many-horned animal called the Elginia.

In Somerset the remains of the first mammals have been discovered. This mammal has been mamed Microlestes (the little thief) and it seems to have belonged to no order now known, but to have been allied at once to the marsupials, the monotremes, and the moles.

Though life was so scanty in England it was more abundant in some other parts of the world, but everywhere cycads, reptiles, and labyrinthodonts were typical of the Triassic Age.

THE REPTILES AND THEIR MONSTER FOOTPRINTS IN THE SAND

The reptiles varied greatly in character. Some resembled lizards, some, like the dinosaurs, walked on their hind legs; some, like the nothosaurs, swam in the sea. The dinosaurs were particularly interesting. They were clumsy, heavy, unwieldy creatures, intermediate in their characters between ostriches and true reptiles. Their footprints show impressions sometimes of three, four, or five toes. Some of the footprints are nearly two feet long.

In the open seas of the Triassic Age animal life was much more abundant than in the inland lagoons. Corals forming coral reefs, foraminifera, sponges, crinoids, and creatures like shrimps and prawns, flourished exceedingly. Particularly numerous were the molluscs, and there are more than a thousand species of cephalopods, including ammonites and the first belemnites. Some of the ammonites were as big as cartwheels.

The Story of Immortal Folk Whose Work Will Never Die

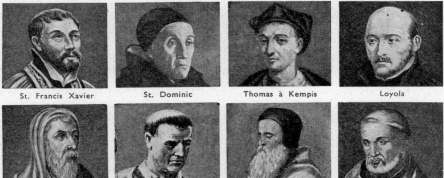

St. Francis Xavier   St. Dominic   Thomas à Kempis   Loyola

St. Athanasius   Roger Bacon   St. Jerome   St. Bernard

FAMOUS MONKS

WE of the English-speaking race have little to do with monasteries and monks. English people, speaking generally, are not of the stuff out of which the monk can be manufactured. It is not their way to shut themselves up from the world, they are more practical than that. The Englishman takes more kindly to making steam-engines, or rabbit-hutches, or a fortune, than to sit still in rapt contemplation.

But the monk is a picturesque figure. He reminds a world too easily vulgar, too easily satisfied with the frolic of Vanity Fair, that life carries an immense responsibility. He is one of the texts of Christ in human form: " What shall it profit a man if he gain the whole world and lose his own soul? " There is more than one way of reading this text, but the monk is at least one rendering of it. He reminds us that, in comparison with eternity, man's life is but a shadow.

There have been bad men in monasteries as well as saints; but chiefly, perhaps, they have been filled with good, quiet, commonplace men, to whom the struggle of life presented either a dull or a terrifying aspect. Still, here and there the records are lighted up by daring, defiant, or revolutionary and heroic figures. One monk, and he was an Englishman, was the first voice lifted up in the interests of science after a silence of fifteen centuries.

Let us begin with the most curious of all monks, hardly meet to be called a monk—the famous Athanasius. A little man, radiant with intelligence, Athanasius was said to be " quick in sympathy, pleasant in conversation, and still more pleasant in temper, effective alike in discourse or in action, assiduous in devotions, helpful to Christians of every class and age, a theologian with the speculative, a comforter of the afflicted, a staff of the aged, a guide of the young." At 30 he was called to be Bishop of Alexandria.

In those days a great controversy tore the Church, and the struggle became at last " the whole world against Athanasius, and Athanasius against it." Again and again he was driven from his bishopric; again and again he returned. Once soldiers rushed in to take him at the altar. He showed no fear. This devoted son of the Church spent the periods of his exile in monasteries, and during those weeks of quiet he wrote some memorable books. He was not a true monk, being as much a statesman as a churchman; but his ideas concerning Christ were devout and sacred, and we owe it to the monasteries in Upper Egypt that some of those ideas

EXPLORERS · INVENTORS · WRITERS · ARTISTS · SCIENTISTS

have come down to us. Born about 296, Athanasius died in 373. The Athanasian Creed is not now believed to be his. The doctrines are those he taught, but the expressions are unlike those he uses, and the best version is in Latin, whereas he wrote in Greek. Moreover, he himself makes no mention of the creed.

BRAVE OLD TELEMACHUS WHO STOPPED THE FIGHTS IN THE COLOSSEUM

A monk whose name deserves to live for ever is that of Telemachus, the Asiatic, of whose brave deed we read among our stories. Leaving the quiet seclusion of his cell, he went to Rome, and in the arena there protested against the bloodthirsty combats of the gladiators. The people were furious and stoned him to death; but from that time—it was in the year A.D. 404—the fearful fights of men and beasts in the Colosseum came to an end.

St. Jerome, another monk, is interesting to us as the Latin translator of the Scriptures. He is also interesting by reason of the picture he presents to us of a man fighting what he considered a dreadful sin —namely, a love of books. Poor Jerome was a scholar and he loved old books, and could only be happy with venerable authors full of tales of long ago. But, brought by sickness to death's door, he reflected on the next world, and came to the conclusion that pagan literature was wicked. Before this time he had been a man who loved to take part in arguments about the Church; now he became a man who wanted to live a Christ-like life.

THE ENGLISH MONK WHO TOOK CHRISTIANITY TO GERMANY

He became a hermit, and lived in the wilderness. But there were books in a monastery there, and soon he was among his temptations again. Called to Rome to help in a dispute, he became a great favourite with ladies, and when he set out to the Holy Land he was followed by a train of admirers. They built three nunneries and a monastery, and Jerome settled down in this monastery at Bethlehem to write the Old Testament in Latin. Jewish Rabbis came to him by night to help him in his work.

But whenever an argument broke out in Rome, off flew Jerome eagerly, for he could not keep himself out of a dispute. He was like the traditional Irishman, always spoiling for a fight. To the end of his life Jerome was a scholar and a dis-

putant. No wilderness and no monastery could ever have held this worthy man without books. He was a good man, and deserved his sainthood. Jerome was born about 342, and died in 420.

It was a monk from England who, in the eighth century, carried Christianity to Germany. His name was Winfrid, and he was born probably at Kirton or Crediton, in Devonshire, the son of a West Saxon chieftain. At seven he was sent to a monastery school in Exeter. The Pope saw him in Rome, commissioned him as a missionary to the Germans, and changed his name to Boniface.

We get a quaint picture of the period in the scene which took place between Boniface and the heathen of Germany to decide between God and Woden. Boniface undertook to chop down their sacred oak. The heathen, thinking he would be struck down by their wrathful god, stood by to watch his destruction. But the oak fell with a crash, and Boniface did not, whereupon the heathen embraced Christianity, and out of the oak Boniface built an oratory to St. Peter.

ST. BERNARD, WHO DENIED HIMSELF PLEASURE AND FOOD AND FRIENDSHIP

But alas for poor Boniface! He was himself to taste the bitterness of a similar defeat. After a life of the most manifold and successful labours he was attacked by a body of pagan plunderers, and, trusting to the relics of saints, he was miserably slain. The old man, frail and delicate, fell before the clubs of savage robbers, and died with the relics clasped in his hand. His life was one of the most useful, hazardous and courageous ever lived by man, and England may be proud of her missionary. Boniface was murdered in 755.

One of the most attractive monks in history is St. Bernard, called the "last of the fathers," so simple was he, so full of faith, so quiet of soul, so touched by the spirit of Jesus. The son of a French knight, he became a Cistercian monk, and set himself to kill all sense of enjoyment, all desire for pleasure in his own soul. He seldom took food till he was on the edge of fainting, and when friends came he would stop his ears with flax in order that he might hear no worldly talk.

He lived the most hard and desolate life, preaching repentance with a rare eloquence. When he was 55, and worn to a thread, he was bidden to bestir Europe for a second crusade. Pale and shrunken, he made a long and exhausting tour of France and Germany, preaching with a success so great that in some districts scarcely one man was left to seven women.

HOW THE GENTLE BERNARD SAVED THE JEWS FROM DEATH

Behind this old man came a young monk stirring people up to massacre the Jews. Bernard turned back, and reproached the monk as " a child of the devil," and sent him to his monastery. " Had not the tender mercy of the Lord sent Priest Bernard, none of us would have survived," said a Jew. That such a tender and beautiful life of fervid piety should have been lived in the twelfth century is a glory of Christianity. He was born in 1091, and died in 1153.

One aspect of St. Bernard brings us in contact with another and far different monk of that period, Peter Abélard. He is not a pretty character. With a brain that used logic as a boy uses a top, he gave himself up to disputing about the most ridiculous things. He passed for a scholar of immense learning. His fame spread. He became a peacock of philosophy, a dandy of theology. He went from town to town airing his knowledge and refuting other teachers. In the height of his fame he fell in love with a girl he was engaged to teach, and he married this Héloïse secretly, lest he should be stopped from advancing in the Church. Then his enemies, stirred up by his pride, came about him. He was persecuted, and had to flee for his life. He was accused of heresy by St. Bernard, who disputed with him. The poor old monk stood up in wordy conflict with this great " scholar."

ABÉLARD AND HÉLOÏSE DIVIDED IN LIFE AND UNITED IN DEATH

We are told that, hearing the eloquence of St. Bernard, Abélard refused to argue, and appealed to Rome. Rome condemned him. He entered a monastery, sick of the world ; his wife went into a nunnery. But his persecutions lasted almost to the day of his death. For Abélard condemned the wicked lives of the monks whose lot he shared, and these men made it hard for him. His reputation as a scholar continued, but he was no longer the swaggering coxcomb seeking to dazzle and attract. He spent his last years in writing rather cold and formal letters of religious instruction to his wife.

When he died, in 1142, his remains were given into the keeping of the faithful Héloïse, and when twenty years later she died, her body was placed in his tomb at the Hermitage at The Paraclete. In 1800 the ashes of both were transferred to Paris, and in 1818 they were buried together in one sepulchre at Père-Lachaise, and there they lie united in death even if separated from each other when alive.

If every person who crosses Blackfriars Bridge in London knew how it came by that name, what a multitude of people would know the extraordinary story of St. Dominic! The name comes to us from one of the best-known figures in the Roman Church—a Spanish priest known as Dominic, who founded an order of friars who wore black robes, and were known, therefore, as the black friars.

He began life with a beautiful and earnest devotion to Christ. As a boy he prayed often; at the university he sold his books to feed the poor, and he offered to go as a slave to Morocco in place of a poor woman's brother who had been captured by the Moors. He was ordained a priest, and soon became known for the rigour of his life and the eloquence of his preaching. But he was sent with his bishop on an embassy to the Danish Court, and on his return stayed for some months in the South of France, where he founded his Order of Preachers, known as the Dominicans.

ST. DOMINIC, THE FRIAR WHO PRACTISED WHAT HE PREACHED

Meeting a magnificent cavalcade from Rome on the same mission, he exclaimed: " How can you expect success with all this secular pomp! These men cannot be touched by words without deeds. Throw aside your splendour and go forth as the disciples of old, barefoot, without purse or scrip, to proclaim the truth."

Dominic practised what he preached, and became a bare-footed, black-robed wandering friar. But, alas! success did not attend his efforts, and he had to say at last: " I have spoken to you with tenderness, with prayers, with tears; but, according to the proverb of my country, where the benediction has no effect the rod may have much. Behold how we rouse up against you princes and prelates, nations and kingdoms, and many shall perish by the sword ! "

Enthusiasts claim for him the distinction, such as it is, of having founded the

SAVONAROLA'S FAMOUS BONFIRE OF VANITIES IN FLORENCE

The power of Savonarola grew until it became greater than that of the rulers of Florence, and galleries were set up in San Marco to hold the crowds that thronged the cathedral. Under his influence the people resolved to burn their vanities, and this picture by F. W. Topham shows the bonfire in the square.

Inquisition; but they are not quite accurate. This tribunal was founded in the twelfth century in Southern France; but nowhere was the Inquisition so terrible in its operation as in its worst years in Spain. Dominic, however, who was the most gentle of men, can be traced in the records of the French Inquisition only in two documents, in each of which he is mentioned as obtaining the release of a condemned heretic. He was born about 1170 and died in 1221.

ROGER BACON, THE ENGLISHMAN WHO WAS SAID TO KNOW EVERYTHING

A great scholar-monk was our English Roger Bacon—" the miracle of the age he lived in." He was said to know everything. He marks for us an interesting place in human history. From the days of Archimedes, about 300 B.C., to the days of Roger Bacon, about A.D. 1200, science made very little progress.

Roger Bacon was the first man to break the long silence. He studied chemistry and astronomy. Under one Pope he was allowed to work unmolested, but soon his knowledge gave offence. He was cast into prison in France, and only came out to drag his weary way to England, where he died—one of the many martyrs of science.

We read elsewhere of this famous Roger Bacon, and elsewhere, also, we read of two monks as famous as he—Thomas Aquinas and Fra Angelico.

Early in the fifteenth century, when Europe was in a state of the greatest confusion—England fighting France, while two Popes, existing at one and the same time, were making a havoc of Church government—there lived in a poverty-stricken monastery in Germany, earning bread for himself and his brother monks by copying books, a kindly, lovable man with soft brown eyes, whose name was Thomas à Kempis.

THE LITTLE MONK WHO WROTE A FAMOUS LITTLE BOOK

That name was then quite unknown outside the monastery walls. Today it is known in practically every language under the Sun. The little monk knew nothing of the political storms in the world. Such things seemed to him unimportant.

He was a deeply religious, profoundly pious man, living a useful and contemplative life. The noise of fighting and the shouts of kings reached his ears like the sounds of children at play. This quiet and simple man, besides copying other people's books, wrote some of his own. One of them, called The Imitation of Christ, which he gave to the world without his name, tells the simple story of the soul in communion with its invisible destiny.

But so sweet, so true, so natural, so golden with the breath of a loving, yearning soul is this little book of the little monk, that it has been translated into many languages.

Little did Thomas à Kempis imagine, while he wrote, that those words of his would become the heart-literature of Europe for centuries. He had been reared in a poor cottage, the son of over-worked peasants, and his name of Thomas Hammerken had been changed at school to "Thomas from Kempen", Kempen being the name of the town where his peasant mother had nursed him. How wonderful is it that this man has sent the name of that humble German town round the whole Earth by just writing down, again and again, that he loved God and desired immortal life ! Thomas à Kempis lived from 1379 to 1471.

SAVONAROLA, THE GREAT FRIAR WHO MADE KINGS TREMBLE

Savonarola, the famous monk of Florence in the second half of the fifteenth century, is one of the picturesque figures of the Middle Ages. In the midst of that gorgeous, wicked, and careless period, we see the shrunken figure and gaunt face of a hooded preacher, whose glowing black eyes, flashing forth judgment and anger, glance like lightning on the crowd from under the shadow of his cowl. Rulers feared him, wicked people maligned him, and the populace was swept like a sea by the tempest of his preaching. He came from his monastery to chastise the world. The world accepted the conflict. Savonarola was raised high in honour, then tried, tortured, hanged, and burned. His ashes were thrown into the river Arno that runs through the lovely city of Florence.

When we look more closely at this great figure we are puzzled by many things. Some people would have us believe that a greater hero never crossed the Earth; others that he was perhaps the grossest impostor who ever lived. Today men read history not to take sides in a fight, but to see the truth of things, and Savonarola appears to us now a strange mixture of nobility and delusion.

He seems to us not a man who sought to deceive, but perhaps himself unconsciously deceived. He believed that evil spirits came and wrestled with him in his cell; that the Holy Spirit settled on his shoulder in the form of a dove, and spoke in his ear. He declared openly that he conversed with God.

All this makes some suggest that the hero-like soul of this good man was afflicted by the distempers of his brain. The preacher who sways a multitude needs a cool head. The severe discipline practised by Savonarola—his brief hours of sleep, his long prayers, his sparing food, his lack of healthy exercise—unfitted him, they say, for politics. He was certainly a very daring man.

THE TRAGIC AND TERRIBLE END OF A MAN OF GREAT COURAGE

But his courage was magnificent. His hatred of vice and luxury was honest. He swayed the people of Florence so that the women came to his great bonfire in the square and threw their vanities into the flames; he persuaded the people to form Florence into a Republic with Jesus Christ as its first President! The wickedness of men and women hurt his noble soul. If ever a man felt the sharp contrast between the simplicity of Jesus and the magnificence and luxury of earthly Courts, it was this fiery prophet of Florence. As he passed to the fire in which he was to be burned—in sight of the cathedral where great crowds had flocked to hear his preaching—a bishop said:

" I separate thee from the Church militant and the Church triumphant."

" Not from the Church triumphant," replied the friar, with quiet confidence. " That is beyond your power."

So Savonarola passed by fire out of the world in which he had been a fiery figure; and we cannot help thinking of him as we read, on another page, the dramatic little poem The Patriot, by Robert Browning.

THE SPANISH SOLDIER WHO FOUNDED THE ORDER OF JESUITS

In 1491 there was born in a Spanish castle a boy destined to become one of the most famous men who ever threw off the world to put on the monk's hood. This was Inigo Lopez de Recalde, known to history as Ignatius de Loyola.

He was a nobleman, and grew up on his father's estate without learning of any kind. He became a page in the Court of Ferdinand, and while following the calling of a soldier he was severely wounded in the right leg. As he lay in his father's castle recovering of this wound, certain books laid hold of his soul.

When he rose from his bed it was to journey to a church, where he hung up his soldier's arms, and vowed himself to live a religious life. He went to Jerusalem, and came back inspired with the idea of founding a new religious society. He put himself to school to learn. While learning he began to influence men. Directly he stated his simple views, however, the hand of Rome came down upon him, and he had to flee. From city to city he went, begging his way, until at last he found freedom in Paris. At the university he drew young men to his side, and at 46 he set out on his preaching mission.

Incredible miracles have been ascribed to Loyola, but the real miracle of Loyola lies in his creation of the Jesuits, a society spread all over the world, and working in many languages to one and the same end. For a man who was not ordained until he was nearly 50, and was fighting at the age of 30, this is a remarkable achievement. Loyola is not responsible for the political power which his society soon gathered; his influence was not political but spiritual.

THE FAMOUS WORDS OF IGNATIUS THAT WON FOR HIM A GREAT DISCIPLE

It is narrated of him that while in Paris he sought to gain the affection of a young student named Xavier, who withstood all the earnest advances of the religious zealot. One day Xavier, having done very well in the class for philosophy, was strutting about in great pride, when Ignatius came to his ear and whispered : " What shall it profit a man if he gain the whole world and lose his own soul ? " Xavier was much struck by the solemn words so aptly spoken, and became the famous Francis Xavier of the Jesuits. Such was the real power of Ignatius—a personal influence on the side of holiness. He died at Rome in 1556, worn out by his labours.

The distinguishing feature of the Jesuit Order that carries on his name is that the members do not retire from the world and shut themselves up in the secluded walls of a monastery. They remain very much in the world, and are active in the homes of men, in the parliaments of nations, and in the councils of Rome.

The Great Stories of the World That Will Be Told for Ever

WILLIAM CLOUDSLEE

THREE outlaws once lived in the forest of Englewood. Their names, which must live as long as the English ballads, were Adam Bell, Clym of the Clough, and William Cloudslee. Their crime was a claim to liberty.

England was oppressed by the wicked Norman forest laws. No one but the King might kill game in the huge woods which stretched across acres of land teeming with deer. These sturdy yeomen had disobeyed the monstrous rule, and their lives were forfeit.

After they had lived in the woods for some time Cloudslee was overcome with a longing to see his wife and children. In spite of the danger and his comrades' entreaties, a day came when he could bear his homesickness no more, and, promising to be back by dawn, he set off for Carlisle.

Cloudslee managed to reach his wife's house unobserved. But while Alice wept for joy and the children climbed over him, laughing, an old woman rose from the chimney corner and crept out. She was a pauper whom Cloudslee had taken under his roof seven years ago. Now she hastened to the Sheriff to betray him.

Suddenly Alice heard a noise outside. The street was filling with armed men. She called to her husband to escape by a back window, but there, too, was a guard.

The little garrison mustered itself in one room. Alice stood at the door with a pole-axe; the children were behind her; William took deadly aim from the window. The soldiers battered on stout doors and shutters in vain.

The Sheriff called on Cloudslee to yield; but Cloudslee's reply to the command was a shower of arrows.

The Sheriff gave orders that the house should be burned.

Cloudslee kissed his wife and children, then he lowered them carefully out of the window with sheets.

" Have you here my treasure," sayde Wyllyam,
  " My wyfe and my chyldren thre:
    For Christé's sake do them no harme,
      But wreke you all on me."

He stayed at his post till the last moment; then he leapt into the crowd and fought till he was overpowered.

He was flung into prison. The gates of Carlisle were locked for fear of rescue. A gallows was set up in the market-place ready for his hanging on the morrow.

A little boy watched the workmen, and asked, " Who is to die? "

The men replied, " A good yeoman, William of Cloudslee."

Everyone detested the forest laws.

The little boy pastured Mistress Cloudslee's swine. He hastened to the city

IMAGINATION · CHIVALRY · LEGENDS · GOLDEN DEEDS · FAIRY TALES

gates; they were locked, but he knew where there was a crevice in the walls. That night he crept through, and brought the news to Adam and Clym in the forest.

They at once determined to rescue their comrade, or die with him. First they prepared a letter with a heavy seal. When they reached Carlisle gates they shouted, " Open to the King's messengers !"

The porter at first refused, but in the end, like the governor of a French town who could not read, he trusted to the seal, and let them in. But they would have to get out again, so they knocked him on the head and took his keys.

Presently two archers mingled with the crowd in the market-place. There was a sullen silence. Here came the cart with Cloudslee lying in it, bound hand and foot. The Justice was there on his horse, the Sheriff was jesting at the gallows' foot. He had promised himself the pleasure of hanging Cloudslee with his own hand. Turning to a youth, he said he should have Cloudslee's clothes for digging his grave.

The Sheriff picked up the noose. Cloudslee's eye ran round the multitude.

Suddenly there was a hiss in the air, and the Sheriff and Justice fell, shot through the heart. The crowd scattered, screaming, in all directions. Adam and Clym seized this moment to reach Cloudslee and cut his bonds. Then the three friends began to fight their way out.

In spite of the Mayor and his soldiery, and because the crowd was for them, they managed to escape. Never were men so glad to enter Englewood as they.

That night Alice joined them in the woods. Peril and hardship were all very well for himself, but Cloudslee could not bear to think of his children living in hiding. He said to his comrades : " Let us go to the King and ask for a pardon."

So after sending Alice and the children to a convent they set out. They gained access to the King, who seemed ready to grant their prayer until he heard what names they bore. Then he cried that it was impossible to forgive such notorious rebels. He ordered his men to hang them without more ado.

" My lord," said the Queen, " when first I came to this house as a bride you promised me any boon I would ask. I have never yet asked for anything."

" That is quite true, madam," answered the King.

" Then I claim the lives of these three yeomen," she said.

The King begged that she would choose anything else :

" Ye myght have askéd towres and townes,
    Parkes and forestes plenté."
" None so pleasant to my pay," she sayde,
" Nor none so lief to me."

He was obliged to keep his oath.

" And Wyllyam bringe me your wyfe,"
    sayde the quene,
" Me longeth her sore to se:
She shall be my chefe gentlewoman
    To governe my nurserye."

The yeomen lived happily thenceforth, and died at peace, and their chronicler ends his song by wishing that we may all take as good aim at Heaven as those three true bowmen of Merry England.

THE LONELY WOMAN OF MOROCCO

SOME time ago there was a poor woman in Morocco who had no children, and she felt very lonely. So she went to the wise man of her tribe and asked him where she could find some merry boys and girls to live with her.

The wise man told her to fill a basket with some dates that were growing on a palm tree in her garden, and then to leave the basket in her kitchen while she went to the church and prayed.

The woman did so, and when she came back she found her house full of young men and maidens and children. So she became very happy with her new family. The young men went out to work and brought her much money, and the maidens kept house for her, and the children laughed and sang to her.

But one morning the children upset a pail of milk, and this made the woman very angry, and she said: " You miserable children of a tree! I wish I had never had anything to do with you."

And she went out in a fury. When she returned all the children of the tree were gone, and the house was lonely.

The woman was now sorry. She went to the palm tree, and saw that all the fruit was growing again; but when she put out her hand to gather the dates once more the dates turned into eyes and stared at her, and she ran away in terror and never went back to the garden again.

THE LAST FIGHT IN THE COLOSSEUM

In the proud days when Rome ruled the world, and the emperor lived in a palace of white marble or in a golden house, the Colosseum was the greatest theatre ever known on the Earth.

There to this day it stands, shattered and broken, but still, perhaps, the most impressive ruin in all the world. In the dark days when Rome was falling from her great place in the world, when Peter and Paul were slain there for their Faith, the little band of Christians hid themselves in great holes in the ground lest they should be tortured and put to death.

To these days we can walk through the catacombs in which the first followers of Jesus hid themselves from Nero, the monster who lived in a golden house inside the city gates.

In those dark and shameful days the great white Colosseum, rising storey after storey from the ground, with enormous galleries inside capable of holding 40,000 people, was a wondrous sight. Here came all Rome to see the great wild beats set loose and tear each other to pieces. Here came the gladiators, strong men trained to fight each other until one of them was killed. Here the Christians were thrown alive to the lions. No place in the world has seen more cruel sights than this.

But slowly Christianity made its way until the very emperor became a Christian. Then these shameful things ceased, and the Colosseum became only a circus.

The Christians had been growing stronger and stronger for four hundred years when there came a terrible day for Rome. Alaric, the leader of the Goths, came thundering outside Rome, which, having only a poor mad boy for its emperor, must have fallen but for a brave general and his men, who put the Goths to flight.

Such rejoicing there was in Rome that day that the people flocked to the Colosseum, cheering the brave general. There was a great hunting of beasts and a wonderful performance, as in the olden time, when suddenly there came out of one of the narrow passages leading into the arena gladiators, with spears and swords. The joy of the people knew no bounds.

Then there happened a strange thing. Into the middle of the arena came an old man, bare-headed and bare-footed, calling upon the people to prevent the shedding of blood. The crowd shrieked at him to stop his preaching and to go away. The gladiators came forward and forced him aside, but still the old man came between them. The gladiators struck him down; a storm of stones fell upon him and the old man perished before the eyes of Rome.

He was a hermit, named Telemachus, one of those holy men who, tired of the wickedness of the world, had gone to live in the hills. Coming to Rome to visit the sacred shrines, he had seen the people flocking to the Colosseum, and, pitying them for their cruelty, had gone out to stop it or to die in the attempt.

He died, but his work was done. All that was best in Rome was stirred by the sight of the hermit slain in the arena, and there was no more slaughter in the great theatre. It was the last fight that was ever held in the Colosseum.

THE SILKIE WIFE OF THE SHETLAND ISLES

The waters around the Shetland Islands are crowded with seals. The islanders call them Silkies, and they tell many strange tales about them.

One night a young fisherman saw two seal-skins lying on the shore. He picked one up, and two beautiful women came swimming toward him crying.

One of them seized the seal-skin on the ground and put it on, and changed into a seal, and disappeared in the ocean. The other remained by the shore and wrung her hands, and begged the fisherman to give her back her skin, so that she could rejoin her companion. In return for this she promised to bring him much treasure.

But the fisherman wanted a wife, and he kept the skin, and spoke so lovingly to the Silkie that she agreed to marry him.

For some years they lived happily in a cottage by the seashore, and the Silkie wife had two charming little children. But one night the fisherman came home tired and hungry after a day's fishing, and as he had caught nothing he was in a bad temper. There was no supper ready.

" This is what comes of marrying a Silkie ! " said the fisherman.

The Silkie wife said no word. She went to the seashore, and took off her clothes and put on her seal-skin; and the fisherman never saw her again.

THE KING OF LEINSTER'S STORY-TELLER

THE King of Leinster had a favourite story-teller, who held a large estate from his Majesty on condition that he told him a new story every night of his life before he went to sleep. But one morning he found himself without a fresh story.

"Well, my dear," said his wife, "order your horses and chariot, and let us take a good long drive, and maybe something will come into your head."

The Story-teller complied, and off they drove for the day in their handsome carriage, drawn by two fine horses, and followed by their three favourite hounds. Toward evening, as they were returning, they saw an old man lying on the ground with a wooden leg beside him.

"Who are you, my good man?" asked the Story-teller.

"Oh, then, 'tis little matter who I am. I'm a poor, old, lame, decrepit, miserable creature, sitting down here to rest awhile."

"Why have you that box and dice in your hand?"

"To be ready for anyone to play a game with me. I have one hundred pieces of gold here in this leather purse."

"Go down and play with him," said the Story-teller's wife, "and perhaps you might have something to tell the King."

Her husband got down, and after a few throws of the dice lost all his money.

"Will you play again?" asked the man.

"Don't talk nonsense; you have all my money."

"Haven't you a chariot and horses?"

"What!" exclaimed the Story-teller. "Do you think for all the gold in Ireland I'd run the risk of seeing my lady obliged to go home on foot?"

"Do play with him, husband," said the lady. "I don't mind walking."

Well, the Story-teller sat down to play again, and lost horses, hounds, and chariot.

"Will you play again?" said the beggar.

"Are you making game of me, man?" said the Story-teller. "What else have I to stake?"

"I'll stake the whole, money and all, against your lady," said the old man.

The Story-teller looked scornfully at the beggar, and was turning away in silence when his wife spoke to him again.

"Do, my dear," said she, "accept his offer. This is the third time, and your luck is sure to turn."

They played again, and when the Story-teller lost his lady walked over and sat down near the ugly old beggar-man.

"Is that the way you are leaving me?" said the Story-teller.

"Sure, I was won, my dear," said the lady. "You would not cheat the poor man, would you?"

"Have you any more to stake?" asked the old man.

"You know very well I have not," replied the Story-teller.

"I'll stake the whole now, your lady and all, against yourself," said the old man.

The Story-teller again agreed, and lost.

"Well," said he, with a desolate look, "you have the whole of us now. And what business have you with me?"

"I'll soon let you know," said the old man, taking out of his pocket a long cord and a wand. "I give you free choice to be turned into a hare, a deer, or a fox."

"My dear," said the wife of the Story-teller, as she looked at her in dismay, "choose to be an honest little hare, and everyone will love you."

He accepted her advice. Then the old man threw a cord around him, struck him with the wand, and turned him into a hare.

Scarcely had he taken a skip or two when his wife called his three hounds and set them after him, clapping her hands, and seeming to enjoy the chase.

At length the hare, panting and weary, ran to his wife's feet, but, to his horror, she unfeelingly kicked him back again toward the dogs. At length the old man struck the hounds, and took the hare into his lap until he had sufficiently recovered his strength. He then placed him on the ground, and, putting the cord around him, struck him again with the wand, on which he immediately reassumed his own form.

"Well," said the old man, "will you tell me how you liked that sport?"

"It might be sport to others," replied the Story-teller, looking at his wife, "but I don't find it very enticing. But who are you that you should enjoy plaguing a poor man in that manner?"

"I am called the Thin Grey Man," replied the stranger, "and if you wish to know anything more of me or my habits come with me on my rambles."

" I'm not my own master to go or stay," replied the Story-teller, with a resigned and melancholy look.

When the stranger heard this he put one hand into the wallet which he carried and drew out of it a middle-aged man, to whom he spoke as follows :

" I command you to take charge of this lady, together with the carriage and horses and all, and have them ready for me whenever I shall require them."

He had scarcely said these words when all vanished from the Story-teller's sight, and he found himself on a sudden transported to the residence of a poet of Leinster, who had been laid up with a broken leg more than eighteen weeks without receiving the least relief, although he had sixteen of the ablest surgeons in Leinster in consultation upon it. Happening to lift up his eyes as he sat before his door, the poet saw the Grey Man and the Story-teller approaching his house.

" Save you, sir," said the Grey Man.

" And you like-wise," replied the poet. " May I ask you what is your profession ?"

" Why," replied the Grey Man, " I am what you may call the makings of a physician from Ulster."

" And what is your name? "

" Call me Cathal, and I will answer to it. I understand you are of a very churlish disposition, and if you changed your conduct I would cure your leg for you."

" I acknowledge my failing," said the poet, " and promise you, if you cure me, that I will conquer it."

While he was speaking the doctors who were in attendance upon him came up, and he told them of the Grey Man's offer.

The doctors looked at the stranger and at the Story-teller, and laughed immoderately.

" Rise up now," said the Grey Man to the poet, " and let me see who can run faster, you or your sixteen physicians."

THE DOCTORS LAUGHED AT THE STRANGER

Up started the poet, and away went the sixteen doctors after their patient; but he left them far behind, and came back in great spirits to his house.

" Now, Sir Poet," said the stranger, " do not be guilty of inhospitality or churlishness from this time forward."

" I promise you I will remember what you say," replied the poet; " and, to make a beginning, come in now and partake of a magnificent banquet which shall be prepared on the instant for you."

Next the Story-teller and his strange master found themselves on a wild heath in Sligo, where they beheld the King of Connaught at the head of a powerful army, with a vast herd of cattle and other spoils which he had driven from Munster.

The Grey Man went up to the King and asked the cause of the expedition.

" You know," replied the King, "that a monarch should always be ready to redress the slightest grievance of his subjects. Now, it happened that a Connaught woman lent a basket to a woman of her acquaintance in Munster, who refused to return it at the proper time. I heard of the injury, and immediately raised an army to avenge it. I am now returning with the spoils, a portion of which I intend to bestow on the poor woman who lost her basket."

"And what will you do with the rest? " inquired the Grey Man.

" I will keep them myself," said the King, " to signalise my victory and enhance the national glory."

" I am afraid it will give you enough to do," replied the Grey Man, " for before you leave this heath you will have more Munster men to meet than there are purple bells growing on it."

" That's what I fear," said the King.

" What will you give me if I help you? " said the Grey Man; " for I have great influence with the Munster men."

"What reward would you require?" asked the King.

"A share of anything you may get while I am with you," replied the Grey Man.

"Agreed!" exclaimed the King.

"Very well," said the Grey Man. "Do you hold on your journey while I coax the Munster men home again."

The King proceeded, and saw nothing of the men of Munster until he reached his own domain, where he arrived before any of his retinue. As he did so he perceived the Grey Man and the Story-teller again by his side. Wearied from the fatigue of the expedition, after welcoming them he entered a cottage, and called for wine. It was brought, and he drank it off without even thinking of the Grey Man.

"I am sorry to see you forget your agreement," said the Grey Man.

"Do you call that trifle a breach of my agreement?" said the King.

"Ah," replied the Grey Man, "it is trifles that show the mind! You went to war for a basket, and you call a cup of wine a trifle!"

The instant he had said this the Grey Man and the Story-teller vanished from the eyes of the King. But what astonished him still more was that not a particle of all the spoils he had driven from Munster remained with his host, nor could anything be found throughout the whole army but an old basket, which the Connaught woman recognised as the one she had lent to the Munster woman.

While all were wondering at these strange events the Story-teller suddenly found himself in company with the Grey Man on the spot where they had first met,

and where his wife and the carriage and horses were awaiting them.

"Now," said the Grey Man, "I will not torment you any longer. There are your carriage and horses, and your dogs, your money, and your lady, and you may take them with you as soon as you please; and I will explain all to you.

"I am Angus of Bruff, for whom you obtained many a favour from the King of Leinster. This morning I discovered by my skill in things hidden that you were in a difficulty, and determined to free you from it. As to your lady, do not blame her for what has passed; I changed the affections of her mind. Go home, therefore; you have a story to tell the King of Leinster."

Saying this, he disappeared; and the lady, bursting into tears, begged her husband's forgiveness, and assured him that she would sooner have died a thousand deaths than have acted in such a manner if some influence had not possessed her.

This explanation proving entirely satisfactory to the Story-teller, they proceeded homeward happily together. Notwithstanding all the speed they could make, it was so late when the Story-teller arrived at the King's palace that his Majesty had already retired to his sleeping chamber. When the Story-teller entered, the King inquired the cause of his delay. Whereupon the Story-teller gave a good account of the adventures of the day.

When it was ended the King laughed heartily, and commanded him never again to go to the trouble of inventing a new story, but to tell him that one every night, for never would he want to listen to any other as long as he lived.

THE BIRD WITH THE GOLDEN WINGS

As Prince Jascha was hunting one day in the Serbian mountains a lovely bird with golden wings fluttered by, and he followed it and came to a high hill covered with white statues. As he was about to ascend a hermit rushed out of a cave, and said:

"Beware! A witch lives on this hill, and she sends out the golden bird to tempt travellers. If she sees you she will change you into a marble statue. But seize her hair before she spies you, and she will be in your power."

Prince Jascha did not follow the bird. Creeping up the hill by another way, he found the witch lying with her back

toward him. He seized her hair, and she shrieked terribly, but he did not let go.

"Well, what do you want, Jascha?" she said at last.

"Give me the golden bird, and bring these statues to life," said the prince.

The witch gave Jascha the bird, and it was so pretty that he kissed it. And as he kissed it it turned into a sweet and beautiful girl. The witch then breathed a blue wind toward the statues, and changed them back into handsome young men. After that Jascha let go of her hair and she disappeared, and all the merry company travelled to Belgrade, where the prince and the bird-girl were married.

Nature's Wonderful Living Family in Earth and Air and Sea

Elks in the snow of North America

THE SWIFT RUNNERS

THE Old Testament men lived near to Nature and were alert observers. From what they saw they exalted the lion as the symbol of power, and the hart as the living expression of speed.

"The young lions roar after their prey, and seek their meat from God," sang Israel's poet king ; and, rejoicing in his own strength and fleetness, he cried, "He maketh my feet like hinds' feet." Isaiah employed the same image of speech in foretelling a time of happiness in which the lame man shall "leap as an hart."

What did these men mean when they spoke of the hart ? It was one of the antelope or deer tribe, and possibly both may have seemed the same to them. Yet we now know that these animals differ from each other on the one hand, and from their allies, the goats and cattle, on the other.

Cattle, sheep, goats, antelopes, and deer all have hoofs, and may be horned. They all have the fourfold stomach of the ruminant. They swallow their food in haste. It is first received into the huge paunch, then is returned to the mouth, a little at a time, is chewed methodically, and transferred to the stomach for leisurely digestion in that and its associated organs.

In that all the cud-chewers agree. Now for differences. The cattle have horns whose cores are composed of honeycombed bone. The antelopes have horns whose cores are practically solid bone. The deer have antlers of true bone, and shed them every year as a tree sheds its leaves, a detail in which they are unique.

Our present group is the ancestral stock from which the more modern cattle and goats arose. Also, from them the great cats, the lion, tiger, leopard, and other animals derive their food.

The carnivores have grown to might and frightfulness nourished by the flesh of these beautiful creatures. The battle is not always to the strong, else there would not be a deer or antelope alive. These animals have specialised in speed to avoid the carnivores, and are unmatched for pace and endurance. But the race is not always to the swift, or the flesh-eaters would long ago have been starved to death.

In this living larder of the lion we witness a marvellous natural balancing of forces. The great cats appear in the world three, four, or five at a birth; the hoofed animals generally one at a time. Yet the peaceful herb-eaters outnumber their enemies by about a thousand to one.

PREHISTORIC LIFE · MAMMALS · BIRDS · REPTILES · FISHES · INSECTS

THE CARIBOU OF THE NORTH

THE NILGAI OF INDIA

THE ELAND OF AFRICA

The giant cats have been a brake on over-multiplication by the deer and antelopes, which would otherwise have overspread the Earth and brought a general famine. There is no animal enemy power enough to thin out the number of lions, tigers, and leopards, so Nature herself interposes and decrees that, though so many are born as to threaten all other animal life, only the few, a sort of standardised number, shall live. Death is thus life's guardian.

To avoid animals as terrible to themselves as lions are to giraffes, lesser creatures have taken to hiding in the earth, in the water, and in the trees. The antelopes and deer have faced life in the open—in the deserts, in the hills, in the forests, and in the marshes.

They have become prime examples of what we call protective resemblance. They have grown to match the colour of sands and rocks, of trees and light-splashed reeds. The hoofs of some are perfect for hill-climbing; those of others ideal for speed over sands; and others, again, are astonishingly lengthened or modified to tread the boggy ways of marshes, of floating masses of vegetation, and of treacherous snow and ice.

From birth to death they live hunted lives. To us such an existence seems appalling. It is not so to them. Agitation and terror are fatal to animal fortunes, and here we have an assembly which has thriven in number of species, in totals of individuals for such species, in size, strength, and beauty.

No; the lives of the hunted are not terrible to these splendid creatures. From birth they have the danger sense highly developed, but with their knowledge that lions are all about them is their consciousness of self-contained protection in the form of sight, scent, hearing, and speed.

Use and instinct are everything. A snail knows that unless he hides himself he may find himself converted into a thrush's breakfast; a rabbit has unchanging views about the sinfulness of stoats; a monkey's nightmare is probably a vision of designing serpents. Yet the world goes well with snails and rabbits and monkeys.

A savage is happy over a lunch of lizard, though surrounding tribes may covet his hut and his head. Civilised men find joy in life in which chimney-pots fall, lightning plays, and highway accidents happen. There is no existence without risk, and a leopard is no worse to a gazelle than a mole to a worm, a toad to a beetle, or a spider to a fly.

The reindeer may meet the wolf-pack; the gnu may find a lion on its back. Both may never see such a foe. If the meeting does occur and is fatal, then the end is swift and merciful ; for Nature demands that if a flesh-eater is to succeed it shall be able to kill or destroy sense and feeling with one paralysing bite. All is strife and battle in the wilds, but the blow is instant and vital, with no lingering agony. The antelopes and deer die at once when attacked, or they escape and celebrate their fortune with jovial appetite whetted by a brilliant gallop.

Speed carries even the lordly eland to safety. King of the antelopes, his height at the shoulders makes a lifeguardsman look short ; for his withers tower six and a half feet above the ground, and a fine bull weighs about 18 hundredweight.

Sight, hearing, speed, horns for defence kept the noble eland safe in Africa until something worse than a lion appeared— a two-handed creature with a gun enabling him to kill at a distance. The very splendour of the animal as a hunter's trophy makes us tremble for its existence. Only rigid laws or its domestication can save the eland. The fact that it succeeds in the milder parts of England is hopeful, but only for the preservation of a few.

The bongo, a forest-keeping antelope, horned in both sexes, is the nearest relative of the eland, and the kudu must once have been a close cousin—a graceful antelope which makes up for deficiency of pace by cunningly plunging into high, rough ground when pursued, there to pick its way with a dexterity impossible to any mounted man.

The peculiar white harness-like markings of their coats give the name of Harnessed Antelopes to the nyala, the situtunga, and the bushbuck. Though their title does not suggest it, they love marshy situations, and the situtunga sinks like a submarine in the water leaving only its muzzle, like a periscope, in the air.

To find a Harnessed Antelope outside Africa we have to cross to India, where the renowned nilgai, prince of all the antelopes on that side of the ocean, is the prize of visiting hunters, but fortunately

THE RED DEER OF ENGLAND

THE WAPITI OF CALIFORNIA

THE WHITE-TAILED GNU

so tameable as often to find its place among Anglo-Indian pets. In the same favoured land is a rarity, the chousingha, or four-horned antelope, sufficiently described by its title.

The addax calls us to the African deserts, and there we find an amazing array of life. Except in rocky, sterile ways the desert has its season of vast gardens, which a later sun burns down like the grass of an English lawn in a heat-wave. There are springs in the desert; there are fluid-bearing melons and bulbs, and with these as a reserve when summer suns are fierce the Oryx group, comprising the gemsbok, the beisa, the Arabian, and white oryx, make a living.

THE GRACEFUL CREATURE THAT WILL FACE A CHARGING LION

Bold horns surmount these fine heads, and not for ornament. A challenged oryx sinks upon his knees, swings his weapons like twin halberds, and it is death if they strike home.

Here is a grim tableau of desert life upon which a hunter stumbled. An oryx and a lion lay fast-locked upon the ground. The lion had sprung ; the oryx had received him full on its horns. The king of beasts died impaled upon that terrific defence ; the oryx died immovably yoked to his bloodthirsty victim, food for vultures both.

The fine sable and roan antelopes, prominent in the books of every gamehunter, must be noted as we pass on to those graceful little desert antelopes, the gazelles. Unlike the generality of antelopes, in which horns are mainly confined to the males, most gazelles of both sexes are horned.

THE LIVING SEA THAT SWEPT THROUGH THE PLAINS OF AFRICA

Numbering over a score of species, the gazelles furnished in the springbucks a genus which can hardly have been exceeded in number by any hoofed animal. Before South Africa became so thickly populated these animals gathered together for their annual migrations in such hosts as to beggar imagination. They moved like a living sea through the plains ; through the openings in the hills they poured as torrents ; in the valleys they were likened to swarms of locusts which darkened the Sun. Nothing could stand in the line of their march. A flock of sheep, a charging lion, a man, were swept away and trodden down by mere numbers. Beasts and birds of prey hovered on their flanks ; many were killed; many sank from exhaustion in the centre of the throngs and were trodden into the earth. It was like a lemming migration—but the springbucks turned with the coming of rain, scattered, and lived.

Names known in the records of travel are borne by some of the gazelles, as, for example, Cuvier's, Kennion's, Loder's, Speke's, Grant's, Thompson's, commemorating the discovery by each of these men of a species not previously described. They are all slight, exquisite creatures, the greyhounds of the tribe, and a tribute to desert fare and conditions.

Returning to the larger animals by way of the handsome Indian blackbuck, famed for its speed, we note the saiga, with its clumsy build and curious swollen nose and extraordinary nostrils ; the waterbuck, which seem to skim up and down the hills, yet are really creatures of the reedy marshes and papyrus clumps ; the klipspringer and rhebok, which occupy the place among African crags of the chamois in Europe. Then we have pygmy antelopes only a foot high ; fantastic little dik-diks, with muzzles suggesting the tapir; and a species so noted for its art of hurried hiding in the reeds that the Dutch called it the duikerbok, which means diving buck.

THE QUAINT ANTICS OF THE GNU IN THE PRESENCE OF THE HUNTER

The gnus follow. They are the most singular of antelopes, with horns like the buffalo, tail and mane suggesting the horse, and the legs of an antelope. Their habits are as strange as their appearance. In the presence of a hunter the bulls leap, caper, butt each other over, dash at the foe and away, perhaps charge home, or fly as if wasps were at their tails.

They have immense speed, power, and endurance, and when all these qualities are concentrated in civilised captivity, they are voted the most dangerous beasts in our zoos. There are two species of gnus, the white-tailed and the brindled, and closely allied are the similarly fashioned hartebeests, melancholy-looking beasts, but in reality less sad than savage.

What is called by Americans the American Antelope is known to science as the prongbuck, a handsome mystery.

The horns are differently shaped from those of other antelopes, and the sheaths are shed yearly, which is an un-antelope-like feature. But the bony cores are not shed, and that is un-deer-like. Thus, they seem to possess characteristics of both groups and to belong to neither.

Until recent years the position of the giraffe was as isolated as the prongbuck's. They stood by themselves, with no near links to connect them with any other existing species. The giraffe is an example

the ground he has to stretch his front legs far apart to bring his head low.

But the life suits the giraffe. He has developed a tongue of tremendous length, and so fine that its tip can enter the hole in a latchkey. His upper lip is as nimble a picker of leaves as a spider monkey's tail. He has magnificent sight in the watch-tower head; he can gallop, though ungracefully, at more than a horse's pace; he can kick with greater force than any other animal, knock a horse over with a

THE OKAPI

SABLE ANTELOPE

THE PRONGBUCK

CUVIER'S GAZELLE

A HERD OF FALLOW DEER IN AN ENGLISH PARK

HARNESSED ANTELOPE

BUSH ANTELOPE

THE RHEBOK

THE KLIPSPRINGER

of giantism, a little species grown monstrous. For the male giraffe may be 18 feet high at the crown of his head! Yet he has exactly the same number of bones in his neck as a pygmy shrew, the tiniest of mammals—seven, but such a seven!

All the antelope group always fed on grass and low-growing herbage; the giraffe took to feeding from trees. For thousands of years he has stretched up to feed thus, till he has grown to what we see.

Deprive him of his lofty acacia trees and he would perish. To drink or eat from

side-swing of his horned head; and can live for months at a time in the desert without water.

The true relationship of the giraffe to the rest of the living animals was revealed early in the present century by the revelation to civilisation of the okapi. Fossil remains of some such animal had been obtained in Africa and India but never a living okapi had been seen. Pygmies of East Central Africa spoke of them; and a piece of skin used by a native as a bandolier was found.

A Dutchman had heard of it and called it a unicorn-like animal. Stanley had heard of it, and when Sir Harry Johnston was going out to Africa, said to him: "If you get a chance, dip into that wonderful Ituri, for you may find there the donkey which the pygmies told me they caught in pitfalls."

How the beast was eventually tracked down and skins sent to England, to prove that it was a primitive member of the giraffe family, is too long to be told here, though it is a splendid story. The okapi is five feet in height, shaped like a giraffe, though shorter in neck and legs, and the male has short horn-like processes on the forehead. As the voiceless giraffe keeps to the sunny open, its loud-voiced cousin keeps to the deepest, darkest forest, and feeds on leaves of banana-like plants.

THE STRANGE BIG NEWCOMER
TO EUROPEAN ZOOS

People never expected to see one alive in Europe but in 1919 one arrived at the Antwerp Zoo. In 1935 the London Zoo's first okapi was presented to it by the Prince of Wales. The strange new animal created great interest, but Congo, as it was called, died in the year of its arrival. The Zoo was then without an okapi until 1937, when the King of the Belgians presented one to King George VI, who deposited it at the Zoo. Buta, as the second okapi was called, took to our climate better than poor Congo had done and became familiar to thousands of visitors year after year.

Now we must glance briefly at the deer, pausing for a moment to emphasise again the unparalleled story of their antlers. These are borne, except in the case of the reindeer, only by the males. As we have seen, these antlers are yearly growths.

Two bony bosses or pedicles appear on the stag's forehead, above and behind the eyes. These are permanent, part of the skull. From these there grows up a mass of bone. It is covered with skin and hair, like the ordinary hide, and richly fed by blood vessels. From the coursing blood bone is deposited, just as it is in the human jaw after a large tooth has been extracted.

The antlers grow, according to the pattern of the species, in a few months. Then a heavy ridge of bone forms round the union between the pedicles and the antlers, shutting off the blood supply. The skin of the antlers, called velvet, dies and peels off in shreds and at last the antlers, rough, rugged, and formidable, appear in naked beauty.

But by this time the antlers themselves are dead bone. The stag carried them through the winter for his battles for mates, then the mighty defences fall off like decayed branches from a tree, and the stag looks like a doe.

HOW THE STAG'S MIGHTY ANTLERS
ARE RENEWED EVERY YEAR

Almost at once new antlers begin to grow, and the entire process is repeated. Every year this happens. At first the young males have small simple antlers; with each increasing year the growth becomes bigger and more branched, until in his prime the fine creature has a spreading frontlet 70 pounds and more in weight.

We may see the wonder every year in our fine red deer parked in England, and wild in great deer forests in Scotland It is a superb breed of animals roaming throughout Europe, Northern Asia, Northern Africa, and North America, though broken up into varying local races.

They have their seasons of ferocity, though generally they are wary and inoffensive. Unless wind brings scent to them, they may be approached openly to within a few score yards without their taking to flight.

Larger antlers than those of the red deer are carried by the wapiti, a noble North American creature which has cousins in Central and North-Eastern Asia. With the larger armament comes larger will and force to use them, so that an angry wapiti is described by hunters as a fiend on four feet.

HOW SOME DEER USE THEIR TEETH
AGAINST THEIR ENEMIES

Smaller, but extremely handsome, is the fallow deer, of which Great Britain possesses two species, the spotted and the uniformly brown unspotted. Deer of this kind were among the food-providers of our old Cave Men, but it is thought that the modern ones were brought in long after the native stock had been exterminated.

What red and fallow deer are to us the chital and sambar deer are to India and South-Eastern Asia. They are the typical woodland and jungle deer. They puzzle us, however, for some of the chitals fail to shed their antlers, and sambar stags are known at times to carry one pair for seasons, which deer would not do.

SWIFT-RUNNING CHILDREN OF THE WILDS

THE WHITE ORYX

A SAMBAR AND ITS BABY

THE YELLOW-BACKED DUIKER   THE CHITAL DEER   THE KUDU

THE GIRAFFE—TALLEST OF MAMMALS   THE LITTLE MUSK DEER

The photographs in these pages are by Messrs. W. S. Berridge, Gambier Bolton, F. Bond, H. Irving, J. Newman, and others

Hoofs and antlers serve to defend these animals, but in the hog deer, the muntjac, and the musk deer, we find sharp, pig-like canine teeth used to gash and lacerate an enemy. But these teeth serve also to grub up roots and bulbs for food.

THE TREMENDOUS VALUE OF THE REINDEER TO THE LAPLANDER

From the tiny musk deer we advance to that fine upstanding animal, the reindeer, which in its wild state has the name of caribou. Widely distributed throughout the northern regions of the Old World and the New, reindeer are an indispensable aid to human life in Siberia, Lapland, Norway, Russia, and Alaska, and their range is being increased by pioneers in new places.

Free, the reindeer feeds in summer in valleys which have no ice ; in autumn they go to the coast to eat seaweed; in winter they find rich food in lichen on the hills.

Their supreme mastery of their wintry surroundings is due, apart from constitutional hardihood, to the beautiful adaptation of their hoofs. Each foot comprises a pair of hoofs in front and a second pair at the sides and rear ; and between the two pairs is a dense patch of coarse hair. The hoofs spread out on the snow like a camel's hoof on the sand ; the hair prevents all slipping on ice.

We all know the immense value of the reindeer in domestication, as a beast of burthen, charger, draught animal, and as provider of milk and meat and clothes. No animal means quite so much to us as the reindeer to the Laplander.

The migrations of the wild species, the caribou, in Siberia and America have often been described. In spite of ages of persecution the herds still move like armies.

THE QUEER-LOOKING ANIMAL WITH ANTLERS SEVEN FEET LONG

The northern migration of the Alaskan caribou in October of 1922 made Dawson, the gold-mining city, the centre of a herd which spread in all directions over an area of 50 square miles. The herds swimming the Yukon River stopped the steamer traffic.

We began with the eland at the head of the Antelopes ; we have in the elk the colossal monarch of the Deer. Here is an animal measuring up to seven feet in height at the withers and with titanic antlers seven feet in span.

But beauty and dignity do not always accompany bulk. The elk, or moose, carries his long neck in a horizontal position, with the head lower than the withers, and the fantastic head and the huge donkey-like ears—perfect for hearing but ruinous to good looks—make this magnificent animal a little grotesque.

He is well fitted to his life in the northern forests. His long legs carry him through deep snow and over fallen trees at a stride; they carry him across flooded rivers, and bear him ahead of the wolf pack. He looks like one of the nightmare creatures long ago extinct, and when bull moose fights bull moose, we get a suggestion of conditions such as raged in wider fields when poor little Man was seeking the way into his kingdom.

Something of elk and reindeer structure is reproduced in the bony structure of our dainty British roebuck, a little native of which we are proud ; and the fighting quality of the moose is there in concentrated form. No animal can do better with antlers and flashing, stabbing hoofs than this native gem of ours.

THE TINY ANCESTORS OF ALL THE DEER AND ALL THE PIGS

Many more species of deer reward the study of the seeker. There are Chinese water deer, which keep to river courses and lack antlers ; and American deer called brockets because their tiny antlers recall those of young red stags, which are termed brockets when sporting their earliest horns.

Finally there are the chevrotains or mouse deer, little creatures of Asia and Africa, hiding in tall grass or among rocks by day and coming timidly out to feed by night. Measuring only from ten to fifteen inches high, they stand alone, living relics of a very ancient past. They are not deer, they are not antelopes. Their history is to be read in extinct forms now fossilised. And that history reveals the astonishing fact that the ancestors of the tiny chevrotains were the ancestors also of all the deer and all the pigs!

Enough has already been said to indicate representative characteristics and species of this great family of swift runners. They have grown to grace and unsurpassed powers among multitudes of ravening enemies, and have prospered as they deserved.

The March of Man from the Age of Barbarism to the United Nations

The Capitol, the great national centre in Rome, as it appeared when the Romans ruled the world

THE RISE OF EUROPE

WHEN Greece was at the height of her glory travellers began to speak of a strange people living in the barbarous west. These strangers were known as Latins, or Romans.

We may imagine the amused smile with which an educated Athenian citizen would suffer some excited chatterbox to tell stories of these barbarians; for history knew nothing of the west. Man's life had risen in the east, and the east was old with civilisations of great wonder and power, old, too, with the names of kings and heroes whose deeds stretched far back into the marvellous past of man's adventure. But the west ! Who could be interested in a world as dark as night? So, perhaps, the Greeks would talk when the travellers came with their marvellous stories.

But Life is more than archaeology; it does not regard itself as the curator of a museum. Glorious might have been the vanished civilisations of the east, but as they had perished Life had nothing more to do with them; nay, the very fact of their disappearance proved that Life had weighed them in the scales of judgment and flung them aside as useless to the purpose of evolution. The east was old and feeble; the west was young and strong. Life turned from the east, turned even from Athens, and pushed its immortal fortunes on the banks of the Tiber.

Rome was a town of humble dwellings built on the seven hills which border the river Tiber. It gathered strength in Italy by successive victories over jealous neighbours. It came to be known outside Italy as the leading State in the country, and enterprising in commerce. Many years of struggle and conquest enabled the republic to grow in power and dignity, till at last it became a matter of great marvel to the farmers of Italy, and a matter of no small envy to foreign countries.

Among these foreign countries the most adventurous and commercial was Carthage, whose merchants soon began to fear the growing power of Rome. And it looked an easy matter to the rich, stay-at-home Carthaginians to storm the city of Rome, for outside the city there was no one to oppose them except farmers and peasants. But the farmers and peasants whom the Carthaginians despised were not only proud of Rome, they loved her, regarding her as their Mother and Protector. For the Romans had brought a new thing into politics. They had beaten the Italians into submission, but they had also won them, by fairness and justice, into co-operation. There was not a peasant in Italy who did not realise that Rome stood between him and slavery.

This method of dealing with other people was destined to have the most powerful

MIGHTY EPOCHS OF THE WORLD & MAN'S WONDERFUL ADVENTURES

consequences in the history of mankind. To us in Britain the Roman method makes particular appeal, not only because we have inherited it, extended it, and applied it successfully to a vast empire greater than anything of which the Romans dreamed, but because we see in the spirit and inspiration of that method our best hope of realising the glorious ideal of a United Nations that shall be world-wide and powerful for good.

Rome shattered the glory of Carthage. For the first time in history the west defeat, to rise up again in undiminished glory, to cross the seas, and burn Carthage to the ground. Victory inspired her with the perilous idea of further conquests. She raised legions which were unconquerable by all the forces of the east. Far from the Italian peninsula those legions marched from victory to victory, their discipline a wonder to behold, their simple dignity a new idea in the world, their conquests an advantage even to the peoples they conquered. The *Pax Romana* became more than a high-sounding phrase.

THE PALATINE HILL ABOVE THE FORUM IN ANCIENT ROME

revealed itself to the east as the heir of the ages. Young Hannibal came from Spain, crossing the Alps with a huge army, and defeated the soldiers of Rome again and again. He overthrew the finest armies of Rome, and annihilated the last levies sent to oppose him. But he never conquered the Italian peasant, and Rome held command of the sea. There he stood in a conquered country, master of all its resources, a tyrant none could withstand; yet powerless. The peasant would have nothing to do with him. He starved in a starving land.

This superb loyalty of the Italians enabled Rome to recover from her terrible For a little while it must have seemed to the eastern philosopher, and perhaps even to the eastern merchant, a great mercy that this new power had come from the west, for where the Romans went peace descended, order reigned, laws were just, and the conditions of life improved. A road made by the Romans was a revelation to the east. Then there were such astonishing things as drains, aqueducts, bridges. Buddha in India, and Confucius in China, might be making many amiable guesses as to the mystery of human existence, but these barbarians from the west were at least extremely useful in smoothing the ways of daily life.

THE ROMAN INCORRUPTIBLE

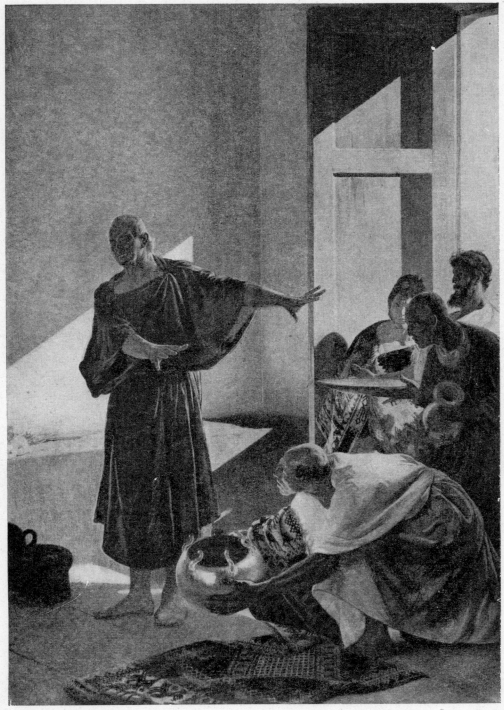

FINDING HIM IN HUMBLE CIRCUMSTANCES, COOKING VEGETABLES IN AN EARTHEN POT, THE ENEMIES OF
ROME TRY IN VAIN TO BRIBE CURIUS DENTATUS, THREE TIMES CONSUL

To the Latin tribes in Italy the Roman held himself as a kinsman and neighbour; to the foreigners whom he conquered he ultimately held himself as a friend and helper. So it came about, in the centuries before the birth of Jesus, that a great new empire appeared upon the Earth, an empire different in spirit and method from all other empires of history; an empire which promised at one time to unify the entire human family.

THE FALL OF THE ROMAN EMPIRE A LESSON TO THE UNITED NATIONS

There are men who look back to the Roman Empire as the greatest experiment in human history, deploring its fall as the most terrible blow ever suffered by civilisation. There are others who see how it happened that the Roman Empire came to grief, and in those causes of downfall discern a lesson of infinite importance for the world at a time when we are seeking to build up the United Nations.

How was it that this mighty Roman Empire crashed to earth, vanishing from the great powers as completely as Babylonia, Egypt, Greece, and Phoenicia ?

Let us begin at the beginning and study the moral character of the Roman.

What sort of human being was this Roman ? How did he differ from the Egyptian, the Grecian, the Carthaginian, and the Chinaman ? First of all, he was both simple and practical. His gods and goddesses, most of them borrowed from Athens, were much more moral than their Grecian originals. They were gods and goddesses who took an active interest in the home, the field, and the market-place.

Moreover, they had a high regard for justice, and lent their heavenly patronage to men who were fearless and law-abiding.

THE HEROIC STUFF OF WHICH THE ROMANS WERE MADE

The Greeks were curious, pliable, uncertain. The Egyptian, the Indian, and the Chinaman were pessimistic : they regarded life as a thing to be suffered and endured, not to be mastered and enjoyed. As for the Carthaginian, he was a materialist, a man who believed in trade, money, and luxury, caring little for things of the mind and nothing at all for things of the spirit.

Here is a story which tells us the difference between the Roman and all the people of the East. A Roman general named Regulus was captured and made prisoner by the Carthaginians. For five years he was separated from his wife and children, from his home, from his native country, from all that made life dear to him. Then the Carthaginians sent him to Rome to arrange a peace, believing that a sight of his wife and his home would make him their best peace advocate. They made him promise to return to captivity if he failed. Regulus went to Rome, and when he arrived there, he bade the Romans continue the war, to continue it till they defeated the Carthaginians. Then, though his wife clung to him and his friends implored him to stay, he returned to Carthage, there to suffer torture and meet a violent death. Such was the heroic stuff of which the best Romans were made. A man's word was his bond. Fear was regarded with contempt. All pain could be endured. Death was better than dishonour.

HOW ROME ROSE IN SIMPLICITY AND PERISHED IN LUXURY

But with this heroic strain there went also a strain of brutality, and we see, when we come to look at the fall of this mighty power, that it was his failure to realise the value of mercy and gentleness which helped to bring the Roman down. For the present let us keep our thoughts on the wonder of this first appearance of the European in world history. To us the Roman is a father. We still walk on his roads. We still keep his laws. And both in our politics and our practical engineering we are following the path he was the first to discover.

Much may be learned from the rise of the Roman Empire, and much from its fall. It rose in simplicity; it perished in luxury. The first Romans lived plainly and hardily. All their notions were simple. They believed in discipline, in loyalty, in faith, in courage. They rejected the idea of kingship, made themselves into a commonwealth, and elected an aristocracy to rule over them from the noblest and most devoted of their citizens. They were willing to learn from the East, and sent little bodies of investigators to Athens that they might report on Athenian culture.

The rise of Europe was an ascension of the human spirit from depravity toward moral grandeur. And these noble Romans carried in their souls the fortunes of the human race.

PICTURE-STORY OF THE MOTOR-TYRE

The compound from which tyres are made is a mixture of rubber itself and many other ingredients, each of which is added to give some particular property. The various ingredients are ground and mixed with rubber by great machines, the compound which emerges being given a final mixing between smooth, heavy rollers as seen in this picture. This process ensures that the compound is finely and evenly mixed.

To be certain that it is of the right quality, every batch of freshly-mixed compound is tested on plastometers, as seen here, and many other machines before it is allowed to pass on to the next operation.

BUILDING UP THE TYRE LAYER BY LAYER

The main structure of a tyre is built up from layers of rubberised material. Each layer consists of cotton, rayon, or nylon cords, each cord being separated from its neighbour by a film of rubber to prevent chafing. In this picture a sheet of tyre cord is seen leaving the machine in which it has been rubberised.

In the tyre-building department the sheets of rubberised cord are cut by this machine into strips of the correct width for a particular tyre. The strips are cut on the angle so that when they are placed on top of each other in tyre building, individual cords will cross each other to give strength in both directions.

GIVING THE TYRE ITS FAMILIAR SHAPE

A motor tyre is made up of many separate pieces, which are skilfully assembled by the tyre builder. In this picture, some of these pieces can be seen stored above the builder, who is here applying one of the final layers of rubberised cord.

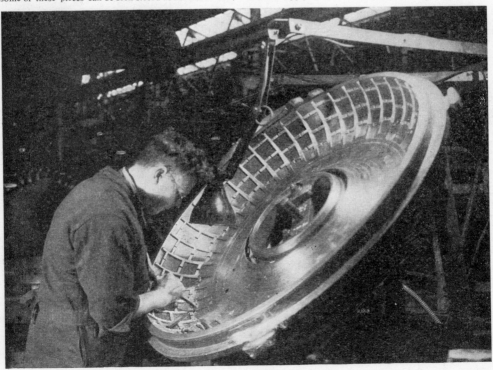

The tread, that patterned surface which enables the tyre to grip the road, is shaped by a mould during vulcanisation, described on the next page. Here we see an engraver cutting out the tread pattern inside a mould.

MOULDING AND TESTING THE TYRE

The assembled tyre leaves the tyre builder as a flat cylinder. It is then given a preliminary shaping by machine and placed in a mould for vulcanisation, as seen here.

Here the freshly-moulded tyre is being removed after vulcanisation. The little "pips" round the edges prove that the rubber compound has entirely filled the mould.

Samples of the finished tyres are always being tested on many kinds of machines to ensure that they are of the highest quality. Here we see how a tyre is tested by being pressed hard against rotating drums to find the strength of the casing portion. This test goes on day and night until the tyre is worn out.

The pictures in these pages are by courtesy of the Dunlop Rubber Company Ltd.

Plain Answers to the Questions of the Children of the World

WHERE DOES THE RAIN GO?

MANY things happen to the rain that sinks in the Earth, and exactly what happens depends largely on what the surface of the Earth is like at that particular place. A great deal of the rain remains in the soil to the depth of some feet, as soil water or ground water. If there is no such water there can be no vegetable life. But in places where rain falls, and the ground holds some of it, there we are sure to find plants of various kinds, that suck up a good deal of this water into themselves by their roots, and then give it back to the air. The soil also contains all sorts of life of other kinds besides green plants, such as various kinds of animals, like worms and insects, and also countless numbers of microbes. All these take up and use for their lives some of the water that the rain gives to the soil.

But still a great deal of the rain is not used up in any of these ways. Much of it is sucked up again into the air by the Sun's heat when the rain stops falling. Much of it also goes on sinking slowly through the Earth until it reaches a layer of something that it cannot sink through. It may be carried on this layer to some lower level, where it may bubble up out of the ground as what we call a spring. In the long run almost all the rain that is not kept by living things, or given back to the air at once, gets into streams and rivers, and into the sea, where the Sun sucks it up to form water-laden clouds and send it on to its round again.

How deep it is possible for rain to sink depends on several circumstances. It might be thought that if rain were constant and copious enough it might sink to any depth, and finally be lost altogether. But, however heavy and continuous rain may be, there are limits set to its penetration. It is certain to reach some impenetrable surface soon. In many cases this is clay. Indeed, except for the clay there would be much less water above the surface and much less under it. The clay acts like a cup and collects the water. Artesian wells are made possible by a layer of clay under chalk, where the rain water accumulates and can be tapped by boring to a considerable depth.

Even if there be no such material as clay, through which water does not pass, the great pressure in the deep crust usually renders it watertight, and at a certain depth the heat of the crust is great enough to convert the water into steam, or to decompose it.

SUN · MOON · STARS · FIRE · WIND · WATER · LIFE · MIND · SLEEP

Why has not Smoke a Force like Steam?

The proper way to find out the answer to a question like this is first to discover why steam has force. When we do this we shall probably find that the important fact about steam to which it owes its force is not true of smoke.

Now, steam is a word which we use in rather different senses; sometimes we use the word steam for the cloud that comes from a kettle, but every engineer knows that that kind of steam is not of much use in his engines—in fact, it has no more force than smoke has.

The steam that *does* work and has force is water-vapour confined in a small space and pressing in all directions outward so as to get more room for itself. It desires to expand, and it is this force of expansion that makes it so useful. When it has got out in the air, and has taken as much room as it pleases, it has no more force. The force is not in the cloud of steam outside the kettle, but in the steam inside that raises the kettle-lid.

Smoke, on the other hand, has no force, because it has no tendency to expand. Smoke is, indeed, not a gas at all, but only a quantity of small pieces of solid matter which, not being very heavy, can be carried in a stream by the gases escaping from a chimney. These gases might have some force if they were confined in a small space, but once we understand where steam gets its force, we shall see there is no reason why smoke should have any force.

Why, with Snow Falling on Them, do Mountains get no Higher?

Plainly something must happen to the snow which falls on mountains, or they would be bound to get higher.

As new snow falls on the old, the old gets pressed from above, and it tends to slide by its own weight down the mountain. In this way it gets very tightly squeezed into ice, and, though we think of snow as a light thing, a mountain-cap of ice many feet thick has a tremendous weight. As it slowly sinks down the mountain side it makes a bed for itself, as water does when it runs along the land; and so there is formed a river of ice which we call a glacier. The glacier may run into the sea and form icebergs, or it may melt when it gets low enough upon the mountain side. Some of the snow, but only a small amount, may form into avalanches, and so be disposed of, and some of the snow even on the top of mountains melts in the Sun and evaporates or runs away.

So we see that the snow that falls on a mountain shares in that endless circulation of water—from sky to Earth and sea, and back to sky again—which is going on always, everywhere.

Why do we Shake a Telephone?

When we are told over the telephone that our voice is faint or indistinct, the hearing of our voice can often be improved if we shake or tap our transmitter or microphone. In speaking into the microphone the air waves set up by our voice strike and vibrate a metal disc behind which are packed numbers of small granules of carbon. The differences in pressure upon these granules, due to the vibration cause changes in the strength of an electric current which passes through the microphone, and it is these changes which go through the telephone line and operate the distant receiver. Sometimes the carbon granules will clog or stick together owing to the continual compression, and it is then that a shake or a tap may free them and improve matters. The condenser microphones and moving coil microphones that are used in wireless transmission are not affected in this way, but owing to its greater sensitiveness the carbon granule transmitter is still used for general telephones, although it does not give quite so faithful a response to the vibrations of the voice in the higher frequencies, which are tremendously important in preserving fidelity of tone in broadcasting.

How Does Still Water Reflect a Distant Scene?

The distance from which the light comes has nothing whatever to do with what happens to it. Still water, like many other surfaces, is a very exact reflector of light. It throws the light-waves back from itself without mixing them up or distorting them. So long as it does this, we can see the image of whatever threw the light. It matters not in the least how far the light has travelled before it reached the water. We can see trees reflected in it, but we can see the moon or the sun reflected in it equally well, though they are scores of millions of miles away.

Why has an Old Clock Four Minute Spaces Instead of Five?

If we look at an old Grandfather Clock, we see that between one hour mark and another there are only four spaces, instead of five as in a modern clock.

The explanation is that the original clocks were made with only one hand, that which we call the hour hand. In the old days, there was no separate long hand to indicate the minutes, and therefore, there were no minute marks such as we have now.

The five divisions between the hour marks in a modern clock represent the minutes ; the four divisions between the hour marks on an old clock represent the division of the hour into quarters.

Our forefathers, when they looked at the clock, read the time by one hand only, and the four divisions told them broadly whether it was a quarter, half, or three-quarters of an hour.

Do Animals Feel Pain as We Do?

This cannot be answered directly; indeed, when we come to think of it, we shall see that no one of us can really compare the amount of pain he feels with what anyone else feels. We cannot feel anyone else's pain, and so we can only judge questions like this indirectly.

Yet it is certain that animals feel pain far less than we do. Different kinds of human beings feel pain differently. Small babies and children are probably much less hurt than grown-up people are by the same thing, though we may be misled by the fact that grown-up people usually control better the results of pain.

Probably women are slightly less sensitive to pain than men. It is well known that, on the average, they can drink fluids hotter, or hold hotter plates, without pain, than men can. The lower races of mankind differ immensely from ourselves in this respect. For instance, a jungle-dweller will cut and mutilate his body, and take little or no notice of it.

So we find that animals feel pain far less than we do. The stroke of a whip, which would hurt us terribly for hours and leave a mark for days, must certainly feel very different to a horse ; and we know that a horse will contentedly eat his food and never move his head in the slightest while a vein or artery is being opened in his body.

Why Has a Postage Stamp a Perforated Edge?

Stamps are printed in large sheets, and the perforations enable them to be torn off singly or in large numbers without any risk of damaging them. Incidentally, the perforations, by marking a conspicuous gap between the stamps, enable large numbers to be counted quickly.

It is interesting to note that, though stamps were brought into use in May, 1840, they were not officially perforated until January, 1854, except in the parliamentary session of 1851, when stamps perforated by a Mr. Archer were issued at the House of Commons, and were so successful that in 1853, the Government paid Mr. Archer £4000 for the patent.

Now many business firms stamp perforated initials on their stamps so that if they are stolen they cannot be sold, for no post office would buy them nor any firm receive such stamps in payment for goods, and if otherwise used they could readily be traced.

Marginal perforations vary in number on stamps of different countries, and are a subject of great interest to stamp collectors, who use a special gauge for measuring and counting them.

When We are Looking at a Rainbow can Other People see the Other Side?

This is a natural question, and, of course, the whole answer to it depends on what a rainbow is. If it is anything like what it appears to be there should be no reason why, when we are looking at one side of it, other people should not be looking at the other side—as if it were, say, the arch of a railway bridge. But it is impossible that anyone can be seeing the other side of the rainbow that we see.

What we call the rainbow is made by the reflection of sunlight from drops of water in the sky. Therefore, to begin with, the rainbow can only appear to us on the opposite side of us to the Sun. Anyone trying to look at the other side of the rainbow would be looking toward the Sun, where, owing to the very nature of a rainbow, one can never be seen. Now, if a rainbow is formed by the reflection of light from drops of water suspended in the sky that are so placed as to have our eyes between them and the Sun, plainly there can be no other side to the rainbow.

Why does Ink Stain while Water does not?

Water does not stain because it contains nothing that can stain. It may produce a mark because, where it falls, it may wash out colouring matter from a fabric, as in the cover of a book, but in water there is nothing melted or hung—dissolved or suspended, to use the proper words—that the water can leave behind where it falls. Milk has a number of tiny balls of oil hung in it, and in falling upon anything it is apt to leave behind a certain number of these balls of oil, which we call cream; and these have a great way of catching dirt, as all oil has.

The case of ink is quite different, for this is water containing a number of coloured things melted in it, among them salts of iron—a metal which has this peculiarity, that nearly all its salts are very highly coloured. There is one peculiar salt, or mixture of salts, of iron that is deeply coloured. It is called prussian blue, and is often used in ink.

Ink stains because when this solution, as it is called, of salts is exposed to the air the water flies away into the air, and the colouring matter is left dry, staining whatever it may have fallen upon.

Do the People at the Poles Spin Round like a Top?

Of course there are no human beings actually living at either the North or South Pole, but that does not make the question about the spinning any less interesting. If we think of a spinning top, we shall see that all parts of it move round in the same time, but that different parts are moving at different speeds, for those near the bulgy part of the top—near its equator—have farther to go in the same time than those near its poles.

Now, in the case of the spinning top that we call the Earth, it is necessarily true that all parts of it complete a revolution in twenty-four hours. This must apply equally to the man standing beside the North Pole, or a man at the Equator, for the Earth moves all in a piece—not like the Sun or Jupiter, different parts of which lag behind the other.

The man at the Equator is being whirled along at the rate of about a thousand miles an hour, but a man actually standing on the North or South Pole, on the point of the very axis of the Earth, is simply being turned completely round once in twenty-four hours, while his brother at the Equator has been whirled through 25,000 miles. So, though at the Poles' people would spin like a top, they would notice nothing, for the spinning would be so slow.

What is Ozone?

Ozone is a gas which is really another form of oxygen, as diamond is another form of carbon. It is blue in colour, and, as its molecule contains three atoms of oxygen, its symbol is O_3.

The gas has a smell something like garlic or chlorine, and when heated it soon breaks up into ordinary oxygen. Formerly it was supposed to occur in small quantities in the atmosphere at the seaside, and people talked about going to the sea to breathe the ozone. But a clever scientist, Dr. Benjamin Moore, proved that the gas at the seaside, which was supposed to be ozone, is mostly another gas called nitrogen peroxide in very minute traces, and other oxides of nitrogen. Ozone is produced in very small quantities from oxygen by ultra-violet light, so that we do get it near the sea and very high up in the air. It is also produced near electrical discharges, and can be smelt near electric motors. It is made by passing air through a glass tube inside and around which are coils of wire carrying a high tension electric current—known as a silent discharge—and is used in many industries for bleaching purposes, and also for sterilising water, as it kills bacteria.

How is a Horse Measured?

We say that a horse stands so many hands high, and this varies from seven to ten hands for a Shetland pony, the smallest of British breeds, to 15 or 17 hands for such magnificent animals as the Shire, the Suffolk, the Hackney, and the thoroughbred. The hand is a measure of length equal to four inches, and is only used for measuring horses. It came into use from the breadth of a man's palm, and it is probable that the placing of palm over palm up the foreleg of a horse to the shoulder once formed a rough-and-ready way of measuring it, much as we can roughly judge a length by spanning it if we know that the distance we can stretch comfortably from the tip of the thumb to the tip of the little finger, is, if we are grown up, about eight inches.

The Story of the Beautiful Things in the Treasure-House of the World

The children of Charles the First, by Van Dyck

THE DUTCH AND THE FLEMINGS

A CURIOUS change came over the art of the Low Countries in the later sixteenth century. Many Flemish artists grew blind to the glories of their native genius, and though they had before them the work of the incomparable van Eycks and their successors they must needs travel to Italy and find a false inspiration in Italian painting.

A period of imitation set in. The idealism and imagination of the Florentines and Venetians was alien to the sturdy and beautiful art of Flanders, and the result of mixing the two strains was a mass of pictures that count for little in European art.

Apart from this fatal following of southern ideals Flanders was suffering from a lack of great men. Genius will rise above all warring elements, and as the seventeenth century set in a man was working in whom the weakness of the period turned to strength. That man was Rubens.

Rubens, who lived between 1577 and 1640, was a giant among artists, and circumstances shaped themselves to his huge growth. He suffered none of the pangs of loneliness or hunger or sorrow that have been the lot of genius in all ages; his life was like a triumphal procession. People vied with each other for the honour of being painted by him; he had friends in most of the princely houses of Europe; he could have filled his studio with pupils a hundred times over.

In the early twenties he went to Italy and stayed there some eight years, bringing back to Flanders a style wherein Italian brilliance played like summer lightning on his powerful compositions. He seemed to paint as other men laughed and talked—naturally, buoyantly, with an extraordinary ease. His figures appear intensely alive, as if with difficulty they could keep still on the canvas. Even his religious subjects like the famous Crucifixion and Descent from the Cross, in Antwerp, are charged with a kind of electric strength; one has a feeling that there must have been a lot of shouting and excitement in his representations of those saddest of all the death scenes of the world.

Rubens was naturally what one might call a gorgeous painter. He was little troubled with problems of character, and his portraits, as studies of men and women, have little merit; as grand compositions, flowing with colour and life, they are stupendous. He was happiest in huge subjects like the Coronation of Marie de' Medici in the Louvre, in a classical story like the flight of Castor and Pollux with the daughters of Leucippus, in the Munich

PICTURES · STATUES · CARVINGS · BUILDINGS · IVORIES · CRAFTS

Gallery. He painted everything he could think of with the same brilliant touch.

Glorious as Rubens is one has a desire that sometimes, somewhere, one of his pictures would be quiet, that someone should stand still. This same exuberance takes from the merits of Rubens' many studies of nude figures; he is rather vulgar and lacks restraint. By this he is ruled out from the company of the great geniuses of the world; but he has his place: a giant among little men.

THE FLEMISH ARTIST WHO BECAME COURT PAINTER TO CHARLES THE FIRST

He left behind between two and three thousand pictures; some of them he had painted entirely himself; he had worked with his pupils on all of them. Over thirty of his pictures and sketches are in the National Gallery.

Another man who stands out among the mediocre artists of the times is Jacob Jordaens. He lived between 1593 and 1678. He is like Rubens, vulgar at times, heartless, but there is a brilliance and strength in his work which gives it a place in the story of art. An interesting study of his is the Three Musicians, in the gallery at Madrid. The Family Banquet, belonging to Dresden Museum, shows his sparkling style and his flourish. The work of this robust painter is also to be seen in the National Gallery.

It is strange to think of Van Dyck, the reserved, aristocratic gentleman, in this boisterous company, strange to think that he was a pupil of Rubens. Van Dyck (1599-1631) was indeed Rubens' best pupil, but he did not imitate his master. A happy fate threw him on the shores of England where he became court painter to Charles the First and his aristocracy. He painted the royal family a great many times, and always he showed the same dignity and restraint, the same low-toned beauty. His portraits of the children of Charles and Henrietta Maria are famous throughout Europe.

THE FINE COLLECTION OF VAN DYCKS IN THE NATIONAL GALLERY

Great strength was never his; he is sometimes charged with womanishness. His art, nevertheless, is to us a precious possession partly because the eye is always pleased by his modesty of treatment, his wonderful delineation of character, his pure drawing, and partly because in his pictures survives the history of a long-dead time. Several of his paintings of the Stuarts are in the Royal Galleries at Windsor. We all know his fine equestrian portrait of Charles in the National Gallery. About twelve of his pictures are in this collection, and they stand out as a group of paintings that are unequalled in their personal dignity and beauty—" A feast to the eyes," very truly says a great French writer on art.

Van Dyck has another special interest for us in that he was the father of English portraiture. In successive generations, when Englishmen began to paint for themselves instead of inviting foreigners to do their portraits, Van Dyck was taken as their model and inspiration.

While this artist was painting industriously in England—he was, in all, responsible for about 1500 pictures—another artist was rising in Flanders whose work was of a very different type. This was Teniers the younger. He was born in 1610, and lived till 1690. He was a follower of Rubens, but his work was more akin to the Dutch. He stands out among a group of small men in Flanders who loved to paint workmen and shops, booths and fairs, still-life pictures.

THE PASSING OF ART IN FLANDERS AND ITS RISE IN HOLLAND

After Rubens' grandiose and florid work the homely pictures of Teniers, painted none the less with strength and brilliance, are very delightful to come upon. They show a style of Flemish art which was unique in its day, and has not been rivalled since. We can see for ourselves in the National Gallery, where about twenty of his pictures are hung, how individual his paintings are, how they stand out in their surroundings.

The work of Teniers has a melancholy interest. Art, which had stayed so long in Flanders and made the Flemish people glorious, was drifting silently away across the little border into the land of dunes and dykes. Teniers was her benediction.

The art of Holland was like one grand hour in her life, a period of great activity which ended abruptly, as it began. It was as if someone opened a door, and for a few generations no Dutchman could escape that door. Then it closed. About 150 years later it opened at the hand of one van Gogh, and closed again.

A most intense interest in this way attaches itself to the art of Holland. It

DUTCHMEN'S PICTURES OF DUTCH LIFE

THE MILL ON THE DYKE, BY JACOB VAN RUYSDAEL

THE AVENUE AT MIDDELHARNIS, BY HOBBEMA

FRANS SNYDERS AND HIS WIFE, BY VAN DYCK

ANDREA BRIGNOLE-SALE ON
HORSEBACK, BY VAN DYCK

LADY READING A LETTER
BY TERBORCH

MAN WITH A SWORD
BY FRANK HALS

was so curiously like the Dutch to drive a wedge through their national life, very much in keeping with their character to work in a solid mass, and then have done.

Perhaps it was because the Dutch did not trifle with their painting, perhaps because they saw no need to experiment and work on " foreign " lines, that their pictures are so very national, so much part of themselves. To take any twelve Dutch pictures is to take a piece of Holland, with its sturdy, clean strength and intense home love. The painters chose for their subjects themselves and their country ; they were gloriously content.

THE LITTLE DUTCH MASTERS AND THE HOMELY SCENES THEY PAINTED

Their independence had cost them dear; there was a saying that every artist in Holland was a son or grandson of the men who had made the republic. Holland being thus their great love and joy they asked nothing more than to mirror her in their pictures.

But it was not only national pride that set the Dutch artists to painting their homely interiors and tranquil landscapes; Holland was staunchly Protestant, and would have nothing to do with carving statues or decorating church walls, painting Madonnas and saints. In the reaction against " Popery " her artists seemed, with a few exceptions, to turn their faces from religious subjects altogether; instead of thinking about the visions and miracles of the saints they thought about everyday people and the doings of the town.

This stay-at-home genius produced an array of pictures without parallel in European art. They are known as the work of The Little Dutch Masters, and they deal with firesides and kitchen tables, butchers' and fishmongers' shops, a working girl's new string of beads, visits to the doctor or the dentist; people eating together, singing, making love; people foolish in their youth, tranquil and wise in their old age.

THE COLOUR PAINTINGS ON THE WALLS OF THE DARK DUTCH HOMES

In addition to these *genre* pictures—a name given to studies of everyday life—the Dutch artists painted a great number of little landscapes, their canals and boats, their fields and trees, and cattle.

Hundreds of these pictures were painted. The walls of Dutch houses, opened out, would have made a very fine set of pano-rama pictures, like those we used to buy of the Lord Mayor's Show. The colours in the paintings gleamed in the houses like jewels against sombre dresses. The homes of the Dutch citizens were rather dark and narrow buildings, inordinately clean and neat; and the light entered from the open doorway or crept through the rather scarce windows, and fell on the rich hues of the canvases on the walls, making them glow.

It is when we realise how intensely these home pictures mattered to the people of Holland, what care and joy was spent on them, that we see the great distance the spirit of art had journeyed, so to speak. It is a far cry from the magnificent frescoes and public paintings of medieval and Renaissant Italy to these little pictures of ordinary people on the walls of ordinary people's houses. Instead of being adored and worshipped from afar, art had come to be lived with and loved at home.

The first of the great Dutch masters—those to be known by name, and not spoken of as a group, like the little islands in an archipelago—was Frank Hals, the artist of Haarlem, who lived from about 1580 to 1666. Next to Rembrandt he was the finest portrait painter Holland produced. He was a merry, jovial person—the laughing artist who imprisoned on canvas human laughter in almost all its forms. From his Laughing Cavalier to the smiling portrait of himself and his wife, Hals ran out a long line of merry people.

THE CHANGE THAT CAME WITH AGE IN THE WORK OF FRANK HALS

But they were not inane under their laughter. This boisterous artist had a shrewd eye; life, thought, and experience are behind the twinkling eyes and smiling lips of the men and women he painted. In addition to his many portraits, he executed from time to time large pictures for the Haarlem Town Hall.

When Hals lost the boisterousness and animal spirits of his youth and middle age, a great change came over his work. He had always had command of a brilliant technique, in some instances rivalling that of Velasquez ; his brush was free and fresh, rioting in colour, seeming to slip about here and there yet all the time recording faultless work. When he was an old man his palette lost its vivid colours and, instead, a beautiful array of greys ranged themselves on either side of black and white. His brush seemed to work of

FAMOUS PICTURES BY RUBENS

A GARLAND OF FRUIT

MOTHER AND CHILD

THE PAINTER'S SONS

itself, with its old freedom, in the narrower lines of his choice.

One of the miracles of art is his Governors of the Hospital, which he painted for the Haarlem Town Hall when he was over 80.

The Haarlem school, which was predominant in Holland until Rembrandt turned everybody's eyes to Amsterdam, produced not only Hals, but the Ruysdaels. These two, Solomon and Jacob, were landscape painters who stamped the art of Holland with their peculiar and individual genius. Jacob Ruysdael (1628–1682) set for his life's work and ideal the rendering on canvas of the light-drenched water of the Dutch landscape.

The rivers, canals, and sky are never separate in the atmosphere of Holland. Water "holds," as the artists say, a tremendous amount of light. You will see on the seashore that when cliffs and sand and town have turned dark the last light of the day is still gleaming on the sea. A great deal of water in a landscape creates a faery illusion, an effect of mist and mirage ; hence the unearthly beauty of the lagoons of Venice.

FRANK HALS' FINE PICTURE OF THE LAUGHING CAVALIER

Something of the same loveliness we see in the flats and waterways of the Norfolk Broads. Ruysdael captured the radiance of light, the beauty of the cool green of a well-watered country in his landscapes.

He can show storm as well as sunshine, as we can see in looking at his picture of Haarlem as a line of soft spires on the skyline, and then at Haarlem "lake," in tempest. His most beautiful picture is called The Marsh, in Leningrad, but many galleries of Europe own Ruysdaels almost as fine. The National Gallery is rich in pictures by the great Dutchman.

Jacob Ruysdael holds the honour of being the greatest landscape painter of Holland. Three or four others did very fine work in the same direction; one of them, Hobbema (1638–1709) the last great Dutch artist, comes sometimes very near the genius of Ruysdael. There are people who think that Hobbema's masterpiece,

The Avenue at Middelharnis, is the greatest landscape picture in the world. That is another of our National Gallery treasures. His fine painting of The Mill, in the Louvre, rivals some of Jacob Ruysdael's work. But it is the Avenue at Middelharnis by which the world will most remember Hobbema and be ever grateful to him.

The picture is reproduced in many ways and is a familiar sight in shops where art prints are shown. People are always buying copies, principally because it is such a beautiful picture to live with. The Avenue is a rough country road set on either side by tall, tremulous poplars. The uneven and fragile lines of the trees run away down the picture so that the eye is continually gratified by their alluring perspective.

It is a little sad to think that an open road was the last great picture painted in Holland, as if the soul of genius had been drawn away to wait for ever between the lovely, wavering lines of the trees.

In the meantime, while the bright day of Dutch art was still clear, there was another man painting fine landscapes, two men at least making pictures of cattle. The first of these was van Goyen, several of whose paintings are in the National Gallery and show us the Holland that he loved, by land and river, in summer and in winter. Van Goyen was a fine painter of snow scenes. The Skaters, in the Orléans Museum, is a wonderful piece of work, showing an icebound river under an immense wintry sky.

The two great animal artists of Holland were Paul Potter (1625–1654), and Albert Cuyp (1620–1691). They stand quite apart from the rest of the animal painters of Europe. There is something very real in the cattle in their pictures—solid, strong, as if the artists had mixed the art of sculpture with that of painting. But the animals have not the coldness of statuary. In Paul Potter's pictures you can almost see the warm, smoking breath coming from the cattle, and the skin is a little wet from contact with the dewy grass.

HOLLAND INDOORS AND OUT

A COUNTRY SCENE, BY SOLOMON RUYSDAEL

A RIVER SCENE WITH CATTLE, BY A. CUYP

SINGING THE OLD SONGS, BY JACOB JORDAENS

THE YOUNG MOTHER, BY GERARD DOU

THE PRODIGAL SON, BY DAVID TENIERS

These pictures are from photographs of the paintings, by Messrs. Alinari. Bruckmann, and Hanfstaengl

Potter is rather more vigorous and real than Cuyp. There is an intense, brute force in his pictures, as if within the horizon of his mind nothing but beautiful strong animals had ever moved, and he painted them naturally—the things he most loved. It seemed that the city he longed to dwell in was the wood at La Haye, a cool, shady place down whose green glades horsemen rode happily and animals wandered.

THE ANIMAL ARTIST WHO AIMED A LITTLE AT BEING A GENTLEMAN

In Cuyp's pictures we see less simplicity and more thought of the setting. Cuyp, like Potter, is intensely Dutch, but Potter's Dutchness is of the powerful peasant, and Cuyp is aiming a little at being a gentleman. One of his finest pictures in the Louvre is of the two horsemen preparing for their ride. The horses are beautiful, sleek and glossy, the riders and the stableman finely posed; but, as in all Cuyp's pictures, the eye goes beyond the animals, cattle or men, to the setting of the groups. His atmosphere is gentle, peaceful, charged with the light of sky and water blended that is peculiar to Holland.

In his great picture, Dutch Landscape with Cattle (National Gallery), it seems that the lovely radiance of the waterside is mysteriously clinging to the animals. They have the look of movelessness, of finality, always found in great pictures. One feels that those cattle were always on that peaceful bank, and always will be.

From the portraits, landscapes, and animal painters of the Dutch artists one turns to the little domestic scenes, and it seems that these are dearest of all. There is a nice and homely intimacy in the art of Holland that appears not to exist in the paintings of any other country. We feel that we are having a glimpse of people's lives, are being allowed to sit in their houses and listen to what they say.

THE MARVELLOUS INTERIORS PAINTED BY PIETER DE HOOCH

Pieter de Hooch who lived from about 1630 to 1677, is the greatest of these magicians; and the next greatest is Jan Vermeer of Delft. Terborch is another. We have Pieter de Hooch's masterpiece, called simply An Interior, in the National Gallery. In this picture it is difficult to know where the finest attraction lies; whether it is the still, statuesque form of the woman whose face is hidden, or the solitary figure in the middle of the picture, or the perfectly drawn tiled floor, or the men sitting by the window, or the beautiful light which envelops the occupants of the room. The whole is flawless, matchless art.

Another of De Hooch's interiors is in Amsterdam, a fine study of light coming into a dark house through a doorway.

These are pictures at which one can look again and again and never tire: pictures to live with, like Hobbema's poplar trees. To live with some of the world's masterpieces would be to feel that there was perhaps too much noise in the room, too much wind, a coldness of very high mountains; we should feel rather uncomfortable. But the pictures of the Dutch Masters are little friends of all the world.

Jan Vermeer (1632–75) and Terborch (1617–81) are among many others to be remembered for that reason. Terborch painted pictures of a little girl having her hair combed, of a woman playing a viol to the accompaniment of a harpsichord—interesting home scenes. He also painted some very fine portraits. Vermeer of Delft has left for the world some of the most beautiful paintings of a courtyard imaginable, La Ruelle, in an Amsterdam gallery.

THE SMALLER MEN WHO ARE PART OF THE ART OF HOLLAND

Another of his fine pictures is that of a girl putting on a necklace; another perfect painting is of the architectural still-life variety—that is to say, there are no people in it. It is merely an interior of a Dutch house, but you *know* someone has just passed by and thrown that silk and ermine cloak on a chair.

Jan Steen, who lived from 1626 to 1679, was a more vigorous painter in this Dutch school—a master more of portrait work and people, of character and emotion. He has not the strength of Hals, but he would like to paint the same kind of pictures. One of his more violent compositions is The Kings, in Brussels. A very quiet and beautiful painting is in the Amsterdam Museum: The Consultation.

The smaller of the men of Holland, Gerard Dou and Mieris, and many more, lost something of strength in their absorption of detail; but we like them, all the same; we could not bear to part with any of them. Like the great Dutch masters, they are part of the art of Holland, a separate and individual creation in the mighty growth of the world's art.

The Wonderful House We Live In, and Our Place in the World

The first drawing shows hair enormously magnified. The others show how the nail grows on the finger, the last one, much magnified, showing the finger as if it were cut across and through the nail.

THE COVERING OF OUR BODIES

SOME of us may think, perhaps, that the skin is not a very interesting part of the body, but that is very far from being the case.

Even if we were only to think of the skin as a material, and were to compare it with silk or indiarubber or paper or cloth, we should find that it is far more wonderful than any of these, and that nothing which human beings can make is equal to it. But it is indeed far more than a material, for it is alive, and besides being the covering of our bodies, it is one of the instruments by which the brain is made acquainted with the outer world.

We know that if we do not have enough light, growth is interfered with, and we become unhealthy. We know, too, that we breathe more deeply under the influence of light; and that in a fixed time animals take in more oxygen and give out more carbon dioxide in the light than in the darkness. This is due to the effect of the light on the brain; but it is not a direct effect, for the brain itself lives in darkness. It is due to the way in which certain nerves running to the brain are affected by light.

These are the nerves of the eyes and the nerves of the skin in general. For instance, an animal does not breathe so well or deeply if its eyes are bandaged.

But the eyes are not alone responsible for helping the brain. The skin, also, has something to do with it, and this is true even though we can see by the eyes and not by the skin. It is good, then, to expose our faces and our hands to the light; and sometimes, when people are ill, they are helped to get well again by taking what are called Sun baths, that is to say, by taking off their clothes and exposing all their skin to the Sun. It is the action of the light on the skin that helps to make bathing in the open air so pleasant and healthful. It is probably rather a drawback to us that we cover up nearly the whole of our bodies so that light cannot play upon the skin; but it is at least well that we should live in the light as much as possible.

We must particularly remember that it is sunlight or daylight to which, through long ages, our bodies have become adapted. It is a great pity we do not use all the daylight we can. We suffer in health and strength through getting up many hours after the Sun, and living by artificial light after the Sun has set. Our bodies were certainly meant to live in the open air and in the light of day. Even the best ventilated building is not as good as open air, and the best kind of artificial light is not as good as daylight.

BODY, MIND, AND SOUL · CITIZENSHIP · ECONOMICS · GOVERNMENT

Now we may pass on to look at the way in which the skin is made, and we may notice some facts about it which we can all see for ourselves.

In the first place, the skin is perfectly elastic. If this were not so we could not move our bodies; for every time we move, the skin is stretched somewhere, and then, by its elasticity, returns to its first position. Anyone can see this for himself by pushing the skin on the back of his hand into folds, and seeing how perfectly it comes back again. One or two cases have been recorded where people had skin which had lost its elasticity, and they found it as difficult to move as if they had been cased in stiff armour with no joints.

WHY OUR FACES TELL SOMETHING ABOUT OUR CHARACTERS

Even the most elastic thing in the world, however, has limits to its power, and this is true of the skin. We notice that as the years pass the skin of the face begins to show lines and folds according to the way in which it has been moved. This depends upon our feelings. The bright and happy person shows his feelings by moving the skin of his face in a particular way; so does the person who is always thinking; so does the person who is gloomy and always worries. In the course of time lasting marks are made in the skin of the face, telling us something about the character of the person. The best kind of beauty of the skin lasts all one's life, and depends upon the kind of life we have lived. Age makes it only more beautiful.

One of the marks of age in the skin is that it loses its elasticity. Often, also, it becomes very thin. In extremely old people the wrinkles in the face often disappear, and the skin becomes thin and smooth. But we must pass to other features of this wonderful living material.

THE MOST WONDERFUL WATERPROOF MATERIAL IN THE WORLD

The skin has a very beautiful texture. This has been compared to velvet, to the skin of a peach, and so on; but there is nothing else which has all the qualities of the surface of the skin when it is well cared for and has not been too much exposed to rough weather. We are so made that this gives us pleasure. Everyone likes to rub his finger against the cheek of a child, for there is nothing else that feels quite so nice. Another most important feature of this material is that it is waterproof, but in one direction only. By means of certain special arrangements, the skin is able to take water from the blood and allow it to escape; but water cannot enter through the skin, not even through the little channels by which the perspiration comes out. It is, of course, most important that the skin should be waterproof, yet it is also most important that it should be able to remove water from the blood, as we shall see. It would be hard to find any other material allowing water to pass through it in one direction, while being perfectly waterproof in the other direction.

The first use of the skin that occurs to anyone is, of course, that it protects all the tissues underneath it from dirt. If the outside of the skin were itself alive, it would be bound to suffer seriously from the dirt which it so often encounters; but almost the most remarkable thing about the skin is that, though it is a product of life, the outside of it is not really alive.

THE OUTER SKIN THAT IS NOT ALIVE AND THE INNER SKIN THAT IS ALIVE

The outside of the skin, indeed, is made of very much the same material as the nails are made of, or the hoofs of a horse, or various kinds of horns. Every time we wash—every time the skin is rubbed at all—a great deal of its outer layer is rubbed off. When we come to study the skin closely we find that it may quite distinctly be divided into two layers, an outer and an inner layer. The Latin name for the skin is *dermis*, and the inner layer of the skin is called the dermis, or true skin. It is really alive; it bleeds when it is pricked, and it hurts when it is touched. The layer that lies outside it is called the *epidermis*— *epi* simply meaning *upon*.

This epidermis is made by the dermis, and is being constantly renewed. It has no feeling in it, for there are no nerves in it, and it can be rubbed off, or can even have a needle passed through it without bleeding, for it has no blood-vessels in it. We know that it is quite easy to pass a needle through the skin at the tip of a finger without feeling anything, and without drawing any blood. The epidermis is very thick there, and we simply pass the needle through that. It is the epidermis that grows over the base of the nails. If you are reading very carefully you will say that anything which grows must be alive, and we have just said that the epidermis is not alive. That is perfectly

WHAT THE SKIN IS REALLY LIKE

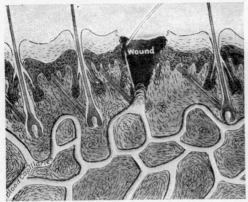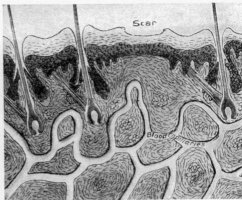

These pictures show how a wound in the skin is healed. In the first picture a capillary is shown growing into the blood clot; in the second picture the scar has formed but a hair is permanently lost.

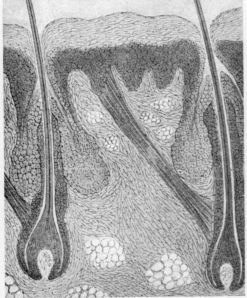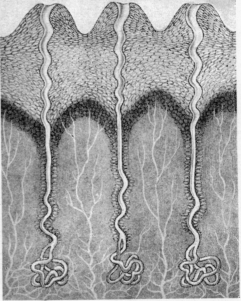

This picture shows the layers of the skin—the horny layer (or cuticle) above and the true skin below. The hairs are seen piercing the cuticle, with glands and with muscles attached to their bulbs.

This picture shows the sweat-glands which begin in twisted coils in the true skin, are continued as long tubes piercing the cuticle, and end in little pores at the top of the little elevations called papillae.

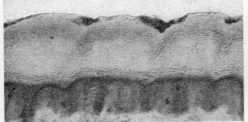

The picture on the left shows the skin of a white man; that on the right shows the skin of a black man. It will be noticed that the dark pigment in the black skin is in the deepest layers of the cuticle.

true. The thin skin that grows on the base of the nail is not alive, and does not grow itself. It is really pushed from behind by the new cells which the true skin is always forming behind it.

HOW THE SKIN CHANGES, AND THE LIVING CELLS PUSH UPWARD AND DIE

The whole skin is made of cells—both the true skin and the outer skin, or epidermis. The cells of the true skin are alive, and when they grow to a certain point they divide into two, and make new cells. This goes on always. It is in the deep layers of the skin that it goes on; and so it happens that the cells which have been already made are pushed upward and outward toward the surface by the young cells formed beneath them. After a time the old cells die; they become thin and flat and horny, and they form the epidermis, or outer skin. They protect the true skin, and the whole of the rest of the body. A great deal of dirt from outside soaks into them, but soon they are rubbed away, and other cells take their places. In this way we are able to keep the surface of the body clean from day to day. The true skin contains much more in it besides the cells which grow and divide and make the epidermis, but the epidermis has no other structures in it.

Any part of the body which has the business of making special fluids is called a gland; glands in the stomach, for instance, make the digestive juices. Now, we find that the true skin contains a large number of glands which have a special purpose; they are called sweat-glands, and consist simply of a long coiled tube, the end of which passes through the epidermis to the surface of the skin.

THE LITTLE TUBES THAT CARRY OFF THE WATER FROM OUR BODIES

These tubes are lined with cells, and outside them is a rich supply of capillary blood-vessels. In every part of the skin we find these sweat-glands, and they are working nearly all the time. We must not think that we perspire only when we can see visible drops standing on the skin. That only happens when the sweat-glands are very actively at work. But even during an ordinary day, when you have not noticed at all that you are perspiring, the skin discharges about 25 ounces of sweat. When we examine the sweat, we find that it is 99 per cent. water; the remaining 1 per cent. is made up of a number of things, including common salt. Sweat is slightly acid when it is produced.

In course of time the watery part of sweat passes into the air as water-vapour, but the solid part is left upon the skin, as the salts of sea-water are left in the sea when the water passes into the air. Even the cleanest skin contains many microbes, and some of these act on the solids that are left from the sweat, so that they are changed into something else that is unpleasant. This is one of the chief reasons for keeping the skin clean.

The production of sweat is one of the most useful things the skin does. Some of the solids of sweat are poisonous substances the body needs to be rid of, so that the skin, through its sweat-glands, is one of the channels by which we dispose of waste products. But we must not think that there is no use in the 99 per cent. of water that is found in sweat. For one thing, it is good in itself that there should be a constant stream of water through the body, because water helps most chemical actions, and because it helps to dissolve and carry away things we do not want. But the water in the sweat has a special use which is of great importance.

HOW OUR BODIES ARE KEPT COOL IN SUMMER AND WARM IN WINTER

It is necessary for the health of all the higher animals, and specially necessary for our health, that the temperature of the body should be kept at a fixed point, no matter whether it is summer or winter, day or night.

There must be some way, then, of regulating the temperature, and this is done mainly by means of the sweat. In very hot weather it is necessary for us to keep cool. The body must lose much heat somehow or its temperature will rise above the fixed point necessary for our health. So we produce a great deal of sweat, as everyone knows, and when the water in it leaves the skin it takes away a great deal of heat from our bodies. The same thing happens even if we put water on the skin from the outside. If, when you wash your hands, you dry only one of them, you will soon find that what we call the evaporation of the water from the wet hand makes it much cooler than the other. Then, on a very cold day, when we need to keep all the heat we can, we perspire only very slightly. Thus, the figure quoted above—25 ounces a day—is only an average figure. The amount of sweat produced depends chiefly upon the body's need for heat.

You must have noticed a dog lying panting, with its mouth wide open, on a very hot day. The dog has sweat-glands only on the skin of the pads of its feet, and so it practically cannot use our method of keeping cool on a hot day. That is why it suffers so much from the heat, and has to breathe quickly to get rid of as much water as possible by its lungs.

WHAT HAPPENS WHEN THE WEATHER IS WHAT WE CALL " CLOSE "

Then again, you must have noticed how uncomfortably hot you become when the weather is what we call " close." On another day the Sun may be hotter, yet we do not feel oppressed at all. The reason is that on the days which we call close, or muggy, there is a great deal of water already in the air. Now, the more water there is in the air, the more slowly can it take up any extra water. Indeed, the air may be so full of water that it will practically take up no more. This means that the sweat cannot evaporate from the skin, and so we cannot become cool in this way. We are as badly off for the time as the dog, which can scarcely sweat at all. But on other days, though the heat of the Sun may be intense, and though the air around us may be just as hot, yet it may happen to contain only a little moisture, and so our sweat evaporates quickly, and we do not find the heat at all oppressive.

THE DRUGS THAT ACT ON THE TINY SWEAT-CENTRE IN THE BRAIN

Now, there must be some way in which the sweat-glands are controlled. There must be some centre which orders them to act as they are needed. This is so. The sweat-centre lies in the lower part of the brain, and from it proceed nerves which carry its orders to the millions of sweat-glands in the skin. Then, when the blood becomes too hot, the sweat-centre in the brain which has the hot blood passing through it gives an order, and the sweat-glands are set in vigorous action. There are various other ways in which the sweat-centre may be disturbed; for instance, a man may sweat in great fear, even though he is quite cold.

Sometimes the sweat-centre is poisoned and does not act properly, yet this may benefit us. In fever, the blood is hot, and the skin hot and dry; but the heat may

kill the germs causing the disease. There are many drugs known which prevent sweating, and some which produce sweating. The most remarkable of these comes from an African plant, and a mere fraction of a grain of it will make the skin simply run with perspiration. A still smaller dose of another drug which comes from the plant called the deadly nightshade will prevent all sweating for many hours. In both cases these doses are so small that they could not possibly act as they do if they had to be spread over all the sweat-glands. But they act on the tiny sweat-centre in the brain, and that is why so little of them can produce such powerful results. A whisper in the king's ear may do more than shouting in the streets!

Something should be said of a few other important facts about the skin. It is one of the great organs of sense or feeling. We are rather apt to confuse the various kinds of sensation that our skin gives us, as if they were all varieties of the same thing, but they are not. There is, first of all, the pressure sense, or sense of touch. This is quite different from the sense of pain, or of temperature.

THE WONDERFUL LITTLE STRUCTURE THAT GIVES US THE SENSE OF TOUCH

If we examine the true skin—especially in the tips of the fingers and toes—we find special structures in it which are there for the purpose of touch. Nerves run to them, and the ends of the nerves spread out within them. Now, wherever these little touch-bodies, as they are called, are most numerous, there our sense of touch is most delicate, and that is why so many of them are found in the tips of the fingers, which must be very sensitive. Many are also found in the skin of the lips, and they also occur in the tip of the tongue. Two points can be felt as two by the skin of the fore-finger when they are very close together, but if the distance between them is increased by twenty times, we can only feel them as one when they are applied to the skin of the back. The skin of the forehead and of the palm of the hand will feel the lightest weight, while the skin of the chin requires the weight to be twenty times as heavy before it can be felt.

The sense of heat and cold is quite distinct from the sense of touch, and has a quite special set of nerves for itself. If you take a cold thing, like the tip of a lead pencil, and pass it over your cheek, you will find that it feels colder at some spots than at others, and the same is true of anything hot. The skin seems to be made up of a host of little spots—pressure spots sensitive to pressure or touch, cold spots sensitive to cold, and not feeling heat at all, and hot spots that are sensitive to heat and do not feel cold at all.

Finally, there is the pain sense. Different parts of the body are differently sensitive to pain, and the skin is far more sensitive in general than the inside of the body. The pain sense has a special set of nerves of its own, and in some people, who have something the matter with these nerves so that the nerves cannot act, the skin of the hand will appreciate heat and cold and touch, but pins can be run into it, without feeling of pain at all.

So we must think of the skin as the organ for three senses—pressure, temperature, and pain. People often say we have five senses, but as a matter of fact we have far more, and three must be put down to the credit of the skin alone.

HOW THE SKIN MAY HELP US TO KNOW THE POSITION OF OUR BODY

Probably, too, we are helped to know the position of our body—where our hands and feet are, and so on—by the amount of stretching of the skin in one part, or loosening of it in another part, which helps the brain to know where the different parts of the body are. So, in addition to everything else it does, the skin contributes to our sense of position—one of the senses we hear little about.

In many parts of the body are special cells in the skin, with power of making certain outgrowths of skin which we all know. Our skin does not produce so many of these as does the skin of many animals, but at any rate it produces two kinds of outgrowth—hair and nails. Our nails are very interesting, for they correspond to the claws of a cat, and to the hoofs of a horse.

For many creatures these outgrowths of the skin at the ends of their fingers and toes are extremely important. Perhaps they catch their prey by them, or walk upon them, or climb by them. But for us these things have lost their importance. Still, our nails remain, though they are too weak and thin to be of much use.

They grow from below, and can be completely removed without destroying the cells which make them. You may have had a nail banged. If it is banged hard, it turns blue. That means that a blood-vessel has been injured, and there has been some bleeding under the nail. A new nail gradually grows up, and in course of time the old nail gets loose, and comes off. But if damage had been done to the special cells which have the power of making the nail, no new nail could ever be formed again.

THE SKIN THAT CAN NEVER BE FORMED AGAIN

Hair is the other thing which our skin produces. The part of the hair showing above the skin is made of much the same kind of material as the epidermis, or outer skin, which is also very much the same as the material that the nails are made of.

Each hair grows from a special place in the true skin. If the true skin is destroyed a scar forms, and we may feel all right again; but nothing can ever form true skin again. A scar is not skin. There are never any hairs to be found growing from a scar, and when the rest of the body is dripping with sweat, a scar will be perfectly dry, for it has no sweat-glands.

The places from which the hairs grow are very complicated and beautifully made. Every hair really consists of six layers, all of which are made by the cells of the little hair-bulb from which the hair grows. But each hair requires to be looked after, or it will become brittle and break off. So there are special glands—usually two to each hair—which produce a kind of oil that keeps the hair soft and pliable, and prevents it from cracking. Also, every hair has a muscle which is attached to its root, and when this tiny little muscle contracts, it pulls on the hair and makes it stand upright. So when we read stories of people whose hair stood on end, it is quite possible that that really might happen though it is not common.

HOW THE CAT MAKES ITS HAIR STAND ON END TO FRIGHTEN ITS ENEMIES

We scarcely ever use these little muscles, and no one can use them by his own will. Like the hairs themselves, they are relics from the past. A cat has them, and everyone who keeps a cat has seen its hair stand on end. A possible use of this is that it may help to clean the skin. But there is a more likely explanation still. When an animal like a cat makes all its hair stand on end, the cat looks much bigger and more alarming. So it is probably useful in helping them to frighten their enemies.

The Story of the Marvellous Plants that Cover the Earth

Nearly all the necessities and luxuries shown in this room come from plants

HOW PLANTS SERVE MANKIND

THE circle of human life runs into that of many different kinds of plants. The relations between the two worlds are manifold, as is plain when we think of wheat, bananas, grapes, olives, cotton, flax, palms, oak, tea, coffee, quinine, mushrooms, yeast, and bacteria. Plants and animals and men have become closely intertwined in the bundle of life.

A general survey of the world shows four great vegetations—the treeless barren grounds of the North; the great zone of pine woods; the dry grasslands or steppes; and the steamy tropical forests. Now it was in transition areas between these great vegetations that man was most successful in his task of cultivation, especially in the eastern end of the Mediterranean area, the Far East, and the warm parts of America. Those places were best where the natural vegetation was not too dense, and where, in the course of the year, there was considerable variation in the rainfall, or in the temperature, or in both. For most cultivated plants flourish best when the seasons are well marked.

Among the food-plants the first place must be given to the cereals like wheat, oats, barley, and rye, which originated from wild grasses. Another very important cereal is rice, which requires abundant water when it is young and a good deal of warmth. It grows well in places that can be flooded or irrigated, as in the basin of the Ganges, and though its cultivation demands much work this is compensated for by its quick growth and its enormous yield. Rice is a difficult plant to grow, and the cultivators have to stand a great deal in the water, but two crops can be raised in a year. Rice-fields bring dense population.

Then there is maize, or Indian corn, which grows so well in warm countries, and has been greatly improved by cultivation. A less valuable cereal is millet, important as a foodstuff in Africa and India, but it does not store well.

The sowing of wheat began many thousands of years ago, as we may infer from what is called the " mummy wheat " of Egyptian tombs and from the little stores found in ancient lake dwellings, and the like; but it must be noted that some of the lowest existing races know nothing about sowing and reaping. The use of fruits and roots is older than all sowing.

When Australia was discovered there were no cultivated plants anywhere on that great island-continent, and the question arises of what the natives found to eat. There were some birds and mammals which clever hunters could kill, but

BOTANY & ITS WONDERS · FLOWERS · TREES · HOW THINGS GROW

theirs must have been a precarious liveli-hood. We must suppose that the women collected leaves and fruits and seeds and roots which could be eaten. Very im-portant among the roots were the yams, twining plants related to daffodils and snowdrops, but with thick fleshy roots, and rich in good food.

THE MEMBER OF A POISONOUS FAMILY VALUABLE AS FOOD

Of course, it would take primitive man a long time to discover what roots, leaves, fruits, and seeds he could safely eat; and then it would probably take him a long time to understand that he must not uproot *all* the yams or gather *all* the seeds if he wished to get more at the same place next year. But the big fact is that before agriculture there was a using of things as they are.

Beside yams must be ranked ordinary potatoes, which flourish well in cool climates, and store up large quantities of starch in the swollen pieces of under-ground stem which we call tubers. As these tubers bear buds or " eyes," they cannot be roots in the strict sense, though for practical purposes they must be included as roots. It is interesting to notice that the potato belongs to a poisonous order— that of the deadly nightshade. The fruits are poisonous, and the tubers become dangerous if they are allowed to " green." Of great value are the rather mysterious life-saving substances called *vitamins*, which are found just under the skin of the potato. If we are to make the most of potatoes, we should have them cooked with their skins on, and not overheated.

THE LITTLE UNDERGROUND STOREHOUSES OF STARCH AND SUGAR

Among the other important root-plants which man uses as food are carrots and turnips, parsnips and artichokes, *sweet* potatoes (belonging to the convolvulus family), and the yams of warm countries. In many cases, like the yams, it is all-im-portant that the roots should be cooked before they are eaten. Another instance of this is the manioc of Brazil and other countries, which furnishes tapioca. It is a vigorous shrub belonging to the spurge family, and very poisonous. The fleshy roots are carefully scraped, and the in-terior is crushed into flour, which is baked in thin layers to drive off the poison. It will be understood that the roots of plants are useful to man because they are par-ticularly rich in starch and sugar, which the plant stores as capital for next year.

It is probable that the plant which feeds most people is the banana. It is an eastern forest plant, with a strong stem bearing enormous leaves, which often get torn into strips by the wind and rain. From among the leaves there hangs down a huge bunch of perhaps hundreds of fruits, and the stem is cut down to get the bananas. The wild bananas of the East have large bitter seeds and rather tasteless pulp, but in remote antiquity man cul-tivated the banana-plant with patience till he reared a stock without seeds and with palatable flesh. The fruit is really a long berry, and it was apparently in its improved seedless state that it was brought to Africa and other countries.

With a little care, the banana plant can be got to bear fruit all the year round, and it is easily propagated by sticking into the soil the shoots which spring up around the base of the cut stem. As long as there is rain enough there is plenty to eat in a banana country, and no need to store or think of the morrow.

THE DATE PALM AND ITS MANY USES FOR MANKIND

The sweet fruits that can be eaten raw are called bananas proper; those that are cooked in an unripe state are called plantains. They are steamed and mashed, then eaten with some flavouring of curry or meat juice. Large quantities of plan-tains, however, are eaten raw by European populations. When we eat a sweet banana it is interesting to remember that its seeds were once big and bitter.

Another of the great fruits of the world is produced by the date palm, a native of North Africa, South-West Asia, and part of India, and cultivated in many other countries. The fruits are very nutritious, and can be stored in a dry state. Date honey is squeezed out from the fruit and can be used as a starting-point for wine; palm wine is also made from the sap; the bud forms palm cabbage; the stones are ground to make a substitute for coffee and they also yield oil; the leaves are made into baskets and mats ; the fibres are wound into string; the wood is used in building huts. There is no tree more useful, except perhaps the coconut, the story of which is told in a later chapter.

There are two kinds of date palm trees: wild ones that produce the fertilising